Routledge Handbook of Japanese Business and Management

The *Routledge Handbook of Japanese Business and Management* provides a comprehensive overview of management and business processes and practices in Japanese companies. The contributors combine theoretical findings and research results with a practical and contemporary view on how corporations and firms are managed in Japan.

The handbook is divided into eight sections, covering:

- historical perspectives on Japanese management;
- structure and theory of the Japanese firm;
- the corporate environment in Japan;
- the Japanese work environment;
- the Japanese market;
- manufacturing and logistics;
- interaction and communication;
- the future of Japanese management.

This book is an essential reference resource for students and scholars working on Japanese companies, the Japanese marketplace, Japanese consumers, or management processes in the Japanese firm. The book also provides an interesting and informative read for managers who need to deepen their knowledge on Japanese business processes.

Parissa Haghirian is the Professor of International Business at Sophia University, Tokyo, Japan.

Routledge Handbook of Japanese Business and Management

Edited by Parissa Haghirian

Routledge
Taylor & Francis Group

LONDON AND NEW YORK

First published 2016 by Routledge

2 Park Square, Milton Park, Abingdon, Oxfordshire OX14 4RN
52 Vanderbilt Avenue, New York, NY 10017

Routledge is an imprint of the Taylor & Francis Group, an informa business

First issued in paperback 2019

British Library Cataloguing in Publication Data
A catalogue record for this book is available from the British Library

Library of Congress Cataloging in Publication Data
Names: Haghirian, Parissa, 1970– editor.
Title: Routledge handbook of Japanese business and management / edited by
    Parissa Haghirian.
Description: Abingdon, Oxon ; New York, NY : Routledge, 2016. | Includes
    bibliographical references and index.
Identifiers: LCCN 2015032336 | ISBN 9780415734189 (hardback) |
    ISBN 9781315832661 (ebook)
Subjects: LCSH: Management—Japan. | Industrial management—Japan. |
    Corporations, Japanese—Management. | Corporate culture—Japan. |
    Japan—Commerce—History.
Classification: LCC HD70.J3 R68 2016 | DDC 658.00952—dc23
LC record available at http://lccn.loc.gov/2015032336

ISBN: 978-0-415-73418-9 (hbk)
ISBN: 978-0-367-86914-4 (pbk)

Typeset in Bembo
by Swales & Willis Ltd, Exeter, Devon, UK

Contents

Contents

Contents

Figures

Tables

Contributors

Editor

Parissa Haghirian is Professor of International Business at the Faculty of Liberal Arts at Sophia University in Tokyo, Japan and a visiting professor in Japanese Management at Waseda Business School, Keio University, and the European Training Programme (ETP) in Japan. Parissa grew up in Austria, where she obtained her MA in Japanese Studies from Vienna University and was awarded an MA and Ph.D. in International Management by Vienna University of Business, Austria. Her research focuses on Japanese management practices, cross-cultural management, and leadership. Since joining Sophia University in 2006, Parissa has taught undergraduate, graduate, and MBA-level classes on the subject of Japanese management, and has researched and consulted on numerous aspects of Japanese business practices with Western and native Japanese companies in Tokyo. She has published several books and articles on the topic and is the author of *Understanding Japanese Management Practices* (2010); *Successful Cross-cultural Management: a Guide for International Managers* (2011); and is the editor of *Innovation and Change in Japanese Management* (2010) and *Japanese Consumer Dynamics* (2011).

Chapter authors

M. Reza Abdi is a faculty member of Bradford University School of Management, UK, and has over twenty years of academic and industrial experience, including research-project supervision and consultancy in the areas of manufacturing system design and modelling, supply chain management, operations management, and decision-support systems, particularly in the areas of computer modelling and simulation, multi-criteria decision modelling, analytical hierarchical process (AHP), analytical network process (ANP), fuzzy logic, and systems dynamics. He has published numerous articles in international peer-reviewed journals, and several book chapters and papers in international conference proceedings.

Bruce Aronson is a professor of Law at Hitotsubashi University's Graduate School of International Corporate Strategy. Bruce's main area of research is comparative corporate governance with a focus on Japan. Major publications include 'The Olympus scandal and corporate governance reform: can Japan find a middle ground between the board monitoring model and management model?,' *UCLA Pacific Basin Law Journal*, 93 (2012), and 'A Japanese CalPERS or a new model for institutional investor activism? Japan's Pension Fund Association and the emergence of shareholder activism in Japan,' *NYU Journal of Law and Business*, 571 (2011). He also acts as an advisor to the law firm of Nagashima Ohno & Tsunematsu in Tokyo.

Stephanie Assmann is a specially appointed professor in the Research Faculty of Media and Communication, Hokkaido University, Sapporo, Japan. Stephanie has obtained professional experience through working for the Japanese company Citizen from 1998 to 1999, and for the Consulate General of Japan in Hamburg, Germany, in 2001. Her recent publications include *Gender Equality in Japan: the Equal Employment Opportunity Law Revisited* (2014), as well as co-editor of *Japanese Foodways, Past and Present*. Her research interests include the study of gender in employment, consumer behaviour, social stratification, food, and nutrition.

Patrick Bessler is currently Director of Communications at the German Chamber of Commerce and Industry in Japan. He is also Editor-in-Chief of the German business magazine *Japanmarkt*, covering market trends and German business activities in Japan. Among his recent main research interests are the globalization of Japan and opportunities for global business relations with Japanese companies, as well as labour market trends and the emergence of the start-up ecosystem in Japan.

Michaela Blahová is a researcher at the Centre of Applied Economic Research at the Faculty of Management and Economics at Tomas Bata University in Zlín, Czech Republic. Recently, she has undertaken her post-doctoral research stay at Sophia University in Tokyo, Japan. Her research interests include finance, management and measurement of corporate performance, and relevant contemporary trends affecting the current business sphere worldwide. Lately, she has been a leader of a research project supported by the Czech Science Foundation focused on creating a strategic performance model framework based on the utilization of the synergy effects of selected management systems and has been an investigator/co-investigator of various international projects.

Harald Conrad is Sasakawa Lecturer in Japan's Economy and Management at the School of East Asian Studies, University of Sheffield, UK. His research focuses on Japanese social policy; human-resource management; the organization of markets; and intercultural business negotiations. His latest journal articles have appeared in the *Social Science Japan Journal*, the *International Journal of Human Resource Management*, and the *Journal of Social Policy*. From 2011 to 2014, Harald was co-editor of the journal *Japan Forum*.

Philippe Debroux is a Belgian citizen who has been resident in Japan since the 1970s. He is Professor of International Management and International Human Resource Management at Soka University, Japan, and a visiting professor at Rennes (France) Chuo (Tokyo), and Sophia (Tokyo) universities. His research focuses on development in human-resource management, innovation and entrepreneurship in Japan and South-East Asia. His main recent publications include *Female Entrepreneurship in Asia* (Chandos, Cambridge, UK); *Asia's Turning Point*, co-authored with Ivan Tselichtchev; and *Innovation in Japan*, co-edited with Keith Jackson.

Makoto Fujii is an Associate Professor at Nihon University, College of Commerce. His research areas are financial accounting and tax law. He is well acquainted with the International Financial Reporting Standards and Corporate Tax Law, not only in Japan, but also in the United States, the United Kingdom, and Germany. He is particularly interested in restructuring and consolidated tax returns. His major publications include: 'Taxable income and tax unit – the influence on reorganization Taxsystem,' *Tax Accounting Research, Japan Tax Accounting Association*, 22 (2011): 17–31.

Tim Goydke is a professor of Japanese Economy and Society at Hochschule Bremen, Germany. Before this, he worked as a consultant for Japan, Korea, and South Asia for the German Asia-Pacific Business Association. Since 2009, he has also been Dean of the International Graduate Center (IGC) of Hochschule Bremen, responsible for all Masters and MBA programmes in the field of further education.

Carsten Herbes is a professor of International Management and Renewable Energy at Nürtingen-Geislingen University (NGU) and Director of the Institute for International Research on Sustainable Management and Renewable Energy, both of these establishments being in Nürtingen and Geislingen an der Steige, Germany. His research interests include marketing and acceptance of renewable energy; Japanese business; and the Japanese economy. Before joining NGU, he worked as a management consultant and board member of a bio-energy company.

Sumiyo Ishii is Assistant Professor in the Faculty of Economics at Daito Bunka University in Tokyo, Japan. Her expertise lies in the field of the history of Japanese economic thought. Her research particularly centres on the relationship between economic thought in Early Modern times and that in Modern times. Specifically, she studies entrepreneurial activities and their thoughts in the nineteenth century. Her most recent publication is *Nihon Keizai Shisôshi: Edo kara Showa* (co-authored, 2015).

Yacob Khojasteh is an Associate Professor of Operations Management at the Graduate School of Global Studies, Sophia University, Tokyo, Japan. He has several years of professional experience in industry and consulting. His research interests include production and operations management; supply chain management; systems modelling and optimization; and lean production systems.

Souichirou Kozuka is Professor of Law at Gakushuin University, Tokyo. He specializes in Commercial Law, Corporate Law, and Comparative Law Studies. His recent publications in English include: 'Law in a changing economy,' in Dimitri Vanoverbeke *et al.* (eds), *The Changing Role of Law in Japan*, and 'Policy and politics in contract law reform in Japan,' (co-authored), in: *The Method and Culture of Comparative Law* (2014). He is a correspondent of UNIDROIT (International Institute of Private Law) and an Associate Member of the International Academy of Comparative Law (IACL).

Hendrik Meyer-Ohle is Associate Professor for Japanese Business and Management in the Department of Japanese Studies at the National University of Singapore. His research focuses on the retail and service industries in Japan, human-resource management, and Japanese business in Southeast Asia. His main publications include *Innovation and Dynamics in Japanese Retailing* and *Japanese Workplaces in Transition* (2003 and 2009).

Mariko Morimoto is Associate Professor of Marketing at Sophia University in Tokyo, Japan. Her expertise lies in the field of advertising and marketing communication. Her research centres on cross-cultural and international advertising, social-media use in marketing, and consumers' privacy concerns on the Internet. She is also currently on the editorial board for the *International Journal of Advertising*.

Emi Moriuchi is currently an assistant professor in Marketing at Fort Hays State University, Kansas, USA. She has studied and conducted research on Japan and Japanese consumers and

SMEs for the last twelve years. She was educated in Singapore, Switzerland, the US, and the UK. Her work has been presented at several international and US domestic conferences. Although she has a Japanese ethnic background, she has worked in several different countries, which allows her to bring in different cultural perspectives on Japanese consumers and the Japanese consumer market.

Luke Nottage is Professor of Comparative and Transnational Business Law at Sydney Law School, founding Co-Director of the Australian Network for Japanese Law, and Associate Director of the Centre for Asian and Pacific Law at the University of Sydney, Australia. His books include: *Product Safety and Liability Law in Japan* (Routledge, 2004) and *Foreign Investment and Dispute Resolution Law and Practice in Asia* (Routledge, 2011). He has had executive roles in the Law Council of Australia, the Australian Centre for International Commercial Arbitration, and the Asia-Pacific Forum for International Arbitration. Luke has also consulted for law firms worldwide, and is founding Managing Director of Japanese Law Links Pty Ltd.

Katsuhiko Okada is Professor of Finance at Kwansei Gakuin University and CEO/CIO of Magne-Max Capital Management Co. Ltd, Japan FSA-registered. He co-founded a hedge-fund management firm (Halberdier Capital) in Singapore in 1997, which later grew to be one of the largest Japan-focused hedge funds in Asia. Katsuhiko sold his stake in 2001 and returned to academia. His research interest is in behavioural finance. Katsuhiko advises financial institutions as a CEO of the investment advisory firm, and serves as a director of academic associations such as ABEF and JFA.

Hiroshi Okano is a professor of Urban Research Plaza, as well as a professor of the Graduate School of Business, Osaka City University, Japan. He is a co-director for Amoeba Management Research Center, Ministry of Finance, China. Research themes include strategic, historical, social, and cultural aspects of strategic management and accounting; financial management for private sectors, public sectors, music and art organizations; and, recently, he has been focusing on strategic and brand management for cities, urban development, poverty management, etc. His publications include *Global Strategy and Accounting* (2003) and *History of Management Accounting in Japan: Institutional & Cultural Significance of Accounting* (2015).

Přemysl Pálka is the Vice-Dean for International Relations and is an academic teaching courses in corporate finance, business valuation, and value-based management at Tomas Bata University in Zlín, Czech Republic. Besides his continuous research interest in the above-mentioned topics, he delivers lectures at the faculty within the course in the Microeconomics of Competitiveness developed by Professor Michael Porter at the Harvard Business School. He has been an investigator/co-investigator in various research projects, as well as educational international projects.

Yumiko Toda is Associate Professor of Marketing at the College of Commerce at the Nihon University, Tokyo. She received her BA in Business Administration from Aoyama Gakuin University (1999), and her MA (2001) and Ph.D. (2007) in Marketing from Keio University. She served as Visiting Scholar at the University of Edinburgh and Coventry University in the UK in 2007, before joining Nihon University. Her primary research interests include the development of marketing theory and the history of marketing practices in Japan, the UK, and the US. She has authored articles on the historical development of the private brand strategies of Marks and Spencer in the UK for various academic journals, and has contributed several chapters to scholarly volumes edited by the Japan Society for the Study of Marketing History. Her recent work on knowledge-transfer practices between Japanese and British retailers was published under the title 'British retail and its influence on the development of private brand strategy at Daiei Incorporated in Japan,' in *Distribution Studies, the Journal of Japan Society for Distribution Sciences* (JSDS), Vol. 35, 2014.

Kazuo Usui is a professor of Marketing, Vice-Dean of the Graduate School of Humanities and Social Sciences and Dean of the Faculty of Economics at Saitama University, Japan, and a visiting professor at the University of Edinburgh, UK. His main research fields include the historical and comparative study of marketing and marketing thought, macro-marketing, marketing, and knowledge management. He is the author of *Marketing and Consumption in Modern Japan* (Routledge, 2014) and *The Development of Marketing Management: the Case of the USA c.1910–1940* (2008), and was awarded the JSDS (Japan Society for Distributive Sciences) Awards in 1999 and 2014.

Franz Waldenberger is Professor for Japanese Economy at Munich University, Germany. He is presently on leave from Munich to head the German Institute for Japanese Studies in Tokyo. His research focuses on the Japanese economy and corporate governance. Recent publications include '"Company heroes" versus "superstars" – executive pay in Japan in comparative perspective,' *Contemporary Japan*, 25 (2013), 189–213, and 'Confronting earthquake risk in Japan – are private households underinsured?,' *Europe Asia Journal*, 11 (2013): 78–91.

Leon Wolff is an associate professor of Law at Queensland University of Technology, and a founding co-director of the Australian Network for Japanese Law (ANJeL). Leon is a comparative lawyer with expertise in Japanese law and society. He is the co-editor and contributing author in a number of edited books, including *Commercial Law in East Asia* (2014); *Community and the Law: A Critical Reassessment of American Liberalism and Japanese Modernity* (2010); and *Corporate Governance in the 21st Century: Japan's Gradual Transformation* (2008).

Introduction

Parissa Haghirian

Japanese management revisited

Based on foundations that date back to the sixteenth century, Japanese corporations have developed a unique management style, with a very strong cultural stamp and a strikingly open-minded attitude towards business practices. Supported by a strong, group-oriented work ethic and a capacity to integrate and improve upon Western ideas, the Japanese economy developed at a tremendous pace after Japan opened up to the world following the Meiji Restoration.

Japan went through the stages of industrialization at tremendous speed. Moreover, even amid the destruction that followed the Second World War, the Japanese managed to restore their economy to pre-war levels within only a few years, and were soon on a par with their Western counterparts. Since then, Japan has become the only truly post-industrial Asian economy.

During this rapid process of development, Japan's corporations developed management practices that are still state-of-the-art today. Foremost among these are its techniques of production management, such as just-in-time inventory management, which enabled Japanese companies to build cars that were cheaper than those of their competitors, yet of higher quality. In recent decades, these techniques have been extended beyond the production of cars to become Japan's premier basis of management expertise. They are not simply copied in other countries – they have become a worldwide standard.

When Japanese companies became role models in the 1980s, this was not simply because of their ability to turn out high-quality products at astonishing speeds. At the same time that they had developed expertise in the management of industrial processes, Japanese corporations had also developed a unique management style strongly rooted in traditional Japanese culture. Japan presented itself as an exotic place of business which was leaving the West behind – an image which held a powerful fascination for Western managers and researchers.

By the 1980s, Japan was overtaking the West in terms of speed of economic development, and Japanese management was widely seen as a role model for the West, if not as a superior management system. There was a great boom in publications on Japanese management as the West tried to emulate the Japanese success. The focus of attention lay in particular on Japanese human-resource management (especially lifetime employment and the principle of seniority), and production technologies. At the same time, Japanese work ethics, knowledge, and innovation management (e.g. 'quality circles') were seen as an underlying driver of their success, and also engendered strong interest within Western corporations.

In the 1990s, after the financial bubble had burst, the image of Japanese management changed. The very same features once seen as the cause of the Japanese miracle were now often portrayed as the reason why Japan could not escape its decade-long recession.

Today, the picture is mixed. Despite the painful restructuring and transformation processes that many Japanese organizations have undergone since the 1990s, many of the old management practices remain intact. The famous Japanese *keiretsu* still retain their traditional management styles; and, while many of these practices are still more successful than Western observers tend to think, others continue to block the process of change and impede competitiveness in global markets. Some companies have failed to adapt to global standards and new customer preferences; others have become more successful than ever.

Many researchers have found the contemporary scene difficult to understand. Few researchers who are not fluent in Japanese have had much success in tracing the major changes in Japanese companies and bringing them to the attention of the world. At the same time, China has become the focus of media and academic interest, and the number of studies on Japanese management written in Western languages has declined, being generally limited to reports from practitioners and managers.

Yet, beyond the transient focus of Western academics and journalists, interest in Japanese management practices has persisted unbroken. For one thing, many Western companies have adopted Japanese management practices, especially as regards production practices and quality-management systems. For managers faced with the practical challenge of sustaining competitiveness within the global trading environment, there have been plenty of occasions to study the background and philosophy of Japanese management.

Furthermore, since the Lehman shock, it has been painfully clear that Western management practices have their own limitations. Japanese management has therefore seen something of a resurgence among Western managers and researchers. The period since the financial crash of 2008 has seen a revival of interest in Japanese management, and the topic has returned to MBA curricula as the business world has sought answers and new inspiration.

About this book

The last decade spent researching management practices in Japan and working in various Japanese organizations has taught me just how little is really known about Japanese management practices in the West. Although managers, students, and researchers may have certain images about how a Japanese company is managed, these images are strongly influenced by stereotypes and myths. Yet, at the same time, there is a strong appetite to know more about how things really work.

This book aims to provide answers to questions about how Japanese management practices have developed and maybe changed over the past decades. It gives a comprehensive overview of modern Japanese management processes. It tries to answer two questions:

1 What do Japanese management practices really look like in the twenty-first century?
2 How have these practices changed over recent years and decades, especially since the recession of the 1990s?

Here, we aim to provide a comprehensive overview of Japanese management in the twentieth and twenty-first centuries, addressing, as far as we can, all aspects and activities of the Japanese corporation. In this attempt, it is the first book of its kind. The book presents 32 chapters on how Japanese management practices have changed over the past decades, and how they function today.

This book does not focus on management sciences alone, but can also be seen as a book in the social-science research tradition. It does not present specific research results comparing Western and Japanese management styles, but tries to offer an overview of current research in each of the major management disciplines. Neither does it touch on economic theories, but rather seeks to describe the processes at work inside Japanese corporations.

Each chapter describes the current state-of-the-art on a topic in Japanese management. This is the first text within the study of Japanese management which seeks to explain *all* the characteristic management practices of such firms. It aims to provide an overview of all the facets of Japanese management, and their current status. At the same time, it also seeks to reflect on the changes that Japanese companies have undergone in the past decade, and to discuss the impact of international economic policies on Japanese management practices.

All the contributors are experts in their respective fields and have many years' experience in researching their topics. They approach each management category from a descriptive perspective, trying to provide an overview at the same time as conveying specific insights. However, the chapters do not focus on presenting specific research results; rather, they are meant to answer all the questions that might arise when dealing with Japanese management.

With this book, we aim to provide interesting and well-researched reading materials for all people interested in modern Japanese management or working in a Japanese corporation. I envisage that the book will be read primarily by researchers and students in the field of international management and Japanese management, as well as in the field of Japanese studies. But, given the accessible nature of the chapters, I entertain hopes that a wider audience, such as interested members of the international business community, and managers working in Japan or for foreign investors in Japan, may also benefit from reading them.

The structure of this book

The first part of the book discusses the historical background of modern Japanese management. Japan had been a sophisticated and functioning market long before the emergence of its distinctive modern management practices. In Chapter 1, Sumiyo Ishii shows how this market functioned, and explains that Japanese corporations were using innovative management practices even before Western ideas and technologies were introduced.

In Chapter 2 on Japanese management after the Second World War, I describe how the Japanese economy recovered after the near-total destruction of the country. The chapter describes the restructuring processes undertaken in the 1950s and 1960s, and sets out which Japanese management practices supported this development.

The second part of the book deals with the structure of the Japanese corporation. In Chapter 3, Franz Waldenberger investigates the *keiretsu* structure, which is still very prominent in the Japanese economy today. He explains the difference between the vertical and horizontal *keiretsu*, sets out the historical background, and explains their relevance for the Japanese economy today.

Many Japanese companies are small- and medium-sized enterprises, and are family-owned. Some have been in business for many hundreds of years. In Chapter 4, Tim Goydke describes their unique features and the challenges that they face in the modern Japanese economy.

In June 2015, Japan introduced a new corporate governance code, which is one part of Shinzo Abe's restructuring programme. In Chapter 5, on corporate governance, Franz Waldenberger describes how Japanese companies are managed and how power is divided within them. He also explains the changes introduced by the new corporate governance code, which are expected to bring greater transparency to the management of Japanese companies in the near future.

In Chapter 6, Carsten Herbes provides an overview of the topic of mergers and acquisitions (M&A). He describes the peculiarities of Japanese M&A and how legal changes in recent years have influenced practices in this area.

The third part of the book investigates the environment in which Japanese companies operate.

Makoto Fujii provides a detailed overview of the Japanese tax system in Chapter 7, looking at corporate income tax, property tax, the consumption tax, and the personal income tax in Japan.

Corporate legislation is the topic of Chapter 8, written by Luke Nottage, Souichirou Kozuka, and Bruce Aronson. They provide an overview of the legal background to Japanese corporate governance and describe how Japanese corporate law is gradually showing more acceptance of the importance of the monitoring function and the monitoring model, even though the pace of development is much slower than in other economies.

Chapter 9 deals with the Japanese stock market. Here, Katsuhiko Okada describes how the Japanese stock market developed and functions. He also describes the ways in which it differs from stock market activities in other economies.

Entrepreneurship in Japan is the subject of Chapter 10. Here, I describe the current status of entrepreneurship and explain why the number of entrepreneurs in Japan is still very low. The number of innovative start-ups is much lower than in other industrialized nations; but, having long focused on companies in the manufacturing industry, the Japanese government has finally realized that young corporations and start-ups could have a positive effect on economic growth. It is currently trying to improve the situation by supporting young entrepreneurs in Japan.

In Chapter 11, Hiroshi Okano provides a description and explanation of Japanese accounting standards. He shows how Japanese accounting standards were developed to support classic Japanese management processes, such as just-in-time and total quality management, using a target-costing approach.

The fourth part of the book deals with the Japanese work environment, dwelling in particular on issues of human-resource processes and relationships within the Japanese firm. In Chapter 12, on Japanese labour law, Leon Wolff investigates the legal background to the institution of lifetime employment, showing that Japanese labour law provides strong protection to employees from being removed from the firm, but that they can be moved around within a company without their consent.

Philippe Debroux discusses Japanese recruitment processes in Chapter 13. He investigates the particular features of recruitment in Japan and explains how recruitment practices have changed over the past decades. He also describes how recruiting in Japan is influenced by global trends and suggests how Japanese companies should react to these changes.

Chapter 14 deals with promotion and compensation processes. Here, Harald Conrad shows how Japanese salaries are constructed and how changes in society and the workforce have forced companies to introduce more achievement-based elements within their compensation systems.

Chapter 15, on the company welfare benefit system, was also written by Harald Conrad and explains the traditional employee-benefit schemes which operate within Japanese firms. Companies also face pressures in this area, and have made dramatic changes in the area of employee-welfare benefits, particularly in the occupational pension field.

Chapter 16 discusses equality in the Japanese firm. Here, Philippe Debroux shows that the classic Japanese employment system favoured male employees in an attempt to support Japanese competitiveness and economic growth. He explains how this system has certain costs for society and the labour market, and describes the changes which would be needed to bring greater gender equality into the Japanese corporate workplace.

Japanese leadership is the topic of Chapter 17. Here, Carsten Herbes and Tim Goydke propose a definition of the concept of leadership as it appears in Japanese firms. They explain the relationship between leadership, company policies, and values in Japanese firms. In contrast to Western leaders, Japanese top managers are chosen for their ability to cooperate and coordinate, not for their aptitude to develop radical strategies and implement change within the organization.

In Chapter 18, Stephanie Assmann investigates the topic of diversity in the Japanese firm. She shows how legal steps to support women, foreign workers, workers with disabilities, and older workers in the Japanese corporation were taken a few decades ago, but still have not shown the expected effects.

In the fifth part we investigate the Japanese market and the distinctive marketing activities found within it.

Chapter 19 deals with Japanese consumer behaviour. Emi Moriuchi explains the particular features of Japanese consumer behaviour and attitudes, such as the preference for Japan-made goods, gift-giving, and luxury products.

In Chapter 20, Mariko Morimoto provides an overview of Japanese consumer rights. She shows how consumer groups have developed over recent decades and how consumer laws have been adapted to the growing demands of Japanese consumers.

Consumer and market research in Japan is the topic of Chapter 21, by Emi Moriuchi. She explains the challenges which non-Japanese people face when doing market research in Japan, and suggests how these can be overcome.

Yumiko Toda provides an overview of Japanese marketing in Chapter 22. She shows that Japanese marketing techniques developed early in the last century, and discusses the development of marketing management practices in the post-war period, from the mid-1950s until the 1980s. She also describes the rise of big retailers, and sets out the development of strategic alliances between manufacturers and retailers from the 1990s to the present day.

Chapter 23, by Kazuo Usui, shows how Japanese retail channels have developed over the past century. He explains the typical Japanese retail channels, such as convenience stores and department stores, and also discusses the recent rise of online retail channels.

The sixth part of the book deals with the most prominent Japanese management practices: production management and logistics.

In Chapter 24, Yacob Khojasteh discusses the key aspects of Japanese production and operations management. He shows which of the characteristic Japanese practices are most popular and how they are being implemented in the Japanese firm.

Chapter 25 looks at how subcontractors operate in the Japanese market. Here, Yacob Khojasteh and M. Reza Abdi show how the Japanese subcontractor supply-management system was a major factor in the success of Japanese manufacturers. They also elaborate on the development of Japanese supply chain management systems and the challenges that they faced after the great earthquake and tsunami of 2011.

In Chapter 26, Patrick Bessler shows how Japanese production has changed in past decades, and describes how Japanese manufacturing companies had to internationalize to stay competitive. The advantages and disadvantages of this phenomenon, called 'hollowing-out', are described.

Kaizen is another famous concept of Japanese management. It refers to the way in which the Japanese manufacturing firm organizes its production processes so as to gradually and steadily improve quality and speed, and decrease production costs. *Kaizen* has generated a great deal of interest among Western managers and researchers. In this chapter, Yacob Khojasteh explains the most important aspects of *kaizen*, and shows, in practical terms, how it is implemented in Japanese firms.

Japanese distribution channels have been considered a major hindrance for Western firms entering the market. Traditionally characterized by the existence of many intermediaries, these distribution channels lead to high product prices. Hendrik Meyer-Ohle describes the classic Japanese trading company and the various Japanese distribution and logistics channels. He explains how they have been affected by recent changes in the Japanese market and how they have adapted to modern market requirements.

The last part of the book deals with interaction and communication in the Japanese corporation.

In Chapter 29, I discuss how Japanese managers negotiate and come to conclusions within the corporation. Japanese negotiation and decision-making processes are strongly related to the sensitive communication style and group orientation which is a distinctive feature of Japanese teams and negotiators.

Another prominent management topic that has also been recognized worldwide is Japanese knowledge management. The creation, transfer, and usage of knowledge in the Japanese firm is discussed in Chapter 30. Here, I show that the corporate structure in Japan has a strong influence on how knowledge and information are communicated and managed. Tacit knowledge plays a more important role in this regard than it does in a Western company.

Strategic management is the topic of Chapter 31. Japanese companies traditionally show a strong orientation towards process. The strategies of Japanese corporations display certain features, such as focusing on relationships with other corporations or differentiating between absolute and relative strengths, which strongly distinguish them from their Western counterparts.

The book ends with a chapter on future topics that will be important for international researchers. This chapter, by Michaela Blahová, Přemysl Pálka, and myself, is the outcome of a joint research project with Sophia University undertaken in 2014. For this project, we interviewed Japanese managers and asked them what topics would be likely to become relevant for Japanese management over the next decade.

The Japanese business environment is currently in a stage of rapid flux; as such, this book can hope only to impart an impression of the status quo. Despite this, I hope that the book will not only provide a concise and comprehensive overview of the most relevant aspects of Japanese management, but that it will also answer many questions that managers and students of International Management may have about the topic.

Personally, I also hope that this book will help readers not only to learn about these very special management practices, but that it will inspire them to further exploration, and perhaps eventually even to implement the unique features of Japanese management in their own management and teaching practice.

Parissa Haghirian
Professor of International Management
Sophia University, Tokyo

Part I
Historical perspectives on Japanese management

1

The historical development of Japanese corporate management: 1603–1945

Sumiyo Ishii
(translated by Yoshitaka Yamamoto)

Introduction

The end of the Second World War in 1945 undoubtedly marked a dramatic turning point in Japanese economic and social history. The policies of the General Headquarters of the Allied Powers (GHQ) initially did not focus on Japan's economic recovery and development. Their urgent goal was to demilitarize and democratize Japan, as was the case for the Five Major Reform Directives that resulted in agricultural land reform; the dissolution of the *zaibatsu*; and the establishment of the trade-union law, labour-standards law, and labour-relations adjustment law. Although the GHQ's policies underwent subsequent changes, the initial directions that they took had a profound impact on Japan's post-war economic structure, and led to a number of modifications being made to the pre-war structure.

Nevertheless, more than a few aspects of the post-war Japanese economic system that are considered to have helped to increase the competitiveness of Japanese firms and made Japan's high economic growth possible were, in fact, inherited from the pre-war economic structure. The distinctive characteristics of the post-war Japanese economic system and corporate management, such as the separation of ownership and management; the prioritization of employee interests; the grouping of enterprises; lifetime employment; seniority-based wages; company-based labour unions; the 'main-bank system'; and the regulation of banks by the Bank of Japan and the Ministry of Finance, are all continuations, in one way or another, of the pre-war economic system. For this reason, in order to make sense of post-war Japanese corporate management, it is crucial to examine what came before.

To be sure, corporate management in pre-war Japan did not transition seamlessly into the post-war period. Yet, at the same time, the end of the war did not signal an absolute break with the past. The history of Japanese corporate management unfolded as a dynamic summation of contrary forces, with continuities and discontinuities taking place side by side. This chapter will examine the development of Japanese corporate management in the years from 1603 to 1945, with a focus on the aspects of pre-war corporate management that survived into the post-1945 period.[1]

The birth of corporate management: 17th century to early 19th century

The Edo period (1603–1868) saw the continuation of economic growth that had begun earlier in the sixteenth century. It must be noted, however, that the more-recent concepts of progress and economic development do not apply to the stationary social conditions in Japan before the Meiji period (1868–1912).[2] Nevertheless, stationary need not mean static. In Edo-period Japan, the rates of economic and population growth were higher than in any of the previous historical periods, and various elements of the socio-economic system that had not existed in medieval times, and were more modern in character, came into existence. This is the reason that this chapter begins with the Edo period.

One example of the new socio-economic developments of this period was the establishment of a class system that resulted in a division of labour and increased trade between farmers in rural areas, and warriors, artisans, and merchants living in castle towns. Another was the governance of provinces by *daimyō* (lords), which caused intra- and inter-provincial markets to form and systems of transportation and financial transactions to develop across Japan. In addition, the Tokugawa shogunate minted Japan's very first unified national currency, allowing the money economy to develop. As standards of education increased across all classes, the literacy and arithmetic skills of the ordinary people improved greatly.[3] Also during the Edo period, as Japan sought an alternative to the Sino-centric rule of East Asia, a Eurocentric worldview was becoming widely shared by the middle of the nineteenth century.[4] Subsequently, more and more Japanese people came to advocate emulating Western ways of bolstering national economic and military strength.

In the seventeenth century, the population grew dramatically as large swathes of land were cleared for cultivation and agricultural productivity soared. Even though the increase in population decreased the size of arable land per capita, a larger labour force resulted in higher productivity, leading to an 'industrious revolution'.[5] These developments in agriculture enabled cities to grow. In particular, the Three Cities (Edo, Kyoto, and Osaka) grew rapidly. Edo developed as the centre of governance and consumption, where *daimyō* on alternate-year residencies and their retainers spent a significant amount of time. Kyoto excelled in the handicraft manufacturing of high-quality silk textiles and other goods produced by highly skilled artisans. Osaka served as a major distribution centre for goods from all over Japan, and as a central node in the Japanese economy.[6]

The nationwide economic growth in the latter half of the seventeenth century provided merchants with big business opportunities. Wholesalers in Edo and Osaka who traded goods from all over Japan found ways to innovate by specializing in a certain type of goods and using their own funds to buy and sell goods. Echigoya (Mitsui) of Ise Province secured its position as one of the largest merchant houses in Japan by first operating a successful wholesale kimono-fabric shop in Edo and venturing into the money-exchanging sector in Edo, Kyoto, and Osaka.

There were also kimono-fabric dealers from Kyoto, such as Shirokiya, that opened new shops in Edo and operated them successfully. After opening new pharmacies, bookstores, and metallurgical shops for silver and bronze in Kyoto, Sumitomo, from Echizen Province, was appointed by the Tokugawa shogunate to oversee the management of metal mining, and also opened money-exchange shops in Edo and Osaka. Merchant houses from Osaka, including sake manufactures and rice wholesalers such as Kōnoike and Kajimaya, began to provide various financial services, including money transfer and financing for *daimyō*. The financial businesses that these merchant houses successfully operated presaged the growth of diversified companies and the expansion of the *zaibatsu* in the Meiji period and onwards.[7]

In the eighteenth century, as the production of agricultural commodities and handicrafts increased in regional areas, regional towns other than the Three Cities also began to prosper. The previously underdeveloped farming villages in the vicinity of Edo began to develop as well, turning Edo into a major distribution centre comparable to Osaka. In the latter half of the eighteenth century and the beginning of the nineteenth century, the volume of trade in Osaka decreased while the volume of trade in Edo and regional towns increased.

Large merchant houses of the Three Cities as well as regional merchants adapted to this shift. The merchant houses of Mitsui, Kōnoike, Daimaru, and Shirokiya, as well as the regional merchants of Ōmi and Ise Provinces, opened and operated regional branches in addition to their main shops in the Three Cities. They put into place a system of product and labour management and finance that was comprised of partly centralized and partly decentralized modes of operation, linking the main stores and the branches. As their businesses continue to expand and the number of employees soared, they set up internal rules for employees regarding hiring, posting, welfare, and retirement.[8]

Moreover, as shops grew larger in scale, the heads of merchant houses could no longer directly oversee their management, and began delegating their managerial roles to head clerks, resulting in the division of ownership and management. Strategic business decisions pertaining to products, finance, and labour management remained under the purview of house-wide rules and policies, however. What was delegated to head clerks consisted of day-to-day operational tasks, and as such, their decision-making power was limited. Also, since merchant houses were managed in the manner of an *ie* (household), a family-like group of tightly knit individuals, the head of a merchant house was also embedded within the larger framework of a going concern that was the *ie* business.[9] Not only the large merchant houses operated in this way, but smaller, regional businesses such as soy sauce manufactures in Noda and Chōshi (in present-day Chiba Prefecture) and the indigo sellers of Awa Province (present-day Kagawa Prefecture), as well as farming houses with large-scale operations, also practised similar forms of business management.[10]

Formation of the *zaibatsu* and entrepreneurial networks: mid-19th century

From the latter half of the eighteenth century and onwards, the Japanese economy grew less agrarian as the non-agricultural sectors increased their output. Then, in the mid-nineteenth century, the opening of ports to foreign trade sent the nationwide system of distribution into disarray, resulting in severe inflation. Amid such drastic changes in the Japanese economy, merchants developed new distribution routes encompassing the newly opened ports of Yokohama and Hyōgo, traded directly with foreign merchants, and brought in high profits through money exchange. On the other hand, many long-established merchant houses and a large number of businesses in the financial sector failed to adapt to the shifting tides in the economy and went into decline at the beginning of the Meiji period. Only a handful of powerful merchant houses, including Kōnoike, Mitsui, and Sumitomo, would weather the turbulent times, although they, too, almost collapsed. In the early years of the Meiji period, Iwasaki (Mitsubishi), who started a shipping business, Ōkura who sold firearms, and other new entrepreneurs operating out of Tokyo and other major cities became prominent players.[11]

From the beginning of the final years of the Edo period, the Tokugawa shogunate, the provinces, and the Meiji government implemented policies to import and develop Western forms of industry, including shipping, shipbuilding, steel, railways, and cotton spinning. The new Meiji government played an important role in adopting Western models and giving the Japanese economy a shape that was most amenable to 'modern' economic growth by reorganizing the paper currency, facilitating industrialization, and creating a more tightly integrated domestic market. Yet, until the turn of the twentieth century, the industrial sectors with the highest volume of production and number of workers were silk spinning, soy sauce production, and tea manufacturing, which were sectors that had already existed since the Edo period and carried on the technology of the earlier times.[12]

These already-existing sectors also benefited from technological advances in the Meiji period, however. The silk-spinning industry provides a telling example. The French- and Italian-style reeling machinery that the Japanese government introduced required large amounts of capital investment, which made them unaffordable for the private sector. Although capital was scarce, there was abundant labour in Japan. Accordingly, adaptations were made to the machinery, including the substitution of wood for the metallic parts in the reeling machines and using porcelain in place of copper pans for immersing the cocoons. Steam power was also substituted by hydropower, so that the overall equipment could be simplified. In addition, consortia were formed to carry out the finishing, packing, and shipping phases of production.[13] The private sector, and not just the government, willingly pushed for industrialization, in part because many considered it an important national objective to maintain Japan's independence by strengthening Japan's economic power and competing successfully with Europe and the United States.[14]

In the newly formed industrial sectors, private companies requiring large amounts of capital turned themselves into stock companies, while many others remained family enterprises. In the early years of the Meiji period, family enterprises tended to join hands with the government in order to acquire business opportunities and profits. Gradually, however, they began to weaken their ties with the government, and around the turn of the twentieth century, formed the *zaibatsu*.

There are various debates surrounding the definition of *zaibatsu*,[15] but the *zaibatsu* refers to a business conglomerate, in which:

1   the main company (a holding company) funded by a family has control over the subsidiaries;
2   business operations are diversified'; and which
3   maintains an oligopoly or monopoly in each industrial sector.

Mitsui and Sumitomo, which originated as large merchant houses in the Edo period, and Mitsubishi, Yasuda, Furukawa, Fujita, Ōkura, and Asano, which became successful after the final years of the Edo period, are the most well-known *zaibatsu*. *Zaibatsu* could be found not only in major cities such as Tokyo and Osaka, but all over Japan in regional locations such as Nagoya, Hanshin, and Kyūshū, and in various sectors such as coal, *sake*, soy sauce, cotton spinning, silk spinning, finance, and machinery.[16]

Meanwhile, in major cities and in regional towns, a number of wealthy landowners and business owners chose not to incorporate their own businesses as family enterprises, and instead, formed networks with other entrepreneurs and jointly founded and managed many companies, or jointly invested in multiple companies and served on their boards of directors. Such non-*zaibatsu* networks of entrepreneurs, sprouting up all across Japan in new as well as long-standing sectors in and after the 1880s, contributed to the nationwide growth of companies and of the Japanese economy.[17] Toward the end of the nineteenth century, these entrepreneurs led the way in establishing chambers of commerce and industry across Japan with the goal of further developing businesses and industries by amassing information, making policy recommendations, and mediating among businesses. Trade associations were also founded in the cotton-spinning and paper-manufacturing sectors.

When companies were just beginning to be founded, the largest stockholders often ran the businesses themselves, and there was no division between ownership and management. Large companies such as Mitsui and Mitsubishi, however, began to hire management specialists who were not owners themselves. Many of them were graduates of institutions of higher education such as Keiō Gijuku, Tokyo Commercial School, and the Imperial College of Engineering.[18] Also, although large merchant houses such as Mitsui had already devised their own systems of double-entry book-keeping by the mid-eighteenth century, other private companies also began to adopt double-entry book-keeping, as the Meiji government encouraged its use. Companies gradually came to put into place proper systems of corporate accounting in response to increases in fixed capital, particularly in the form of factory equipment, and as companies began to take depreciation into account as a tax-saving strategy.

Companies in the cotton- and silk-spinning industries competed fiercely for female factory workers. In the heavy industries, companies had to depend on older, skillful workmen for the recruitment of new hires, since the older workmen served as masters who hired young workmen to work for them and managed all aspects of technical training, as well as day-to-day life. Workmen in this period did not stay at the same company for long, frequently moving to a different company. During this period, there was scarcely any system of labour management in today's sense.

Growth of heavy and chemical industries and advances in labour management and technology: early 20th century

The First World War (1914–1918) gave Japan the opportunity to become one of the 'Five Great Powers', and the Japanese began to see themselves as members of a 'first-class' nation.[19] The war also brought significant changes to the Japanese domestic economy.

The textiles industry played a major role in the early years of industrialization in Japan in the 1890s. Within the textiles industry, the newly established cotton spinning sector was the leading sector. After the Second World War broke out, however, demand in the munitions sector increased as imports of heavy and chemical industrial products came to a halt, and, as a result, the heavy and chemical industries began to expand rapidly in the 1920s, now becoming the top players in Japan's economic development. On the flipside, the post-war recession lasted for almost ten years. These changes in Japan's industrial structure and the business climate affected the sizes of Japanese companies, as well as their corporate structures.

The economic downturn prodded mergers and consolidations of companies in cotton spinning, paper manufacturing, mining, and banking, leading to formations of larger companies. These large-sized companies sought to maintain their monopolistic positions in the market by streamlining their own business operations. They also sought to streamline their own industries as a whole by forming cartels, with the goal of preventing companies from competing for workers, jointly buying and shipping raw materials, increasing product sales, raising funds under favourable conditions, and collecting and disseminating information.

The recession also widened the gap between the successful *zaibatsu* and the not so successful ones, which resulted in the four *zaibatsu* of Mitsui, Mitsubishi, Yasuda, and Sumitomo dominating the market.[20] Strategic decisions regarding the diversification of business operations that had been made during the wartime boom largely determined the fate of each *zaibatsu*. As the banking businesses of Furukawa and Asano were operating on a relatively small scale, these banks lost the trust of their depositors as the recession hit, causing a significant portion of the deposits to be withdrawn. On top of that, lending stagnated due to their subsidiaries floundering or failing. In the end, the banking businesses of Furukawa and Asano collapsed. Subsequently, the government beefed up its monitoring of banks, including non-*zaibatsu* banks, and induced the consolidations of small and medium-sized banks, eventually leading to the emergence of the so-called 'convoy system' in 1927 amidst the Showa Financial Collapse. *Zaibatsu* trading companies such as Suzuki Shōten, Furukawa Shōji, and Kuhara Shōji that expanded their businesses during the wartime boom plunged into the red as their speculative ventures failed when the recession hit. The end of the First World War saw the collapse of economic bubbles in the shipping, shipbuilding, and steel industries, which negatively affected the *zaibatsu* that had expanded into these industries.[21]

On the other hand, in 1909, Mitsui, one for the four major *zaibatsu*, established by Mitsui Gōmei Kaisha, a main holding company funded entirely by the Mitsui *zaibatsu* family. Its banking, general trading, and mining businesses, which had previously been under direct management, were now reorganized as separate limited liability companies, whose stocks were owned exclusively by the holding company. The holding company also exercised comprehensive control over these companies. This was how the *Konzern* (combine) system came to be formed. Under this system, the *zaibatsu* family owned a majority of the main company's stock, and the main company owned the stock of its direct subsidiaries, which in turn owned the stock of their subsidiaries. This type of *zaibatsu* thus had a pyramidal structure. Other *zaibatsu* followed Mitsui's example in setting up holding companies and adopting the *Konzern* system, strategically seeking to save on taxes; to use the ownership of stock as collateral when taking out loans; and also to increase the number of executive positions.[22] Even while most companies and the general public suffered from the recession, the *zaibatsu* companies with abundant capital continued to remain powerful, inviting criticisms and eventually prodding the government to place certain restrictions on their activities.

The growth of the heavy and chemical industries gave rise to new corporate entities. Although the iron, shipbuilding, and machinery sectors led the heavy and chemical industries in the 1910s, they suffered the blow of the recession. In the 1920s, new sectors such as electrical machinery, electric cable, synthetic ammonium sulphate, rayon, rubber, and automobiles came to constitute important parts of the heavy and chemical industries. The main players in these sectors included companies like Nihon Sangyō (Nissan), Nihon Chisso Hiryō (Nitchitsu), Nihon Sōda (Nissō), which newly formed *zaibatsu* in the 1930s. The new *zaibatsu* of the 1930s, in contrast to the existing *zaibatsu*, generally did not have a holding company, and instead collected funds by going public or taking out bank loans. They also strengthened ties with the Japanese military, which looked unfavourably at the existing *zaibatsu*, and actively expanded their businesses to the Japanese colonies.[23]

The early twentieth century also saw a number of foreign heavy and chemical industrial firms, including Dunlop of Britain and Ford of the United States, expand their businesses to Japan. Some Japanese companies partnered up with foreign manufacturers through capital or technological tie-ups and increased their competitiveness. Yet the Japanese government and private companies also learned from their experiences during the First World War, when foreign technology was no longer readily available, that they needed to develop their own technology domestically. The Japanese government established research institutes such as the Institute of Physical and Chemical Research and the Institute of Aeronautical Research where fundamental research was conducted, and companies in the private sector increasingly hired university-educated engineers. Researchers, as well as research institutions, also partook in business ventures. One such example was the establishment of the Toyoda Automatic Loom Works after the shuttle change automatic loom was invented.[24]

As companies grew larger and their levels of activity soared during and after the First World War, companies changed how they hired employees and workmen. As companies increased in size and their organizations became more complex, the demand for management specialists rose higher. Such specialists were often graduates of institutions of higher education, and were hired in great numbers.[25] A seniority-based system of promotion was also put in place, which enabled larger numbers of highly educated employees to work their way up to top management. Because of this, companies that adopted the *Konzern* (combine) system sought to increase the number of executive positions.

On the other hand, due to changes in technology and also due to labour movements, there was a serious shortage of skilled workmen. Large companies countered this trend by improving their systems of labour management. They abolished the long-standing system in which older workmen hired and managed younger workmen, and, instead, hired and managed all workers directly. They also began to train workmen to acquire skills that were most useful to the types of technology and the system of production that the companies had put in place. Consequently, new graduates came to be hired at regular intervals, and lifetime employment became the norm. Also, promotions and regular salary raises based on seniority, i.e. the number of years in continuous service, were institutionalized. In addition, companies began to provide severance and retirement payments and other forms of welfare, and labour relations and factory committees were formed.[26] It became normal for employees and workmen of larger companies to be continually employed by the same company for an extended period of time.

Company managers often upheld the notion that a company ought to be run like a household-like collective unit. Managers, acting in the capacity of parents or the head of a family, would find benevolent ways to look to the needs of their employees, while employees, in turn, would be expected to return the favor by contributing wholeheartedly to the life and growth of their company. Companies such as Kanegafuchi Bōseki (Kanebō), Ōji Seishi (Ōji Paper), and Kokuyūtetsudō (the National Railway) that grew in size through mergers and consolidations at the beginning of the twentieth century articulated these values with the hope of uniting the disparate parts of their companies, and other companies followed suit.[27] Companies also adopted systematic methods of management, such as Frederick Winslow Taylor's 'scientific management'.

At the same time, gaps in the rate of growth, productivity, and wages widened between agricultural and industrial sectors, as well as between large and smaller companies. A 'double' dual economic structure thus took shape in the early twentieth century.

Wartime production, labour, and technology: mid-20th century

In 1930, Japan plunged into the so-called Showa Depression. To alleviate the negative effects of recession, the Japanese government led the way in reorganizing existing cartels in order to strengthen them, and also in forming new cartels in a variety of industrial sectors such as iron, energy, coal, and electrical machinery. In addition, large companies in spinning, paper manufacturing, banking, iron, and sugar sectors underwent large-scale consolidations and mergers.[28] In the *zaibatsu*, the major subsidiaries that had grown larger in size increased their autonomy, leading to decentralization. The first half of the 1930s also saw the rapid growth of newly formed *zaibatsu*, and Nissan became the third largest *zaibatsu* after Mitsui and Mitsubishi.

In the mid-1930s as Japan entered war, *zaibatsu* subsidiaries grew in number and came to make up a larger fraction of the Japanese economy.[29] *Zaibatsu* industrial companies such as Mitsubishi Heavy Industries and Sumitomo Heavy Industries cooperated with Japan's national policy of amassing military strength by manufacturing naval vessels and aircraft. During the Pacific War (1941–1945), as access to European markets was cut off and with tighter regulations in Japan, general trading companies such as Mitsui Bussan and Mitsubishi Shōji shifted their focus to the Chinese mainland and the Japanese occupied areas in Southeast Asia and the Pacific, and supplied the raw materials and equipment industrial companies needed, thus playing an important role in supporting the business activities of *zaibatsu* companies. New *zaibatsu*, on the other hand, suffered from the increased difficulty in acquiring raw materials and competitions with the long-established *zaibatsu*.

During wartime, *zaibatsu* companies raised funds primarily by borrowing from the financial institutions within their own *zaibatsu*. As a result, equity ratios of *zaibatsu* companies plummeted, and lending was now centred around the large *zaibatsu* banks, instead of the holding companies as was the case previously. Munitions companies developed strong ties with the banks, which were subsequently institutionalized in 1944 by the Designated Financial Institution System for Munitions. The *zaibatsu* banks financing other companies of the same *zaibatsu* became the prototype for the post-war main bank system.

Also, as the Japanese wartime economy shifted from a market economy to a planned economy, the Japanese government introduced a system through which company managers could freely decide to increase production without being held in check by stockholders. In the meantime, companies underwent further consolidations and reorganizations. Light industries were forced to downsize or close down, while, in the heavy and chemical industries, subcontractual relationships between large and smaller companies were further strengthened. The spread of subcontractual relationships in this period laid the foundation for the emergence of the post-war subcontractual system.[30]

In the first half of the 1930s, company-trained workers generally continued to work for the same company, and the worker turnover rate remained low at large companies. As the economy improved and the gap in compensation between full-time and temporary workers widened, the full-time workers' allegiance to their companies grew stronger. Not all full-time workers received equal treatment, however, as there was a clear wage gap among the employees, with office workers earning up to six times as much as factory workers in some cases. As the labour market faced increasingly difficult conditions as the war wore on, and companies competed for scarce labour, the turnover rate of workers soared. In order to counter this situation, regulations for bringing labour and wages under control were implemented, leading to tighter measures for the posting of workers and wage levels. These measures led companies to bolster the system of promotions even further.

Factory committees became prevalent in the 1930s, and, during wartime, they became part of the industrial mobilization movement, which called on capital and labour to cooperate in order to serve the state. They were subsequently merged with the Association of Industrial Mobilization, the central organization of this movement. The ability of factory committees to mediate in labour-management issues declined, and instead, their primary role became the mobilization of materials and workers in service of the state. Yet, at the same time, the industrial mobilization movement saw workers as important contributors to the state alongside managers, and thus sought to elevate their social standing.[31]

Companies streamlined their management structures further, and business administration greatly improved as the idea of 'scientific management' came to be widely shared across many industries. The use of cost conversion analysis and the introduction of the 'forwarding' (*zenshin*) method of assembly-line operation, whereby the machinery being assembled passed through each process within a fixed amount of time, were both examples of the rationalization of corporate management and operations.[32] The government and the private sector, primarily the munitions sector, jointly carried out research and development to devise and put into practice such improvements. As war halted the imports of foreign equipment, machinery, and technology into Japan, new and existing domestic research institutes rapidly expanded their activities, and significantly larger numbers of university and occupational school graduates in science and technology were hired.

Nevertheless, under wartime governmental control of the economy, advancements in product and labour management and technology were limited in scope, owing to the scarcity of raw materials; larger numbers of unskilled workers; and requests from the military for changes in product design, among other factors. At the same time, however, the knowledge and expertise in product and labour management, as well as design and manufacturing technology, along with the managers, workers, and engineers who had gained them, were passed on to the post-war period.

Notes

1 Unless otherwise noted, this chapter draws on the following sources: Shigeaki et al. (eds), *Nihon Keieishi*, Vols 1–4 (Iwanami Shoten, 1995); Nishikawa et al. (eds), *Nihon Keizai no Nihyaku-nen* (Nihon Hyōronsha, 1996); Ishii et al. (eds), *Nihon Keizaishi*, Vols 1–4 (University of Tokyo Press, 2000–2007); Ōta et al., *Nihon Keizai no Nisen-nen* (Keisō Shobō, 2006, revised edition); Miyamoto et al., *Nihon Keieishi: Nihon-gata Kigyō Keiei no Hatten, Edo kara Heisei e* (Yūhikaku, 1998); Miyamoto et al. (eds), *Kōza Nihon Keieishi*, Vols 1–4 (Minerva Shobō, 2009–2011); Sugiyama, *Nihon Keizaishi: Kinsei-Kindai* (Iwanami Shoten, 2012).
2 Hayami et al. (eds), *Nihon Keizaishi 1: Keizai Shakai no Seiritsu* (Iwanami Shoten, 1988), p. 44.
3 Dore, R. P. (Matsui, Hiromichi, trans.), *Edo Jidai no Kyōiku* (Iwanami Shoten, 1970), 1–27. [Original text: Dore, R. P. *Education in Tokugawa Japan* (London: Routledge and Kegan Paul, 1965).]
4 Satō, Hirō (ed.), *Gaisetsu Nihon Shisōshi* (Minerva Shobō, 2007), pp. 203–207.
5 Hayami et al. (eds) (1988), pp. 36–37.
6 Saitō, Osamu, *Edo to Ōsaka: Kindai Nihon no Toshi Kigen* (NTT Shuppan, 2002), pp. 28–37.
7 Ishii, Kanji, *Keizai Hatten to Ryōgaeshō Kinyū* (Yūhikaku, 2007), pp. 232–233.
8 Miyamoto et al., *Nihon Keieishi: Nihon-gata Kigyō Keiei no Hatten, Edo kara Heisei e* (Yūhikaku, 1998), pp. 53–74.
9 Sakane, Yoshihiro, *Nihon Dentō Shakai to Keizai Hatten: Ie to Mura* (Nōsan Gyoson Bunka Kyōkai, 2011), pp. 187–191.
10 Irie, Hiroshi, *Kinsei Shomin Kakun no Kenkyū: 'Ie' no Keiei to Kyōiku* (Taga Shuppan, 1996), pp. 353–364.
11 Miyamoto, Matao, *Nihon no Kindai 11: Kigyōka-tachi no Chōsen* (Chūō Kōronsha, 1999), pp. 48–79.
12 Nakamura, Takafusa, *Meiji Taishō-ki no Keizai* (University of Tokyo Press, 1985), pp. 177–185.
13 Miyamoto et al. (Yūhikaku, 1998), pp. 112–113.
14 Kawaguchi, Hiroshi, 'Joshō: Nihon no Keizai Shisō Sekai'. In: Kawaguchi, Hiroshi (ed.), *Nihon no Keizai Shisō Sekai: 'Jūkyū-seiki' no Kigyōsha, Seisakusha, Chishikijin* (Nihon Keizai Hyōronsha, 2004), pp. 16–21. Kinmonth, E. H. (Hirota Teruyuki, trans.), *Risshin Shusse no Shakaishi: Samurai kara Sararīman e* (Tamagawa University Press, 1995), pp. 73–76. [Original text: Kinmonth, H. E., *The Self-Made Man in Meiji Japanese Thought: From Samurai to Salary Man* (University of California Press, 1981).]
15 Regarding questions such as whether the *zaibatsu* is oligopolistic or monopolistic and the influence of main companies on subsidiaries, Shigeaki Yasuoka, Hiroshi Matsumoto, Kanji Ishii, and Haruhito Takeda have expressed views that differ from those of Hidemasa Morikawa, Takeo Kikkawa, Jurō Hashimoto, and Tetsuji Okazaki.
16 Shibutani, Ryūichi, Katō, Ryū, and Okada, Kazunobu (eds), *Chihō Zaibatsu no Tenkai to Ginkō* (Nihon Hyōronsha, 1989), pp. 10–38.
17 On entrepreneurial networks of this period, see: Tanimoto, Masayuki, Dōki to shiteno 'Chiiki Shakai': Nihon ni okeru 'Chiiki Kōgyōka' to Tōshi Katsudō. In: Shinozuka, Nobuyoshi, Ishizaka, Akio, and Takahashi, Hideyuki (eds), *Chiiki Kōgyōka no Hikakushiteki Kenkyū* (Hokkaido University Press, 2003). Teranishi, Jūrō, *Nihon no Keizai Hatten to Kinyū* (Iwanami Shoten, 2004). Ishii, Kanji and Nakanishi, Satoru (eds), *Sangyō-ka to Shōka Keiei: Beikoku Hiryōshō Hiromi-ke no Kinsei, Kindai* (Nagoya University Press, 2006). Suzuki, Tsuneo, Kobayakawa, Yōichi, and Wada, Kazuo, *Kigyōka Nettowāku no Keisei to Tenkai: Dētabēsu kara Mita Kindai Nihon no Chiiki Keizai* (Nagoya University Press, 2009). Nakanishi Satoru, *Umi no Fugō no Shihon Shugi: Kitamaebune to Nihon no Sangyōka* (Nagoya University Press, 2009).

Sumiyo Ishii

18 Amano, Ikuo, *Gakureki no Shakaishi: Kyōiku to Nihon no Kindai* (Shinchōsha, 1992), pp. 256–257. Kawaguchi *et al.* (Keisōshobō, 2015), *Nihon Keizai Shisōshi: Edo kara Showa*, pp. 198–206.
19 Kawaguchi, Hiroshi, *Joshō: Nihon no Keizai Shisō Sekai* (Nihon Keizai Hyōronsha, 2004), pp. 21–24.
20 Takeda Haruhito, *Zaibatsu no Jidai: Nihongata Kigyō no Genryū Saguru* (Shinyōsha, 1995), pp. 197–219.
21 Miyamoto *et al.* (Yūhikaku, 1998), pp. 163–164.
22 On the four major *zaibatsu*, see: Matsumoto, Hiroshi, *Mitsui Zaibatsu no Kenkyū* (Yoshikawa Kōbunkan, 1979). Mishima Yasuo (ed.), *Nihon Zaibatsu Keieishi: Mitsubishi Zaibatsu* (Nihon Keizai Shimbunsha, 1981). Sakudō, Yōtarō (ed.), *Nihon Zaibatsu Keieishi: Sumitomo Zaibatsu* (Nihon Keizai Shimbunsha, 1982). Kikkawa Takeo, *Nihon no Kigyō Shūdan: Zaibatsu tono Renzoku to Danzetsu* (Yūhikaku, 1996). Yasuoka, Shigeaki, *Zaibatsu no Keieishi* (Shakai Shisōsha, 1990).
23 On the new *zaibatsu*, see: Udagawa, Masaru (ed.), *Nihon Zaibatsu Keieishi: Shinkō Zaibatsu* (Nihon Keizai Shimbunsha, 1984). Saitō, Satoshi, *Shinkō Kontserun Riken no Kenkyū* (Jichōsha, 1987).
24 On technological partnerships between Japanese and foreign companies, and technological research and development in Japan, see: Minami, Ryōshin and Kiyokawa, Yukihiko (eds), *Nihon no Kōgyōka to Gijutsu Hatten* (Tōyō Keizai Shinpōsha, 1987). Chokki Toshiaki, *Nihon no Kigyō Keiei: Rekishiteki Kōsatsu* (Hōsei University Press, 1992).
25 On the hiring of new graduates in the context of corporate management, see: Morikawa, Hidemasa, *Nihon Keieishi* (Nihon Keizai Shimbunsha, 1981); Morikawa, Hidemasa, *Keieisha Kigyō no Jidai* (Yūhikaku, 1991).
26 Hazama, Hiroshi, *Nihonteki Keiei no Keifu* (Bunshindō, 1989), p. 116.
27 On discussions and debates surrounding the so-called 'keiei kazoku shugi' (translated as 'managerial paternalism', or more literally, 'family-like corporate management'), see: Enoki, Kazue, Kindai nihon no keiei patānarizumu. *Ōhara Shakai Mondai Kenkyūjo Zasshi,* Vols 611–612, September and October 2009, pp. 29–39.
28 On the strengthening of cartels and consolidations of companies, see: Okazaki Tetsuji, Kigyō shisutemu. In: Okazaki, Tetsuji and Okuno, Masahiro (eds), *Gendai Nihon Keizai Shisutemu no Genryū* (Nihon Keizai Shimbunsha, 1993). Miyajima, Hideaki, Sangyō gōrika to jūyō sangyō tōseihō. In: Kindai Nihon Kenkyūkai (ed.), *Nenpō Kindai Nihon Kenkyū,* Vol. 6 (Yamakawa Shuppansha, 1984).
29 On an in-depth analysis of the *zaibatsu* in the 1930s, see: Hashimoto Jurō, Zaibatsu no Kontserunka. In: Hōsei Daigaku Sangyō Jōhō Sentā, Hashimoto Jurō, and Takeda Haruhito (eds), *Nihon Keizai no Hatten to Kigyō Shūdan* (University of Tokyo Press, 1992).
30 Ueda Hirofumi, *Senjiki Nihon no Shitauke Kōgyō: Chūshō Kigyō to 'Shitauke=Kyōryoku Kōgyō Seisaku'* (Minerva Shobō, 2004).
31 On the industrial mobilization movement, see: Saguchi, Kazurō, *Nihon ni okeru Sangyō Minshu Shugi no Zentei* (University of Tokyo Press, 1991). Ōkado, Masakatsu, *Kindai Nihon to Nōson Shakai* (Nihon Keizai Hyōronsha, 1994).
32 Yamamoto, Kiyoshi, *Nihon ni okeru Shokuba no Gijutsu Rōdōshi: 1854–1990-nen* (University of Tokyo Press, 1994), pp. 252–253, 260–265.

References

Amano, Ikuo (1992). *Gakureki no Shakaishi: Kyōiku to Nihon no Kindai*, pp. 256–257. Tokyo: Shinchōsha.
Chokki, Toshiaki (1992). *Nihon no Kigyō Keiei: Rekishiteki Kōsatsu*. Hōsei University Press.
Dore, R. P. (Matsui, Hiromichi, trans.) (1970). *Edo Jidai no Kyōiku*, pp. 1–27. Iwanami Shoten. (Original text: Dore, R. P. (1965). *Education in Tokugawa Japan*. London: Routledge and Kegan Paul).
Enoki, Kazue (2009). Kindai nihon no keiei patānarizumu. *Ōhara Shakai Mondai Kenkyūjo Zasshi*, Vols 611–612, September and October 2009, pp. 29–39.
Hashimoto, Jurō, (1992). Zaibatsu no kontserunka. In: Hōsei Daigaku Sangyō Jōhō Sentā, Hashimoto, Jurō, and Takeda, Haruhito (eds), *Nihon Keizai no Hatten to Kigyō Shūdan*. Tokyo: University of Tokyo Press.
Hayami, Akira and Miyamoto, Matao (eds) (1988). *Nihon Keizaishi 1: Keizai Shakai no Seiritsu*, pp. 36–37, 44, Iwanami Shoten.
Hazama, Hiroshi (1989). *Nihonteki Keiei no Keifu*, Tokyo: Bunshindō, p. 116.
Irie, Hiroshi (1996). *Kinsei Shomin Kakun no Kenkyū: 'Ie' no Keiei to Kyōiku*, pp. 353–364, Tokyo: Taga Shuppan.
Ishii, Kanji (2007). *Keizai Hatten to Ryōgaeshō Kinyū*, pp. 232–233. Tokyo: Yūhikaku.

18

Ishii, Kanji, Hara, Akira, and Takeda, Haruhito (eds) (2000–2007). *Nihon Keizaishi*, Vols 1–4. Tokyo: University of Tokyo Press.

Ishii, Kanji and Nakanishi, Satoru (eds) (2006). *Sangyō-ka to Shōka Keiei: Beikoku Hiryōshō Hiromi-ke no Kinsei, Kindai*. Nagoya: Nagoya University Press.

Kawaguchi, Hiroshi (2004). Joshō: Nihon no Keizai Shisō Sekai. In: Kawaguchi, Hiroshi (ed.), *Nihon no Keizai Shisō Sekai: 'Jūkyū-seiki' no Kigyōsha, Seisakusha, Chishikijin*. Nihon Keizai Hyōronsha, pp. 16–21, 21–24.

Kawaguchi, Hiroshi, Ishii, Sumiyo, Gramlich-Oka, Bettina, and Liu, Qunyi (2015). *Nihon Keizai Shisōshi: Edo kara Showa*. Tokyo: Keisōshobō, pp. 198–206.

Kikkawa, Takeo (1996). *Nihon no Kigyō Shūdan: Zaibatsu tono Renzoku to Danzetsu*. Tokyo: Yūhikaku.

Kinmonth, E. H. (Hirota Teruyuki, trans.) (1995). *Risshin Shusse no Shakaishi: Samurai kara Sararīman e*, pp. 73–76. Tamagawa University Press. (Original text: Kinmonth, E. H. (1981). *The Self-Made Man in Meiji Japanese Thought: From Samurai to Salary Man*. University of California Press.

Matsumoto, Hiroshi (1979). *Mitsui Zaibatsu no Kenkyū*. Yoshikawa Kōbunkan.

Minami, Ryōshin and Kiyokawa, Yukihiko (eds) (1987). *Nihon no Kōgyōka to Gijutsu Hatten*. Tokyo: Tōyō Keizai Shinpōsha.

Mishima, Yasuo (ed.) (1981). *Nihon Zaibatsu Keieishi: Mitsubishi Zaibatsu*. Tokyo: Nihon Keizai Shimbunsha.

Miyajima, Hideaki (1984). Sangyō Gōrika to Jūyō Sangyō Tōseihō. In: Kindai Nihon Kenkyūkai (ed.), *Nenpō Kindai Nihon Kenkyū*, Vol. 6. Tokyo: Yamakawa Shuppansha.

Miyamoto, Matao (1999). *Nihon no Kindai 11: Kigyōka-tachi no Chōsen*. Tokyo: Chūō Kōronsha, pp. 48–79,

Miyamoto, Matao, Abe, Takeshi, Udagawa, Masaru, Sawai, Minoru, and Kikkawa, Takeo (1998). *Nihon Keieishi: Nihon-gata Kigyō Keiei no Hatten, Edo kara Heisei e*, pp. 53–74, 112–113, 163–164. Tokyo: Yūhikaku.

Miyamoto, Matao, Kasuya, Makoto, Abe, Takeshi, Nakamura, Naofumi, Sasaki, Satoshi, Nakabayashi, Masaki, Shiba, Takao, and Okazaki, Tetsuji (eds) (2009–2011). *Kōza Nihon Keieishi*, Vols 1–4. Kyoto: Minerva Shobō.

Morikawa, Hidemasa (1981). *Nihon Keieishi*. Tokyo: Nihon Keizai Shimbunsha.

Morikawa, Hidemasa (1991). *Keieisha Kigyō no Jidai*. Tokyo: Yūhikaku.

Nakamura, Takafusa (1985). *Meiji Taishō-ki no Keizai*, pp. 177–185. Tokyo: University of Tokyo Press.

Nakanishi, Satoru (2009). *Umi no Fugō no Shihon Shugi: Kitamaebune to Nihon no Sangyōka*. Nagoya: Nagoya University Press.

Nishikawa, Shunsaku, Odaka, Kōnosuke, and Saitō, Osamu (eds) (1996). *Nihon Keizai no Nihyaku-nen*. Tokyo: Nihon Hyōronsha.

Ōkado, Masakatsu (1994). *Kindai Nihon to Nōson Shakai*. Tokyo: Nihon Keizai Hyōronsha.

Okazaki, Tetsuji (1993). Kigyō Shisutemu. In: Okazaki Tetsuji and Okuno Masahiro (eds), *Gendai Nihon Keizai Shisutemu no Genryū*. Tokyo: Nihon Keizai Shimbunsha.

Ōta, Yoshiyuki, Kawaguchi, Hiroshi, and Fujii, Nobuyuki (2006, revised edition). *Nihon Keizai no Nisen-nen*. Tokyo: Keisō Shobō.

Saguchi, Kazurō (1991). *Nihon ni okeru Sangyō Minshu Shugi no Zentei*. Tokyo: University of Tokyo Press.

Saitō, Osamu (2002). *Edo to Ōsaka: Kindai Nihon no Toshi Kigen*, pp. 28–37. NTT Shuppan.

Saitō, Satoshi (1987). *Shinkō Kontserun Riken no Kenkyū*. Tokyo: Jichōsha.

Sakane, Yoshihiro (2011). *Nihon Dentō Shakai to Keizai Hatten: Ie to Mura*, pp.187–191. Tokyo: Nōsan Gyoson Bunka Kyōkai.

Sakudō, Yōtarō (ed.) (1982). *Nihon Zaibatsu Keieishi: Sumitomo Zaibatsu*. Nihon Keizai Shimbunsha.

Satō, Hirō (ed.) (2007). *Gaisetsu Nihon Shisōshi*. Kyoto: Minerva Shobō, pp. 203–207.

Shibutani, Ryūichi, Katō, Ryū, and Okada, Kazunobu (eds) (1989). *Chihō Zaibatsu no Tenkai to Ginkō*. Tokyo: Nihon Hyōronsha, pp. 10–38

Sugiyama, Shinya (2012). *Nihon Keizaishi: Kinsei-Kindai*. Tokyo: Iwanami Shoten.

Suzuki, Tsuneo, Kobayakawa, Yōichi, and Wada, Kazuo (2009). *Kigyōka Nettowāku no Keisei to Tenkai: Dētabēsu kara Mita Kindai Nihon no Chiiki Keizai*. Nagoya: Nagoya University Press.

Takeda, Haruhito (1995). *Zaibatsu no Jidai: Nihongata Kigyō no Genryū wo Saguru*. Tokyo: Shinyōsha, pp. 197–219.

Tanimoto, Masayuki (2003). 'Dōki to shiteno 'Chiiki Shakai': Nihon ni okeru 'Chiiki Kōgyōka' to Tōshi Katsudō' in Shinozuka Nobuyoshi, Ishizaka Akio, and Takahashi Hideyuki (eds), *Chiiki Kōgyōka no Hikakushiteki Kenkyū*. Sapporo: Hokkaidō University Press.

Teranishi Jūrō (2004). *Nihon no Keizai Hatten to Kinyū*. Tokyo: Iwanami Shoten.

Udagawa, Masaru (ed.) (1984). *Nihon Zaibatsu Keieishi: Shinkō Zaibatsu*. Tokyo: Nihon Keizai Shimbunsha.

Ueda, Hirofumi (2004). *Senjiki Nihon no Shitauke Kōgyō: Chūshō Kigyō to 'Shitauke=Kyōryoku Kōgyō Seisaku'*. Kyoto: Minerva Shobō.

Yamamoto, Kiyoshi (1994). *Nihon ni okeru Shokuba no Gijutu Rōdōshi: 1854–1990-nen*, pp. 252–253, 260–265. Tokyo: University of Tokyo Press.

Yasuoka, Shigeaki (1990). *Zaibatsu no Keieishi*. Tokyo: Shakai Shisōsha.

Yasuoka, Shigeaki, Amano, Masatoshi, Miyamoto, Matao, Abe, Takeshi, Yui, Tsunehiko, Daitō, Eisuke, Yamazaki, Hiroaki, and Kikkawa, Takeo (eds) (1995). *Nihon Keieishi*, Vols 1–4. Tokyo: Iwanami Shoten.

2
Japanese management in the twentieth century

Parissa Haghirian

Introduction

Japan's economic success and rapid development is a unique phenomenon. As early as the Edo period (1603–1868), when the Japanese nation was still mostly isolated from the rest of the world, the Japanese people had a well-developed and independent internal market. Japanese corporations had developed distinctive and innovative marketing activities; traded products all over the country; and had a sophisticated monetary system.

After the Meiji Restoration, Japan was quick to embrace Western technology, and initiated a rapid process of industrialization. At this time, major corporations developed, and Japan began to engage in international trade. By the Second World War, Japan had developed into an industrial nation that had to import its raw materials from overseas. The dependency on these imports led to an aggressive policy during the Second World War, as Japan invaded a number of neighbouring countries to secure its access to their resources.

After the defeat in 1945, the country was devastated, but economic reconstruction quickly gathered pace after the start of the Korean War. A phase of long economic booms and high growth rates followed. Although the oil shock of the 1970s interrupted this process, by the beginning of the 1980s, Japan was already on a par with Western industrialized economies. The rapid development of the Japanese economy was supported by a set of characteristic management practices underpinned by economic policies that the government implemented very early on.

The collapse of the so-called bubble economy, which was followed by a long recession, put an end to this development process. The recession saw the start of massive restructuring programmes, both in the economy at large, and within the corporations themselves; as a result, the corporate landscape today is markedly different from what existed even two decades ago.

Today, at the beginning of the twenty-first century, Japan has been trying to keep pace with globalization and maintain its supremacy in Asia. These efforts were rudely interrupted by the massive earthquake in March 2011 and the problems at the nuclear power plant in Fukushima. It was only in January 2013, at the beginning of Prime Minister Shinzo Abe's second term of office, that hope seemed to be re-emerging. Abe presented a comprehensive restructuring plan, but there remains strong political awareness that the problems of the Japanese economy and its companies are founded on structural challenges such as the declining workforce, outdated management structures, and increasing competition on international markets.

This chapter describes the history of Japan's phenomenal economic success after the Second World War, describing how Japanese corporations developed their own management styles, leading to a corporate success story which is unprecedented in history.

Resurrection after the Second World War

As the Second World War came to an end, Japanese corporations faced numerous challenges. After their victory in 1945, the Occupation Authorities implemented a number of changes to Japan's corporate governance structures, as well as in the legal foundations of Japanese firms (Okazaki 1999). The political system was restructured; the traditional structure of the *zaibatsu* was dissolved; and the American forces imposed rationing, controlled Japan's international trade, and implemented land reforms (Smitka 1998). Another major change was the enactment of the Labor Union Law in 1945, which allowed unions to be formed and employees to demand their rights within a corporation (Okazaki 1999). Foreign capital participation in Japanese firms was strictly controlled (Ōmae 1982). At the same time, the Occupation Authorities raised the status of employees in the Japanese firm and lowered the status of the shareholders (Okazaki 1999).

The Korean War, which broke out in 1950, was a turning point for the Japanese economy after years of poverty (Smitka 1998). The war was an external factor in Japan's recovery, since US offshore procurement became a strong stimulus for the Japanese economy (Reischauer and Jansen 2005).

The 1950s and 1960s: rapid economic development

The economic recovery became evident in the 1950s (Reischauer and Jansen 2005). By 1955, the economy had grown to its pre-war level (Smitka 1998). Changes in society led to new business opportunities for manufacturing corporations. In pre-war times, household electrical products had not been the focus for the large manufacturers of electric goods. In the 1950s they started to become more and more popular, and many manufacturing companies turned to the increasingly profitable market of electrical domestic goods. The competition among these manufacturers increased, as did their marketing efforts, and they tried to stimulate sales by setting up efficient retail channels (Usui 2014).

Alongside the light-industrial plants focusing on textiles and food which already existed before the war, Japan now developed heavy industries which produced machinery, chemicals, ships, steel, and semi-conductors. Having conquered the domestic market, household electrical appliances now began to be exported (Okazaki and Okuna-Fujiwara 1999). By the late 1960s, Japan had become one of the most important trading partners of almost every country, flooding the world with its products (Reischauer and Jansen 2005). After Prime Minister Ikeda introduced the 'double income plan' (according to which incomes should double in the following ten years) in 1960, the following decade saw growth at an average of 9 per cent per year during the 1960s (Smitka 1998).

Changes in the economy also produced social changes. The number of workers in the manufacturing and service sector increased, which led to many people moving to the cities and caused the tremendous growth of Tokyo and Osaka (Haghirian 2015a). The proportion of Japanese citizens living in cities swelled from 37.3 per cent in 1950, to 56.1 per cent in 1955 (Usui 2014). This shift in the workforce is considered as one of the reasons why Japanese productivity at that time rose so quickly. The young people moving to the city were better educated and willing to work for less than the previous generation, leading to high productivity per unit of wage (Drucker 1979).

Starting with Tokyo and Osaka, Japanese cities started to grow in a way that offered relatively little opportunity for social activities in public spaces. Japanese families focused on their homes and workplaces, and enjoyed the new comfortable domestic lifestyle. A new middle class developed (Francks 2009). These developments, and the decreasing number of traditional three-generation families, also led to the adoption of a new urban lifestyle, and the Japanese became the primary consumers of products made in Japan. The consumption of modern consumer goods changed their daily lives. From the late 1950s, the 'three sacred treasures' – washing machine, refrigerator, and black-and-white TV – became a common sight in many Japanese households (Usui 2014). Car ownership soared from around 150,000 in 1955 to over 14 million by 1973 (Townsend 2013).

This rapid development also had an effect on the Japanese manufacturing firm, which became highly competitive in the late 1960s, looking for new business opportunities by introducing technologies from Western companies and beginning to develop new products, such as the personal computer, while increasingly diversifying their existing products (Usui 2014).

What caused Japan's rapid economic development?

The rapid development of the Japanese economy after the war can be attributed to a number of cultural and structural factors. For example, the complete destruction of the pre-war economic facilities, perversely, became an opportunity for rapid recovery. Factories destroyed during the war were replaced with state-of-the-art plants, which often proved to be superior to facilities in Europe and the United States (Reischauer and Jansen 2005).

The Japanese attitude towards work is also considered to have been a major influence factor. The traditional farming life in a small and populous country with few natural resources had forced the Japanese to work hard to survive (Misumi 1990). Long exposure to natural forces such as the weather and periodic violent earthquakes had made the typical Japanese worker both sensitive and adaptable. The high rate of household savings after the war also supported economic development (Coates 1988).

Government support and intervention also contributed to Japan's development. From the 1960s, the Japanese government adopted policies intended to foster the development of a prosperous and sustainable economy. Economic growth was firmly guided and strongly encouraged by the government, focusing on certain key industries (Holroyd 2008) and the formation of industrial groupings in the form of *keiretsu* (Coates 1988); all this was framed by a strong sense of cooperation between the business sector and the government. The Japanese government tried to avoid the danger of business failure and consequent unemployment by controlling the private sector via a number of measures. Each industry was supervised separately by a government authority, which was empowered to use administrative measures to guide and support development in the particular field. The Ministry of International Trade and Industry, for example, had a supervising role in the manufacturing industry, whereas the Ministry of Finance controlled the finance industry (Okazaki and Okuno-Fujiwara 1999). However, government intervention did not encompass production schedules or targeted sales and profits. The government developed strategies which were highly supportive of the economy and the business sector, but did not interfere in their decision-making processes. This combination created the best environment for growth (Craig 1975).

Management and industry organizations therefore played an entirely different role in Japan from that of their counterparts in Western countries. They planned and implemented government policies to support the development of certain industries, and, at the same time, collected information about management activities from the companies and the company shop-floors. They acted as an information agent between the government and corporations, and, alongside the government and the *zaikai* (business world), comprised the third main force or player in the development of the Japanese economy after the Second World War. As well as information gathering, they also conferred greater power to individual companies in each industry and eased the implementation of government policies and regulations (Yonekura 1999, p. 181). Favourable tax and regulatory conditions for key sectors, as well as major national investment programmes, were further supportive of rapid growth (Holroyd 2008).

On top of this, the Japanese corporate structure was a powerful driver of the development of new management systems. Japanese corporations display the characteristics of the traditional Japanese family system, i.e. a patriarchal stamp and an awareness of social responsibility. In this, they resemble the small family shops and agricultural organizations of traditional Japan (Levine 1955, p. 61). Many observers assume that the *keiretsu* formed after the war and were intended to restore the old *zaibatsu*, but this is not the case. The *zaibatsu* had been under the control of a central holding company, which was owned by the founder family. These holding companies did not have the same power as holding companies in the West, but often only owned 10 per cent of the smaller corporations. Power was executed via the dependency of the smaller affiliates and the switching and interlocking of executives (Reischauer and Jansen 2005). Before the war, Japanese companies mainly relied on direct financing to raise capital. This was done by issuing shares in companies, but these shareholders had more power than shareholders do today, and also had a supervisory function as regards management (Okazaki and Okano-Fujiwara 1999).

On the other hand, the *keiretsu* structure, which was established after the war, often centres on a bank which already holds an average of 30 per cent of the shares. Indirect financing is the rule, as money is mainly being lent from financial institutions which monitor the corporation. This way of financing limits the power of shareholders, and encourages the lending organizations to make a long-term commitment to the welfare of the firm (Okazaki and Okano-Fujiwara 1999). The division between ownership and management was another driver of growth (Coates 1988).

The *keiretsu* also had strong ties with their suppliers. Manufacturing *keiretsu* could rely on exclusive, decades-old relationships with their key suppliers, and could buy products at prices that were non-competitive. They also often held shares in the supply companies (Aoki and Lennerfors 2013).

The *keiretsu* are powerful units in the Japanese economy; they not only provide support for directly affiliated companies, but also promote the economic development of the country through their economies of scale; highly integrated and reliable vertical structures; financial opportunities to invest overseas; and general reliability (Keys *et al.* 1994). The term *keiretsu* refers to 'clusters of independently managed firms maintaining close and stable economic ties, cemented by a governance mechanism such as presidents' clubs, partial cross-ownership, and interlocking directorates' (Grabowiecki 2006, p. 1).

The development of unique Japanese management practices

Certain modern management practices, which are unique to Japan, are another factor that has a close and interdependent relationship with Japan's fast economic development. Japanese management practices are strongly based on traditional Japanese values, work ethic, and cultural and social structures. Foremost are production and operations management activities – both areas in which Japanese corporations became world leaders in cost-effective and high-quality production. Up until the 1970s, Japanese corporations aggressively used Western technology through licensing agreements, and were even called 'copyists' during that period. This strategy of using existing technology was supported by a strong interest in developing effective production processes, quality control, and continuous improvement in technology and production processes (Ōmae 1982).

The Japanese production and manufacturing systems that were developed during that period include: just-in-time manufacturing and inventory control; total quality control (TQC); and the use of employee suggestion systems and quality circles (Young 1992, in Keys *et al.* 1994).

The just-in-time production system is intended to produce only what has been ordered by customers. Demand is what drives the production processes, assembly and subassembly schedules, and raw-material deliveries (Heiko 1989). Just-in-time is the perfect coordination of all these purchasing and production processes with consumer demand and volume of orders. Its main goal is to produce products with the highest cost efficiency and quality, and to reduce all forms of waste, such as unused inventory items, overproduction, or neglect of employee creativity (Liker 2004).

Management concepts such as just-in-time production and *kaizen* have now become a global standard. The suggestions system is used worldwide to leverage employees' knowledge and ideas, and quality-control activities such as quality circles (in which teams of workers meet outside of work time to develop ideas to improve production processes) are an important element in the Japanese production system (Kenley and Florida 1995), but also in non-Japanese companies around the globe.

Another relevant practice, which was only later seen as a main driver of rapid economic development, is human-resource management. Japanese corporations (often in the production field) grew very quickly during the boom years, and hired large numbers of workers. These workers often moved to Tokyo from the Japanese countryside, leading to rapid urban growth. Unique Japanese human-resource practices, which are still in use today, are seen as one of the keys to Japanese economic success (Firkola 2006, p. 115). These developments went hand in hand with increasing enrolment in compulsory education facilities such as primary and lower secondary schools; the advancement to upper secondary schools; and the establishment of new universities and junior colleges. The same period saw a rapid growth in the number of research institutions, both private and university-based. The consequent human-capital accumulation can be seen as another major factor supporting the fast growth of the Japanese economy (Kimura 2013).

Special practices emerged within firms to leverage this human-resource capital. The most famous practices are lifetime employment and the seniority principle. Lifetime employment or *shūshin kōyō* is still in place in many Japanese corporations today, notably in the *keiretsu*, and has been seen as a major supporter of the competitive advantage of Japanese businesses (Keys *et al.* 1994). Under *shūsuhin kōyō*, full-time employees in Japanese companies enjoy a certain protection against dismissal (see Chapter 12 on Japanese labour law). Lifetime employment is said to have its origins in the rice-growing tradition that had dominated the Japanese economy and culture for two millennia. Farmers growing rice not only needed to work in teams to bring in the harvest, but also needed to persevere and plan for the following season. Working in groups provided all members of the family or village with support in times of hardship, and even in the Tokugawa period the working relationships were usually established for life (Tudor *et al.* 1996). During the Edo period, villagers had little opportunity to travel and often spent their entire life in a village. As Firkola remarks, '[I]n this environment, the best way to ensure prosperity for oneself was to dedicate one's life to the prosperity of the village. This is a possible origin of the modern practice of lifetime employment' (Firkola 2006, p. 116).

Lifetime employment is seen as one of the main reasons why Japanese corporations and the Japanese economy were able to grow so quickly. Employees felt secure, and dedicated themselves fully to the company. Long-term projects could easily be undertaken, without fear of a destabilizing change in staff members. Loyalty to the company would also increase.

The lifetime employment and seniority-based system was strongly supported in *keiretsu* firms. Here, the long-term commitment of the financial institution supporting the corporation allowed companies to establish long-term relationships with their employees. The *keiretsu* consists of many different but related corporations, and these subsidiaries and subcontractors function as a buffer for the parent company in accepting staff transfers, so supporting the system of long-term employment (Okazaki and Okano-Fujiwara 1999). Lifetime employment also supported company growth, because many low-cost younger workers could be hired. These workers would stay in the company to be trained, and talented workers could then be assigned to long-term projects (Firkola 2006, p. 120).

Since Japanese employees are supposed to stay in a company for many years, lifetime employment and the seniority principle (*shūshin kōyō*) are generally inextricable. The seniority principle refers to the difference in the treatment of employees according to the length of their membership in the organization. Salaries are increased every year; promotions are often also based on the time spent in the corporation (Haghirian 2010a). Again, the seniority principle also has historical roots. During the Tokugawa period, there was an apprenticeship system in which young apprentices lived with their master and developed a strong emotionally dependent relationship with them (Tudor *et al.* 1996), not dissimilar to Japanese corporations of the twentieth and twenty-first centuries.

Lifetime employment and the seniority principle have a strong effect on the Japanese corporation. First, Japanese companies have a tendency to develop generalists instead of specialists. Employees in the *keiretsu* have common responsibilities because their individual job assignments are not clearly defined. This supports collective actions and general commitment to work, and encourages cooperation among employees. Consequently, Japanese employees also engage in efforts that go beyond their formal work assignments (Wang 2011). The lifelong membership in an organization also provides employees with a sense of prestige (Okada 1999) and a feeling of oneness that increases their feeling of motivation.

Knowledge management is another management practice that has also played an important role in organizational development, although it only became prominent in business studies in the 1990s. Japanese employees practising lifetime employment share more knowledge than employees in Western corporations, which eases new product development and engenders a feeling of unity. Whereas Western knowledge-management practices focused on technology tend to abstract knowledge away from the individual company member, Japanese organizations focus on tacit knowledge and knowledge creation (Nonaka and Takeuchi 1995).

The 1970s: the end of high growth

By 1968 the Japanese economy was overtaking the German economy, and in 1970 Japanese workers and employees attained the same level of income as workers in European economies (Smitka 1998). The high rate of growth came to an end in the 1970s, but Japanese success was evident. Within 30 years, Japan had transitioned from a low-technology and low-wage economy into a leading industrial nation that was renowned for innovation in various fields, including computers, automobiles, consumer appliances, and the development of industrial robots (Holroyd 2008). Japanese companies started to compete with Western firms in many markets (Lehmberg *et al.* 2013), and in some cases defeated them; and this led to the first scientific investigation of the Japanese 'model' and its relationship to Japanese culture and society. The rapid increase in Japanese foreign investment during the 1970s and 1980s led to rising interest in Japanese management styles and practices (Kenney and Florida 1995). This was the time when Western managers and researchers started to show a deeper interest in the Japanese economy and its traditional management styles (Van Wolferen 1989; Jackson 1993; Abbeglen and Stalk 1996).

The 1980s: the bubble economy

After the Plaza Accord, the value of the dollar dropped from 240 to 160 yen, and the Japanese government loosened its monetary policy. Credit became easily available, leading to a new Japanese management practice called *zaitech*, in which more money could be made by investing money in land and assets than from traditional business activities (Vaszkun and Tsutsui 2012). The so-called Japanese bubble economy had begun to inflate. In these years, Japanese companies borrowed massively from Japanese banks (which had obtained their funds from the high levels of saving by Japanese households). Ongoing inflation enabled the companies to pay their loans back without problems until 1990.

The bubble economy also had a strong influence on Japanese lifestyles. At that time, consumption became a hobby and a lifestyle, and foreign travel became very popular among Japanese consumers (Haghirian 2015b). Japanese consumers became known for their willingness to pay for the best quality and brands (Francks 2009). This led to an increasing number of foreign brands and corporations entering the Japanese consumer market (Haghirian 2015b). At the same time, Japanese companies tried to apply international standards within the workplace. One aspect of this was the position of women in Japanese firms. The Equal Employment Opportunity Law, passed in 1985, was largely meant to placate international opinions. It did not have the effect it was intended to have, namely to prohibit discrimination in hiring or promotions. Indeed, many companies introduced a system that was based on separating the management (*sōgōshoku*) from the administrative or clerical tracks (*ippanshoku*). In doing this, they developed a legal cover for the continuing practice of gender discrimination (Weathers 2006).

The 1990s: 'the Lost Decade'

In the 1990s, the bubble burst. Real estate purchased at bubble prices was no longer able to pay for itself, putting pressure on the businesses that owned it, and the banks that were left with bad loans either went bankrupt or turned to the government for support (Kobayashi 2006). A period of deflation and economic downturn followed, from which Japan has yet to fully emerge (Lehmberg *et al.* 2013). The long recession that mired the Japanese economy in the 1990s has led to that period being named the 'Lost Decade'. Growth rates were low, deflation pervasive, public debt was rising, and asset prices were weak. The Japanese government attempted a number of measures to stop the downward trend (Sharma 2014), but the performance of the economy could not return to the level of 1989. Real GDP growth fell from 5–10 per cent to 1–2 per cent in 1990. At the same time, unemployment rose from 2.1 per cent to a peak of 5.4 per cent in 2002. Land and stock prices both plummeted: the index of land prices in the six major cities declined from 100 in 1990 to 30.4 in 2002 (Vaszkun and Tsutsui 2012).

The economic crisis also led to stagnation in the Japanese *keiretsu*, which had to accept foreign investors to survive (e.g. Nissan) (Aoki and Lennerfors 2013). Japanese corporations also had to deal with the emergence of new challengers – South Korea, Taiwan, Hong Kong, and then China – which now offered inexpensive labour and high-quality products. Japan's competitive position in global trade and industrial production became vulnerable (Vaszkun and Tsutsui 2012).

At the same time, the practice of lifetime employment, which had supported Japanese development since the 1950s, suddenly became an obstacle to meeting the new challenges. Since

Japanese employees are highly protected, the only way to control labour costs is to reduce the number of graduates being recruited. At the same time, the number of older and more costly employees is growing (Firkola 2006, p. 121). The stable workforce that Japanese companies could boast of in past decades is suddenly not so stable. Short-term and part-time positions are increasing in number (Lehmberg *et al.* 2013). Corporations have tried to reduce costs by increasing the number of irregular employees: lower-paid, disposable non-regular (*hiseiki*) workers; part-timers, *arubaito* (side-job workers, often students); temporary agency workers; and contract workers. Although they have lower status and pay than the regular workers, in many cases they do equivalent work (Weathers 2006).

Large companies are increasingly stressing merit based on performance, and are downplaying the relevance of seniority for promotion and wages (Firkola 2006, p. 123). In 1984, 84.7 per cent of employees were *seishain* (full-time employees), whereas, in 2010, this number had decreased to only 65.6 per cent (Yoshida *et al.* 2013). This has had an influence on incomes and the standard of living in Japan, and, at the same time, these employees have lower chances of a proper career (Lehmberg *et al.* 2013).

The recession has also affected Japanese consumer behaviour. Traditionally, the Japanese were known for being consumers with very high expectations for quality, design, ease of use, and service. These attitudes received a major setback during the 'Lost Decade'. Consumers started to accept cheaper products, provided that they still offered good quality (Lehmberg *et al.* 2013).

The end of economic growth

After almost two decades of economic recession, it has become evident that the problems of the Japanese economy are multifaceted (Sharma 2014). The Japanese economy and the Japanese business world are facing numerous challenges, and these need to be addressed through structural reforms, as well as via attitude changes within companies and on the part of employees themselves.

One very pressing issue is inequality in the workplace and the shrinking labour force. Japanese employees were traditionally full-time, male, and enjoyed a number of perks from the corporation. Due to economic pressure, in the 1990s companies changed their employment practices and dramatically increased the number of part-time employees. This has led to inequality in the workplace and a growing number of Japanese who cannot earn enough to support themselves. Non-regular workers are generally paid by the hour, and, in principle, are not required to work overtime (many, of course, work irregular hours) (Weathers 2006). They do not receive the benefits of full-time, regular employees (working full-time with a contract that does not curtail the date of employment) such as lifetime employment, automatic promotion based on length of service, and large retirement pay (Nishiyama 2000). In addition, non-regular workers typically receive few or no social-security benefits, and their salaries are not part of the seniority system, whereas regular workers still tend to receive some form of seniority pay (Weathers 2006). Despite these differences, irregular workers and employees still work side-by-side with full-time employees and still undertake the same tasks. Thus, while irregular workers are finding it increasingly difficult to provide for their financial needs, Japanese companies are having to deal with a shrinking workforce and an ageing society.

Galapogization, globalization, and international competition

Japanese companies still tend to operate in an ethnocentric manner (Lehmberg *et al.* 2013). The press have named this the 'Galapagos Syndrome', or the 'Galapogization of Japan', referring to the fact that many Japanese products are extremely advanced but cannot be used outside Japan – much in the same way as the species on the Galapagos Islands evolved on their own separate path that was superior to the rest of the world, but remained isolated on their island (Inagaki and Ito 2012). Japanese mobile phones, which are highly sophisticated but dependent on Japanese infrastructure for their operation, were a typical product of this trend. Despite being trendsetters from the start (email capabilities since 1999, camera phones in 2000, third-generation networks in 2001, full music downloads in 2002, electronic payments in 2004, and digital TV in 2005), they became a 'little too clever', and did not succeed in overseas markets (Tabuchi 2009). Japanese mobile phones have thus become the most prominent example of a product which is only popular in Japan, and cannot convince an international audience. By focusing too much on perfectionism and hardware, many Japanese companies are losing out in the international consumer-product markets.

Abenomics and its effects

After taking office in December 2012, Prime Minister Shinzo Abe introduced a new programme, which has been named Abenomics by Japanese and international media. 'Abenomics' is a deflation-busting programme comprising the 'three arrows' of radical monetary easing from the Bank of Japan; fiscal spending; and attempts at structural reforms, including radical deregulation in new 'special economic zones' spread across the country. These efforts triggered a sharp drop in the yen and big stock gains, benefiting big exporters and the wealthy (Tachikawa 2014; *The Economist* 2013). The Abe government has found a solution that had already been proposed by Western observers (e.g. Weathers 2006, p. 42): women should increasingly take over management positions and fill the missing positions in Japanese corporations, and this is evident in the new attempts to increase the number of women in Japanese corporations.

At the same time, the Abe government set out some clear signs. It introduced an increase in the consumption tax from 5 to 8 per cent in 2014, and it plans to increase it further to 10 per cent (*Asahi Shimbun* 2014). In 2015, Abe announced that the Japanese corporate tax will be reduced from a top rate of 35 per cent to a rate of 25–27 per cent (Sharma 2014). The Abe government also introduced a new government code in 2015, which requires dramatic changes such as the introduction of two external and neutral directors in Japanese company boards (Benes 2015).

Conclusions

Based on unique cultural foundations, Japanese corporations managed to develop their own management practices and styles, many of which became international standards and still intrigue Western managers and scholars today. This chapter has explained how Japanese corporations were able to develop the particular management practices which supported (and in turn were supported by) Japan's rapid and unprecedented development after the Second World War. Japan became the only Asian country to have gone through a similar process of industrial development to its Western counterparts, and today is a post-industrial market and economy.

The need for change is understood in Japanese corporations and among Japanese managers. Japan is facing the questions of whether it prefers a stable and protected economic environment, or whether it should take a risk and develop a more liberal, market-oriented economy, which may also expose it to strong global competition (Vaszkun and Tsutsui 2012).

The past decade has shown not only that Japanese companies can change, but also that they have understood the necessity to change and adapt to the new globalized business world. The

Abe government promised change and implemented reforms, which are thought to be having a strong influence on corporations and Japanese management (including the support for entrepreneurship in Japan, and a new corporate governance code). But *major* structural reforms such as the deregulation of Japan's strongly protected health-care and agricultural industries; female equality and female participation in the Japanese workplace; and opening the country to more foreign labour, have so far not been on the Abe agenda. The question remains of how and in what form they will adapt, and whether these changes will have an effect on the traditional Japanese management styles.

References

Abbeglen, J. C. and Stalk, G. J. (1996). *Kaisha: the Japanese Corporation*. Tokyo: Tuttle Company.

Aoki, K. and Lennerfors, T. L. (2013). The new, improved keiretsu. *Harvard Business Review*, September 2013: 109–113.

Asahi Shimbun (2014). Government to delay consumption tax rate hike to 2017. *Asahi Shimbun*, 15 November 2014. http://ajw.asahi.com/article/behind_news/politics/AJ201411150032, last accessed online on 2 October 2015.

Benes, N. (2015). Japan's new code of conduct; defining new principles and practices for the way companies do business. *Wall Street Journal*, 2 June 2015, http://www.wsj.com/articles/japans-new-code-of-conduct-1433262245, last accessed 3 November 2015.

Coates, N. (1988). Determinants of Japan's business success: some Japanese executives' views. *The Academy of Management Executive (1987–1989)*, 2(1): 69–72.

Craig, A. M. (1975). Functional and dysfunctional aspects of government bureaucracy. In: Vogel. E. (ed.), *Modern Japanese Organization and Decision Making*. Tokyo: Tuttle Company, pp. 3–33.

Drucker, P. (1979). Economic realities and enterprise strategies. In: Vogel, E. (ed.), *Modern Japanese Organization and Decision Making*. Tokyo: Tuttle Company, pp. 228–248.

The Economist (2013). Time to get started: Shinzo Abe is giving new hope to Japan's unappreciated entrepreneurs. *The Economist*, 31 August 2013.

Firkola, P. (2006). Japanese management practices past and present. *Economic Journal of Hokkaido University*, 35: 115–130.

Francks, P. (2009). *The Japanese Consumer: an Alternative Economic History of Modern Japan*. Cambridge, UK: Cambridge University Press.

Grabowiecki, J. (2006) *Keiretsu Groups: Their Role in the Japanese Economy and Their Reference Point (or Paradigm) for Other Countries*. Institute of Developing Economies, Japan External Trade Organization, VRF Series, No. 413, March 2006.

Haghirian, P. (2010a). *Understanding Japanese Management Practices*. New York: Business Expert Press.

Haghirian, P. (2010b). Historical development of Japanese consumerism. In: Haghirian, P. (ed.), *Japanese Consumer Dynamics*, London: Palgrave, pp. 3–17.

Haghirian, P. (2015a). Japanese business and management. In: James D. Babb (ed.), *The SAGE Handbook of Japanese Studies*. Chapter 28, p. 654.

Haghirian, P. (2015b). Japanese consumers and consumerism. In: Babb, James D. (ed.), *The SAGE Handbook of Japanese Studies*. Chapter 29, p. 669.

Heiko, L. (1989). Some relationships between Japanese culture and just-in-time. *The Academy of Management Executive (1987–1989)*, 3(4): 319–321.

Holroyd, C. (2008). Reinventing Japan Inc.: twenty-first century innovation strategies in Japan. *Prometheus*, 26(1): 21–38.

Inagaki, K. and Ito, T. (2012). Japanese M&A: beating the Galapagos Syndrome. Wall Street Journal Business Blog, 30 May 2012. http://blogs.wsj.com/japanrealtime/2012/05/30/japanese-ma-beating-the-galapagos-syndrome/, last accessed 16 October 2015.

Jackson, T. (1993). *Turning Japanese: the Fight for Industrial Control of the New Europe*. London: HarperCollins.

Kenley, M. and Florida, R. (1995). The transfer of Japanese management styles in two US transplant industries: autos and electronics. *Journal of Management Studies*, 32(6): 789–802.

Keys, J. B., Denton, L. T., and Miller, T. R. (1994). The Japanese management jungle revisited. *Journal of Management*, 20(2): 373–402.

Kimura, F. (2013). *Japan's Model of Economic Development; Relevant and Nonrelevant Elements for Developing Economies*. Research Paper No. 2009/22. Tokyo: United Nations University: UNU-WIDER, World Institute for Development Economics Research.

Kobayashi, K. (2006). *The Japanese Economy*. Tokyo: IBC Publishing.

Lehmberg, D., Dhanaraj, C., and Funai, A. (2013). What do we make of Japan? *Business Horizons*, 56: 219–229.

Levine, S. B. (1955). Management and industrial relations in postwar Japan. *The Far Eastern Quarterly*, 15(1): 57–75.

Liker, J. K. (2004). *The Toyota Way: 14 Management Principles from the World's Greatest Manufacturer*. New York: McGraw-Hill.

Misumi, J. (1990). The Japanese meaning of work and small group activities in Japanese industrial organizations. *International Journal of Psychology*, 25: 819–832.

Nishiyama, K. (2000). *Doing Business with Japan: Successful Strategies for Intercultural Communication*. Honolulu, Hawaii: University of Hawaii Press.

Nonaka, I. and Takeuchi, H. (1995). *The Knowledge Creating Company: How Japanese Companies Create the Dynamics of Innovation*, New York: Oxford University Press.

Okazaki, T. (1999). Corporate governance. In: Okazaki, T. and Okuno-Fujiwara (eds), *The Japanese Economic System and Its Historical Origins*. Oxford, UK: Oxford University Press.

Okazaki, T. and Okuno-Fujiwara, M. (1999). Japan's present-day economic system and its historical origins. In: Okazaki, T. and Okuno-Fujiwara, M. (eds), *The Japanese Economic System and its Historical Origins*. Oxford, UK: Oxford University Press.

Ōmae, K. (1982). *The Mind of the Strategist*. New York: McGraw-Hill.

Reischauer, E. O. and Jansen, M. B. (2005). *The Japanese Today: Change and Continuity*. Tokyo: Tuttle Publishing.

Sharma, S. D. (2014). Abenomics gamble and the Japanese economy: the risks and opportunity. *Journal of International Economics*, 5(2): 103–113.

Smitka, M. (1998). *Japanese Economic History, 1600–1960*. Volume 4. The textile industry and the rise of the Japanese economy. New York and London: Garland.

Tabuchi, H. (2009). Why Japanese cellphones haven't gone global? *New York Times*, Online edition. 19 July 2009. http://www.nytimes.com/2009/07/20/technology/20cell.html?_r=0, last accessed 2 October 2015.

Tachikawa, T. (2014). 2015: make or break year for 'Abenomics'? *Japan Times*, 28 December 2014.

Townsend, S. C. (2013). The 'miracle' of car ownership in Japan's 'era of high growth', 1955–73. *Business History*, 55(3): 498–523.

Tudor, T., Trumble, R., and George, G. (1996). Significant historic origins that influenced the team concept in major Japanese companies. *Journal of Applied Business Research*, 12(4): 115–127.

Usui, K. (2014). *Marketing and Consumption in Modern Japan*. Abingdon, Oxford, UK: Routledge.

Van Wolferen, Karel (1989). *The Enigma of Japanese Power*. London: Macmillan.

Vaszkun, B. and Tsutsui, W. M. (2012). A modern history of Japanese management thought. *Journal of Management History*, 18(4): 368–386.

Wang, Y. (2011). Examining organizational citizenship behavior of Japanese employees: a multidimensional analysis of the relationship to organizational commitment. *The International Journal of Human Resource Management*, 26(4): 425–444.

Weathers, C. (2006). Equal opportunities for Japanese women? What progress? *The Japanese Economy*, 33(4): 16–44.

Yonekura, S. (1999). The functions of industrial associations. In: Okazaki, T. and Okuno-Fujiwara, M. (eds), *The Japanese Economic System and its Historical Origins*. Oxford, UK: Oxford University Press.

Yoshida, T., Yashiro, K. and Suzuki, Y. (2013). Intercultural communication skills: what Japanese businesses today need. *International Journal of Intercultural Relations*, 37: 72–85.

Young, S. M. (1992). A framework for successful adoption and performance of Japanese manufacturing practices in the United States. *Academy of Management Review*, 17(4): 677–700.

Part II
Structure and theory of the Japanese firm

3

Keiretsu

Franz Waldenberger

Structures (once) characteristic of Japan's industrial organization

Besides '*kaizen*', the Japanese way of continuously improving processes, products, and services, the term '*keiretsu*' is probably the second-most common Japanese word used in management and industrial organization literature. Whereas '*kaizen*' describes a management practice (Imai 1986), the term '*keiretsu*' refers to structural characteristics of Japanese industrial organization (Aoki 1988: 204–257; Miyashita and Russel 1994; Lincoln and Gerlach 2004: 15–27). The horizontal *keiretsu* describe company networks that span different manufacturing and service industries. The vertical *keiretsu* characterize inter-firm structures along the value chain, and can be further distinguished in upward supplier–buyer and downward manufacturer–distributor relations.

The different types of *keiretsu* share the common characteristic of stable inter-firm linkages. The different *keiretsu* types are connected in so far as large manufacturing firms, which are members of horizontal groups, often spearhead vertical *keiretsu*. However, horizontal, supply, and distribution *keiretsu* differ with regard to their origins, functions, and evolution (McGuire and Dow 2009: 334). They will therefore be discussed in separate sections below. Nevertheless, the literature review will be guided by the same set of questions. What are the defining characteristics? When and how did the structural characteristics develop? What functions did they fulfil during the course of Japan's economic development? What changes did they undergo and by what forces were these transformations necessitated and shaped? What relevance do *keiretsu* bear today for Japan's industrial organization?

The fuzzy boundaries, as well as the varied and changing forms and functions of *keiretsu*, have always invited controversy about what they actually are, what function they fulfil, and what economic implications they carry (Miwa and Ramseyer 2001; Miwa and Ramseyer 2002). There is little disagreement that they have lost much of their once-recognized relevance (Lincoln and Shimotani 2009: 2). The disputed evidence relates to when *keiretsu* started to dissolve and to what extent their importance has diminished. The final section will argue that, nevertheless, *keiretsu* research has more than just historic value. Seen from a broader perspective, it provides insights into industrial organization that continue to be of relevance.

Horizontal *keiretsu*

Defining characteristics

Horizontal *keiretsu* (*kigyō shūdan*), also known as conglomerate, financial, or industrial group-ings, consist of companies from different industries. Due to the conglomerate character of the group, there is, on average, little direct business among members. However, some mem-bers provide services to all or most other firms in the same *keiretsu*. This is especially true for the group's financial institutions, and here again above all for its so-called main bank, and for its general trading company (*sōgō shōsha*). There is no central strategic unit steering the network (Odagiri 1994: 175–180). Group companies are legally and economically independ-ent. They are linked by shareholdings, often mutually in the form of cross-shareholdings, but the amount of stock held among group companies does not grant any owner a controlling interest.

Core members of groups held monthly president meetings and some still do so today.[1] The nature and importance of these gatherings is disputed (Miyashita and Russel 1994: 61–66; Odagiri 1994: 184–185; Lincoln and Gerlach 2004: 16–17). Some saw the meetings as an opportunity for discussing group-related strategic issues. Others interpreted them as purely formal events for exchanging information about general political and economic issues and for fostering personal ties among business leaders. The truth is likely to lie somewhere in the middle, and is bound to have varied according to circumstances, but has, overall, declined over time.

Research has generally focused on the big six horizontal *keiretsu*. Mitsubishi, Mitsui, and Sumitomo are direct descendants of pre-war *zaibatsu*, with Mitsui and Sumitomo having roots in pre-Meiji Japan. The Fuyo, Sanwa, and Daiichi Kangyō groups also have partial *zaibatsu* origins, but were newly formed and named after the Second World War. They were less-tightly organized, which is also proven by the fact that they had core members in common. For example, Hitachi was a core member of all three groups. Kobe Steel, Nissho Iwai, and Nippon Express belonged to both the Sanwa and the Daiichi Kangyō Group.

Table 3.1 lists the industry affiliations of the members of the groups' respective president meetings as of 1997. These core members belonged to a wide range of industries representative of Japan's economic structure during the high-growth period from 1955 to 1973. The groups' attempt to mimic the economy's overall industrial set-up has been termed 'one set principle' (Lincoln and Shimotani 2009: 5). Even in the case of the three direct *zaibatsu* descendants, presi-dent club members did not necessarily carry the group's name, like Toyota and Toshiba in the case of the Mitsui Group, or Kirin, Asahi Glass, and Nikon in the case of the Mitsubishi Group, or NEC in the case of the Sumitomo Group.

The president meetings defined the core members per group. To delineate the overall cor-porate network of a horizontal *keiretsu*, empirical research normally looked at linkages with the group's main bank. A company would be considered a member if the group's main bank was its largest lender of capital. Share ownership by the main bank would sometimes be considered as an additional criterion. Under the wider definition, networks of horizontal *keiretsu* comprise a much larger number of companies (Miyashita and Russel 1994: 48–49).

Historical background

Horizontal *keiretsu* have their roots in the pre-war *zaibatsu*. The *zaibatsu* were family-owned conglomerates organized and controlled hierarchically within a holding-company structure

Table 3.1 Industry affiliation of president-club members of six major horizontal *keiretsu*

	Mitsui	*Mitsubishi*	*Sumitomo*	*Fuyo*	*Sanwa*	*DKB*
Finance	4	4	4	4	3	6
Trading	2	1	1	1	4	6
Forestry	0	0	1	0	0	0
Mining	2	0	1	0	0	0
Construction	2	1	1	1	4	1
Food	1	1	0	3	2	0
Textile	0	0	0	2	1	0
Paper	1	1	0	1	0	1
Chemicals	4	5	2	3	8	8
Petroleum	0	1	0	1	1	1
Rubber	0	0	0	0	1	1
Stone, etc.	1	1	2	1	1	1
Steel	1	1	1	1	4	3
Metal	1	4	3	0	1	3
Machinery	0	1	1	2	1	3
Electronics	1	1	1	3	5	5
Vehicles	3	2	0	1	3	3
Precision instruments	0	1	0	1	1	1
Real estate	1	1	1	1	0	0
Logistics	2	2	1	3	3	3
Other	0	1	0	0	1	2
Total	26	29	20	29	44	48

Source: Based on Japan Fair Trade Commission (1994: 17)

(Hashimoto 1992). Their growth and success was closely related to Japan's process of industrialization. They consequently entertained a close relationship with the government and benefited from Japan's colonial expansion into China and South-East Asia. The Allied Powers saw them as an important element in Japan's military industrial complex and decided to dissolve them as part of their demilitarization, democratization, and deconcentration policies (Nakamura 1995: 24–27; Hoshi and Kashyap 2001: 67–72). The concrete and lasting measures taken included the break-up of the holding companies; the general prohibition of holding-company structures in the Antimonopoly Act of 1947;[2] the forced sales of *zaibatsu* family owners' shares to the general public; and the purging of top managers from their companies.

The new *keiretsu* structures formed during the high-growth period (Kikkawa 1992). The high-growth period that set in the mid-1950s created financing needs that by far surmounted the cash flow of post-war corporations. The decision of the government to favour a financial system based on banks instead of capital markets meant that companies had to turn to loans as the major source of funding. They naturally grouped around their former *zaibatsu* banks. These banks, having also been freed from *zaibatsu* control, became the main banks of the new corporate networks.

Soon after the re-opening of the Tokyo Stock Exchange in 1949, the share of equity held by private households declined, whereas share ownership by the domestic corporate sector steadily increased (Baum 1997: 1273–1299). The trend accelerated after a small stock market bubble in the early 1960s (Okazaki 1992). When, in the mid-1960s, Japan committed to capital liberalization, fears arose that Japanese industry would become a takeover target of financially strong foreign firms. As a precautionary measure, members of horizontal *keiretsu* further increased cross-shareholdings and strengthened ties with so-called stable shareholders. No shareholder would own a controlling stake, but, in sum, the cross- and stable-shareholder packages precluded the possibility of hostile takeovers. By the end of the 1960s, the big six horizontal *keiretsu* had achieved their final form, characterized by main-bank finance and governance; stable shareholding structures including cross-shareholdings; and president club meetings.

Functional interpretation and implications

The main business relations among horizontal *keiretsu* members were with financial institutions, and here especially the group's main bank, and with the general trading companies providing access to international markets. The centrality within the network put main banks and trading companies in the position of an information hub (Odagiri 1994: 184–185). The trading companies played a unique role in Japan's economic development (Young 1979; Yonekawa 1990) and they continue to do so today, although in a quite different form. Their influence, which extended well beyond their position within a horizontal *keiretsu*, and the transformation of their business model, which helped them survive when demand for their services by group members declined, have made them an object of research on their own merits (Tanaka 2012).

The characterization of horizontal *keiretsu* as financial business groups underlines the importance of the main bank and points to the allocation of financial capital as a core function. The importance of the main bank was dictated by four conditions (Hoshi and Kashyap 2001: 91–112).

- the scarcity of internal sources of finance after the war;
- the high growth potential resulting from Japan's stage of economic development;
- the suppression of capital markets by regulatory means;
- a regulatory framework of the banking sector based on the belief that stability of the financial system could only be achieved by excluding competition.

The allocation of financial capital was complemented by related functions such as risk diversification and governance. Various empirical studies showed that *keiretsu* groups achieved income smoothing via credit channels. Financially strong companies would pay an interest premium that allowed banks to help weaker companies to overcome situations of financial distress. For members of horizontal *keiretsu*, the return on capital would on average be lower, but more stable (Nakatani 1984; Hoshi 1994; Dow and McGuire 2009; Kwak *et al.* 2009; Chen *et al.* 2010).

Main banks were a central actor in the insider model of governance characteristic of Japan until the late 1990s (see Chapter 8). The governance function was not comparable with that of a major shareholder. It was the contingent kind of governance performed by a lender who only steps in when credit positions are at risk (Aoki *et al.* 1994). Given the increasingly high leverage of Japanese corporations, including those listed on stock markets and the relatively short maturity of loans, top management and banks were, nevertheless, in regular and close contact. In addition, banks held minor, but non-negligible, equity positions and would also take seats on the board of directors, especially when companies faced harsh times. Many case studies demonstrate the role of the main bank in monitoring, resolving financial distress and restructuring (Sheard 1994). However, there are also counter-examples, where such support was not granted

(Miwa 1996: 113–119; Hoshi and Kashyap 2001: 179–180), indicating that main banks were not able and not willing to provide unconditional support.

The cross-and stable-shareholding structures protected *keiretsu* members from hostile takeover threats. Taken together, the stable financing relations and shareholding structures complemented the companies' commitment to long-term employment and to the in-house careers of management up to board positions (Aoki 1988: 99–101).

The 151 non-financial president-club members of the six business groups accounted for 13 per cent of the total paid in capital, 11 per cent of total assets, and 11 per cent of total sales in the Japanese economy in 1999 (Japan Fair Trade Commission 2002, part 2, chapter 8-3). The figures had continuously declined since the collapse of Japan's stock-price bubble in 1990, when the non-financial core members had combined 17 per cent of the country's equity capital, 16 per cent of total assets and 13 per cent of sales. But how should such figures be evaluated? They definitely underline the then-prevalent 'network structure' of Japanese industry. It would, however, be misleading to interpret them as signs of a high concentration of economic power or collusion (Weinstein and Yafeh 1995). The six groups were big enough to have the Japanese Fair Trade Commission regularly report on them from 1977 onwards until 2002. But, given the internal structure and the lack of a central locus of strategic control, they could hardly be interpreted as single organizations, and neither would the six taken together represent any meaningful economic entity.

Horizontal *keiretsu* recruited their core members from industries that played an essential role in Japan's economic development. *Keiretsu* financing enabled the accumulation of capital necessary for Japan's economic catch, and it also supported the allocation of funds needed for changing Japan's industrial structure. Whether the existence of horizontal *keiretsu* enhanced the effectiveness of Japan's 'developmental' policies directed toward economic catch-up cannot be unambiguously discerned. The bank-centred financial system might have provided the government with more control over capital allocation, but the replication of industrial structures implied by the 'one set principle' must have been considered as wasteful under MITI's industrial policy plans focusing on the concentration of production capacities to exploit economies of scale (Tsuruta 1988: 63–64).

Change and relevance today

As the allocation of financial capital through bank lending was the core function of the horizontal *keiretsu*, the rationale for their existence and viability rested on the corporate sector's dependence on external finance and on lack of access to capital markets. After the end of the high-growth period in 1973, both conditions were less and less met. For the corporate sector, the accumulation of capital slowed down, while the capability to fund projects internally steadily increased. At the same time, the slow but profound transformation of Japan's financial system provided larger companies with access to capital markets. All these developments reduced the importance of bank finance, and consequently placed the existence of horizontal *keiretsu* into question (Hoshi and Kashyap 2001: 219–259).

The collapse of the stock market and real estate bubble at the beginning of the 1990s and the ensuing financial crises resulted in a fundamental reshuffling of the banking industry (Japanese Bankers Association 2006: 13–15). In 2000, the Fuji Bank, the Dai-Ichi Kangyō Bank, and the Industrial Bank of Japan became integrated into the Mizuho Bank. The Sumitomo and the Mitsui Bank (then named Sakura Bank), the main banks of the two *keiretsu* with the oldest roots, merged in 2001 to form Sumitomo Mitsui Banking. In the same year, the Sanwa Bank ended up in the UFJ Group that four years later was taken over by the Tokyo Mitsubishi Bank. So, by

2005, the main banks of the six major horizontal *keiretsu* had been reorganized into three financial conglomerates. Cross-*keiretsu* consolidation via merger also occurred in other industries, but there was no 'merging of business groups'. It was rather their dissolution that occurred.

As a result of the transformation of the financial system, and accelerated by the financial crisis, cross- and stable-shareholdings were steadily reduced, bringing about a fundamental change in the ownership structures of listed firms (see Chapter 8). Horizontal *keiretsu* were not unaffected by these developments. By 1999, the portion of cross-held shares among core members had declined to 20 per cent on average (Japan Fair Trade Commission 2002: figure 2).

It is worth noting that the ban on holding companies, which had been prescribed by the Allied Powers and which had been decisive for the decentralized structure of the newly forming horizontal *keiretsu*, was lifted in 1997 (Thorson and Siegfanz 1999). There were fears among anti-trust experts that this might spur the revival of the old pre-war *zaibatsu*. It did not. Holding companies helped reorganize and consolidate Japan's industry, but that could neither reverse nor stop the dissolution of the business groups.

Vertical *keiretsu*

Supplier keiretsu: *characteristics and historical origins*

A typical vertical supply *keiretsu* consisted of a large manufacturer sourcing from smaller, dedicated suppliers. The pyramid-like structure often extended over several stages of production. Vertical supplier *keiretsu* were especially prominent and pronounced in assembly industries, like those for cars, electronics, machinery, or precision instruments, where the final product is made out of hundreds, if not thousands, of components. Interestingly, it was in these industries that Japan achieved a very strong comparative advantage after the end of the high-growth period (Waldenberger 1999: 182–183). The share of assembly industries in total exports increased from 40.6 per cent in 1964–1973 to 71.3 per cent in 1990–1993. Respective import shares remained low until the mid-1980s, when they picked up as Japanese companies started sourcing from low-cost suppliers in South-East Asia. The shift to international sources of supply implied a fundamental change in supplier–buyer relations.

Descriptions of vertical *keiretsu* relations typically emphasize the following characteristics (Waldenberger 1996; Hemmert 1999):

- Relationships are long-term.
- Relationships are exclusive in the sense that suppliers dedicate a major portion of their productive capacity to one buyer.
- This in turn implies a strong concentration of turnover on one buyer.
- Buyers guarantee a purchasing volume that matches the dedicated capacity, although they might source from more than one supplier.
- Products and services transacted in such relations are not standardized commodities, but tailor-made solutions based on buyer specifications. This is why vertical *keiretsu* are also often discussed under the term 'subcontracting' (*shitauke*). In the following, the two terms will be used interchangeably.[3]
- Buyers are typically much larger than their suppliers, so that their demand is sufficient to ensure the financial viability of their suppliers.
- Buyers offer suppliers financial support, but, more importantly, technical and management support through personnel training, temporary dispatches of personnel, and transfers of experienced top managers.

The historic origin of vertical *keiretsu* dates back to the pre-war period of Japanese industrialization. Subcontracting became widely used under the wartime economy in heavy and machinery industries facing rapid increases in demand (Nishiguchi 1994: 28–34). The predominance of subcontracting, especially in assembly industries during the high-growth period (1955 to 1973), was not only induced by strong demand, but also by the fact that Japanese manufacturers, being in a late-comer position, could not rely on existing parts and components suppliers. In addition, strong import and foreign-exchange controls, combined with restrictions on foreign direct investment, precluded purchases from foreign suppliers. Manufacturers were therefore forced to nurture their own supply base. These quasi-proprietary structures were naturally exclusive. This still leaves open the question of why they did not fully integrate the supply stage.

Interpretations and underlying rationale

Vertical *keiretsu* relations represent an organizational form located between a free market transaction and vertically integrated production (Hemmert 1999). Their long-term and exclusive nature distinguishes them from an open-market setting where partners to a transaction can easily be exchanged. The fact that the transacting parties remain legally independent entities differentiates subcontracting from vertical integration.

The pyramid-like structure of value chains in assembly industries – a few end products at the top; a larger number of components at the next layers; and many smaller parts towards the bottom – is independent of the organizational form. The lower vertical integration of Japanese manufacturers meant that they had to deal with fewer first-tier suppliers than their integrated Western counterparts. The exclusive nature implied a mutual interdependence, which fostered, and in turn depended on, trust (Sako 1992). The long-term, trust-based relationship supported the knowledge transfer from the manufacturer to the supplier. The transfer of knowledge was especially important during the infant phase of the supply industry and in the context of technological catch-up. Vertical *keiretsu* allowed a close integration of processes across firm boundaries. They played an essential part in the 'lean production' system (Womack *et al.* 1990: chapter 6). Knowledge transfers and process integration, combined with tailor-made supply solutions, implied a high level of relation-specific investments. The consequently high entry and exit barriers shielded the relationship from short-term price competition.

The strong economic dependence of subcontractors on their major buyers and the comparatively low wage level of their employees created the impression of a dual structure, within which the large end producers on the top of the pyramid exploited the smaller, lower-tier suppliers. However, such an interpretation was in many respects misleading. It ignored the mutual interdependence – buyers were similarly dependent on exclusive suppliers. It also ignored the fact that the differences in wage levels were in line with differences in the level of skill and capital intensity (Nakamura 1995: 162–182). Finally, the exploitation explanation did not account for the knowledge transfer and support that especially first-tier suppliers received from their major customer. Statistical analysis also showed that buyers did not fully pass on market risk, but absorbed part of the variance in final demand (Okamuro 2001). Suppliers were nevertheless indirectly exposed to the competitive pressures that their customers experienced in end-product markets. They were effectively controlled and incentivized to steadily raise productivity and reduce cost to support the competitiveness of the vertical group as a whole.

The historical context briefly sketched above does not answer the question as to why manufacturers did not fully integrate the upstream stages of production like their Western counterparts, but instead established a quasi-integrated structure. The key to this answer is to be found in the segmentation of the Japanese labour market implied by company-based training and career paths that evolved in parallel with the subcontracting system (Nishiguchi 1994: 19–49).

Company-based training and career paths imply high costs with regard to the development and management of human resources. More generally, the commitment to offer a lifetime career to core employees as such puts a high burden on companies. It is therefore understandable that they aim to keep the number of core employees as small as possible. To do so without sacrificing market shares in end-product markets is to outsource labour-intensive production processes along the value chain. The personnel-management cost-driven outsourcing strategy can explain both the general predominance of small and medium-sized enterprises in Japan, and the pronounced wage gap between large and small companies (Waldenberger 1996).

Vertical *keiretsu* ties did not only allow large manufacturers to avoid high personnel costs; they also provided smaller companies with an opportunity to overcome the structural disadvantages implied by a segmented labour market with regard to the recruitment of skilled labour. They would receive training and skilled labour through knowledge transfer and the dispatch of personnel from their major customer. In this context, the transfer of elderly skilled engineers and managers to suppliers was likely to be a win–win arrangement. Suppliers received highly qualified personnel. Buyers could dispose of top personnel whom they would not be able to promote to limited higher in-house ranks. The transfer would at the same time strengthen the underlying business tie.

Change and relevance today

Vertical *keiretsu* structures provided an organizational solution to Japanese industries in a specific economic and institutional environment. While the institutional environment – especially the segmentation of labour markets – has so far remained more or less unchanged, the economic setting fundamentally changed, partly as a result of the success of *keiretsu* structures themselves.

Japan's successful economic catch-up was achieved by an impressive absorptive capacity with regard to foreign technology. Vertical *keiretsu* structures greatly supported the diffusion of technology. The technological base thus created laid the foundations for further improvements and innovation across firm boundaries. During this process, first-and second-tier suppliers established their own research and development capabilities. Their growth enabled them to accumulate not only technical expertise, but also internal sources of finance. It also enhanced their ability to recruit and train talented graduates. As a result, their dependence on their major customer with regard to financial support, as well as knowledge and personnel transfer, declined (Sato 1980). Surveys among manufacturers enquiring about the benefits that they derive from subcontracting showed a clear tendency for supplier technological know-how becoming more important than access to cheap labour (Waldenberger 1999: 171–172).

The internal evolution just described did not weaken *keiretsu* ties *per se*, but rather put them on a more-equal footing. The more fundamental change resulted from the internationalization of the supply chain that started in the mid-1980s. This was spurred on the one hand by high domestic labour costs, a strong yen, and intensified international competition, and, on the other hand, by an economic and political transformation of South-East Asia that made countries in the region an attractive destination for foreign direct investment. Both factors induced a rapid shift in the regional and commodity structure of Japanese imports. Between 1990 and 1996, Japanese imports of parts and components in assembly industries increased 2.3-fold (Waldenberger 1999: 171). South-East Asia became Japan's extended factory. Smaller subcontracting firms did not survive the 'hollowing-out' of domestic supply chains. The stronger ones went abroad by themselves, thus expanding the existing domestic customer ties on to an international scale.

Over the last twenty years, global competition has continued to push towards a further emancipation of suppliers and buyers, with the former looking for new business abroad and the latter for alternative global purchasing channels. Given the high share of value added contributed by parts and components, the competitiveness of auto makers depended to a large extent on how effectively they managed their supply chains. Sticking to vertical *keiretsu* ties may still have been by far the most preferred arrangement, but it no longer guaranteed the best match. Japanese electronics firms gave up the production of lower-end consumer products and became increasingly global suppliers of high-value components. Progressive maturation and standardization of business processes reduced the relation-specific investments that once formed the economic rationale for long-term exclusive *keiretsu* ties. In addition, the highly competitive and dynamically changing environment increased the cost of committing to a long-term business partnership and made such a commitment less credible. Close, long-term and personalized business relations are still important in Japan today, especially in the automotive industry. There, they have, however, become less exclusive, more competitive, and more diverse overall (Aoki and Lennerfors 2013).

A note on distribution keiretsu

Vertical *keiretsu* relations can also extend into distribution channels, although they have never drawn the same level of attention as subcontracting along supply chains. They were especially pronounced for cars, home electric appliances, cosmetics, and pharmaceuticals (Maruyama 1993: 34). They were in many respects similar to supply *keiretsu*, but also had distribution-specific structural characteristics (Itō 2000; Utaka 2003):

- *Keiretsu* distribution channels provided manufacturers with exclusive access to retail outlets.
- It would at times extend over several stages from national through regional wholesalers to retail shops.
- The manufacturer would be much larger than the wholesale and retail companies.
- Manufacturers would provide various kinds of support to *keiretsu* retailers, like training, dispatch of sales staff, or marketing.
- They would also protect retailers from competition, provide margins and volume rebates to encourage sales, and accept the return of unsold products.

Distribution *keiretsu* served several functions (Shimotani 1995; Kikkawa and Takoka 1998; Itō 2000). They effectively coped with the shortcomings of the special structural characteristics of the Japanese distribution system, which, at the time, was dominated by very small family businesses. The high degree of urbanization, combined with a lack of motorization, implied a very high shop density at the retail level and two or more wholesale layers. It was only through the establishment of a *keiretsu* distribution that manufacturers were able to control the flow, pricing, and promotion of their goods. The exclusive nature of *keiretsu* sales channels ensured that training, promotion, and other support measures provided by the controlling manufacturer would not spill over to competing products. Support measures were especially important for products like cars, home electric appliances, cosmetics, and pharmaceuticals, which required well-trained sales personnel. Last, but not least, distribution *keiretsu* not only supported differentiation and branding, but also increased the entry barriers for newcomers, including foreign brands, which would need to establish their own distribution network to compete in the Japanese market (Flath 2005).

Distribution *keiretsu* did not fully overcome the high costs of the traditional Japanese distribution system that were caused by geographical conditions, consumer behaviour, and regulations that prevented the expansion of larger-scale discounters in order to protect the income interests of small-shop owners. As the distribution system modernized, the advantages of *keiretsu* channels vanished. Trends were already visible in the 1970s and 1980s (Maruyama 1993: 29–30). The main drivers of modernization were the motorization of Japanese society and the deregulation of the retail sector, combined with a stricter application of the Japanese Antimonopoly Act with regard to vertical restraints. Deregulation and stricter anti-monopoly enforcement had been strongly pressured by the US and the EU in bilateral trade negotiations toward the end of the 1980s and in the early 1990s (Kikkawa 1998: 101–102). The more liberal regulatory environment allowed larger stores and retail chains to rapidly expand. Innovative entrepreneurs exploiting advances in transportation as well as information and communication technology further streamlined distribution channels (Maruyama 2005). Given the improved economies of scale in a modernized, open distribution system, manufacturer-controlled *keiretsu* channels proved in many cases too expensive. However, they did not fully disappear (Wako and Ōta 2005). The automotive industry still relies on *keiretsu* channels, whereas home electronic appliances are now mainly sold through large independent retail chains, especially in the metropolitan areas. Cosmetics and pharmaceuticals have moved to a hybrid system, combining both open and controlled channels.

Conclusions

Keiretsu present an organizational form between full integration and full independence. As such, they are not limited to Japan, but can also be found in other countries, especially in emerging Asian economies (Hemmert 2007). In Japan, they were most prominent during the high-growth and successful technological catch-up period following the Second World War. *Keiretsu* organization on the one hand offers relational stability, while on the other hand it reduces the complexity and rigidity of large integrated bureaucratic organizations.

Both horizontal and vertical *keiretsu* provided organizational solutions adapted to the Japanese regulatory environment and the state of economic development. Horizontal *keiretsu* were a response to the dissolution of the pre-war zaibatsu. They allowed for fast capital accumulation, risk sharing, and governance in the context of politically suppressed capital markets. Vertical *keiretsu* overcame market deficiencies in the supply of industrial goods and in the distribution of new, service intensive consumer products. Supply *keiretsu* supported the absorption and diffusion of imported technology and domestic innovations, especially in assembly industries. They complemented the segmentation of labour markets created by the predominance of company-based careers.

As the Japanese economy developed, financial markets were deregulated and liberalized; supply channels were globalized; and the distribution system was modernized, the *keiretsu* lost much of their competitive advantage. They have, in many cases, given way to shorter-term, open market relations or more fully integrated organizational forms. Still, they have not completely vanished. Long-term, personal relations continue to be the preferred mode of structuring business in Japan. So, as long as short-term market transactions are not clearly superior, Japanese companies will stick to traditional ways. In new and highly dynamic industries facing complex cross-firm coordination problems, the intermediate organizational form continues to have a competitive advantage, as could be seen in the introduction of the mobile Internet, where the Japanese approach of forming exclusive strategic alliances led by the mobile network operator proved more effective in solving the various coordination problems than the open European approach (Haas and Waldenberger 2005). However, the advantage was limited to the first years of the mobile Internet. Japan's mobile telecommunication industry has, in the meantime, moved to an open system.

The example above shows that intermediate organizational forms, while no longer representing a dominant structural characteristic of industrial organization in Japan, remain a strategic option that can be advantageous in a specific industry for a specific development phase. As such, they also bear relevance outside of Japan.

Notes

1 See, for example, the Mitsubishi Group (www.mitsubishi.com). Group identity is maintained beyond president club meetings. For example, some groups still entertain joint public-relations committees, like the Mitsui Group (www.mitsuipr.com/en/index.html).
2 The ban was lifted in 1997 (Thorson and Siegfanz 1999).
3 Vertical *keiretsu* are based on subcontracting relations, but subcontracting relations can also be found in industries like textiles that do not have pronounced vertical supply *keiretsu*.

References

Aoki, K. and Lennerfors, T. T. (2013). Whither Japanese keiretsu? The transformation of vertical keiretsu in Toyota, Nissan and Honda 1991 to 2011. *Asia Pacific Business Review*, 19: 70–84.

Aoki, M. (1988). *Information, Incentives, and Bargaining in the Japanese Economy*, Cambridge, UK: Cambridge University Press.

Aoki, M., Patrick, H., and Sheard, P. (1994). The Japanese main bank system: an introductory overview. In: Aoki, M. and Patrick, H. (eds), *The Japanese Main Bank System: Its Relevance for Developing and Transforming Economies*. Oxford, UK: Oxford University Press.

Baum, H. (1997). Börsen- und Kapitalmarktrecht in Japan. In: Hopt, K. J., Rudolph, B., and Baum, H. (eds), *Börsenreform. Eine ökonomische, rechtsvergleichende und rechtspolitische Untersuchung*. Stuttgart: Schäffer-Poeschel, pp. 1265–1395.

Chen, C. R., Guo, S., and Tay, N. S. P. (2010). Are member firms of corporate groups less risky? *Financial Management*, 39: 59–82.

Dow, S. and McGuire, J. (2009). Propping and tunneling: empirical evidence from Japanese keiretsu. *Journal of Banking and Finance*, 33: 1817–1828.

Flath, D. (2005). Distribution keiretsu, foreign direct investment, and import penetration in Japan. *The Japanese Economy*, 33: 26–53.

Haas, M. and Waldenberger, F. (2005). Strategic alliances and innovative performance in network industries: the case of the mobile internet in Japan and Europe. In: Sudoh, O. (ed) *Digital Economy and Social Design*, Tokyo: Springer, pp. 126–151.

Hashimoto, J. (1992). Zaibatsu no kontserun-ka (Transformation of zaibatsu into a multi-corporate enterprise). In: Hashimoto, J. and Takeda, H. (eds), *Hōsei Daigaku Sangyō Jōhō Sentaa, Nihon Keizai no Hatten to Kigyō Shūdan* (Japan's economic Development and Business Groups), Tokyo: Tokyo University Press, pp. 91–148.

Hemmert, M. (1999). Intermediate organization revisited: a framework for the vertical division of labor in manufacturing and the case of Japanese assembly industries. *Industrial and Corporate Change*, 8: 487–517.

Hemmert, M. (2007). The competitive potential of Asian business groups: a comparative analysis of Kigyō Shūdan and Chaebol. In: Yau, O. H. M. and Chow, R. P. M. (eds), *Harmony Versus Conflict in Asian Business*, New York: Palgrave Macmillan, pp. 186–208.

Hoshi, T. (1994). The economic role of corporate grouping and the main bank. In: Aoki, M. and Dore, R. (eds), *The Japanese Firm: Sources of Competitive Strength*, Oxford, UK: Oxford University Press, pp. 285–304.

Hoshi, T. and Kashyap, A. (2001). *Corporate Finance and Governance in Japan: the Road to the Future*, Cambridge, MA: MIT Press.

Imai, M. (1986). *Kaizen: the Key to Japan's Competitive Success*, New York: McGraw-Hill.

Itami, H., Kagono, T. and Itō, M. (eds) (1993). *Nihon no Kigyō Shisutemu. Dai 4-kan. Kigyō to shijō* (The Japanese Company System. Volume 4. Firms and Markets), Tokyo: Yūhikaku.

Itō, M. (2000). Competition in the Japanese distribution market and market access from abroad. In: Ito, T. and Krueger, A. O. (eds), *Deregulation and Interdependence in the Asia-Pacific Region*, Chicago, IL: University of Chicago Press, pp. 139–156.

Japanese Bankers Association (2006). *The Banking System in Japan*, Tokyo: Research Department Japanese Bankers Association.

Japan Fair Trade Commission (JFTC) (1994). *Nihon no Roku Dai-kigyō Shūdan no Jittai* (Actual situation of the six large business groupings), Tokyo: Tōyō Keizai Shinpōsha.

Japan Fair Trade Commission (JTFC) (2002). *Heisei 14nenpan Kōsei Torihiki Iinkai Nenji Hōkoku. Dokusen Kinshi Hakusho* (Annual Report Japanese Fair Trade Commission 2002. Anti-monopoly White Paper), Tokyo: Kōsei Torihiki Kyōkai, www.jftc.go.jp/info/nenpou/h13/13kakuron00002-8.htm, last accessed 17 October 2015.

Kikkawa, T. (1992). Sengo-gata kigyō shūdan no keisei (Formation of post-war type business groups). In: Hōsei Daigaku Sangyō Jōhō Sentaa, Hashimoto, J. and Takeda, H. (eds), *Nihon Keizai no Hatten to Kigyō Shūdan* (Japan's Economic Development and Business Groups), Tokyo: Tokyo University Press, pp. 255–304.

Kikkawa, T. and Takoka, M. (1998). A new perspective on the Japanese distribution system: structure and trade practices. *Social Science Japan Journal*, 1: 101–119.

Kimino, S., Driffield, N., and Saal, D. (2012). Do keiretsu really hinder FDI into Japanese manufacturing? *International Journal of the Economics of Business*, 19: 377–395.

Kwak, W, Lee, H. and Mande V. (2009). Institutional ownership and income smoothing by Japanese banks through loan loss provisions. *Review of Pacific Basin Financial Markets and Policies*, 12: 219–243.

Lincoln, J. R. and Gerlach, M. (2004). *Japan's Network Economy: Structure, Persistence, and Change*. Cambridge, UK: Cambridge University Press.

Lincoln, J. R. and Shimotani, M. (2009). *Whither the Keiretsu, Japan's Business Networks? How Were They Structured? What Did They Do? Why Are They Gone?*, IRLE Working Paper No. 188-09, http://irle.berkeley.edu/workingpapers/188-09.pdf, last accessed 17 October 2015.

McGuire, J. and Dow, S. (2009). Japanese keiretsu: past present, future. *Asia Pacific Journal of Management*, 26: 333–351.

Maruyama, M. (1993). A study of the distribution system in Japan. *OECD Economics Department Working Papers*, No. 136, http://dx.doi.org/10.1787/150587255461, last accessed 17 October 2015.

Maruyama, M. (2005). Japanese distribution channels. *The Japanese Economy*, 32: 27–48.

Miwa, Y. (1996). *Firms and Industrial Organization in Japan*, Basingstoke, UK: Macmillan.

Miwa, Y. and Ramseyer, J. M. (2001). Rethinking relationship-specific investments: subcontracting in the Japanese automobile industry. *Michigan Law Review*, 98: 2636–2667.

Miwa, Y. and Ramseyer, J. M. (2002). The fable of the keiretsu. *Journal of Economics and Management Strategy*, 11: 169–224.

Miyashita, K. and Russel, D. (1995). *Keiretsu: Inside the Hidden Japanese Conglomerates*. New York: McGraw-Hill.

Nakamura, T. (1995). *The Postwar Japanese Economy: Its Development and Structure 1973–1994*, Tokyo: University of Tokyo Press, 2nd edn.

Nakatani, I. (1984). The economic role of financial corporate groupings. In: Aoki, M. (ed) *The Economic Analysis of the Japanese Firm*. Amsterdam: North Holland, pp. 227–258.

Nishiguchi, T. (1994). *Strategic Industrial Sourcing: the Japanese Advantage*, Oxford, UK: Oxford University Press.

Nishitateno, S. (2014). *Network Effects on Trade in Intermediate Goods: Evidence from the Automobile Industry*, Australian National University, Arndt-Corden Department of Economics, Departmental Working Papers, https://crawford.anu.edu.au/acde/publications/publish/papers/wp2014/wp_econ_2014_09.pdf, last accessed 17 October 2015.

Odagiri, H. (1994). *Growth through Competition, Competition through Growth. Strategic Management and the Economy in Japan*, Oxford, UK: Clarendon Press.

Okamuro, H. (2001). Risk sharing in the supplier relationship: new evidence from the Japanese automotive industry. *Journal of Economic Behavior and Organization*, 45: 361–381.

Okazaki, T. (1992). Shihon jiyūka ikō no kigyō shūdan (Business groups after capital liberalization). In: Hōsei Daigaku Sangyō Jōhō Sentaa, Hashimoto, J., and Takeda, H. (eds), *Nihon Keizai no Hatten to Kigyō Shūdan* (Japan's Economic Development and Business Groups), Tokyo: Tokyo University Press, pp. 305–335.

Sako, M. (1992). *Prices, Quality and Trust. Inter-Firm Relations in Britain and Japan*, Cambridge, UK: Cambridge University Press.

Sato, Y. (1980). *Teiseichōki ni Okeru Gaichū Shitauke Kanri* (Purchase- and Subcontract-Management in Times of Low Growth). Tokyo: Chūō Keizaisha.

Sheard, P. (1994). Main banks and the governance of financial distress. In: Aoki, M. and Patrick, H. (eds), *The Japanese Main Bank System: Its Relevance for Developing and Transforming Economies*. Oxford, UK: Oxford University Press.

Shimotani, M. (1995). The formation of distribution keiretsu: the case of Matsushita Electric. *Business History*, 37: 54–69.

Tanaka, T. (2012). *Sōgō Shōsha no Kenkyū* (Research on General Trading Companies), Tokyo: Tōyō Keizai Shinpōsha.

Thorson, A. H. and Siegfanz, F. (1999). The 1997 deregulation of Japan's holding companies. *Pacific Rim Law and Policy Journal*, 8, 261–349.

Torii, A. and Nariu, T. (2004). On the length of wholesale marketing channels in Japan. *Japanese Economy*, 32: 5–26.

Tsuruta, T. (1988). The rapid growth era. In: Komiya, R., Okuno, M., and Suzumura, K. (eds), *Industrial Policy of Japan*, New York: Academic Press, pp. 49–87.

Utaka, A. (2003). An economic analysis of Japanese distribution systems. *Managerial and Decision Economics*, 24: 411–416.

Wako, T. and Ōta, H. (2005). Who benefits from corroding keiretsu? *Pacific Economic Review*, 10: 539–556.

Waldenberger, F. (1996). The influence of transaction costs in labor markets on the organization of industry – a comparative analysis of Japanese industrial organization. In: Picot, A. and Schlicht, E. (eds), *Firms, Markets, and Contracts. Contributions to Neoinstitutional Economics*. Heidelberg: Physica-Verlag, pp. 59–75.

Waldenberger, F. (1999). *Organisation und Evolution arbeitsteiliger Systeme. Erkenntnisse aus der japanischen Wirtschaftsentwicklung*. Munich: Iudicium Verlag.

Weinstein, D. E. and Yafeh, Y. (1995). Japan's corporate groups: collusion or competitive? An empirical investigation of keiretsu behaviour. *Journal of Industrial Economics*, 43: 359–376.

Womack, J. P., Jones, D. T., and Roos, D. (1990). *The Machine That Changed the World*, New York: Free Press.

Yonekawa, S. (ed.) (1990). *General Trading Companies: a Comparative and Historical Study*, Tokyo: United Nations University Press.

Young, A. K. (1979). *The Sōgō Shōsha: Japan's Multinational Trading Companies*, Boulder, CO: Westview Press.

4

Japanese family businesses

Tim Goydke

Introduction

In the past, Japan has been recognized mainly for its large corporate enterprises and its business groups (*keiretsu*). Little attention has been paid to Japan's small- and medium-sized companies (SMEs)[1], and especially to family businesses, although SMEs, which are in most cases family-owned, constitute 99.7 per cent of the total of 4.3 million Japanese enterprises. The SMEs contribute to almost 70 per cent of total employment and have a similarly high share of the value added to the economy as compared with SMEs in other developed countries (Economist Intelligence Unit 2010).

Japan also has a long tradition of long-lived family businesses. Until recently, Japan was home to the oldest-known family enterprise in the world, a construction company which closed in 2006 after more than 1,400 years of existence (Hutcheson 2007).

Also, today's large, multi-industry conglomerates like Sumitomo, Mitsui or Mitsubishi have their roots in the pre-war holdings run by single capitalist families or clans.[2] Ten per cent of Japan's large corporations are still run by a member of the founding family, the best-known being Toyota (Morck and Nakamura 2003).

While Japanese family firms have long remained unrecognized by the academic world inside and outside of Japan, recently, a growing number of scholarly contributions have been dealing with the subject. Asaba (2012) demonstrates that family firms in the electrical machinery industry between 1995 and 2006 showed a more aggressive and sustainable investment strategy than non-family firms. Allouche *et al.* (2008) proved that family businesses perform better in terms of profitability and financial structure than non-family firms, and that the level of family control is strongly correlated with the performance. Similarly, Saito (2008) found that family firms outperformed non-family firms in the 1990s (1990–1998). In a study on family business in Japan over the last forty years, Mehrotra *et al.* (2013) came to the conclusion that companies led by non-blood heirs outperform those led by biological heirs. According to Kurashina (2003), family businesses perform better than non-family businesses in twenty-one of thirty-three industries, whereas in only seven is the performance worse.

This chapter aims to shed some light on family businesses in Japan, its background, tradition, management approach, etc. First, definitions of family firms and its perception in Japan from a scholarly perspective will be introduced. The second section provides an overview of the characteristics of family firms in Japan. In the third section, a discussion of recent challenges for family businesses will be provided.

Definition of family firms

There exists a multiplicity of definitions of family businesses in literature.[3] Most authors, however, agree on the dominance of a family over the company in terms of management, ownership, and control as a decisive factor, and the influence of more than one generation on the company's strategy and vision (e.g. Chua *et al.* 1999: 25; Astrachan *et al.* 2006: 169; Eisenmann-Mittenzwei 2006: 18).

To understand family businesses, it is helpful to consider these entities as the intersection of two social systems, i.e. the family and the company, with different values and goals. These relations, supplemented by ownership as the third component, can be shown in a three-circle model (Figure 4.1). Every person involved can be assigned to one of these three circles or to one of the intersections between the fields in this model. Thus, family members have either no direct relationship with the company; are only passive owners of shares; or are involved in the enterprise as managers and/or owners. Since the management has a central role, it is again specified as a nuclear element in the company.

In Japan, family businesses are called *dōzoku gaisha* (family firm) or *daidai kagyō* (family-like business/multi-generation business), but the terms *kazoku keiei* (family management) or *dōzoku keiei no kigyō* (family-led enterprise) are also frequently used (Yamashiro 1997: 39; Bosse 2003: 33).

The Japanese corporation-tax law (*hōjinzei hō*) provides a legal definition for family firms, in which the ownership structure is of special importance: a company is regarded a family firm (*dōzoku gaisha*) if a family holds more than 50 per cent of the shares.[4] However, Kamei (2008) argues that, unlike many Western countries, families in Japan often possess only a minority share in their business, which is explained by the high inheritance tax (up to 70 per cent before the

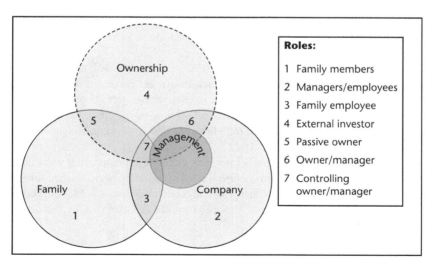

Figure 4.1 Three-circle model of family firms

Source: Authors' figure, following McCracken (2000: 11)

reform in 2002 and now up to 50 per cent). As a result, the retention rate for capital held by the founding family decreased considerably after several generations.

According to Kurashina (2003), three types of Japanese family businesses can be distinguished:

1   Family members are major shareholders and they keep the leading positions (president, vice president, and general manager).
2   The founding family is the major shareholder, but no one from the family occupies a higher management position. Family members are simply members of the board.
3   The founding family is not the major shareholder. However, they participate in the top management.

Characteristics of Japanese family firms

Size, number, and legal form

Family firms in Japan strongly differ in size and legal form. They can be both private firms (kojin kigyō) and statutory corporations (hōjin kigyō), both large-scale companies and small and medium-sized enterprises (SME).

In the case of small enterprises, the entrepreneur usually unites management and ownership in their person, so that generally these enterprises can be ranked among the family firms. On the other hand, large-scale enterprises in particular tend towards a form of business organization where the influence of the owner family is not so clearly visible.

Aoi *et al.* (2012) differentiate three types of Japanese family firms:

1   Small businesses not publicly traded, which have survived over 300 years. The majority of these firms are independent hotels, restaurants, and craft makers.
2   Firms which were mostly started before the Second World War in heavy industries, transportation, transportation equipment, and electric appliances (e.g. Tobu Railroad, Toyota, Nakayama Steel).
3   Firms in newer high-tech industries mostly listed at the stock exchange but still run by the founding families (e.g. Square-Enix, Omron, Kyocera).

For the latter, two peaks of initial public offering (IPO) can be observed, i.e. between 1949 and 1950 and between 1961 and 1964. After the stock exchanges reopened in 1949, around 450 pre-war listed firms went public again, of which only approximately 22 per cent were family-owned. However, after the opening of the second section of the stock exchange in 1961, a number of relatively young firms appeared (625 firms) of which approximately 60 per cent were family firms (Shim and Okamuro 2011: 194).

Similarly, Kurashina (2003) finds that 43 per cent of the listed companies were family businesses. It is no surprise that, with increasing firm size, the ratio of owner-managed firms is lower; however, even among firms with more than 1,000 regular employees it is 34.7 per cent, and, for firms with over 5,000 regular employees, 19.4 per cent are still managed by the owner family (Morikawa 2008: 5f).

Family system

Many Japanese authors (e.g. Kitano 1970; Nakane 1970; Kumagai 1992) have linked the patterns and behaviour observed in Japanese industrial organizations to the traditional construct of the Japanese 'family system' (*ie-seido* or *iemoto-seido*). *Ie* can be directly translated as 'household', but its implications go beyond this simple meaning: *ie* includes the tangible possessions of the family, i.e. the material assets, as well as the intangible organization of the group to which the people belong, i.e. their class and ranking in society. *Ie* embodies the family values of the Japanese feudalism with its strong roots in Confucianism: especially seniority and social relations characterized by mutual rights and obligations and in which trust has a higher value than achievements. The traditional *ie* is characterized by a network of hierarchical ties among people within an *ie* and between households. Rights and duties in the *ie* were based on the principles of *ko* – duty to parents – and *on* – reciprocal obligations between family members (Kitaoji 1971: 1036; Bhappu 2000: 410f; Horide 2009).

Even today, the values of the family culture play a substantial role in many family firms. The importance of these values for business becomes particularly clear in traditional enterprises, whose establishment often dates back to the Tokugawa (Edo) period, but also can be found in companies established after the Second World War. One visible example is the family codex (*kakun*) which can be found in many family firms, particularly in traditional trading firms. In the *kakun*, the most important rules of behaviour – often on the basis of religious values or the rules of the *samurai* class – are written down. These codices cover admonishments to the employees to work diligently, to be frugal, to obey the government, and to retain the reputation of the house. The more-modern codices reflect social responsibility in the reconstruction of the Japanese economy and society in the post-war period. Many enterprises cite common values in their firm slogan instead of profit orientation, and thereby promote the motivation of their employees. These basic values have a significant influence on the decisions of the entrepreneur, ranging from personnel and management to succession regulation, and thus on central aspects of management (Ramseyer 1979: 217; Picken 1987: 138; Goydke and Smailus 2009).

Succession

One central function of the *ie* system was the continuance of the house. Therefore, succession is a key aspect of the *ie* system. Succession basically means the transfer of an enterprise to a successor. In the broadest sense, all forms of the transfer of leadership and financial responsibility are included (Kollmann 2005: 410).

Succession in the traditional family implies the occupation of the position as head of the household (*shōtai nushi*). Particularly in patrilinear families in the agricultural sector, the successor was usually the oldest son. In families in the commercial/trading sector, the successful continuation of the house took a higher value than the continuation of the blood-related line. If no male descendant was available, adoption was quite common, and it still is today.

Although there is a lack of comparative data, most authors agree that adoption has been far more popular in Japan than in most other industrialized countries (e.g. Paulson 1984; O'Halloran 2009; Mehrotra *et al.* 2013). Child adoption was only introduced by the Americans after the Second World War, whereas the traditional form of adoption in Japan has been adult adoption, known as *yōshi engumi* or *futsū yōshi* (ordinary adoption). *Yōshi engumi* is a contract by mutual consent whereby the (usually male) adoptee agrees to carry forward the name of the adopting family and pledge allegiance in return for inheritance. He also often marries a daughter of the patriarch or is already a son-in-law, making him a so-called *muko yōshi* (husband-brother). However, if a potential candidate is already married, it is not uncommon to adopt the couple together. The displaced biological heirs are normally not cast out of the family, but get treated as second best, often pursuing the life of the idle rich (Mehrotra *et al.* 2013: 842ff).

No overall data on succession by non-blood heirs exists, but Mehrotra *et al.* (2013) found from their research data on approximately 1,200 family firms that 10 per cent are run by non-consanguineous heirs. Goydke and Smailus (2009), in their research on family businesses in the furniture industry found that in the SME academy (*chūshō kigyō daigakkō*), a training institute for entrepreneurs, one out of twenty-five participants is normally adopted.

Apart from succession within the family (*shinzoku nai shōkei*), the Japanese literature (e.g. JCBS 2006: 15) differentiates between two further forms of succession: the succession by a manager from outside the family, who is recruited, for example, among the company's own employees, and the sale or the fusion (mergers and acquisitions, M&A) with another company. Both forms have gained increasing importance recently.

Longevity

Longevity is one of the most striking characteristics of Japanese family firms. In comparison with American family firms, which are, on average, twenty-four years old, Japanese companies are, on average, fifty-two years old. There are 15,000 companies in Japan that are more than 100 years old; around 400 have a history of more than 300 years; and seven companies date back more than 1,000 years. Until 2006, the oldest enterprise in the world was also a Japanese company with a history of 1,421 years (*Chosun Online* 2007; Hutcheson 2007; Shizuoka Sangyō Shien Saito 2007).

According to Goto (2006), the longevity of Japanese firms can be explained by:

1 the relatively stable and secure environment during the period of Japan's self-imposed isola-tion under the Tokugawa shogunate (1603–1867);

2 management practices derived from the traditional household system of the *ie*, such as sepa-ration of ownership and management, personal management, accounting system, and risk management; and

3 the influence of the Tokugawa period's *shingaku* movement – a mix of Shintoism, Zen Buddhism, and Confucianism, which provided a system of ethics for merchants and arti-sans, encouraging devotion to work, frugality, honesty, obligations to society, etc.

The longevity of Japanese firms is often referred to the tradition of the *shinise*, literally meaning 'companies/shops of long standing'. *Shinise* originally described traditional families of merchants and artisans from Kyoto, but, today, generally refers to companies or stores which have existed for more than 300 years (Suekane 2009). Among the 400 *shinise* still existing, the largest number are *sake* (liquor) manufacturers (57), inns (31), and pastry shops (19). Almost 50 per cent are in the manufacturing sector, and the largest numbers can be found in Kyoto and Tokyo (see Table 4.1).

Table 4.1 Distribution of *shinise* by region (top five prefectures) and business type

Prefecture	No. of shinise	Business type	Percentage
Kyoto	55	Manufacturers	46.2%
Tokyo	34	Wholesalers	19.0%
Aichi	19	Service	16.4%
Osaka	17	Retailers	14.2%
Hyogo	15	Construction	4.0%

Source: Suehara (2009: 2)

The roots of *shinise* are seen in the managerial creed of Edo period merchants from *Ōmi* province (today part of Shiga Prefecture near Kyoto). Their distinctive feature was peddling trade throughout Japan. Their business was based on the behavioural principle of *sampo yoshi*, describing a three-way relationship between buyer, seller, and the society. For *Ōmi* merchants, all participating parties should benefit from an interaction, and revenues should be generated ethically and fairly (Sakai 2013). Core characteristics of *shinise,* therefore, were quality- and customer-orientation, sound business practices (e.g. management without debt, cash-flow-based management), and horizontal networks with other firms (Kamei 2008: 9).

One good example is the ITOCHU Corporation, which was founded in 1858 by Itō Chubei (1842–1903), an *Ōmi* merchant, as a linen trading company. Since its foundation, ITOCHU evolved into one of Japan's large general trading companies (*sōgō shōsha*). In 1872, Chubei established a 'store law' as a very first ethical code. As part of this management philosophy, the store's net profit was divided between the store owner, the store's reserve fund, and the employees (ITOCHU 2008). Even today, ITOCHU refers to the managerial creed of the *Ōmi* merchants as its CSR core principle:

> Ever since Chubei Itoh I originally founded ITOCHU, we have followed the Ohmi merchant philosophy of 'sampo yoshi' [. . .], and continually apply it in our daily business activities. [. . .] If returns are generated for both customers and a company, and people become more affluent and comfortable, leading to the realization of a sustainable society, then the company will enjoy stable returns as a natural result. The ITOCHU Group corporate philosophy of 'Committed to the Global Good' expresses this 'sampo yoshi' spirit on a large scale.
>
> *(ITOCHU 2012: 2)*

Several authors also link the longevity of Japanese family firms to the practice of adoption, as it does not only solve the problem of a missing heir but also the issue of a lack of leadership capacity among existing heirs (e.g. Kondo 1990; Bhappu 2000). Adoption allows the continuation of the lineage tradition of the house on a long-term basis. As a result, unlike the US, where the company is regarded as property that can be bought or sold, family firms in Japan remain in the family for generations (Picken 1987: 138; Howorth *et al.* 2006: 2, 31).

Entrepreneurship

Although Japan has a long history of entrepreneurship, comparably few people today take the initiative to start their own business in Japan. According to the Global Entrepreneurship Monitor 2013, Japan ranks last in the Total Early-Stage Entrepreneurial Activity (TEA) index, which covers individuals both in the process of starting a business and running new businesses less than three and a half years old, while the United States has the highest TEA score. Together with Russia, Japan has the lowest entrepreneurial intention rates; less than 2 per cent of Japanese people aged between eighteen and sixty-four are actively working to establish their own business, while in the US the ratio is 4.9 per cent. The 2009 Global Entrepreneurship Monitor revealed that Japan is the most risk-averse country among twenty innovation-based advanced economies. Moreover, Japan has the lowest number of people who see opportunities in setting up their own business or could consider a career in an entrepreneurial business: only 6 per cent of the Japanese people asked in a survey saw opportunities for starting a business, and only 9 per cent believed that they personally have the necessary skills (Amorós and Bosma 2013; *The Economist* 2013; Karlin 2013).

The reasons for these low figures may be manifold. Karlin (2013) sees the major reason as the comparably high risks of setting up a business in Japan. Debt financing for start-ups carries a major personal risk for the entrepreneur, as the assets of the company and the individual are collateralized. Moreover, debt is transferable, i.e. if the venture fails, the guarantor and/or family of the founder may be held liable for the debt, and, even in case of the founder's death, the family is still responsible for the unpaid debt. However, entrepreneurs do not have many other options for capitalization. Due to a fairly even distribution of wealth, Japan lacks the super-rich venture capitalists who often fund business start-ups in other countries.

Because of the low prestige in which entrepreneurship is held in Japan, entrepreneurs are unable or unwilling to ask family or friends for financial support. As such, it is even difficult to find a financial guarantor. New entrepreneurs also cannot count on financial assistance from the first generation of successful entrepreneurs. Unlike the US, where entrepreneurs often set up a number of start-ups, many of which fail, Karlin (2013) describes the older generation of Japanese entrepreneurs as 'one-hit wonders' who are quite risk-averse and prefer conservative investments, such as Japanese or US government bonds. Many former employees dare to make the leap into independence only after leaving a large enterprise. As a result, the average age of entrepreneurs is already high when they start their business (Storz 1997: 36; Bosse 2003: 71f; SMEA 2007: 27, 39).

The low number of start-ups also prevents the development of a venture-capital market, and foreign venture-capital firms do not regard Japan as an interesting market. As a result, almost no foreign venture-capital firms are active in Japan. In turn, the lack of venture-capital funding may prevent potential entrepreneurs from setting up a business (Karlin 2013).

Until recently, almost no spin-offs from universities or incubators occurred, basically because universities in Japan are mainly considered job training centres or springboards for a career in large companies. Also, it has been more common for an employer – quite often a large *keiretsu* group – to establish a new but dependent entity integrated into the *keiretsu* group (so-called 'corporate venturing' or 'intrapreneurship'), rather than inventors leaving the company to set up their own business. However, the situation has now started to change. A growing number of incubators were set up recently at Japanese universities, and large companies such as the real estate giant Mitsubishi Estate started their own incubators with support functions for start-ups (Haghirian 2014: 21).

Many authors emphasize that many successful entrepreneurs have studied abroad. One example is Hiroshi Mikitani, the founder and CEO of the Internet and e-commerce service company Rakuten Inc., who earned an MBA at Harvard. Mikitani quit his job at the Industrial Bank of Japan to start a consulting business, and later founded Rakuten. He is frequently featured in the media as role model for Japanese entrepreneurs (Sasagawa 2012; Karlin 2013).

Table 4.2 provides a summary of the perception of Japanese family firms and family-like businesses (*kagyō*) in contrast to the (large) non-family enterprises.

Challenges for family firms

One of the major challenges for traditional family businesses in Japan is the rapid ageing of the Japanese population. The 'baby boomers' (*dankai sedai*) merit special attention. Since 2007, these people have been reaching the age of sixty, which is the official retirement age in Japan. The age of the managing directors in SMEs (enterprises with a capital of under 10 million yen) has increased by more than five years in the past twenty years, while in large-scale enterprises (which hold capital of more than one billion yen) it remained relatively constant at approximately sixty-two to sixty-three years. Entrepreneurs are, on average, over fifty-seven years old,

Table 4.2 Forms of management in Japanese companies

Family-like businesses	Non-family (large) enterprises
Old-fashioned	Modern
The logic of kinship; the concept of the *ie* group	The logic of property and of capital
Blood family; company; local relationship	Capitalist entrepreneur; owner entrepreneur
Closed group with emotional ties	Economic unit
Family head; patriarchal structure	Management under the control of capital
Obligations and honour; emotion; means of subsistence; growth in inherited property	Economic profit maximization
Tradition of mutual assistance; service to the company; bottom-up decisions	The principle of the individualistic entrepreneur
Kinship ties between the 'in group'; foreigners regarded as the 'out group'	A society in which its members are in competition

Source: Yamashiro (1997: 49)

and, with an average resignation age of sixty-seven years, the succession problem has recently become one of the most important challenges (Kohlbacher 2006: 109).

For small enterprises in particular, in which the entrepreneur has a central role and is the so-called 'value driver', sudden death or illness can have devastating effects, even resulting in bankruptcy. According to a study by Harada (2007), the most frequently mentioned causes for closing down a company are pessimistic future expectation for the business (37.9 per cent) and the age and illness of the managing director (20 per cent). This applies in particular to those enterprises in which the managing director is older than sixty-five years (68 per cent of the responses) (Harada 2007: 403f).

Many small businesses have not been created with the intention of continuing for many years. In particular, in the case of private firms without additional employees, the business activity is often terminated with the retirement of the entrepreneur. For all other companies, early succession planning is of strategic importance (Bosse 2003: 71f, JCBS 2006: 10).

Conclusions

It has been shown that Japanese family businesses have unjustifiably gained little attention from scholars and the public, as they provide a considerable contribution to the Japanese economy. Although family businesses have been overlooked, they form the backbone of the Japanese industry. Japan has a tradition of long-lived family-owned businesses, and is host to some of the oldest firms in the world. Their business ethos stems from the tradition of merchant families who developed a value system of reciprocal obligations and mutual benefits. Despite its long tradition of family businesses, today, Japan lacks innovative start-ups, due to unfavourable support networks and a certain public disdain for entrepreneurship. The major challenge that family businesses face is the question of succession. Many Japanese family firms can reflect upon a long tradition in which a very specific management creed has formed which highlights corporate social responsibility and the aims of reciprocity, mutual obligations, and benefits. Although Japanese family businesses have been quite pragmatic in finding successors outside the founding family and, by adopting promising heirs, many companies face difficulties in finding a heir. It seems somewhat unique to Japan that it has been and still is not uncommon to secure succession by adopting a non-consanguineous heir. Nevertheless, many family firms face the challenge that no successor can be found.

Notes

1 In Japan, SMEs (*chūshō kigyō*) are officially defined by their capital and the number of employees, with reference to the respective industrial sector: i.e. the manufacturing and processing industry, up to 300 million yen capital and three hundred employees; wholesale, up to 100 million yen capital and one hundred employees; services, up to 50 million yen capital and one hundred employees; and the retail trade, up to 50 million yen and fifty employees (Chūshōkigyō-chō 2005).
2 The pre-war family-controlled conglomerates were dissolved under the US Occupation and transformed into public companies with no controlling shareholder (Morck and Nakamura 2003).
3 For an overview see Chua *et al.* (1999: 21), Viehl (2003: 18), and Eisenmann-Mittenzwei (2006: 19).
4 See Japanese corporation-tax law, book 1, chapter 1, paragraph 2, 10.

References

Allouche, J., Amann, B., Jaussaud, J., and Kurashina, T. (2008). The impact of family control on the performance and financial characteristics of family versus nonfamily businesses in Japan: a matched-pair investigation. *Family Business Review*, 21: 315–329.

Amorós, J. and Bosma, N. (2013). *Global Entrepreneurship Monitor: 2013 Global Report – Fifteen Years of Assessing Entrepreneurship Across the Globe*. London: Global Entrepreneurship Research Association.

Aoi, M., Asaba, S., Kubota, K., and Takehara, H. (2012). *Family Businesses and Corporate Social Performance: an Empirical Study of Public Firms in Japan*. Paper presented at the 12th Annual IFERA World Family Business Research Conference, University of Bordeaux IV, France, 26–29 June.

Asaba, S. (2012). Patient investment: a study on the behavior of the listed family business in the Japanese electric machinery industry. *Asia Pacific Journal of Management*, 30(3): 697–715.

Astrachan, Joseph H., Klein, Sabine, and Smyrnios, Kosmas X. (2006). The F-PEC scale of family influence: a proposal for solving the family business definition problem. In: Poutziouris, P., Smyrnios, K., and Klein, S. (eds), *Handbook of Research on Family Business*, Cheltenham, UK Edward Elgar Publishing, pp. 167–179.

Bhappu, A. (2000). The Japanese family: an institutional logic for Japanese corporate networks and Japanese management. *Academy of Management Review*, 25(2): 409–415.

Bosse, Friederike (2003). *Nachfolgeregelung im japanischen Mittelstand*, Hamburg: IFA.

Chosun Online (2007). *Chūshōkigyō no Jigyō Shōkei wo Shien Suru Nihon to Doitsu* (Support for successors in Japan and Germany). http://www.chosunonline.com/article/20071205000043, no longer available, last accessed 15 March 2008.

Chua, J. H., Chrisman, J. J., and Sharma, P. (1999). Defining the family business by behavior. *Entrepreneurship: Theory and Practice*, 23(4): 19–39.

Chūshōkigyō-chō (2005). *FAQ chūshōkigyō no 'teigi ni tsuite'* (Frequently asked questions on 'the definition of SME'). www.chusho.meti.go.jp/faq/faq01.html, no longer available, last accessed 20 November 2007.

The Economist (2013). Entrepreneurs in Japan – time to get started, 31 Aug 2013, http://www.economist.com/news/business/21584328-shinzo-abe-giving-new-hope-japans-unappreciated-entrepreneurs-time-get-started, last accessed 20 October 2015.

Economist Intelligence Unit (2010). *SMEs in Japan – a New Growth Driver?* http://www.economistinsights.com/sites/default/files/EIU_Microsoft_JapanSMEs_FINAL-WEB.pdf, last accessed 1 November 2015.

Eisenmann-Mittenzwei, A. (2006). *Familienunternehmen and Corporate Governance*, Hamburg: Verlag D. Kovač.

Goto, T. (2006). Longevity of Japanese family firm. In: Poutziouris, P., Smyrnios, K., and Klein, S. (eds), *Handbook of Research on Family Business*, Cheltenham, UK: Edward Elgar Publishing.

Goydke, T. and Smailus, H. (2009). Erfolgsfaktoren und Herausforderungen der Nachfolge in japanischen Familienunternehmen am Beispiel der Möbelindustrie. (Success factors and challenges in management succession in Japanese family firms). In: Pohl, M. and Wieczorek, I. (eds), *Japan: Politik, Wirtschaft und Gesellschaft*. Berlin: VSJF, pp. 149–168.

Haghirian, P. (2014). Japanische Start-ups – ein Randphänomen? (Japanese start-ups – a marginal phenomenon?). *JapanMarkt*, April 2014: 20–21.

Harada, N. (2007). Which firms exit and why? An analysis of small firm exits in Japan. *Small Business Economics*, 29, pp. 401–414.

Horide, I. (2009). *The Ethics of Buddhism and the Ethos of the Japanese Management: the Spirit of Ji-Hi*, Reitaku University, Department of Economics and Business Management, Working Paper Series, 22 June 2009.

Howorth, C., Rose, M. and Hamilton, E. (2006). Definitions, diversity and development: key debates in family business research. In: Casson, M., Bernard, Y., Anuradha, B., and Wadeson, N. (eds), *The Oxford Handbook of Entrepreneurship*, Oxford: Oxford University Press.

Hutcheson, O. (2007). *The End of a 1,400-Year-Old Business*, Bloomberg Business, 16 April 2007, http://www.bloomberg.com/bw/stories/2007-04-16/the-end-of-a-1-400-year-old-businessbusinessweek-business-news-stock-market-and-financial-advice, last accessed 1 November 2015.

ITOCHU (2008). *ITOCHU Corporation's 150th Anniversary and the Roots of CSR, Sampo Yoshi*, ITOCHU Corporation CSR Report 2008. Tokyo: ITOCHU.

ITOCHU (2012). *ITOCHU Corporation CSR Digest*, October 2012. Tokyo: ITOCHU.

JCBS (Japanese Conference of Business Succession) (2006). *Jigyō shōkei gaidorain* (Guide for company succession). Online: http://www.jcbshp.com/achieve/guideline_01.pdf, last accessed 20 October 2015.

Kamei, K. (2008). *Tradition and Innovation in Japanese Family SME*. Paper presented at conference. Innovation, Competitiveness, Growth and Tradition in SMEs, 1–3 September, St Gallen, Switzerland.

Karlin, A. (2013). *The Entrepreneurship Vacuum in Japan: Why It Matters and How to Address It*. http://knowledge.wharton.upenn.edu/article/the-entrepreneurship-vacuum-in-japan-why-it-matters-and-how-to-address-it/, last accessed 20 October 2015.

Kitano, S. (1970). Dozuku and kindred in a Japanese rural society. In: Hill, R. and Konig, R. (eds), *Families in East and West: Socialization Process and Kinship Ties*, The Hague, Netherlands: Mouton.

Kitaoji, H. (1971). The structure of the Japanese family. *American Anthropologist*, New Series, 73(5): p. 1036.

Kohlbacher, F. (2006). Nisennana nen mondai: Bedeutung and Auswirkungen einer alternden Bevölkerung and Belegschaft für Firmen. *Japan: Politik, Wirtschaft und Gesellschaft*, Berlin: VSJF.

Kollmann, T. (2005). Unternehmensgründung. In: Kollmann, T. (2005) *Gabler Kompakt-Lexikon*, Wiesbaden, Germany: Gabler.

Kondo, D. (1990). *Crafting Selves: Power, Gender, and Discourses of Identity in a Japanese Workplace*, Chicago, IL: University of Chicago Press.

Kumagai, F. (1992). Research on the family in Japan. In: UNESCO (eds), *The Changing Family in Asia*, Bangkok: UNESCO, pp. 159–237.

Kurashina, T. (2003). *Family Kigyō no Keieigaku* (Management studies on family business), Tokyo: Tokyo Keizai Shimbunsha.

Mehrotra, V., Morck, R., Shim, Y., and Wiwattanakantang, Y. (2013). Adoptive expectations: rising sons in Japanese family firms. *Journal of Financial Economics*, 108: 840–854.

Morck, R. and Nakamura, M. (2003). *Been There, Done That – the History of Corporate Ownership in Japan*. European Corporate Governance Institute (ECGI) – Finance Research Paper Series No. 20/2003. Brussels: ECGI.

Morikawa, M. (2008). *Productivity and Survival of Family Firms in Japan: an Analysis Using Firm-Level Microdata*. Research Institute of Economy, Trade and Industry (RIETI) Discussion Paper Series 08-E-026, July 2008. Tokyo: RIETI.

Nakane, C. (1970). *Japanese Society*, Berkeley, CA: University of California Press.

O'Halloran, K. (2009). *The Politics of Adoption – International Perspectives on Law, Policy and Practice*. Dordrecht, Netherlands: Springer.

Paulson, J. (1984). *Family Law Reform in Post War Japan: Succession and Adoption*. Ph.D. Dissertation, Department of History, University of Colorado.

Picken, S. (1987). Values and value related strategies in Japanese corporate culture. *Journal of Business Ethics*, 6(2): 137–143.

Ramseyer, J. (1979). Thrift and diligence. house codes of Tokugawa merchant families. *Monumenta Nipponica*, 34(2): 209–230.

Saito, T. (2008). Family firms and firm performance: evidence from Japan. *Journal of the Japanese and International Economies*, 22: 620–646.

Sakai, Y. (2013). *Information and Distribution: the Role of Merchants in the Market Economy with Demand Risk*, Shiga University, Faculty of Economics, Center for Risk Research, Discussion Paper No. A-6, July 2013. Shiga, Japan: Shiga University.

Sasagawa, A. (2012). Entrepreneurship in Japan: taking on the Big Boys, *The Tokyo Weekender*, 26 March 2012. www.tokyoweekender.com/2012/03/entrepreneurship-in-japan-how-can-the-land-of-big-business-produce-the-next-mikitani/, last accessed 20 October 2015.

Shanker, M. C. and Astrachan, J. H. (1996). Myths and realities: family businesses' contribution to the US economy – a framework for assessing family business statistics. *Family Business Review*, 9(2): 107–119.

Shim, J. and Okamuro, H. (2011). Does ownership matter in mergers? A comparative study of the causes and consequences of mergers by family and non-family firms. *Journal of Banking and Finance*, 35: 93–203.

Shizuoka Sangyō Shien Saito (2007). *Bijinesu Shien Kōza 9* (9th Seminar on Business Support). Online: http://www.hanjyou.jp/~b-nest/doc/school/seminor/bis_semi_07l09.html, not available, last accessed 19 March 2008.

SMEA (Small and Medium Enterprise Agency) (2007). *Share of SMEs in the Japanese Economy*. http://www.chusho.meti.go.jp/sme_english/outline/07/01.html, last accessed 20 October 2015.

Storz, C. (1997). *Der mittelständische Unternehmer in Japan*, Baden-Baden, Germany: Nomos.

Suekane, A. (2009). *An Analysis on Long Standing Companies in Japan: Why They Can be Sustainable?* Paper presented at the International Symposium of the Society for Social Management Systems 2009, Kochi University of Technology, Japan.

Viehl, P. (2003). *Familieninterne Unternehmernachfolge – Eine Ex-Post-Analyse aus Nachfolgersicht*, Münster, Germany: LIT.

Yamashiro, A. (1997). *Japanische Managementlehre*, Munich: Oldenbourg Verlag.

5

Corporate governance

Franz Waldenberger

Definition and outline

The UK Cadbury Report of 1992 defines corporate governance as 'the system by which companies are directed and controlled'.[1] Typical core institutions are stock markets, ownership structures of listed companies, supervisory boards, and remuneration packages of top executives. The broader system encompasses corporate law, bankruptcy procedures, disclosure rules, and takeover regulations, as well as the more general economic and market environment (OECD 2004: 11–12).

The starting point of the corporate governance debate is the separation of ownership and control typical of listed stock companies (Tricker 2012: 6–9). Although listed firms account for only a small fraction of the total number of companies, they employ a substantial amount of financial and human capital and invest heavily in research and development. Corporate governance therefore affects not only shareholder wealth; it also impacts the functioning of stock markets, risk allocation, and the investment in and productive employment of an important portion of an economy's resources (OECD 2004: 11).

Research on corporate governance in Japan has been inspired and driven by comparative institutional and system analysis (Dore 2000; Aoki *et al.* 2007; Whittaker and Simon 2009). What characterizes the corporate governance of Japanese listed stock companies? How can differences be explained? What implications do they carry? Do we see convergence towards a 'global standard'? Moreover, there are many studies focusing on the role of important actors or the design and functioning of specific elements of the system, like the main bank, institutional investors, boards of directors, executive compensation, or the market for corporate control.

The sections that follow will review the respective findings. However, we will first examine the role of stock markets and the ownership structure of listed stock companies. Next, we will summarize the research on the Japanese 'stakeholder' or 'insider' model and its main characteristics up to the mid 1990s. Then we will take a closer look at how the major changes in the legal and economic environment affected essential elements of the system, i.e. the shareholders, the market for corporate control, boards, and compensation. The final section will summarize the findings and, based on these, comment on the most recent efforts by the Japanese government to use corporate governance reform as part of its 'new growth strategy'.

The separation of ownership and control

The separation of ownership and control characteristic of listed companies bears important benefits in terms of risk diversification and liquidity. However, it also confronts a severe governance problem, because outside shareholders have no contractual income rights. They only have a residual claim on the profits or losses realized after all the contractual income rights of the other stakeholders have been served. The severity of the control problem explains why most companies are owner-managed. Only for the largest companies do the benefits of separating ownership and control seem to outweigh the costs. Japan counted 1.7 million incorporated enterprises in 2012, but only 3,540 companies, or 0.2 per cent, were listed on the country's stock exchanges.[2]

The advantages of stock market listings are likely to increase as an economy develops, and its companies grow larger and engage in riskier ventures. International comparisons show that high-income countries have a significantly larger number of listed companies per million of population. In Japan, too, the number of listed companies and the market capitalization relative to GDP increased from 1961 to 2011 as the economy developed (Table 5.1). Today, both indicators are slightly above the respective averages for high-income economies. This can be interpreted as evidence for the fact that the stock market in Japan is well developed, which also means that the corresponding governance problems are equally well controlled.

The advantages of separating ownership and control continue to increase with the degree of ownership dispersion. A higher degree of dispersion enhances risk diversification and liquidity. However, it also aggravates the governance problem, because dispersed ownership implies the absence of a controlling shareholder.

Ownership in listed stock companies in Japan is relatively dispersed when compared to continental European and other Asian economies (Dietl 1998; La Porta et al. 1999; Claessens et al. 2000). The data-sets are almost twenty years old, but there is no evidence that the distribution has become more concentrated.[3]

Compared with other advanced economies, Japan takes more advantage of the separation of ownership and control. Slightly more domestic companies are listed on its stock exchanges, and the listed equity is more widely dispersed. The last fact indicates that, like their US counterparts, Japanese companies rely little on direct monitoring by controlling shareholders. This raises the question as to how they resolve the ensuing governance problem, i.e. what other means they apply to protect the interests of non-controlling outside shareholders.

Table 5.1 Stock markets in Japan in international perspective, 2011

	GDP/head (2005 US dollars)	Listed companies per million of population	Market capitalization as percentage of GDP
Japan 1961	7728	13.4	33.3%
Japan 2011	36161	31.0	68.6%
High-income economies	30695	29.4	50.9%
Middle-income economies	2623	4.4	25.3%
Low-income economies	403	1.4	22.9%

Source: The World Bank, Global Financial Development Database, http://data.worldbank.org/data-catalog/global-financial-development, last accessed 9 November 2015. Numbers for Japan 1961 taken from TSE (2012) and national accounts statistics, see http://www.esri.cao.go.jp/en/sna/data/kakuhou/files/1998/12annual_report_e.html, last accessed 5 May 2014

Characteristics of the post-war system

Stakeholder orientation

To whom does a listed stock company belong? In the mid-1990s, this question was posed to top managers in five leading economies. The answers differed strongly between Japanese, continental European, and US and UK respondents (Figure 5.1).

Whereas managers of firms headquartered in the US and the UK felt that they should give first priority to shareholder interests, managers in Japan, Germany, and France claimed to pay more attention to employee interests. Other national surveys conducted in the mid-1990s revealed that Japanese top management ranked shareholder interests below those of customers, employees, suppliers, labour unions, industry associations, banks, or even the government (Teramoto 1997: 102).

Of course, managers in all countries have to serve the interests of all stakeholders if they want their companies to stay in business. The distinction between shareholder- and stakeholder-orientation, therefore, cannot mean that specific groups are neglected. Stated or observed priorities rather reflect differences in the constraints that managers confront in dealing with various stakeholders. Such constraints are defined by the legal framework and by the market environment.

Company-bound careers as a major control mechanism

Japan's system of corporate governance evolved during the period of economic growth between the early 1950s and the early 1970s. Its core element is the internal labour market or, more specifically, the in-house careers of highly skilled employees, including management (Aoki 1988: 49–86). It meant that top management positions and boards of companies would routinely be filled with people who had successfully survived a twenty-five- to thirty-year-long in-house competition. Having been selected out of the ranks of employees, the board's highest priority was to ensure that the next generation could equally enjoy a successful lifetime career. This implied long-term strategies focusing on the return on human rather than financial capital and oriented more towards growth than profit maximization (Abegglen and Stalk 1985; Odagiri 1992).

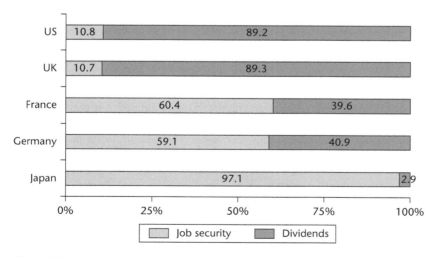

Figure 5.1 Employee versus shareholder interests

However, sufficient profitability was, in any case, needed to ensure the stability of employment and the ability to offer good career prospects to talented recruits.

Internal labour markets tied the long-term career interests of employees to the success of their company. For those who finally reached board positions, career horizons were naturally shortened. However, they would be monitored by younger colleagues, whose career prospects depended on how well the company did, and, apart from general reputational concerns, older board members would still be exposed to the threat of losing lucrative post-retirement rewards in cases where their performance did not meet expectations (Dore 2007).

Japanese corporate governance neither relied on direct monitoring by a controlling shareholder (as in continental Europe), nor on the disciplining role of hostile takeover threats (as in the US). Profitability would be ensured by the career concerns of in-house-grown managers. The different mechanisms of direct, market, and internal control nevertheless functioned quite similarly. Japanese board members would be exchanged just as quickly in response to bad performance as would their US counterparts (Kaplan 1994).

Stable shareholders and main banks as complementary parts

Japan's model of internal control was complemented and supported on the financing side by dispersed – but stable and patient – shareholders, and by the so-called main-bank system. Stable shareholdings started to arise during the 1960s when Japan's commitment to capital-market liberalization sparked fears of takeovers by capital-rich foreign companies (Okabe 2002: 4). Until the mid-1990s, stable shareholdings made up around 45 per cent of all listed stock in value terms. Banks and insurance companies accounted for two-thirds of the value of stable shares. The remaining one-third was held by non-financial corporations. Less than half of stable ownership occurred in the form of cross-shareholdings (NLI 2004). Stable institutional shareholders would normally not interfere with management. They would, however, get involved, when companies faced financial difficulties, by sending their own representatives to boards and dismissing incumbent members (Kaplan and Minton 1994).

In the high-growth environment, the corporate sector depended heavily on external funds. The regulatory framework strongly favoured bank borrowing over equity and bond financing. As a consequence, bank loans became the major financing channel even for listed companies (Ueda 1994; Hoshi and Kashyap 2001: 91–128). To secure stable financing, firms would seek long-term relationships with a main bank (Aoki *et al.* 1994). The main bank would generally be the largest lender, operate the company's settlement accounts, and provide an array of other financial services, including the coordination of borrowings from other financial institutions. It would also be one of the stable shareholders, and would often dispatch managers and directors to client firms.

Operationalizations of main-bank relations in empirical studies differed, but their existence as such was undisputed (Miwa 1996: 100–101). Opinions, however, diverged with regard to the functional interpretation of the relationship. For some observers, the main bank formed an essential complementary part of the insider-controlled stakeholder model (Aoki *et al.* 1994; Hoshi and Kashyap 2001: 145–183). Due to its informational advantages, the main bank would be the exclusive monitor on behalf of other lenders. It stepped in in times of financial distress, providing fresh capital, deploying bank representatives to boards, and arranging the restructuring process. Main-bank relations provided a contingent governance mechanism. The primary goal was not the protection shareholder interests. Interventions occurred when the position of lenders was endangered. Main-bank-led restructuring avoided formal bankruptcy procedures and protected the lifetime careers of employees.

Proponents of the above view corroborated their theoretical interpretation with descriptions of bank–firm relations and case studies of main-bank intervention in financially distressed firms (Sheard 1994). They could also refer to statistical evidence that firms with main-bank relations had better and cheaper access to capital when encountering severe business conditions (Hoshi et al. 1990; Kawai et al. 1996). However, other researchers studying bank–firm relations have criticized the governance interpretation as overgeneralizing and an idealization.[4] Main-bank relations were never as stable as the model would have suggested (Horiuchi et al. 1988; Miwa 1996: 101–107). Main banks did not always come to the rescue of failing firms (Miwa 1996: 113–119; Hoshi and Kashyap 2001: 179–180). Firms depending on main-bank finance had higher financing costs (Weinstein and Yafeh 1998); main-bank intervention proved not always successful (Hoshi and Kashyap 2001: 180), and its monitoring function seems not to have been appreciated by listed companies.[5]

The common denominator in the debate might be summarized as follows. Main banks existed. They were important and influential lenders during the high-growth period, but less so afterwards (see below). They had a legitimate interest in safeguarding their loans, when borrowers faced financial distress. As arrangers of loans from other lenders, they bore monitoring and governance responsibilities. Whether, how, and how successfully they intervened was not predetermined by their position as the main bank *per se*, but depended in addition on specific circumstances causing variations in behaviour and outcomes.

The insider system and the dark side of the post-war model

Although ownership structures of companies listed on Japanese and US stock markets resembled each other, outside shareholders in Japan were much less informed about the actual financial conditions of the companies that they had invested in. The lack of disclosure did not interfere with Japan's insider-control-based governance system. Main banks did not have to rely on publicly disclosed information. Stable shareholders could be informed privately if necessary.

In an insider system, outside investors rely on signals in order to guess whether there is trouble. In Japan, important signals that were interpreted as indicating hidden difficulties were the lowering of dividend payments, but also the length of annual shareholder meetings.[6] To avoid bad signalling effects, Japanese companies applied a more conservative and stable dividend policy than US listed companies (Ujiie 2002: 225). Many of them also made illegal payments to so-called 'sokaiya', who threatened to disturb and therefore prolong shareholder meetings, or who promised to keep other potential troublemakers quiet (Milhaupt and West 2004: 109–144).

Adjustments in the low-growth era

Changes in the economic and legal environment

The Japanese model of governance was established in the context of a high-growth environment. Growth started to slow down rapidly after the first oil crisis in 1973. Annual growth rates of real GDP had, on average, been 9.7 per cent between 1955 and 1970. They declined to 4.2 per cent per year between 1970 and 1990, and to 1.3 per cent between 1990 and 2012.[7]

Low growth, combined with the development of domestic capital markets and international capital liberalization, reduced the dependence of large companies on bank credit (Horiuchi 1999: 76). The ratio of the sum of short-term and long-term bank loans to total assets declined from its peak of 39 per cent at the end of March 1975, to 17 per cent at the end of March 2008.[8] Financial system transformation was further driven by deregulation and a banking crisis that, while being ignited by the collapse of the stock market bubble in 1990 and the real estate bubble in 1992, only reached its full impact in 1998 (Waldenberger 2000). The introduction of new accounting standards improved transparency and supported the shift from a bank-based to a market-based financial system (Shishido 2004: 18–19).

Taking advantage of capital liberalization and the fragility of Japan's financial institutions, foreign (mainly US-based) institutional investors looking for diversification of their portfolios on a global scale started to steadily increase their share in Japanese stock from 7 per cent in 1985 to 28 per cent in 2012 (see Table 5.2).

Finally, the last twenty years have seen a number of legal reforms that have directly affected important parts of the corporate governance system (Jackson and Miyajima 2007: 17). Their implications and the impact of the aforementioned changes in the economic and market environment will be assessed in the following section.

The decline of the main-bank system

The financial system transformation, culminating in the banking crisis at the end of the 1990s, fundamentally undermined the bank relationships of listed companies (Aoki 1994; Arikawa and Miyajima 2007; Jackson and Miyajima 2007). Firm–bank relationships became more diverse. Financially healthy firms turned to capital markets, while weaker firms continued to rely on main banks (McGuire 2009).

The conservative and protective nature of main-bank intervention remained visible in the slower speed of restructuring observed in main-bank-dependent firms (Arikawa and Miyajima 2007; Xu and Zhang 2009). Improved bankruptcy regulations, introducing a 'debtor in possession system', reduced the restructuring responsibility of the main bank (Xu 2007).

The financial bubble and its aftermath laid open the downside of close firm–banking relationships (Yao and Ouyang 2007). Powerful banks wanting to expand business had pressured clients to borrow beyond their needs. When projects failed, they continued to extend credit further, weakening their own financial condition (Konishi and Yasuda 2003; Peek and Rosengren 2005).

Shareholder activism and the market for corporate control

Indices of 'anti-director rights' attest to Japan's very high level of shareholder rights.[9] On a practical level, the main concerns are the still-high concentration of shareholder meetings on a single day and the short release time of proxy statements (ISS 2013: 103–105). Both increase the cost of preparing and attending meetings.

Until the early 1990s, individual shareholders would, at times, sue directors for alleged wrongdoings, but the number of such derivative suits was negligible (Milhaupt and West 2004). This changed when, in 1993, the filing fees were radically reduced to a flat fee of 8,200 yen. The number of cases rapidly increased. Although, like in other countries, very few of them succeeded, they nevertheless prompted the introduction of director and officer liability insurance and upper limits for director liability.

In the post-war system, friendly institutional shareholders would raise their concerns, if at all, outside of shareholder meetings. Publicly visible shareholder activism appeared when stable and cross-shareholding structures started to unwind and ownership structures changed (Table 5.2). The most important trends after 1995 are the decline of financial institutions' share, the shift within financial institutions from banks to trust banks, and the growing presence of foreign investors.

Table 5.2 Shareholding structure 1985 to 2012

	1985	*1995*	*2005*	*2012*
Financial institutions	39.8	41.1	30,9	28.0
*Banks**	*20.9*	*15.1*	*4.7*	*3.8*
Trust banks	*N/A*	*10.3*	*18.0*	*17.7*
Others	*20.8*	*15.7*	*8.2*	*6.5*
Corporations	28.8	27.2	21.3	21.7
Individuals	22.3	19.5	19.9	20.2
Foreign investors	7.0	10.5	26.3	28.0
Others†	2.2	1.7	1.6	2.2

Notes:
* City banks and regional banks.
† Government and securities companies.

Source: Tokyo Stock Exchange, 2–5 transition in shareholding ratio/shareholding at market value by investor category, see http://www.tse.or.jp/english/market/data/shareownership/index.html, last accessed 5 May 2014

The unwinding of cross-shareholdings between banks and corporations occurred more or less simultaneously. Statistical analysis suggests that decisions on whose shares to sell were based on the strength of the relationship; stronger relationships would be maintained, rather than on portfolio optimization criteria. As a consequence, banks retained investments in the stock of poorly performing firms (Miyajima and Kuroki 2007).

Foreign institutional investors focused their investments on larger companies with high export ratios and promising growth opportunities (Ahmadjian 2007; Miyajima and Kuroki 2007). They would demand corporate governance reforms, especially the appointment of outside directors, and dividend pay-out levels in line with a company's financial conditions and investment opportunities. Investors pursuing a long-term investment strategy would communicate their principles of investment and views on corporate governance; tie up with local investment partners; talk with management; and support non-profit organizations in Japan to lobby for regulatory reform (Jacoby 2009). Investors focusing on short-term financial returns were more confrontational. Both groups found followers among Japanese institutional investors (Buchanan and Deakin 2009).

A number of studies looking at the effect of foreign ownership on listed companies in Japan were able to discern a variety of patterns (Ahmadjian 2007; Hamao *et al.* 2010; Mizuno 2010). A higher share of foreign institutional ownership would go along with higher dividend pay-outs, more outsiders on boards, better transparency, and speedier restructuring, but also with a higher likelihood of takeover defence measures. Interestingly, companies with higher shares of foreign ownership were also more actively promoting women (Kawaguchi 2009). The effects on long-term performance were, however, mixed (Hamao *et al.* 2010; Mizuno 2010).

The advent of shareholder activism changed the style of annual shareholder meetings. They had been ritual gatherings, perfectly organized and orchestrated, and ideally finishing within 30 minutes (Milhaupt and West 2004: 131). Now they became platforms where proxy statements would be publicly opposed by shareholders who would, at times, also bring in their own proposals. Voting results reveal that one-fourth of proxy statements had opposition rates of over 10 per cent in 2011 and 2012, but no shareholder proposal succeeded (ISS 2013: 105–125). Incumbent management was therefore still in control, although it faced a less friendly audience.

Voicing criticism is not the only option. Dissatisfied and unheard shareholders can sell, with negative effects on share prices. The fact that foreign investors account for 40 to 50 per cent of trading[10] means that their market influence is significantly larger than their presence as owners would suggest.

The most radical way to push one's demands is by acquiring a controlling stake in a company. Under dispersed ownership, the stock market functions as a market for corporate control (Manne 1965). Bad management will prompt shareholders to sell, causing the firm's stock price to fall. Investors, who are convinced that they can do better, will buy the undervalued shares, take over control, and replace the incumbent team. The threat of being taken over will, by itself, exert a disciplining effect on management.

Hostile takeover threats were not credible in Japan's post-war governance system. Listed stock was dispersed, but was generally held by so-called stable and friendly owners. The situation changed as stable shareholdings dissolved. Unsolicited tender offer bids started to appear in the year 2000 (Gilson 2004; Buchanan and Deakin 2009). The bidders were not only from abroad, but also from Japan. Among them were corporations pursuing long-term strategic goals, as well as investment funds seeking short-term profits.

Within a few years, hostile takeover threats had become a reality in Japan (Milhaupt and West 2004: 198). However, the various fights over control also revealed that the regulatory framework was not well equipped to deal with the new situation. Japanese industry, alarmed by a business conduct that seemed incompatible with the high esteem for harmony characteristic of Japanese business culture, lobbied for reforms. The Companies Act of 2005 provided relief in the form of legal instruments and procedures against hostile bids. The Financial Instruments and Exchange Law of 2006 added regulations for tender offers. The latest step in the attempt to create more cooperative relations between institutional investors and management was the release of a Stewardship Code in February 2014. Following the UK model, the Code defines principles of investment and governance considered as adequate for enhancing corporate value, and invites institutional investors to disclose whether they adhere to the principles or to otherwise explain why not.[11]

The changes in the legal framework did not fully do away with unfriendly takeover threats, but allowed sufficient protection for Japan's 'community firm' (Hayakawa and Whittaker 2009). 'Poison pills', i.e. defence measures against hostile takeover bids, need to be approved by shareholder meetings and have, in fact, become a regular agenda item. Some 523, or 14.6 per cent of all listed companies in Japan, had respective provisions in 2012. The number is below the peak of the 570 provisions (15.0 per cent) counted in 2008 (ISS 2013: 106).

Boards – the prevailing influence of in-house careers

Like the US, Japan has a one-tier board system. Directors are formally appointed and dismissed by the shareholder meeting. They have fiduciary duties similar to their colleagues in the US. However, despite their formal resemblance, Japanese boards differed in many respects (Miwa 1996: 204–205; Learmount 2002: 125–129; Dore 2007). They tended to be larger, comprising on average 20 members,[12] mainly Japanese men beyond the age of fifty-five, who would not consider themselves as representing primarily shareholder interests. Board membership meant the final stage of a successful in-house career. Board size reflected the need to offer this reward to a sufficient number of qualified, hard-working managers. Monitoring or strategic decision-making were of less concern. The former was felt to have been sufficiently 'socialized' and 'internalized' by lifetime company careers. The latter one was reserved to a smaller informal circle within the board, the so-called *jōmu-kai*, but was, in any case, also shared with lower ranks as part of consensus building.

Legal board reforms in 1981, 1993, and 2001 focused on the role of statutory auditors (Shishido 2001: 666–667; Shishido 2007). Statutory auditors are a specific Japanese governance institution. They are appointed by shareholders to monitor and report on the legal compliance of the board as well as the soundness of internal control systems. To fulfil their duties, they must attend board meetings and must have access to relevant documents; they do not, however, participate in board decisions.[13] The first two reforms introduced plural, full-time, and outside auditors. The 2001 reform clarified that an outsider must have never worked for the company, and required that at least half of the auditing board must be outsiders. The responsibilities of statutory auditors cover only part of the functions that an independent director representing the interests of minority shareholders would be expected to perform. The governance implications of the reforms were therefore limited.

The most fundamental board reform was the introduction of the 'company with committee' system by the 2002 revision of the Commercial Code (Shishido 2007). The new board structure does away with statutory auditors. Instead, boards are obliged to set up nomination and compensation and audit committees, each staffed with a majority of outside directors. The new system resembles the US board model by more clearly separating monitoring and management functions. As far reaching as it is, it is only an option. Listed companies can stay with the old statutory auditor system, and 97.8 per cent continued to do so in 2012 (TSE 2013: 15). This might have been one reason why the most recent corporate governance reform taking effect in 2015 introduced a third model, the so-called company with audit and supervisory committee. It provides a kind of golden mean between the two former solutions. The audit and supervisory committee is less powerful as in the company with committee structure, but, being fully equipped with director rights, it has more influence on the board than the statutory auditors (Nakamura 2015).

In particular, foreign institutional investors have long been pressuring for more outsiders on Japanese boards and for outsiders that are more independent. Japan ranks lowest in international comparisons with regard to board independence (ISS 2013: 107). The most recent corporate governance reform also introduced stricter independence critera for outside directors, together with the requirement for companies to appoint at least one independent director, or else to explain why if they do not (Goto 2013). Japan's Corporate Governance Code, released in March 2015, goes even further by asking for at least two independent directors.[14]

Meanwhile, Japanese companies had themselves undertaken measures to improve the efficiency of their boards (Dore 2007). They slimmed down board size by reserving monitoring functions for the board and moving daily management functions to a group of executive officers.[15] They established outside advisory boards and/or internal committees to support decision-making processes or to streamline and strengthen specific management functions. The measures show that the statutory auditor system has been flexible enough to realize some of the benefits of the committee system without having to fully adopt it. This at least partly explains the reluctance of companies to opt for the company with committees model.

Some studies tried to sort out the characteristics of companies that adopted the board with committee structure. One important factor was the presence of a parent company or major shareholder (Dore 2007). They took advantage of the new system, as it allowed them to better monitor the companies under their control. This, however, was not the original intention of the new law, as outside directors were meant to represent the interests of minority shareholders. Companies with committees also tended to have a highly diversified and modular business structure, as opposed to one focused around a core business (Miyajima 2007); had a higher foreign ownership share; and were more likely to be cross-listed on the New York Stock Exchange (Chizema and Shinozawa 2012).

Other studies looked at the causes and implications of board size and board composition. They generally found that board size or board composition had no significant effect on performance (Miwa and Ramseyer 2005, Uchida 2011). Japanese board size adjusted to company characteristics in a way similar to patterns observed in the US. The main difference was the low number of outside directors (Aman and Nguyen 2012). Board reforms, while responding to specific needs, like a more effective monitoring structure for parents and controlling shareholders or more transparent and speedier decision-making processes, did not imply a fundamental shift away from the insider control model (Dore 2007; Uchida 2011; Ahmadjian and Yoshikawa 2013). The large majority of board seats remain to be reserved for employees who successfully completed a twenty-five to thirty-year-long in-house career. Outside recruitment of executive board members continues to be the rare exception (Favaro *et al.* 2010). The predominance of in-house promotions and the corresponding absence of external hiring is reflected in low turnover rates for employees in higher managerial positions. During the 2000s, respective turnover rates were as low as 1 per cent – significantly lower than the 4 per cent to 5 per cent for employees in general (Naganuma 2014).

Executive compensation

If the general absence of independent outsiders on Japanese boards was an indication of a severe governance problem, we might expect Japanese top executives to pay themselves excessively high compensation. The opposite is, in fact, true. Total compensation for Japanese top executives amounts, on average, to about one-fifth of what their US counterparts take home (Nakazato *et al.* 2011; ISS 2013: 114; JACD 2013: Appendix 1). Executive pay can be conceived as the price for top management services. In the US, the price seems to be the outcome of competition among corporations for the best talent in the market. Theoretical analysis and empirical research suggest that the main driver of CEO compensation is the asset size of companies (Edmans *et al.* 2009). Given the dominance of in-house careers and in-house appointments in Japan, executive pay is not determined by external market processes, but the outcome of a multi-stage internal tournament competition. It is not driven by asset size, but by employment size. The fact that the employment-to-asset ratio declines as companies grow larger may – apart from the fact that shareholders in Japan have always had a say on pay – explain why Japanese CEO compensation levels are so much lower than in the US (Waldenberger 2013).

Japanese pay packages for top managers are not only relatively low, but they are also less performance sensitive (ISS 2013: 1141–1120; JACD 2013: Appendix 1). Again, the difference may not be a lack of incentives *per se*, but the outcome of different constraints and control mechanisms present in the Japanese internal-control model (Waldenberger 2013).

Outlook

How to combine shareholder and stakeholder perspectives

Changes in the economic and legal environment transformed Japan's corporate governance model that had been formed during the post-war high-growth period. Most listed companies no longer rely on main-bank financing. They can no longer count on being protected by stable and friendly shareholders. They apply international accounting rules and engage in investor relations. They have boards of a smaller size with a clearer separation of monitoring and management functions. However, the vast majority of executive directors continue to be appointed from among the ranks of male employees with a life-long in-house career. Independent non-executive directors remain rare. Japan's new system of corporate governance is more market-based, more transparent, but basically still insider-controlled.

The mixing of elements from the market-based US-type governance model with the insider-control structure of the post-war system seems to contain a basic dilemma. How can Japanese boards protect the work-places of their core employees from rapid and fundamental restructuring measures, while at the same time serving the profit interests of less patient institutional investors? There are several possible ways: trying to re-establish stable shareholding structures; accumulating cash to prolong restructuring processes; having defence measures in place to fend of hostile takeovers; strengthening investor relations; appointing independent directors to gain the understanding and trust of institutional investors; or actually shifting towards shareholder orientation at the expense of employee protection.

The relevance of the last 'solution', i.e. the shift from stakeholder to shareholder orientation, has been investigated by several studies. Tanaka (2006) shows that Japanese listed companies no longer unanimously stick to the stakeholder model as in the case of Yoshimori's survey conducted in the early 1990s. On average, they have become indecisive as to whether the company belongs to shareholders or to long-term employees. The statistical analysis by Kubo (2011) reveals that there are, in fact, two groups of companies. Traditional companies with a low share of foreign ownership sticking to traditional board structures continue to keep employment stable, to the detriment of dividend payouts, whereas companies that reformed their board and had an above-average ratio of foreign share ownership tended to give higher priority to dividend payouts and were more likely to reduce employment during business downturns.

The above research findings suggest that it is hard to strike a compromise between shareholder and stakeholder orientation within a corporation. It is achieved, rather, in the composition of corporations, where some are more shareholder-oriented and others more stakeholder-oriented. The Japanese system seems flexible enough to accommodate both types of corporate cultures.

Governance reform as growth strategy

The high number of Japanese companies listed on domestic stock exchanges, the high degree of ownership dispersion, and the moderate pay levels of top executives, all indicate that Japan's system of corporate governance structures functions well. It makes full use of the benefits of market-based equity financing and risk diversification, while effectively containing the income aspirations of top executives. However, the hoarding of cash accompanied by a low level of return on equity (Aoyagi and Ganelli 2014; OECD 2015: 25); the low degree of internationalization (Waldenberger 2008); and the persistently low growth in productivity (Kalantzis *et al.* 2012; Fukao 2013), suggest that the resources at the disposal of Japan's large corporations are not managed in the most productive way. This combines with and is partly caused by a low propensity to take on risk; slow decision-making processes due to a strong consensus orientation; a lack of cross-company mobility of resources; and a lack of diversity in management teams and boards.

Although there is no directly visible deficiency in Japan's corporate governance hampering the functioning of stock markets, policy makers have increasingly come to perceive corporate governance reform as a means to change the way that Japanese corporations are managed and to tap yet-unexploited potentials of productivity growth. As a result, corporate governance reform has become one of the main pillars of the so-called new growth strategy, the 'third arrow of

Abenomics'. The key words are 'growth-oriented' governance.[16] The Corporate Governance Code finalized in March 2015 forms a central element. Whereas corporate governance reform in other countries has largely been driven by the need to constrain excessive risk-taking, the Japanese code explicitly states that it:

> does not place excessive emphasis on avoiding and limiting risk or the prevention of corporate scandals. Rather, its primary purpose is to stimulate healthy corporate entrepreneurship, support sustainable corporate growth and increase corporate value over the mid- to long-term.[17]

Whether the Code can fulfil these expectations will to a large extent depend on the engagement of shareholders, especially institutional investors. They will need to actively incorporate the principles in their interaction with boards and top management as envisaged by the Stewardship Code released in February 2014. Another more structural condition is the persistence of in-house careers that have so far formed the backbone of Japanese governance structures and management styles. Will lifelong in-house careers stand in the way of any fundamental reform; will they become victim of such a reform; or will they be able to accommodate a new, more-entrepreneurial and risk-friendly governance structure? These are questions that will have to be addressed by future research.

Notes

1 http://www.ecgi.org/codes/documents/cadbury.pdf, last accessed 27 October 2015.
2 The number of incorporated enterprises is taken from Japan Statistical Yearbook 2014 (www.stat.go.jp/english/data/nenkan/index.htm), table 6–7, accessed 20 October 2015. The number of listed companies is given in the 2012 Share Ownership Survey (TSE et al. 2012: 3).
3 Excluding listed subsidiaries that are by definition controlled by a parent company, 76 per cent of the companies on the first section of the Tokyo Stock Exchange had no shareholder owning more than 20 per cent of shares (as of September 2012; my own calculations based on data from TSE 2013: 6–9). Although the sample is similar to the ones used by Claessens et al. (2000). and Dietl (1998), it should be noted that the older studies focus on the concentration of voting rights, which does not fully coincide with the concentration of share ownership, as, in Japan (as elsewhere), one share does not necessarily correspond with one vote.
4 Most forcefully, Miwa and Ramseyer (2002). See, as a critique of their critique, Puchniak (2013).
5 In a survey conducted among companies listed on the Tokyo Stock Exchange by Fuji Sogo Kenkyujo in 1993, only 11.1 per cent of respondents considered the main bank as an entitled monitor (Scher 1997: 126–127).
6 Thirty minutes was considered a normal length for a smooth meeting. Longer meetings had statistically significant negative effects on the share price of the respective company (Milhaupt and West 2004: 131).
7 Own calculations based on national accounts statistics.
8 Own calculations based on Ministry of Finance, Financial Statements Statistics of Corporations by Industry.
9 Japan receives 4.5 to 5 points out of a maximum of 6, which is equal to the US and one point above the UK value (Spamann 2010: 475).
10 Own calculation for 2008 to 2011, based on figures in TSE (2012: 5).
11 See www.fsa.go.jp/en/refer/councils/stewardship/20140407.html, accessed on 20 October 2015.
12 The mean of the samples of Miwa and Ramseyer (2005), comprising more than 1,000 companies listed on the Tokyo Stock Exchange for each of the years 1985, 1990, and 1995.
13 Outside auditors are, nevertheless, often counted as 'outside directors' in official statistics.
14 Principle 4.8. The Code is to be applied by companies listed on the major Japanese stock exchanges. It is based on a 'comply or explain' rule and is to be implemented jointly by the Tokyo Stock Exchange (TSE) and the Financial Services Agency (FSA).

15 The first company to introduce the so-called 'executive officer system' was Sony in 1997.
16 The original Japanese term '*seme no gabanānsu*' literally means 'aggressive governance'.
17 Japan's Corporate Governance Code (Final Proposal), provisional translation, www.fsa.go.jp/en/refer/councils/corporategovernance/20150306-1.html, para 7, last accessed 20 October 2015.

References

Abegglen, J. and Stalk Jr, G. (1985). *Kaisha: the Japanese Corporation*. New York: Basic Books.

Ahmadjian, C. (2007). Foreign investors and corporate governance in Japan. In: Aoki, M., Jackson, G., and Miyajima, H. (eds), *Corporate Governance in Japan: Institutional Change and Organizational Diversity*. Oxford, UK: Oxford University Press, pp. 125–150.

Ahmadjian, C. and Yoshikawa, T. (2013). Killing two birds with one stone: board reforms in the Japanese electronics industry. *Columbia Business School, Center on Japanese Economy and Business Working Paper Series*, No. 315.

Aman, H. and Nguyen, P. (2012). The size and composition of corporate boards in Japan. *Asian Business and Management*, 11: 425–444.

Aoki, M. (1988). *Information, Incentives and Bargaining in the Japanese Economy*, New York: Cambridge University Press.

Aoki, M. (1994). Monitoring characteristics of the main bank system. In: Aoki, M. and Patrick, H. (eds), *The Japanese Main Bank System: Its Relevance for Developing and Transforming Economies*. Oxford, UK: Oxford University Press, pp. 109–141.

Aoki, M., Jackson, G., and Miyajima, H. (eds) (2007). *Corporate Governance in Japan: Institutional Change and Organizational Diversity*. Oxford, UK: Oxford University Press.

Aoki, M., Patrick, H., and Sheard, P. (1994). The Japanese main bank system: an introductory overview. In: Aoki, M. and Patrick, H. (eds), *The Japanese Main Bank System: Its Relevance for Developing and Transforming Economies*. Oxford, UK: Oxford University Press, pp. 1–50.

Aoyagi, C. and Ganelli, G. (2014). Unstashing the cash! Corporate governance reform in Japan. *IMF Working Paper* WP/14/140.

Arikawa, Y. and Miyajima, H. (2007). Relationship banking in post-bubble Japan: coexistence of soft- and hard-budget constraints. In: Aoki, M., Jackson, G., and Miyajima, H. (eds), *Corporate Governance in Japan: Institutional Change and Organizational Diversity*. Oxford, UK: Oxford University Press, pp. 51–78.

Buchanan, J. and Deakin, S. (2009). In the shadow of corporate governance reform: change and continuity in managerial practice at listed companies in Japan. In: Whittaker, D. H. and Simon, D. (eds), *Corporate Governance and Managerial Reform in Japan*, Oxford, UK: Oxford University Press, pp. 28–69.

Chizema, A. and Shinozawa, Y. (2012). The company with committees: change or continuity in Japanese corporate governance? *Journal of Management Studies*, 49: 77–101.

Claessens, S., Djankov, S., and Lang, L. H. P. (2000). The separation of ownership and control in East Asian corporations. *Journal of Financial Economics*, 58: 81–112.

Dietl, H. M. (1998). *Capital Markets and Corporate Governance in Japan, Germany and the United States: Organizational Responses to Market Inefficiencies*, London: Routledge.

Dore, R. (2007). Insider management and board reform: for whose benefit? In: Aoki, M., Jackson, G., and Miyajima, H. (eds), *Corporate Governance in Japan. Institutional Change and Organizational Diversity*. Oxford: Oxford University Press, pp. 370–397.

Edmans, Alex, Gabaix, Xavier, and Landier, Augustin (2009). A multiplicative model of optimal CEO incentives in market equilibrium. *Review of Financial Studies*, 22(12): 4,881–4,917.

Favaro, K., Karlsson, P., and Neilson, G. L. (2010). CEO succession 2000–2009: a decade of convergence and compression. *Strategy and Business*, 59, reprint at www.booz.com/media/file/CEO_Succession_2009.pdf, last accessed 20 October 2015.

Fukao, K. (2013). Explaining Japan's unproductive two decades. *Asian Economic Policy Review*, 8: 193–213.

Gilson, R. (2004). *The Poison Pill in Japan: The Missing Infrastructure*, Stanford Law and Economics, Working Paper 244, https://www.law.stanford.edu/publications/the-poison-pill-in-japan-the-missing-infrastructure, last accessed 20 October 2015.

Goto, G. (2013). The outline for the Companies Act reform in Japan and its implications. *Journal of Japanese Law*, 35: 13–38.

Hamao, Y., Kutsuna, K., and Matos, P. P. (2010). *Investor Activism in Japan: The First Ten Years*, Marshall Research Paper Series, Working Paper FBE 06-10, http://ssrn.com/abstract=1573422, accessed 20 October 2015.

Hayakawa, M. and Whittaker, D. H. (2009). Takeovers and corporate governance: three years of tension. In: Whittaker, D. H. and Simon, D. (eds), *Corporate Governance and Managerial Reform in Japan*, Oxford, UK: Oxford University Press, pp. 70–92.

Horiuchi, A., Packer, F., and Fukuda, S. (1988). What role has the 'main bank' played in Japan? *Journal of the Japanese and International Economies*, 2: 159–180.

Hoshi, T. and Kashyap, A. (2001). *Corporate Finance and Governance in Japan: The Road to the Future*, Cambridge, MA: MIT Press.

Hoshi, T., Kashyap, A., and Scharfenstein, D. (1990). The role of banks in reducing the costs of financial distress in Japan. *Journal of Financial Economics*, 27: 67–88.

ISS (2013). *2012 Proxy Season Review. World Markets.* Institutional Shareholder Services, place of publication not given.

JACD (2013). *Guidelines on Executive Compensation 2013 and Requests for Revisions of Regulations and Tax Systems 2013.* Japan Association of Corporate Directors, http://www.jacd.jp/en/resources/130412_guidelines-on-executive-compensation2013.html, last accessed 20 October 2015.

Jackson, G. and Miyajima, H. (2007). In: Aoki, M., Jackson, G., and Miyajima, H. (eds), *Corporate Governance in Japan: Institutional Change and Organizational Diversity.* Oxford, UK: Oxford University Press, pp. 1–49.

Jacoby, S. M. (2009). Foreign investors and corporate governance in Japan. In: Whittaker, D. H. and Simon, D. (eds), *Corporate Governance and Managerial Reform in Japan*, Oxford, UK: Oxford University Press, pp. 70–92.

Kalantzis, Y., Kambayashi, R., and Lechevalier, S. (2012). Wage and productivity differentials in Japan: the role of labor market mechanisms. *Review of Labour Economics and Industrial Relations*, 26 (4): 514–541.

Kaplan, S. N. (1994). Top executive rewards and firm performance: a comparison of Japan and the United States. *Journal of Political Economy*, 102: 510–546.

Kaplan, S. N. and Minton, B. A. (1994). Appointments of outsiders to Japanese boards: determinants and implications for managers. *Journal of Financial Economics*, 36: 225–258.

Kawaguchi, A. (2009). Corporate governance by investors and the role of women. *Japan Labour Review*, 6: 72–90.

Kawai, M., Hashimoto, J., and Izumida, S. (1996). Japanese firms in financial distress and main banks: analyses of interest-rate premia. *Japan and the World Economy*, 8: 175–194.

Konishi, M. and Yasuda, Y. (2003). Evidence on a cause of Japan's prolonged banking crisis. *Applied Letters*, 10: 853–855.

Kubo, K. (2011). Haitō seisaku to koyō chōsei (Dividend policy and employment adjustment). In: Miyajima, H. (ed) *Nihon no kigyō tōchi – sono saisekkei to kyōsōryoku no kaifuku ni mukete* (Japan's corporate governance – towards its redesign and the regaining of competitiveness). Tokyo: Tōyō Keizai Shinpōsha.

La Porta, R., Lopez-De-Silanes, F., and Shleifer, A. (1999). Corporate ownership around the world. *The Journal of Finance*, 54: 471–517.

Learmount, S. (2002). *Corporate Governance: What Can Be Learned from Japan?* Oxford, UK: Oxford University Press.

McGuire, P. (2009). Bank ties and firm performance in Japan: some evidence since fiscal 2002. *Monetary and Economic Studies*, 27: 99–141.

Manne, H. G. (1965). Mergers and the market for corporate control. *Journal of Political Economy*, 73: 110–120.

Milhaupt, C. J. and West, M. D. (2004). *Economic Organization and Corporate Governance in Japan: The Impact of Formal and Informal Rules.* Oxford, UK: Oxford University Press.

Miwa, Y. (1996). *Firms and Industrial Organization in Japan*, Basingstoke, UK: Macmillan.

Miwa, Y. and Ramseyer, J. M. (2002). The fable of the keiretsu. *Journal of Economics and Management Strategy*, 11: 169–224.

Miwa, Y. and Ramseyer, J. M. (2005). Who appoints them, what do they do? Evidence on outside directors from Japan. *Journal of Economics and Management Strategy*, 14: 299–337.

Miyajima, H. (2007). The performance effects and determinants of corporate governance reform. In: Aoki, M., Jackson, G., and Miyajima, H. (eds), *Corporate Governance in Japan: Institutional Change and Organizational Diversity.* Oxford, UK: Oxford University Press.

Miyajima, H. and Kuroki, F. (2007). The unwinding of cross-shareholding in Japan: causes, effects, and implications. In: Aoki, M., Jackson, G., and Miyajima, H. (eds), *Corporate Governance in Japan: Institutional Change and Organizational Diversity*. Oxford, UK: Oxford University Press, pp. 79–124.

Mizuno, M. (2010). Institutional investors, corporate governance and firm performance in Japan. *Pacific Economic Review*, 15: 653–665.

Naganuma, S. (2014). *Kou sukiru rōdōsha no tenshoku kōdō* (Job change behaviour of high skilled workers), Bank of Japan Working Paper Series, 14-J-3, http://www.boj.or.jp/research/wps_rev/wps_2014/index.htm/, last accessed 20 October 2015.

Nakamura, N. (2015). *Amendment of the Company Law and Corporate Governance Reform of Listed Companies*. Tokyo: Waseda University Institute of Comparative Law, http://www.waseda.jp/hiken/en/jalaw_inf/topics2013/topic/002nakamura.html, last accessed 3 November 2015.

Nakazato, M., Ramseyer, J. M., and Rasmusen, E. B. (2011). Executive compensation in Japan: estimating levels and determinants from tax records. *Journal of Economics and Management Strategy*, 20: 843–885.

NLI (2004). Kabushiki Mochiai no Jōkyō Chōsa. 2003 Nendo-ban (Survey on the situation of cross-shareholdings. Fiscal 2003 edition), NLI Research Institute, http://www.nli-research.co.jp/consulting/misc/mochiai03.pdf, last accessed 20 October 2015.

Odagiri, H. (1992). *Growth Through Competition, Competition Through Growth,* Oxford, UK: Clarendon Press.

OECD (2004). *OECD Principles of Corporate Governance*. Paris: OECD.

OECD (2015). *OECD Economic Surveys Japan*. Paris: OECD.

Okabe, M. (2002). *Cross Shareholding in Japan: A New Unified Perspective on the Economic System*, Cheltenham, UK: Edward Elgar Publishing.

Peek, J. and Rosengren, E. S. (2005). Unnatural selection: perverse incentives and the misallocation of credit in Japan. *The American Economic Review*, 95: 1144–1166.

Puchniak, D. W. (2013). A skeptic's guide to Miwa and Ramseyer's 'The Fable of the Keiretsus'. *Journal of Japanese Law*, 24: 273–290.

Scher, M. J. (1997). *Japanese Interfirm Networks and Their Main Banks*, Basingstoke, UK: Macmillan.

Sheard, P. (1994). Main banks and the governance of financial distress. In: Aoki, M. and Patrick, H. (eds), *The Japanese Main Bank System: Its Relevance for Developing and Transforming Economies*. Oxford, UK: Oxford University Press, pp. 188–230.

Shishido, Z. (2001). Reform in Japanese corporate law and corporate governance: current changes in historical perspective. *The American Journal of Comparative Law*, 49: 653–678.

Shishido, Z. (2004). *Changes in Japanese Corporate Law and Governance: Revisiting the Convergence Debate*, University of Berkeley, eScholarship Repository, http://escholarship.org/uc/item/9376480h, last accessed 20 October 2015.

Shishido, Z. (2007). The turnaround of 1997: changes in Japanese corporate law and governance. In: Aoki, M., Jackson, G., and Miyajima, H. (eds), *Corporate Governance in Japan: Institutional Change and Organizational Diversity*. Oxford, UK: Oxford University Press, pp. 310–329.

Spaman, H. (2010). The 'Antidirector Rights Index' revisited. *The Review of Financial Studies*, 23(2): 467–486.

Tanaka, K. (2006). Kabunushi shuken to jūgyōin shuken – nihon no jōjō kigyō ni miru jiremmā (Shareholder supremacy versus employee supremacy – the dilemma of Japanese listed stock companies). *RIETI Discussion Paper Series* 06-J-036, Tokyo: RIETI.

Teramoto, Y. (1997). *Nihon Kigyō no Kōporeeto Gabanansu* (Corporate Governance of Japanese Firms), Tokyo: Seisansei Shuppan.

Tricker, B. (2012). *Corporate Governance: Principles, Policies, and Practices*, Oxford, UK: Oxford University Press.

TSE (2012). *Factbook 2012*, Tokyo: Tokyo Stock Exchange, www.tse.or.jp/english/market/data/factbook/index.html, last accessed 20 October 2015.

Uchida, K. (2011). Does corporate board downsizing increase shareholder value? Evidence from Japan. *International Review of Economics and Finance*, 20: 562–573.

Ueda, K. (1994). Institutional and regulatory framework for the main bank system. In: Aoki, M. and Patrick, H. (eds), *The Japanese Main Bank System: Its Relevance for Developing and Transforming Economies*. Oxford, UK: Oxford University Press, pp. 89–108.

Ujiie, J. (2002). *Nihon no Shihon Shijō* (Japanese financial markets), Tokyo: Tōyō Keizai Shimposha.

Waldenberger, F. (2000). Institutional change – lessons from the Japanese banking crisis. In: Riekeberg, M. and Stenke, K. (eds), *Banking 2000. Perspektiven und Projekte*. Wiesbaden, Germany: Gabler, pp. 79–95.

Waldenberger, F. (2013). 'Company heroes' versus 'superstars' – executive pay in Japan in comparative perspective. *Contemporary Japan*, 25: 189–213.

Weinstein, D. E. and Yafeh, Y. (1998). On the cost of a bank-centered financial system: evidence from the changing main bank relations in Japan. *The Journal of Finance*, 53: 635–672.

Whittaker, D. H. and Simon, D. (eds) (2009). *Corporate Governance and Managerial Reform in Japan*, Oxford, UK: Oxford University Press.

Xu, P. (2007). Corporate governance in financial distress: the new role of bankruptcy. In: Aoki, M., Jackson, G. and Miyajima, H. (eds), *Corporate Governance in Japan. Institutional Change and Organizational Diversity*. Oxford, UK: Oxford University Press, pp. 179–204.

Xu, M. and Zhang, C. (2009). Bankruptcy prediction: the case of Japanese listed companies. *Review of Accounting Studies*, 14: 534–558.

Yao, J. and Ouyang, H. (2007). Dark-side evidence on bank–firm relationship in Japan. *Japan and the World Economy*, 19: 198–213.

Yoshimori, M. (1995). Whose company is it? The concept of the corporation in Japan and the West. *Long Range Planning*, 28: 33–44.

6

M&A in Japan

Carsten Herbes

Introduction

Mergers and acquisitions (M&A) are important strategies for companies around the world (Kling *et al.* 2014). With M&A, companies pursue goals such as fast entry into foreign markets, acquisition of new technologies, and cost reduction through economies of scale or elimination of overcapacities in the market, but management hubris also plays an important role (Jensen and Ruback 1983; Trautwein 1990; Andrade *et al.* 2001; Nguyen *et al.* 2012; Svetina 2012). 'Merger' can mean the combination of two or more companies, of which only one survives or which form a new legal entity (Piesse *et al.* 2013). However, the term 'merger' is also often used to imply a combination of equals. Acquisition denotes a transaction whereby the acquirer controls the acquired firm (target) through purchasing shares representing more than 50 per cent of the voting rights, or whereby the acquirer buys a certain portfolio of assets of a firm (asset deal). M&A often has profound effects on the companies involved, especially the target company in the case of an acquisition. Being acquired can have positive effects on the target's productivity, survival, and growth (Sufian and Habibullah 2014). However, it also often means a reduction of the workforce (Krishnan *et al.* 2007) and replacing top management (Walsh and Ellwood 1991; Krug *et al.* 1997; Krug *et al.* 2014). Realizing synergies in purchasing often involves volume bundling and a consolidation of the supplier base, which can severely hurt the current suppliers' position (Herbes 2006). But shareholder value is also affected. Shareholders may benefit from a price premium over the current stock price offered by the acquirer (Laamanen 2007). If they receive the shares of the acquirer in exchange for their shares in the acquired company, then they may also benefit from a value increase following a successful M&A deal that delivers on the planned synergies. But, according to many studies (Lubatkin 1983; Ficery *et al.* 2007), M&A deals often fail and, therefore, shareholders receiving shares of the acquirer run the risk of being negatively affected by post-merger problems.

We have seen that all stakeholders of a company are affected by an M&A deal, either positively or – and this is a widespread concern of many stakeholders – negatively. Looking beyond single firms, M&A can also bring about big changes on an industry or national level. It can lead to consolidation of formerly dispersed industries (Shin *et al.* 2003; Esteve-Perez 2012; Mehta and Schiereck 2012) or be a means for foreign acquirers to gain a foothold in the domestic market, or even establish a dominant position there (Cheng 2006). With these far-reaching effects of M&A, it comes as no surprise that how companies and nations deal with M&A – whether they approve of it and foster it or whether they disapprove of it and try to impose far-reaching regulation – is to a large extent a matter of cultural values. Cultural values are far from being just a 'soft factor', but become manifest, e.g. in M&A legislation, shareholder structures and managers', and employees' behavior. If a culture is more in favour of a market approach and perceives companies rather as assets, then M&A meets rather favourable conditions. However, if a culture perceives companies as communities of people, then selling a company is like selling people, and acquirers face a much more difficult environment. In particular, hostile takeovers tend to make these fundamental differences in the approach towards M&A often visible.

M&A activities around the world have been increasing throughout the last decades, with notable peaks around 2000 and 2007 (Kengelbach *et al.* 2013), and the percentage of cross-border deals within total M&A volume has increased significantly (Erel *et al.* 2012). Although the Japanese numbers have increased as well, Japan has remained a special case with regard to M&A. In relation to its economic power, the number of M&A deals is remarkably low (Erel *et al.* 2009). In particular, out–in-deals where foreign acquirers buy Japanese firms are an exception, and also the volume of foreign direct investment in general is rather negligible (Pilat and Beltramello 2011).

This chapter will proceed as follows. After giving a short overview of the historical development and peculiarities of Japanese M&A in the next section, we will discuss a number of legislative, structural, and cultural factors influencing M&A activities in Japan. In the subsequent section, we will analyse the peculiarities of post-merger integration, which most often follows the M&A deal and is decisive in making a deal a success. The chapter will close with a brief conclusion. Although the macroeconomic effects of M&A are an important subject, this topic will be omitted here since this book focuses on processes within and between firms rather than on the Japanese economy at large.

Historical development and peculiarities of M&A in Japan

After a number of deals in the 1950s in the course of re-grouping firms from the former *zaibatsu*, which had been dissolved after the Second World War, and some more in the 1960s aiming at cost efficiency and preventing foreign takeovers in the steel and car industry, domestic and in-bound M&A did not play a major role in Japan until the end of the 1990s (Miyajima 2007; Muramatsu 2007). However, in outbound M&A, Japanese companies were very active in the 1980s as a consequence of the bubble economy, acquiring companies and other assets around the world (Muramatsu 2007: 72; Thomas 2008: 56) (see Figure 6.1).

From 2001 until around 2007 there was another upswing in overall M&A activity in Japan embedded into a global surge in M&A (Taguchi and Yanagawa 2013). In terms of deal numbers, the peak was 2007; in terms of transaction value, it was 2005 (Metwalli and Tang 2013). While some of the drivers such as technological development and deregulation have been similar to M&A waves in other industrialized countries; at the same time, there are also some driving factors specific to Japan: first, overcapacities had been building up throughout the prolonged recession of the 1990s. Reversing the overly strong diversification from the bubble period and the strong fragmentation, especially in the financial industry was another driver specific to Japan (Jackson and Miyajima 2007: 10; Miyajima 2007: 6). Structural factors and legal reforms gave rise to hopes that M&A would surge further in the coming years (Thomas 2008). However, from 2008 onwards, M&A activity was rather sluggish due to the global recession, and has only picked up recently. Recent M&A activities of Japanese

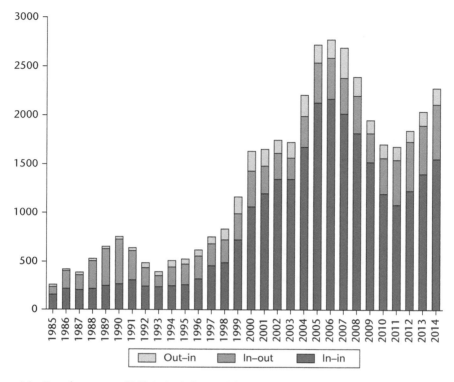

Figure 6.1 Development of M&A deals from 1985 to 2014

Source: Recof Corporation (2015)

companies in South-East Asia receive support from the Japanese government (Grant and Soble 2013). But, overall, the number and volume of M&A deals remains low in relation to Japan's economic power.

Looking at deals in the decade from 2000 to 2010, the following characteristics of the Japanese M&A market become clear (Metwalli and Tang 2013): first, 91 per cent of target firms and 94 per cent of acquiring firms were Japanese; the market is, thus, essentially a domestic market. This is a marked difference from the late 1980s and 1990s when the majority of deals were cross-border outbound (Thomas 2008: 56). In the small segment of foreign acquirers, US firms were most prominent (1.6 per cent), followed by firms from the UK (0.5 per cent) and Germany (0.2 per cent). An analysis by transaction type reveals that the biggest group was asset deals (35 per cent of transaction value and 42 per cent of deals), followed by an acquisition of partial interest and acquisition of majority interest. Another important feature of the M&A market is that a big share of all transactions are intra-group. For the period from 1994 to 2004, intra-group activities accounted for nearly half of all deals (Thomas 2008: 58). Looking at M&A by industry, the three biggest deals in the first decade of the millennium took place in the financial industry, with the Bank of Tokyo–Mitsubishi and UFJ Holdings merger in 2005 being on top of the list with a transaction volume of US$41 billion (Metwalli and Tang 2013). Current drivers of outbound M&A include the strong yen and limited domestic growth opportunities for Japanese companies due to the ageing population and the ongoing recession (Metwalli and Tang 2013). One peculiarity of M&A in Japan is that even if one partner is clearly bigger or stronger than the other, both parties often make a point of treating each other as equals (Kondo 2005; Herbes and Vaubel 2007), going as far as decoupling the share swap ratio from company values (Nakamura 2002). Acquirers had often held stakes in the target for a longer period before the acquisition took place (Miyajima 2007:14). As for the outcome for shareholders, it has been found that M&A deals in Japan very often do not create value for the shareholders of the seller or of the buyer (Mehrotra *et al.* 2011).

Hostile takeover attempts have been less frequent than in other countries; deals are often brought about by private negotiations (Komoto 2000; Miyajima 2007). But, after 2000, the number of tender offers has risen sharply, with the combined number for 2002 and 2003 surpassing the cumulative number of the three decades until 2000 (Colcera 2007).

Hostile takeovers had been unknown in Japan until 2000, and the number of deals is still considerably lower than in most other countries (Miyajima 2007). Foreign financial investors like Steel Partners Japan Strategic Fund were the first to attempt hostile takeovers of Japanese firms, but, in 2006, Oji Paper was the first domestic industrial company to launch a hostile takeover bid for Hokuetsu Paper, thus breaking a dam in the Japanese M&A culture. Already, in 2004, the attempt of US financial investor Steel Partners to take over Soto had sparked a heated public debate (Herbes and Vaubel 2007). Even more than the Oji Paper–Hokuetsu deal, the attempt of Livedoor to take over NBS in 2005 is considered as a 'watershed' (Whittaker and Hayakawa 2007: 16), with this takeover battle being fought in public and a court finally ruling that a part of NBS's defence measures were unlawful. Livedoor's takeover attempt aroused vast public interest and sparked a heated debate over M&A and especially defensive mechanisms with far-reaching effects: 'The fierce debate which was generated about legitimate anti-takeover measures produced a flurry of reports, guidelines and legislation, seeking to curb management entrenchment on the one hand, and to discourage destructive corporate raiders on the other' (Whittaker and Hayakawa 2007: 16). But, despite the recent springing up of hostile takeovers, Japan remains different from Anglo-American markets with its 'preference for mutual consensual transactions between the concerned parties' (Miyajima 2007: 4) and widespread condemnation for hostile takeover bids (Whittaker and Hayakawa 2007).

Summarizing, one can say that Japan has seen a number of M&A waves in the last decades, but that overall numbers remain relatively low. Moreover, M&A is a domestic phenomenon dominated by intra-group and friendly deals, rather than an international phenomenon.

Influencing factors

In this section, we will look at three major influencing factors for M&A in Japan. First, we will examine the legal environment. Then we will analyse structural factors such as cross-shareholdings. The last part of this section is dedicated to cultural factors, although one can argue that both legal and structural factors are also influenced by culture (see Figure 6.2).

When examining drivers of increasing M&A, deregulation in the legal environment is a frequent object of study. Deregulation can affect M&A activities in four ways: first, it can do this indirectly by changing the legal environment in certain industries and thereby bringing about changes in competition and strategies that may make M&A an interesting option or strategic necessity in these industries. Second, deregulation may affect company practices such as accounting, which, for example, alter the level of transparency for foreign investors and thus foster M&A. Third, it may affect regulation of the financial markets, e.g. concerning announcements that have to be made. And fourth, there is deregulation of legal provisions relating directly to M&A processes. For many years, the legal environment in Japan was very unfavourable for M&A: 'Japanese corporate law is full of restrictive rules that impede

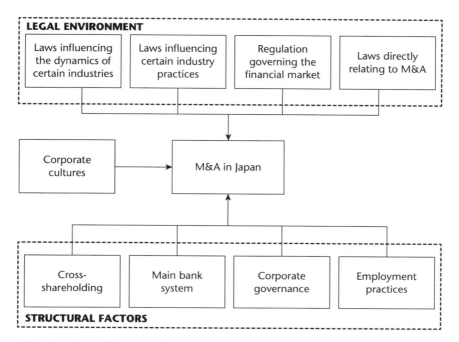

Figure 6.2 Overview of factors influencing M&A in Japan

Source: author's own illustration

corporations from acquiring each other and from changing their corporate structure' (Poe *et al.* 2002: 76), but since 2001 and the revision of the Company Act, a lot has changed.

In the first category, i.e. deregulation as a driver of changes in competition, Japan has experienced deregulation, especially in the public-transport, telecommunications, and financial industries, as well as in retail (Okada 1999; Kim 2002; Herbes and Vaubel 2007; Miyajima 2007; Choo 2010; Kushida 2012; Sakai and Takahashi 2013; Lopez and Spiegel 2014). In the second category, transparency of financial information by companies was greatly improved by legal reforms in 1999. While, before the reforms, the liabilities of companies resulting from their relations to their often numerous subsidiaries were a constant threat to any investor, consolidated financial statements since the reforms offer a much more reliable basis for assessing a target's financial risks (Miyajima 2007). Moreover, companies became more prone to sell subsidiaries performing poorly in the M&A market (Higgins and Beckman 2006). Other important reforms were the lifting of the ban on holding companies in 1997 (Shimotani 2012), although banks are still not allowed to hold more than 5 per cent of the shares of another company (Suzuki and Yamada 2013).

In the legal environment directly affecting M&A activities, various procedures, such as notification of creditors as well as rules governing shareholders' meetings before and after the merger, were facilitated in 1997 (Poe *et al.* 2002). The introduction of a stock-swap system in 1999 (Colcera 2007: 93), which allowed acquirers to pay their acquisition using their own shares, was important. This was an attractive option, especially for younger companies with high growth prospects but limited cash resources (Miyajima 2007). The squeeze-out of minority shareholders was facilitated in the same year, and a mechanism for corporate spin-offs was created in 2000 (Poe *et al.* 2002: 76). Moreover, in 2007, triangular mergers opened up further opportunities for foreign investors, allowing them to use their own shares to acquire companies in Japan (Colcera

2007; Herbes and Vaubel 2007). The introduction of the triangular merger option had been preceded by a heated public debate, which led to a postponement of about two years for this measure that had originally been planned for 2005 (Thomas 2008).

A very important part of the legal environment concerns defensive measures against takeovers. Especially in the context of Livedoor's takeover attempt of NBS in 2005, defence mechanisms were discussed vigorously in Japan.

Anti-takeover measures included cross-shareholding, increasing the volume of authorized shares, a staggered board, and others (Colcera 2007: 202).

A 2006 reform of the company law increased opportunities for managers to set up defence measures against takeovers, among others, by introducing special-class stocks. They can, for example, introduce new rights that can be exercised by all shareholders but the bidder or so-called 'golden shares' grant special rights, e.g. the right to appoint directors (Whittaker and Hayakawa 2007). At the same time, the new law requires a higher degree of transparency on the side of the management concerning anti-takeover measures, and several court-rulings have been issued ordering companies to abandon certain measures (Whittaker and Hayakawa 2007). In 2012, around 20 per cent of all companies listed on the TSE had adopted anti-takeover measures, slightly less than in the last survey two years prior (Tokyo Stock Exchange 2013). Bigger companies and those with a foreign shareholding of 20–30 per cent were most prone to introduce defensive measures (Tokyo Stock Exchange 2013: 95–96).

Structural factors

Cross-shareholding and the high share of so-called friendly, stable, or insider shareholders, especially but not only in the context of the big corporate groups or *keiretsu*, have been considered to be an important barrier to M&A (Milhaupt and West 2001; Colcera 2007; Herbes and Vaubel 2007). The nature of these stable shareholdings can be described as being: 'based on long-term business relationships, and supported by an implicit agreement between respective managements to stay out of the affairs of the firms they invest in, and to protect shareholdings from hostile third parties' (Miyajima and Nitta 2014: 2). Investors do not seek to maximize financial returns, but rather to underscore and stabilize their relationship to the firm in which they hold shares.

However, it must be said that the entire concept of *keiretsu* does not go uncontested (Miwa and Ramseyer 2002), and that a far-reaching change was brought about by the banking crisis at the end of the 1990s: 'the corporate ownership structure in Japan veered from an insider-dominated to outsider-dominated structure' (Miyajima and Nitta 2014). The cause–effect-relationship of changes is bidirectional here. While the decreasing importance of stable shareholders, as well as the increasing share of financial investors in corporations, have facilitated takeovers of Japanese companies, the acquirers (especially those of foreign origin) tend to sell the targets' shareholdings in other Japanese companies, such as in the Renault–Nissan case, and thus reinforce the trend. The unlocking of cross-shareholding also had a profound effect on the relative importance of different types of shareholders. While the importance of industrial companies and banks as shareholders decreased, the pension funds, other institutional investors, and also foreign shareholders, became more prominent. Cross-shareholdings and the relative importance of insider shareholders declined from the early 1990s, and especially after 1997 and up until 2006. This development was driven by the banking crisis of 1997, but also by the introduction of consolidated accounts in 2000. From 2007 onwards, however, Japanese firms started to re-establish these ties in order to protect themselves from foreign activist investors, while foreign shareholders sold parts of their Japanese investments in the course of the global financial crisis (Miyajima and Nitta 2014). But, with the system having been transformed to a more outsider-dominated scheme, it is questionable if this kind of move has any chance to unfold protective effects (Miyajima and Nitta 2014) (see Figures 6.3 and 6.4).

A second important mechanism that served as a stabilizing factor was the so-called main bank system. A main bank in the Japanese system is the main lender, as well as a shareholder, of its client, and they also played an important role as monitors in the Japanese corporate governance system (Aoki and Patrick 1994). A main bank's role included rescuing financially ailing clients. While potentially protecting firms from takeovers, main banks also seem to play an active role in domestic M&A. Mehrotra *et al.* (2011) have shown that, for deals where the acquirer and target

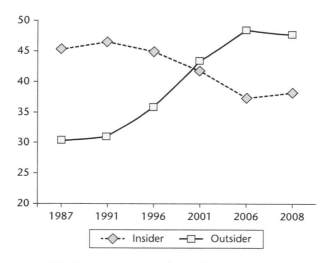

Figure 6.3 Percentage of insider and outsider shareholdings 1987–2008

Source: Miyajima and Nitta (2014: 34)[1]

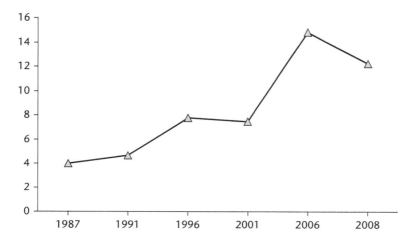

Figure 6.4 Percentage of foreign shareholders 1987–2008

Source: Miyajima and Nitta (2014: 36)

share the same main bank, it was more likely that a financially strong and a weak partner were involved and that the deal did not create wealth for the shareholders of either of them. This hints at the main bank being a main beneficiary of those deals. However, with the liberalization of the Japanese capital markets, and especially during the bubble economy, companies started to rely more on equity financing via the capital markets than lending from the main bank (Weinstein and Yafeh 1998). Moreover, after the banking crisis, the main banks faced their own financial challenges and became increasingly reluctant to perform the rescuer role (Miyajima 2007). On top of this, a number of bank mergers subsequent to the bank crisis in Japan blurred the hitherto clear-cut allocation of one main bank to one group of companies (Lee and Nagano 2008).

Corporate governance regulations as a structural influencing factor for M&A are a long-standing battleground for advocates and opponents of increasing M&A activity in Japan (for a review of players' positions in corporate-law reform, see Poe *et al.* 2002). Corporate governance mechanisms have long been regarded as a major obstacle, especially for foreign acquirers.

The virtual absence of outside directors on most boards in Japan gave rise to worries that directors would not act in the best interest of shareholders, but would rather represent employees and the current management's interest in the case of a takeover bid or other attempts of buying the company (Poe *et al.* 2002). While the 2002 reform of the Companies Act has introduced a choice for companies to switch to a unitary board system with committees modelled on the US legislation, most Japanese companies stick with the traditional system. In the current company-law reform process, corporate governance is, again, one of the main points, and the role of outside directors is a bone of contention between other stakeholders and *Keidanren*, which is strongly opposing any further strengthening of outsiders (Goto 2013). Under the current law, companies can choose between a two-tiered system with a *kansayakukai* (board of statutory auditors) and a one-tiered system with committees in the board of directors. When following the *kansayakukai* system, half of the statutory auditors have to be outsiders, but the position of the *kansayakukai* is rather weak, with no voting rights on the board of directors and no power in electing or removing directors (Goto 2013). Under the committee system, companies have to create a nomination committee; a compensation committee; and an audit committee, each of which has to consist of at least three directors with outsiders holding the majority of seats (Goto 2013). Of all listed companies on the Tokyo Stock Exchange, only around 2 per cent have adopted the committee system with its rather strong position of outside directors. There are also companies staying with the statutory auditor system that have appointed outside directors on a voluntary basis (Tokyo Stock Exchange 2013), but these are not necessarily independent, since they may come from a mother company (Goto 2013). There is a clear connection between the corporate governance system and the importance of foreign shareholders for a company: companies with a committee system have a markedly higher share of foreign shareholders; 31 per cent of them have a foreign ratio of more than 30 per cent, while this is only the case for 7 per cent of companies with a statutory auditor system (Tokyo Stock Exchange 2013). The reforms of the company law now underway only take a soft-law approach to the outside director issue, but, according to Goto (2013), the generally positive stance of the draft underway on the effect of outside directors is already a step forward.

The last structural factor that we examine is employment practices. Employment practices in Japan, with their focus on long-term employment of a large core workforce, tended to deter investors, due to the related financial risks in the case of a downswing. Again, the cause–effect relationship with M&A is two-sided. The increase of a peripheral workforce not experiencing or benefiting from life-time employment (Yu 2012); the shortening of tenures (Kawaguchi and Ueno 2013); and the increasing acceptance of Japanese companies dismissing members of the core workforce sent positive signals to potential investors, especially from abroad. On the other hand, financial and foreign investors are more likely to cut the workforce to improve the target's financial performance in the case of M&A.

M&A and corporate culture

Culture is frequently mentioned by practitioners and in academic research as an important barrier to M&A, especially involving foreign buyers (Kester 1991; Muramatsu 2007). But what are these cultural barriers? They mainly constitute the following factors:

- A strong tendency among small and medium-sized businesses to perceive the sale of a business as entrepreneurial failure (Nakamura 2002).
- The deep-rooted belief that a company is a community of stakeholders rather than an asset that can be bought and sold (Miyajima 2007).
- The sale of a company is equated to a sale of people (Crabb 1987).
- A strong wish to preserve the specific culture of one's own company (Miyajima 2007).

However, several surveys among Japanese business leaders, as well as among employees, show that reservations about M&A, and especially hostile takeovers, are waning (Colcera 2007). A long-standing relationship and a step-by-step approach can be a way to overcome cultural barriers on the side of Japanese targets. The Merck–Banyu case and the Roche–Chugai case are considered as examples of successful cross-border acquisitions (Kester 1991; Colcera 2007).

In a recent survey by the Tokyo Stock Exchange (TSE), c.80 per cent of all companies did not have anti-takeover measures in place, and many of those providing reasons for non-adoption stated that maximizing corporate value is the most effective measure against takeovers. Some who had adopted anti-takeover measures in the past considered abandoning them, and 'reasons for that include the company believing that shareholders should be the ones to decide whether takeover defence measures' are necessary (Tokyo Stock Exchange 2013: 101). These very recent developments are another indicator of a change in the thinking about corporate control in Japan.

Post-merger integration

Although public interest is highest when a deal is being announced, and often fades quickly afterwards, it is often not until much later that the success or failure of a deal becomes clear. Whether a deal succeeds depends, crucially, on the activities after the closing, i.e. the post-merger-integration (PMI) phase (Datta 1991; Epstein 2004; Herbes and Vaubel 2007; Hopkins 2008; Hernandez Barros and Lopez Dominguez 2013). There are acquisitions which do not aim at integrating the target into the acquirer's operations, and, in this case, integration may be mostly limited to financial reporting. In most cases, however, the acquirer tries to integrate the target by, for example, combining sales forces, or implementing joint procurement, or a group-wide human-resource management including the target. PMI can comprise strategy, processes, organizational structure, human resources, and culture. Without PMI, it is difficult to achieve synergies, and, without synergies, most deals will not create value.

PMI in Japan, just as with M&A, exhibits a number of peculiarities:

- a 'strong tendency to preserve the independence of target firms' (Miyajima 2007: 3–4);
- slow speed in integration;

- continuing the treatment of partners as equals even if size and economic power differ considerably (spirit of equality: '*taitō no seishin*') (Ōta and Sato 2003);
- combining boards of directors instead of integrating them, which leads to inflated board sizes (Herbes and Vaubel 2007).

Conflicts around the differences in corporate cultures can be so strong that even deals that had already been announced were called off in the past. When the acquirer is a foreign firm that wants to integrate the Japanese target into its global operations, problems tend to be especially strong, as culture is an important factor in post-merger integration (Cartwright and Cooper 1993; Weber *et al.* 1996; Barmeyer and Mayrhofer 2008; Edwards and Edwards 2012). Below is a non-exhaustive list of problems and resulting conflicts in some important areas of PMI:

- Joint procurement and changing to an arm's length principle in supplier dealings endangers traditional, relational Japanese supplier relationships. This may meet strong resistance by suppliers, who often focus on one or a few customers, and by employees, who feel an obligation towards their suppliers (Herbes 2008).
- Changing the remuneration and evaluation systems in human-resource management from a seniority-based system towards a performance-based pay and promotion scheme may provoke resistance by employees. This is because this move devalues the investments that older employees have made by accepting comparably low pay in their younger years, and they can only be sure to recoup the money if their wages keep rising according to the seniority system (Herbes 2008).
- Changing the acquired company's name may harm the identity and reputation of Japanese employees. While changing a company's name after an acquisition is a controversial issue in all cultures, it is especially threatening for Japanese employees, who have their identities and reputations closely tied to those of their employers (Herbes and Vaubel 2007).

Conclusions

M&A numbers in Japan are comparatively low. Moreover, M&A is a rather domestic phenomenon dominated by intra-group and friendly deals. Legal, structural, and cultural impediments have been partly removed in the last decades. Some, however, like cross-shareholding, have recently been on the rise again after years of decline. But then again, the planned introduction of IFRS rules will further heighten awareness of the risks of cross-shareholdings, and, thus, probably contribute to further unwinding (Miyajima and Nitta 2014). Still, foreign acquirers may find it more difficult to buy a company in Japan than in other parts of the world.

Note

1 'Insiders' include cross-shareholdings, holding companies, holdings by directors, and family control. 'Outsiders' include institutional investors, small individual investors, and foreign firms.

References

Andrade, G., Mitchell, M., and Stafford, E. (2001). New evidence and perspectives on mergers. *Journal of Economic Perspectives*, 15(2): 103–120.
Aoki, M. and Patrick, H. T. (1994). *The Japanese Main Bank System: Its Relevance for Developing and Transforming Economies*. Oxford, UK; New York: Oxford University Press.

Barmeyer, C. and Mayrhofer, U. (2008). The contribution of intercultural management to the success of international mergers and acquisitions: an analysis of the EADS group. *International Business Review*, 17(1): 28–38.

Cartwright, S. and Cooper, C. L. (1993). The role of culture compatibility in successful organizational marriage. *Academy of Management Perspectives*, 7(2): 57–70.

Cheng, Yung-Ming (2006). Determinants of FDI mode choice: acquisition, brownfield, and greenfield entry in foreign markets. *Canadian Journal of Administrative Sciences/Revue Canadienne des Sciences de l'Administration*, 23(3): 202–220.

Choo, Y. Y. (2010). Economies of scale in the non-life insurance industry in Japan: did deregulation enhance economies of scale? *Journal of Insurance Regulation*, 29(2): 47–71.

Colcera, E. (2007). *The Market for Corporate Control in Japan: M & AS, Hostile Takeovers and Regulatory Framework*. Berlin, New York: Springer.

Crabb, K. C. (1987). The reality of extralegal barriers to mergers and acquisitions in Japan. *The International Lawyer*, 21(1): 97–128.

Datta, D. K. (1991). Organizational fit and acquisition performance: effects of post-acquisition integration. *Strategic Management Journal*, 12(4): 281–297.

Edwards, M. R. and Edwards, T. (2012). Company and country effects in international mergers and acquisitions: employee perceptions of a merger in three European countries. *Economic and Industrial Democracy*, 33(3): 505–529.

Epstein, M. J. (2004). The drivers of success in post-merger integration. *Organizational Dynamics*, 33(2): 174–189.

Erel, I., Liao, R. C., and Weisbach, M. S. (2009). *World Markets for Mergers and Acquisitions*, NBER Working Paper Series No. 15132, Cambridge, MA. www.nber.org/papers/w15132.pdf?new_window=1, last accessed 20 October 2015.

Erel, I., Liao, R. C., and Weisbach, M. S. (2012). Determinants of cross-border mergers and acquisitions. *The Journal of Finance*, 67(3): 1045–1082.

Esteve-Perez, S. (2012). Consolidation by merger: the UK beer market. *Small Business Economics*, 39(1): 207–229.

Ficery, K., Herd, T., and Pursche, B. (2007). Where has all the synergy gone? The M&A puzzle. *Journal of Business Strategy*, 28(5): 29–35.

Goto, G. (2013). The outline for the Companies Act reform in Japan and its implications. *Zeitschrift für japanisches Recht/Journal of Japanese Law*, 35, 13–38.

Grant, Jeremy and Soble, Jonathan (2013). Japan leads field of M&A in southeast Asia. *Financial Times*, 23 July 2013, http://www.ft.com/cms/s/0/c5f52c86-f37d-11e2-942f-00144feabdc0.html#axzz3qLh03dYj, last accessed 2 November 2015.

Herbes, C. (2006). *Post-Merger-Integration bei europäisch–japanischen Unternehmenszusammenschlüssen: Konflik-torientierte Analyse am Beispiel des Lieferantenmanagements*. Gabler Edition Wissenschaft Schriften zum europäischen Management. Wiesbaden, Germany: Gabler.

Herbes, C. (2008). Schneider Electric – digital electronics: a successful case of foreign M&A in Japan. *Japan Aktuell – Journal of Current Japanese Affairs*, 2008(4): 33–66.

Herbes, C. and Vaubel, D. (2007). On the importance of successful post merger integration for M&As in Japan. *Japan Aktuell – Journal of Current Japanese Affairs*, 2007(3): 43–62.

Hernandez Barros, R. and Lopez Dominguez, I. (2013). Integration strategies for the success of mergers and acquisitions in financial services companies. *Journal of Business Economics and Management*, 14(5): 979–992.

Higgins, H. N. and Beckman, J. (2006). Abnormal returns of Japanese acquisition bidders –impact of pro-M&A legislation in the 1990s. *Pacific-Basin Finance Journal*, 14(3): 250–268.

Hopkins, H. Donald. (2008). Cross-border mergers and acquisitions: do strategy or post-merger integration matter? *International Management Review*, 4(1): 5–10.

Jackson, G. and Miyajima, H. (2007). *Varieties of Capitalism, Varieties of Markets: Mergers and Acquisitions in Japan, Germany, France, the UK and USA*, RIETI Discussion Paper Series No. 07-E-054. Tokyo: RIETI.

Jensen, M. C. and Ruback, R. S. (1983). The market for corporate control. *Journal of Financial Economics*, 11(1–4): 5–50.

Kawaguchi, D. and Ueno, Y. (2013). Declining long-term employment in Japan. *Journal of the Japanese and International Economies*, 28: 19–36.

Kengelbach, J., Klemmer, D. C., and Roos, A. (2013). *The Global M&A Market Remains in a Deep Freeze*. https://www.bcgperspectives.com/content/articles/mergers_acquisitions_alliances_joint_ventures_global_m_and_a_market_remains_deep_freeze/, last accessed 20 October 2015.

Kester, W. C. (1991). *Japanese Takeovers: The Global Contest for Corporate Control*. Boston, MA: Harvard Business School Press.

Kim, J.-Y. (2002). Deregulation reconsidered: protecting internet speech in the United States, Germany, and Japan. *Communications and the Law*, 24(1): p. 53.

Kling, G., Ghobadian, A., Hitt, M. A., Weitzel, U., and O'Regan, N. (2014). The effects of cross-border and cross-industry mergers and acquisitions on home-region and global multinational enterprises. *British Journal of Management*, 25: S116.

Komoto, K. (2000). *The Present Status of Takeover Bids (TOB) and Their Effect on Stock Prices*, NLI Research No. 147, www.nli-research.co.jp/english/economics/2000/eco0012a.pdf, last accessed 20 October 2015.

Kondo, H. (2005). Why Does M&A in Japan Go Wrong? (first part) (Nihon de no M&A ha naze umaku ikanai ka [sono ichi]), *Nikkei Business Publications*, online, http://nikkeibp.jp/sj2005/contribute/02/index.html, last accessed 20 October 2015.

Krishnan, H. A., Hitt, M. A., and Park, D. (2007). Acquisition premiums, subsequent workforce reductions and post-acquisition performance. *Journal of Management Studies*, 44(5): 709–732.

Krug, J. A. and Hegarty, W. Harvey (1997). Postacquisition turnover among U.S. top management teams: an analysis of the effects of foreign vs. domestic acquisitions of U.S. targets. *Strategic Management Journal*, 18(8): 667–675.

Krug, J. A., Wright, P., and Kroll, M. J. (2014). Top management turnover following mergers and acquisitions: solid research to date but still much to be learned. *Academy of Management Perspectives*, 28(2): 143–163.

Kushida, K. E. (2012). Entrepreneurship in Japan's ICT sector: opportunities and protection from Japan's telecommunications regulatory regime shift. *Social Science Japan Journal*, 15(1): 3–30.

Laamanen, T. (2007). On the role of acquisition premium in acquisition research. *Strategic Management Journal*, 28(13): 1359–1369.

Lee, M. H. and Nagano, M. (2008). Market competition before and after bank merger wave: a comparative study of Korea and Japan. *Pacific Economic Review*, 13(5): 604–619.

Lopez, J. A. and Spiegel, M. M. (2014). Foreign entry into underwriting services: evidence from Japan's 'big bang' deregulation. *Journal of Money, Credit and Banking*, 46(2–3): 445–468.

Lubatkin, M. (1983). Mergers and the performance of the acquiring firm. *Academy of Management Review*, 8(2): 218–225.

Mehrotra, V., van Schaik, D., Spronk, J., and Steenbeek, O. (2011). Creditor-focused corporate governance: evidence from mergers and acquisitions in Japan. *Journal of Financial and Quantitative Analysis*, 46(4): 1051–1072.

Mehta, R. and Schiereck, D. (2012). The consolidation of the global brewing industry and wealth effects from mergers and acquisitions. *International Journal of Business and Finance Research*, 6(3): 67–87.

Metwalli, A. M. and Tang, Roger Y. W. (2013). Mergers and acquisitions in Japan: an update. *Journal of Corporate Accounting and Finance*, 24(6): 25–34.

Milhaupt, C. J. and West, M. D. (2001). *Institutional Change and M&A in Japan: Diversity Through Deals*. Columbia Law School, The Center for Law and Economic Studies, Working Paper No. 193, New York: Columbia Law School.

Miwa, Y. and Ramseyer, J. M. (2002). The fable of the keiretsu. *Journal of Economics and Management Strategy*, 11(2): 169–224.

Miyajima, H. (2007). *The Comparative Features and Economic Role of Mergers and Acquisitions in Japan*, RIETI Discussion Paper Series No. 07-E-056, Tokyo: RIETI.

Miyajima, H. and Nitta, K. (2014). *Does ownership matter?: The causes and consequence of changing ownership structure in Japan under the globalization*. Retrieved from www.worldbhc.org/files/full%20program/C8_DoesOwnershipmattertheroleofinstitutionalinvestorsver2.pdf, last accessed 20 October 2015.

Muramatsu, S. (2007). M&A in Japan – past and present. In: Bebenroth, R. (ed.), In the wave of M&A: Europe and Japan. München: Iudicium, pp. 70–93.

Nakamura, R. (2002). *Preliminary Report on the Current State of Mergers and Acquisitions in Japan*, Working Paper No. 140, Stockholm: the European Institute of Japanese Studies, Stockholm School of Economics, http://swopec.hhs.se/eijswp/papers/eijswp0140.pdf, last accessed 20 October 2015.

Nguyen, H. T., Yung, K., and Sun, Q. (2012). Motives for mergers and acquisitions: ex-post market evidence from the US. *Journal of Business Finance and Accounting*, 39(9–10): 1357–1375.

Okada, Y. (1999). Path dependent globalization: the state and financial deregulation in Japan. *Humanomics*, 14–15(4–1): 19–48.

Ōta, N. and Sato, T. (2003). The tasks of the human resources department in M&A (M&A ni okeru jinjibu no shimei). *Jinzaikyōiku*, September 2003: 14–24.

Piesse, J., Lee, C.-F., Lin, L., and Kuo, H.-C. (2013). Merger and acquisition: definitions, motives, and market responses. In: Lee, C.-F. and Lee, A. C. (eds), *Encyclopedia of Finance*, Wiesbaden, Germany: Springer, pp. 411–420.

Pilat, D. and Beltramello, A. (2011). *Opening Japan – Comparisons with Other G20 Countries and Lessons Learned from International Experience: BBL Seminar Handout*. Tokyo. www.rieti.go.jp/en/events/bbl/11062301.pdf, last accessed 30 October 2015.

Poe, M., Shimizu, K., and Simpson, J. (2002). Revising the Japanese Commercial Code: a summary and evaluation of the reform effort. *Stanford Journal of East Asian Affairs 2002*, Spring 2002, Volume 2: 71–95.

Recof (2015). Numbers sent by Recof Data through e-mail on 27 January 2015.

Sakai, H. and Takahashi, Y. (2013). Ten years after bus deregulation in Japan: an analysis of institutional changes and cost efficiency. *Research in Transportation Economics*, 39(1): 215–225.

Shimotani, M. (2012). Japanese holding companies: past and present. *Japanese Research in Business History*, 29: 11–28.

Shin, G., Fraser, D. R., and Kolari, J. W. (2003). How does banking industry consolidation affect bank–firm relationships? Evidence from a large Japanese bank merger. *Pacific-Basin Finance Journal*, 11(3): 285–304.

Sufian, F. and Habibullah, M. S. (2014). The impact of forced mergers and acquisitions on banks' total factor productivity: empirical evidence from Malaysia. *Journal of the Asia Pacific Economy*, 19(1): 151–185.

Suzuki, K., and Yamada, K. (2013). Blockholder and firm performance: quasi-experiment using Japanese bank mergers. *SSRN Electronic Journal Working Paper*.

Svetina, M. (2012). Managerial motives in mergers: propensity score matching approach. *Managerial and Decision Economics*, 33(7–8): 537–547.

Taguchi, H. and Yanagawa, T. (2013). The dynamic impacts of M&A on employment in Japan. *Journal of Management and Governance*, 17(2): 511–533.

Thomas, I. (2008). *Grenzüberschreitende Mergers and Acquisitions: Erfolg und Erfolgsfaktoren internationaler Unternehmenszusammenschlüsse in Japan. Schriften zur Wirtschaft Asiens*, Vol. 5. Marburg, Germany: Metropolis-Verlag.

Tokyo Stock Exchange (2013). *TSE-Listed Companies White Paper on Corporate Governance 2013*. www.tse.or.jp/english/listing/cg/b7gje60000003y6y-att/b7gje6000001fy2s.pdf, last accessed 20 October 2015.

Trautwein, F. (1990). Merger motives and merger prescriptions. *Strategic Management Journal*, 11(4): 283–295.

Walsh, J. P. and Ellwood, J. W. (1991). Mergers, acquisitions, and the pruning of managerial deadwood. *Strategic Management Journal*, 12(3): 202–217.

Weber, Y., Shenkar, O., and Raveh, A. (1996). National and corporate cultural fit in mergers/acquisitions: an exploratory study. *Management Science*, 42(8): 1215–1227.

Weinstein, D. E. and Yafeh, Y. (1998). On the costs of a bank-centered financial system: evidence from the changing main bank relations in japan. *Journal of Finance*, 53(2): 635–672.

Whittaker, D. H. and Hayakawa, M. (2007). Contesting 'corporate value' through takeover bids in Japan. *Corporate Governance: an International Review*, 15(1): 16–26.

Yu, W.-H. (2012). Better off jobless? Scarring effects of contingent employment in Japan. *Social Forces*, 90(3): 735–768.

Part III

The corporate environment in Japan

7

The Japanese tax system

Makoto Fujii

Introduction

There are over fifty types of taxes in Japan, and the tax on corporate income is remarkably complicated. Therefore, it is not an easy task to understand the full scope of the tax system in Japan. In this chapter, first, I will describe corporate-income tax, and then, briefly, property tax, consumption tax, and personal-income tax in Japan.

The Japanese accounting system

Since corporate-income tax is closely tied to the accounting system, I will provide an overview of the accounting system prior to discussing corporate-income tax. In accordance with the provisions of the Company Law, all companies must prepare financial statements, such as a balance sheet and an income statement. If the corporation has affiliates and subsidiaries, then it must prepare not only individual but also consolidated financial statements. For the companies listed on the securities market, disclosures of more-detailed financial statements are required in accordance with the Financial Instruments and Exchange law. Accounting standards in the Financial Instruments and Exchange Law are substantially similar to the International Financial Reporting Standards (IFRS), and a fair-value evaluation is partially performed to calculate the comprehensive income, based on the asset and liability view. The Financial Instruments and Exchange Law also requires companies to prepare individual financial statements and consolidated financial statements.

Corporate-income tax

General

Corporate-income tax, corporate-residence tax, and business tax are imposed on the income that is derived from the business activities of a corporation. On the one hand, both corporate-residence tax and business tax are local taxes, which are basically calculated in accordance with the corporate-income tax. On the other hand, corporate-income tax is a national tax.

Tax rate

The corporate-income tax rate is a fixed rate of 23.9 per cent. The reduced tax rate of 15 per cent is applied to income of up to eight million yen for small and medium-sized corporations whose capital is 100 million yen or less. Moreover, the standard corporate-residence tax rate is 17.3 per cent, which consists of 3.2 per cent for the prefecture, 9.7 per cent for the municipality, and 4.4 per cent for the prefecture and the municipality. However, a local government has the authority to apply an excess rate over these standard rates. Since the corporate-residence tax is calculated based on the amount of the corporate-income tax, it takes 4.1347 per cent. Apart from these two taxes, a business tax is also imposed. The effective tax rate on the income is 32.34 per cent in Tokyo. The current effective tax rate on corporate income is comparatively high when compared to the worldwide average; therefore, the Japanese government is considering lowering it.

Tax base and general rules for the computation of taxable income in each fiscal year

The tax base of corporate-income tax is the income amount of each fiscal year (Corporation Tax Law, article 21), and the taxable income is calculated by deducting gross expenses from gross revenue for each fiscal year (Corporation Tax Law, article 22).

In calculating the taxable income in each fiscal year for a corporation, the amount to be included in gross revenue in the accounting period shall, unless otherwise provided for, be the amount of revenue from the sales of assets; onerous or gratuitous transfer of assets; or rendering of service; or gratuitous acquisition of assets other than capital transactions (Corporation Tax Law, article 22(2)). Unless otherwise specified, gross revenue is basically the same as the revenue in the income statement, and it is recognized by the realization principle.

The amount to be included in gross expenses in the accounting period, unless otherwise provided for, shall be the amount prescribed in the following list (Corporation Tax Law, article 22(3)):

1   The amount of the cost of sales, the cost of completed construction work, and other similar costs with regard to the revenue in that particular fiscal year.
2   The amount of expenses involved in selling; general and administrative expenses; and other expenses in that particular fiscal year (excluding expenses that are concerned with liabilities that are not definite until the last day of the fiscal year).
3   The amount of the loss in that particular fiscal year from transactions except transfer of the capital.

In other words, the provisions of the tax law takes priority over the accounting standards on gross income and gross expenses. Corporate-income tax focuses on the income of the corporation, therefore, the capital transactions and the dividends are excluded (Corporation Tax Law, article 22(5)). Taxation on dividends has been discussed in relation to the choice between debt and equity of financing in Japan and the United States (Block 2001: 37; Ishi 2001: 182).

Relationship between corporate tax law and the accounting standards

The amount of revenue and expense shall be calculated in accordance with the general accepted accounting standards (Corporation Tax Law, article 22(4)). The taxable income for each fiscal period, which is the tax base of corporation tax, is the amount calculated by deducting the amount of expenses from the gross revenue. The Corporation Tax Law adopts the principle of final settlement of accounts (Corporation Tax Law, article 74). Specifically, the amount of income is calculated by adjusting (adding or deducting) based on the accounting profit on a commercial income statement, which is calculated according to the generally accepted accounting principles (GAAP), on the attachment schedule No. 4 of the tax return form (Gomi and Honjo 2015: 115 (see Figure 7.1).

The accounting profit is the net income that is displayed in individual financial statements under the Company Law. Consolidated financial statements are not used in calculating the taxable income, even if it is to apply the consolidated tax return. This system is similar to the authoritative principles in Germany (Maßgeblichkeitsgrundsantz). This Maßgeblichkeitsgrundsantz operates in Germany, France, Belgium, and many other countries, with some variations (Nobes and Parker 2008: 34). However, there is a difference between Japan adopting a method of correcting the income statement and Germany adopting a method of correcting the balance sheet (Knobbe-Keuk 1993: 17).

Dividend

When the corporation receives a dividend, the dividend is excluded from the gross revenue in principle because, if the Corporation Tax Law does not make any adjustment, corporate-income tax is levied on multiple taxation. For example, when a corporation establishes a subsidiary, it is taxed twice on the same income, and this would violate the principle of neutrality. The purpose of the neutrality principle is that it promotes economic efficiency and is fair to the tax-payer (Musgrave 1989: 33). However, because there is an element of investment in the shares held by a corporation, the tax law may not completely adjust the double taxation. Provisions are described as follows (Corporation Tax Law, article 23):

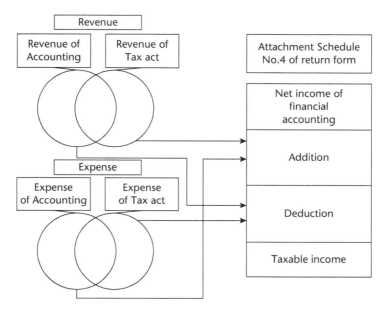

Figure 7.1 Conceptual diagram of the taxable income calculation

1   dividends from a wholly owned subsidiary or related corporation (the proportion of the shareholding is more than 33.3 per cent): 100 per cent exclusion;
2   dividends in the case where the proportion of the shareholding is from 5 per cent to 33.3 per cent: 50 per cent exclusion;
3   dividends in the case where the proportion of the shareholding is 5 per cent and less: 20 per cent exclusion.

Foreign tax-credit

The Corporation Tax Law classifies every corporation into a domestic corporation and a foreign corporation. While the domestic corporation is a corporation having its head office or principal office in Japan, the foreign corporation is defined as a non-domestic corporation (Corporation Tax Law, article 2 (iii, iv)).

The domestic corporation is taxed on income earned worldwide, but the foreign corporation is taxed only on domestic source income (Corporation Tax Law, articles 5, 9). The provisions above are based on the principles of both the capital export neutrality and the capital import neutrality (Fujii 2007: 48). The capital-export neutrality is a principle that tax law should be neutral with respect to the corporation's decisions on where to export the capital. Furthermore, the capital-import neutrality requires that a domestic corporation and a foreign corporation shall do business activities under the same competitive conditions. While this taxation system satisfies both principles, it has a major problem. That is, there is the problem of the double taxation of corporate-income tax in Japan and in a foreign country. In order to solve this problem, the foreign tax credits system is adopted (Corporation Tax Law, article 69).

The following is an example of the foreign tax credit: a corporation earned 2,000 units of domestic source income and 1,000 units of foreign source income. It is assumed that the tax rate in Japan is 23.9 per cent and the foreign tax rate is 20 per cent. In this case, since 200 units of corporate-income tax to be paid in the foreign country will be double taxation, an adjustment is necessary. First, add the tax paid in a foreign country in the process of calculating the taxable income, and then subtract the same amount in the process of tax calculation (see Figure 7.2).

Depreciation

With respect to depreciation, there are no detailed standards or regulations in the Japanese GAAP. Since the depreciation is an internal transaction, a manager can manipulate income through an arbitrary depreciation. The Corporation Tax Law and regulations stipulate exactly the acquisition cost, depreciation method, and depreciation rate, corresponding with the useful lives of products. However, the principle is not that the tax authorities incorporate the depreciations into expenses of their own accord, while a corporation does not include such depreciations, but that the authorities judge the amount to be included in gross expenses in calculating taxable income, based on the amount of depreciation incorporated by the corporation into expenses (Gomi and Honjo 2015: 155). For assets of less than 100,000 yen, it is allowable to write this off immediately.

Reserve

As mentioned above, the Corporation Tax Law adopts the definite liability principle on the expenses. Therefore, no reserve is included in calculating expenses as a general rule (Arai and Narimichi 2004: 27). Some reserves used to be allowed as a deductible item, but it is hardly ever

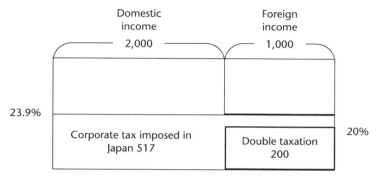

Item	Amount
Net income in the income statement	2,800
Adding the adjustment of foreign corporation tax	200
Taxable income	3,000
Amount of corporate tax before adjustment	717
Foreign corporation tax credit	200
Amount of corporate tax after adjustment	517

Figure 7.2 Example of foreign tax credit

allowed now, since the tax rate has been reduced. An allowance for bad debts is only permitted for small and medium-sized corporations (Corporation Tax Law, article 52). In addition, corporations engaged in publishing can include a deductible reserve for sales returns (Corporation Tax Law, article 53).

Net loss

In the case where there is a net loss arising in the accounting periods beginning within ten years before the first day of each accounting period of a corporation, the amount shall be included in gross expenses when calculating the taxable income (Corporation Tax Law, article 57). Both carry-over and carry-back are allowed with respect to net loss. While carry-over is allowed a ten year period, carry-back is limited to only a one year period as a rule, and this application has been suspended currently (Corporation Tax Law, article 80, Act on Special Measures Concerning Taxation, article 66–13).

Reorganization

Since the company law defines reorganization, such as the types described below, under the condition that the corporations involved in the transaction meet the certain requirements, the Corporation Tax Law stipulates 'tax-free' provisions (Corporation Tax Law, articles 62–2, 62–3, 62–5). This term 'tax-free' does not mean tax exemption, but the deferral of tax.

Types of reorganization

1 merger;
2 separation-type corporate separation; the method is used for creating a sister company by dividing an existing company;
3 subsidiary-type corporate separation; the method is used for creating a subsidiary by dividing an existing company;
4 investment in kind;
5 distribution in kind;
6 stock exchange (the method is used for acquiring a company);
7 stock transfer; the method is used for establishing a holding company.

In applying tax-free provisions for reorganization, the delivery of assets other than shares should not be carried out in cases where cash is paid, i.e. the capital gain is deemed to be realized in the reorganization, and also one of the following requirements must be met:

1 there is reorganization of a group of companies that is under complete shareholder control, i.e. where the proportion of the shareholding is 100 per cent;
2 there is reorganization of a group of companies under a controlling interest of more than 50 per cent. However, the group also has to satisfy conditions that allow continuation of the business activities and employment of more than approximately 80 per cent of the employees;
3 there is reorganization to establish a joint business under certain conditions, while there is no capital relationship.

Group taxation

Inter-company transactions among corporations which have full controlling interests are substantially similar to internal transactions, and such transactions often result in tax avoidance. For this reason, gains and losses on inter-company transactions are deferred until the asset goes out of the group (Corporation Tax Law, article 61–13). The assets that are affected by this provision are property worth 10 million yen or more.

Consolidated tax return

If the full controlling relationship exists between the parent company and the subsidiaries, such corporations can apply the consolidated tax return (Corporation Tax Law, article 61–13). The capital relationship of 100 per cent is required in this system, because there is no need to consider the minority shareholders, and it is taking into account the neutrality of the parent–subsidiary company and the head–branch-office relationships. If a corporation applies the consolidated tax return, then the parent company will combine the income of the subsidiaries with its own income. Consequently, if one corporation has a net loss, then it is offset against the income of the other corporation. In addition, gains and losses on transactions between consolidated corporations are excluded from revenues and expenses in this system.

International taxation

Transfer pricing rule

When a corporation deals with foreign group corporations, this is possible by manipulating the transaction price, in order to transfer the income overseas. The fact that the corporate-tax rate in Japan is higher than in other countries is the background to this. This provision shall deem that transactions between foreign group corporations have been done at the arm's length price (market price) (Law on Special Measures Concerning Taxation, article 66–4).

Tax haven rule

There are cases where a corporation establishes a paper company in the tax haven region or country, and then the corporation suspends the income there. In this case, it is not possible for the tax authorities to levy tax on the corporation semi-permanently. Therefore, the authorities shall deem that income, which is reserved to the paper company, is distributed to the corporation (Law on Special Measures Concerning Taxation, article 66–6). This tax system does not combine the income of the corporation in Japan and of the foreign paper company. So, the income of the paper company is summed up, but the loss is ignored.

Thin capitalization rule

When a corporation is a subsidiary of a foreign corporation, in some cases, corporations aim to reduce the tax burden by borrowing money from the parent company instead of investment. The fact that the interest expenses are deductible, but dividend payments are excluded from the expenses, can lead to such a situation. If both of the following ratios are more than 300 per cent, interest expenses corresponding with an amount more than 300 per cent of the amount of investment by the foreign parent company are not deductible.

1   amount of loans from foreign parent company/amount of the equity of foreign parent company;
2   amount of debt required to pay interest/amount of equity capital.

Disallowance of manipulated transaction or computation

Since the ownership and management are not separated in the family corporation, governance does not function well. Therefore, tax evasion often occurs. In addition, since the consolidated tax system and reorganization tax system are very complex, it is necessary to deal with tax avoidance, which the laws do not seem to assume.

If the district director accepts the transactions or book entries of the corporations, this would result in an improper decrease in the burden of corporation tax. The district director may calculate the tax base according to his/her recognition, notwithstanding the transactions or book entries by the corporations (Corporation Tax Law, article 132). This provision only applies to the following corporations:

1   a family corporation;
2   a corporation that has made the reorganization;
3   a corporation that has selected the consolidated tax return.

The principle of substance over form and the principle of fair taxation lay behind this provision. The principle of substance over form is found in the Internal Revenue Code in the United States (Bittker and Eustice 2000: 1–20) and in Germany as well.

Makoto Fujii

Foreign corporation

When a foreign corporation has a permanent establishment, for example, a branch office, it is taxed on only its domestic source income (Corporation Tax Law, articles 4(3), 138). The income of the foreign corporation is calculated in accordance with the income calculation of domestic corporations. The principle of no taxation without permanent establishment is common all over the world (Fujimoto 2005: 87).

Withholding system

Along with the provisions of the Income Tax Law, a certain amount is withheld for interest, dividends, remuneration, and salary (Income Tax Law, articles 181–189). As a result of this withholding system and the year-end adjustment that companies carry out, most businesspeople need not declare a final tax return. Since the withholding system is widely adopted in Japan, tax evasion hardly occurs. The withholding system is originally intended for individuals, but would also apply to the dividends and interest that corporations receive. In this case, the corporation must pay the income tax that they should not bear. Therefore, in order to solve this problem, an income tax credit is permitted, as it is the same as the foreign tax credit.

Corporate-resident tax

In addition to the corporate-income tax, a corporation must pay the corporate-resident tax. Corporate-resident tax is levied not only on income, but also on a per capital basis using the amount of the corporation's capital and the number of employees (Local Tax Law, article 23, 292) (see Table 7.1).

When a corporation has offices in two or more prefectures and/or municipalities, it is necessary to pay the tax in each region.

Business tax

For corporations with capital of more than 100 million yen, pro forma standard taxation is levied based on income, added value, and the capital as the taxable base (Local Tax Law, articles 72(2)). Each tax rate is as shown in Table 7.2.

Table 7.1 Amount of corporate-resident tax

Amount of capital		Number of employees	Resident tax
From:	Up to:		
–	10,000,000 yen	Up to fifty	70,000 yen
		More than fifty	140,000 yen
10,000,000 yen	100,000,000 yen	Up to fifty	180,000 yen
		More than fifty	200,000 yen
100,000,000 yen	1,000,000,000 yen	Up to fifty	290,000 yen
		More than fifty	530,000 yen
1,000,000,000 yen	5,000,000,000 yen	Up to fifty	950,000 yen
		More than fifty	2,290,000 yen
5,000,000,000 yen	–	Up to fifty	1,210,000 yen
		More than fifty	3,800,000 yen

Table 7.2 Standard rate of business tax

Taxable base		Corporation with 100 million yen or less in capital	Corporation with more than 100 million yen in capital
Income	Less than 4,000,000 yen	5%	3.8%
	4,000,000 yen to 8,000,000 yen	7.3%	5.5%
	More than 8,000,000 yen	9.6%	7.2%
Value added		–	0.48%
Capital		0.2%	0.2%

There are some cases where tax rates differ among local governments. Until the completion of the fundamental reform of the tax system, including the consumption tax, a portion of the business tax is replaced tentatively by the special local corporate tax. This tax is intended to alleviate the uneven nature of tax-revenue distribution among local governments.

Property tax

A corporation must pay the property tax based on the market value of the fixed assets (land, buildings, machine, and equipment, etc.) owned. The standard tax rate is 1.4 per cent and is notified by the municipality. The taxable base of the property tax is a fair market price (Kaneko 2011: 571).

Personal income tax

General

Individuals, based on the comprehensive income concept, are required to pay personal income tax for all their income. The taxable period is the calendar year. All the income can be classified into ten categories:

Classification of income (Income Tax Law, articles 23–35)

1 Interest income is the interest on bank deposits.
2 Dividend income is a dividend in accordance with the investment and equity. Interest related to debt incurred in order to buy shares is deductible.
3 Real estate income is the income obtained by the real estate lending, and the related expenses are deductible from the income.
4 Business income is the income obtained from business activities, and the related expenses are deductible from the income.
5 Salaries income is the income that an employee earned as compensation for labour provided.
6 Retirement income is the income earned when an employee is retired.
7 Capital gain is the income earned by the transfer of assets.
8 Timber income is the income earned by the sale of standing trees. In calculating the timber income, first of all, one should divide the income by five, and then multiply the amount of tax five times, which is calculated by applying the tax rate.
9 Temporary income is the income earned temporarily, and 50 per cent of the income is the taxable income.
10 Other income, including pension income, includes all other types of income that are not categorized above.

Taxation

All the types of income described above are subject to comprehensive taxation in principle. However, there are exceptions, such as the following:

1   Uniform withholding taxation. Interest income is, in many cases, taxed upon uniform withholding tax by a personal-income tax rate of 15 per cent and a personal-resident tax rate of 5 per cent.
2   Separate taxation is applied for the purpose of reducing the tax burden, i.e. on retirement income, timber income, and capital gains relating to land and buildings. For retirement income and timber income, additional measures are taken to reduce the tax burden.

Fictional theory of the corporation

Japanese tax law adopts so-called corporate fictional theory. Therefore, in order to eliminate the double taxation of personal-income tax and corporate-income tax, a dividend credit system is provided. This system partially eliminates double taxation and it is similar to the half-income method (Halbeinkünfteverfahren) in Germany (Djanani *et al.* 2007: 219).

Tax rate

As shown in Table 7.3, the tax rate is applied with progressive rates from 5 to 45 per cent. In addition to the normal personal income tax, a special reconstruction income tax (2.1 per cent of the personal income tax) was introduced in 2013. This reconstruction tax will be imposed for twenty-five years from the time of introduction. The tax will pay for reconstruction following the Great East Japan Earthquake that occurred in March 2011. While the personal-income tax and the special reconstruction income tax are national taxes, the individual resident tax at a flat tax rate of 10 per cent, is also imposed and this is a local tax.

Consumption tax

General

Consumption tax is intended to impose a tax for the consumption of goods and services, and is similar to the value-added tax found in Europe and the United States. Most of the tax revenue

Table 7.3 Personal income-tax rate, special reconstruction income-tax rate, and resident-tax rate

Amount of income		Income-tax rate	Special reconstruction-tax rate	Resident-tax rate
From:	Less than:			
0 yen	1,950,000 yen	5%		
1,950,000 yen	3,300,000 yen	10%		
3,300,000 yen	6,950,000 yen	20%		
6,950,000 yen	9,000,000 yen	23%	2.1%	10%
9,000,000 yen	18,000,000 yen	33%		
18,000,000 yen	40,000,000 yen	40%		
40,000,000 yen	–	45%		

Note: The bracket for an income-tax rate of 45 per cent is expected to be introduced from January 2015; while personal-income tax is a national tax, residence tax is a local tax used to be from the direct taxes, such as corporate-income tax and personal-income tax, but the proportion of contributions from indirect taxes such as consumption tax is now increasing.

Tax rate

The current consumption tax rate is 8 per cent (Consumption Tax Law, article 29, Local Tax Law, articles 72–83) which is lower than in European countries. However, there are plans to raise the tax rate to 10 per cent after April 2017. A reduced rate is not available at the moment, but there have been discussions on whether or not to introduce it, bearing in mind the problems of the regressive nature of the consumption tax when the 10 per cent rate is applied.

When the consumption tax was introduced in April 1989 for the first time, the tax rate was 3 per cent; it rose to 5 per cent in April 1997, and to 8 per cent in April 2014. Due to the following two reasons, the consumption tax rate is rising gradually (Mizuno 2011: 757):

1 To solve the chronic budget deficit;
2 To cover the social-security costs that are being increased by the ageing population in Japan.

In addition to these reasons, there is also a need to compensate for the shortfall in tax revenue due to the reduction in the corporate-income tax rate and the personal-income tax rate.

Input tax credit

The corporation or private concern actually pays the consumption tax, but the last person to pay this tax burden is the consumer. Therefore, the method for inputting the tax to the consumer is important.

The tax base of the consumption tax is the transfer of assets and the provision of services (Consumption Tax Law, article 4). However, transactions without charge are excluded from the taxable base. Moreover, the transfer of assets and the provision of services carried out by individuals for non-business purposes are tax-free.

In order to eliminate the accumulation of taxation, it is necessary to implement the tax credit (Consumption Tax Law, article 30). In the following illustrative example, four parties are assumed: material supplier, manufacturer, distributor, and consumer. First, a material supplier sells materials to a manufacturer for 1,000 yen. Then, the manufacturer sells products to a distributor for 1,200 yen. At the end, the distributor sells products to a consumer at 1,500 yen. It is assumed that 10 per cent consumption tax is levied on all transactions.

In this case, the amount of consumption tax that each company should pay to the government is as follows. Needless to say, the one who bears the weight of the consumption tax is the consumer at the end of the chain.

1 material supplier: 100 yen (= 100 yen – 0 yen)
2 manufacturer: 20 yen (= 120 yen – 100 yen)
3 distributor: 30 yen (= 150 yen – 120 yen)
4 total: 150 yen.

In this way, each company should pay the government after deducting the consumption tax paid from sales tax.

In Japan, the tax credit is carried out based on book-keeping, while value-added tax in European countries is carried out based on the invoice.

Conclusions

In many cases, Japanese tax law is very similar to German tax law. Since Japan is a country of written law, its provisions of tax law are very complex. In addition, it is a characteristic that the corporate tax is closely related to the accounting system. On the other hand, in introducing a consolidated tax payment system and the tax-free reorganization tax system, the Internal Revenue Code of the United States is used as a reference. Furthermore, there are large numbers of specifically Japanese systems, such as the group tax system. As compared with other countries, Japanese corporate-income tax has a tendency to be imposed on the corporate group.

Bibliography

Arai, M. and Narimichi, H. (2004). *Zeimukaikeiron* (Tax Accounting). 3rd edn, Tokyo: Chuoukeizai-sha.

Bittker, B. I. and Eustice, J. S. (2000). *Federal Income Taxation of Corporations and Shareholders*, 7th edn. New York: Warren, Gorham and Lamont.

Block, C. D. (2001). *Corporate Taxation*, 2nd edn. New York: Aspen Law & Business.

Djanani, D., Brähler, G., and Lösel, C. (2007). *German Income Tax*. Frankfurt am Main, Germany: Verlag Recht und Wirtschaft GmbH.

Fujii, M. (2007). Denshi-Shōotorihiki ni Kakawaru Hōjinshotokuzeihō no Mondaiten (Problems of taxation on e-commerce). *Zeikeitsuishin*, 62(14), 42–51.

Fujimoto, T. (2005). *Kokusai Sozeihō* (International Tax Law Theory and Practice). Tokyo: Chuōkeizai-sha.

Gomi, Y. and Honjo, T. (2015) *Corporation Tax Act 2012*. Tokyo: Sozeishiryokan.

Ishi, H. (2001). *The Japanese Tax System*, 3rd edn. Oxford, UK: Oxford University Press.

Kaneko, H. (2011). *Sozeihō* (Tax Law), 16th edn. Tokyo: Kobundo.

Knobbe-Keuk, B. (1993). *Bilanz-und Unternehmenssteurrecht neunte Auflage*. Köln: Dr Otto Schmidt KG.

Musgrave, R. A. and Musgrave, P. B. (1989). *Public Finance in the Theory and Practice*, 5th edn. New York: McGraw-Hill.

Mizuno, T. (2011) *Sozeihō* (Theory of Tax Law in Japan), 5th edn. Tokyo: Yūhikaku.

Nobes, C. and Parker, R. (2008) *Comparative International Accounting*, 10th edn. London: Pearson Education.

8

Corporate legislation in Japan

Bruce Aronson, Souichirou Kozuka, and Luke Nottage

Introduction

Until the 1990s, the success of the Japanese corporation (J-Firm) was generally perceived as having little relationship to Japan's corporate law or the formal legal system. Rather, Japan's system was characterized as strongly preferring informality over law – an economic system based on close, informal government–industry cooperation, and governance at J-Firms focused on informal ties with a variety of stakeholders such as main banks, lifetime employees, and *keiretsu*-affiliated companies (Milhaupt and West 2004: 14; Kozuka and Nottage 2014).

Although every modern corporate law provides the board of directors with the dual roles of both advising management (and making significant corporate decisions) and supervising management, in Japan, the board of directors was expected to focus on day-to-day management of the company. Its additional legal role of monitoring or supervising management was instead presumed to be performed informally in the form of internal monitoring by stakeholders, particularly by main banks.

The extent of this system, and its actual functioning, was always subjects of debate (Milhaupt 2002). For example, bank monitoring was contingent, and arguably conducted on behalf of the bank itself as a creditor rather than on behalf of shareholders or stakeholders generally. In addition, by the 1990s, there was clear evidence of a long-term overall weakening of this system, with a shrinking (but still significant) core of lifetime employees, less bank shareholding, a reduced importance of *keiretsu*-affiliated companies, and a relative increase in the importance of general shareholders (Nottage *et al.* 2008).

The bursting of Japan's economic bubble in the early 1990s caused a re-examination of many of the assumptions of the post-war system and created strong pressures for wide-ranging reform. In a broad sense, reform measures initiated from the mid-1990s sought to shift the economy's emphasis from informal bureaucratic coordination to greater private market initiatives based on legal rules and their interpretation. Corporate and securities law, as well as corporate governance more widely, were very much on the reform agenda, generating a large literature even in Western languages (Baum *et al.* 2013: 47–51, 282–327). Reformers aimed to increase the international competitiveness of Japanese corporations as well as to increase investor returns and the attractiveness of the stock market, against the backdrop of a rapidly ageing population and pressures on the pension system.

The twin concerns of economic competitiveness and attractiveness to investors resulted in numerous corporate law amendments in the decade from the mid-1990s that contained two separate, and sometimes contradictory, components: providing corporate management with greater flexibility than traditionally granted under Japan's Commercial Code to finance and structure corporate activities (e.g. permitting spinoffs, stock options, etc.) and, to a lesser degree, providing greater protection for the interests of shareholders (e.g. the debate over a legal requirement for 'outside' directors in the 2000s) (Milhaupt 2006; Shishido 2007). Most reforms enhanced management flexibility, so were welcomed by big business groups (such as *Keidanren*) and easily undertaken. Measures to protect shareholders, generally opposed by business groups, constituted a minority of the reforms and were undertaken at a much slower pace.

Numerous amendments to reform specific corporate law provisions of Japan's Commercial Code during the decade from the mid-1990s to the mid-2000s (listed in Nottage *et al.* 2008: 13–20) culminated in the enactment of a new Companies Act in 2005 (Law No. 86 of 2005, as amended). The first amendment of the Companies Act occurred in 2014 (Kozuka 2014). The Companies Act generally modernized Japan's corporate law and further codified a number of ongoing trends such as the distinction between public companies and privately held companies. Special rules for 'large companies' initiated originally in 1974 (now art. 2, no. 6, Companies Act) and subsequent developments also provided for separate treatment for public companies (art. 2, no. 5, Companies Act).

One distinguishing feature of Japanese corporate reform was allowing companies to select among a number of different corporate structures. The Companies Act provided a new array of structuring options for smaller private entities (Hashimoto 2007). Since 2002, public companies were given a choice: they could retain the 'traditional' Japanese corporate form with the German-inspired features of a *kansayaku* board (board of audit) and a representative director as the CEO, or adopt a new option of an 'American-style' structure that replaced the board of audit with three committees on the board of directors (audit, compensation, and nomination committees, with a majority of outside directors required for each committee) and a new class of executive officers headed by the chief representative officer (Gilson and Milhaupt 2005).

In addition to these two choices of a company with *kansayaku* board and a company with nomination and other committees (art. 328 (10), Companies Act; prior to 2014 referred to simply as a 'company with committees'), the 2014 amendment to the Companies Act added a third option: a company with an audit and supervisory committee. This new form essentially replaced the traditional *kansayaku* board with a 'one-committee' system; it requires only an audit committee, with a majority of outside directors as a committee of the board of directors.

Corporate legislation was supplemented by extensive amendments that overhauled existing securities laws in 2006 (Law No. 25 of 1948, as amended; renamed the Financial Instruments and Exchange Act (FIEA) in 2006). The FIEA contains several provisions relevant to corporate governance, primarily related to information disclosure and reporting requirements. It required, for example, a new system of quarterly reporting for listed companies (art. 24-4-7, FIEA).

Reform legislation in Japan can thus be characterized as representing gradual, but significant, evolutionary change (Kozuka 2008; Nottage *et al.* 2008). During the first decade of reform, this approach disappointed some critics who, impressed by the apparently successful American post-industrial model and the possibility of global 'convergence' towards the American model, looked for a more far-reaching transformation in Japan from a stakeholder-oriented system to a shareholder-oriented system (Milhaupt 2006).

The US model did, in fact, serve as the main inspiration during the first decade of reform in Japan, as seen, for example, in the structural option of an 'American-style' company with nomination and other committees that was provided to Japanese companies. However, following the 2008 financial crisis, the UK approach, featuring mainly 'soft law' corporate governance codes with 'comply or explain' disclosure provisions for listed companies, has gained increasing influence over the US 'hard law' approach exemplified by the Sarbanes–Oxley Act of 2002.

Functions of the board of directors: management model and monitoring model

The dual board roles of management and monitoring raise the issue of their relative importance in board functioning. The traditional role of directors in Japan, focused on the management function, is referred to as the management model of the board. The United States, which evolved over decades to emphasize independent directors supervising management, is often referred to as representing the monitoring model of the board. Much of the ongoing debate concerning the reform of corporate governance in Japan has focused on the extent to which Japan will move towards, or incorporate elements of, the monitoring model.

Even under the traditional *kansayaku* board, directors in Japan are also charged with monitoring the CEO (art. 362 (2), Companies Act). Monitoring by the board (then generally consisting of only executive or 'inside' directors) was first introduced in 1983 in response to the problem of dictator-like CEOs who made important decisions on their own without consulting the board. Specifically, corporate law required board approval of major business decisions, such as sales of significant assets, making of significant loans, or appointment of senior employees (now art. 362 (4), Companies Act). There has gradually been greater acceptance in Japan of the importance of the monitoring function and greater recognition of the monitoring model, even among traditional companies with a *kansayaku* board (e.g. a distinction between executive and non-executive directors was introduced in 2002 under art. 363 (1) of the Companies Act). However, most Japanese companies still tend to view themselves as forming a 'company community' (Buchanan *et al.* 2012; Osugi 2014).

The company with nomination and other committees structure was based on the US monitoring model. The board has three mandatory committees (nomination, audit, and compensation) that are each required to have a majority of outside directors (art. 400 (3), Companies Act) and executive officers (art. 418, Companies Act. However, in practice, only a handful (2 per cent) of Japanese listed companies adopted this structure (TSE White Paper 2013: 10). In addition, some of the companies utilizing the nomination and other committees structure are listed subsidiaries of large companies who already monitor their subsidiary's performance and operations, and arguably may have less need of monitoring by independent directors than would truly independent companies. Thus, this committee structure may sometimes have been used for the purpose of entrenching group control rather than for the protection of general shareholder interests (Gilson and Milhaupt 2005).

Monitoring in the 'company with audit and supervision committee' structure is conducted by the sole audit and supervision committee, which must have a majority of outside directors (art. 331 (6), Companies Act). It is a new structural option for Japanese listed companies, and its function is not yet clear (Goto 2013). The question remains whether it will turn out to be simply a variation of the traditional *kansayaku* board structure dressed up to appeal to institutional investors and others who are demanding more independent directors, or whether it will be a new hybrid model that usefully combines aspects of the management board and monitoring board models.

Board members

Differences between the managing board and monitoring board models are reflected in a long and ongoing debate in Japan over the extent to which there should be legal requirements for outside and/or independent directors, and for the use of executive officers to undertake day-to-day management.

Outside directors are not required for the traditional company with *kansayaku* board. For other corporate structures (the company with nomination and other committees and the company with audit and supervision committee), the Companies Act requires that outside directors constitute a majority of each board committee. In practice, such companies are therefore required to have at least two outside directors, because each committee must have at least three directors, with the majority (i.e. two) being outside directors.

The Companies Act originally defined 'outside' directors simply as non-executive directors, i.e. a 'director who is not, or has not been, an executive director, officer or employee of the company or its subsidiary' (art. 2, no. 15, Companies Act). Directors employed by parent companies therefore qualified as 'outside' directors of the subsidiary. The legislative intent was to ensure that directors would perform their monitoring role properly and not be intimidated by the CEO. The 2014 amendment to the Companies Act changed the definition of outside director to focus on director independence more broadly. It now excludes employees, directors, and officers of parent and sister companies (although in all cases it now permits former employees, etc. who have not acted as such for a period of 10 years to become outside directors) and of controlling shareholders, and also their close family members (art. 2, no. 15, Companies Act after 2014 amendments). However, the definition of outside director does not exclude persons from trade partners, such as main banks, which is a significant issue in Japan.

Nonetheless, since 2010 the Tokyo Stock Exchange (TSE) rules have required that each listed company must have one director or *kansayaku* who meets a stricter definition of independence. And, in a separate provision in February 2014, the TSE strongly recommended having at least one such independent director (rather than a *kansayaku*). Independence is generally defined as a quality that is unlikely to give rise to conflicts of interest with general shareholders. Yet, like many definitions of independence outside Japan (and like the Companies Act definition of outside director), it focuses on excluding persons in certain categories and does not contain a positive requirement for independence.

'Executive officers' were first developed in 1996 by Sony Corporation, and were not based on any provision of the Companies Act or its predecessors. At that time, the traditional *kansayaku* board was the only permissible legal structure for large, listed companies in Japan. The reasons for this development include a desire by some larger Japanese companies to delegate day-to-day management downward from the board to officers. This approach can leave the board to focus on more important decisions and on monitoring management. At the same time, it can also speed up daily management decisions and result in more efficient management.

Most Japanese companies now have executive officers: some are required by statute (in the case of companies with one of the two alternative corporate structures involving board committees) and some are voluntary (i.e. for traditional companies with a *kansayaku* board). In the latter case, officers operate on an informal (non-legal) basis and, for example, do not have established fiduciary duties under corporate law.

Kansayaku

Kansayaku are an important feature of Japanese companies, as some 97.8 per cent of listed companies have retained their structure of a company with *kansayaku* board (TSE White Paper 2013: 15), but their actual role remains controversial. Although many countries in Asia have some kind of audit or supervisory board, only in Japan has corporate law reform sought to strengthen their function to serve as a possible substitute for independent directors. For example, the *kansayaku*'s term of office has been gradually extended to four years, longer than the two years for directors, in an effort to protect the *kansayaku* from CEO pressure and ensure their independence (art. 336 (1), Companies Act).

Kansayaku are required only for a company with *kansayaku* board. In a 'large' public company, there must be three or more *kansayaku* (art. 328 (1), Companies Act), and at least half of them must be outside *kansayaku* (art. 335 (3), Companies Act). Their traditional authority under the Companies Act is to 'audit' for illegality (*ihōsei*); there is also a debate concerning the extent to which *kansayaku* should go beyond instances of illegality to audit for acts that are unsound or not in the best interests of the corporation (*datōsei*). The *kansayaku*'s role has been criticized by foreign investors as being essentially a compliance function, as they lack the legal authority to supervise management: they have a duty to attend board meetings and to intervene when necessary (art. 383 (1), Companies Act), but have no right to vote and also cannot fire the company president of directors (Asian Corporate Governance Association 2008: 18).

Kansayaku do, however, have important powers of their own, including the power of investigation and enquiry at their company (art. 381 (2), Companies Act), and also at their company's subsidiaries (art. 381 (3), Companies Act), and the right to request a court injunction when a manager (director) commits an unlawful act (art. 385 (1). In addition, each *kansayaku* can exercise his or her powers individually, and some of the *kansayaku* are full-time insiders with thorough knowledge of the company (comparing *kansayaku* and independent directors, see Asian Corporate Governance Association 2013).

Kansayaku often claim that their role, in practice, is generally becoming broader than compliance and is focusing more on risk management, although it is difficult to measure or judge actual practice. In recent years, *kansayaku* have been assigned an important role in controlling conflicts of interest (such as approval for limiting the liability of directors). On the other hand, the board was also given a more specific role in the *kansayaku*'s traditional field of compliance. Under the Companies Act, the board of directors must make decisions on the establishment of a company's internal control system (art. 362 (4) no. 6, Companies Act) and, under the FIEA, such board decisions must be publicly disclosed (art. 24-4-4, FIEA).

Shareholders and general shareholders' meeting

In Japan, shareholders have always had a relatively broad range of rights, which are exercised primarily at general shareholders' meetings and secondarily through shareholder derivative suits. In addition to the election of directors and *kansayaku*, shareholders' rights exercised at general shareholders' meetings include decisions on directors' compensation (art. 361, Companies Act).

Even when a matter is within the decision-making authority of the board, it can be delegated to the general shareholders' meeting through an amendment to the corporate charter (art. 295 (2), Companies Act). A prominent example of this approach occurred in one of the most famous hostile takeover attempts in Japan. In the Bulldog Sauce case, the issuance of share options (the power of the board of directors under the default rule: art. 240 (1), Companies Act), as part of a 'poison pill' defence against would-be foreign acquirer Steel Partners, was delegated to the general shareholders' meeting and approved by 80 per cent of the shareholders. As mentioned below, shareholder approval became an important basis for the Supreme Court's affirmation of the validity of Bulldog Sauce's defence (art. 240 (1), Companies Act).

Large minority shareholders have several additional rights, including the right to make shareholder proposals at the general shareholders' meeting (1 per cent or 300 units or more of the voting rights required: art. 303 (2), Companies Act); the right to inspect the company's accounting books (3 per cent or more of the voting rights or 3 per cent or more of the outstanding shares required: art. 433, Companies Act); and the right to request appointment of an inspector of the company's operations (3 per cent or more of the voting rights or 3 per cent or more of the outstanding shares required: art. 358, Companies Act).

Since 1950, originally inspired by Illinois corporate law, individual shareholders have the right to file derivative suits (art. 847, Companies Act). Derivative suits began to increase in number and importance following further reforms in 1993. The most important derivative suit was the Daiwa Bank case, decided in 2000 (Aronson 2003). It established that, as part of a director's duty of oversight, the board must establish a system of internal controls. This duty was subsequently reflected in provisions of the Companies Act and FIEA.

In a derivative suit, the shareholder alleges a director's breach of fiduciary duty (including the duty of care and duty of loyalty, see arts. 330 and 355, Companies Act). In the case of the duty of care, Japanese courts apply a version of the business judgment rule and will not find liability if the director conducted a careful examination of information in advance and made a decision that was not 'extremely unreasonable' (Supreme Court's Judgment of 15 July 2010; Puchniak and Nakahigashi 2012).

In the past, Western literature on general shareholder meetings in Japan ignored formal rights under corporate law and consistently focused on the informal and unusual role of *sōkaiya* ('shareholder meeting racketeers') in Japan, who, at one time, dominated general shareholder meetings. *Sōkaiya* were described as part of a system in which Japanese companies tried to closely manage general shareholder meetings, and cared only about keeping meetings short, adhering to the meeting's 'script', and avoiding any questions from shareholders (West 1999).

This may have been largely true up until the early 2000s, but in the last decade this situation has completely changed. Due to both greater information disclosure and a crackdown on *sōkaiya* activities, general shareholder meetings in Japan today closely resemble those in the United States and other Western countries. There are no *sōkaiya* at general shareholder meetings; companies do not focus on the length of the meetings; and companies expect, and even welcome, questions from shareholders (Iwatani and Taki 2010).

A general shareholders' meeting must be held at least once a year (art. 296 (1), Companies Act), and it must be within three months from the end of the fiscal year (art. 124 (2), Companies Act). As the fiscal year of many listed companies is 31 March, a large number of companies hold their meetings within a few weeks in late June. In the past, Japanese companies were encouraged to hold their meetings on the same day to make it more difficult for *sōkaiya* to attend many meetings. However, as *sōkaiya* influence has waned, the trend in recent years is for meetings to be spread out among different dates to allow institutional shareholders to attend as many meetings as possible, although there remains more concentration than in some other major economies.

As in other countries, resolutions approved by shareholders may still be subject to attack on the grounds that shareholders were not provided with adequate information. In Japan, the Companies Act provides that directors have a duty to respond sufficiently to shareholders' questions (art. 314, Companies Act). Failure to provide an adequate response can be a cause for annulment of a resolution passed by the general shareholders' meeting if it is determined that the resolution was adopted 'by an extremely unfair procedure' (art. 831 (1), no. 3, Companies Act).

Most shareholder voting takes place prior to the general shareholders' meeting. Voting by mail has been in use since 1983 (art. 301, Companies Act), and electronic voting is also available (at the option of the issuing company) (art. 302, Companies Act). Proxy voting is utilized to obtain support from large shareholders (art. 310, Companies Act). Although they are rare, proxy contests are provided by law (for their regulation, see art.194, FIEA, and the Ministerial Order on Proxy Solicitation), and any shareholder has the right to copy the list of shareholders (to send out proxy solicitation letters) (art. 125 (2), Companies Act).

Mandatory disclosure of the actual voting results of proposals made at general shareholders' meetings was introduced in 2010 (art. 24-5 (4), FIEA and art. 19 (2), no. 9-2, Ministerial Order on Corporate Disclosure). Such disclosure has had a significant influence on listed companies to become more responsive to the voices of shareholders (in particular, institutional investors).

Regulation of takeovers

Hostile takeovers have been very rare in post-war Japan. However, shareholder activism, including takeover attempts, has increased substantially since the late 1990s. A complicated jurisprudence has developed concerning defensive measures against takeovers, featuring both government guidelines and court decisions. There is debate in characterizing Japanese takeover law between those who stress the influence of Delaware law (Milhaupt 2005), others who look to the example of the UK takeovers panel, and observers who detect a hybrid approach (Nottage 2008 et al.). There is similar debate on how to evaluate Japan's approach, with some arguing that it is overly protective of management, while others see shareholder activism more broadly as helping to ensure corporate value by imposing a partial constraint on management.

Although some new Japanese shareholder activists were initially welcomed in the early 2000s as potentially leading to more innovative and responsive Japanese companies, the Livedoor case in 2005 rocked Japanese industry and led to the widespread introduction of poison-pill defensive measures. Livedoor, led by a brash young entrepreneur, Takafumi Horie, secretly amassed a large holding in a Fuji Television subsidiary (Nippon Broadcasting System or NBS) in after-hours trading, and NBS responded to this threatened takeover by issuing a large number of share options to Fuji and other shareholders (excluding Livedoor) that would greatly raise Fuji's holdings in NBS and dilute the holdings of Livedoor.

Livedoor's request for an injunction against NBS' issuance of stock options was granted by the Tokyo District Court and upheld by the High Court. Existing case law followed a primary purpose rule, under which the issuance of stock would be enjoined if such options were issued primarily for the purpose of affecting a contest for corporate control rather than for financing the company's activities or other legitimate business purpose, since such issuance constituted an 'extremely unfair method' under corporate law (arts 210, no. 2, and 247, no. 2, Companies Act). In the Livedoor case, the Tokyo High Court decision extended this approach to the issuance of stock options (Fujita 2012). It noted that the issuance of stock options for control purposes would be permitted in exceptional cases to defend against 'abusive' bids that would clearly harm shareholder interests, provided that the company's defence was proportional to the threat.

The Livedoor decision was the first case law on poison pill defences against takeovers. It seemed to open the door to hostile takeovers, potentially including those by foreign acquirers.

This occurred at a time (2005) when the new Companies Act, which also appeared to encourage takeovers, was in the process of being enacted. Concerns of business groups prompted a government review and the issuance of METI/MOJ Guidelines by its Corporate Value Study Group, which focused on how companies could adopt 'legitimate' takeover defences to improve corporate value by obtaining the approval of shareholders.

This emphasis on shareholders' approval developed into the controversial Supreme Court ruling in the 2007 Bulldog Sauce case. The High Court decision in that case had labelled the aggressive foreign bidder, Steel Partners, as an 'abusive acquirer'. While the Supreme Court refrained from similar name-calling, it nevertheless substituted approval of the shareholders for a determination that the bidder would harm the shareholders' collective interests if it successfully acquired control of the target company. It also essentially permitted a 'greenmail' payment by corporate management to Steel Partners, which arguably harmed the interests of general shareholders (Oda 2012). Shareholder approval of defensive measures is a feature of the English law tradition, rather than US law (allowing greater deference to incumbent management), but against the backdrop of particularly active institutional investors in the UK as well as the outright prohibition of various defensive measures (Armour *et al.* 2010).

The Corporate Value Study Group published another report the following year, in 2008, attempting a modest rollback of the Supreme Court's approach by pointing to the danger that excessive emphasis on shareholders' approval would encourage inefficient (re-)building of cross-shareholding (Kanda 2010). Nevertheless, the lesson of the Bulldog Sauce case for some foreign hedge funds and private equity funds was that the nascent movement towards a more open market for hostile takeovers in Japan would not come to fruition, as numerous Japanese companies rapidly adopted poison pills as defenses to any potential hostile takeovers.

Japanese law has also faced challenges in dealing with potential conflicts of interests in friendly takeover cases, particularly in the area of management buyouts (MBOs). METI's MBO Guidelines require not only compensating the share's value prior to the MBO, but also distributing a part of the premium (synergies) generated by the MBO. This approach was affirmed by the Supreme Court in the leading case of Rex Holdings (per concurring opinion of Justice Tahara) (Saito 2012; Tanaka 2011).

A standard no-shop clause (ensuring an exclusive right to negotiations), and judicial refusal to allow an injunction to enforce it, became an issue in another well-known case involving Japan's three megabanks (Taylor 2009). UFJ signed a deal for the sale of UFJ Trust Bank to Sumitomo Trust; however, UFJ subsequently entered into talks with Mitsubishi Tokyo Financial Group and agreed to a new sale in violation of the no-shop clause in the original deal with Sumitomo Trust. An unprecedented lawsuit involving the three major banking groups resulted in the Supreme Court denying provisional injunctive relief to Sumitomo Trust in its attempt to enforce the no-shop provision, although the case focused more on the lack of a need for provisional relief than on the merits.

A cash-out of the minority shareholders remaining after a takeover has long been cited as an important issue in need of reform, since a fear of discriminatory low payments to 'hold-out' shareholders could have the effect of coercing them to accept a takeover offer. Prior practice often used the 'shares subject to full call' technique (art. 171, Companies Act) (issuing new shares of large value in (art. 171, Companies Act) (issuing new shares of large value in exchange so that a remaining shareholder receives only a fraction of one share, which must be compensated in cash (art. 234, Companies Act)). A new cash-out procedure was introduced by the 2014 amendment to the Companies Act (articles 179 to 179-10) that was similar to the procedure for the issuance of new shares, including advance disclosure, an injunction remedy against coercive bids, and voiding such bids in extreme cases.

Soft law and corporate practice

In addition to substantial new corporate legislation, in recent years, the increased significance of soft-law approaches and voluntary corporate practices has also had an important impact on the evolution of Japanese corporate governance.

During much of the post-war era in Japan, US business law, including corporate law and corporate governance, was the main model for reform. This remained true even as the US model of corporate governance evolved into a monitoring model, resulting in vast differences between the US monitoring model and traditional Japanese practices. The US model also increasingly focused on hard law, such as the Sarbanes–Oxley Act that established a legal requirement that all public companies in the US have a majority of independent directors. Japan found it difficult to follow or compromise with this model, and progress was slow even when compared with other countries hesitant about this approach.

The dominance of the US model ended with the financial crisis of 2008. In recent years, Japan has focused more on soft-law approaches, more characteristic of the UK tradition (although that itself has slowly added various mandatory requirements to its corporate law system). This perspective emphasizes gradual reform through corporate practices and market pressures, rather than immediate legislative requirements. The main mechanism comprises a corporate governance code or principles from self- or co-regulated organizations such as stock exchanges, requiring listed companies to adopt specified perceived best practices (such as a minimum proportion of independent directors), or else to explain the reasons for any divergence.

Over the past several years, Japan has utilized some aspects similar to this approach in a number of areas, including TSE rules requiring one independent director or *kansayaku*; METI/MoJ guidelines and TSE rules on takeover defences; the adoption of a Stewardship Code in February 2014; and the ruling Liberal Democratic Party's first official recommendation that Japan adopt a corporate governance code as part of its growth strategy (announced in June 2014). Such soft-law reforms still encounter business opposition, but are arguably both less objectionable and a better 'fit' with the overall evolutionary approach of corporate governance reform.

Voluntary corporate governance reforms at leading Japanese companies are also significant as a sign of increasing acceptance of important aspects of the monitoring model. One example is the substantial reduction in the average number of board members of listed companies to 8.13 members as of 2013 (TSE 2013: 22), which is a reform that was not mandated by law or stock-exchange rule. More importantly, a number of large, complex, and increasingly global leading Japanese companies have an interest in reforms to focus the board of directors on strategic issues such as capital allocation among their various lines of business. Such an approach also contains the potential for a more useful role for outside directors who may not be knowledgeable about day-to-day management issues.

These recent voluntary reform efforts may be described as a hybrid approach in which Japanese companies seek to build on their traditional strengths (including *kansayaku*) and incorporate a greater element of monitoring by voluntarily adding a number of outside directors and board committees (particularly a nomination committee) (Aronson 2012). Such efforts try to combine insiders' information with outsiders' independence to achieve more effective board functioning. The challenge for Japanese corporate governance is to find a way to standardize and spread these emerging best practices by, for example, utilizing a corporate governance code that is implemented through a comply-or-explain or similar 'soft law' approach.

Conclusions

Japanese corporate law is gradually evolving towards a greater acceptance of the importance of the monitoring function and the monitoring model, although this evolution has proceeded more slowly than in other major economies. The limits of this evolution are clearly illustrated by the strong persistence of the *kansayaku* system, despite complaints from international institutional investors and others that it is not an effective substitute for independent directors and does not sufficiently represent shareholder interests.

Since the mid-1990s there has been a gradual, but significant, evolution in Japanese corporate law and corporate governance. Although reform centred on corporate legislation in the early stages, in recent years soft-law approaches and voluntary adaptation in corporate practices have also had a significant impact. This may serve to moderate some of the rigid requirements of current structuring options for corporations that tend to emphasize form over substance, such as requirements for the 'American-style' company with nomination and other committees (mentioned in the Introduction to this chapter) and the definition of outside director. Whereas such an approach tended to be viewed suspiciously by outside observers before the 2008 financial crisis, there is now more acknowledgement of its advantages.

The continuation of these trends of an emphasis on soft law and voluntary changes in corporate practices, for example by the enactment in Japan of a wide-ranging corporate governance code enforced through a comply-or-explain mechanism, will likely have a significant influence on the future development and direction of Japanese corporate governance.

Bibliography

Armour, J., Jacobs, J., and Milhaupt, C. J. (2011). The evolution of hostile takeover regimes in developed and emerging markets: an analytical framework. *Harvard International Law Journal*, 52: 219–285.

Aronson, B. (2003). Reconsidering the importance of law in Japanese corporate governance: evidence from the Daiwa Bank shareholder derivative case. *Cornell International Law Journal*, 36: 11–47.

Aronson, B. (2012). The Olympus scandal and corporate governance reform: can Japan find a middle ground between the board monitoring model and management model? *Pacific Basin Law Journal*, 30: 93–148.

Asian Corporate Governance Association (2008). *White Paper on Corporate Governance in Japan*, available at: www.acga-asia.org/public/files/Japan%20WP_%20May2008.pdf, last accessed 15 October 2015.

Asian Corporate Governance Association (2013). *The Roles and Functions of Kansayaku Boards*, www.acga-asia.org/public/files/ACGA_Paper_Kansayaku_Audit_Committees_October_2013_English_Final.pdf, last accessed 15 October 2015.

Baum, Harald, Thier, Markus, Nottage, Luke, and Rheuben, Joel (2013) *Japanese Business Law in Western Languages: An Annotated Selective Bibliography*, 2nd edn, New York: Hein.

Buchanan, J., Chai, D. H., and Deakin, S. (2012). *Hedge Fund Activism in Japan: the Limits of Shareholder Primacy*, Cambridge, UK, and New York: Cambridge University Press.

Fujita, T. (2012). Case No. 29. In: Bälz, M., Dernauer M., Heath, C., and Petersen-Padberg, A. (eds), *Business Law in Japan – Cases and Comments*, Alphen aan den Rijn, Netherlands: Kluwer.

Gilson R. and Milhaupt, C. J. (2005). Choice as regulatory reform: the case of Japanese corporate governance. *American Journal of Comparative Law*, 53: 343–377.

Goto, G. (2013). The outline for the Companies Act reform in Japan and its implications. *Journal of Japanese Law*, 18: 13–38.

Hashimoto, K., Natori, K., and Roebuck, J. C. (2007). Corporations. In: Gerald McAlinn (ed.), *Japanese Business Law*, The Hague, Netherlands: Kluwer.

Iwatani, M. and Taki, T. (2010). Evolution of general shareholders' meetings in Japan. *Nomura Journal of Capital Markets*, http://ssrn.com/abstract=1423723, last accessed 15 October 2015.

Kanda, H. (2010). Takeover defenses and the role of law in Japan. *University of Tokyo Soft Law Review*, 2: 2–9.

Kozuka, S. (2008). Conclusions: Japan's largest companies, then and now. In: Nottage, L., Wolff, L., and Anderson, K. (eds), *Corporate Governance in the 21st Century: Japan's Gradual Transformation*, Cheltenham and Northampton, UK: Edward Elgar.

Kozuka, S. (2014). Reform after a decade of the Companies Act: why, how, and to where? *Zeitschrift für Japanisches Recht (Journal of Japanese Law)*, 37: 39–50.

Kozuka, S. and Nottage, L. (2014). Japan. In: du Plessis, J. J., Hargovan, A., and Bagaric, M. (eds), *Principles of Contemporary Corporate Governance*, 3rd edn, Melbourne, Australia: Cambridge University Press.

Milhaupt, C. J. (2002). On the (fleeting) existence of the main bank system and other Japanese economic institutions. *Law and Social Inquiry*, 27: 425–437.

Milhaupt, C. J. (2005). In the shadow of Delaware? The rise of hostile takeovers in Japan. *Columbia Law Review*, 105: 2171–2216.

Milhaupt, C. J. (2006). A lost decade for Japanese corporate governance reform? What's changed, what hasn't, and why. In: Blomstrom, M. and La Croix, S. (eds), *Institutional Change in Japan*, London and New York: Routledge.

Milhaupt, C. J. and West, M. D. (2004). *Economic Organizations and Corporate Governance in Japan*. Oxford and New York: Oxford University Press.

Nottage, L., Wolff, L., and Anderson, K. (2008). Introduction: Japan's Gradual transformation in corporate governance. In: Nottage, L., Wolff, L., and Anderson, K. (eds), *Corporate Governance in the 21st Century: Japan's Gradual Transformation*, Cheltenham and Northampton, UK: Edward Elgar.

Oda, H. (2012). Case No. 30. In: Bälz, M., Dernauer, M., Heath, C., and Petersen-Padberg, A. (eds), *Business Law in Japan – Cases and Comments*, Alphen aan den Rijn: Kluwer.

Osugi, K. (2014). Stagnant Japan? – why outside (independent) directors have been rare in Japanese companies. In: Shishido, Z. (ed.), *Enterprise Law: Contracts, Markets and Laws in the US and Japan*, Cheltenham and Northampton, UK: Edward Elgar.

Puchniak, D. and Nakahigashi, M. (2012). Case No. 21. In: Bälz, M., Dernauer, M., Heath, C., and Petersen-Padberg, A. (eds), *Business Law in Japan – Cases and Comments*, Alphen aan den Rijn, Netherlands: Kluwer.

Saito, M. (2012). Case No. 28. In: Bälz, M., Dernauer, M., Heath, C., and Petersen-Padberg, A. (eds), *Business Law in Japan – Cases and Comments*, Alphen aan den Rijn, Netherlands: Kluwer.

Shishido, Z. (1997). The turnaround of 1997: changes in Japanese corporate law and governance. In: Aoki, M., Jackson, G., and Miyajima, H. (eds), *Corporate Governance in Japan: Institutional Change and Organizational Diversity*, London and New York: Oxford University Press.

Tanaka, W. (2011). Going private and the role of courts: a comparison of Delaware and Japan. *University of Tokyo Soft Law Review*, 3: 12–23.

Taylor, V. (2009). Japanese commercial transactions and sanctions revisited: Sumitomo v. UFJ. *Washington University Global Studies Law Review*, 8: 399–426.

Tokyo Stock Exchange, Inc. (2013) TSE-Listed Companies White Paper on Corporate Governance, www.tse.or.jp/rules/cg/white-paper/b7gje60000005ob1-att/b7gje6000003ukm8.pdf, last accessed 15 October 2015.

West, M. D. (1999). Information, institutions, and extortion in Japan and the United States: making sense of sokaiya racketeers. *Northwestern University Law Review*, 93: 767–817.

9

The Japanese stock market

Katsuhiko Okada

Overview

Japan has always been unique from the standpoint of Western norms. Its economy is based on capitalism, as Western economies are; however, it also possesses significant institutional and cultural traits that distinguish it from the West. The Japanese stock market is unique in many ways. There are distinct differences in the way the market is organized, as described later in this chapter, which led to differences in market functions. The peculiarities of the Japanese stock market could be viewed as forms of different investor behaviour that present different market patterns. This chapter focuses on these peculiarities regarding market structure, market functions, and stock market behaviour.

The structural uniqueness of the Japanese stock market

Financial markets develop to meet the needs of investors. Although the structure of the Japanese stock market is roughly the same as in the United States, there are several important differences.

Lack of specialist markets

There are four types of markets: direct-search markets, brokered markets, dealer markets, and auction markets. The direct-search market is the least organized market. Buyers and sellers must seek each other out directly. An example of a transaction in such a market is a classified ad in the newspaper.

The next level of organization is a brokered market, in which brokers find it profitable to offer search services to both buyers and sellers. A good example is the real estate market, where economies of scale in searches for available homes and for prospective buyers make it worthwhile for participants to pay brokers to conduct their searches.

An increase in trading interest in a particular type of asset will lead to more frequent transactions. A dealer market addresses this issue. Dealers specialize in various assets, purchase them for their own accounts, and later sell them from their inventory for a profit. Traders in dealer markets save on search costs because market participants can easily look up the prices at which they can buy from or sell to dealers. In the New York Stock Exchange (NYSE), trading in each security is managed by a specialist responsible for that security. The Tokyo Stock Exchange (TSE), however, has no specialists quoting bids and offers for traders.

The most integral market is an auction market, in which all traders converge in one place (either physically or online) to buy or sell an asset. An advantage of auction markets over dealer markets is that one need not search across dealers to find the best price for a product. If all participants converge, then they can arrive at mutually agreeable prices and narrow the bid–ask spread. The TSE is a continuous auction market, as opposed to periodic auctions such as those in the art world.

The saitori system

The TSE is the largest stock exchange in Japan, accounting for more than 80 per cent of total trading. The TSE has no specialist system. Instead, a *saitori* maintains a public limit order book, matching market and limit orders, and is obliged to follow certain actions to slow down price movements when the simple matching of orders would result in price changes above exchange-prescribed minima. In their clerical role of matching orders, *saitori* are somewhat similar to specialists on the NYSE. However, *saitori* do not trade for their own accounts and are therefore quite different from either dealers or specialists in the United States.

Because the *saitori* performs an essentially clerical role, there are no dealers or specialists who provide market-making services of liquidity to the market in Japan. The limit-order book is the primary provider of liquidity. On the TSE, however, if order imbalances result in price movements across sequential trades that the exchange considers too extreme, the *saitori* can temporarily halt trading and advertise the imbalances in the hope of additional trading interest in the weak side of the market. Under *saitori* systems, incidents such as flash crashes are unlikely.[1]

Stock market indexes

The daily performance of the Nikkei 225 Stock Average (Nikkei 225) is a staple of the evening news. The Nikkei 225, which averages 225 representative corporations in Japanese industry, has been computed since 1971, replacing the stock market average that had been computed by the TSE since 1950. The Nikkei 225 is calculated as the simple average of the 225 stocks included in the index, that is, the summation of those 225 stocks divided by 225. The percentage change in the Nikkei 225 is, then, the percentage change in the average price of the 225 shares. Because the Nikkei 225 measures the return (excluding dividends) on a portfolio that holds one share of each stock, it is called a price-weighted average. Although the Nikkei 225 is the best-known measure of the performance of the Japanese stock market, it is only one of several indicators. Other more broadly based indexes are also computed and published daily.

Among other indicators, the Tokyo Stock Price Index (TOPIX) is commonly used and represents an improvement over the Nikkei 225 in two ways. First, it is a more broadly based index of all the stocks listed in the first section of the TSE. Second, it is a market value-weighted index. If a firm X has market capitalization (market price times the number of shares outstanding) double the size of firm Y, the TOPIX would give X twice the weight given to Y. The TOPIX is computed by calculating the total market value of the firms in the first section of the TSE (1867 firms as of March 2015) and their total market value on the previous day of trading. The percentage increase in the total market value from one day to the next represents the increase in the index.

In 2014, the TSE released another market value weighted index, the JPX-Nikkei Index 400 (JPX-Nikkei 400), where the exchange and Nikkei Inc. select 400 stocks from the first and second sections of the TSE, Mothers, and JASDAQ indexes. The TSE explains the role of the new index as follows:

> JPX-Nikkei 400 is composed of companies with high appeal for investors, which meet the requirements of global investment standards, such as the efficient use of capital- and investor-focused management perspectives. The new index will promote the appeal of Japanese corporations domestically and abroad, while encouraging continued improvement of corporate value, thereby aiming to revitalize the Japanese stock market.
>
> *(www.jpx.co.jp/english/markets/indices/jpx-nikkei400/index.html)*

Whether the new index becomes the representative stock index of the Japanese market remains to be seen.

Separation of ownership and management

Many businesses are owned and managed by the same individual. Such a simple structure is well suited to small businesses and, in fact, is still the most common form of business organization in terms of numbers of firms in Japan.[2] However, there are a quite a few enormous global corporations with highly developed business operations around the world. For example, in 2014, Toyota had a market capitalization of 28 trillion yen, with 350,000 employees. Such a large group of individuals obviously cannot actively participate in the day-to-day management of the firm. Instead, they elect a board of directors, which in turn hires and supervises the management of the firm. This structure means that the owners and managers of the firm are different parties, which provides the firm stability that an owner-managed firm cannot achieve. For example, if some stockholders decide they no longer wish to hold shares in the firm, they can sell these to other investors, with no impact on the firm's management. Thus, financial assets and the stability to buy and sell these assets in the financial markets allow for easy separation of ownership and management.

The separation of ownership and management in Japanese corporations has been less clear than in the West, however. One of the reasons may be that large, traditional Japanese corporations are generally committed to lifetime employment and the internal promotion of top management. New members of these companies are recruited once a year, among college graduates, and it is relatively rare to hire personnel who already have a few years of work experience. Generally speaking, Japanese firms have traditionally valued growth over profitability or efficiency, and their employment system has been well suited for this purpose. US firms usually focus on profitability and short-term shareholder value; high personnel turnover and outside recruiting are therefore necessary to achieve those goals. Shareholders in Japan were also generally more stable and less active than in the West until the mid-2000s.

The other reason for the unclear separation of ownership and management may be Japan's unique monitoring system, called the main-bank system. The main bank system was designed to stabilize the financial system in an environment of high macroeconomic volatility. Since managers have more information about the firm than shareholders do, information asymmetry exists between them. The conflict of interest between managers and shareholders eventually leads to a deadweight loss, which is called the agency cost. The most important benefit of the main-bank system is the reduction of this agency cost through bank monitoring. It is common for the lending bank to hold equities or sending new board of directors in times of financial distress.

Lack of a market for corporate control

In Western markets, bad performers are subject to the threat of takeover. If the board of directors is lax in monitoring management, unhappy shareholders can, in principle, elect a different board. They can do so by launching a proxy contest in which they seek to obtain enough proxies (i.e. the right to vote the shares of other shareholders) to take control of the firm and vote in another board. However, this threat is usually minimal. Shareholders who attempt such a fight must use their own funds, while management can defend itself using its corporate coffers. Most proxy fights fail. The real takeover threat is from other firms or activist funds. If activist shareholders observe a firm underperforming, then they can acquire shares from the market or existing shareholders at a premium and take over the firm. In the United States, the hostile takeover market is viewed as an effective venue for corporate control; however, in Japan, there is no such market, and few hostile takeovers succeed (see Figure 9.1).

Uniqueness of the Japanese stock market's performance

US stock market

Investors invest in anticipation of future returns, but these can rarely be predicted precisely. Risk is almost always associated with investment. Actual returns will almost always deviate from expected returns anticipated at the start of the investment period. For example, in 1990 (the worst calendar year for the market since 1945), the Japanese stock market lost 43 per cent of its value. In 1933 (the best year), the stock market gained 54 per cent. Investors certainly did not anticipate such extreme performance at the start of either of those years.

Naturally, if all else could be held equal, investors would prefer investments with the highest expected return.[3] However, the 'no free lunch' rule in financial markets tells us that all else cannot be held equal. If you want higher expected returns, you have to pay a price in terms of extra risk. If higher expected returns can be achieved without bearing extra risk, there will be a rush to buy the high-return assets, thus driving up the price. Individuals considering investing in

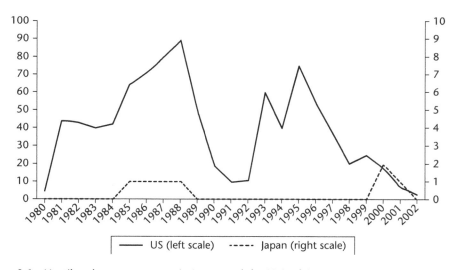

Figure 9.1 Hostile takeover attempts in Japan and the United States
Source: Thomson Financial

the asset at the now higher price will find the investment less attractive. If one buys at a higher price, one's expected return is lower. The asset will be considered attractive and its price will continue to rise until its expected return is no more than commensurate with risk. At this point, investors can anticipate a 'fair' return relative to the asset's risk, but no more.

Similarly, if returns were independent of risk, there would be a rush to sell high-risk assets. Their prices would fall and their expected return would rise until these assets eventually became attractive enough to be included again in investors' portfolios. This relation between expected return and risk is called the risk–return tradeoff in the financial market, with higher-risk assets priced to offer higher returns than lower risk assets are.

Figure 9.2 illustrates the dollar value growth of investment from 1900 to 2010. As shown, equity investment has been the most lucrative investment in the United States. One dollar invested in the US stock index in 1900 has grown to 18,317 dollars by 2010. After inflation is considered over this period, equity investment has been by far the most lucrative investment over the long run. Even the worst timer who bought stocks at their peak before the Great Depression (i.e. the stock market crash in October 1929) would have recouped all buy and hold strategy losses by 1949. Investors who bear the risk of asset-value volatility are able to achieve high returns over the long run. Treasury bond/bill investors bear no risk because the coupon and the principal payments are guaranteed by the government. Investors in such riskless assets generate much lower returns, as shown in Figure 9.2. This risk–return trade-off is solidly ensconced in the stock market.

Japanese stock market performance

The Japanese stock market outperformed the West in the post-war period. In 1990, the Japanese stock market's capitalization almost equalled that of the United States (see Figure 9.3). In the late 1980s, on the heels of a three-decade-long 'economic miracle', Japan experienced its infamous bubble economy in which stock and real estate prices soared to stratospheric heights, driven by excessive liquidity. Overconfidence nurtured by high post-war economic growth and the

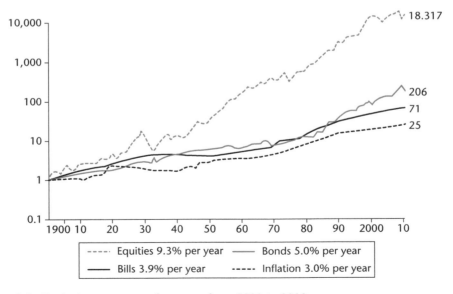

Figure 9.2 Equity investment performance from 1900 to 2010

Source: Dimson *et al.* (2010)

Bank of Japan's loose monetary policy in the mid- to late 1980s led to aggressive speculation in domestic stocks and real estate, pushing the prices of these assets to previously unimaginable levels. From 1985 to 1989, Japan's Nikkei stock index tripled to 38,900 and accounted for more than one-third of the world's stock market capitalization. Real estate prices experienced similar manic action, with prices in Tokyo's prime neighbourhoods rising to levels that made them 350 times more expensive than comparable land in Manhattan (Investopedia 2009). The land underneath Tokyo's Imperial Palace was estimated to have been worth as much as the entire state of California in the same year (Impoco, 2008).

By 1989, Japanese regulators and central bankers became increasingly concerned with the country's growing asset bubbles, and the Bank of Japan decided to tighten its monetary policy. Soon after, the Nikkei stock bubble burst and the index plunged by nearly 50 per cent, from approximately 38,900 to 20,000 during 1990, hitting 14,300 by 1992. Japan's imploding stock bubble also burst the country's real estate bubble, creating *zaitech*[4] in reverse and throwing the country into a deep financial crisis, halting the three-decade-old economic miracle dead in its tracks. Japan's deteriorating competitive edge against other Asian exporters, including China and South Korea, and its steadily deflating stock and property prices during the 1990s and 2000s, also contributed to this period being called the lost decades. During this time, many unprofitable and debt-ridden companies were kept afloat through frequent government bail-outs, leading to

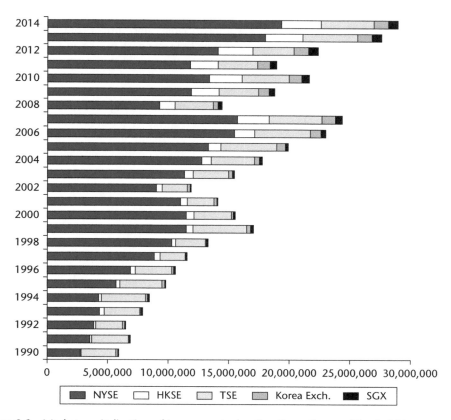

Figure 9.3 Market capitalization of Japanese stocks after the collapse of the bubble economy

Source: World Federation of Exchange

their nickname 'zombie companies'. By 2004, residential real estate in Tokyo was worth only 10 per cent of its peak in the late 1980s, while the most-expensive land, in Tokyo's Ginza business district, had fallen back to just 1 per cent of its 1989 level (Barsky 2009). Similarly, that year, the Nikkei stock index plummeted below 10,000, a quarter of its all-time high.

Japanese stock market anomalies and characteristics

Efficient market hypothesis (EMH) and market anomalies

Some market practitioners may believe there is a predictable pattern to stock market movement and that, if one could determine it, one would be able to capitalize on it. Many academic researchers and practitioners have examined this proposition, but with little convincing success so far. In 1953, Maurice Kendall examined this proposition for the first time, and could identify no predictable patterns in stock prices: stock prices seem to evolve randomly, and are as likely to go up as to go down on any particular day, regardless of past performance. At first, these findings were disturbing to some financial economists. They seemed to imply that the stock market is dominated by erratic market psychology. The result was interpreted to confirm market irrationality. On further reflection, however, economists came to reverse that interpretation. It soon became apparent that random price movements indicated a well-functioning, efficient market. The EMH embodies the notion that stocks already reflect all available information. Stock prices change in response to new (unpredictable) information, and new information is, by definition, unpredictable; therefore, the stock market is unpredictable. Since prices contain all available information, in a perfectly efficient market, there is nothing much left for the professionals to do.

It is not surprising that the EMH does not arouse enthusiasm in the community of professional portfolio managers, since it implies that a great deal of their activity is, at best, wasted effort. Consequently, the EMH has never been widely accepted among professionals, and debate continues to this day on the degree to which security analysis can improve investment performance. Meanwhile, some academicians who believe in the irrationality of the stock market have documented various stock market behaviours that are apparently inconsistent with the EMH view, called anomalies. In the next section, we look at some common global market anomalies and some that are unique to the Japanese stock market.

Size and book-to-market anomalies

One way of providing evidence against market efficiency is to demonstrate that a subset of stocks systematically perform well or worse than average, regardless of their risks. The so-called size or small-firm effect, originally documented by Banz (1981), shows that average annual returns are consistently higher in small firm portfolios. The difference in average returns between the portfolios of firms in the largest and the smallest deciles is 8.52 per cent annually between 1928 and 2011. Of course, smaller firm portfolios tend to be riskier but, even when returns are adjusted for risk, there remains a consistent premium for smaller-firm portfolios. Imagine earning a premium of this magnitude on a billion-dollar portfolio. It is indeed remarkable for a simple rule to enable an investor to earn excess returns. If the market is efficient, such an obvious money-making rule, once known to the public, would be practised by many investors, thus eliminating the excess return.

Fama and French (1992) show that a powerful predictor of returns across stocks is the ratio of the book value of the firm's equity to the market value of equity. The authors stratify firms into 10 groups according to book-to-market ratios and examine the average monthly rate of return of each of the ten groups. The decile with the highest book-to-market had an average annual return of 16.87 per cent, while the lowest-ratio decile averaged only 10.92 per cent for 1926–2011. This indicates that the stock market return depends on the book-to-market ratio. In other words, stocks with a high book-to-market ratio are systematically underpriced for long periods, which is, again, inconsistent with the market efficiency argument. Fama and French find that, after controlling for size and book-to-market effects, the riskiness of a business has no effect in explaining average stock returns. Many researchers have investigated the Japanese market and confirm that size and book-to-market anomalies persist in Japan.

Momentum anomalies throughout the world and in Japan

Another way of discerning trends in stock prices is by measuring the serial correlations of stock market returns. Such serial correlations refer to the tendency for stock returns to be related to past returns: a positive serial correlation means that positive returns tend to follow positive returns (a momentum type of property) and a negative serial correlation means that positive returns tend to follow negative returns (a reversal property). While broad market indexes demonstrate only weak serial correlation, there appears to be stronger momentum in performance across market sectors exhibiting the best and worst recent returns. In an investigation of intermediate-horizon stock-price behaviour (using three- to twelve-month holding periods), Jegadeesh and Titman (1993) find a momentum effect in which the good or bad recent performance of particular stocks continues over time. They conclude that, while the performance of individual stocks is highly unpredictable, a portfolio of the best-performing stocks in the recent past appears to outperform the portfolios of other stocks with enough reliability to offer opportunities for profit.

Markets do exhibit occasional anomalies – for instance, small stocks outperform in January, or the stock market generally performs poorly in the summer months – that may be too small or unreliable to exploit. In contrast, the momentum effect is large and persistent in the long term. Dimson, Marsh, and Staunton (2010) looked at the one hundred largest stocks in United Kingdom since 1990 and found that the twenty best performers in the previous twelve months outperform the twenty worst performers by 10.3 percentage points annually. The authors apply the same methodology and investigate twenty countries and find the momentum effect

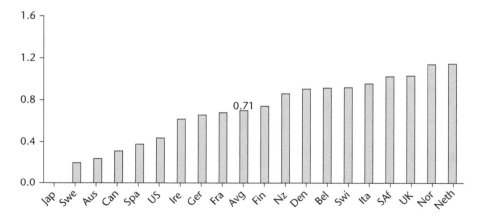

Figure 9.4 International momentum effect comparison

Source: Dimson *et al.* (2010)

in nineteen countries. Figure 9.4 shows each country's winner-minus-loser (WML) returns between 1975 and 2009. The average WML return over this period is 0.71 per cent per month. Momentum investing was therefore profitable in most countries except for Japan, which had a WML return of zero.

Momentum investing involves a stock-rotation strategy. Winners do not remain winners forever. The composition of a winner portfolio changes rapidly, as does that of a loser portfolio. This result is difficult to explain based on risk, but the strategy has been very profitable. Unfortunately, no such money-making opportunity exists in the Japanese stock market.

Stock market seasonality and Japan's dekansho-bushi *effect*

Every year, usually in May, the financial press refers to the old saying 'Sell in May and go away and come back on St Leger Day'. This well-known trading adage warns investors to sell their stock holdings in May to avoid a seasonal decline in the equity markets. The investor who sells his or her stock holdings in May and gets back into the equity market only in November, thereby avoiding the typically volatile May–October period, will be much better off than an investor who stays in equities throughout the year. This strategy is based on the historical underperformance of stocks in the six-month period commencing in May and ending in October, compared to the six-month period from November to April. Although this seasonality is repeatedly cited in the media, it has largely been ignored in academic circles. Nonetheless, a comprehensive empirical study by Bouman and Jacobsen (2002) shows that this seasonal pattern, indeed, occurs in 36 out of 37 stock markets across the world. History shows the pattern emerged in the UK stock market in the seventeenth century (1694).

Sakakibara, Yamasaki, and Okada (2013) investigated the Japanese stock market in depth and found that the market yields a slightly different seasonal pattern from that of other countries. It tends to perform well up to June and then turn sour from July on. During 1950–2008, the widely quoted Nikkei 225 showed a cumulative gain of 3887.4 per cent for a buy-and-hold strategy during the first half of the year and a gain of a mere 102.2 per cent for the second half.

Sakakibara *et al.* (2013) stratify the stocks into twenty-five portfolios based on size quintiles and book-to-market ratio quintiles to investigate whether this seasonality is independent of firm characteristics. Between 1978 and 2008, most categories of portfolios demonstrated good performance in the first half of the year and poor performance in the second half. Figure 9.5 indicates the average returns of the size and book-to-market portfolios for every calendar month. As shown, the majority of these 25 portfolios demonstrate a strongly positive average return from January through June. It is noteworthy that June is a particularly good month for the Japanese stock market, yielding the highest average return in the year. This seasonality is called the *dekansho-bushi* effect,[5] as opposed to the 'sell in May effect', after a traditional Japanese ballad, because the pattern matches what the folk song advocates: fund managers, like the farmers in the ballad, should work only the first half of the year.

Conclusions

A dogmatic belief in the EMH can paralyse the investor and make it appear that research effort cannot be justified. This extreme view is probably unwarranted. There are enough empirical anomalies in the prior studies to justify the search for underpriced securities, which that clearly continues. One of the frontiers in such an effort is the search for behavioural biases in the financial market.

Based on the peculiarities of the Japanese stock market, its anomalous behaviour is partially attributable to investors' cultural and behavioural biases combined with the unique market

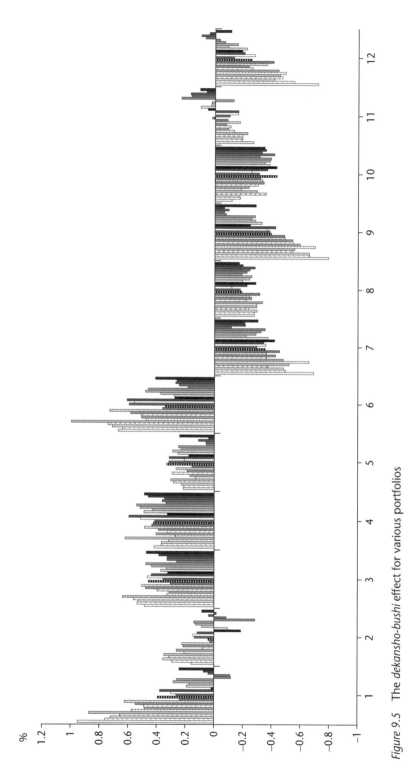

Figure 9.5 The *dekansho-bushi* effect for various portfolios

Source: Sakakibara et al. (2013)

structure. Behavioural finance focuses on systematic irrationalities that characterize investor decision-making. Japan's unique 'behavioural shortcomings' described in this chapter could therefore be consistent with several Japanese anomalies.

Notes

1 On the afternoon of 6 May 2010, American share and futures indexes went into a seemingly inexplicable tailspin, falling by 10 per cent in a matter of minutes, with some large-capitalization stocks trading at a penny, only to recover most of the lost ground before the end of the trading day. This happened because the automated trading systems used by market makers and other large liquidity providers paused as they were designed to do when prices move beyond certain thresholds.
2 A total of 99.7 per cent of Japanese corporations are small businesses and have less than 300 million yen (roughly 2.7 million dollars) in capital.
3 The expected return is not the return investors believe in, or even their most likely return. It is the result of averaging across all possible outcomes, recognizing that some outcomes are more likely than others. It is defined as the average rate of return across all possible economic scenarios.
4 *Zaitech* refers to risky investments by corporate Japan, which was flush with excessive cash in the late 1980s and the early 1990s.
5 *Dekansho-bushi* is a well-known folk song that was traditionally sung by farmers since the Edo era (1603–1868) in the Sasayama district, in the western part of Japan. It celebrates a lifestyle of labouring only during the first half of the year and spending the rest of the year at one's leisure.

References

Banz, R. W. (1981). The relationship between return and market value of common stocks. *Journal of Financial Economics*, 9: 3–18
Barksy, R. B. (2009). The Japanese bubble: a 'heterogeneous' approach. *NBER Working Paper Series*, DOI 10.3386/w15052.
Bouman, S., and Jacobsen, B. (2002). The Halloween indicator, 'sell in May and go away': another puzzle. *American Economic Review*, 92: 1618–1635.
Dimson, E., Marsh, P., and Staunton, M. (2010). *Credit Suisse Global Investment Returns Sourcebook*. Zurich: Credit Suisse.
Fama, E. F. and French, K. R. (1992). The cross-section of expected stock returns, *Journal of Finance*, 47: 427–465.
Kendall, M. (1953). The analysis of economic time series, part I: prices, *Journal of the Royal Statistical Society*, 116: 11–34.
Impoco, J. (2008). Life after the bubble: how Japan lost a decade. *New York Times*, 16 March 2012.
Investopedia (2009). 5 Steps of a Bubble, Investopedia. www.investopedia.com/articles/stocks/10/5-steps-of-a-bubble.asp#axzz1p5r28bBE, last accessed 15 October 2015.
Jegadeesh, N. and Titman, S. (1993). Returns to buying winners and selling losers: implications for stock market efficiency. *Journal of Finance*, 48: 65–91.
Sakakibara, S., Yamasaki, T., and Okada, K. (2013). The calendar structure of the Japanese stock market: the 'Sell in May Effect' versus the '*Dekansho-bushi* Effect'. *International Review of Finance*, 13: 161–185.

10

Entrepreneurship in Japan

Parissa Haghirian

Modern Japan is not a country known for entrepreneurs and dynamic start-ups. Even if the country's wealth was built by famous and successful entrepreneurs such as Sōichirō Honda or Akio Morita, the percentage of entrepreneurs in much lower than in other industrialized countries (Weston 2002).

There are number of reasons for the low number of entrepreneurs in Japan: the preference for being a member of a strong and successful organization; the fact that entrepreneurship is considered as a high-risk adventure; and the scandals, such as the case of well-known entrepreneurs like Takafumi Horie (who was accused of insider trading in 2006 and sentenced under enormous hype to several years in prison) which had a negative effect on the image of start-ups in Japan as well as on the number of new entrepreneurs in Japan. It is particularly true that many younger people follow their parents' example and try to seek lifetime employment in a Japanese company.

In this chapter I will discuss and present the current situation of entrepreneurs and start-ups in Japan. The reasons for the low rates will be explained, and different types of business founder will be introduced. We will then have a look at new government initiatives to increase the number of start-ups, to spur innovation, and to create an entrepreneur-friendly environment for aspiring entrepreneurs in Japan.

Entrepreneurship in Japanese history

Despite our current discussion about how to increase the numbers of entrepreneurship, the history of post-war Japan has had many capable entrepreneurs. Many famous Japanese companies that drive economic success now are the result of enthusiastic and creative entrepreneurship. Before the Meiji Restoration new companies were already being founded. One of the most famous cases is the story of the Mitsui Corporation, which was founded by Mitsui Hachirobei Takatoshi in the seventeenth century. The Mitsui family produced a number of talented managers, who made the company into one of the most powerful and successful *keiretsu* in the Japanese economy (Weston 2002). Today, it is one of the most influential Japanese companies. At the beginning of the twentieth century, visionaries like Kōnosuke Matsushita founded new enterprises. And, also during the time of economic growth after the Second World War, the

Japanese economy was supported by entrepreneurs, such as Sōichirō Honda, the founder of Honda, and Akio Morita who founded Sony. The Japanese government during that time, however, focused on growing industrial businesses, and the focus was not on entrepreneurship as such. During the decades of Japanese economic development, entrepreneurship was not considered as a relevant economic policy objective, but as a mere by-product of economic growth and development (Debroux 2010). The success and rapid growth of big Japanese organizations changed the attitudes of many young Japanese (see Figure 10.1) The strength and size of these companies made lifetime employment very interesting for Japanese graduates, who increasingly focused on becoming a member of one of these organizations rather than founding their own.

Development in the past twenty years

Despite the changes in attitude and in the economy, the actual number of small and medium-sized enterprises in Japan is not that much lower than in other countries. 'Small and medium-sized enterprises' in the Japanese context refers to companies with twenty to three hundred employees and with a stated capital of 300 million yen or less. Within this group, we find small enterprises which have up to twenty employees. Japan had about 3.853 million SMEs in 2014, which employ 32.17 million employees (3.343 million of which are small enterprises which employ 11.93 million people). In contrast to this, we find only 11,000 large enterprises in Japan. However, they do employ about 13.97 million employees nationwide. The majority of Japanese companies are very small; 86.5 per cent of Japanese enterprises fall into the category of small enterprises (METI 2014)

What does differ from the West is the number of newly founded small and medium-sized enterprises in Japan. The number of newly founded companies is still very low compared with other industrialized countries. Thus, the start-up rate in Japan is only 4.5 per cent, whereas it is 9.3 per cent in the United States, and in the United Kingdom it is as high as 10.2 per cent (Haghirian 2014).

The yearly survey conducted by the Global Entrepreneurship Monitor (GEM) showed results that portray the low level of entrepreneurial activity in Japan. In 2012 the Global Entrepreneurship Monitor put Japan in joint last place out of twenty-four developed nations for levels of entrepreneurial activity (*The Economist* 2013). One factor investigated is the total early-stage entrepreneurial activity (TEA). This includes individuals who are currently in the process of starting a venture and individuals who are running a new business less than three years old. Generally, this measure tends to be the highest amongst the adult population (18–64 years old) in factor-driven economies (economies which rely on the use of unskilled labour and production to increase national wealth), and declines in economies with higher GDP. Amongst innovation-driven economies such as Japan, the highest total early-stage entrepreneurship activity rates are found in the United States (13.8 per cent), Australia (13.1 per cent), and Canada (13.0 per cent). Japan, with 3.8 per cent, and Italy, with 4.4 per cent, have the lowest share of early-stage entrepreneurs amongst their respective adult populations (Singer *et al.* 2014). These numbers are consistent with the data from previous years, where the total early-stage entrepreneurial activity ranked 3.7 per cent in 2013. In the US and UK, one out of ten companies is a start-up; in Japan it is one out of twenty (Makinen 2015). Generally wealthier economies like Japan, the Republic of Korea, and Singapore show lower than average opportunity and capability perceptions towards entrepreneurship than earlier-development-stage economies like China, Pakistan, and Thailand (Xavier *et al.* 2012).

The most striking result here is that Japan ranks lowest amongst the innovation-driven economies. The figure reflects the low number of new entrepreneurs. In past years, a significant

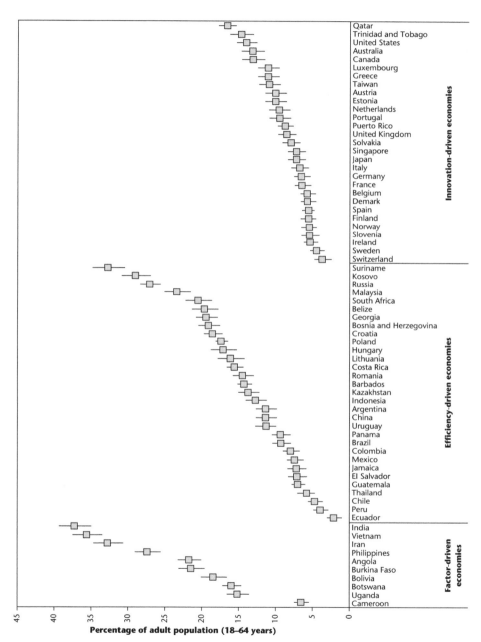

Figure 10.1 Total early-stage entrepreneurial activity (TEA) in the GEM economies in 2014, by phase of economic development (Singer *et al.* 2014)

decrease in people intending to start businesses (which nearly halved from approximately 1.6 million to approximately 0.8 million) could be observed. However, the number of entrepreneurs has remained almost the same, with 0.2 to 0.3 million entrepreneurs newly emerging every year (METI 2014).

Reasons for low entrepreneurship

The question which arises automatically is why Japan has such low levels of actual start-ups. There have been rumours that Japanese entrepreneurs face a lot more challenges than aspiring founders in other countries. In fact, Japanese entrepreneurs have to face the same challenges as entrepreneurs in other countries. They struggle with initial funding and marketing their business ideas to their first customers. They often struggle when growing a firm. Nevertheless, there are some specifics when starting a new enterprise in Japan (Haghirian 2014). Furthermore, we can find a number of structural and country-specific factors that have led to the slow growth of entrepreneurship.

Factors specific to Japanese business culture

Some relevant factors are the traditional Japanese business culture and its characteristic features such as lifetime employment and the seniority system attached to it (Helms 2003). The dominance of the big Japanese multinationals and their traditional *keiretsu* structure has influenced the attitude of young Japanese towards entrepreneurship. Since the 1990s, a job, preferably a full-time job that comes with lifetime-employment expectations, has been the major goal of Japanese university graduates, and also their parents (Haghirian 2014). Big companies can provide security and status, and so can attract and retain the best and the brightest employees (Feigenbaum and Brunner 2002). This is not only reflecting negatively on the number of entrepreneurs, but also on the number of highly talented people that a start-up can hire.

Attitudes towards entrepreneurship

Other factors are tight governmental regulations related to the establishment of new businesses and a high risk aversion amongst Japanese employees when it comes to founding new enterprises (Helms 2003). Fear of failure is generally higher in the Asia-Pacific and South-Asia region, with Vietnam having the highest rate at 56 per cent, followed by Japan and Thailand at 49 per cent (Singer 2015).

One reason for this attitude is the Corporate Reorganization Law, which provides specific guidelines that need to be met for a firm to declare bankruptcy. In Japan, creditors have more rights than the firm and are allowed to attempt to collect their debts while the incumbent management is forcibly replaced. This often leads to the fact that SME declaring bankruptcy are being liquidated and entrepreneurs who fail can face personal bankruptcy as well (Kushida 2001). This is not the case in other industrialized countries, where failure does not need to have a long-term effect on a career. Bankruptcy laws protect the personal possessions of the entrepreneur, and founders of failed companies can get jobs with a start-up or an established company, where their experience and knowledge is often cherished. Furthermore, they can innovate with another idea and try again (Feigenbaum and Brunner 2002).

In addition, many new graduates are not very interested in founding new companies, but would rather enter a preferably big corporation right after graduation. In Japan, the recruiting and hiring system is rather rigid and gives preference to fresh graduates who can be trained

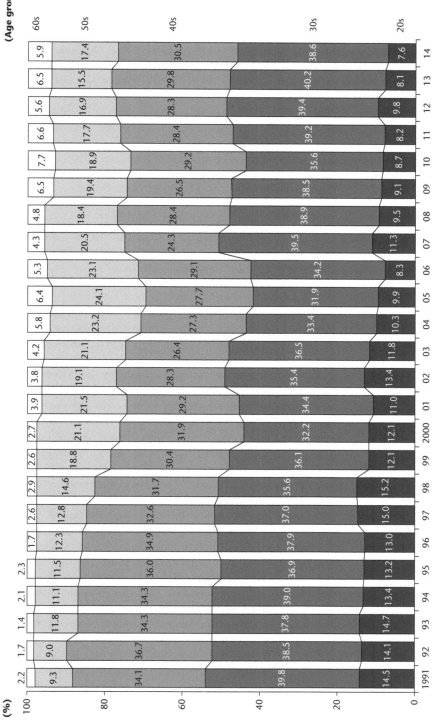

(Age group)

	60s	50s	40s	30s	20s
14	5.9	17.4	30.5	38.6	7.6
13	6.5	15.5	29.8	40.2	8.1
12	5.6	16.9	28.3	39.4	9.8
11	6.6	17.7	28.4	39.2	8.2
10	7.7	18.9	29.2	35.6	8.7
09	6.5	19.4	26.5	38.5	9.1
08	4.8	18.4	28.4	38.9	9.5
07	4.3	20.5	24.3	39.5	11.3
06	5.3	23.1	29.1	34.2	8.3
05	6.4	24.1	27.7	31.9	9.9
04	5.8	23.2	27.3	33.4	10.3
03	4.2	21.1	26.4	36.5	11.8
02	3.8	19.1	28.3	35.4	13.4
01	3.9	21.5	29.2	34.4	11.0
2000	2.7	21.1	31.9	32.2	12.1
99	2.6	18.8	30.4	36.1	12.1
98	2.9	14.6	31.7	35.6	15.2
97	2.6	12.8	32.6	37.0	15.0
96	1.7	12.3	34.9	37.9	13.0
95	2.3	11.5	36.0	36.9	13.2
94	2.1	11.1	34.3	39.0	13.4
93	1.4	11.8	34.3	37.8	14.7
92	1.7	9.0	36.7	38.5	14.1
91	2.2	9.3	34.1	39.8	14.5

Figure 10.2 Changes in the average age of Japanese entrepreneurs starting their own business over the past twenty-four years (Matsuda 2015)

and easily adapted to company wishes These practices do not leave a lot of freedom for young Japanese people to experiment with different types of working or entrepreneurial freedom or take a year off after graduation. In most industrialized countries, young people can start their own company after graduation, and if they fail then they can still find a job a few years later. Also, many companies even value employees with an entrepreneurial flair. However, in Japan, this is not the case, and there is a very high risk of never finding a full-time position (Haghirian 2014). The success of the big companies born out of Japan's great period of post-war entrepreneurialism has, over the last few decades, discouraged graduates from joining newer ventures (*The Economist* 2013). Since the risks involved in becoming an entrepreneur are considered to be very high, Japanese entrepreneurs tend to be highly conservative, and young professionals shun entrepreneurship (Feigenbaum and Brunner 2002). The total entrepreneurship activity amongst the 20 to 24 and the 25 to 29 age bracket is the lowest worldwide (Debroux 2010). Figure 10.2 provides an overview of the average age at which entrepreneurs set up companies in Japan.

Venture capital

Risk aversion has a negative effect not only on innovative entrepreneurship but also on the intention to invest in new ventures. Japanese firms attract around one-twentieth of the venture-capital money that start-ups in America pull in (*The Economist* 2013). In the US, venture-capital investment amounts to 0.17 per cent of GDP; in Japan, the total is just 0.03 per cent (Makinen 2015).

Another unusual feature is the fact that Japanese venture capital often evolves from branches of large companies (Kushida 2001). Corporate venturing or 'intrapreneurship' means that a company is founded by the employees of a corporation, who either have a particularly good product idea or are interested in a new technology or industry. Instead of leaving the firm and looking for an outside investor, these employees found the new company themselves but are supported and funded by their original employer.

Large companies have a greater ability to connect start-ups to networks and provide support in Japan. Japanese corporations have a strong group orientation, and employees who move horizontally across multiple firms are extremely scarce. It is difficult for groups of people to leave large corporations and look for outside capital, so many newly founded companies are not financially independent, and their employees are salaried company employees who do gain directly from good venture business performance (Kushida 2001). The classic Japanese company hierarchies support these processes. Often, new technologies or new business ideas are developed by younger employees who cannot be promoted to the head of a business unit without disturbing the harmony and structure of the traditional seniority-based organizations. In these cases, it is easier to found a new and venture-based business unit and let the younger members of the organization work on the new business idea or technology more independently. To keep the traditional structure intact, a new company is founded and integrated into the *keiretsu* structure. This company provides a fresh start for the founders. They can set up their own new hierarchy, not depending on age; they can take leadership roles; and they can focus on developing a new technology and business. However, these companies are usually incorporated into the *keiretsu* business structure. The young company is not fully independent, but is still connected to the parent company. This comes with both benefits and costs. On the one hand, this relationship provides financing and the first customers, but, on the other hand, it also controls the development of the new venture and ensures that the venture is not becoming too independent (Haghirian 2014). Kono 1992 reports that internal venture teams, which can be formed by an individual who has developed a new idea and brings it to the market level on a more autonomous basis are not so common in Japanese companies (Kono 1992b). All of these factors lead to a business culture that can be called 'entrepreneur unfriendly' (Helms, 2003).

Who is founding new enterprises in Japan?

Generally, there are two types of founders. New companies are often founded by young, motivated personalities (often students and in university) creating a company with an innovative technology-oriented business model. Their businesses are often part of a university research project and set up with the help of an incubator, business angel, or investor. These types of founders have not been a dominant force in Japan in the past few decades. Until recently, Japanese universities did not focus on supporting their students to found businesses, but perceived themselves as purely teaching organizations. Japanese students also do not need to pursue Master's or doctoral programmes to boost their careers, and they are not as involved in research as students in other industrialized countries, e.g. students in the European Union. Japanese students see their university years primarily as a starting point for a career in an established Japanese company (Haghirian 2014).

The second group of entrepreneurs is mid-career managers with a desire for independence (Haghirian 2014). Also, in Japan, new ventures are founded mostly by entrepreneurs who are mature businesspeople or researchers when they start their own businesses. Like their Western counterparts, they start with technical or managerial skills and a good business network (Debroux 2010). Some 70 per cent of early-stage entrepreneurs in Japan are motivated by improvement-driven opportunities (Singer *et al.* 2015). For example, there are managers with many years of specific experience in a certain industry, who have a desire for responsibility or independence and typically leave their jobs between the ages of forty to fifty years to found their own businesses. Often, these entrepreneurs have many years of industry knowledge, and use their former corporate contacts to find their first customers. Their business models mostly cater to the needs of a very particular customer group. Depending on the overall intentions of the founders, these businesses often grow, but, frequently, do not expand over a certain size (Haghirian 2014). Feigenbaum and Brunner (2002) see the reason for this approach in the limited funding through outside investors, because usually they are under pressure to turn a small amount of capital into a profit as quickly as possible. With little capital to begin with, these start-ups cannot afford the high investment which is needed in creating innovations, so they decide to take a safer road and return to low-risk, low-return business models (Feigenbaum and Brunner 2002). And the numbers of this type of entrepreneur are still lower than in other countries.

Next to limited funding, there are other factors keeping enthusiastic managers from founding their own firm, thus remaining of their companies and having little intention to leave them. Many of these employees have invested many years of their careers in a big Japanese company, and this is a personal investment that they are careful not to endanger.

The second reason is the fact that leaving a Japanese company, especially a well-known and successful one, is not viewed as an attempt to lead a fulfilled life, but often as a sign of something being wrong (Haghirian 2014). The media name this reaction the 'Mother-in-Law Factor'. Experienced managers are seldom keen to leave large companies. Wives, mothers, and mothers-in-law exert a strong influence on men not to join risky start-ups (*The Economist* 2013). Kushida (2001) reports that: 'The community ostracizes those who fail, and their careers are permanently tainted' (p. 91).

So often the 'classic' founders in many industrialized countries stay in their jobs in Japan. If they have good ideas then they use them within their company but not to found their own enterprise. It is a Japanese phenomenon that the rate of innovative start-ups in Japan is so low, even though the number of patents registered are the highest in the world. In Japan, big companies provide space and money for creativity and new product development, and focus on it as part of their competitive strategy (Kono 1992a). However, this only happens in the traditional working environment, and it strengthens the power of the existing *keiretsu* – the huge Japanese business conglomerates. It does not support the Japanese economy to develop more variety and new business models. Also, academic entrepreneurship is affected by the strength of the large Japanese corporations. As for the entrepreneurial context, Japanese academia has a long history of strong connections with industry, and university scientists traditionally had close, although usually informal, ties with industry through various channels, such as receiving donations, cooperating with corporate researchers in their laboratories, and sharing patent rights to industry partners (Shibayama *et al.* 2012).

What kind of businesses are founded in Japan?

Many Japanese companies are not started because a new and lucrative business opportunity is recognized, but to fulfil a small and often very specific niche in a local market (Haghirian 2014). The local business model is a lot more dominant in Japan than in other industrialized countries, and can be called a low-risk and low-return business, unlike those in the United States, for example, which have a preference for high-risk, high-return start-ups (Feigenbaum and Brunner 2002). These low-risk Japanese companies are not busy promoting innovation and creating jobs, but they always perform services in their local area, such as small laundries or free real estate agents. Japanese company founders tend to be older than founders in other nations (Debroux 2010). Usually, their companies provide one job (for the founder) and maybe one or two more for part-timers. These little shops can be seen anywhere in Japan, even in Tokyo. They play a very important role in local neighbourhoods. Also, the high number of small restaurants in Japan contributes to these numbers (Haghirian 2014). Considering the preference for working in a big company and enjoying the status and benefits of being a member of it, it is not surprising that Japanese SMEs and micro-enterprises name securing human resources as one major challenge in new business development (METI 2014). On the other hand, we can (as in most industrialized countries) find a growing number of so-called SOHO-type entrepreneurs (small office, home office), which represent freelancers, professional specialists, and teleworkers in recent years. There are 5 million of these in Japan is (Debroux 2010).

Japanese start-ups as drivers of the economy?

Like so many things in the Japanese economy, however, the situation of small and medium-sized enterprises in Japan does not quite compare with that of SMEs in other developed countries. Although the majority of Japanese small and medium-sized enterprises provide jobs, they do not have a positive effect on the innovation capacity of the Japanese economy. Even when providing necessary services for local communities and their attempts to provide more independence for their founders and employees, they do not have a strong effect on the long-term development of the Japanese economy. In the entrepreneurship phase, they tend to focus on safety-oriented activities and the low-risk, low-return start-up business models mentioned above. Newly founded SMEs choose early profitability over up-front investment and can therefore not grow big enough or fast enough to revitalize an entire economy (Feigenbaum and Brunner 2002).

First, they do not foster innovation, because of low innovation business models. The number of SMEs conducting research is also decreasing in the past decades, despite the fact that small and medium-sized companies that involve themselves in research activities show a higher rate of productivity. Figure 10.3 shows the ratio of Japanese small and medium-sized companies involved in research and development in the past decades (Nomi 2015).

Second, they grow only beyond a certain size. The number of start-ups based on innovative business models which grow quickly and provide jobs and have a strong impact on their industry is still very low in Japan. On top of this, many of these small mum-and-pop-stores are not very professionally managed. Low management knowledge and, in many cases, a reluctance to use new technologies are characteristic of many of these companies. In a survey by the Japanese SME Agency, only 48 per cent of the surveyed small businesses agreed to the question of whether they successfully use modern information technology. In medium-sized enterprises, the answers were more positive, with 59 per cent already using IT (METI 2014).

However, the challenges faced by these particular companies are obvious. They survive because they serve a local neighbourhood with a very specific demand and neither expand their business within Japan nor overseas. They are only partially successful. The number of these companies that are left in Japan is about the same as the those newly established in the market (Haghirian 2014). However, in order to realize continual growth of a company, entrepreneurship with a risk-oriented management strategy is required (Ma 2006).

Entrepreneurship in Japan today

Traditionally, the Japanese government focused on supporting big companies in their growth and development efforts, and has pursued innovation policy mainly for large firms up to now, because large firms account for 94.0 per cent of business domestic expenditure on R&D (Nomi 2015). Next to establishing new structures, another issue provides challenges for the Japanese economy. The rapid ageing of Japanese population also has an effect on small enterprises and

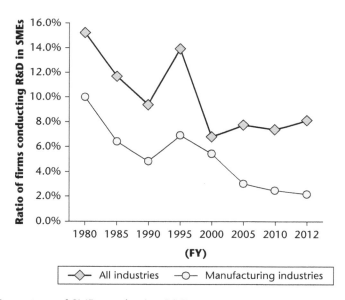

Figure 10.3 Percentage of SMEs conducting R&D

Source: Report on the Survey of Research and Development by the Ministry of Internal Affairs and Communications (Nomi 2015)

SMEs. Many Japanese enterprises are owned by older individuals, who often find it difficult to find successors for their company. While 87 per cent of these business were taken over by relatives in 1987, this number shrank to around 42 per cent in 2012. At the same time, the number of outside managers taking over the business rose from 5 per cent to 13 per cent. It has become a challenge for many older entrepreneurs to continue a small business. This is also the reason that business closures and company dissolutions have been increasing recently. As reasons for deciding to close the business, approximately 50 per cent of respondents cited the ageing and health problems of the manager in charge (METI 2014).

Public authorities realized that the process needed to stimulate Japan's economy does involve new entrepreneurs and new successful start-ups. There are a substantial number of government policies designed to promote entrepreneurships comparable to those in other industrialized countries (Yasuda 2004). The first attempts to improve the situation had already been started during Prime Minister Junichiro Koizumi's term of office, when the Lower House of the Japanese parliament approved an economic stimulus package for distressed small and mid-sized companies (Kunii 2003). Only 1.8 per cent of Japanese employees were new entrepreneurs in 2003, a strong decline from 5.2 per cent in 2001. At that time, 10.5 per cent of the American working population and 14.5 per cent of the South Korean working population considered themselves entrepreneurs being in business for less than forty-two months (Kunii 2003). At that time, it took about 10 million yen to create a *kabushiki kaisha* (or joint-stock corporation) (Kushida 2001). The first changes could be seen with the new corporate law in May 2006. The creation of a limited company changed this amount to 1 yen, and made founding a company more accessible to younger entrepreneurs.

In addition, the government of Shinzo Abe stated that entrepreneurship is a means to support economic growth. One attempt to change the attitude of young people towards the topic is giving more attention to successful Internet entrepreneurs such as Hiroshi Mikitani, the founder of Rakuten, an online-commerce giant, who is now chairing committees in the Japan Association of New Economy. Mikitani has been brought in to advise the government on its deregulation efforts (*The Economist* 2013).

New developments

Despite all the discussions and investigations about new enterprises in Japan, a small but rather active new start-up scene developed in Japan. Another Japanese rarity is the fact that big companies are acting as venture-capital firms. Whereas in Europe the state or provincial agencies try to boost the number of start-ups by means of subsidies and competitions, in Japan, *keiretsu* take this role. So one of the most famous Japanese incubators was established by real estate giant Mitsubishi in Marunouchi. The company provides free office space for a start-up in one of Tokyo's most prestigious business locations. KDDI is sponsoring a start-up competition (Haghirian 2014). In 2015, Dentsu, Japan's biggest advertising company, launched a capital venture fund with a volume of 5 billion yen targeting global companies as well as promising business support (Dentsu 2015).

Conclusions

Although many large and famous Japanese companies were founded after the war, not enough companies have been founded since 1990. Other industrialized countries have a higher rate of entrepreneurship and companies that drive innovation and create new jobs. However, companies founded in Japan do not resemble start-ups in other Western countries. They are usually providing local services, such as dry-cleaning shops or restaurants, and many of them do not apply modern management practices and technology. The number of start-ups driving innovation, creating jobs, and influencing the Japanese economy has traditionally been very low. The *keiretsu* structure in Japan is still very dominant. Other reasons for low rates entrepreneurship are the fear of insecurity, as well as a non-existent safety net for entrepreneurs.

Although the situation has improved somewhat for founders in Japan, it is still challenging for young entrepreneurs to get their idea to market. It remains to be seen whether the current wave of new entrepreneurs leads to a lasting change for the Japanese economy in the coming years. Younger and more flexible firms can react more easily to change, use modern technology more easily, and can adapt their business models faster if necessary. Necessary changes in the economy and in the government economic policy are not only needed to improve the situation of young companies in Japan, but for all enterprises.

Nevertheless, many business models have been developed specifically for the Japanese market, and these benefit from traditional Japanese attitudes and ways of working. Another important aspect is the fact that many of the new young companies not only create some jobs; they take risks; they develop profitable strategies; but they also develop a more contemporary Japanese style of management.

References

Amoros, J. E. and Bosma, N. (2014). *Global Entrepreneurship Monitor 2013 Global Report.* http://www.gemconsortium.org/, last accessed 15 October 2015.

Debroux, P. (2010). *Female Entrepreneurship in East and South-East Asia: Opportunities and Challenges.* Oxford, UK: Chandos Publishing.

Dentsu Inc. (2015). *Dentsu to Establish 'Dentsu Ventures' Corporate Venture Capital Fund.* Press Release, http://www.dentsu.com/news/release/2015/pdf/2015036-0415.pdf, last accessed 15 October 2015.

The Economist (2013). Time to get started; Shinzo Abe is giving new hope to Japan's unappreciated entrepreneurs. *The Economist*, 31 August 2013.

Feigenbaum, E. A. and Brunner, D. J. (2002). *The Japanese Entrepreneur: Making the Desert Bloom.* Tokyo: Nihon Keizai Shimbun.

Haghirian, P. (2014). Entrepreneurship in Japan – a new wave? *Japan Spotlight*, July/August 2014.

Helms, M. M. (2003). Challenge of entrepreneurship in a developed economy: the problematic case of Japan. *Journal of Developmental Entrepreneurship*, 8(3): 247–263.

Kono, T. (1992a). *Strategic Management in Japanese Companies.* Oxford: Pergamon Press.

Kono, T. (1992b). *Long-Range Planning of Japanese Corporations.* Berlin, New York: de Gruyter.

Kunii, Irene M. (2003). Don't stifle your entrepreneurs, Japan. *Business Week Online*, http://joi.ito.com/weblog/2003/02/10/business-week-a.html, last accessed 6 January 2015.

Kushida, Kenji (2001). Japanese entrepreneurship: changing incentives in the context of developing a new economic model. *Stanford Journal of East Asian Affairs*, 1: 76–95.

Ma, J. (2006). Entrepreneurship, innovation and growth of venture businesses in Japan. *Far Eastern Studies*, 5: 15–33.

Makinen, J. (2015). A subculture of entrepreneurship hatches in Japan. *LA Times*, 29 March 2015. www.latimes.com/world/asia/la-fg-japan-entrepreneurs-20150329-story.html#page=1, last accessed 15 October 2015.

Matsuda, N. (2015). Is entrepreneurship a privilege reserved for the young? RIETI (Institute of Economy, Trade and Industry), Column 306: Entrepreneurship and Aging. http://www.rieti.go.jp/en/columns/a01_0417.html, last accessed 28 October 2015.

METI (Ministry of Economy, Trade and Industry) (2014). *2014 White Paper on Small and Medium Enterprises in Japan*, http://www.meti.go.jp/english/press/2014/0425_01.html, last accessed 28 October 2015.

Nomi, T. (2015). Rising expectations for small and medium enterprises for promoting innovation. RIETI (Research Institute of Economy, Trade and Industry), *Reforming the Innovation System with Small and Medium Enterprises.* http://www.rieti.go.jp/en/columns/s15_0003.html, last accessed 27 October 2015.

Shibayama, S., Walsh, J. P., and Baba, Y. (2012). Academic entrepreneurship and exchange of scientific resources: material transfer in life and materials sciences in Japanese universities. *American Sociological Review*, 77(5): 804–830.

Singer, S., Amoros, J. E., and Arreola, D. M. (2014). *Global Entrepreneurship Monitor Global Report 2014*. http://www.gemconsortium.org/, last accessed 28 October 2015.

Weston, M. (2002). *Giants of Japan: the Lives of Japan's Greatest Men and Women*. New York: Kodansha America Inc.

Xavier, S. R., Kelley, D., Kew, J., and Herrington, M., and Vorderwülbecke, A. (2013). *Global Entrepreneurship Monitor 2012 Global Report*. http://www.gemconsortium.org/, last accessed 28 October 2015.

Yasuda, T. (2004). Post-startup growth rates, entrepreneurs' attributes, startup types and motives: the case of Japan. *Entrepreneurial Studies*, 1: 79–95.

11

Accounting in Japanese corporations

Cost designing for product development

Hiroshi Okano

Introduction

During the 'Lost Decade' following the collapse of Japan's economic bubble in the early 1990s, one Japanese company after another made a shift in personnel evaluation to systems centring on individual performance, e.g. merit-based pay systems, and pushed through accounting reforms. Another set of major reforms was conducted during the economic crisis stemming from the subprime mortgage meltdown in the United States. Having long played an unsung role since the end of the Second World War, management accounting is now being taken advantage of by various players as a form of *technology* to give direction to reforms. One may well wonder what other roles management accounting will assume from here on.[1]

Okano and Kobayashi (2015) have shed light on the interpenetration process between the practice and theory of Japanese management accounting, using mostly historical methods. Japanese management accounting can be characterized by the fact that, while paying attention to one aspect of accounting, i.e. 'invisibility', it not only emphasizes the management of entities, such as JIT, cell-type production systems, other production control systems, and *kaizen* activities, but also attempts to resolve 'invisibility' as a part of upstream management through both the 'combined use' and '*zurashi* (displacement)' of target costing, *kaizen* costing, and cost maintenance.[2] In this way, it has become possible to extract the shapes of 'reforms', as well as the Japanese notion of 'acceptance' (Okano 1995, 2009, 2015).

This chapter deals with some historical *features* of management accounting, while at the same time using methods within cultural and organizational aspects to depict the state of 'Japanese management accounting' as something that 'forms' or 'composes' itself independently at private enterprises and academic societies (Hopwood 1987; Hopwood and Miller 1994; Okano 2009). In other words, by discussing the continuity and discontinuity of Japanese management accounting and considering the process of target costing's institutionalization in light of the multi-layered structure of Japanese culture, the author attempts to identify the distinctive features (cross-functional management, *gemba* and *gembutsu* principles, emphasis on voluntarism, causal management) and archetypes of the Japanese management system, and then describes the process in which independent *technology* is formed as such features interrelate with each other.

Cultural and organizational significance of management accounting in Japan

Since the Meiji Restoration in 1868, Japan experienced 'contact' with the European and American systems on two occasions (Okano and Suzuki 2007). The first was at the time of the Restoration itself, with the major influences coming from European countries such as the UK, Germany, and France, while the second major influence came from the US, during its occupation of Japan in the aftermath of the Second World War.

The 'Japanese-style management system' arose in a different form from the 'American system' outlined in the preceding section. One of the characteristics of the system is a focus on causal management that does not confine itself to the production site, but extends back to such processes as design and product development; in addition, its features include the construction of a company-wide system to support this, which transcends individual departments, as well as the reintegration of implementation processes with the planning that makes this possible.

As has already been pointed out, in order to examine the characteristics of Japanese-style management accounting, it is necessary to analyse not only the *accounting* system, but also the *management* system of the form of organization, including the relationship between power and responsibility, as well as the social system that underpins these two systems (Okano 1995, 2002, 2003). Furthermore, with regard to the connection between managerial accounting and the organization, it is necessary to examine America's comptroller system.

The comptroller system was introduced to Japan before the Second World War, but the announcement of Internal Controls in Companies by the Industrial Rationalization Council in 1951 can be cited as having provided the momentum for its actual introduction in Japanese companies (Kato 1991). At NEC, which was an international joint venture with Western Electric, the founding company positioned the accounting staff as American-style comptrollers. At Matsushita Electric Industrial as well, which was the first Japanese company to implement a departmental system, the accounting staff were treated as staff in charge of management administration, accountable to the company president and head office, and the accounting staff system, working separately from the departmental director management system, is still in force even today (Sakurai 1997).

In contrast, it should be noted that the function of accountants within Japanese companies was mainly a regulatory one, and the substantive planning and control functions were delegated to the business divisions, factories, and manufacturing subsidiaries, which were rather autonomous. As well as delegating the manufacture of its mass-produced goods to subsidiary production companies in each region in the mid-1960s, the aforementioned NEC has gradually separated its cost control activities, which focused on operating efficiency, from the core of the accounting division, and entrusts them to the autonomous activities of its business divisions (Koike 1993). This can be said to be a crucial point where the system differs from common practice in US companies, where management activities revolve around the controller or comptroller. In the following, let us examine the characteristics of the Japanese-style management system.

Characteristics of the Japanese-style management system

Cross-functional management and policy management

After the war, TQC (total quality control) was systemized by the American quality-control scholar A. V. Feigenbaum. To be more specific, it can be described as a self-sustaining quality-control system using specialist personnel, which took as its basis the statistical methods that incorporated Shewhart's ideas about quality management.

At the same time, in Japan, it was developed as CWQC (company-wide quality control) involving all employees, thanks mainly to the efforts of a variety of practitioners involved with institutions such as the Union of Japanese Scientists and Engineers and the Japanese Standards Association, who were assisted by Japanese academics and American quality-control experts such as W. E. Deming and J. M. Juran.

One of the key concepts of this was *cross-functional* management, which is distinguished from departmental/functional management. What should be noted here is that the semantic content of the word 'function' is not the same 'function' as in Europe and America, which presupposes a 'department', but encompasses such critical factors in management as quality, cost, reliability, delivery dates, etc. (Ishikawa 1984; TQM Committee 1998).

This Japanese-style cross-functional management is a mechanism for promoting factors important to the management of a company, such as quality functions, cost functions, and overseas functions, by means of their cross-sectional coordination with related organizations, and implies horizontal organizational management. Historically, it was formed amidst the process of introducing Japanese-style TQC (total quality control). It is antithetical to the 'functional management' of Europe and America, which consists of departments' systems of responsibility and authority.

In other words, it is closely linked to the characteristics of Japanese-style quality control, which creates an overlap between the functions of each organization and emphasizes cross-functional activities. There was a loose relationship between business and people, and, by overlapping the work itself and getting all employees to commit themselves, the system induced them to take on responsibility.[3]

Cross-functional management was introduced in the early 1960s, around the time when TQC was beginning to take place. At the time, there were strong vertical links in organizations, with hierarchical relationships, for example within the manufacturing division and the sales division, and there were barriers to horizontal relationships, due to sectionalism, so communication was difficult. Cross-functional management involves setting up cross-functional committees or conference structures relating to issues such as quality assurance or cost controls, and seeking to supervise and improve these functions by promoting them within each department, in order to deal with problems that are related to the horizontal organization, which cannot be solved by one department within the vertical organization (Kurogane 1993).

Gemba *and* gembutsu *principles*

The *gemba* (*genchi*) principle is a concept under which specific, individual problems become clear for the first time by experiencing the phenomena that occur at each site (the '*ba*' of '*genba*'), and can be seen uniformly in production and sales by Japanese companies. In particular, in plant management, it has come to be regarded as the cornerstone of efforts to eliminate ideas and management systems that have become isolated from a sense of the workplace.

This also corresponds with the fact that in-house training programmes, focusing mainly on OJT (on-the-job training) are commonplace (Odaka 1993; Hisamoto 1998). The results that have emerged from Japanese-style production systems such as the aforementioned CWQC and JIT (just-in-time) can be reduced to these *gemba* and *gembutsu* principles.

At the same time, the *gemba* and *gembutsu* principles are utilized in the logic used when eliminating cost accounting, which emphasizes basic unit management focusing on physical measurements, and is a form of currency unit management. In other words, the accounting that was limited to monetary measures was eliminated in order to avoid accounting invisibility, and, although it seems paradoxical, Japanese-style management accounting was created.

As a result, cost-management techniques characteristic of each company are developed. Examples of this include NEC's two-stage standard cost accounting (Nakayama 1963) and Toyota's target costing and *kaizen* costing. As can be seen from the observations of Taiichi Ōno, who formulated Toyota's production system, the *gemba* and *gembutsu* principles were of great significance in the elimination of accounting invisibility (Ōno 1988).

Emphasis on voluntarism

Practices at companies such as NCR and Ford were used as the models for introducing suggestion schemes, bearing names such as small-group and QC circle activities, to Japanese companies, but there were major differences. To be specific, while the main aim in US companies was to elicit ideas from employees that would lead to cost reductions or an increase in profits, with evaluations of those responsible for the implementation of the system being made according to the figures in the company's books, the aim in Japanese companies was participation in the system by the company employees, with evaluations of those in charge of the scheme being decided according to the degree of participation by employees (Robinson and Stern 1997). In other words, it was positioned as a voluntary management activity in which the group was organized by workers at the same workplace, voluntary targets were set in a forum for discussion that had at its core a leader chosen from amongst that group, and efforts were made to achieve these.

Of course, this QC circle was promoted as part of the CWQC movement, and one could not really say that the workers organized themselves voluntarily. Nevertheless, one should take note of the fact that 'the term "voluntary management activity" indicates its origins in small-group activities, which arose as a means of making use of employees' voluntarism' (Hyodo 1997). The fact that most QC circle activities initially took place outside working hours demonstrates this.

At the same time, with regard to relationships with suppliers, a voluntary forum for improvement activities that focuses on production processes can be created. Toyota's Jishuken voluntary study group and Supplier Support Center are examples of this. At the Supplier Support Center in Kentucky, care is taken to ensure that individual information, such as which suppliers are conducting activities regarding what kind of themes, is not disclosed to Toyota via formal routes. Naturally, by emphasizing the fact that it is voluntary, they are ultimately trying to avoid lagging behind their competitors and are hoping that this will actually have the effect of increasing its coercive power, but it is first and foremost not compulsory, and it is important to maintain its voluntary nature.

Built-in quality and costs, and causal management

Quality- and cost-control activities that take place in Japanese companies have been positioned as activities involving the entire company that are carried out by both staff and line organizations based on *gemba* and *gembutsu* principles. This is due to the thorough implementation of causal management, which takes the view that quality and costs are built in on site, based on awareness that quality and costs are decided prior to the design stage.

This point differs completely from practice in America, which is centred on staff (comptrollers, etc.) who are experts in quality control and cost control, and many methods of quality engineering, such as QFD (quality function deployment) have been devised. In VE (value engineering) too, the intention is to implement not only *second-look* VE at the production stage, but also *first-look* VE, which extends to the design stage, and even *zero-look* VE, which goes all the way back to the product planning stage.

Moreover, the aim of the guest engineer system, which commonly takes place as part of the product design process, is not to reduce costs through negotiating prices, but to increase the effectiveness of VE and *kaizen* costing and build a long-term win–win relationship by ensuring that engineers working for the manufacturer and suppliers share a common awareness of the link between costs (design costs) and specific individual improvement activities. This creates trust between the manufacturer and suppliers, and it can be said to be a device for communication about costs rather than prices, taking place on the basis of this trust (Sako 1992).

In addition, although it is necessary to observe prior processes from the next process perspective in order to build in quality and costs, JIT, which is referred to as the *pull formula*, is generated by an awareness that 'the next process is our customer'. It is well known that the foundations of this concept originate in the ideas of Taiichi Ohno and others, who asked whether it would not be possible to use the supermarket formula, which many participants in a delegation visiting America after the war had admired, in factory management.

Theoretical framework of target costing

Cost management, which is a type of strategic planning, has been interpreted in a variety of ways. In particular, interpretation varies in the West; some literature points out its similarity to standard cost, some emphasizes its aspect as a strategic tool.

This chapter describes the basic theory of target costing, including mechanism, process, characteristics, and the basic implementation rule, by taking examples from Toyota Motor Corporation, and then explores the direction where strategic accounting will go, by referring to various theories concerning relations between the strategy and target costing.[4]

The mechanism and process of target costing: Toyota's case

Mechanism

There are three characteristics of cost management practised in Toyota: *vertical* and *horizontal* management; management by part/unit; and the chronological cost-management system (target costing, cost maintenance, *kaizen* costing). In this framework, target costing can be described as a profit-and-loss management by product (automobile in this case). It is a vertical management as well as a profit-and-loss management by segment. It is one of the cost-management activities, incorporating management by part/unit, and carried out before the start of production.

The characteristics of this mechanism are: management by type of vehicle; management by objective; activities in the entire organization; and the differential cost-management system. Toyota has been basically practising management by type of vehicle, although there was a change in the system, from the project-leader (*shusa*) system to the chief-engineer system (Okano 1995, 2003; Fujimoto 1999). This management is based upon an understanding that aggregation of profit and loss by type of vehicle comprises the total profit and loss of the company. Here it is important to calculate the target profit by type of vehicle, based upon the total profit goal of the company.

A distinct feature of the target costing adopted by Toyota has been the differential cost-management system between the current and new models of vehicle. This method is also used for setting a sales price in addition to setting the target cost. The reasons for these are: to increase the accuracy of the estimate by estimating only the cost of the parts for which the engineering design change takes place; to ensure accuracy in determining prices of purchased parts; and to decrease the number of processes and time required for making an estimate, by limiting the items to be managed.[5]

In addition, this system is helpful in involving all the divisions and departments concerned. Although target costing is an activity lead by the design and the production-engineering divisions, it requires the cooperation of all the divisions in the company from a development stage, in terms of the number of cars produced, prices, and the amount of investment, etc. Cooperation from the suppliers is also necessary. This is true of the quality control as well. Therefore, the management by function and the management by objective illustrated above can be described as a system to involve all the divisions concerned in the company.

The target costing process

Examining the outline of the target profit

Target costing starts with the examination of the outline of target profits. It is calculated based upon the target profit guideline by the type of vehicle, which is set following the mid- and long-term target profits, as well as considering the current status of the operating profit and marginal profit of the relevant model.

However, prior to that, it is necessary to decide the type of vehicle that is subject to target costing. In the past, the 'basic type', which is a standard type of the model, and the 'representative type', which is a hot-selling line of the model, were chosen.

Setting postulates

At the stage of conceptualizing a product plan, many things are uncertain. Basic items that have not been decided are decided as *postulates* of target costing, by getting approval from the respective sections involved. Such items include sales price; the number of cars subject to target costing; investment in plant and equipment; number of processes; and plants.

Estimating cost

After setting postulates, the differential cost from the current cost is calculated, based upon the specification assumed and the postulates set, and the estimated cost of a new model is quoted. Responsibilities for estimating the cost and following up are shared amongst the design and production-engineering divisions.

The roles of estimating cost are also divided: cost engineers are responsible for the design cost in the first stage of the development (macro-estimate, zero-order estimate); in the following stages (primary, tertiary estimates, estimate for the mass-production trial), the accounting division is responsible for estimating the cost of the internally produced products; the procurement division estimates the cost of the purchased goods; and the accounting division estimates the processing cost and calculates the total cost per car.

Deciding target profit/target cost

After calculating the estimated cost of the new model, the cost that needs further reduction is calculated based upon the difference between the target profit and the target cost calculated. When the target cost of the vehicle as a whole is decided, the targets are set by design cost and by processing cost. The design cost is further deployed into the calculation of target cost by the design group and the target cost by part.

Cost engineers are staff involved in cost management at a development centre. They are engaged in:

1   making a macro- and zero-order estimate;
2   making a target-cost instruction by part;
3   grasping the progress of design–cost achievement; and
4   supporting VE promotion.

They are divided into people in charge of products and those in charge of function.

Cost-reduction activities (VE activities)

When the target cost is deployed, an improvement committee is formulated and cost-reduction activities (VE) are promoted, led by chief engineers.

Follow-up of the target

The *kaizen* costing committee meeting by model is held after the primary trial production, mass-production trial, and line-off, respectively, to support and follow up the cost-reduction activities.

Organizational learning and inter-company organization

The system that provides learning opportunities at an organizational level in Toyota can be divided into three parts. The first one is the Toyota Production System Independent Study Meeting (*jishuken*). This study group was established in October 1976, for the purpose of spreading the ideas of the Toyota Production System (TPS), in Toyota and its suppliers' plants (Nishiguchi 1994; Sako 1996; Dyer 2000). The members consist of *keiretsu* (suppliers within the industrial group) and independent suppliers. The meeting is held once a week for two months. It is aimed at sharing knowledge amongst suppliers and learning how to make a diagnosis for work improvement, and to carry out follow-up activities in specific work areas.

The second part involves individual and group guidance given by the procurement (purchase) division to disseminate *total quality control* (TQC), to suppliers. It is an integral part of the management improvement scheme for respective suppliers, and guidance has been given on the cost management and investment plan. It is aimed at improving suppliers' comprehensive management ability and their ability to synergize TPS and TQC.

The third part involves the seminars and presentation meetings hosted by Kyohokai, which is an organization established to foster suppliers. In 1971, in order to improve the constitution of the member companies of Kyohokai, two committees: the quality committee and the cost committees, were established in Kyohokai. In 1976, to respond to the age of low growth, Kyohokai convened the Toyota Production System Workshops by inviting Taichi Ōno, then vice-president of Toyota, as a lecturer (Toyota Motor Corporation 1987). What forms the basis of this are the long-term relative transactions with suppliers (Hashimoto 1996; Japan Society for Production Management 1996).

Characteristics of target costing

Target costing makes a clear distinction with ordinary accounting, both in terms of accounting structure and the way that the system is managed. The features can be summarized as follows:

Basic unit and rate: separation between target costing and capital-investment planning

The first characteristic is that the cost subject to the target accounting is the basic unit (physical unit) multiplied by a rate in its accounting logic. In particular, target costing is considered to be an activity led by design engineers to reduce the basic unit itself through design drawing improvement. Take spot welding, for example, where efforts are made to reduce the number of welding shots from three to two.

On the other hand, capital investment planning is an activity that reduces the cost of a basic unit by cutting the rate (cost figures for each particular measure) through the efficient use of the facility. Here, production engineers play a leading role. For example, the cost per welding shot is cut by sharing equipment or by effectively using the existing facilities.

The movement to separate target costing and capital-investment planning accelerated in 1980s, as capital investment increased sharply with the rapid introduction of Factory Automation and Computer Integrated Manufacturing. However, recent globalization and intensified competition started to make Toyota review this separation again, as described in Chapter 8 of this book. In other words, it has become increasingly necessary to carry out target costing as an integral part of the product development in the entire organization.

Two dimensions of cost: incurred cost *and* committed cost

The second characteristic is that target costing focuses upon committed cost instead of incurred cost, which used to be the focus of calculation in the existing cost accounting. Cost management at a committed level is conducted prior to the production. It is a fictitious calculation that adopts a special cost concept or design cost, and the basis of the calculation has been shifted from the calculation of 'place' to that of 'goods'.

Specifically, target costing allows the calculation to be finalized at the design stage, by aligning design postulates between the new and existing products, and by eliminating uncertain elements, relevant to production and suppliers, in the calculation. On the other side, a huge separation between the calculations at a production stage and those at a design stage can be avoided by making an alignment between the two after the start of production.

Beneath the focusing on the committed cost lies the recognition that there is a need to control a process in which cost is *committed* instead of the process in which the cost is *incurred*. In other words, it is an idea to try to project a target cost at a draft level before the design drawings of a part are finalized, and to try to strike a balance between the cost of a product as a whole and the cost at a part level, within the framework of making a profit.

In the same way, suppliers are expected to follow the similar process. This method has been meaningful for both the assembly manufacturer and suppliers. This is because, in Japanese business practice, suppliers often undertake major design and seek approval from the manufacturer. The assembly manufacturer can enjoy a certain cost reduction via a proposal made by the supplier, even if the assembly manufacturer does not have data relevant to the cost. On the part of the supplier, working and studying together with the engineers of the assembly maker makes it much easier for them to sell their products to other assembly manufacturers. The approved drawing and the drawing for loan have a different cost structure, and it is safe to say that such a difference was brought about by the unique relationship between manufacturers and suppliers in Japan.

In the example of target costing cited above, a different concept of cost was created before mass production (design cost) and after mass production (real cost/standard cost). Even prior to mass production, a difference in the cost concept could occur in various processes, including preparation for production and product design; product design and process design; and quality control and production control.

The occurrence of such a gap is inevitable in some sense. The more the company is oriented to the source management, the more often the gap arises. It is, therefore, necessary to establish an accounting method that suits respective purposes. There is the accounting done before mass production (for instance, at the development stage), and the accounting made after mass production becomes self-contained, and each process rotates the PDCA (plan–do–check–action) cycle without being related to each other from a calculation point of view.

Take an example of target costing and *kaizen* costing. They are not related to each other in terms of calculation; target costing is a 'calculation by product' using a technical and cost-engineering approach, or design cost, whereas *kaizen* costing is a calculation by segment that uses an accounting (financial) approach, an approach which mainly consists of a period (week or month) profit-and-loss calculation. The difference exists not only from a computation system viewpoint, but also at organizational activity level. It effectively illustrates the way that various relationships prescribe the calculation structure, and the calculation structure prescribes various relationships. It is a challenge to figure out how and which theory can link them.

The company-wide activities built into the organization: the distributed accounting system

The third feature of target costing is that it simultaneously manages quality, cost, delivery date, and efficiency (excluding environmental conservation), as well as cost. A system is established in each process of target costing, where relevant organizations make commitments by function, such as quality and cost, in the Japanese-style 'functional management structure'. This has caused a conflict/interrelationship between the engineering and accounting divisions, as asserted in the study of the history of management accounting. In addition to this, the function of management accounting (the accounting function) was distributed amongst the design; production engineering; purchase; and sales and marketing divisions. In particular, it is distinctive that, besides the design and development departments, the purchase, accounting, production engineering, and sales divisions also make a commitment at an early stage. It is important to note that a 'rugby' style (by using a scrum, maul, ruck or cross-functional team) is emphasized instead of a 'relay race' style in the methodology for research and development. It gives greater importance to the process than the result. It is built in accordance with a specific issue in the process management, such as design development and preparation for production.

Target costing is also characterized by long-term budget management and budget management by product. Clark (1923) asserted that there are 'different costs for different purposes'. Target costing has an important implication in the history of management accounting. However, for Toyota, the concept of target costing far exceeds Clark's idea. Cost is not regarded as a cost that is subject to objective calculation of the results of activities. Toyota regards cost as something to be created to conform to specific purposes.

In particular, target costing in Toyota emphasizes the calculation of the technical cost according to the purpose, using the differential cost-estimate method. Important points in comparing cost are:

1   alignment of postulates and calculation methods so that the cost-calculation method meets the purpose;
2   adjustment of the classification method; the account headings; and the depreciation and calculation methods, in comparing cost between companies; and
3   comparison of the cost under the standard load.

From the observations given above, it can be understood that target costing up to now carried an essential quality of the Japanese management system. The cross-functional organization system, which is a postulate for the target-costing system, is the deployment of the management by function. It is an idea from a workplace and an idea based upon a principle that makes much of actual goods, and which focuses on costs at a committed level in order to avoid accounting visibility; it mainly uses costs at a technical level. Learning opportunities provided in (amongst) organizations postulated an emphasis on voluntary activities. Here, we can find ideas of source management and ideas that quality/cost must be built in through their focus on the relationship between incurred cost and committed cost.

Basic rules in implementing target costing

For effective implementation of target costing, it is necessary to start the activities when the cost is committed instead of at the time when the cost is incurred. The basic idea of target costing in this statement is clear. However, many problems emerge when it comes to specific methods and effective implementation measures while trying to foster cooperation amongst different organizations. The important point is how to solve this issue within the organization. Here, it becomes necessary to establish rules of target costing. This aspect will be delved into from three perspectives: philosophy and fundamental principles; operating standards; and evaluation rules.

Philosophy/fundamental principles

Philosophy/fundamental principles are the fundamental/universal ideas of the company relevant to target costing: how the company thinks about the cost management; its relations with respective subsystems (budget, *kaizen* costing, and capital investment plan) including target costing; and the purpose and the ultimate goal of target costing.

Specifically, the following idea: that ensuring the target profit is the most important to ensure the profit plan, should be shared. This includes information about the target profit, target cost, and calculation basis, and their postulates.

Operating standards

Operating standards are often the standard of the calculation system, including timing to measure cost; rules of making an estimate; rules to change premises; and rules for setting target profit. They also include the items that may change depending on the corporate strategies, such as items subject to target costing, organizational structure, meetings with division members mainly in charge of target costing, and deciding the tools to achieve the target.

As far as the timing for measuring cost is concerned, if the differential cost between the current and the new models is adopted, then the base cost is the latest cost at the time of the trial and follow-up time, and the differential cost uses the cost when the target cost is set. This is because if the timing for setting the cost is different between the target and estimated cost, elements other than the designing difference come in, and an adequate judgement cannot be rendered.

The feature of the differential cost system is that the cost is divided into the cost that is incorporated into the target costing and the cost that is not incorporated into target costing. In other words, the costs relevant to the design and the production engineering activities are included in target costing, but cost fluctuations due to the following factors: changes in the production location; changes in the management environment such as inflation and deflation; and the purchase policy, are not reflected in target costing.

Rules for change in the postulates are rules for specifications; the number of cars planned; the foreign-exchange rate; and the internal and external production. Rules for setting the target profit emphasize the alignment with the mid- and long-term profit goals, and rules are decided, following the guidelines of the target profit by the type of the vehicle, which conform to the mid-and long-term profits.

Evaluation rules

The evaluation rules are designed to deal with specific problems that may arise in operating a project. They include rules in setting targets; rules of calculation; efforts to divert use of equipment; the effects of reducing the types of components; sharing dies during trial production; responses to dealers; and measures regarding reducing emissions and noise and increasing car safety. Without these rules, a gap will occur between the target-costing activities and the calculation systems, and this will not lead to the achievement of the target profit even if target-costing activities are carried out, and then the target costing will become a dead system. Amongst the evaluation rules, the range of necessary cost reductions with regard to the estimated cost; the range of VE; and the range of reserve costs for chief engineers, are all of importance.

Imprinting rules

The above rules are not necessarily shown explicitly to all the members of the organization at the time of introduction of the target costing. Very often, they are embedded into the organization, and nurtured implicitly through trial and error. As the paradigm of the competition within the organization changes, it is inevitable for these philosophies/principles and evaluation rules to be changed. However, it is also possible that some of the rules only continue to exist due to inertia within the company.

When target costing is carried out at an overseas subsidiary and the Japanese head-office, it should be made clear what kind of change must be made in the rules, and the nature of the element that is hindering that change.

Meetings with the top management of the suppliers are the place to explain the purchase policy of the assembly manufacturer, as well as the place to 'imprint' the development strategy, including target costing, to suppliers. Target costing is also transferred implicitly and explicitly to the supplier in the daily designing routine through various programmes, including 'the guest engineer system' that allows the supplier's engineers to take part in the development team of the assembly manufacturer.

Concluding remarks

As is apparent from the above discussions, target costing has changed from a means or technique for VA- or VE-oriented cost-reduction activity to a total cost-management-oriented conceptual device to simultaneously achieve cost, quality, delivery term, and reliability requirements, as the interrelationship between the environment and the organization changes. Through this evolutionary process, cost designing has today reached the stage where it is accepted as an important product-development management process by deepening the inter-company relationships centred around *keiretsu* affiliation and undergoing a series of developmental reorganizations. While the specific styles differ from one company to another, the dispersion and integration of accounting functions were undertaken in parallel and concurrent ways in this process.

Notes

1 On financial accounting and accounting policy, see Okano and Kudo (2011).
2 This book was published with the support of design engineers and designers at Toyota Motor Corporation.
3 Even with Honda's 'big room', the aim can be described as the exchange of information both formally and informally in processes that result in decisions being made, rather than aiming to create an overlap between formal responsibilities.
4 See Kato (1993a, 1993b), Monden (1993), Tanaka (1993), Tani *et al.* (1994), Bhimani and Okano (1995), Bonzemba and Okano (1998, 1999), Nishimura (2003), and Ansari *et al.* (2007).
5 However, Toyota stopped the differential cost-estimate system recently, and introduced the absolute cost-estimate system in the early 2000s. This means an important turnaround took place in target costing.

References

Ansari, S. L., Bell, J. E., and Okano, H. (2007). Target costing: uncharted research territory. In: Chapman, C., Hopwood, A. G., and Shields, M. D. (eds), *Handbook of Management Accounting Research*, Vol. 2, Elsevier, pp. 507–530.
Bhimani, A. and Okano, H. (1995). Target excellence: target costing at Toyota in the UK. *Management Accounting* (UK), 73(6): 21–27.
Bonzemba, E. and Okano, H. (1998). The effects of target costing implementation on an organizational culture in France. *Proceedings, the Second Asian Pacific Interdisciplinary Research in Accounting Conference*, Osaka City University, 4–6 August 1998.
Bonzemba, E. and Okano, H. (1999). Target cost management: Japanese–French comparison of suppliers' involvement, presented at *Accounting, Organizations and Society International Accounting Symposium 1999*, City University of Hong Kong, 4–5 January 1999.
Clark, J. M. (1923). *Studies in the Economics of Overhead Costs*, Chicago, IL: University of Chicago Press.
Dyer, J. H. (2000). *Collaborative Advantage: Winning Through Extended Enterprise Supplier Networks*. Oxford, UK: Oxford University Press.
Fujimoto, T, (1999). *Evolution of a Manufacturing System at Toyota*, Oxford, UK: Oxford University Press.
Hashimoto, T. (1996). History of face-to-face bargaining in Japan. In: Hashimoto, T. (ed.), *Enterprise System after World War II in Japan*. Tokyo: University of Tokyo Press.
Hisamoto, N. (1998). *Kigyō nai Roshi Kankei to Jinzai Keisei (Industrial Relations Inside Companies and Cultivating Human Resources)*, Tokyo: Yūhikaku.
Hopwood, A. G. (1987). The archaeology of accounting systems. *Accounting, Organizations and Society*, 12(3): 207–234.
Hopwood, A. G. and Miller, P. (1994). *Accounting as a Social and Institutional Practice*, Cambridge, UK: Cambridge University Press.
Hyodo, T. (1997). *Rōdō no Sengoshi (History of Labour after WWII)*. Tokyo: University of Tokyo Press.
Ishikawa, K. (1984). *Nihon teki Hinshitsu Kanri* (Japanese Quality Control), Tokyo: JUSE (1st edn published in 1980).
Japan Society for Production Management (1996). *Toyota Production System*. Tokyo: Nikkan Kogyō Shimbunsha.
Kato, N. (1991). *Komentaru Nihon Keieishiryo Taikei* (Collected Materials on Business History in Japan), Vol. 7 (Accounting), Tokyo: San-ichi Shobo.
Kato, Y. (1993a). *Genka Kikaku: Senryaku-teki Cost Management* (Target Costing: Strategic Cost Management). Tokyo: Nihon Keizai Shimbunsha.
Kato, Y. (1993b). Target costing support systems: lessons from leading Japanese companies. *Management Accounting Research*, 4 (March): 25–35.
Kurogane, K. (1993). *Cross-Functional Management: Principles and Practical Applications*. Tokyo: Productivity Press.
Koike, A. (1993). *Nihon Denki no Rieki Kanri Hoshiki* (The New Way of Profit Management at NEC), Chuokeizai-sha.
Monden, Y. (1993). Genka kikaku, genka kaizen, genkaiji no kigen to hatten, (origin and development of target costing, kaizen costing and cost maintenance). *Kigyo Kaikei* (Accounting), 45(12): 26–32.
Nakayama, R. (1963). *Jissen Hyojungenka Keisan* (Standard Costing in Practice: Dual System). Tokyo: Chūōkeizaisha.

Nishiguchi, T. (1994). *Strategic Industrial Sourcing: The Japanese Advantage*, Oxford, UK: Oxford University Press.

Nishimura, A. (2003). *Management Accounting: Feed Forward and Asian Perspectives*. London: Palgrave Macmillan.

Odaka, K. (1993). *Kigyōnai Kyoiku no Jidai* (The Age of the Education System Inside Companies) Tokyo: Iwanami Shoten.

Ōno, T. (1988). *Toyota Production System: Beyond Large-Scale Production*. Tokyo: Productivity Press (Japanese edition 1978).

Okano, H. (1995, 2002). *Nihon-teki Kanrikaikei no Tenkai: Genka Kikaku eno Rekishi-teki Shiza*. (Japanese Management Accounting: Institutional and Historical Perspective). Tokyo: Chūōkeizaisha.

Okano, H. (2003). *Global Senryaku Kaikei: Seihin Kaihatsu Cost Management no Kokusai Hikaku* (International Comparison on Product Development Cost Management), Tokyo: Yūhikaku.

Okano, H. (2009). Nihonteki Kanrikaikei no Renzokusei to Hirenzokusei (Continuity and Discontinuity of Japanese Management Accounting). *Kaikei (Accounting)*, March 2009: 1–12.

Okana, H. (2015). *History of Management Accounting in Japan: Institutional & Cultural Significance of Accounting* (Studies in the Development of Accounting Thought), Bingley: Emerald Group Publishing.

Okano, H. and Kobayashi, H. (eds) (2015). *Kosuto Dezain: Toyota/Kenkyusha no Jissen Komyuniti* (Cost Designing for Product Development: in Search of Creative Management) (supported by Toyota Motor Corporation), Osaka: Osaka Municipal Universities Press.

Okano, H. and Kudo, E. (2011). Japan. In: Previts, G., Walton, P., and Wolnizer, P. (eds), *A Global History of Accounting, Financial Reporting and Public Policy: Asia and Oceania*, New York: Emerald, pp. 171–185.

Okano, H. and Suzuki, T. (2007). A history of Japanese management accounting. In: Chapman, C., Hopwood, A. G., and Shields, M. D. (eds), *Handbook of Management Accounting Research*, Vol. 2, Oxford, UK: Elsevier, pp. 1,119–1,137.

Robinson, A. G. and Stern, S. (1997). *Corporate Creativity: How Innovation and Improvement Actually Happen*, San Francisco, CA: Berrett-Koehler Publishers.

Sako, M. (1992). *Prices, Quality and Trust: Inter-firm Relations in Britain and Japan*. Cambridge, UK: Cambridge University Press.

Sako, M. (1996). Suppliers' association in the Japanese automobile industry: collective action for technology diffusion. *Cambridge Journal of Economics*, 20(6): 651–671.

Sakurai, M. (1997). *Wagakuni no Keiri Zaimu Soshiki* (Accounting and Finance Organizations in Japan), Tokyo: Zeimu Keiri Kyokai.

Tanaka, T. (1993). Target costing at Toyota. *Journal of Cost Management*, 7(1) (Spring): 4–11.

Tani, T., Okano, H., Shimizu, N., Iwabuchi, Y., Fukuda, J., and Cooray, S. (1994). Target cost management in Japanese companies: current state of the art. *Management Accounting Research*, 5: 35–46.

Toyota Motor Corporation (1987). *Sozo Kagirinaku: History of Toyota Motor Corporation for 50 years*, Toyota City: Toyota Motor Corporation.

TQM Committee (1998). *TQM: 21Seiki no Sogo 'Shitsu' Keiei* (Total Quality Management: Towards an Integral System for the 21st Century), Tokyo: Japan Union for Scientists and Engineers.

12

Japanese employment law

Leon Wolff

The marginal relevance of law to Japanese social and economic life is an enduring theme in the comparative law literature on Japan. At its starkest, the thesis is that, 'in a word, Japanese do not like law' (Noda 1976: 170). They are reluctant to sue (Kawashima 1963); ambivalent about rights (Kim and Lawson 1979); and privilege informal dispute resolution over litigation (Port 1994: 659–670). This is contrasted with the supposed excessive legalism of the United States – a society with 'too much law, too many lawyers, and too little justice' (Rhode 2002: 1348). A similar message underpins commentary on Japanese employment relations. In particular, lifelong employment – a distinctive Japanese-style employment model that is central to Japan's model of corporate governance (Roe and Gilson 1999; Konzelmann 2005: 593–594) – is, according to many, a practice lacking a legal foundation (Araki 2007); a 'social norm' (Jackson 2007: 282); a 'moral imperative' (Ahmadjian and Robinson 2001: 624); an 'unwritten . . . guarantee' (Dore 2000: 107); or an implicit political bargain struck between management and labour (Boyer and Juillard 2000).

Law, however, *does* matter in Japan. Such, writes Haley (2002), is the 'consensus' in the literature. The work of successive generations of Japanese and non-Japanese scholars alike, both in law and the social sciences, clearly shows that legal rules, legal processes, legal actors, and legal institutions play important roles in social and economic ordering in Japan. Scholars reach this same conclusion regardless of the particular empirical method deployed – whether institutional history (e.g. Haley 1998); rational-choice theory and regression analysis (e.g. Ramseyer and Nakazato 1999); ethnography (e.g. Johnson 2002); narrative analysis (e.g. Burns 2005); communitarianism (e.g. Tanase 1995a, 1995b); or neo-institutionalism (e.g. West 2006).

So, too, law matters in employment. To be sure, lifelong employment is neither constitutionally enshrined nor explicitly legislated. Neither does it constitute a term in any employment contract; form part of a company director's fiduciary duties; or qualify as an insurable risk under any corporate insurance policy (Miwa and Ramseyer 2002). Indeed, the Labor Standards Act (Law No. 49 of 1947), by express statutory language, permits employers to discharge an employee without cause upon four weeks' notice. Despite this, Japanese employment law erects a regulatory framework that constrains the exercise of this express right and, by so doing, supports the lifelong employment system (Foote 1996; Yamakawa 2001; Araki 2005, 2007). And this regulatory structure is still intact even though, since the turn of the century, the Japanese parliament, the Diet, has enacted sweeping amendments to a suite of Japanese labour statutes, and Japanese judges have unveiled some important new directions in employment-rights jurisprudence. This is because these legal developments evince a mix of *both* deregulatory and re-regulatory measures and, as such, do not fundamentally reconfigure the key regulatory design underscoring permanent employment relations in Japan.

The purpose of this chapter is to illustrate how employment law patterns permanent employment relationships. To put the argument in context, the chapter begins with a brief description of lifelong employment in Japan; its importance to post-war Japanese corporate governance and capitalism; and empirical evidence of its survival despite a deregulatory turn in Japanese law and politics. The chapter proceeds to explore *direct* law on employment relationships, noting that constitutional, corporate, contract, and even labour law provides no explicit guarantee of employment security. It proceeds to outline how employment law statutes and judicial decisions, however, create an *indirect* regulatory structure facilitating Japan's system of lifetime employment. It does so through a regulatory trade-off, balancing expectations of security for employees with flexible deployment of the workforce for employers. This model of regulation is dubbed 'flexicurity' (Foote 1996; Yamakawa 2001; Araki 2005, 2007).

Employment relationships in Japan

A distinctive trait of Japanese employment is the implicit promise of a job for life: lifetime employment. Championed as one of the 'three sacred treasures' in Japanese industrial relations, along with seniority-based wages and enterprise unions, lifelong employment is said to be the key to Japan's 'practice-dependent, stakeholder model of corporate governance' (Araki 2007). It holds shareholder primacy in check by privileging the interests of employee welfare. As such, it exemplifies Japan's kinder, more benign – and normatively superior – brand of capitalism, variously described a 'proletarian paradise' (Coates 2000: 131), the 'communitarian firm' (Inagami and Whittaker 2005), or 'human capitalism' (Ozaki 1991).

Lifetime employment assumes that employees enter a firm immediately upon graduation and remain until retirement. Resignations and mid-career hires are rare. During their tenure, employees receive in-house training, secure promotions and wage increases in line with their length of service, and enjoy welfare provisions (such as health-care coverage) from their firms (Jacoby 2005a, 2005b, 2005c). Employees do not necessarily perform the same task for their entire careers; indeed, many employees take advantage of internal opportunities – either within the firm or in related entities – to extend their skill-sets. However, job-hopping from firm to firm or from industry to industry is unusual (Dore 1993: 68).

Lifetime tenure brings lifelong commitment. Employees strongly identify with their firms and are loyal to their employers. Many even derive self-esteem and social prestige from their association with their firms (Ahmadjian and Robinson 2001: 623–624; Blanpain *et al.* 2007: 526–527; McAlinn 2007: 403–407). Workplace relationships are like family (Inagami 2005), a recurring theme in Japanese popular culture (Dissanayake 2012: 194). This loyalty secures specific economic advantages. The relational ties between employer and employee promote investment, skills-development and strategic business planning by the firm. For example, the long-term attachments make it worthwhile for firms to invest in the technical training of their workforce in a planned and coordinated way. Early-career employees can be rotated throughout the different divisions within the firm or enterprise group in order to acquire a broad set of company-specific skills. When companies decide to embark on new business strategies requiring new skills, they have the incentive to re-train their mid-career personnel (Lazonick 1992: 144).

Employees, too, are more likely to be industrious, to cooperate with their colleagues, and to limit wage demands to reasonable levels (Coates 2000: 127–128).

Although often referred to as a 'system' or an 'institution' (Hiwatari 1999: 275; Marshall 2005: 103–104; Ono 2007), lifelong employment, according to the empirical evidence, is not a ubiquitous practice. On the contrary, it is reserved for a core workforce of mostly white-collar and blue-collar male workers in large companies or major institutions such as government ministries and agencies; schools; and banks. At best, according to Ono (2007: 33), it applies to about 20 per cent of the Japanese workforce. The remaining 80 per cent, therefore, fall into one of two groups. The first are full-time workers in smaller enterprises, with lower wages and poorer working conditions. The second are 'atypical' workers: part-time employees on fixed-term contracts; casual workers (*arubaito*) without any contractual protections; freelance workers (*furiitā*) who usually work on several jobs simultaneously; and temporary workers dispatched by secondment agencies. To the extent that it exists, lifelong employment disproportionately benefits men over women (Lazonick 1994: 144). Evidence of gender stratification is clear from data on the share of workers in certain categories of tenure. Based on wage census figures in 2000, women are over-represented in the category of less than one year and under-represented in the longer-term categories. Thus, while 51.0 per cent of men enjoy a tenure of ten years or more, and 25.9 per cent twenty years or more, the corresponding figures for women are 32.7 per cent and 11.0 per cent respectively (Ono 2007: 23–24, 47).

A debate is currently taking place over the endurance of lifelong employment in modern deregulating Japan. McAlinn (2007: 408), for example, reports an upward trend in job mobility in Japan in the early twenty-first century, and an apparent decline of generic skills-training in favour of more focused specialities, such as in-house legal practice. Some survey data lends support to this anecdotal evidence of a declining commitment amongst large firms to long-term employment practices (Ahmadjian and Robinson 2001; Mouer and Kawanishi 2005: 250, 259; Moriguchi and Ono 2006: 167, 172; Jackson 2007: 286–287). However, these conclusions sit uneasily with other empirical evidence. For example, Abe and Shimizutani (2007: 347), cite recent studies indicating a general *increase* in job tenure for full-time workers until the mid-1990s – and even until 2000. Further, a series of surveys on hiring practices amongst large Japanese corporations show that lifetime employment practices are continuing (Yamakawa 2001: 630; Jackson 2007: 283). This conflict in empirical studies suggest that 'dead-or-alive' assessments of lifelong employment are too extreme: on the one hand, lifelong is not yet on its deathbed; on the other, it has not emerged from the Heisei recession (the post-bubble recession of the 1990s) unscathed by economic dislocation. Certainly, the 'Lost Decade' witnessed significant shifts in the Japanese labour market, including unprecedented levels of unemployment and the ongoing casualization of the workforce. But this does not necessarily mean that Japan is now converging to a market-based, dismissal-at-will system of labour regulation. Instead, as this chapter will demonstrate, lifelong employment remains underpinned through an existing regulatory framework of 'flexicurity' (Wilthagen and Tros 2004).

Direct legal framework

Japanese law offers no direct legal guarantee of lifelong employment. Take constitutional law, for example. Article 27 of the Japanese Constitution provides that all citizens have the 'right and duty' to work. The right to work, however, is not absolute. The Supreme Court (Judgment of 10 September 1958), for example, has ruled that the state must not unreasonably restrict a citizen's freedom in choosing an occupation, but it is not under an obligation to provide unfettered access to – or, by necessary inference, security of tenure of – employment. The Tokyo District

Court (Judgment of 13 July 2000) has extended this general principle to private employers, ruling that a firm-wide policy of compulsory retirement at age 55 – despite the industry norm of 60 or older – is not inconsistent with a worker's constitutional right to work. The judicial interpretation of article 27, therefore, is that employment opportunity is more a state policy objective rather than an enforceable individual right.

Corporate law also largely ignores the rights and interests of workers. This is despite frequent claims in the literature that lifelong employment is a cornerstone of Japanese corporate governance (e.g. Jaboy 2005a, 2005b, 2005c). Dore (2000), for example, distinguishes Japanese corporate governance from its American counterpart by employing the imagery of the clan. The Japanese company, he writes, is a 'transcendental entity'; managers are more 'elders of an enterprise community' than 'the agents of shareholder principals'; and employees have a 'relationship with their firm comparable to a soldier's sense of regimental loyalty' (Dore 2000: 107). However, as Araki (2007: 26) rightly observes, Japanese corporate law enshrines the principle of shareholder primacy just as unambiguously as in Anglo-American law. As the Tokyo District Court held in *Ikenaka v Tabuchi* (Judgment of the Tokyo District Court, 16 September 1993, 1469 *Hanrei Jiho* 25 at 25):

> Corporations are entities that pursue profits by entrusting their operations to directors elected at the general meetings of shareholders. Thus, in principle, the decision of legally elected directors shall be respected where such [a] decision was made within their authority and in the best interests of the company, so that the directors may concentrate on management without being inhibited. In this way, corporations can expect to make profits.

Furthermore, as Miwa and Ramseyer (2002) note, contract law is invariably silent on employment tenure. Despite the principle of freedom of contract, Japanese employment contracts do not typically include clauses explicitly guaranteeing permanent employment. Corporate insurance policies, similarly, do not generally define as an insurable risk the losses that might accrue due to maintaining a permanent workforce in times of economic downturn.

Japanese labour legislation, too, offers no assurance of permanent employment. In fact, the opposite is true: the express statutory language of the Labor Standards Act (article 20 of Law No. 49 of 1947) permits an employer to discharge an employee for any reason upon four weeks' notice (or four weeks' pay in lieu). As this chapter will explain, however, the courts have read into this statutory language an equitable constraint on the 'abusive' exercise of this right, thereby creating an unwritten law protecting workers against unjust dismissal (Foote 1996; cf. Kettler and Tackney 1997). Even so, the point still stands: there is no statutory guarantee of security of employment in Japan's employment statutes.

Indirect legal framework

So how does the law underpin Japan's model of lifelong employment, despite the absence of *direct* regulation in constitutional, corporate, contract, and labour law? Japanese employment law achieves this through an *indirect* regulatory regime – one that protects employees from arbitrary termination and, as a quid pro quo, grants employers powers of flexible deployment of staff. This framework creates dynamic of 'flexicurity' – a regulatory marriage-of-convenience between employee security and employer flexibility (Foote 1996; Yamakawa 2001; Araki 2005, 2007). Security is achieved by vesting employees with a general right against unjust dismissal; flexibility is accomplished by arming employers with broad discretionary powers to alter working conditions, effect internal rotations and external transfers, build a casual workforce, and control working times. A recent mix of 'deregulatory and reregulatory measures' during and since the Lost Decade (Araki 2007: 278) has reinforced this original design as well as paved the way for re-aligning the security–flexibility balance (Yamakawa 2001: 632). Thus, the protections on job tenure remain largely in place. Indeed, they are bolstered by recent initiatives to keep pace with evolving social values about privacy, gender equity, whistle-blowing and work–life balance (Araki 2007: 273–274, 277–278). Conversely, a spate of deregulatory moves has broadened the powers of employers to deal flexibly with working conditions.

Security

Security of employment tenure exists because of the judicial doctrine protecting vulnerable workers against unfair dismissal (Foote 1996; cf. Kettler and Tackney 1997). This doctrine provides indirect support for employment security: rather than *positively* upholding a 'default' of permanent employment, it *negatively* prevents employers from arbitrarily terminating employment. It is a powerful defence, because employees do not simply have a remedy for economic loss; they can also petition for injunctive relief to restore their employment. The doctrine seems unusual because it seems to defy the express text of the Labor Standards Law (No. 49 of 1947), which, by article 20, empowers dismissal without cause. This seems contrary to the doctrine of parliamentary sovereignty, a key value in most legal systems under which statutory law prevails over judge-made law.

However, it is explicable on the basis that Japanese courts have interpolated into the statutory language a requirement against the abusive exercise of this right. This is a common technique amongst the judiciary worldwide to adjust the apparent harsh operation of a legislative instrument, either by subjecting it to an interpretation that better reflects its apparent policy objective or by imposing equitable constraints on legal powers so that they are exercised in good faith, for a proper purpose or so as not to offend public policy. In the Japanese case, after a string of lower-court decisions, the doctrine was first endorsed by Japan's highest court in a 1975 Supreme Court decision in which the bench held that it was against the 'common sense of society' to permit an employer to dismiss an employee without 'reasonable grounds' (judgment of 25 April 1975, 29–4 *Minshu*, p. 456).

Subsequent courts have strictly scrutinised the legitimacy or otherwise of termination decisions. The high-water mark was reached in the widely cited Supreme Court decision (Judgment of 31 January 1977, 268 *Rōdō Hanrei*, p. 17) invalidating the dismissal of a presenter of an early-morning news bulletin who had overslept twice in a fortnight, once missing the entire broadcast and another missing half of the programme. The company argued that the employee was irresponsible and his actions had harmed the reputation of the station. However, the Court ruled that the dismissal was unduly harsh and unreasonable. This was because the radio station did not take steps – such as by offering a wake-up call service – to assist the announcer to arrive in time for his early-morning shifts. Two years later, the Supreme Court (Judgment of 20 July 1979, 33–5 *Minshu*, p. 582) further invalidated as abusive the withdrawal of a provisional offer of employment to a university graduate whom the personnel director later thought was too 'gloomy' for the position.

The doctrine against abusive dismissals is not limited to terminations due to employee misconduct, incompetence or poor character; it extends to economically motivated retrenchments. In one decision, the Niigata District Court (Judgment of 26 August 1966, 17–4 *Rominshu*, p. 996) held that a company had abused its right to dismiss by reducing its workforce simply to improve profitability and enable dividend payments to shareholders. The Court held that retrenchments of this type should be a last resort in the face of persistent, not temporary, trading difficulties. Following this decision, the courts have developed a stringent four-part test for determining the validity of adjustment-related dismissals:

1 there must be a compelling business need to reduce staffing levels;
2 management must have duly considered other options for coping with its business problems and resorted to adjustment-related dismissals only as an unavoidable last step;
3 the selection of staff for retrenchment must be objectively reasonable; and
4 employers must make a bona fide effort to consult with the union or worker group about the necessity, timing, scale, and method of any dismissals.

This four-part test explains why lifelong employment is more strongly embedded in larger than smaller firms.

Since larger firms have greater financial capacity to cope with business downturns and more tools available to them to regulate surplus labour (such as secondments to other related entities, early retirements and new-hire freezes), the onus of satisfying the four-part test is much greater than for SMEs.

However, in 2000, in a controversial case, the Tokyo District Court (Judgment of 21 January 2000, 782 *Rōdō Hanrei*, p. 23) appeared to have liberalized the test even for larger companies. The Court held that the four-part test for economically motivated dismissals must be evaluated holistically; each prong was a 'factor' rather than an independent legal requirement. The decision sparked furious criticism amongst pro-labour lawyers, but it has been confirmed in subsequent judicial decisions. The new standard is thought to ease the burden on larger firms seeking to restructure during economic downswings, but it does not go so far as to judicially sanction at-will discharges (Araki 2005: 38).

In 2003, the Labor Standards Act was amended to incorporate the judicial doctrine against unjust dismissal. Article 18(2) now provides: 'Where a dismissal lacks objectively rational grounds and is not considered to be appropriate in general societal terms, it shall be null and void as an abuse of right'. The employer must also give 30 days' notice of the dismissal (art. 20) and, if requested, provide reasons to the employee (art. 22). The government had initially proposed to incorporate a provision confirming the right of an employer to dismiss, but this was dropped from the bill after objections from labour unions, the opposition parties, the Japan Federation of Bar Associations, and other groups (Araki 2005: 40).

Although the amendments to the Labor Standards Act merely codify the judicial doctrine against unfair dismissal, rather than significantly modify or clarify its scope, other legislative reforms have strengthened job security for employees in line with changing social values. For example, the Whistleblowers Protection Act (No. 122 of 2004) prohibits dismissal by reason of whistle-blowing in the public interest (art. 3). The Equal Employment Opportunity Act (No. 45 of 1985) was amended in 1997 and 2006 to strengthen the rights of working women, including prohibiting dismissals attributable to direct or indirect discrimination and sexual harassment. Further, the Child Care and Family Care Leave Act (No. 76 of 1991), revised in 2004, prohibits an employer from dismissing or treating a worker disadvantageously by reason of the worker applying for or taking eligible child-care leave (art. 10), family-care leave (art. 16), or leave to care for a sick or injured child (art. 16(4)).

Flexibility

To accommodate the restrictions on employee dismissals, Japanese law affords employees with a number of tools to ensure flexible working practices. These tools roughly divide into two types: (1) those that empower management to command labour; and (2) those that allow the outsourcing of work (Mouer and Kawanishi 2005: 111). Recent legislative amendments have mostly operated to increase these powers.

First, Japanese corporate and competition law affords firms considerable freedom to structure their businesses into an enterprise group. The longstanding prohibition on holding companies since the end of the war was lifted by 1997 reforms to the Anti-Monopoly Act (No. 54 of 1947, amended by No. 87 of 1997). Subsequent reforms to the Commercial Code in 1999 and 2000, retained in the new Company Act (No. 86 of 2005), facilitated the creation of holding companies and corporate divisions by obviating the need for the individual consent of creditors. This reform has allowed firms to create more distinct business units through which they can rotate their personnel (Inagami and Whittaker 2005: chapter 6). Corporate restructures, however, cannot be used unilaterally to streamline staff numbers. By virtue of the Labor Contract Succession Act (No. 103 of 2000), workers' labour contracts are automatically transferred to the new entity in the event of a corporate division.

Second, the Labor Standards Act authorizes employers to unilaterally alter working conditions, including specifications about the type and place of work. This frees up Japanese companies to transfer redundant staff above their objections to other divisions or affiliated businesses. Although the Act provides that the employment contract must specify the conditions of work, including the location and required duties, it also allows employers to promulgate work rules that apply across the whole organization (art. 89). Employers are expected to consult with worker representatives, but are not required to obtain their consent. Employers typically reserve in their work rules a right to transfer staff, and the courts have generally not interfered with the exercise of this right.

Third, a range of judicial and legislative developments permits employers to weaken working conditions to protect their firms against souring business conditions. For example, the Supreme Court (Judgment of 25 December 1968, cited in Araki 2007: 251) held that companies may make an unfavourable modification of their work rules, provided that they are reasonable in the circumstances. In addition, although the Labor Standards Act states that contractual working conditions cannot be inferior to the work rules (art. 93), the judiciary has allowed the converse – namely, work rules that are inferior to contractual conditions. Furthermore, 1998 amendments to the Labor Standards Act have introduced a discretionary work scheme for most white-collar workers. This defines working time by reference to the tasks completed rather than the hours worked. Since this separates overtime entitlements from actual hours worked, this amendment allows companies to control their overtime budgets as well as foster increased competition amongst workers and intensified working practices (Mouer and Kawanishi 2005: 111).

Fourth, Japanese law has increased the power of firms to casualize their workplaces. Under former law, the legal maximum limit for an employment contract was one year. However, the 2003 amendment to the Labor Standards Law has increased this upper limit to three years. This is attractive to managers for two reasons. One is that it allows them to 'lock in' a casual workforce rather than rely on annual contract renewals. The other is that it provides an opportunity to make strategic, medium-term hires of professional staff or skilled technicians and thereby externalise some of the costs of training. Today, Japan has a three-tiered workforce comprising elite core workers, medium-term skilled workers, and shorter-term workers engaging in repetitive labour (Mouer and Kawanishi 2005: 115). Moreover, the Worker Dispatching Act (No. 88 of 1985) has been dramatically deregulated. Originally restricting legal dispatch of temporary workers to sixteen highly specialized occupation categories, the number of categories was lifted to twenty-six in 1996. In 1999, the in-principle prohibition on worker dispatch was removed and the supply of temporary labour became available for most occupational fields (Mouer and

Kawanishi 2005: 115; Araki 2007: 276). In 2003, the prohibition on dispatching workers to production sites was removed altogether.

Conclusions

Japanese employment law, therefore, offers indirect support for Japan's system of lifetime employment. Through the principle of 'flexicurity', Japanese law both protects workers against harsh dismissals as well as granting employers significant discretion to command their workforce. This post-war regulatory model remains in force despite the shift towards deregulation in Japanese law and politics in twenty-first-century Japan. If anything, legal amendments have intensified 'flexicurity' by, on the one hand, reinforcing employment security norms by codifying the law against abusive dismissals, but, on the other, widening the discretionary options for employers to deal flexibly with their workforce, such as by restructuring corporate organization; commanding transfers and reassignments; unilaterally altering work conditions; and making greater use of casual labour to replace departing staff. The net effect of this is to re-adjust – without abandoning altogether – the balance between flexibility and security in employment relations.

References

Abe, N. and Shimizutani, S. (2007). Employment policy and corporate governance – an empirical comparison of the stakeholder and the profit-maximization model. *Journal of Comparative Economics*, 35: 346–368.

Ahmadjian, C. L. and Robinson, P. (2001). Safety in numbers: downsizing and the deinstitutionalization of permanent employment in Japan. *Administrative Science Quarterly*, 46: 622–654.

Araki, T. (2000). A comparative analysis: corporate governance and labour and employment relations in Japan. *Comparative Labor Law and Policy Journal*, 22: 67–96.

Araki, T. (2002). Labor law scholarship in Japan. *Comparative Labor Law and Policy Journal*, 23: 735–748.

Araki, T. (2005). Corporate governance reforms, labor law developments, and the future of Japan's practice-dependent stakeholder model. *Japan Labor Review*, 2(1): 26–57.

Araki, T. (2007). Changing employment practices, corporate governance, and the role of labor law in Japan. *Comparative Labor Law and Policy Journal*, 28(2): 251–281.

Blanpain, R., Bisom-Rapp, S., Corbett, W. R., Josephs, H. K., and Zimmer, M. J. (2007). *The Global Workplace: International and Comparative Employment Law – Cases and Materials*, New York: Cambridge University Press.

Boyer, R. and Juillard, M. (2000). The wage labour nexus challenged: more the consequence than the cause of the crisis. In: Boyer, R. and Yamada, T. (eds), *Japanese Capitalism: A Regulationist Perspective*, London: Routledge.

Burkett, P. and Hart-Landsberg, M. (1996). The use and abuse of Japan as a progressive model. In: Panitch, L. (ed.), *The Socialist Register 1996*, London: Merlin Press, pp. 62–92.

Burns, C. (2005). *Sexual Violence and the Law in Japan*, London and New York: Routledge-Curzon.

Coates, D. (2000). *Models of Capitalism: Growth and Stagnation in the Modern Era*, Cambridge, UK: Polity Press.

Dissanayake, W. (2012). Asian television dramas and Asian theories of communication. *Journal of Multicultural Discourses*, 7(2): 191–196.

Dore, R. (1993). What makes the Japanese different? In: Crouch, C. and Marquand, D. (eds), *Ethics and Markets: Co-operation and Competition within Capitalist Economies*, Oxford: Blackwell Publishers and the Political Quarterly Publishing Co. Ltd.

Dore, R. (2000). Will global capitalism be Anglo-Saxon capitalism? *New Left Review*, 6: 101–119.

Foote, D. H. (1996). Judicial creation of norms in Japanese labor law: activism in the service of stability? *UCLA Law Review*, 43: 635–709.

Haley, J. O. (1998). *Spirit of Japanese Law*, Athens, GA: University of Georgia Press.

Haley, J. O. (2002). Litigation in Japan: a new look at old problems. *Williamette Journal of International Law and Dispute Resolution*, 10: 121–142.

Inagami, T. and Whittaker, D. H. (2005). *The New Community Firm: Employment, Governance and Management Reform in Japan*, Cambridge, UK: Cambridge University Press.

Jackson, G. (2007). Employment adjustment and distributional conflict. In: Aoki, M. Jackson, G. and Miyajima, H. (eds), *Corporate Governance in Japan: Institutional Change and Organizational Diversity*, Oxford and New York: Oxford University Press.

Jacoby, S. M. (2005a). Corporate governance and society. *Challenge*, 48(4): 69–87.

Jacoby, S. M. (2005b). Business and society in Japan and the United States. *British Journal of Industrial Relations*, 43(4): 617–634.

Jacoby, S. M. (2005c). *The Embedded Corporation: Corporate Governance and Employment Relations in Japan and the United States*. Princeton, NJ: Princeton University Press.

Johnson, D. T. (2002). *The Japanese Way of Justice: Prosecuting Crime in Japan*, Oxford and New York: Oxford University Press.

Kawashima, T. (1963). Dispute resolution in contemporary Japan. In: von Mehren, A. (ed.), *Law in Japan: the Legal Order in a Changing Society*, Boston, MA: Harvard University Press.

Kettler, D. and Tackney, C. T. (1997). Light from a dead sun: the Japanese lifetime employment system and Weimar labor law. *Comparative Labor Law and Policy Journal*, 19: 1–41.

Kim, C. and Lawson, C. M. (1979). The law of the subtle mind: the traditional Japanese conception of law. *International and Comparative Law Quarterly*, 28(3): 491–513.

Kitamura, Y. (2000). Regulatory enforcement in local government in Japan. *Law and Policy*, 22(3–4) 305–318.

Konzelmann, S. J. (2005). Varieties of capitalism: production and market relations in the USA and Japan. *British Journal of Industrial Relations*, 43(4): 593–603.

Marshall, S. (2005). Hedging around the question of the relationship between corporate governance and labour regulation. *Australian Journal of Labour Law*, 18: 97–105.

Miwa, Y. and Ramseyer, J. M. (2002). The myth of the main bank: Japan and comparative corporate governance. *Law and Social Inquiry*, 27(2): 401–424.

Moriguchi, C. and Ono, H. (2006). Japanese lifelong employment: a century's perspective. In: Blomstrom, M. and La Croix, S. (eds), *Institutional Change in Japan*, Oxford and New York: Routledge.

Mouer, R. and Kawanishi, H. (2005). *A Sociology of Work in Japan*, Cambridge, UK: Cambridge University Press.

Noda, Y. (1976). *Introduction to Japanese Law*, trans. A. H. Angelo, Tokyo: University of Tokyo Press.

Ono, H. (2007). Lifetime employment in Japan: concepts and measurements, *SSE/EFI Working Paper Series in Economics and Finance*, 624: 1–58.

Port, K. (1994). The case for teaching Japanese law at American law schools. *Depaul Law Review*, 43: 643–671.

Ramseyer, J. M. and Nakazato, M. (1999). *Japanese Law: An Economic Approach*, London and Chicago: University of Chicago Press.

Rhode, D. L. (2002). Legal scholarship. *Harvard Law Review*, 155: 1327–1361.

Roe, M. J. and Gilson, R. J. (1999). Lifetime employment: labor peace and the evolution of Japanese corporate governance. *Columbia Law Review*, 99: 508–540.

Schaede, U. (2008). *Choose and Focus: Japanese Business Strategies for the 21st Century*. Ithaca, NY, and London: Cornell University Press.

Tanase, T. (1995a). Kataritoshite no ho enyo – ho no monogatari to bengoshi rinri (1). *Minshoho Zasshi*, 111(4): 677–706.

Tanase, T. (1995b). Kataritoshite no ho enyo – ho no monogatari to bengoshi rinri (2). *Minshoho Zasshi*, 111(6): 865–903.

West, M. D. (2006). *Law in Everyday Japan: Sex, Sumo, Suicide, and Statutes*, Chicago and London: University of Chicago Press.

Yamakawa, R. (2001). Labor law reform in Japan: a response to recent socio-economic changes. *American Journal of Comparative Law*, 49: 627–651.

Part IV
The Japanese work environment

13

The recruitment processes in the Japanese firm

Philippe Debroux

Changes in the legal, business, and societal environments are now leading many Japanese companies to more radically reassess their recruitment philosophy, policy, and practices. In the post-war era, the practices of recruitment in large companies were based on recruitment of new graduates within a long-term perspective. Lifetime employment is a practice that supported the growth of Japanese firms. It evolved over time, but had proved resistant in its fundamental tenets up until the last decade. Over the past few decades, Japanese companies have not discarded their long-term perspective, because they still believe that it is the source of sustainable competitive advantages. However, companies have started to recruit a growing number of non-regular workers of different status, and they are expected to continue to do so. Moreover, recruitment is also likely to include more women and foreigners in the years to come. Facing a different environment, Japanese companies are adopting new modes of recruitment in order to respond to their need for more diversified human resources. They are rethinking the advantages and disadvantages of recruiting regular employees almost solely from a pool of new graduates. In many industries, the long-term acquisition of firm-specific skills may not be as relevant as before, reinforcing the needs of mid-career recruitment and a diversified workforce to meet the demands of an increasingly globalized business environment.

Introduction

Social belonging and the psychological rewards of membership have always been important aspects of company life for Japanese workers, and they are likely to continue to be so, albeit in different ways from before. However, on the whole, relationships between employers and workers can be expected to be more contingent than before, and Japanese companies must take into account the changing understanding and expectations about the jobs and careers of a heterogeneous group of prospective recruits.

Japanese companies must devise more attractive monetary and non-monetary packages to recruit and retain capable workers from other corporations while retaining their own workers (Nakata and Miyazaki 2011). Many of them still focus their recruitment on new graduates, but few young Japanese people envision staying in their entry organization during their entire professional life.

Changes in the Japanese labour market have been manifold. The external labour market for professionals willing to change jobs is growing, and capable individuals are gradually able to build their own careers by changing employers. Name value may not be sufficient to recruit the best prospects and remain an employer of choice. Therefore, higher job mobility is bound to be part of the recruitment and selection strategy. Employee–company mismatch and an increase in the opportunistic behaviour of regular and non-regular employees have become concerns. An increasing number of employees have been quitting their jobs within a few years of being recruited, just when the population decline is becoming a threat to securing human resources.

Successive reforms of employment practices since the 1980s have aimed to gradually increase external financial, functional and temporal flexibility in human resource management. In streamlining and enlarging diversity in employment, they have made it possible to recruit non-regular workers of diverse types, such as dispatched workers, temporary workers, and part-time workers with less constraints (The Japan Institute for Labour Policy and Training 2013). In so doing, they have allowed companies to somehow escape from the rigidities of the internal labour market while keeping intact the status of their core regular workers.

It is argued that these reforms have been the harbinger of a new normality in employment relationships (Ministry of Health, Labor and Welfare 2010). However, the drastic increase of non-regular work since the 1980s has done nothing to change the idea that regular employment is the ideal norm and that other forms of employment should be considered temporary or reflect specific circumstances (family care for example). Non-regular employment is connected with below-par working conditions and not as a stepping stone towards regular employment. Therefore, to gain legitimacy, the alternative employment status must dispel the worries of those eager to have more choice of employment but who are scared by the prospect of income instability and poor-quality working conditions that employment mobility might entail.

Historical and cultural background

Permanent employment was not the employers' and employees' ideal of employment relationships in the aftermath of the Second World War. It was more of a temporary policy that large companies used to recruit and retain scarce skilled labour in the high-growth period (1955–1973). Even during that period, 50 to 80 per cent of recruits were mid-career workers. While large companies were indeed eager to recruit new graduates, most small concerns were not able to do so until after the 1980s. The stability of the employment system until the 1970s was largely the result of the growing job opportunities offered inside large and small companies because of rapid economic growth and the subsequent expanding demand for labour.

However, over time, long-term employment started to become institutionalized. Labour-management consultation mechanisms allowed stable industrial relations that facilitated the smooth adoption of new technologies and innovative production processes. The integrated mode of production in key industries such as automobile manufacturing and electronics required knowledge of a tacit nature and constant exchanges of information, requiring the long-term presence of core human resources. A long-term job guarantee fitted in with the need for income stability for the large segments of population that were entering the consumer society. Thus, although unlimited lifetime employment with a single organization never really described most careers, especially in small companies, norms about the social and productive labour–capital relationship, i.e. norms that favour long-term employment, spread throughout the entire business system. However, since the beginning, these norms have been based on three specific features of Japan's division of labour that have driven recruitment philosophy and practices since then:

1   A gap in terms of wages, fringe benefits, and social prestige that makes employment in a large company much more attractive than in a small one.
2   An insider–outsider type of division of labour based on status with, on the one hand, regular employment unlimited in duties or duration and *de facto* 'permanent' until retirement, and, on the other hand, non-regular employment of various kinds,[1] where employees are recruited with limited-term contracts or working schedules, thus by definition with a 'non-permanent' status.
3   An acceptance of taken-for-granted segregated gender roles in the workplace, drastically reducing women's prospects of regular employment.

The socio-economic order created by this division of labour was legitimized (using economic and socio-cultural arguments), by the most influential stakeholders, e.g. policy makers, large companies, business associations, and organized labour. The projected image of large companies was that of organizations that should be considered as public goods, launching socially useful products on the market while being responsible for job creation, stable long-term income, and employee welfare (Sugimoto 2010). The privilege of becoming an insider was seen as a reflection of the results of a meritocratic educational competition. In the minds of all parents and children, the idea was constantly reinforced that regular employment in a large organization was the ideal to be reached, and that it was worth the important sacrifices required (money, time, the social life of children) (Rohlen 1974). In so doing, it shaped the philosophy of the whole educational system (what, how, and for which purpose the learning process should be organized) and contributed to building the intricate relations between recruitment policy and education that continue to exist up to the present day.

However, despite the institutionalizing of long-term employment in the 1970s, recruitment practices were never so clear-cut, and their diversification had already started during the same period. With the end of the high-growth period, companies started to have difficulty delivering enough internal jobs and to offer appropriate career development in the seniority-based promotion and reward system (Whittaker 1990). The strong risk-stabilizing mechanisms of the employment system that the state had created through public-works projects started to fade away. The whole HR system became unsustainable in terms of cost, despite labour externalization through the use of contingent non-regular labour and transfers in subcontracting and associated companies. When the financial bubble burst in the early 1990s, companies accelerated the move away from a purely internal-labour-driven recruitment strategy (Keizer 2005). Applying the concept of employment portfolio promoted by business associations (Nikkeiren 1995), gradual drawdown of regular employees was engineered, combined with recruitment of part-timers and contract workers, as well as the use of the external labour market in order to have access to specialized expertise that they could not nurture internally.

A more-fluid labour market has emerged with gradual loosening of the rules concerning non-regular workers since the 1980s. The Law for Dispatch Workers enacted in 1985 has increased the opportunity to offer and utilize short-term employment contracts. The scope was enlarged to all types of jobs, including in manufacturing, in 2003 (Hisano 2007). Since 1998, the Labor Standards Law has contained an amendment introducing the so-called discretionary type of employment (*sairyō rōdō*) under which workers are recruited within strict performance criteria on clear objectives on a contractual basis, but can freely utilize their time as long as they achieve the negotiated results. It allows companies to control their overtime budgets while responding to the need to accommodate a diverse life- and working-style and to satisfy the demand for short-term and specific expertise. Since 2003, the legal maximum limit for an employment contract has been three years instead of one. It gives the opportunity to achieve strategic, medium-term recruitment of skilled workers while partly externalizing the costs of training (Wolff 2011).

The traditional practices of recruitment

In the internal labour market, recruitment is seen as the beginning of a long-term relationship between companies and employees. The criteria of recruitment are focused on academic credentials, values, and attitudes. This fits in with the objectives of integrating the new recruits in the corporate culture and having them acquire professional firm-specific skills of a conceptual, technical, intellectual, and relationship-based nature (Ouchi 1981). Employees are not recruited for specific jobs, because skills are acquired through company on-the-job training (Haak and Pudelko 2005). The applicants have to take a number of written tests, but the interviews are regarded as the most important part of the selection process. The priorities when selecting new graduates (more specifically in the social sciences) have traditionally focused on personal qualities, namely communicative ability, drive, and enthusiasm; acceptance of challenges; and drive for self-improvement. Recruiting and selecting in giving importance to the presence of those personal qualities is in line with the idea that education denotes something more than skills in the context of the Japanese internal labour market. Education connotes learning and internalization of appropriate social norms and values such as team spirit, altruism, enthusiasm, dedication, and motivation that are necessary prerequisites before recruitment.

The recruitment process is based on a schedule spanning more than a year. This early recruitment process is referred to as 'aotagai' (buying rice before it is harvested), since students are recruited far in advance of graduation (Jackson and Tomioka 2004). Intellectual achievement is considered a critical factor in recruitment, in the sense that students who entered universities with more difficult entrance examinations are considered as deserving the most the material, prestige, and power-related rewards that are offered in large public and private organizations (Dore 1987). Thus, job-seekers are motivated to enhance their marketability through higher academic credentials or entering into prestigious institutions. To make their choice, they have at their disposal qualitative and quantitative information giving all kinds of details about schools and universities. This has created a huge hierarchical pyramid of educational institutions, with relative strengths, weaknesses, and prestige, and their guarantee of a specific 'standard quality' of graduate. The hierarchy of institutions was seldom challenged until very recently, and the rewards of graduation from a given institution can be evaluated more automatically than in the Western world (Glazer 1976). Conversely, it allows companies to minimize the risk of unfitness of the new recruits and the cost of monitoring inside the organization. Accepting a candidacy only after receiving a recommendation letter from the university used to be the norm until recently, and most students know that many companies still continue to recruit only from certain institutions (Firkola 2011). Natural-science applicants, in particular, are still often recommended to companies by their professors. Thus, up until now, reflecting the general Japanese attitude towards education, the ability of an individual has been translated directly in terms of academic credentials (Nakane 1970).

A key characteristic of recruitment in Japan has been that companies offer the same entry salary to all new recruits. Moreover, almost all companies of the same size in the same industry offer about the same entry financial conditions. This is a far cry from what is observed in the Western world, but also in China, for example, where entry conditions may be very different from company to company and from individual to individual (Yano 2013). This Japanese characteristic is deeply engrained in the egalitarian spirit that is a cornerstone of traditional Japanese management. Nevertheless, Japanese companies will have to consider this issue, as well as others that call into question their usual practices, in case they become unable to attract the best Japanese and foreign workers in the market.

Like companies, Japanese educational institutions are still able, by and large, to recruit according to the value that their name carries. The consequence of this internal-labour-market logic is that, prior to the last ten years, universities did not need to devise specialized programmes connected to professional life for undergraduate and post-graduate students (Rohlen 1974) (although this is a must for natural-science students). However, the situation is rapidly changing now, with the diversification of recruitment patterns that start to value more specialized education in Japan and in foreign institutions. Educational institutions are also requested to better prepare their students for entry into professional life, in order to reduce mismatch and high turnover amongst new workers. The development of a new curriculum, with specialization increasingly leading to the acquisition of certification, is required from educational institutions in order to expand recruitment choice.

The need for change in recruitment policies and practices

In general terms, the recruitment process is so strongly linked to economic conditions that it becomes dysfunctional and wasteful of human resources in periods of high market instability. For instance, from 2003 to 2007, the better economic conditions and the baby-boomers' retirement created a seller market that drove companies to rush to recruit talented students, although afterwards they could not deliver career opportunities to many of them. At the opposite end, the market became a buyers' one after the financial crisis in 2008, preventing equally talented people from enjoying similar job prospects. Overall, large companies recruit fewer regular employees, but job-hopping and the vagaries of the economic situation push some of these companies to factor in employee turnover when recruiting. In doing so, they deprive other companies, including many smaller companies struggling to secure human resources, of the possibility of recruiting talented new graduates.

The distinction between regular employees who perform core tasks and non-regular employees who perform routine tasks no longer reflects the situation on the ground. The increased vagueness in the horizontal division of labour and the emergence of sub-categories of workers calls for a clear framework and rules to streamline their status (Ishida and Sato 2011). Fixed-contract employees can be a purely buffer-type workforce who cover the need for numerical, temporal, and financial flexibility in performing unspecialized jobs. They can be recruited directly in the external labour market or through brokers. They are often underpaid, and have poor career possibilities. As a result, they are difficult to motivate and their productivity is lower than that of regular workers (Weathers 2009).

However, there are also types of 'core' non-regular workers that companies permanently need for an array of non-specialized, specialized, and/or firm-specific tasks. In some sectors, e.g. retailing, the food/drink business, hotels, and transportation, it is very difficult to secure a stable basis for recruitment, even for non-specialized occupations.

The ageing of population and the increase in the pensionable age has made recruitment with the status of regular employee an increasingly costly and risky policy. As a result, about one-fifth of non-regular employees want regular employment but cannot find it (Ministry of Health, Labor and Welfare 2013). Conversely, people eager to limit their commitment and avoid transfers and long working hours, often have little choice but to accept low-paid jobs with few career perspectives. Therefore, the reforms are presented as aiming to create employment that decreases the constraints for both parties while offering access to a living wage, training, career prospects, and stability in a clear legal framework. They are expected to fit in with the stronger tendency of the Japanese people to seek 'self-realization' (Sugimoto 2010). The currently envisioned reforms that put emphasis on individuals' control over their career, employability, and empowerment are said to appeal to the most dynamic segments of the population, especially the young professionals, while responding to the need of business for innovative thinking, drive, and risk-taking behaviour and attitudes.

Instability of business conditions makes traditional regular employment unrealistic for workers in many services sectors. This is also the case for the 'hybrid' workers used in manufacturing. Business strategy does not justify their recruitment on a regular basis, but they are often *de facto* 'internalized' and 'semi-regular'. While recruitment on a non-regular basis is explained by the need for lower costs, the use of these 'hybrid' workers also responds to the functional need for flexibility. They work in positions normally occupied by regular workers. Therefore, they are expected to acquire the same skills and demonstrate the same level of teamwork as regular employees (Hirano 2011).

Although the treatment of the 'hybrid' workers and of the 'core' non-regular workers in service sectors is generally better than that of the short-term non-regular workers, they do not receive a reward commensurate with the level of their work. The gap in remuneration and fringe benefits as compared with regular workers is often wide. Apart from the issues of business ethics and the potential deterioration in organizational efficiency, the current situation is likely to become a structural problem. It is likely to add to the cost and unpredictability of the whole process of recruitment and retention if better working conditions are not offered. Therefore, there is a need for intermediate types of job status. In view of the difficulties in finding and keeping fixed-term contract workers, companies have to offer limited regular status to stabilize their HR management (*Asahi Shimbun* 2014). That is also why a growing number of companies are now integrating some of those core hybrid skilled workers into their regular staff (Debroux 2013).

Unemployment and changing jobs

Today there are about as many jobs as job-seekers in Japan, and the main measure of unemployment puts it at around 4 per cent (Japan Institute for Labour Policy and Training 2014). As mentioned above, this could strengthen the positions of the new entrants. Nevertheless, competition for good, regular positions is bound to remain harsh in many sectors (Uenishi 2013). Opportunities to move from non-regular to regular status do exist, but they concern only some groups of non-regular workers. For example, a number of dispatch workers are recruited under the 'temp to perm' system. Although the number is likely to increase, access to regular status will probably remain limited to specific types of skills where there is a labour shortage, such as in the information and communication technologies (ICT), retail, eating/drinking, and amenities businesses (Japan Institute for Labor Policy and Training 2015).

If non-regular employment is frowned upon, it also appears that some positions, while regular, are also not satisfactory because they are not well paid and do not offer good career opportunities. This explains the growing job-hopping of young employees, even those with a regular status, and the wide discrepancy amongst industries between offer and demand. Overall, only about 40 per cent of available jobs are regular positions (*Mainichi Shimbun* 2014). There is a glut of candidates for fewer general administrative jobs. Conversely, the shortage in the manufacturing, construction, and amenities businesses mentioned above is likely to worsen with the decline in the young population, and this is starting to have negative consequences. Companies are forced to renounce contracts because they cannot find staff, and others may even have to close shops or curtail opening times (*Asahi Shimbun* 2014).

An unbalanced job market

The imbalance in the labour market results notably from the shortcomings of professional education at the level of schools and adult training. As a by-product of the internal labour market, Japan did not (and still does not, actually) invest enough in public training and is far below the OECD average in this regard (OECD 2009). But the imbalance is also due to the type of companies to which university students continue to apply. Despite the decline in recruitment; the flattening of the hierarchy that makes it unlikely for the majority of the new recruits to reach managerial level in many of them; and the decline of welfare corporatism, the vast majority of students still prioritize applications to the prestigious large companies. They often do not devote enough time to job-searching in smaller and medium-sized companies which are also looking to recruit new graduates. It is often after having failed to secure a job in a large company that they look down, by default, at smaller concerns. Because they often do this without sufficient knowledge about the working environment, this results in failure and a rapid move to another company. The situation is gradually changing, because smaller companies that offer desirable working conditions are able to attract more new graduates than before. But, overall, there is still an oversupply of applicants to large, famous companies and a shortage of applicants to small and medium-sized companies, even if many of them offer working conditions on a par with and sometimes even better than large companies.[2]

Towards diversification of recruitment policies and practices

The current reforms are part of the shift from protection of employment to labour mobility matching labour supply and demand, in a kind of Japanese-style 'flexicurity' system giving preference to employability over the defence of current jobs (Ministry of Health, Labor and Welfare 2010). Limited regular employment (*gentei seiki koyō*) and labour mobility are proposed as solutions to the class polarization and the rising number of non-regular workers. A 'trampoline-style society' is envisioned, with a safety net that would protect those who lose their job. They would then be retrained and launched back in the labour market in good condition. Workers' position in the labour market would come from their expertise and experience and not from their status at recruitment time. Marketable skills are expected to give them the opportunity to find a decent job, i.e. not necessarily 'permanent' in the traditional sense, but making possible long-term career progress while respecting work–life balance.

Companies would enjoy more flexibility in HR management thanks to further steps towards deregulation of the labour market. New changes are expected in the dispatch worker law, eliminating almost all limits on using temporary staff. The period of time before which non-regular workers with specialized ability and/or high salaries of a certain level would have the right to apply to transition to regular worker status could pass from five to ten years. Provisions would limit the working hours for some workers; strengthen efforts to get workers to take paid leave; and expand discretionary labour for workers in occupations where hours are difficult to calculate (Ministry of Health, Labor and Welfare 2013).

Inclusiveness with a clear legal framework

Many women who are pushed off the career track in the over-demanding current environment are expected to relish the status of limited regular worker, especially if it provides the opportunity to change (reverse) status according to specific situations (giving birth and caring of young children, or taking care of parents) whose impact on work-life is temporary. Smaller businesses are already successfully tapping the talent of women who had entered the managerial track but had decided to take a career break after giving birth. In the case of elderly workers, limited regular employment may give companies the opportunity to optimize these workers' experience and knowledge while allowing them to continue working under good working conditions (wages, working hours), but at a lower cost, until they are entitled to receive a pension.[3] In the case of the young workers, limited regular employment is a response to the negative effects of internal-labour-market logic at a time when large companies are reducing their recruitment of new graduates. It would offer a second chance to those who have not been able to find a regular job just after graduation and have limited access to specialized skills. Rules could be devised that would allow time during which workers could have the opportunity to build competency, while companies could see how well they work out (Debroux 2013).

Regular employment statutes that are limited by location (one location, no transfers); by job (limited duties); or by hours of work (no or low overtime); have been in use since the 1980s. Since then, there has been an increase in the number of companies that allow new recruits to work in a particular city of their choice (Natsume 2007). In the past, this policy was limited to a few sectors such as retail and finance, and massively targeted female employees. It is more widespread now in many sectors and an increasing number of male employees opt for that status (Namikawa 2013). Airline and railway companies and travel agencies that are popular amongst university students have, for a long time, also adopted schemes based on a kind of contract employment. In those cases, the applicants are recruited as contract workers for a number of years, and then after this fixed period they can become regular workers.

Those examples show that the recruitment process has increasingly taken into account the diversity of the workforce. It is also observed that, in the past, the workers who had been recruited in one location were given limited promotion opportunities. This is not necessarily the case now: some workers recruited for a specific location are given the opportunity to enter the career track (and possibly shift to unlimited status later on). Nevertheless, legal problems have emerged because of the ambiguity of the status of many of the schemes described here above. Work in air transportation and tourism is demanding (long working hours), and the pay is not attractive. Thus, the drop-out rate has tended to be high. In business where it is difficult to differentiate the tasks (in an aeroplane, for example), it is difficult to motivate non-regular workers receiving a salary and fringe benefits significantly lower than those of regular workers, especially if the prospect of shifting to regular status is uncertain and based on subjective criteria. Therefore, establishing a clear legal framework for limited regular employment is necessary in order to reduce the uncertainties and risks for both parties: unfair treatment in the case of employees; and legal liability and loss of reputation in the case of the organization. This is expected to reduce companies' current reluctance about expanding recruitment other than atypical precarious employment. New employees could be recruited from the start as limited regular employees, and current non-regular workers could gradually be given the opportunity to shift to a regular (or limited regular) status.

New approaches of the new graduates

It is argued that, in order to create products with unique features, long-term relationships with internal and external partners and cultivation of broad integrative skills and problems-solving abilities have to remain at the centre of the HRM and knowledge-management strategy (Itami 2011). On the one hand, this calls for keeping the internal-labour-market logic and to continue to focus on recruitment of new graduates. In the first decade of this century, there was a trend toward recruiting more mid-career workers, even in large companies. However, since 2008, stagnation in the recruitment of mid-career human resources has been observed. It seems that the recruitment of new graduates has again been given preference. Fundamentally, the idea in large companies is still to recruit human resources and to nurture leadership internally over a long-term perspective (Nagano 2014). On the other hand, companies do look for more diversified types of human resources. Individual characteristics are said to be more important than before in the recruitment process (Firkola 2011). Hence, some companies are ready to recruit new graduates with unconventional profiles, in addition to the traditional reliable and diligent type of candidate. They decided to abolish the university recommendation system and to open the recruitment pool to all graduates, without asking for academic credentials. At the same time, some companies are rethinking the need to recruit only once a year, in order to cope with the growing number of Japanese returnees (Japanese who lived and/or studied abroad) and the influx of foreign applicants.[4] Admittedly, enlarging the pool of candidates' profiles entails a higher risk of mistakes in the recruitment process. Moreover, with an emphasis placed on employability and empowerment, higher in–out mobility can be expected. The problem of mismatch is compounded by the fact that most of the early stages of the recruitment process have gone online and become impersonal (Uenishi 2013).[5]

Amongst companies there now appears to be an acceptance of labour mobility amongst students. Allowing more choice and flexibility is deemed necessary to attract outstanding talent. Traditionally, applicants used to receive little input with regard to their future job or work location. In particular, in the case of natural-science graduates, some companies introduce a job-matching system that determines in advance which divisions the applicants should target (Natsume 2007). Some companies offer a number of specific career courses from which to choose. For example, it is observed that Panasonic offers a choice of sixteen career courses (Firkola 2011). Some companies give graduates the opportunity to list their own preferences for the first job placement. Conversely, supervisors can select their future subordinates. This reflects the growing role of line managers in the recruitment process and the concomitant decline of the direct role of the human-resource department (Debroux 2013).

Even for humanities-oriented HR, some companies now provide a space on their job application forms for 'key areas of academic achievement', and enquire about areas of expertise.[6] Companies now recruit people who graduated in the past three years if they can show that they have been doing things that could be useful to the organization (Nagano 2014). This may give graduates time to study overseas and develop a variety of skills before entering the workforce, hence reducing the reluctance of young Japanese people to go abroad in case they cannot find a regular job when they return. Likewise, the introduction of internships that lead directly to employment has also been observed, in contrast to the current status of internships as not being directly related to job-seeking. This type of internship is also a way of avoiding mismatching of employees and jobs (Nagano 2014). In some cases, internships become a prerequisite for applying to a company.

The recruitment of foreign human resources

A consensus is developing in favour of greater immigration of skilled foreign workers. Indeed, the number of professional workers from abroad has been rising during the last five years (Nabeta 2011). This group can be expected to increase further with the shift towards recognition of merit in the evaluation and reward systems, and also thanks to the social-security agreements that Japan has concluded with foreign countries. The need to have a pool of globally competent recruits with a global mindset is now the leitmotiv shared by the public authorities, business, and the academic world (Nabeta 2011). The war to capture talent, not only in Japan, but also in the whole East and South-East Asian region, requires an active talent strategy that is based on the enlargement of the recruitment pool and the selection of the Japanese and foreign workforce (The Economist Group 2010). Recently, almost all large Japanese companies started increasing the recruitment of foreign students. They are generally thought of as a bridge between Japan and their home countries. However, more and more companies recruit them for the purpose of boosting managerial expertise and knowledge diversity within the organizations. A growing number of foreign applicants are offered global careers on a par with Japanese employees (Nabeta 2011).

For the time being, Japanese companies do not have a good record regarding the retention rate of their foreign employees, and they are not very attractive in the eyes of the young global elite (The Economist Group 2010). Higher transparency about the evaluation criteria, the reward system, the acquisition of skills, and the career prospects is required. The possibility of a choice of a more limited organizational commitment than expected from traditional regular status is appealing to inherently mobile foreign professionals. Limited commitment could favour the recruitment of employees (Japanese and foreigners) with fresh ideas and drive but also a high engagement level, if they think that the monetary and non-monetary reward package is attractive.

However, it remains to be seen whether Japanese companies are ready for cross-fertilization, i.e. the in–out flow of high-level Japanese and foreign employees.[7] Even if globally competent/minded human resources become available in Japan in larger numbers than before, they are unlikely to contribute to the success of Japanese companies in cases where they are not allowed to fully utilize their special skills and abilities. Precisely because they are globally competent, these human resources are likely to be eager to make careers in globally competent organizations. Unless Japanese companies are able to achieve global competence at the organization level, the efforts to recruit globally competent/minded individuals could result in moves away (Japanese and foreign alike) to other organizations, making their recruitment costly and unattractive.

Conclusions

It is too early to form a definitive opinion about the most-recent reforms, especially about the projected limited regular employee status. Those reforms that are now envisioned are not limited to a cost strategy as was the case for reforms since the 1980s that have centred almost exclusively on non-regular workers. Because they may entail changes in the status of the regular workers, their impact could be broader and deeper than the previous ones. Their proclaimed objective is to offer alternative employment status that could open new career opportunities to all categories of workers, especially to those that have been left behind during the last two decades (Sato 2013). Indeed, if the reforms are not directly calling the traditional regular employment norms into question for the time being, the indirect argument is that those norms neither respond appropriately to the needs of some categories of population nor to the needs of business. In the long term, they may transform the mutual expectations of employees and management in the workplace, namely the role of companies as key intermediate bodies in the Japanese socio-economic fabric as providers of welfare and stable employment.

Opponents see the proposed reforms as a new step toward dismantling Japan's already weakening long-standing social compact. They argue that limited regular employment contains inherent contradictions. If the reforms are implemented just to lower the institutional cost of 'normal' regular employment in loosening the social and legal constraints on companies' right to lay-off workers and to undermine the regular status, then it will lead to the emergence of second-class regular workers (Scott 2014). Even if this situation can be controlled in large companies, it may not be the case in small companies. Working hours could end up being as long as before, because the same availability will be required from the limited regular workers – whatever the negotiated agreements. But wages and fringe benefits could remain lower than for the regular workers. As a result, far from correcting the imbalance between regular and non-regular workers, the reforms could further impede the career opportunities of those that they are supposed to benefit. However, good or bad, in any case the reforms are likely to exert an impact on the regular employees' group. First, the introduction of the scheme may reduce their number even further. If limited regular employment becomes widespread, then companies will not have to recruit as many regular employment workers as now. Second, provided that the treatment offered (financial, training, and career opportunities; relatively high employment stability) of the limited regular workers is significantly better than the current non-regular status (and it has to be in order to gain legitimacy and attract enough candidates), it may lead to a deeper reconsideration of the status (and concept) of the regular employees. Unlimited duties and control of one's career by the company (investment relating to the acceptance of restrictiveness by the employees) may become difficult to promote if it is no longer associated with significantly better treatment.

In a tight labour market, workers' bargaining power is likely to be enhanced, and companies could be under pressure to improve working conditions in circumstances where they have problems recruiting and retaining workers as Japan's declining population drives up labour demand. In addition, expanded corporate welfare (more attuned to diversified life-styles than the traditional welfare-corporatist schemes), training, and care, may become necessary inducements for recruiting good workers. A number of issues have been raised regarding present and future recruitment practices. The extent of diversification in terms of flexibility, choice for applicants, and increased recruitment of foreign recruits, should be examined further. The emergence of socially and economically plausible work alternatives to Japanese-style regular employment is likely to transform the very concept of work in Japanese society. As such, the current debate has important implications for employment ethics, contractual norms, and relations in production, as well as for lives and careers and the viability of companies. It will be interesting to know what will become the new benchmarks of the recruitment system amongst Japanese companies in such circumstances.

Notes

1 There are four main types of non-regular workers: fixed-term contract worker, part-time worker, dispatched worker, and outsourced worker. Fixed-term contract and part-time workers are recruited directly by employers or through intermediaries. Part-time work is broadly defined as 'regular wage employment in which the hours of work are less than "normal"' (Kalleberg 2000). Specifically, Araki (2002) takes thirty hours a week as the dividing line.

2 In 2013, the ratio of job offers to applicants was 0.65 for companies with over 1,000 employees; it was 1.86 in the case of companies with less than 1,000 employees; and it was 3.35 in the case of companies with less than 300 employees (Uenishi 2013).

3 The reforms are in line with the need to rebalance the social-security account. The retirement age is planned to increase to 65 years old by the year 2025. Therefore, pressure is mounting on companies to control the cost of the elderly employees that they have to keep on their payroll.

4 Educational institutions are still the major sources of recruitment and development of human resources. They are obliged to follow the trend towards more flexibility in recruitment. That is why some of them now offer the possibility of graduating in September and not only at the end of March.

5 It should be noted that drop-out rates are still lower in larger companies than in smaller concerns. There is also a large discrepancy according to sector. In the case of 2009 graduates, the yearly drop-out rate was 48.5 per cent in the accommodation, eating, and drinking sectors, compared with 15.6 per cent in manufacturing (Uenishi 2013). Labour turnover is a major concern for companies that have had to devote time

and resources recruiting and then training these new recruits during their first years of employment. This leads to the factoring in of the drop-out rate that was mentioned earlier in this chapter.

6 This is especially useful in the recruitment and selection process of foreign employees

7 Although the external labour market is growing, many companies still often offer their mid-career recruits a salary that is fundamentally based on the length of service and achievement in the company in which they are currently employed. It does not fully (or does not at all) take into account the experience and achievements elsewhere, and neither is there any attempt to measure the workers' job capability (*shokuno*) so that the starting salary could be adjusted accordingly.

Bibliography

Araki, T. (2002). *Labor and Employment Law in Japan*, Tokyo: Japan Institute of Labor.

Asahi Shimbun (2014). Jinzai busoku kigyo ga himei (Shortage of manpower, the scream of companies). *Asahi Shimbun*, 2 May 2014, p. 3.

Debroux, P. (2013). Human resource management in Japan. In: Varma, A. and Budhwar, P. (eds), *Managing Human Resources in Asia-Pacific*. London: Routledge, pp. 105–128.

Dore, R. (1987). *Taking Japan Seriously: A Confucian Perspective on Leading Economic Issues*. Stanford, CA: Stanford University Press.

Economist Group (2010). *Talent Strategies for Innovation: Japan*. London: Economist Intelligence Unit.

Firkola, P. (2011). Japanese recruitment practices – before and after the global financial crisis. *Economic Journal of Hokkaido University*, 40: 59–71.

Glazer, N. (1976). Social and cultural factors in Japanese economic growth. In: Patrick, H. and Rosovsky, H. (eds), *Asia's New Giant*, Washington, DC: The Brookings Institution.

Haak, R. and Pudelko, M. (2005). *Japanese Management: The Search for a New Balance between Continuity and Change*, London: Palgrave Macmillan.

Hirano, M. (2011). Diversification of employment categories in Japanese firms and its functionality. In: Bebenroth, R. and Kanai, T. (eds), *Challenges of Human Resources in Japan*, Abingdon, UK: Routledge.

Hisano, K. (2007). Employment in transition: changes in Japan since the 1980s. In: Burgess, J. and Connell, J. (eds), *Globalisation and Work in Asia*. London: Chandos Publishing.

Ishida, M. and Sato, A. (2011). The evolution of Japan's human-resource management. In: Miyoshi, H. and Matanle, P. (2003). *Japanese Capitalism and Modernity in a Global Era: Re-Fabricating Lifetime Employment Relations*, London and New York: Routledge-Curzon.

Itami, H (2011). Restoring Japanese-style management rudder. *JapanEchoWeb*, 5, February–March 2011, http://www.japanpolicyforum.jp/archives/economy/pt20110207140508.html, last accessed 15 October 2015.

Jackson, K. and Tomioka, M. (2004). *The Changing Face of Japanese Management*, London, Routledge.

Japan Institute for Labour Policy and Training (2013). *Transition in Diversification of Employment III: 2003/2007/2010*, JILPT Research Report No. 161, English summary at http://www.jilgo.jp/, last accessed 4 November 2015.

Japan Institute for Labour Policy and Training (2014). *Japanese Working Life Profile 2013/2014*, Tokyo: Japan Institute for Labor Policy and Training.

Japan Institute for Labour Policy and Training (2015). *Labor Situation in Japan and its Analysis: Detailed Exposition 2014/2015*. Tokyo: Japan Institute for Labor Policy and Training.

Kalleberg, A. L. (2000). Nonstandard employment relations: part-time, temporary and contract work. *Annual Review of Sociology*, 26: 341–365.

Keizer, A. (2005). *The Changing Logic of Japanese Employment Practices: A Firm-Level Analysis of Four Industries*. Rotterdam, Netherlands: Erasmus University Press.

Mainichi Shimbun (2014). Koyo seisaku no minaoshi: seishain tōnoku kennen (Rethinking employment policy: small worry for regular employees) 2 February 2014, p. 5.

Ministry of Health, Labor and Welfare (2010). *Yokuyaku Kano na Katsuyaku aru Shakai o Jitsugen suru Keizai. Koyo System* (An Economic and Employment System to Enable Continuous Social Activity), Tokyo: Ministry of Health, Labor and Welfare.

Ministry of Health, Labor and Welfare (2013). *Hiseiki Koyo no Genjo* (Non-regular Employment, Current Conditions), Ministry of Health, Labor and Welfare.

Nabeta, S. (2011). Gaikokujin shinsotsu saiyo no saishin jijo (Latest news about recruitment of foreigners). *Rosei Jiho*, 3805, 9 September: 10–47.

Nagano, H. (2014). Trends in corporate hiring of recent graduates: focus on developments since the global financial crisis. *Japan Labor Review*, 11(2), Spring 2014: 23–36.

Nakane, C. (1970). *Japanese Society*, Berkeley, California: University of California Press.

Nakata, Y. and Miyazaki, S. (2011). The labor market for Japanese scientists and engineers: is the labor market externalized? What has happened at their workplace? *Japan Labor Review*, 8(3): 95–118.

Namikawa, K. (2013). *Nihon No Work Life Balance*. Rōdō Keizai Kenkyukai, Monthly Meeting, 8 November 2013. Tokyo: Rōdō Keizai Kenkyukai.

Natsume, K. (2007). *New Recruit White Paper 07/08* (in Japanese), Tokyo: Labor Productivity Information Center.

Nikkeiren (1995). *The Current Labor Economy in Japan*, Tokyo: Japan Federation of Employers' Associations.

OECD (2009). *Jobs for Youth, Japan*, Paris: OECD.

Ouchi, W.G. (1981). *Theory Z: How American Business Can Meet the Japanese Challenge*, Reading, MA: Addison-Wesley.

Rohlen, T. (1974). *For Harmony and Strength: Japanese White Collar Organization in Anthropological Perspective*, Berkeley, CA: University of California Press.

Sato, H. (2013). Muki koyo no tagenka to kigyo no jinzai katsuyō no kadai (Diversification of regular employment and issues of the use of human resources in companies). *Tōkyō Daigaku Jōhō Gakkyo*, April 2013: 1–4.

Scott, N. (2014). Limited regular employment and the reform of Japan's division of labor. *The Asia-Pacific Journal*, 12(1): 1–10.

Sugimoto, Y. (2010). *An Introduction to Japanese Society*, Cambridge, UK: Cambridge University Press.

Uenishi, M. (2013). Employment of new graduates. *Japan Labor Review*, 10: 80–89.

Weathers, C. (2009). Non regular workers and inequality in Japan. *Social Science Japan Journal*, 12: 143–148.

Whittaker, D. H. (1990). The end of Japanese-style management? *Work, Employment, and Society*, 4: 321–347.

Wolff, L. (2011). Lifelong employment, labor law and the lost decade: the end of a job for life in Japan. In: Haghirian, P. (ed.), *Innovation and Change in Japanese Management*, Basingstoke: Palgrave Macmillan, pp. 77–99.

14

Promotion and compensation

Harald Conrad

Introduction

Japanese firms' compensation practices have undergone significant changes over the last two decades, while promotion systems have been fairly stable. The purpose of this chapter is to outline what we might like to call 'traditional' promotion and compensation practices as they were prevalent until the 1990s, and then discuss the changes that we have been witnessing over the last two decades. The chapter is structured as follows. In order to set the stage for an analysis of recent changes in promotion and pay practices, we will first take a brief look at the historical development of the modern pay systems and introduce some of the key explanatory factors in the second section. This is followed by an overview of the traditional practices in the third section, and a discussion of the driving factors for reform in the fourth section. The fifth section describes and analyses recent changes before the chapter closes with a short conclusion.[1]

Historical developments and interdependencies

Seniority-based pay (*nenkō joretsu chingin*), which is closely linked to seniority-based promotion, has often been described as one of the so-called 'three pillars of the Japanese employment system', the two others being lifetime employment (*shūshin koyō*) and in-house company unions (*kigyōbetsu kumiai*) (e.g. OECD 1977; Debroux 2003). How did seniority-based pay develop and what were the key explanatory factors for this development? During the late nineteenth century, Japanese wage systems in the private sector were basically characterized by a combination of day wages and payment by the job or the piece, but many companies had already started to construct wage ladders of greater or lesser complexity to encourage white-collar workers to rise in rank and pay within the enterprise. Yet, the fact that regular 'seniority wage increases' became nearly universal in the heavy industry sector and other sectors of the economy by the end of the Second World War was primarily the result of government regulation and informal government pressure during the war economy of the 1930s and 1940s. The authorities at the time aimed to restrict labour movement and improve industrial productivity through job security and wages that met livelihood or life-cycle needs, with age as the best single proxy for need (Gordon 1985: 43–45, 257–298).[2]

After the Second World War, employers hoped to move away from these livelihood wages. The emerging management–labour compromise thus saw the establishment of wage systems, which consisted of several components reflecting mostly livelihood factors like age, educational background, and gender, but also production quota and incentive pay factors (Gordon 1985: 374–386). Following the slowdown of the economy at the end of the catch-up period, and as a result of mounting employers' pressure in the later 1960s, the weight of the living-cost and seniority elements was gradually reduced, while work-related elements increased. At the centre of these changes was the so-called skill-grading system (*shokunō shikaku seido*), which aimed to link employees' skills to pay levels, a system that was actively promoted by Nikkeiren from the mid-1960s onwards (NNKK 1969; Rebick 2005). Thus, wages were, for the most part, no longer directly linked to age or tenure, but, since employees' skills were judged to increase with longer tenure, the new systems were (as we will discuss later), in practice, still very much seniority-oriented.

The fact that seniority-oriented wages became widely accepted in the post-war period cannot only be attributed to a political compromise or ideological factors. These practices did not only satisfy perceived societal needs, but fitted in well with the emerging Japanese production system. In particular, Aoki (1988, 1990, 1994) has highlighted the institutional complementarities between human-resource management practices and the production system of Japanese companies. He has shown how many, especially larger, Japanese production facilities have developed operation modes where horizontal mutual coordination amongst operating units is of utmost importance. In this way, planning and implementing operations are not strictly hierarchically structured, and rotation of employees between engineering and workshop personnel is practised frequently. This team-work approach, where operating units are expected to mutually coordinate their tasks, requires an incentive mode, which allows individual workers to commit themselves fully to the team-work process without fear of losing compensation. Since workers are expected to cope independently with the needed changes or problems in the production process, they need autonomous problem-solving capabilities, which are nurtured by frequent job rotations. Such rotations familiarize workers with various jobs and enhance their ability to process and communicate information back into the production process. The immediate use of on-site information in quality control and production planning – such as the famous *kanban* system – has become a key explanatory factor for the competitive strength of many Japanese manufacturers.

According to Aoki, the production mode described above requires distinctive incentives to ensure that individual workers commit themselves to a team-based effort. Japanese companies have therefore designed incentives that are not tightly related to a specific job category, but that motivate wide-ranging job experience amongst employees. At the centre of their incentive schemes are rank hierarchies – with separate rank hierarchies for blue-collar workers, white-collar workers, and engineers, as well as for supervisory and managerial employees. Each rank is usually associated with a certain range of pay, which consists – as will be discussed in more detail later – of several pay elements. Employees of the same educational background and tenure cohort (*nenji*) start their company careers with identical pay, and for some years – usually until they are in their thirties – they are promoted at an equal speed. A comparative study of the Japan Institute of Labor (RSKKK 1998) shows that the first real selection for promotion amongst members of the same tenure cohort is held 7.9 years after recruitment, substantially later than in the United States (3.4 years) and Germany (3.7 years). Japanese workers, thus, only start to compete for promotions in positions around their mid-thirties. At this stage, it is usually a competition about promotion to section chief (*kachō*), while those falling behind still have another chance to be promoted in later years. It is only in their early forties that Japanese workers lose their chances of being promoted. At this stage, promotions are typically a competition by tournament over department chief (*buchō*) posts. Only winners of these competitions can subsequently be promoted to higher positions.

The central criteria for promotions are the number of years of continuous employment and merit. According to the underlying skill-grading system, merit does not so much depend on a particular job or output, but is broadly defined by problem-solving and communication skills, as well as other qualifications. Thus, employees are neither rewarded for achieving a given well-defined objective nor in respect of a subjective evaluation of their performance. Frequent appraisals assess potential ability based on adaptability to technical changes, as well as soft skills such as loyalty and the ability to cooperate well with other workers. It is also important to note that speed of promotion does vary in an employee's later years – with some reaching higher ranks only shortly before the mandatory company retirement age, whereas others proceed to supervisory ranks in mid-career – and that those who do not show continuous progress might be posted to minor subsidiaries or affiliated companies.

Overview of traditional compensation practices

The last section outlined the important relationship between the promotional rank-hierarchy system and compensation practices. However, while *promotion* systems have not changed fundamentally over the last two decades, *compensation* practices have been substantially transformed. In order to understand this, it is important to note that compensation is not simply a function of rank. In fact, pay systems have been, and for the most part remain, highly complex, and take into account numerous factors. Table 14.1 gives an overview of typical pay components in Japanese companies.

According to the General Survey on Working Conditions, which covers establishments with more than 30 employees, total compensation can be divided into 78.9 per cent monthly cash payments and 21.1 per cent twice-yearly bonuses. At 67.6 per cent, base pay makes up the largest portion of total compensation. Furthermore, various allowances for the family, commuting, housing, etc., make up another 5 per cent of the total compensation (Rebick 2005: 45).

Base pay closely reflects the position of employees in the rank-hierarchy, and is a function of ability/skills (*shokunōkyū*), age (*nenreikyū*), and performance (*seisekikyū*). However, the latter has so far played only a marginal role, whereas ability/skills and age have been the most important determinants.[3] Most companies used to have a pay component which was explicitly and directly linked to age, but ability/skills as criteria for the evaluation in the skill-grading system have in principle been the most important factors for base pay.

Bonuses have traditionally been paid bi-annually. Although there might be the expectation that they have been a kind of profit-sharing scheme, academic opinion on this issue has been divided, with some stressing the profit-sharing aspect (e.g. Freeman and Weitzman 1987), but

Table 14.1 Typical pay components in Japanese companies

Standard pay (*kijunnai chingin*)	Base pay (*kihonkyū*)
	• Age pay (*nenreikyū*)
	• Ability/skill pay (*shokunōkyū*)
	• Performance pay (*seisekikyū*)
	Family pay (*kazokukyū*)
	Work-site allowance (*gengyōteate*)

most others downplaying it (e.g. Ohashi 1989; Brunello 1991; Morishima 2002). Bonus payments have usually been negotiated twice a year between employers and labour unions, and the latter have, at least until recently, considered bonuses as part of regular pay, which should not be linked to company profits. Kato and Morishima (2003) confirm that only about one in four publicly traded firms use profit-sharing plans (PSP), where the total amount of bonuses is linked to a measure of firm performance, such as profit.

Pressures for change

During the latter half of the 1990s, the above-described promotion and pay practices have come under increasing critique. Underlying this critique are various challenges that will be shortly reviewed in this section.

Probably the single most important challenge is the ageing of Japanese society and the resulting increase in the number of older employees. The percentage of people over fifty in the Japanese labour force increased from 18 per cent in 1985 to 28.4 per cent in 2012 (the most recent data available) (Sōmuchō Tōkeikyoku 2014). Given the age-related compensation and promotion practices, this has led to a quasi-automatic increase in labour costs and a need to create more managerial positions, although a worsening business climate and a general trend towards organizational structures with fewer managerial layers and flatter hierarchies would, on the contrary, indicate that steps should be taken in the opposite direction. Since the mid-1990s, companies have therefore striven to reduce overall personnel expenditure and to turn fixed expenditure into variable costs (Ogoshi 2006).

However, as Abe (2007) points out, rising labour-management costs alone cannot explain the shift to the new salary systems, because there were also periods in the past, especially in the 1970s and early 1980s, during which labour costs surpassed company income, but which did not lead to any fundamental changes. Technological innovations also seem to have played an important role in recent reforms. Innovation in information and communications technology has led to a mismatch between the skills of many older white-collar workers and the sort of skills that are actually required. The new pay systems try to address this problem with a new incentive structure (Abe 2007).

Overall, the fast-changing business environment and the use of IT have made it harder to rely on continuous long-term technological progress and generalist skills, which have so far been the comparative strengths of Japanese companies (Miyamoto and Higuchi 2007). Related to this point is the problem that the skill-grading system assumes a constant accumulation of skills and, in principle, does not take into account whether certain skills may have become obsolete due to technological changes (Shakai Keizai Seisan Honbu 2000: 45).

Empirical evidence of changes and their analysis

As a result of the pressures described, in the 1990s a growing number of Japanese companies started to look for new incentive tools. Due to a growing diversity of pay systems across and within companies, generic features are nowadays much harder to identify than in the past, when companies often followed similar models. Nevertheless, we might try to summarize the general trend in the pay-system reforms as far as they relate to the core labour-force (excluding the growing ranks of part-time workers) as follows (based on Ishida 2006; Nakamura 2006; NRSKKK 2006): pay systems of managers (section or department managers and above) show the greatest changes, whereas changes for rank-and-file employees remain more limited, but are also significant. Generally, the number of pay components is decreasing.

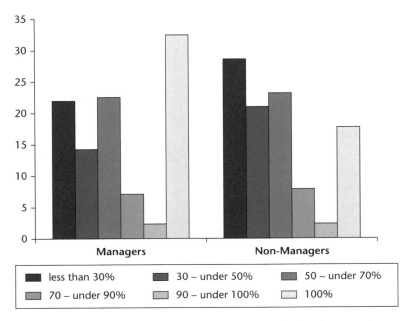

Figure 14.1 Weight of the role/job pay component (*yakuwarikyū*) in base pay in per cent
Source: Shakai Keizai Seisansei Honbu (2006: 13)

More and more companies are eliminating or at least reducing age-based pay (*nenreikyū*), as well as the different allowances (for good examples see the cases discussed by Shibata 2000 and Nakajima, Matsushige, and Umezaki 2004). For management positions, ability/skill pay (*shokunōkyū*) is often abolished, whereas it continues to play an important but also diminishing role for rank-and-file employees. Accordingly, the surveys of the Japan Productivity Center for Socio-Economic Development indicate that between 2000 and 2005, the percentage of companies that claimed to have ability/skill pay declined from 82.4 per cent to 57.5 per cent for managers, and from 87 per cent to 70.1 per cent for non-managers (Shakai Keizai Seisansei Honbu 2006: 19).[4]

For workers in managerial positions, regular pay rises, which formed the core of the seniority-based wage system, have more or less been abolished. For these workers, ability/skill pay is often replaced with a pay component that reflects a particular job class or hierarchical role that an employee fulfils in an organization (*yakuwarikyū*). As can be seen in Figure 14.1, in over 30 per cent of companies, role/job pay for manager-class workers makes up 100 per cent of base pay.

Frequently, this job or role pay-component consists of a fixed amount and a performance-related part, resulting in a monthly salary range. Managers within each class, thus, receive different and fluctuating salaries, depending on the assessment of their performance.

Although role/job pay also plays an increasingly important role for non-managerial workers, the overall weight of this component, and, consequently, the significance of performance for pay determination, still remain limited. Table 14.2 indicates how the weighting of the different pay components might change over an employee's career course.

Table 14.3 summarizes the direction of the current pay reforms for the most important pay components, excluding welfare benefits.

Table 14.2 Model of the relative importance of different wage components over the course of a career

	Non-managerial workers	Lower managers	Section chief	Department chief
	20s	30s	40s	50s
Age pay (nenreikyū) Seikatsushugi	OO	O	–	–
Ability/skill pay (shokunōkyū) Nōryōkushugi	O	OO	OO	O
Role/job pay (yakuwarikyū) Seikashugi	–	–	O	OO

Source: Shakai Keizai Seisansei Honbu (2002: 17)

What is being evaluated as performance varies amongst companies, and is commonly a combination of individual and/or team performance. With regard to the performance appraisals, it is important to note that performance is only rarely assessed in terms of simple quantitative results such as sales, profits, or cost reductions, etc. Such an approach might possibly work for sales personnel (where sales commissions are commonly found as a top-up for a fixed minimum pay), but, in general, it is not regarded as suitable, because it neglects various factors which are beyond the influence of individual sales people. The new performance systems focus generally on what Nakamura (2006; 2007) calls process-oriented, performance-based salary systems (*purosesu jūjigata seika shugi*). Here, performance is evaluated not only in terms of the degree of success in achieving quantitative goals, but also in terms of the process of achieving those goals. Although performance has, thus, gained in importance as a determining variable for pay, skill factors have not been abolished, and skill-grading systems still play a large role – at least for rank-and-file employees. However, whereas companies used to operate with an all-embracing concept of skills, which included personal attributes such as educational background and age (with a focus on 'capable of doing'), the evolving systems focus more strongly on work-related, usable skills and performance (with a focus on 'doing'), with much less emphasis on the age factor. In line with this transformation, the rather vague assessment of skills in the past has been replaced with more objective 'management by objectives' appraisal systems. Despite the continuation of skill-based pay systems for rank-and-file employees, this change in skill assessment has, in principle, capped age-related wage increases as they were found in the past.

Probably the most visible change affecting all types of workers can be witnessed in the handling of bonus payments. Bonuses used to be paid as a certain number of months' worth of base pay, usually not strongly reflecting personal or company performance. Although there are still differences in arrangements for manager-class and rank-and-file employees, the new bonus systems are commonly split into at least two parts. One part is still paid as a certain multiple of base pay (which, as already described, now depends more strongly on individual performance in the case of managers, whereas it is still very much skill-based for rank-and-file employees). The other part depends on the employees' performance, with a stronger emphasis on the end results for the managers, and more emphasis on proven abilities for the rank-and-file workers. Furthermore, some companies add a bonus payment component that is explicitly linked to company performance over the past year.

Table 14.3 Common changes in pay systems in companies that have introduced performance-based pay

	Past	Present/future	Type of workers affected
Base pay	– A function of age pay (*nenreikyū*), ability/skill pay (*shokunōkyū*), and – performance pay (*seisekikyū*) with different weightings depending on the career stage	– Greater weight attached to the performance pay component, while ability/skill pay and age pay components are reduced or eliminated – In some cases, base pay is transferred to: annualized pay schemes where the part of the annual salary that is comparable with the old base pay remains more or less unchanged, while the part comparable with the twice-yearly bonus depends on individual and/ or firm performance	– All types of regular workers, while the performance-orientation is strongest for managerial workers – Annualized schemes are usually limited to managerial and specialist workers
Allowances	– Various livelihood allowances reflecting the idea of a 'living wage' based on the different stages of life	– Livelihood allowances are often transferred to base pay	– All types of regular workers – Especially workers in upper management positions and specialists who are being paid by an annual salary scheme
Bonuses	– Usually paid semi-annually as a defined number of months' worth of base pay with little consideration of firm or employees' performance	– More and more companies split their bonuses into various components, including a fixed amount and a flexible amount linked to firm, individual, and/ or group performance	– All types of regular workers, although the bonuses of managerial workers tend to have a larger performance-based component
Employees' appraisal	– Focus on latent skills, with a strong seniority orientation	– Stronger focus on proven and relevant skills, with less seniority orientation – Many companies have introduced management-by-objective schemes and use the concept of competency (involving behavioural assessment)	– All types of regular workers

Note: This table highlights some stylized facts about those companies that have introduced performance-based pay. It needs to be kept in mind that there are major differences in the way that companies introduce and mix the different measures

Source: The author based this table on the work of Sasajima Yoshio and Shakai Keizai Seisansei Honbu (2000, 2002, 2003, 2004, 2007); Rebick (2005); and JILPT (2009)

How common are these new performance-based salary systems? In terms of the statistical definitions, companies are assumed to have introduced pay-for-performance systems if they assess and reflect an individual's performance in his/her wage, regardless of how much weight is attached to the performance-related part and how performance is measured. Based on such a broad definition, the General Survey on Working Conditions (KDKTJ 2012), covering 6,128 companies with more than 30 employees and a response rate of 71.1 per cent, reports that 42.2 per cent of companies are reflecting performance factors in base pay. However, there are marked differences depending on company size. Whereas 60.4 per cent of companies with more than 1,000 employees claim that they reflect performance factors in base pay, only 38.3 per cent of companies with 30–99 employees state the same.

How successful have the reformed systems been? In general, performance-related pay systems are introduced with the expectation of increased performance. The most common explanation, stemming from 'agency theory' in personnel economics, is that such systems can improve employee motivation, which in turn can increase productivity and profits. Other factors that can influence productivity include effects on the willingness to collaborate in groups, to increase competence, or to focus on strategic tasks (see, for example, Prendergast 1999 for a comprehensive review of the theoretical issues).

Unfortunately, cross-sectional statistical analyses on the effects of the new pay-for-performance systems on labour productivity and labour costs are rare, and have rather limited validity because they are not entirely based on firm-level data. However, one study by Miyamoto and Higuchi (2007), which compares firm-level data about the introduction of pay-for-performance systems with industrial-level data about labour costs in 481 firms, highlights some interesting issues. Their regression analysis reveals that labour productivity and firm performance (measured as return on sales) has increased only in firms where the introduction of the new pay systems was accompanied by suitable measures of procedural fairness. Only companies which disclosed their appraisal standards and results to their employees; which had a grievance system for employees to express their unhappiness; and which had appropriate communication in the decision-making process, showed a statistically significant, yet still weak, improvement in terms of labour productivity and firm performance after the introduction of pay-for-performance systems. In other words, the introduction of pay-for-performance systems *per se* does not seem to have improved firm performance if these systems are not operated in a fair manner – an issue to which I will return (Miyamoto and Higuchi 2007).

Overall, actual wage effects have not been as radical as the term '*seika shugi*' might suggest. One factor contributing to this finding is probably that companies are still in the process of adjusting their pay practices after the initial changes often had negative repercussions on organizational effectiveness. In particular, survey results indicate that the most difficult aspects of the new systems have been problems with the personnel evaluation systems (Rōmu Gyōsei Kenkyūjo 2005; KDKTJ 2007). These sorts of problems have also been at the heart of the criticism that was voiced in popular books on the topic, such as those by Jō (2004) and Takahashi (2004). Jō (2004) identified a number of problems at Fujitsu, one of the forerunners in the introduction of performance-based pay, that Meyer-Ohle's (2009) analysis of employees' Internet blog entrees showed not to be restricted to Fujitsu: a decline in morale due to grouping in predetermined performance bands; a split in the workforce and a decline in productivity due to the setting of contradictory objectives; a focus on narrow objectives to the detriment of irregular but important or strategic tasks; and an increase in unpaid overtime.

Many companies had to concede that they opted prematurely for an increase in performance-based pay without establishing clearly the criteria for what was relevant to performance, and without institutionalizing the evaluation processes which trained managers and allowed them to discuss evaluation results with subordinates. Morishima (1997), Fujimura (1998) and Tsuru (2001) have stressed the importance of fairness in adjustments of employee-evaluation systems, and clarity in evaluation in order to ensure that employees accept the new performance-based systems, while Genda, Kanbayashi, and Shinozaki (2001) have shown that combining such systems with education and training programmes increases employees' motivation.

Numerous companies are, thus, still fine-tuning their reward and appraisal systems to meet such challenges. Finding clear criteria for individual performance is, however, not always easy, because job descriptions in operational types of work are usually not very clear, and the lines between individual job and team activities are frequently blurred. For this reason, a number of companies focus not only on individual but also on team performance.

Conclusions

This chapter has sought to shed light on the ongoing transformation of Japanese promotion and compensation practices. While promotion practices have not changed fundamentally since the 1990s, it is clear that many companies are currently experimenting with new compensation practices and that performance-related pay components are becoming increasingly popular. However, these changes do not affect workers on all hierarchical levels in the same way, and tend to apply more to managerial than non-managerial workers. Moreover, the particular understanding of what performance-based pay means, how to measure performance, and whether and to what degree to focus on individual and/or group performance, varies across firms.

As for the future, we have strong reasons to assume that the adoption of performance-based pay practices is irreversible. In particular, legal regulations concerning the minimum mandatory retirement age (e.g. the Law Concerning the Stabilization of Employment of Older Persons) are expected to strengthen the reliance on performance-based pay. As the Japanese state is likely to require Japanese firms to employ their older workers for longer years in order to address higher life expectancies and rising public-welfare expenditures, more companies will have an incentive to flatten their age–wage profiles in the future.

Notes

1 Parts of this chapter are based on earlier contributions of this author, namely Conrad (2010) and Conrad (2013).
2 For a detailed account of the history of the seniority-based wage system, see also Magota (1970).
3 For a detailed example of a traditional pay system, see Shibata (2000).
4 However, it should be noted that the numbers from the different surveys are not directly comparable, because the responding firms are not necessarily identical. The surveys, conducted yearly amongst 2,300–2,700 stock-listed firms, have had response rates from the years 2000 to 2005 varying between 9.2 per cent and 13.3 per cent.

References

Abe, Masahiro (2007). Why companies in Japan are introducing performance-based treatment and reward systems – the background, merits and demerits. *Japan Labor Review*, 4(2): 7–36.
Aoki, Masahiko (1988). *Information, Incentives and Bargaining in the Japanese Economy*, New York and Melbourne: Cambridge University Press.
Aoki, Masahiko (1990). Toward an economic model of the Japanese firm. *Journal of Economic Literature*, 28(1): 1–27.

Aoki, Masahiko (1994). The Japanese firm as a system of attributes: a survey and research agenda. In: Aoki, Masahiko and Dore, Ronald (eds), *The Japanese Firm: The Sources of Competitive Strength*, Oxford, UK; and New York: Oxford University Press, pp. 11–40.

Brunello, Giorgio (1991). Bonuses, wages and performances in Japan: evidence from micro data. *Ricerche Economiche*, 45(2–3): 377–396.

Conrad, Harald (2010). From seniority to performance principle – the evolution of pay practices in Japanese firms since the 1990s. *Social Science Japan Journal*, 13(1): 115–135.

Conrad, Harald (2013). Converging to a new type of human resource management? – compensation system reforms in Japan since the 1990s. In: Kushida, Kenji, Shimizu, Kay, and Oi, Jean C. (eds), *Syncretism: the Politics of Economic Restructuring and System Reform in Japan*, APARC/Brookings Institution, Washington DC, pp. 173–197.

Debroux, Philippe (2003). *Human Resource Management in Japan: Changes and Uncertainties*, Hampshire, UK: Ashgate.

Freeman, Richard B., and Weitzman, Martin L. (1987). Bonuses and employment in Japan. *Journal of the Japanese and International Economy*, 1(2): 168–194.

Fujimura, Hiroyuki (1998). Kanrishoku ni yoru hyōka seido no unyō – sa wo tsukeru jinji seido ha kano ka. (The operation of an appraisal system by managers – is a personnel system seeking disparity possible?) *Nihon Rōdō Kenkyū Zasshi*, 460: 17–27.

Genda, Yuichi, Kambayashi, Ryo, and Shinozaki, Takehisa (2001). Seikashugi to nōryoku kaihatsu: kekka toshite no rōdō iyoku. (Performance-related pay and skill development: the resulting motivation to work) *Soshiki Kagaku*, 34(3): 18–31.

Gordon, Andrew (1985). *The Evolution of Labor Relations in Japan – Heavy Industry, 1853–1955*, Cambridge, MA: Harvard University Press.

Ishida, Mitsuo (2006). Chingin seido kaikaku to rōshi kankei. (Wage system reform and industrial relations). In: Rengō Sōgō Seikatsu Kaihatsu Kenkyūjo (ed.), *Chingin Seido to Rōdō Kumiai no Torikumi ni Kan Suru Chōsa Kenkyū Hōkokusho*. (Report on a Survey about the Wage System and Labour Union Response). Tokyo: Rengō Sōgō Seikatsu Kaihatsu Kenkyūjo, pp. 11–49.

JILPT (Japan Institute for Labour Policy and Training) (2009). *Labor Situation in Japan and Analysis: Detailed Exposition 2009/2010*, Tokyo: JILPT.

Jō, Shigeyuki (2004). *Uchigawa Kara Mita Fujitsu – 'Seika Shugi' no Hōkai* (An Inside Look at Fujitsu – the Collapse of the Performance-based Pay System.) Tokyo: Kōbunsha.

Kato, Takao and Morishima, Motohiro (2003). The nature, scope and effects of profit sharing in Japan: Evidence from new survey data. *The International Journal of Human Resource Management*, 14 (6): 942–955.

KDKTJ (Kōseirōdōshō Daijin Kanbō Tōkei Jōhōbu) (2007). *Heisei 19-nenpan Shūrō Jōken Sōgō Chōsa* (2007 General Survey on Working Conditions). Tokyo: Rōdō Kōsei Kenkyūjo.

KDKTJ (Kōseirōdōshō Daijin Kanbō Tōkei Jōhōbu) (2012). *Heisei 24-nenpan Shūrō Jōken Sōgō Chōsa*. (2012 General Survey on Working Conditions), Tokyo: Rōdō Kōsei Kenkyūjo.

Magota, Ryōhei (1970). *Nenkō Chingin no Ayumi to Mirai: Chingin Taikei 100-Nenshi*. (The Development of Seniority-oriented Pay and its Future – a 100-year History of Wages), Tokyo: Sangyō Rōdō Kenkyūjo.

Meyer-Ohle, Hendrik (2009). *Japanese Workplaces in Transition – Employee Perceptions*, Basingstoke, UK: Palgrave Macmillan.

Miyamoto, Dai and Higuchi, Junpe (2007). Paying for success: performance-related pay systems and its effects on firm performance in Japan. *Asian Business and Management*, 6: 9–31.

Morishima, Motohiro (1997). Kigyōnai chingin kakusa no soshikironteki inpurikeshon. (Organizational implications of firm-level wage disparities). *Nihon Rōdō Kenkyū Zasshi*, 449: 27–36.

Morishima, Motohiro (2002). Pay practices in Japanese organizations: changes and non-changes. *Japan Labor Bulletin*, 1 April: 8–13.

Nakajima, Tetsuo, Matsushige, Hisakazu, and Umezaki, Osamu (2004). Chingin to satei ni mirareru seika shugi dōnyū no kōka – kigyō nai maikurodeta ni yoru bunseki. (The effect of the introduction of performance-based pay on wages and assessment – an analysis based on firm-level data). *Nihon Keizai Kenkyū*, 48: 18–33.

Nakamura, Keisuke (2006). *Seika Shugi no Jijitsu* (The Truth about Performance-based Pay), Tōkyō: Tōyō Keizai Shinpōsha.

Nakamura, Keisuke (2007). Seika shugi to jinji kaikaku. (The performance-based salary system and personnel management reforms in Japan). *Nihon Rōdō Zasshi*, 560: 43–47.

NNKK (Nikkeiren Nōryōkushugi Kanri Kenkyūkai) (1969). Nōryōku Shugi Kanri: Sono Riron to Jissen (Administration of Skill-based Pay – Theory and Practice), Tokyo: Nihon Keieisha Dantei Renmei Kōhōbu.

NRSKKK (Nihon Rōdō Seisaku Kenkyū Kenshū Kikō) (2006). Gendai nihon kigyō no jinzai manejimento (The contemporary management of Japanese companies). *Rōdō Seisaku Kenkyū Hokokusho*, 61.

OECD (1977). *The Development of Industrial Systems: Some Implications of the Japanese Experience*, Paris: OECD.

Ogoshi, Yonosuke (2006). Current Japanese employment practices and industrial relations: the transformation of permanent employment and seniority-based wage system. *Asian Business and Management*, 5: 469–485.

Ohashi, Isao (1989). On the determinants of bonuses and basic wages in large Japanese firms. *Journal of the Japanese and International Economy*, 3(4): 451–479.

Prendergast, Canice (1999). The provision of incentives in firms. *Journal of Economic Literature*, 37(1): 7–63.

Rebick, Marcus (2005). *The Japanese Employment System – Adapting to a New Economic Environment*. Oxford, UK: Oxford University Press.

Rengō Sōgō Seikatsu Kaihatsu Kenkyūjo (2005). *Chingin Seido to Rōdō Kumiai no Torikumi ni Kan Suru Chōsa Kenkyū Chūkan Hōkokusho* (Intermediate Report on a Survey About the Wage System and Labour Union Response). Tokyo: Rengō Sōgō Seikatsu Kaihatsu Kenkyūjo.

Rōmu Gyōsei Kenkyūjo (2005). *Seika Shugi Jinji Seido no Dōnyū Kōka to Mondaiten*. (The Results and Problems in the Introduction of Performance-based Pay Systems). Tokyo: Rōmu Gyōsei Kenkyūjo.

RSKKK (Rōdō Seisaku Kenkyū Kenshū Kikō) (1998). *Kokusai Hikaku – Daisotsu Howaitokara no Jinzai Kaihatsu, Koyō Shisutemu – Nichi, Bei, Ei, Doku no Daikigyō*. (An International Comparison of Human Resources Development and Employment Systems in Japan, US, UK and Germany) http://db.jil. go.jp/db/seika/zenbun/E2000014381_ZEN.htm, last accessed 16 October 2015.

Sasajima, Yoshio and Shakai Keizai Seisansei Honbu (2000, 2002, 2003, 2004, 2007). *Seika Shugi Jinji Chingin IV, V, VI, VII, IX* (Performance-based Pay – Examples from Various Companies). Tokyo: Shakai Keizai Seisansei Honbu Seisansei Rōdō Jōhō Sentā.

Shakai Keizai Seisansei Honbu (2000, 2002, 2006). *Nihonteki Jinji Seido no Genjō to Kadai*. (Actual State and Issues of the Japanese Human Resource Management System). Tokyo: Shakai Keizai Seisansei Honbu Seisansei Rōdō Jōhō Sentā.

Shibata, Hiromichi (2000). The transformation of the wage and performance appraisal system in a Japanese firm. *The International Journal of Human Resource Management*, 11(2): 294–313.

Sōmuchō Tōkeikyoku (2014). *Heisei 26-nen Nihon tōkei nenpo* (Japan Statistical Yearbook 2014), Tokyo: Sōmushō Tōkeikyoku.

Takahashi, Nobuo (2004). *Kyomō no Seika Shugi – Nihon-Gata Nenkosei Fukkatsu no Susume* (The Delusion of the Performance-based Pay System – the Revival of the Japanese-style Seniority-based System), Tokyo: Nikkei BP.

Tsuru, Tsuyoshi (2001). Jinji hyōka to chingin kakusa ni tai suru jugyōingawa no hannō: aru seizōgyō kigyō no jirei bunseki. (The response of employees to personnel appraisal and wage disparity: analysis from a manufacturing company). *Keizai Kenkyū*, 52(2): 143–156.

Company welfare benefit systems

Harald Conrad

Introduction

Given that monthly salaries and bonuses make up over 80 per cent of a typical Japanese employee's compensation package, it is not surprising that most observers have tended to focus primarily on changes to these pay components in discussions of changes from seniority-oriented to performance-oriented compensation systems since the 1990s. However, Japanese companies have traditionally been known for very comprehensive welfare benefit systems (*fukuri kōsei seido*), which have also undergone substantial changes in recent years. A full understanding of compensation system reforms thus requires a thorough understanding of the characteristics of and recent changes in these schemes. After an overview of the different types of employee-welfare benefits in the next (second) section of this chapter, the third section focuses briefly on pressures for change, while the fourth section discusses the nature of recent changes. The chapter finishes with a short conclusion.[1]

A strong tradition of comprehensive employee-welfare benefits

Japanese firms have long been noted for institutional features that set them apart from their counterparts in Western industrialized countries (e.g. Abegglen 1958). These unique features have been found in inter-firm relationships, finance, and corporate governance patterns, as well as in employment practices (e.g. Aoki 1988; Vogel 2006). In particular, the academic literature has frequently made references to the so-called 'three pillars of the traditional Japanese employment system', namely 'seniority-based pay', 'lifetime employment', and 'enterprise labour unions' (e.g. Debroux 2003). While recent studies have shown that pay systems have become more performance-oriented during the last two decades, far less is known about changes in Japanese employee-benefit systems, which form an integral and important part of traditional compensation practices.

Table 15.1 gives an overview of the wide variety of employee-welfare benefits that large Japanese firms have traditionally offered.

We have to note here that Japanese observers commonly differentiate between welfare benefit schemes (*fukuri kōsei*) and occupational pensions (*kigyō nenkin*). The principal reason

Table 15.1 Traditional employee-benefit schemes of Japanese firms

Housing support

– Housing allowance and rent aid
– Company housing (for families; company-owned or contracted out)
– Company housing (for bachelors; company-owned or contracted out)
– Loan and/or financial-support scheme for the acquisition of employee-owned housing

Medical support

– Yearly medical examination (in addition to statutory requirements)
– Medical examinations for lifestyle-related illnesses
– Monetary aid for out-of-pocket medical expenses
– Mental-health consultation
– Income compensation system for non-working employees with long-term disabilities
– Monetary assistance for fertility-related medical expenses

Child-care support

– Child-care and baby-sitter support
– Nursery (company-owned or contracted out)
– System of child-care leave and/or shorter working hours during child-care
– Information system to keep employees on child-care leave updated about work
– Web-based bulletin board for employees on child-care leave
– Income support for employees on child-care leave

Financial assistance

– Monetary gifts for celebrations (e.g. marriage, childbirth, school entrance)
– Monetary gifts for condolences and hospital visits
– Informational support for private insurance
– Workers' asset accumulation or internal financial deposit system
– Employee stock-ownership plans
– Employee stock options
– Mutual aid insurance
– Financial assistance for employees' cafeteria food consumption
– Support system to pay private insurance contributions directly out of employees' monthly pay

Pension benefits

– Lump-sum retirement payment for dependants of a deceased employee
– Survivors' pensions, orphans' pensions, and orphans' educational grants
– Defined benefit pension plan
– Lump-sum retirement benefit
– Defined contribution pension plan (401k-plan)

Long-term care support

– Dispatch of long-term care helper (including financial assistance)
– Income support for employees on long-term care leave

Recreational benefits

– Workplace cafeteria
– Leisure facilities (company-owned or contractual-type: resort and sports facilities)
– Financial support of club activities
– System to facilitate taking a longer vacation once a year (longer than one week)
– Organization or support of workplace vacations

– Organization or support of company sports' days
– Organization or support of meetings to acknowledge someone's achievements (e.g. group drinking events)
– Organization or support of company competitions

Education support

– Life-planning courses/seminars
– Financial-planning courses/seminars
– Preparatory education for soon be to retired employees
– System to facilitate external studies (at foreign or domestic colleges or companies)
– Support for acquisition of official qualifications and correspondence courses
– Long-term leave system for personal development/refreshment

Note: In the 1980s some companies introduced so-called 'cafeteria plans', which offer a wide variety of the benefits listed here and allow employees to choose freely from those benefits up to a designated point value
Source: the author based this table on Meiji Yasuda Seikatsu Fukushi Kenkyūjo (2008)

for this is that pension benefits, regardless of their financing mode, have been considered largely as a form of deferred wages, while this has not been the case for the other types of employee benefits. However, in this chapter we do not follow this Japanese convention but rather international practice, according to which occupational pension benefits are commonly considered to be an integral part of employee-welfare benefit systems (e.g. Dulebohn *et al.* 2009).

As can be gathered from Table 15.1, large Japanese employers have traditionally offered a large array of welfare benefits to their employees. Such benefits include housing support, medical support, child-care support, financial assistance, pension benefits, long-term-care support, recreational benefits, and education support. While non-regular workers have, to a large extent, been excluded from these benefits, regular employees are commonly and comprehensively covered. Overall, these benefits have been part of a human-resource management system that one might characterize as paternalistic: seniority-based pay with comprehensive benefit packages, high employment security, extensive on- and off-job training, and comparatively little employee influence.

As Table 15.2 indicates, occupational pensions make up the largest part of voluntarily offered welfare benefits, regardless of company size.

Most large, but also many medium-sized, Japanese companies have traditionally offered a defined-benefit (DB) occupational pension and/or final lump-sum retirement payments that

Table 15.2 Composition of average monthly labour costs in 2011 (all industries; in Japanese yen)

Company size (employees)	Total labour costs	Total wages (including bonus)	Legally mandated welfare benefits (social-security contributions)	Occupational pensions	Other: voluntary welfare benefits
Over 1,000	477,136	379,854	49,130	31,509	13,042
300–999	411,721	335,680	44,000	22,034	7,017
100–299	379,210	313,841	43,315	14,469	5,579
30–99	350,911	296,013	39,939	8,795	4,587

Source: Kōseirōdōshō (2011)

mirrored the seniority-oriented pay structure of employees' base pay. In DB plans, employees are promised an eventual pension benefit that is determined by a pre-specified pension formula, typically reflecting a worker's age, pay, and/or service level. The strong link between pension benefits and seniority has meant that leaving one's job voluntarily has been associated with high opportunity costs, since pension benefits increase disproportionately during the latter part of one's career. The major advantage of DB plans from the employee's perspective is that they provide a stable replacement rate of final income. As real wages change, employers have to adjust their funding rates and, thus, bear the investment risks in these plans (Logue and Rader 1998).

Pressures for change

Recent changes to welfare benefit systems have been driven to a large extent by cost considerations. As can be seen in Figure 15.1, Japanese companies have faced a more or less continuous rise in public social security contributions since the 1980s. This trend, which is linked to the rapid ageing of the Japanese society and an associated rise in public-pension and health-care costs, can be expected to continue in the future, even though public-pension and health-care reforms have been passed to limit future contribution increases. While Japanese companies have very limited power to reduce costs related to public social-security contributions, changes to voluntary employee-welfare benefit systems do present opportunities for cost cutting. From this perspective, the continued rise in occupational-pension contributions arguably has presented Japanese companies with the biggest challenge. This rise is primarily linked to the depressed Japanese stock market and declining interest rates following the collapse of the bubble economy in the early 1990s. These developments forced companies to increase their contributions to

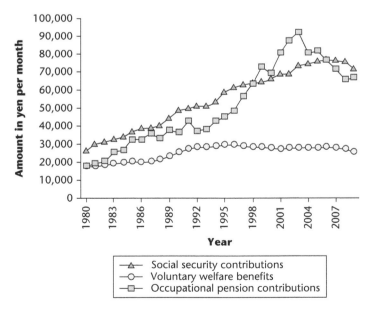

Figure 15.1 Development of social security contributions, voluntary welfare benefits, and occupational-pension contributions in predominantly large firms

Source: NKDR (2012)

prevent an underfunding of the prevailing DB plans, as they, as was explained above, shoulder the investment risks of these types of plans.

Data from the Pension Fund Association show that, in the period 1989–2003, the average return on assets managed by Employee Pension Funds (EPFs) was just 2 per cent in nominal terms, while the government-set guaranteed rate was 5.5 per cent (Kigyō Nenkin Rengōkai 2003). Furthermore, the new accounting standards that were introduced in April 2000 made these unfunded pension liabilities for the first time visible on companies' balance sheets and damaged their stock market valuations (Kigyō Nenkin Kenkyūkai 2007; Shiniapuran Kaihatsu Kikō 2004).

In response to these problems, in the 1990s, firms lobbied for new pension-benefit options which would allow them to rid themselves to some extent of the investment risks associated with the prevailing DB plans. Such new options were eventually introduced by the 2001/2002 occupational-pension reform laws (Kigyō Nenkin Kenkyūkai 2007) and set off a wave of pension restructuring which will be addressed in more detail below.

Changes since the 2000s

As one might expect from the above discussion of pressures for change, the area of employee welfare benefits where companies have made the most dramatic changes is the occupational-pension field. However, other welfare benefit systems have also been reformed in recent years, even though aggregate spending has not changed fundamentally. Before discussing changes in occupational pensions, we address first the changes in other voluntary welfare benefits.

Table 15.3 shows that housing benefits have made up about half of all voluntary welfare benefits in Japanese companies (excluding pensions) since the early 2000s. Less comprehensive but longer-term data from Nikkeiren (NKDR 2012) confirm the same pattern since the mid-1960s, and show that housing benefits have hardly changed in absolute terms since the early 1990s.

However, despite this stability in aggregate numbers, research interviews conducted by this author in October 2010 and November 2011 highlight an interesting dichotomy among responding firms: housing benefits fall into three categories, namely housing for families, housing for bachelors, and monetary housing support. While some companies have outsourced the maintenance of employee dormitories to specialized providers after the collapse of the bubble economy, all but one responding firm continued to use such facilities. However, we can distinguish here two groups of firms: one group of firms considers that dormitories (company-run halls of residence) for bachelors and families are still indispensable for the socialization of new staff members and the nurturing of strong ties among them. In a few cases, the responding firms were even in the process of reintroducing such benefits to enhance employee socialization, which reportedly suffered after prior cost-cutting in this area. These companies stress, in line with their labour unions, the important welfare-enhancing role of dormitories and monetary housing benefits in high-cost urban centres (*fukushiyō shataku*). Another group of firms, while in principle maintaining the different kinds of housing benefits, has cut back on general housing for families and/or monetary housing support, and now focuses more strongly on the maintenance of dormitories for workers on job rotations or transfers to subsidiaries or affiliated companies, as they are especially common in the manufacturing sector (*gyōmuyō shataku/ tenkinyō shataku*).

Our interviews showed that the issue of housing benefits is, at least in part, related to the finding that so-called 'cafeteria plans' do not play a large role in employee-welfare provision in Japan. Cafeteria plans allow employees to choose among various benefits up to a predefined value. They were first introduced in the United States in the late 1970s, and gained popularity there as a means to control health-care-related expenditures and to realize tax savings

Table 15.3 Voluntary welfare benefits in companies with over 1,000 employees

	2002		2006		2011	
Housing benefits	8,844	(55.1%)	7,816	(57.2%)	7,038	(54.0%)
Medical benefits	1,247	(7.8%)	1,137	(8.3%)	1,605	(12.3%)
Meals benefits	1,573	(9.8%)	1,116	(8.2%)	854	(6.5%)
Cultural and educational benefits	1,056	(6.6%)	794	(5.8%)	506	(3.9%)
Private-insurance benefits	611	(3.8%)	449	(3.3%)	490	(3.8%)
Additional accident-insurance benefits	71	(0.4%)	158	(1.2%)	97	(0.7%)
Child-care benefits	466	(2.9%)	391	(2.9%)	323	(2.5%)
Savings support benefits	596	(3.7%)	344	(2.5%)	250	(1.9%)
Other benefits	1,580	(9.8%)	1,465	(10.7%)	1,880	(14.4%)
Total benefits	16,044	(100%)	13,670	(100%)	13,042	(100%)

Source: Kōseirōdōshō (2002 and later years of the same survey)

(Nishikubo 2004). The latest, most comprehensive Japanese survey on cafeteria plans stems from 2002, and shows that only 3.2 per cent of companies with more than 1,000 employees had adopted such plans (Kōseirōdōshō 2002). The less comprehensive Nikkeiren survey put the number for 2002 somewhat higher at 4.3 per cent, but has since reported yearly increases, reaching 12.3 per cent in 2010 (NKDR 2012). Our informants pointed out that cafeteria plans do not offer any particular tax benefits in Japan; require additional administrative work; and altogether lack the advantages that make them so popular in the United States. In particular, they highlighted the difficulty of including existing housing benefits in such plans. Not all employees could be given a housing option, while monetizing housing benefits would lead to expenditure increases. Not surprisingly, therefore, cafeteria plans are mainly found in companies that have either abolished or never offered housing benefits, or manage this particular kind of benefit outside a cafeteria plan.

Despite the fact that all responding firms continued to use a wide range of benefits, all but one firm had experienced gradual small cuts in their overall voluntary welfare expenditures. Asked about noteworthy changes since the 1990s, many respondents stressed that there had been a reorientation in emphasis on non-monetary aspects of welfare provision. Informants stressed two areas receiving special attention: mental health and family support, including child-care and long-term care support.

Mental-health problems, caused by depression or various forms of harassment, have increased considerably over the last two decades, and several informants regarded this as a 'major' problem. The Labor Contract Law from 2008 made it a legal obligation for employers to consider related work-safety issues and not least, due to this requirement, all the respondents' firms offer now counselling services, either in-house or outsourced.

Family support, as part of a wider work–life-balance agenda, is another important arena for changes to voluntary welfare benefits. While few companies have actually increased monetary benefits in this area, many informants stressed that family support, especially child-care and long-term care support, had become fields where companies were strengthening their non-monetary activities, primarily by accommodating employees' needs for shorter working hours, flexitime or work breaks to take care of children or ageing parents. Child-care issues have gained in importance, in so far as companies are nowadays much more reliant on qualified female workers. In companies with an increasing average age of employees, respondents pointed to the need to provide better assistance for employees to look after their ageing parents in need of long-term care.

Finally, let us turn to changes in occupational pensions. As was already mentioned, prior to the new pension legislation enacted in 2001/2002, Japanese occupational retirement benefit systems were predominantly of the defined-benefit (DB) type: internally managed lump-sum payments through Book-Reserve Plans (BRPs), and externally managed annuities or lump-sum payments from Tax-Qualified Pension Plans (TQPP) or Employee Pension Funds (EPF). EPFs have a semi-public character, as they are closely linked with the public Employees' Pension System by substituting a part of the public pension in return for lower social-security contributions with the rebate rate. Following the 2001/2002 changes in pension legislation, which introduced new options for DB and DC pensions, the mix of retirement benefits offered by companies has changed significantly, while overall employee coverage has declined. In 1997, 99.5 per cent of firms with more than 1,000 employees paid retirement benefits, while this percentage decreased slightly to 95.2 per cent in 2008. Today, 84 per cent of Japanese companies with more than 30 employees pay retirement benefits. The number of active participants has declined from 20.1 million in 2001 to 16.6 million in 2012. Despite lower employee coverage in absolute terms, DB benefits remain, in relative terms, the dominant form of retirement benefit (Figure 15.2).

While the number of EPFs and TQPPS has declined substantially (TQPPS were phased out in 2011) since the early 2000s, these plans were, to a large extent, compensated for by newly introduced DB and DC plans (Table 15.4).

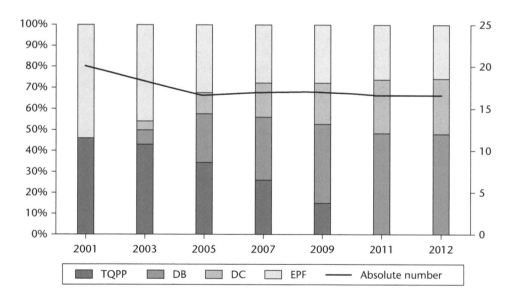

Figure 15.2 Occupational pension-plan participants (relative and absolute numbers)

Note: Absolute number of members in millions (right scale); relative numbers in percentages (left scale). After 2001, companies started to introduce multi-layered occupational pension schemes, where employees are frequently enrolled in a combination of DB and DC schemes. The absolute number of pension plan participants, as reported by the Japanese Ministry of Health, Labor and Welfare, does not account for these multiple memberships and thus exaggerates the number of employees in occupational pension plans.

Source: Kōseirōdōshō (2014)

From the 1,737 EPFs with 10.87 million participants in 2001, only 515 plans with 3.98 million members remained in mid-2014. About 50 per cent of former EPFs were converted into new DB plans, a process during which the companies returned their obligations for the contracted-out portion of the public Employees' Pension Insurance back to the government (Kōseirōdōshō Nenkinkyoku 2009). This has had the effect of removing large pension liabilities from corporate balance sheets and has fundamentally altered the state–enterprise welfare mix, since almost all large companies have now left the semi-public EPFs, with only smaller companies remaining.

All of the informants agreed that cost considerations were the most important factor driving employers' pension restructuring efforts. However, while employers in liberal-market economies like the United States or the United Kingdom have drastically reduced DB plans in the last two decades to minimize companies' costs and risk exposure (US Department of Labor 2008; Office for National Statistics 2008), this has clearly not been the case in Japan. Here, large employers have, instead, often created new multi-layered retirement-benefit systems in which DB benefits continue to play a dominant role. Some 47 per cent of large companies have adopted DC plans *in addition* to the existing DB plans, replacing DB benefits only partially by DC benefits. The percentage of DC benefits within the new retirement benefit packages varies, but does usually not exceed 10 per cent to 25 per cent.

What explains this resilience of DB plans in Japan? While Japanese employers have undoubtedly succeeded in reducing their cost and risk exposure since the early 2000s, they have been careful not to alienate long-term employees by toppling existing incentives. Such social constraints, whether real or perceived, have shaped the institutional innovation of the newly evolving multi-layered retirement systems. As part of a careful reform approach, Japanese employers have reduced their direct costs and risks by partially replacing DB with DC benefits, and, in some cases, even by tying the existing DB benefits closer to employees' performance factors. The latter change reflects the general trend towards stronger performance-oriented pay.

While companies have, thus, maintained fairly comprehensive pension benefit packages for their regular workers, they have, at the same time, realized cost reductions by drastically increasing the proportion of non-regular workers who are not covered under any of these schemes. The percentage of such non-regular workers in the Japanese labour force has increased substantially from 18.3 per cent in 1988 to 35.1 per cent in 2012 (JILPT 2014).

There can be no doubt that government regulation has played a large role in shaping companies' options for pension restructuring. In fact, some foreign observers have claimed that the resilience of Japanese DB plans is the result of the low tax-free contribution ceilings. According to Huh and McLellan (2007: 10), 'the low contribution caps set forth in the DC legislation prevented many Japanese firms from fully converting their existing DB plans to DC plans'. However, based on the available statistical evidence and the assessment of the informants, this statement cannot be said to reflect the overall complexity of the issue.

The regulatory environment has undoubtedly exerted a considerable impact on the way that companies have restructured their pension plans since 2001/2002, and explains to a certain extent the continued popularity of DB plans. However, many of the informants stated that these factors alone could not explain the resilience of DB plans.

It is true that the DC law is rather inflexible and prevents an unlimited transfer to DC plans because it does not allow companies to pay voluntarily taxable contributions beyond the tax-free amounts. Since contributions are, in most cases, paid as a percentage of wages, which increase still very much in line with tenure, it is usually the contributions of older workers that can reach the maximum contribution ceilings. Accordingly, many companies have adopted overall contribution rates that allow their highest wage earners to stay within these ceilings.

Table 15.4 Indicators of major Japanese occupational pension plans (1998–2014)

Name of plan	Nature of plan	Year	Number of plans	Number of members (in millions)
Employees' pension-fund plans (EPF)	DB	2001	1,737	10.87
		2003	1,357	8.35
		2005	687	5.31
		2007	626	4.78
		2009	608	4.56
		2011	577	4.37
		*2014	515	3.98
Tax-qualified pension plans (TQPP)	DB	2001	73,582	9.2
		2003	59,162	7.8
		2005	45,090	5.7
		2007	32,826	4.4
		2009	17,184	2.5
		2010	8,051	1.3
		2011	0	0
Corporate DB plan	DB	2003	316	1.35
		2005	1,430	3.84
		2007	3,098	5.06
		2009	7,407	6.47
		2011	14,989	8.01
		2012	14,697	7.96
Corporate DC plan	DC	2002	70	0.09
		2003	361	0.33
		2005	1,402	1.26
		2007	2,313	2.19
		2009	3,043	3.11
		2011	3,705	3.71
		2013	4,247	4.39
		†2014	4,434	4.64

Note: All numbers are for fiscal years ending at the end of March.
* As of 1 July 2014.
† As of 31 March 2014.

Sources: Life Design Kenkyūjo (2000); Nomura Research Institute (2007); Kigyō Nenkin Kenkyūkai (2008); Kigyō Nenkin Rengōkai (2008); Kōseirōdōshō (2014)

In practice, however, only 29 per cent of DC plans have chosen amounts that reach the legal maximum contributions (Kigyō Nenkin Rengōkai 2008). In other words, 70 per cent of companies seem not to be directly affected by the tax framework. According to several informants, this underlines that the corporate commitment to DB benefits is real and not solely a function of the tax framework. According to this view, DB pensions are widely regarded as a tax-advantaged way to manage externally what used to be internally managed lump-sum benefits (BRP). Higher tax ceilings for DC pensions would not address the fundamental problem that DC pensions are not a suitable vehicle to replace DB-type lump sum benefits.

However, other informants voiced the opinion that the contribution ceilings are posing a problem, and that many large companies would in fact like to transfer more DB into DC benefits (e.g. *Nihon Keizai Shimbun* 20 June 2008). The business community has been requesting higher contribution ceilings for some years now, but any major increases or the adoption of a tax framework considering lifetime contributions like, for example, in the UK seem, however, unlikely.

Conclusions

This chapter has presented an overview of employee welfare benefit systems as they are commonly found in large but also a lot of medium-sized Japanese companies. In terms of coverage and spending on voluntary welfare benefits (excluding pensions), there have not been any fundamental changes in recent years. Occupational pension arrangements, however, have undergone considerable changes since the early 2000s. Companies have realized some cost and risk reductions by introducing multi-layered occupational pension systems that frequently combine DC pensions with existing or newly introduced DB pensions. The resilience of DB pensions, and their strong weighting among the new multi-layered systems, shows that Japanese companies continue, at least for the meantime, to take long-term responsibility for the welfare of their employees and are prepared to shoulder the investment risks which are associated with DB pensions. The institutional innovation of these multi-layered plans lies in stark contrast to developments in many other countries, where DB pensions have been disappearing quickly in recent years. Whether Japanese companies will continue to provide DB pensions in the future depends on various factors, such as the long-term recovery of the Japanese stock market and companies' willingness to pursue long-term employment policies in the future.

Note

1 Parts of this chapter are based on the earlier contributions of the author, namely Conrad (2011) and Conrad (2013).

References

Abegglen, James C. (1958). *The Japanese Factory*, Glencoe, IL: Free Press.
Aoki, Masahiko (1988). *Information, Incentives and Bargaining in the Japanese Economy*, Cambridge, UK: Cambridge University Press.
Conrad, Harald (2011). Change and continuity in Japanese employment practices: the case of occupational pensions since the early 2000s. *International Journal of Human Resource Management*, 22(15): 3051–3067.
Conrad, Harald (2013). Converging to a new type of human resource management? – compensation system reforms in Japan since the 1990s. In: Kushida, Kenji, Shimizu, Kay and Oi, Jean C. (eds), *Syncretism: The Politics of Economic Restructuring and System Reform in Japan*, Washington DC: APARC/ Brookings Institution, pp. 173–197.
Debroux, Paul (2003). *Human Resource Management in Japan: Changes and Uncertainties*, Hampshire, UK: Ashgate.
Dulebohn, James, Molloy, Janice C., Pichler, Shaun M., and Murray, Brian (2009). Employee benefits: literature review and emerging issues. *Human Resource Management Review*, 19, 86–103.
Huh, Elmer and McLellan, Sarah (2007). A tale of two pension reforms: a US–Japan comparison. *Pension Research Council Working Paper*, 2007–01.
JILPT (Japan Institute for Labour Policy and Training) (2014). *Labour Situation in Japan and its Analysis, Chapter 2: Labour Market*. www.jil.go.jp/english/lsj/general/2013-2014/chapter2.pdf, last accessed 15 October 2015.
Kigyō Nenkin Kenkyūkai (2007). *Kigyō Nenkin Seido no Shikō Jōkyō no Kenshō Kekka – An – Shiryō 1* (Results from a Review into the Enforcement of the Corporate Pension System – Proposal – Material no. 1). Tokyo: Kōseirōdōshō, 10 July 2007.
Kigyō Nenkin Kenkyūkai (2008). *Tekikaku Taishoku Nenkin no Ikō no Genjō Oyobi Torikumi – Shiryō 2* (The Current Situation of the Transfer of the Tax-Qualified Pension Plans – Material no. 2), Tokyo: Kōseirōdōshō. 21 October 2008.

Kigyō Nenkin Rengōkai (2003, 2008). *Kigyō Nenkin ni Kan Suru Kiso Shiryō* (Basic Data about Corporate Pensions), Tokyo: Kigyō Nenkin Rengōkai.

Kōseirōdōshō (2002, 2006, 2010, 2011). *Shūrōjōken Sōgō Chōsa* (General Survey on Working Conditions). www.e-stat.go.jp/SG1/estat/NewList.do?tid=000001014004, last accessed 15 October 2015.

Kōseirōdōshō (2014). *Kigyō Nenkin Seido no Genjō Nado ni Tsuite* (About the Current Situation of the Occupational Pension System), Dai 5-kai Shakai Hōsho Shingikai Kigyō Nenkin Bukai, Heisei 26-nen, 6-gatsu, 30-nichi, Shiryō 1, http://www.mhlw.go.jp/file/05-Shingikai-12601000-Seisakutoukatsu-kan-Sanjikanshitsu_Shakaihoshoutantou/0000049599.pdf, last accessed 15 October 2015.

Kōseirōdōshō Nenkinkyoku (2009). *Kigyō Nenkin Seido – Heisei 21-nen 4-gatsu, 13-nichi* (The Occupational Pension System 13 April 2009), Tokyo: Kōseirōdōshō Nenkinkyoku, internal document.

Life Design Kenkyūjo (2000). *Heisei 12-nenban Kigyō Nenkin Hakusho* (Occupational Pension White Paper 2000). Tokyo: Life Design Kenkyūjo.

Logue, Dennis E. and Rader, Jack S. (1998). *Managing Pension Plans: A Comprehensive Guide to Improving Plan Performance*, Boston, MA: Harvard Business School Press.

Meiji Yasuda Seikatsu Fukushi Kenkyūjo (2008). *Fukuri Kōsei Shisaku no Aratana Hōkōsei* (Towards a New Plan for Employee Welfare Benefit Systems), Tokyo: Meiji Yasuda Seimei.

Nihon Keizai Shimbun (2008). Firms pursue more affordable, sustainable pension schemes. *Nihon Keizai Shimbun*, 20 June 2008.

Nishikubo, Koji (2004). *Nihongata Fukuri Kōsei no Saikōzō* (The Restructuring of a Japanese-style Employee Benefit System), Tokyo: Shakai Keizai Seisansei Honbu.

NKDR (Nihon Keizai Dantai Rengōkai) (2012). *Fukuri Kōseihi Chōsa Kekka Hōkoku* 2010-nendo (Report on the Findings of the Company Welfare Benefit Survey for the Fiscal Year 2010), Tokyo: Nihon Keizai Dantai Rengōkai.

Nomura Research Institute (2007). *Japan's Asset Management Business (Summary)*. Lakyara, Vol. 28.

Office for National Statistics (2008). *Occupational Pension Schemes Annual Report*, Newport, UK: Office for National Statistics.

Shiniapuran Kaihatsu Kikō (2004). *Taishokukin – Kigyō Nenkin Seido Kaikaku no Shinchoku Jōkyō to Kongo no Hōkō ni Kan Suru Chōsa Kenkyū* (Research Report on the Progress and Future Direction of Retirement Benefits and Occupational Pensions), Tokyo: Shiniapuran Kaihatsu Kikō.

US Department of Labor (2008). *Private Pension Plan Bulletin Historical Tables*, http://www.dol.gov/ebsa/pdf/privatepensionplanbulletinhistoricaltables.pdf, last accessed 15 October 2015.

Vogel, Steven K. (2006). *Japan Remodeled*. Ithaca, NY: Cornell University Press.

16

Equality in the Japanese firm

Philippe Debroux

Introduction

The legitimacy of the concept of equality at workplaces in Japan was built on the economic success in the post-Second World War period. Until the 1990s, the employment system was considered as the cornerstone of the dynamics of efficiency and effectiveness that had contributed to generate corporate growth and profitability. Its egalitarian characteristics were thought to have been instrumental in assuring widespread redistribution of wealth and social protection through private mechanisms. Moreover, this was done while keeping public finances in balance. This explains why the employment system had been widely accepted up until the 1990s, despite the fact that its tenets translated into a privileged position for the male regular employees in large companies and the subordination (forced or accepted because of socio-cultural and/or institutional norms) of the interests and welfare of specific human resources, especially women, non-regular workers, and workers in small companies. Those features are now considered as unjustifiable and unsustainable ethically, socially, and economically in a low-growth economy and ageing society where women do not have the social and economic positions commensurate to their educational level. This calls for the revamping of a social compact that would be more inclusive in order to fit with the need of the economy and the aspiration of the working population. In view of the limits of a social compact only centred on companies and family, the development of such inclusive basis of equality may require a public–private mix of policies with a stronger direct and indirect intervention of the state.

The Japanese employment system

In the post-war period, the dominant stakeholders, e.g. the public authorities, large companies, and in-house unions shaped the modes and practices of functioning of the labour market and employment system. This was done through political, legal, societal, and economic instruments of power, backed up by specific incentives, guidance, and management tools of control. The norms and values of equality on which the systems are based were legitimized, supported and/or imposed by the dominance of the national interest, i.e. the competitiveness of Japanese industry. Based on those premises, first, large companies played a critical role in creating privileged arrangements for their own regular workers; second, in forcing their subcontractors and affiliated companies to adapt to their structures and relations; and third, in building their goals and procedures directly into society as institutional rules (Meyer and Rowan 1977).

Based on a social contract centred on companies and families as intermediate institutions, the idea of Japanese companies as altruistic 'communities of fate' (*unmei kyodotai*) was constantly reinforced but, conversely, they became self-sustained and self-contained type of organizations, very selective in terms of belonging and keeping outsiders at arm's length. In doing so, large companies, alongside the state, were instrumental in creating a dual labour market characterized by an internal labour market for regular workers and sharply different working conditions according to employment status, size of the company, and gender.

The creation of sustainable virtuous circles

The legitimacy of the social compact

Up until recently, it had been pointed out that policy makers were more likely to opt for transferring the costs of labour market reform to the non-regular workers. This is despite the fact that most of them had been already excluded from the privileges of the internal labour market in favour of regular workers (Song 2014). But, in a political structure where its input in the labour reforms was almost inexistent, the political left did not exert pressure on the state to develop social protections in order to absorb the costs of adjustments for those affected by reforms. In-house unions have been reluctant, up until the last decade, to integrate non-regular workers in their ranks (Nakamura 2009). Male non-regular workers have always been more likely to prefer to shift from non-regular to regular employment, as opposed to the relaxation of employment protection for regular workers to equalize job security, working conditions, and wages with their own working conditions.

In large companies, women entered the labour market as regular workers (mostly in routine types of administrative job), but they were not supposed to stay in the company after marriage. Young women (middle-school and high-school graduates) played an important role as blue-collar workers (mostly) in small- and medium-sized companies, first of all in the textile industry in the 1950s and 1960s, and afterwards in the electronics industry. Many of them were also quitting at marriage as full-time regular workers, but, for those who were staying, the fact that they had little access to training and career development explains why their age profile of wages was flatter compared with male workers (Ueshima 2014). Women were not part of the skill-based seniority-driven egalitarian employment system, and, to compound this, there was no strong constituency to defend their rights.

In the context of the large-company-centred economic structure in Japan, company size has been a critical factor in determining the workers' careers, because of the different levels of job security, wages, and social protection between regular workers in large companies and those in the small ones. Workers in small concerns were always utilized as a buffer labour force. This was a consequence of the integrated production model[1] that made manufacturing companies prefer to hoard their regular workers even during economic downturns. Transferring the cost of labour adjustments to small companies was preferable, lest companies lose the benefits from production strategies and labour-management practices developed on the basis of acquisition of firm-specific skills.

Nevertheless, although the role of the yearly 'Spring Offensive' (*shunto*) negotiation between the unions and management was never to reduce the wage gap across companies of all sizes, the centralization of wage negotiation and the strength of *keiretsu* relationships up until the 1990s

Philippe Debroux

helped to equalize wage-increase rates over the entire economy. Regular workers in small companies gained access to a similar range of wage increases, and were able to enjoy some level of job protection (albeit much lower than in large companies) and corporate welfare.

As at 1990, Japan's secondary market amounted to about 10 per cent of the workforce. It was mostly composed of middle-aged part-time and temporary female workers concentrated in a small number of sectors, such as the retailing, amenity, and food and drink businesses. The small number of non-regular male workers provided external numerical and financial flexibility in the construction industry and in small manufacturing companies. They were mostly excluded from the coverage of collective bargaining at the company level, and received around 60 per cent of the wages of male regular workers. However, although it was a forced choice for the majority of them (Gordon 1998), they were able to somehow secure a decent life, thanks to the wealth redistribution assured by the subcontracting relationships. Therefore, the issue of the working poor was not considered as an important problem, and initiatives from civil society remained muted until the last decade – all the more so because the number of poor single-parent (overwhelmingly women) households that account for a sizeable share of the working-poor population was still very small at that time

So, despite its lack of inclusiveness, the employment system remained sustainable as long as it could deliver enough well-paid regular work in large and small companies while remaining cost efficient in terms of welfare. At the same time, the gender-segregation of the labour force had to continue to be the accepted societal norm; the structure of the family had to remain stable; and the number of workers completely excluded from the system had to remain small.

The historical and cultural background of the employment and welfare system

In the post-war period, the same message of harmonious labour–capital relationships in business was constantly conveyed, especially after the collapse of militant trade-unionism at the beginning of the 1950s. Emblematic figures such as Konosuke Matsushita and Akio Morita advocated a humanistic and egalitarian management approach, presented as going beyond a capital-driven paternalism favouring of the strong over the weak (Debroux 2014). This mantra was reinforced by the circumstances in the aftermath of the Second World War. High inflation and subsequent poverty triggered the unions to demand that companies take responsibility for the 'reproduction costs' of labour – the amount required to sustain a decent standard of living for the worker and their family. Thus, the *living wage* became the basic component of the wage package and the cornerstone of the concept and perception of what is equality and social fairness at work (Takahashi 2013).

The egalitarian feeling was reinforced by the connection between education and management. Japanese people have traditionally accepted the fairness of the entrance-examination system, because it is believed to be an open and meritocratic one, offering equal opportunities to all (Sugimoto 2010).[2] Dore made the point that education in a Japanese context influenced by Confucianism does not mean only acquisition of skills. Intellectual achievement and moral excellence go hand in hand to foster legitimacy in management (Dore 1976). As a result, the seniority principle can justify wage differentials and the selection of those who are promoted. Dore explains how seniority understood as 'service seniority' and 'age seniority' is one of the most egalitarian of all principles of status allocation. Through 'service seniority', the merits and rewards of the workers who have faithfully fulfilled their subordinate roles with dedication and patience in a long-term perspective are recognized (Dore and Whittaker 2001). The age dimension of seniority is justified partly on the basis that family expenses increase naturally

198

with age (the living-wage concept), and partly on the assumption that the prospect of a regular wage increase and predictable promotion increases workers' satisfaction, which is likely to boost motivation and engagement (Dore 1973).

In such contexts, experienced workers are likely to transfer their skills to the younger ones in good faith. Workers have no reason to consider themselves as rivals, to hoard information, and to compete with each other. Thus, seniority, from an internal-labour-market perspective, becomes the best indicator of the mastering of firm-specific skills, and the natural basis of equality and fairness. On-the-job training (OJT) has seldom been considered up until recently as a cost that could not be recouped later on in one way or another. In essence, the acquisition of new skills was thought to be something good for the organization and the workers (Debroux 2013). In view of the high level of informality and ambiguity of OJT, it would have been difficult to measure its effect very precisely, but, in any case, it was considered that there was no need to assess OJT. Wages at different ages are never equal to productivity in such a system, but it is not considered as unfair in a long-term perspective, because there are internal intergenerational transfers when wages are determined.

Nearly thirty years ago, it was found (Koike 1988) that the age–wage profiles of regular workers conformed to the living-wage idea. They fitted in with the life stages and living costs of the model households. Overall, this remained true until the end of the 1990s. Even now, despite the shift toward the pay for performance system, it is observed that the livelihood-related part of the wage (*seikatsukyu*) is still maintained for non-managerial positions in most companies (Sasajima 2012). Likewise, the tournament-based promotion system is yet another example of the egalitarian principle based on meritocracy (Aoki and Dore 1994). It is presented as rewarding the best and giving promotion opportunities to all employees up to the top of the hierarchy. While increasing nowadays, it is not yet common for Japanese companies to recruit outside board members. Although this masks growing compensation differentials in some sectors – ICT and finance for example – resulting from the creation of more explicit fast tracks, the compensation differential remains low compared with other advanced countries. The variable part of remuneration is increasing in some companies (for example, in the finance industry) through stock options and other financial incentives. However, it remains less common than in the Anglo-Saxon world, and access to capital-based fringe benefits is broader, including average employees in many cases (Debroux 2013).

The 'white-collarization' of blue-collar workers through integration in the same in-house union enlarged their career opportunities and facilitated their entry into the middle class (Koike 1988). It was instrumental in reinforcing the message of the egalitarian and hard-working 'one hundred million middle-class-based society' (*ichi oku sochuryu shakai*). Until the 1990s, Japan was able to efficiently manage its social compact without injecting massive public funds. Workfare was preferred to welfare, with male full employment in regular jobs being the key objective of labour policy. Japan did not socialize the cost of labour adjustment and welfare like social-democratic European countries. Fitting better with the traditional socio-economic roles and responsibilities of business in society, the institutionalization of job security, wages, and welfare at company level has always been considered more important than formal rules and regulations defined by legal frameworks.

Institutional loss mechanisms built into the system prevented regular workers from easily leaving the organization. The complete availability demanded by employers intruded on their private life (overtime work, few holidays, frequent transfers to other work locations). But they were able to express their voice through the unions, and their job was protected thanks to the mediation of the state. Welfare corporatism adopted as alternative mechanisms of social protection provided crucial social protections to complement the small state-funded welfare programmes (Estevez-Abe 2008).

The crumbling of the virtuous circles and the need for change

Inequality and employment status

Between 1990 and 2013, the number of non-regular workers jumped from 10 million to 20 million (just under 40 per cent of the entire working population), while the number of regular workers declined by 5 million (Ministry of Health, Labor and Welfare 2013). The proportion of Japan's female non-regular workers, whose largest contingent was made up of part-time workers in the service sector, increased from 37 per cent to 55 per cent of the female workforce between 1987 and 2007. The proportion of male non-regular workers rose from 9.1 per cent to 19 per cent during the same period (OECD 2010).

The presence of 'full-time part-timers', mostly middle-aged women in retailing and small-scale manufacturing, has been acknowledged for a long time. Many of them make a whole career in one company to the point that they are *de facto* regular employees. It is observed that about 30 per cent of part-time workers work as many hours as full-time workers (Jones and Urasawa 2011). As pointed out by Keizer (2008), a distinct feature of the retail industry is that non-regular workers, including a large majority of women, play central roles. But the same feature is observed in the fast food and food and drink sectors, where non-regular workers sometimes assume managerial positions.

However, although those workers work long hours and extend their responsibilities in the workplace, they do not receive commensurate treatment, because their wage and fringe benefits are determined by their job status and not their occupation (Tachibanaki 2005). Likewise, some of the non-regular workers in manufacturing, the so-called *hybrid workers*, are fully integrated in teams, have access to training, and are involved in complex tasks to the point that they could also be considered as semi-regular employees. However, they also do not benefit from the same wage and traditional welfare corporatism programmes, and are not given the same career-development opportunities as the regular workers (Hirano 2011).

Non-regular employment now includes a growing number of highly educated young people, women, and elderly people. Nearly half of non-regular workers, including many women, are the main breadwinner for their family (Ministry of Health, Labor and Welfare 2011). This means that below-par treatment of larger, younger, and more-educated segments of the working population is becoming structural – a casual fixture of the Japanese socio-economic system on which companies base their competitive advantage. The status of regular worker gives a significantly better access to welfare programmes, such as the Employment Insurance Program, the Public Pension Program and National Health Insurance (Ministry of Health, Labor and Welfare 2012), partly because (mostly small) companies evade payment for social-insurance premiums.[3]

A large number of non-regular workers may never find a well-paid job in the current labour environment. Almost 80 per cent of them (this includes part time workers, however) are paid less than 200,000 yen (about $2000) a month, while 86 per cent of regular workers earn more than that amount (Jones and Urasawa 2011). Some of them are likely to remain working poor during their entire career. They may not be able to satisfy basic aspirations such as marriage and access to decent social life, and to optimize their potential as producers and consumers. In the longer term, many are unlikely to be able to maintain decent standards of living on their own when they leave the labour market. Therefore, they are bound to become a burden for the state finances and/or face a drastic decline in living standards.

The priority given to workfare means that the Japanese social system (including training opportunities) is not designed to cope with long-term unemployed (or underemployed) people, especially the younger ones. Unemployment allowances were purposefully kept meagre. This fitted in with the self-reliance mindset engrained in the workfare-based traditional work ethic. But, when unemployment and the scarcity of regular jobs become structural, then the internal-labour-market logic starts to have perverse effects. The short-term tenure of non-regular workers reduces the incentive for companies to invest in training them. It leaves significant segments of population (including highly educated people) without access to professional training, a situation that induces a spiral of relative poverty.

Starting from a high homogeneity of income with a Gini coefficient on a par with Scandinavian countries in the 1990s, among the developed economies, Japanese society has seen the strongest increase in unequal wages during the last 15 years (OECD 2013). The lack of sufficient public compensating policies for those most affected by labour market reform could still accelerate labour market inequality and dualism, despite business initiatives. Japan suffers from a shortage of job-training facilities that would give the opportunity for young people to have access to professional training. For the time being, Japan's public spending on training is less than one-third of the OECD average (OECD 2009).

Some companies integrate non-regular skilled workers, but, in Japan, a non-regular job is seldom a stepping-stone into regular employment (Jones and Urasawa 2011). Surveys show that the main objective of companies in utilizing a non-regular workforce is cost reduction (Yamaguchi 2013). Most of them have little incentive to change their stance in the current environment, except in sectors such as retailing and food and drink, where a labour shortage and overly high workforce mobility may become detrimental to business activities (*Asahi Shimbun* 2014). It is pointed out that the configurations of industrial relations affect the degree of increasing labour market inequality and dualism along the lines of employment status, by facilitating or obstructing the expansion of social protections, as a compensation mechanism in the politics of reform (Song 2014). Up until recently, neither the companies nor the in-house unions were likely to support the development of social protections for those affected by labour market reform. The case of the pension reform in 2004 raised by Song (2014) is typical in this regard. In view of the increase in part-time workers, the government attempted to have them covered by the Employees' Pension Insurance. However, because it entailed the additional contribution of premiums to help the government to restore the financial stability of the pension programme, the companies and unions opposed the proposal because of rising labour costs (Song 2014).

Inequality and company size

The role of *shunto* as wage-coordination mechanism declined sharply during the recession that followed the bursting of the financial bubble. The pressure from business grew to decentralize wage bargaining. As a result, the coordination mechanisms almost disappeared in the late 1990s and 2000s (Nakamura 2005). As pointed out, under conditions of decentralized industrial relations, employers and unions focus narrowly on economic interests at the company and workplace level (Song 2014). The trickle-down effect disappears, and large companies no longer fulfil the role of benchmarks in wage bargaining on behalf of small companies. As a result, the dualism of the labour markets becomes even stronger than before. A widening wage differential across companies according to size was observed during the last decade (Ministry of Health, Labor and Welfare 2011). More than 75 per cent of Japanese businesses are not making a profit. Delocalization of industry, and the subsequent decline of the *keiretsu*, added to the desire of large companies to keep a strategic core of regular workers, leads to increasing pressure on small businesses to lower costs in adjusting down wages and welfare.

Inequality and changes in the basis of competitive advantage

The importance of firm-specific skills is losing its relevance in the innovation and production process. On-the-job training is not completely discarded, and manufacturers still need workers with organizational flexibility, technical, conceptual, and relational skills (Fujimoto 2007), but the required number is smaller. The internal market has tended to decline even in manufacturing, because the higher market volatility requires more external numerical and financial flexibility. Regular workers are replaced by different categories of non-regular workers – recruited on the basis of cost on the external labour market – who are not expected to acquire high-level skills.

Moreover, the remaining core workers are managed according to the concepts of equality and fairness that are separated from the concept of seniority. Job descriptions are less ambiguous for many tasks, because of the shift towards product modularization. Individual performance is more easily assessed, and occupational skills become more important than firm-specific skills. A similar evolution is observed in manufacturing and service industries for technical and managerial jobs. Companies no longer want to base internal equity on seniority in the absence of empirical measurements of the effects of job training. Equality in the treatment of workers has to be based on actual measurable performance, with acceptance of higher wage differentials and explicit career fast-tracks. Companies' needs for diversification of skills and the benefit of cross-fertilization means that broad job experience and expertise increasingly drives recruitment, wages, and career development. In order to become the employers of choice, companies have to offer the best possible monetary and non-monetary reward package. Welfare benefits have declined during the last two decades. Companies outsource welfare or remove it for managers. Attracting and retaining outstanding workers requires a welfare policy, but one that is no longer linked to a 'community of fate'-based egalitarian concept. Complete availability and devotion versus long-term job guarantee and egalitarian treatment are likely to be replaced by variable benefits based on performance and work–life balance in the new psychological contract.

Inequality and the institutional position of the regular workers

The Japanese government has created institutional arrangements to legitimize non-regular employment during the last twenty years, in relaxing the regulations concerning some categories of workers, notably the dispatched workers and those working on fixed contracts in manufacturing (Araki 2002). But, conversely, the Labor Contract Succession Law and the revision of the Labor Standards Law in 2007 further strengthened employment protections for regular workers, heading in the opposite direction from labour market liberalization. This was done in return for the acceptance by the unions of performance-driven evaluation and rewards systems and lower wages expectations. In so doing, companies intended to respond to the unions' fear of a complete drift towards a neo-liberal model represented by easing hiring and firing practices. As a result, just over 60 per cent of workers have remained under an implicit (albeit increasingly shaky) guarantee of employment protection (Ministry of Health, Labor and Welfare 2013).

The traditional model of regular employment is still supported by business in industries where the integrated production model is relevant. But, it is argued that business and policy makers will not as easily form a coalition as before with regard to selective labour market reforms benefiting regular workers and with the persistence of the same high level of protection (Song 2014). Further shrinking of the number of the regular workers in the traditional sense, i.e. employees bound through a relational-type of psychological contract to one company, can be expected. However, this does not mean that the overall number of regular workers, i.e.

those benefiting from a certain level of job protection, will not increase. On the one hand, companies are less likely to make the same commitments to job security and welfare, since they do not expect returns as high as before from investing in workers' firm-specific skills. On the other hand, however, the increase in non-regular workers also creates problems of motivation, employee retention, and communication in the workplace that are bound to affect business profitability. This is particularly the case in the service industries. For example, skilled workers in the retail industry tend to change employers to build their careers. The female workforce is younger, more mobile, and less committed to work and the company (Keizer 2008). So, if they want to attract and retain the best workers, companies have to offer better working conditions (*Asahi Shimbun* 2014).

For these reasons, companies and government are more likely to promote labour market reform for a broader range of workers. It could be done thanks to reforms of the labour market targeting priority type of workers, notably women and young people, that aim to legitimate intermediary categories of 'limited' (location, working time, scope of occupation) regular workers. Some kind of job security and welfare would be assured and they would receive a higher wage than current non-regular workers. Conversely, it can be expected that employers would have more flexibility to lay them off because their commitment would also be 'limited' (closing of a particular shop or factory, or disappearance of a specific job leading to termination of the contract, for example). It could also be done through legal initiatives to improve job security of some specific categories of workers. After 2008, in view of the deterioration of the labour market, a law was enacted to reduce the required period of enrolment for the Employment Insurance Programs. Similarly, with the revision of the Labor Contract Law in 2013, companies are obligated to offer indefinite-duration employment contracts to any worker whose length of employment at the company exceeds five years (Yamaguchi 2013). At the same time, unions at last recognize the economic importance of the non-regular workers and the role they could play in the unions' revival. They now attempt to integrate them with the intention of reconstructing the internal labour market in a more inclusive way, with the hope of regaining bargaining power thanks to a broader constituency basis (Hashimoto 2012). Inevitably, all those changes will result in equalization of conditions between the different categories of workers, improving the status of some but downgrading the status of the regular workers in relative terms.

The state and companies remain ambiguous, though. The 2008 revision of the Part Time Labor Law introduced the concept of 'balanced treatment' between regular and non-regular workers. It was done to discourage companies from using fixed-term contract workers for the sole purpose of reducing labour costs. However, the term of 'balanced treatment' is vague, and many interpretations are possible. So far, there is little evidence that the differences in treatment between regular and non-regular workers are more 'balanced' than before. A large discrepancy is still observed in the absence of penalties on companies that fail to provide equal treatment, even in cases of the same job description, job rotation, and type of labour contract as regular workers (OECD 2013).

Care should be taken to avoid unintended consequences triggered by businesses' cost aversion towards measures in favour of the non-regular workers. Restrictions on their use may just mean even more overtime for regular workers; more automation and delocalization; and not more recruitment. The Labor Contract Law revision in 2013 is an example of well-intended policy that already seems to produce negative outcomes. Workers whose specific technical and organizational skills and knowledge are deemed necessary may get access to regular status (Debroux 2013). But, the revision could have negative consequences for the non-core semi-regular employees. In order to keep financial flexibility, it may induce companies to terminate employment contracts within five years, thus making the fixed-term contract status even more precarious (Yamaguchi 2013).[4] Likewise, the moves to reform the tax and benefit system to remove disincentives to work by secondary earners[5] have to be considered with circumspection. Considered as a remnant of the male breadwinner ideology, and thus a symbol of women's economic dependence, removal of the system should be considered a step forward to gender equality. The aim of removing obstacles to female work is indeed commendable, but it makes many households uneasy because it may mean a decline in income for many of them. Many women are not eager to look beyond their current non-regular job, and, even if they wanted to find another one, the possibilities are limited for the majority of them.

The gender dimension of equality

The most blatantly discriminatory policies (obligation to resign at marriage time, limited access to training, a flatter wage curve, etc.) have gradually faded away. However, the gender gap in economic activities in Japan is one of the biggest among developed countries. Of the 135 countries in the Global Gender Gap Index compiled by the World Economic Forum in 2013, Japan ranked very low (105d) in the category of 'economic participation and opportunity'. The rate of Japanese women's labour-force participation is far lower than those of Northern European countries and the United States, despite the increase of women with higher education since the 1970s (World Economic Forum 2013). The percentage of female university graduates in the labour market is about 10 per cent lower than the OECD average (Jones and Urasawa 2011).

Growing women's employment has been accompanied by changes in household structures with a greater number of dual-earner couples, and more single-person and single-parent households. Japanese middle-class women tend to stay in the labour force as full-time worker more than before with the weakening gender segregation of occupation and an expansion of women in higher education. In part, this reflects a slow shift away from a traditional male breadwinner model and the growing aspirations for economic equality at home and at work expressed by Japanese women (Namikawa 2013).

Non-regular or 'non-career' employment is not always a 'forced choice'. It often fits with the needs of married women who prefer a temporary or part-time employment status for various reasons, e.g. flexible working time and favourable social-welfare benefits. Non-regular employment for married women was promoted for the purpose of the aforementioned social-welfare and tax benefits. Non-career employment may be the preferred choice of qualified women for reasons linked to lifestyle, i.e. they want to preserve one facet of their organizational autonomy that they consider central. For many of them, economic autonomy is not the only form of autonomy that they valorize. They do work, but without career ambitions. They prefer to devote their time to volunteering, raising their children, cultivating hobbies, or studying something, rather than to make more money. In other words, they understand independence less in financial terms than in organizational terms. A sizeable number of highly educated Japanese women who could have been business managers (and sometimes have been managers before quitting their position) manage NGOs and NPOs that are active at grassroots level, while having a non-regular job (Namikawa 2013).

At the same time, non-regular employment is, indeed, a 'forced choice' at both ends of the spectrum. The growth of the female labour-force during the last 20 years largely reflects the rise of non-regular labour in the service industries (OECD 2010). Nowadays, women account for less than 30 per cent of regular workers (Ministry of Health, Labor and Welfare 2012). The majority of women with non-regular work have an unrewarding and unsecure job that does not offer any prospect of improvement. They work out of necessity, i.e. their husband's income is low, or they have to support themselves on their own. Women managing a single household, for instance, have limited mobility when it comes to work transfers, and would relish the limited regular worker status in a specific location and with flexible working times.

It is also a forced choice for those who would prefer a full-time regular job fitting their professional qualifications but do not find it or enter the managerial track, and later on decide to drop out because it is too demanding in terms of time and energy. When it comes to women's participation in the labour force at managerial level, Japan ranks low on the list of advanced countries. The ratio of women in managerial positions is about 10 per cent, compared with ratios in the range of 30 per cent to 40 per cent in United States and some European countries (Ouchi 2014). Gradual progress of women up the hierarchy of organizations can be observed, but it appears that, in many companies, access to the most promising positions remains difficult for female managers. They are often confined in specific jobs and divisions with more limited career prospects than their male counterparts. Those who have children are put in less challenging kind of 'Mummy track', facing difficulties in returning to the main managerial track if they wish to do so (Ouchi 2014). This reinforces the need for public policies and management practices to reconcile job and care commitments, otherwise women will continue to have difficulties holding down a full-time job. It could be argued, for example, that priority should be given to availability of affordable and high-quality child-care facilities. The Childcare and Family Care Leave Law in 2010 offers expansion of child-care leave (from twelve to fourteen months) and shorter work hours during child-rearing. It is pointed out that equality policies and flexible working arrangements are related, since the development of flexible working arrangements may be adopted precisely in order to promote the objective of gender equality, and it is observed that both types of policies are responsive to the increase in women's labour force participation (Yamada 2013).

The Equal Employment Opportunity Act (EEOA) was enacted in 1986, followed in 1999 by the Basic Law for a Gender-Equal Society. The Work–Life Balance Charter was adopted in 2007 to develop systems that enable men to participate more in housework and child-care. Since 2007, through the Law on Child Care Leave system, measures are taken to help achieve compatibility between work and child-rearing based on the Act on Advancement of Measures to Support Raising Next-generation Children. However, the 1999 Basic Law has been criticized for lacking specificities in its application of employment protection. Likewise, although it aimed to guarantee gender-equality, the EEOA did not earnestly tackle key factors of inequality, including indirect instances of discrimination, before its latest revision in 2006.

Now, any disadvantageous treatment toward a female worker that applies a criterion other than the worker's gender 'except in a case where there is a legitimate reason' is considered as indirect discrimination. However, it is pointed out that this definition does not indicate any clear-cut criterion for these 'legitimate reasons'. Therefore, practices with an unclear intention of discrimination have not been regarded as indirect discrimination. This is notably the case for the double career-track system separating routine and managerial jobs. Although a growing number of women enter in the managerial track, the double-track system is thought to remain gender-biased in many companies. In that sense, it may still be a factor of unequal outcome between male and female workers (Yamada 2013). So, as a result of the ambiguity of the text, government initiatives may again end up having limited impact. In some cases, they can even be potentially counterproductive. This is, for example, the case for the above-mentioned revised Childcare and Family Care Leave Law. It may have the unintended consequences of justifying different treatment for a 'legitimate' reason because it makes women a more costly and (supposedly) less reliable workforce because of longer time devoted to childcare.

In any case, the EEOA alone is insufficient to change the situation. Its objective is to offer equal opportunity, i.e. to eliminate discriminatory treatment. It does not require employers to implement initiatives beyond the law. For instance, it has no provisions to encourage them to make efforts to achieve work–life balance (Yamada 2013). The shortcomings of the law justified the launching of incentive-driven initiatives that would induce companies to favour women's work. In this line of thought, the Family-friendly Companies Awards was initiated in 1999, with gender equality as its main objective. The idea was to give awards to companies that provide support for achieving compatibility between work and family opportunity. The objective is to help create corporate role models that would emulate other companies to go beyond the law. The initiative is linked with the Corporate Awards for the Promotion of Gender Equality that was introduced at the same time. If a number of cases of advanced companies have indeed emerged, it appears that the large majority of companies are barely trying to comply with the law. Overall, it is observed that the impact of those initiatives is limited (Kawaguchi 2013).

Conclusions

Japan must rebuild its social compact, and this means that a new compromise must be concluded between the key stakeholders. Since the 1990s, the dualism of the labour market that was centred on the dichotomy between large versus small companies has not disappeared, but the relative importance of the dualism centred on gender and employment status has grown. In view of the severe consequences on the fabric of the Japanese economy and Japanese society, the integration of some categories of non-regular workers, namely women and young qualified people, into some form of regular employment is recognized as a necessity. It can be expected that measures will be taken by business, but this cannot be done on the same premise as before. Business can no longer be expected to fulfil the social responsibilities that should be assured by the family and/or the public authorities. Nowadays, Japanese companies are not a 'community of fate', and traditional welfare corporatism no longer fulfils economic and societal needs.

Labour and social issues are interconnected, but they should be dealt with separately. Japan has already started the reform of its social security system, including health care, pensions, and the help given to elderly people. It is bound to be under growing strain because of the ageing population, but it is quite an egalitarian system that currently operates efficiently and is financially effective (Lechevalier 2011). Japan has to deal with the labour issues in the same way. It is possible to manage human resources with different types of job status, corresponding with the different needs and expectations of both labour and business in a sensible way for both parties. There are already examples of companies abandoning the double-track system or adapting it flexibly, so that they can optimize their female labour capital. Likewise, we have seen that retailers offer better working conditions to non-regular workers – out of necessity. The envisioned development of intermediary employment status indicates that business and government want to find a solution that would create more flexibility and offer more choice to both labour and business, while keeping down the cost of the reform for public finance and companies.

However, in view of the companies' reluctance to invest in human capital, it is difficult to see how they could develop a craving for flexibility that would also induce them to invest in employability for the bulk of the non-regular workers. The worry concerning the current reforms is that they may not be inclusive enough and will leave those at the bottom of the labour market under-protected. Quality of work is closely related to education, because regular jobs for low-skilled people will be in short supply. So, first of all, the issue of equal access to the best education should be addressed rapidly, lest it develop into a situation where young people from low-income families start with a handicap in the labour market. It has to be done alongside more adult education schemes that would compensate for the decline of the internal labour market.

Finally, time is ripe for issues such as work–life balance to be tackled in a broader sense. It seems that both male and female workers want to reconcile family and work, thanks to a balance between the material and organization dimensions of autonomy. The economic autonomy of women is generally considered a prerequisite to equality between the sexes in Japan, as elsewhere. Therefore, measurements of family–work conciliation aimed at encouraging families with two economic providers are perceived as a decisive step towards equality between men and women.

Nevertheless, it may be important to conceive individual autonomy from a more androgenic point of view, so as to integrate it into the reality and economic and social responsibilities of both genders. The privileged access of male workers to the labour market went with the sacrifice of the organizational dimension. Male workers have equal rights to enjoy a normal social life. Therefore, the idea of equality based on two spouses having a full-time job may be unattainable without a drastic change in male work patterns towards reduction of working hours and limited company transfers. This has to be done while eschewing gender equality purely understood and measured in terms of the number of female managers and gender-related wage differentials. The sustainability of the employment system depends on the balance between the social and economic interests of both genders.

Notes

1 The archetypal Japanese employment system is found in manufacturing sectors, with product development based on integral architecture, such as automobile and heavy industries. Each component is functionally incomplete and is interdependent with other components functionally and/or structurally. This architecture requires close coordination amongst workers and the acquisition of conceptual, technical, and relational skills that can only be nurtured over time (Fujimoto 2007).
2 The reform of the educational system since the 1980s has aimed to shift from a system said to be focusing too much on academic credentials – criticized for being purely examination-driven (thus impeding creativity and critical thinking) – towards a learning-capital-driven educational system more attuned to the need for creativity and respect for individuality. It is argued that the transformation in school structure and diversification in learning that it has created has mainly benefited children from the middle and upper classes. It has made the educational system more open and dynamic, but also less egalitarian than before (Kariya 2009), with the risk of creating barriers to access accessing the best education, based on family income.
3 It is observed that, so far, Japanese public authorities have been rather tolerant towards companies in this regard. This calls for public interventionism, for example in unifying the collection of taxes and social-insurance contributions (Jones and Urasawa 2011), and in imposing more transparency and accountability on business with regard to social issues.
4 The situation is not clear-cut in terms of the attitudes of workers towards regulation of non-regular types of work. In 2004, female part-timers opposed the increase in the financial contribution to the Employment Insurance scheme because most of them can take advantage of the coverage of their husband if they earn less than 1.3 million yen a year (Song 2014). In general, regular workers strongly support stricter rules on the use of non-regular workers, who could substitute for them. Conversely, in the absence of a realistic possibility of moving into a regular job, most non-regular workers are generally opposed to restrictions on non-regular work. Following this line of thought, regular workers are bound to oppose the limited regular workers scheme envisioned by government.
5 Spouses with annual pay below 1.03 million yen are exempt from income tax, and this can be claimed as a tax deduction by the primary earner. Companies pay many family allowances based on this threshold.

Bibliography

Aoki, M. and Dore, R. (1994). *The Japanese Firm*, Oxford, UK: Oxford University Press.
Araki, T. (2002). *Labour and Employment Law in Japan*, Tokyo: Japan Institute of Labor.
Asahi Shimbun (2014). Jinzai busoku kigyō ga himei (Shortage of manpower, the scream of companies). *Asahi Shimbun*, 2 May, p. 3.

Debroux, P. (2013). Human resource management in Japan. In: Varma, A. and Budhwar, P. (eds), *Managing Human Resources in Asia-Pacific*. London: Routledge, pp. 105–128.

Debroux, P. (2014). Spiritualism and social compact in Japan. *Soka Keiei Ronshu*, 38(2–3): 51–66.

Dore, R. (1973). *British Factory, Japanese Factory: The Origins of National Diversity in Industrial Relations*, Berkeley, CA: University of California Press.

Dore, R. (1976). *The Diploma Disease*, Berkeley, CA: University of California Press.

Dore, R. and Whittaker, D. H. (2001). *Social Evolution, Economic Development and Culture*, Cheltenham, UK: Edward Elgar.

Estevez-Abe, M. (2008). *Welfare and Capitalism in Postwar Japan*, Cambridge, UK: Cambridge University Press.

Fujimoto, T. (2007). Theory of open manufacturing and its application, Tokyo: RIETI.

Gordon, A. (1998). *The Wages of Affluence: Labor and Management in Postwar Japan*, Cambridge, MA: Harvard University Press.

Hashimoto, S. (2012). Unionization of non-regular workers by enterprise unions. *Japan Labour Review*, 9 (1): 25–43.

Hirano, M. (2011). Diversification of employment categories in Japanese firms and its functionality. In: Bebenroth, R. and Kanai, T. (eds), *Challenges of Human Resources in Japan*. Abingdon, UK: Routledge.

Jones, R. S. and Urasawa, S. (2011). *Labour Market Reforms in Japan to Improve Growth and Equity*. Paris: OECD, Economics Department Working Papers, No. 889, pp. 1–29.

Kariya, T. (2009). From credential society to 'learning capital' society: a rearticulation of class formation in Japanese education and society. In: Ishida, H. and Slater, D. (eds), *Social Class in Contemporary Japan*, London: Routledge.

Kawaguchi, A. (2013). Equal employment opportunity act and work–life balance: do work–family balance policies contribute to achieving gender equality? *Japan Labor Review*, 10 (2): 35–56.

Keizer, A. (2008). Non-regular employment in Japan: continued and renewed dualities. *Work, Employment and Society*, 22(3): 406–425.

Koike, K. (1988). *Understanding Industrial Relations in Modern Japan*, New York: St Martin's Press.

Lechevalier, S. (2011). *La Grande Transformation du Capitalisme Japonais*, Paris: Sciences Po Les Presses.

Meyer, J. W. and Rowan, B. (1977). Institutionalized organizations: formal structure as myth and ceremony. *American Journal of Sociology*, 83: 340–363.

Ministry of Health, Labor and Welfare (2011). *Shugyo Keitai no Taiyoka ni Kansuru Sogo Jittai Chosa* (General Survey on Diversified Types of Employment), 2011, Tokyo: Ministry of Health, Labor and Welfare.

Ministry of Health, Labor and Welfare (2012). *Shugyo Keitai no Taiyoka ni Kansuru Sogo Jittai Chosa* (General Survey on Diversified Types of Employment), 2012, Tokyo: Ministry of Health, Labor and Welfare.

Ministry of Health, Labor and Welfare (2013). *Heisei 25 White Paper on Labour Economics*, Tokyo: Ministry of Health, Labor and Welfare.

Nakamura, K. (2005). Kaikaku no naka no itsudatsu (Deviation inside the reform). In Institute of Social Science (ed.), *Ushinawareta 10 Nen o Koete 2: Koizumi Kaikaku no Jidai* (Beyond the Lost Decade, Volume 2: the Koizumi Reforms), Tokyo: University of Tokyo Press.

Nakamura, K. (2009). *Kabe wo Kowasu* (Tearing Down Walls), Tokyo: Daichi Shorin.

Namikawa, K. (2013). Nihon no Work Life Balance, Rōdō Keizai Kenkyukai, Monthly Meeting, 8 November 2013.

OECD (2009). *Jobs for Youth, Japan*, Paris: OECD.

OECD (2010). *Employment Outlook*, Paris: OECD.

OECD (2013). *OECD Economic Survey of Japan*, Paris: OECD.

Ouchi, S. (2014). Kigyo wa honki de josei o sogoshoku toshite sodatete kita ka (Did companies really nurture the talent of women as managers?) *Nihon Romu Gakkaishi*, 15(1): 97–106.

Sasajima, Y. (2012). Nihon no chingin seido: kako, genzai soshite mirai. (Japan's wage system: past, present, and future). *Meiji Gakuin Daigaku*, 145(1): 23–32.

Song, J. (2014). *Inequality in the Workplace – Labour Market Reform in Japan and Korea*, Ithaca, NY, and London: Cornell University Press.

Sugimoto, Y. (2010). *An Introduction to Japanese Society*, Cambridge, UK: Cambridge University Press.

Tachibanaki, T. (2005). *Confronting Income Inequality in Japan*, Cambridge, MA: MIT Press.

Takahashi, K. (2012). *Influences of Institutional and Labor Market Characteristics on Careers in Japanese Companies*. University of California Riverside, Electronic Thesis and Dissertations, http://escholarship.org/uc/item/02d8b4j6, last accessed 15 October 2015.

Ueshima, Y. (2014). High economic growth and human capital: conditions for sustained growth. *Japan Labor Review*, 11(3): 5–34.

Yamada, S. (2013). Equal employment opportunity act, having passed the quarter-century milestone. *Japan Labor Review*, 10(2): 6–19.

Yamaguchi, K. (2013). Considering the potential side effects of employment system reforms. *RIETI*, 24 July 2013.

World Economic Forum (2013). *The Global Gender Gap Report*, Geneva: World Economic Forum, http://www3.weforum.org/docs/WEF_GenderGap_Report_2013.pdf, last accessed 4 July 2014.

17

Leaders and leadership in Japanese companies

Carsten Herbes and Tim Goydke

Introduction

Leadership is an important element both of management research and management practice. Leadership in Japanese companies has become an object of interest from two perspectives: first, both Western academics and managers have come to see it as a key driver of the success of Japanese companies in the 1980s and later as a potential reason for their failure. And second, the increasing numbers of Japanese companies setting up their offices around the world raised the question if and how Japanese leadership could be transferred to other cultures.

Leadership cannot be separated from the people that assume leadership positions. These people, their values, their education, and their career paths crucially influence the way that leadership is practised in Japan. For this reason, we will devote a reasonable part of this chapter to exploring the identities of the leaders in Japanese companies.

We will start the chapter with a brief overview of academic literature on Japanese managers. We will then explore the influencing factors of Japanese managers' leadership behaviour, starting with their values and goals and further depicting their education and career paths. Following that, we will outline the basic principles and techniques of leadership in Japan, as well as the influence of corporate culture on this.

Literature on Japanese managers and leaders – an overview

Research on 'Japanese management' or 'management in Japan' is abundant (e.g. Dirks *et al.* 1999; Jackson and Tomioka 2004; Haak and Pudelko 2005; Abegglen 2006; Baden-Fuller 2009). So is literature on the 'Japanese employee' or 'salaryman' (e.g. Chiba *et al.* 1997, Kato 2001; Iida and Morris 2008). Compared with these two streams, research on the Japanese manager as an employee of a certain hierarchical level in the organization is relatively scarce. But why is this?

A part of the answer may be found in the fact that, in Japan, managers and 'ordinary' employees are not as clearly separated as in Europe or the US. Unlike these two regions, the concept of a managerial elite earns little support in Japan: 'Contemporary Japanese society [. . .] discourages overt elitism, which suppresses many of those potential leaders from demonstrating their leadership capabilities' (Duke 1991: 31).

The role of top management is played down in the literature in three ways: first, research on Japanese managers tends to stress the role of a broad middle-management layer (Kase *et al.* 2005) and the importance of ordinary employees (Kobayashi 1998), rather than the role of top management. Second, although not undisputed by academic research, Japanese managers often emphasize the existence of equal opportunities, i.e. that any of their young employees could become president of the company in principle (Maury 1991; Kroek *et al.* 1999). And third, the impact of a change in top management on company behaviour is qualified as negligible (Nonaka and Johansson 1985: 185). Kase *et al.* go as far as saying 'CEOs are even seen as expendable or fungible' (Kase *et al.* 2005: 2). Consequently, because of this denial of managers as a class of their own, there is not even a generic term for 'manager' in Japanese (Dutton 1987: 24). The perception of managers or top managers as not being so important for a company's fate, and the difficulty of separating them from the rest of the staff, are probably the most important reasons why 'Japanese managers' and 'Japanese leaders' have not been as popular a subject of research as 'Japanese management'. Besides Kase *et al.* (2005), only Hasegawa (2010) recently focused on top leaders in Japan, but, provides only anecdotal case evidence based on a relatively small population.

Within the literature on leaders in Japan, leaders' values and goals have been a clear focus of research and have been described by many scholars in the last 40 years.[1] Another popular topic has been careers, with a special emphasis on education as a driver for promotion. We found some literature on this subject, but, compared with research on values and targets, there were relatively few contributions on training managers during their managerial career, on leadership behaviour, and other issues.

Given these observations, it is not a big surprise that few contributions on leadership theory from Japanese authors can be found. Ouchi's 'Theory Z' stresses collective responsibility and decision-making and a more informal and implicit control with few formalized explicit measures as key characteristics of Japanese managers and leaders (Ouchi 1981). Misumi's 'Performance-Maintenance (PM) Theory of Leadership' concludes that typical Japanese leaders best combine the two dimensions 'performance', i.e. the leader's behaviour toward the achievement of group goals and problem resolution, and 'maintenance', i.e. the self-preservation of the group and the maintenance of social processes (Misumi 1990 1995).

Factors influencing Japanese managers' leadership behaviour

We have grouped managers' behaviour into three categories: decision-making, leading, and monitoring.[2] Many authors see decision-making as the core of management (Robbins and Coulter 1999; Martinsons and Davison 2007). In addition, leading is one of the manager's duties that holds a pivotal place in management literature (e.g. Kroek *et al.* 1999). The manager's activities are subject to both the leeway and constraints of their position, as well as the characteristics of the manager as a person. The manager's position is part of the management system of the company, which strongly influences the manager's decision-making via task allocation and standard practices (Simon 1976). The manager's personal characteristics can be grouped into values and skills. The influence of values on managers' activities have been widely described in both the general literature (Hofstede 1980) as well as in studies on Asian and Japanese managers (Ralston *et al.* 1997, Giacomino *et al.* 2001). Skills, again, can be divided into domain-general skills by training while in a management position.

This section is dedicated to the influencing factors, and covers values, training, and education, as well as careers. Then, we will cover the items at the centre: leadership and decision-making.

Values, goals, and stakeholders

We will start with three topics that are closely intertwined: first: values, i.e. a core set of common beliefs, second: goals, and, third: the question of which stakeholders are most important for Japanese managers. Values as basic beliefs and the relative importance of different stakeholder groups determine, amongst others, managers' leadership styles.

Most studies relate Japanese leadership values to Confucianism, collectivism, and paternalism. Confucianism was made the official ethical philosophy in Japan under the Tokugawa Shogunate (1603–1867), promoting persistence, frugality, and commitment to the society as key values for business leaders. One of the core concepts is '*ningen kankei*' (human relationships), written with the same characters as the Chinese 'guanxi' but with a different meaning. While '*guanxi*' may involve non-family relations but is basically concerned with family relations, '*ningen kankei*' in Japan is basically achieved through socialization, and there is a stricter distinction between business relations and family (Picken 1987).

A close tie between superiors and their subordinates is manifested in Japan in the relationship between '*sempai*' (mentor or senior) and '*kōhai*' (protégé or junior). This includes paternalistic behaviour of the leader and requires respect and obedience from the subordinates. But, moreover, it gives the leader a responsibility to care for their subordinates – even for their private lives (Dorfman *et al.* 1997).

Several authors have underlined the collectivistic nature of the Japanese business culture, emphasizing collective decision-making and collective responsibility (e.g. Ouchi 1981; Pascale and Athos 1981). One central concern of Japanese leaders is to maintain harmony within the organization by applying a bottom-up decision-making process (Wu 2006). The individual is regarded as part of the group, with human existence exclusively defined by group membership (Picken 1987). These collectivistic values are frequently connected with the Japanese concept of '*wa*', often translated as 'group harmony', but better explained as the desire for mutual cooperation and community cohesion. '*Wa*' also implies that group members are expected to subordinate their personal interests under those of the group (e.g. Ouchi and Jaeger 1978; Alston 1989; Kroek *et al.* 1999).

In his pioneering study, Ouchi (1981) revealed that, in Japan, leadership is egalitarian to a greater extent than in American companies, and is based on strong interpersonal trust. Ouchi reasons that the high level of trust has its roots in the fact that more emphasis is given to the employees' commitment to work than on a strict assessment of individual performance. In the realm of values, it has been found that work gives a meaning to the life of Japanese employees, and that leaders see their employees rather as family members (Maury 1991). However, the will to 'work hard and contribute to their company's prosperity' (Okabe 2012: 1221) decreased considerably between 1995 and 2009. Moreover, the reason for working hard shifted from promotion prospects to liking the job.

After these more general considerations of values related to leadership in Japan, we now turn towards the leaders as persons and the values that they harbour. What are the values that have been identified as most important for Japanese leaders, and where do they differ from leaders of other nations? A first noteworthy aspect is that Japanese leaders are obviously ready to give their own personal values second priority, and are strongly influenced by company values (Nakano 1999: 335). This makes them vulnerable to unethical behaviour in cases where their companies lag behind in institutionalizing business ethics, or in cases where they believe that unethical behaviour is in the companies' interest. Choi and Nakano (2008) point out that, recently, Japanese managers tend to base their decisions more on the situation, while company interests are no longer dominant, even if the company policy is still comparatively important (Choi and

Nakano 2008). If ethical behaviour can be a problem, what role does education play in this field? Business ethics education in tertiary education in Japan is not as developed as in comparable institutions in Europe or the United States (Yang *et al.* 2011). Many Japanese people seem to take it for granted that because Japanese management is less profit-centred it is more humanistic *per se*, i.e. ethical. And, even among academics, this notion is not completely rejected: 'To a certain extent, it is true that Japanese business has always valued the importance of business's human aspect' (Yang *et al.* 2011: 327). However, the multitude of scandals in which Japanese businesses were involved over the last few decades, from Minamata to Olympus, makes it hard to believe that the alleged employee focus of Japanese companies is to be equated with ethical behaviour. Moreover, looking at the numbers, it becomes more than clear that this employee-focus is really a focus on a a privileged minority consisting of male core employees. Therefore, Japanese managers and management students would benefit from business-ethics courses, just like their counterparts in Europe or the United States.[3]

Out of a set of instrumental value dimensions, 'Cheerful, Forgiving, Helpful, and Loving' as well as 'Clean, Obedient, Polite, Responsible, and Self-Controlled' were more important to Japanese managers than to any other nation. On the other hand, 'Broad-minded, Capable, and Courageous' were much less important than to the average of the other nations (Bigoness and Blakely 1996). This corresponds with collective decision-making and close, personal ties between superiors and employees, which are attributed to Japanese managers and their leadership styles.

In the ranking of stakeholders, the order of shareholders and employees is the most interesting aspect. Japanese managers, such as Shoichi Saba, the former CEO of Toshiba, tend to emphasize that 'the employees are the true owners of [*sic*] corporation' (Saba 1989: 7). Many surveys support the high priority of employees in Japanese managers' thinking (e.g. Noda 1998; Tachibanaki 1998; Witt and Redding 2009), which clearly should have repercussions on their leadership style. Overall, it becomes clear that employees are still at least as important as shareholders, if not more important.

Tachibanaki finds primary goals of top executives to be: 'the stability of the firm, the safeguarding of jobs' (Tachibanaki 1998: 20). These goals, in turn, are often volume-oriented rather than profit-oriented. In Buecher's (1994) survey, the 'well being and safety of employees', as well as 'increase in sales and profit', are ranking first among the managers' goals (Buecher 1994: 33).

Training and education

Besides values, the skills that managers acquire through their pre-career education, as well as training throughout their career, are important influencing factors. It is widely known that training of Japanese leaders is mainly done in-house, although the faculty may partly comprise external trainers, e.g. professors from well-known universities. Japanese companies spend more resources on in-house training than Western firms (Chen *et al.* 2004), and they do not appreciate external training measures, since these are not suitable for enhancing loyalty towards the company. Another important instrument besides internal training is '*shukkō*',[4] i.e. a temporary secondment to affiliates in order to enable the gathering of additional experience. Nonaka and Johansson point out the 'relative lack of professional education exhibited by Japanese management' (Nonaka and Johansson 1985: 184). The job rotation system equips the managers with broad skills, and thus produces generalists rather than specialists (Kroek *et al.* 1999). Nevertheless, Mujtaba and Isomura (2012) point out that an increasing number of Japanese companies have introduced selective education of candidates for leadership positions recently.

Due to the strong emphasis on in-house training in Japan, executive education at universities has long played an unimportant role (Dutton 1987). Moreover, Japan has, for a long time, leaned towards the German model, focusing on technical education rather than quickly adopting the North American business school model like other countries in East Asia. Warner summarizes: 'The absence of North America-style business schools in Japanese universities is remarkable; there are only a few comparable to the US model' (Warner 2013: 254).

In 1978, Keio Business School set up Japan's first MBA programme (Isomura and Huang 2012). Since the 1990s, an increasing number of American-style business schools have started operating in Japan. But in the QS top MBA ranking, among the top 200 business schools in the world, there is only one Japanese school: Waseda. And even that school ranks rather low compared with other Asian business schools (Lavelle and Kahn 2015). Moreover, the reactions from HR departments of Japanese companies have been controversial, since teaching US business concepts may be of limited practical value in Japan. Companies that dispatch their future leaders into MBA programmes want the candidates to accumulate 'stimulating experiences' (Kambayashi et al. 2007), rather than to acquire specific skills or management techniques. Also, international experience was one of the goals of companies who dispatched employees to foreign business schools (Isomura and Huang 2012). However, in recent years, the number of Japanese students studying at foreign business schools has dropped, while the numbers at the c.30 domestic business schools have increased, which corresponds with the increasing numbers of part-time students (Isomura and Huang 2012). Despite the government's efforts to expand the professional graduate school system, MBA holders are still a small minority among managers in Japan, and a high presence of MBAs in Japan's future boardrooms is not very probable, as opposed to the US, where a high percentage of CEOs holds an MBA (Kambayashi et al. 2007). The main growth driver of MBA programmes in Japan are not employees sponsored by their companies, but self-sponsored students (Isomura and Huang 2012), reflecting the still low recognition of MBA education in Japanese HR departments.

Careers

Before studying the career patterns of Japanese managers, we need to make ourselves aware of two Japanese peculiarities that make it difficult to compare the results with research on the careers of Western managers. Firstly, the object of investigation is a rather homogeneous group: all individuals in this group have a college degree, very few have external work experience, and almost all of them are male (see Spilerman and Ishida 1995: 6–7 for their panel; see Yuasa 2005 on female managers). This, however, may be regarded as a weakness *per se*: 'The management structure consisting of Japanese permanent male employees with bachelor's degrees may be weak in terms of global competitiveness' (Keizai Doyukai 2009). Second, managers in most cases spend their entire career with one employer.

General employment patterns

Permanent employment is more widespread among managers than among non-managerial employees (Beck and Beck 1994). Job changes have mostly been taking place 'through socially acceptable methods like *amakudari* and *shukkō*'[5] (Beck and Beck 1994: 86). Reasons not to change are uncertainty about the future of the new company; opposition from the family; and worries about personal relationships in the new company (Beck and Beck 1994). Especially in their younger years, Japanese managers experience cross-functional career steps within their company (Yashiro 2013), but changes across companies are difficult: new managers in a company face opposition, and Japanese managers who have lived abroad are seen as being 'tainted with foreignness' (Beck and Beck 1994), at least in large companies. Outside experience does not count as much as tenure when it comes to promotion decisions, and 'the accumulation of firm-specific skills is more essential for promotion to top management in large firms' (Noda 1998: 42). Comparative surveys of top-managers' career patterns show that the vast majority of Japanese top managers are 'experienced insiders', a pattern found in no other country that was surveyed (Biemann and Wolf 2009).

Nevertheless, job changing is an increasing phenomenon. This is also reflected in the lower levels of organizational commitment of younger managers as compared with older managers, and a declining commitment to stay with the company until retirement (Okabe 2012). When it comes to promotions, there are three major factors to be found in the literature: seniority, education, and personality (and to a lesser degree the department where young employees have spent their first years with the company). However, traditional career patterns are more and more challenged. Japanese companies have de-layered in the last years and, therefore, opportunities for vertical promotion have been reduced (Hassard *et al.* 2012).

Seniority principle

The first important factor for promotion is experience, i.e. the tenure with the firm. Seniority still plays a large role in promotion, although this practice is generally subject to change. There are two aspects to the logic of promotion according to seniority. A long tenure with the company signals organizational loyalty, and that in turn is used to rate a manager's suitability to fulfil a leadership position. Moreover, practical experience is preferred over theoretical knowledge, and this experience can only be accumulated over the years. Only relatively late in their career does competition among Japanese managers start with regard to the speed of promotion, and only even later is the competition between managers about whether someone is promoted to the next level or not. However, in recent years, the speed of promotion in Japanese organizations has increased (Kroek *et al.* 1999; Chen *et al.* 2004; Hassard *et al.* 2012; Yashiro 2013).

Evaluation and promotion is traditionally slow in Japan in order to socialize employees and to avoid a lack of motivation in the lifetime employment system. However, according to Mujtaba and Isomura (2012), especially large companies increasingly adopt fast selection and promotion systems for employees.

The frequently-described high level of interpersonal trust in Japanese companies is also rooted in the traditional seniority system. It is still a common belief among most Japanese executives that only employees who have served the company for years are 'mature' enough to resume a leadership position. In other words, only those who have proved their loyalty to the company will be promoted to the top ranks. Thus, seniority is a decisive factor for the selection of leaders in Japanese companies (Von Glinow *et al.* 1999).

Gender

The number of female Japanese managers has been traditionally low by international comparison and, as a result, very few can be found in leadership positions. Bozkurt (2012, 226) states a 'near-absence from managerial posts' and Nemoto speaks of a 'vertical sex segregation' (Nemoto 2013b: 155) Although more than ten years ago the Japanese government had already set an ambitious target of having 30 per cent of leadership positions filled by women by the year 2020 (Bando 2007) and initiated numerous legislative changes (Nemoto 2013b, Weathers 2005), not a lot has happened (Bozkurt 2012). As of 2014, women occupied only 1.6 per cent of the seats on the boards of directors of public companies in Japan (Catalyst 2015). The 1972 Equal Employment Opportunity Law (EEOL) in Japan has been criticized for relying too much on voluntary compliance, and the Japanese government was suspected to have passed the law to avoid international pressure rather than out of conviction (Cooke 2013).

The reasons for the low numbers of female managers are seen in the fact that many female employees still choose not to be promoted, or leave their job because of their attitude towards family responsibilities, that female managers who have to take care of children at home are systematically assessed lower in terms of their willingness to sacrifice their life for the company (Nemoto 2013a), and that women who return to work after a break are usually classified as part-time workers who are generally not promoted into management positions (Steinhoff and Tanaka 1993; Yuasa 2005). Combining a management position with having a family seems to be especially difficult. One practical issue is that women anticipate difficulties in finding suitable child-care facilities (Aarsman 2014). But an even stronger barrier is maybe the fact that women are expected to temporarily withdraw from the workforce when giving birth and have to re-enter the workforce after some months or years. This is difficult, because the Japanese labour market is generally unfavourable towards people switching jobs or re-entering the labour market (Aarsman 2014), and, because of their years outside the company, they lose seniority. The expectation of women of leaving the workforce to take care of their children results in what Bando (2007) calls a vicious circle: 'On the one hand, for statistical reasons, employers are reluctant to give women positions with responsibilities or opportunities to develop their careers. On the other hand, women are discouraged from working because of their limited prospects' (Bando 2007: 4–5). Moreover, in the 1980s, Adachi (1989) had already found that women do not receive the same level of managerial training as their male colleagues. Moreover, working in managerial positions in Japan in most cases means long working hours that are difficult to combine with having a family (Bando 2007, Nemoto 2013a), and thus many women managers tend to emulate masculinity, embrace longer working hours, and decide not to marry (Nemoto 2013b). Boyles and Shibata (2009) investigated the drop in job satisfaction arising from a gap between actual and desired work time. Not only when it comes to promotion into managerial ranks, but long before, women are disadvantaged by the track hiring system (Nemoto 2013b) or dual-track system (Weathers 2005). Much more often than their male colleagues, they work as temporary or part-time employees and do not become part of the regular workforce from which future managers are selected (Futagami 2010; Nemoto 2013b). Above and beyond the above-mentioned structural factors, Nemoto (2013b) uses the concept of organizational masculinity, and finds masculine beliefs and practices to be a major barrier for women's careers in Japanese companies. But it is not just the content of the values (strong masculinity) that act as a barrier, but also the 'tightness', i.e. the strengths of these values and the related sanctions (Toh and Leonardelli 2012). Similarly, Wu *et al.* (2000) revealed in a comparative study of American, Taiwanese, and Japanese female managers that Japanese women in leadership positions have the highest problems with their social and gender roles in the male-dominated corporate environment. As a result, female leaders are more risk-averse and tend to make decisions only after consultation with colleagues. They also favour harmonious relationships and a transactional leadership style (Wu *et al.* 2000).

A marked exception to the general trend are foreign companies in Japan, which are not only very popular employers among young Japanese women, but also offer opportunities for managerial careers that Japanese companies do not (Duignan and Iaquinto 2005; Bozkurt 2012). For foreign employers, on the other hand, women have for a long time been a reserve to draw on when it is difficult to lure their male colleagues out of careers in Japanese companies (Lansin and Ready 1988).

When women achieve management positions in Japan, their career paths seem to differ from those of their male colleagues. Bando (2007) states that women more often than men take the risk of joining new businesses that are founded, for example, by their former boss. Since new businesses have difficulties in attracting good personnel, the women have better chances of getting into management positions.

The strong gender inequality is not limited to management or executive positions, but is a marked characteristic of the entire Japanese employment system (Bozkurt 2012). However, more and more well-educated women do enter the labour market (Nemoto 2013b), and the imminent demographic challenge may force Japanese companies in the future to increasingly open up managerial careers and better employment conditions in general to women (Levonian 2013).

University background and recruiting

Education, i.e. the university from which a candidate has graduated, has a strong influence on the propensity to be promoted, and thus on the earnings of Japanese managers (Tachibanaki 1987; Kato and Rockel 1992; Noda 1998). In Tachibanaki's sample, half of the executives surveyed were graduates of just twelve universities. According to Kato and Rockel (1992), almost 30 per cent of Japanese CEOs have graduated from the University of Tokyo, most commonly from the Economics and Business Departments (36 per cent). But what are the employers appreciating about these graduates? It is not so much their superior intellectual abilities as their determination and their willingness to make a determined effort (Tachibanaki 1998, Beck and Beck 1994). Moreover, they benefit from strong alumni networks both within their companies and outside (Ohashi 1998; Ishida *et al.* 1995).

Leadership behaviour

Having identified and described the most important factors influencing leadership in Japan, we will now turn to leadership behaviour itself.

Participative leadership

Authors frequently emphasize that the main tasks and activities of Japanese top managers are motivating their employees, maintaining harmony in the company, and creating consensus, as well as enabling their members to come forward with creative ideas and to listen to the employees and their complaints (Dutton 1987; Buecher 1994; Kroek *et al.* 1999; Pearson *et al.* 2003). Pearson *et al.* (2003) characterize the Japanese manager's role as being 'to tap into the everyday knowledge capital through untiring link-building of formal and informal interactions' (Pearson *et al.* 2003: 102). Often, Japanese managers' listening qualities are mentioned (Kroek *et al.* 1999; Yancey and Watanabe 2009). Buecher emphasizes the paternalistic role of Japanese managers. Managers in her sample frequently fulfil social tasks such as attending the funerals and wedding ceremonies of their employees (Buecher 1994). More than 60 per cent state that they are holding the role of a father figure (Buecher 1994). Dutton characterizes Japanese managers as 'a coordinator of the network' (Dutton 1987).

Many authors argue that Japanese leaders tend to use a participative leadership communication style, where managers encourage and facilitate the flow of information and generate consensus among organizational members. Thus, Japanese team leaders focus on people-oriented communication in order to maintain group harmony. Leading in Japan means a more people-oriented than task-oriented mentoring. Leadership is therefore more focused on relationships than on tasks (Hirokawa 1981; Kroek *et al.* 1999; Tang *et al.* 2000; Kuncora 2007). Although managers often have the authority to decide on their own, Kroek *et al.* (1999) observe an implicit agreement that leaders consult with their team members before exerting their authority. Rao and Hashimoto (1997) underline that leadership in Japan is strongly based on reciprocity, i.e. leaders offer their subordinates friendship, respect, and esteem in exchange for compliance. In a comparative study, Martinsons and David found that 'Japanese business leaders employed decision-making processes that involved comparatively more people and more subjective elements that their counterparts in the U.S. and especially China' (Martinsons and Davison 2007: 293). Ishikawa (2012) describes leadership in Japan as 'Shared Leadership' or 'Gatekeeping Leadership', characterized by the tasks of directing, motivating, and supporting other team members. Unlike the Western concept of transformational leadership, shared leadership is regarded as a collective construct, with a focus on interaction between team members and the sharing of leadership responsibilities. Similarly, Pohl and Wolframm (2014) argue that the role of leaders in Japan is more the collection, handling, and communication of ideas between middle management and the supervisory board, instead of guidance with a strong hand and individual decision-making. Leaders are expected to maintain harmony and consensus, thus enabling the best possible solution for all persons involved.

Charisma

Duke emphasizes that '[f]ew Japanese . . . can be described in Western terms as charismatic leaders who stand out by demonstrating unique qualities that attract others to follow. It is simply not part of the cultural tradition of the society' (Duke 1991: 30). Others also state that Japanese managers do not stand out from the group (Kroek *et al.* 1999; Pearson *et al.* 2003).

Keiza Doyukai's *16th Whitebook* summarizes the role of the ideal leader (i.e. top manager) of a Japanese company as an 'evangelist of corporate philosophy', as somebody who gives HR development priority, as a good communicator (Keizai Doyukai 2009).

New developments in Japanese leadership

Case-based research on the occupational careers of Japanese leaders by Hasegawa (2010); Pohl and Wolframm (2014), and by the authors, suggests that a new type of leader has entered into top positions in some Japanese companies. Unlike the traditional Japanese leaders, these new leaders have not served their whole career in the company in which they have been appointed into the top position. Moreover, these new leaders often have experience abroad, either from job assignments or from academic studies. However, these leaders can often be found in companies related to the Internet, mobile telecommunications, or computer games, i.e. industries which cannot be regarded as traditional Japanese industries. Moreover, although many others believe that these leaders also pursue a different leadership style, there is an obvious lack in empirically founded evidence.

Conclusions

Literature on Japanese leaders draws a picture of men (because women are still a rare species in management ranks in Japan) who do not form a class of their own, but who are an integral part of the workforce of their company, from which they usually have developed into management positions.

They harbour values like loyalty, paternalism, and collectivism. Their foremost tasks are to motivate employees; maintain harmony; listen intensively; and help their employees to develop and voice their ideas. The ideal Japanese leadership style is based on indirect discussion, implicit consensus and non-verbal communication, where the typical leader provides only the overall objectives and broad group assignments and leaves it to the subordinates to find a solution within the group.

Promotion into management ranks is still often a matter of seniority. What is striking, however, is the continued strong influence of the name of the school from which the management candidates have graduated. Looking at these numbers, the mainstream perception of top managers as merely 'another important employee' (Dutton 1987: 24) and the denial of a 'manager class' seems doubtful.

Although the importance of Japanese managers, especially top managers, has been downplayed by researchers and managers, likewise, in the past decades, there seems to be a growing perception of their impact in the last few years.

Notes

1 Also, in the general literature on Japanese management, values and attitudes have been a dominant focus of research (Godkin and Endō 1995: table 3, p. 89).
2 See Mintzberg (1999) for a review of the aspects of a manager's role most emphasized in the literature.
3 The PRME initiative (principles of responsible management education) provides a widely accepted international framework for business schools to advance responsible management education in line with the ten principles of the United Nations Global Compact (UN PRME 2015). Of the more than 500 signatories (business schools around the world), only five are from Japan (UN PRME 2015).
4 See Herbes (2009) for other purposes of *shukkō*.
5 *Shukkō*: temporary secondment, often to an affiliate (Herbes 2009), *amakudari*: second career at an affiliate after retirement (Herbes 2006).

References

Aarsman, Mieke (2014). *What Women Want: Exploring Perceptions and Desires of Japanese Women Regarding Work and Family Planning*. Master's Thesis in Asian Studies (120), Japanese track, Universiteit Leiden, Leiden.

Abegglen, J. C. (2006). *21st-century Japanese Management: New Systems, Lasting Values*, Basingstoke: Palgrave Macmillan.

Adachi, Kazuhiko (1989). Problems and prospects of management development of female employees in Japan. *Journal of Management Development*, 8(4): 32–40.

Alston, J. (1989). Wa, Guanxi, and Inhwa: managerial principles in Japan, China, and Korea. *Business Horizons*, 32(2): 26–31.

Baden-Fuller, C. (2009). *Special Issue: Japanese Management, Long Range Planning*, 42(4): 423.

Bando, M. (2007). *A Comparison of Women Executives in Japan and the United States*, USJP Working Paper 07–03, 1–30. Cambridge, MA: Harvard University

Beck, J. and Beck, M. N. (1994). *The Change of a Lifetime: Employment Patterns Among Japan's Managerial Elite*, Honolulu, Hawaii: University of Hawaii Press.

Biemann, T. and Wolf, J. (2009). Career patterns of top management team members in five countries: an optimal matching analysis. *International Journal of Human Resource Management*, 20(5): 975–991.

Bigoness, W. J., Blakely, G.L. (1996). A cross-national study of managerial values. *Journal of International Business Studies*, 27(4): 739–752.

Boyles, C. and Shibata, A. (2009). Job satisfaction, work time, and well-being among married women in Japan. *Feminist Economics*, 15(1): 57–84.

Bozkurt, Ö. (2012). Foreign Employers as relief routes: women, multinational corporations and managerial careers in Japan. *Gender, Work and Organization*, 19(3): 225–253.

Buecher, S. (1994). *Topmanager im japanischen Unternehmen – eine empirische Untersuchung*, Bochum, Germany: Universitätsverlag Dr N. Brockmeyer.

Catalyst (2015). Women in Japan. http://www.catalyst.org/knowledge/women-japan, last accessed 30 October 2015.

Chen, Z., Wakabayashi, M. and Takeuchi, N. (2004). A comparative study of organizational context factors for managerial career progress: focusing on Chinese state-owned, Sino-foreign joint ventures and Japanese corporations. *International Journal of Human Resources Management*, 15(4–5): 750–774.

Chiba, H., Sawaji, O., and Tikubo, R. (1997). Salaryman today and into tomorrow. *Compensation Benefits Review*, 29(5): 67–75.

Choi, T. H. and Nakano, C. (2008). The evolution of business ethics in Japan and Korea over the last decade. *Human Systems Management*, 27(3): 183–199.

Cooke, F. L. (2013). Gender and management in East Asia. In: Warner, M. (ed.), *Managing Across Diverse Cultures in East Asia: Issues and Challenges in a Changing Globalized World*, London and New York: Routledge, pp. 153–167.

Dirks, D., Huchet, J. F. and Ribault, T. (eds) (1999). *Japanese Management in the Low Growth Era: Between External Shocks and Internal Evolution*, Berlin: Springer.

Dorfman, P., Howell, J. P., Hibino, S., Lee, J. K., Uday, T., and Bautista, A. (1997). Leadership in Western and Asian countries: commonalities and differences in effective leadership process across cultures. *Leadership Quarterly*, 8(3): 233–274.

Duignan, R. and Iaquinto, A. (2005). Female managers in Japan: early indications of career progression. *Women in Management Review* 20(3): 191–207.

Duke, B. C. (1991). *Education and Leadership for the Twenty-First Century: Japan, America and Britain*, New York: Praeger.

Dutton, R.E. (1987). The Japanese manager: a coordinator of the network. *Business Forum* 12(2): 21–24.

Futagami, S. (2010). *Non-standard Employment in Japan: Gender Dimensions*. International Institute for Labour Studies Discussion Paper. Geneva, Switzerland: IILS Publications, pp. 1–19.

Fujimoto, T. (2007). Architecture-based comparative advantage – a design information view of manufacturing. *Evolutionary and Institutional Economics Review*, 4 (1): 55–112.

Giacomino, D. E., Akers, M. D. and Fujita, A. (2001). Personal values of Japanese business managers. *Business Forum*, 241(2): 9–14.

Godkin, L. and Endō, M. (1995). An analysis of Japan-Focused cross-cultural management research: 1981–1990. *Journal of Education for Business*, 71(2): 87–91.

Haak, R. and Pudelko, M. (eds) (2005). *Japanese Management: The Search for a New Balance Between Continuity and Change*, Basingstoke, UK: Palgrave Macmillan.

Hasegawa, Y. (2010). *Rediscovering Japanese Business Leadership: 15 Japanese Managers and the Companies They're Leading to New Growth*, Hoboken, NJ: John Wiley and Sons.

Hassard, J., Morris, J., and McCann, L. (2012). 'My brilliant career?' New organizational forms and changing managerial careers in Japan, the UK, and USA. *Journal of Management Studies*, 49(3): 571–599.

Herbes, C. (2006). *Post-Merger-Integration bei europäisch-japanischen Unternehmenszusammenschlüssen: Konfliktorientierte Analyse am Beispiel des Lieferantenmanagements*, Wiesbaden, Germany: Deutscher Universitäts-Verlag.

Herbes, C. (2009). Restructuring of Japanese enterprises – programs for a special institutional environment. In: Haghirian, P. (ed.), *Innovation and Change in Japanese Management*, Palgrave Macmillan.

Hirokawa, R. Y. (1981). Improving intraorganizational communication: a lesson from Japanese management. *Communication Quarterly*, 30: 35–40.

Hofstede, G. (1980). *Culture's Consequences: International Differences in Work-Related Values*, Beverly Hills, CA: Sage Publications.

Iida, T. and Morris, J. (2008). Farewell to the salaryman? The changing roles and work of middle managers in Japan. *International Journal of Human Resource Management*, 19(6): 1072–1087.

Ishida, H., Spilerman, S., and Su, K.-H. (1995). *Educational Credentials and Promotion Prospects in a Japanese and an American Organization*, New York: Columbia Business School, Center on Japanese Economy Working Paper No. 92, pp. 1–27.

Ishikawa, J. (2012). Transformational leadership and gatekeeping leadership: the roles of norm for maintaining consensus and shared leadership in team performance. *Asia Pacific Journal of Management*, 29(2): 265–283.

Isomura, K. and Huang, P. (2012). Exploring the future direction of Japan's MBA education, *Asia Pacific and Globalization Review* 2.1, not paginated.

Jackson, K. and Tomioka, M. (2004). *The Changing Face of Japanese Management*, London: Routledge.

Jones, R.S. and Urasawa, S. (2011). *Labour Market Reforms in Japan to Improve Growth and Equity*. OECD Economics Department Working Papers, No. 889, OECD Publishing.

Kambayashi, N., Morita, M., and Okabe, Y. (2007). *Management Education in Japan*, Oxford, UK: Chandos Publishing.

Kase, K., Sáez-Martínez, F. J., and Riquelme, H. (2005). *Transformational CEOs: Leadership and Management Success in Japan*, Cheltenham and Northampton, UK: Edward Elgar.

Kato, T. (2001). The end of lifetime employment in Japan?: evidence from national surveys and field research. *Journal of the Japanese and International Economies*, 15(4): 489–514.

Kato, T. and Rockel, M. (1992). The importance of company breeding in the U.S. and Japanese managerial labour markets: a statistical comparison. *Japan and the World Economy*, 4: 39–45.

Keizai Doyukai (2009). *The 16th Corporate White Paper: Creating a New Style of Japanese Corporate Management*, www.doyukai.or.jp/en/, last accessed 17 October 2015.

Kobayashi, Y. (1998). Path to becoming a manager: promotion, advancement and incentives for office workers. In: Tachibanaki, T. (ed.), *Who Runs Japanese Business? Management and Motivation in the Firm*, Cheltenham and Northampton, UK: Edward Elgar.

Kroek, G., Von Glinow, M. A., and Wellinghoff, A. (1999). *Revealing Competencies for Global Managers: Using Decision Room Technology to Identify and Align Management Competence with Corporate Strategy*, Miami: Florida International University, Working Paper.

Kuncora, S. (2007). *Culture and Team Leadership Communication Effectiveness: A Cross-cultural Study from Japanese and German Leadership Communication Literature*, New Zealand: Unitec.

Lansing, P. and Ready, K. (1988). Hiring women managers in Japan: an alternative for foreign employers. *California Management Review*, 30(3): 112–127.

Lavelle, L. and Kahn, D. (2015). *QS Global 200 Business Schools Report*, www.topmba.com/why-mba/publications/200-global-business-schools-report-201415/thank-you, last accessed 17 October 2015.

Levonian, M. (2013). *Contemporary Women's Employment in Japan: The Effects of State-Mandated Gender Roles, Wars, and Japan, Inc.* Claremont McKenna College Senior Thesis, Paper 618.

Martinsons, M. G. and Davison, R. M. (2007). Strategic decision making and support systems: comparing American, Japanese and Chinese management. *Decision Support Systems*, 43: 284–300.

Maury, R. (1991). *Die japanischen Manager – Wie sie denken, wie sie handeln, wie sie Weltmärkte erobern*, Wiesbaden, Germany: Gabler.

Mintzberg, H. (1999). The manager's job. In: Mintzberg, H., Quinn, J. B., and Ghoshal, S. (eds), *The Strategy Process, Revised European Edition*, Harlow, Essex: Pearson Education.

Misumi, J. (1990). The Japanese management of work and small group activities in Japanese industrial organizations. *International Journal of Psychology*, 25: 819–832.

Misumi, J. (1995). The development in Japan of the performance-maintenance (PM) theory of leadership. *Journal of Social Issues*, 51(1): 213–218.

Mujtaba, B. G. and Isomura, K. (2012). Examining the Japanese leadership orientations and their changes. *Leadership and Organization Development Journal*, 33(4): 401–420.

Nakano, C. (1999). Attempting to institutionalize ethics: case studies from Japan. *Journal of Business Ethics*, 18(4): 335–343.

Nemoto, K. (2013a). Long working hours and the corporate gender divide in Japan. *Gender, Work and Organization*, 20(5): 512–527.

Nemoto, K. (2013b). When culture resists progress: masculine organizational culture and its impacts on the vertical segregation of women in Japanese companies, *Work, Employment and Society*, 27: 153–169.

Noda, T. (1998). Determinants of top executives' promotion and remuneration. In: Tachibanaki, T. (ed.), *Who Runs Japanese Business? Management and Motivation in the Firm*, Cheltenham and Northampton, UK: Edward Elgar.

Nonaka, I. and Johansson, J. K. (1985). Japanese management: what about the 'hard' skills? *The Academy of Management Review*, 10(2): 181–191.

Ohashi, I. (1998). Does the name of the university matter? In: Tachibanaki, T. (ed.), *Who Runs Japanese Business? Management and Motivation in the Firm*, Cheltenham and Northampton, UK: Edward Elgar.

Okabe, Y. (2012). Changes in Japanese managers' work values and attitudes: a comparison of 1995 and 2009. *International Journal of Human Resource Management*, 23(6): 1216–1225.

Ouchi, W. (1981). *Theory Z: How American Business Can Meet the Japanese Challenge*, Reading, MA: Addison-Wesley.

Ouchi, W. and Jaeger, A. (1978). Type Z organization: stability in the midst of mobility. *Academy of Management Review*, 3: 308–311.

Pascale, R. and Athos, A. (1981). *The Art of Japanese Management: Applications for American Executives*, New York: Warner Books.

Pearson, Cecil A. L., Chatterjee, S. R., and Okachi, K. (2003). Managerial work role perceptions in Japanese organizations: an empirical study. *International Journal of Management* 20(1): 101-108.

Picken, S. D. B. (1987). Values and value related strategies in Japanese corporate culture. *Journal of Business Ethics*, 6(2): 137–143.

Pohl, Y., Wolframm, J. (2014). Japans CEOs: Zwischen den Stühlen (Japan's CEOs: between the chairs). *Japan Markt*, February: 6–14.

Ralston, D. A., Gustafson, D. J., Elsass, P. M., Cheung, F., and Terpstra, R. H. (1992). Eastern values: a comparison of managers in the United States, Hong Kong, and the People's Republic of China. *Journal of Applied Psychology*, 77: 664–671.

Ralston, D. A., Holt, D. H., Terpstra, R. H., and Kai-Cheng, Y. (1997). The impact of national culture and economic ideology on managerial work values: a study of the United States, Russia, Japan, and China. *Journal of International Business Studies*, 28(1): 177–207.

Rao, A. and Hashimoto, K. (1997). Universal and culturally specific aspects of managerial influence: a study of Japanese managers. *Leadership Quarterly*, 8(3): 295–312.

Robbins, S. P. and Coulter, M. (1999). *Management*, 6th edn, Upper Saddle River, NJ: Prentice-Hall.

Saba, S. (1989). *The Japanese Corporation and its Management*, Working Paper No. 26, New York: Columbia Business School, Center on Japanese Economy.

Simon, H. A. (1976). *Administrative Behavior: a Study of Decision-Making Processes in Administrative Organizations*, 3rd edn, New York: Free Press.

Spilerman, S. and Ishida, H. (1995). *Stratification and Attainment in a Large Japanese Firm*, Working Paper No. 91, New York: Columbia University, Graduate School of Business, Center on Japanese Economy and Business.

Steinhoff, P. G. and Tanaka, K. (1993). Women managers in Japan. *International Studies of Management and Organization*, 23(2): 25–48.

Tachibanaki, T. (1987). The determination of the promotion process in organizations and of earnings differentials. *Journal of Economic Behavior and Organization*, 8(4): 603–616.

Tachibanaki, T. (1998). Road to the top and executive management goals. In: Tachibanaki, T. (ed.), *Who Runs Japanese Business? Management and Motivation in the Firm*, Cheltenham and Northampton, UK: Edward Elgar.

Tang, T., Kim, J., O'Donald, D. (2000). Perceptions of Japanese organizational culture: employees in non-unionized Japanese-owned and unionized US-owned automobile plants. *Journal of Managerial Psychology*, 15(6): 535–559.

Toh, S. M. and Leonardelli, G. J. (2012). Cultural constraints on the emergence of women as leaders. *Journal of World Business*, 47(4), 604–611.

UN PRME (2015). www.unprme.org/about-prme/index.php, last accessed on 17 October 2015.

Von Glinow, M. A., Huo, Y. P., and Lowe, K. (1999). Leadership across the Pacific Ocean: a trinational comparison. *International Business Review*, 8: 1–15.

Warner, M. (2013). Management education and training in East Asia: China, Japan and South Korea. In: Warner, M. (ed.), *Managing across Diverse Cultures in East Asia: Issues and Challenges in a Changing Globalized World*. London and New York: Routledge, pp. 246–260.

Weathers, C. (2005). Equal opportunity for Japanese women: what progress? *Japanese Economy*, 33(4): 16–44.

Witt, M.A. and Redding. G. (2009). The reasons for the existence of the firm: Germany and Japan compared. *The Academy of Management Proceedings*, Annual Meeting Proceedings, DOI 10.5465/AMBPP.2009.44260241.

Wu, M.-Y. (2006). Compare participative leadership theories in three cultures. *China Media Research* 2(3): www.chinamediaresearch.net, last accessed 17 October 2015.

Wu, W., Lin, C., and Lee, L. (2000). Personal characters, decision-making patterns and leadership styles of female managers: a comparative study of American, Taiwanese, and Japanese female managers. *Cross Cultural Management – an International Journal*, 7(4): 18–32.

Yancey, G. B. and Watanabe, N. (2009). Differences in perceptions of leadership between U.S. and Japanese workers. *The Social Science Journal*, 46: 268–281.

Yang, B., Ding, D., Umezu, M., Siegenthaler, C. P., Okamatsu, A. and Park. Y. (2011) Humanistic management education in Asia: management education in Asian business schools for the changing era (cases from China, Japan, and Korea). In: Amann, W., Pirson, M., Dierkmeier, C., von Kimakowitz, E., and Spitzek, H. (eds), *Business Schools Under Fire: Humanistic Management Education as the Way Forward*, Palgrave Macmillan, pp. 323–339.

Yashiro, A. (2013). Selection and promotion of managers in Japanese companies: present and future perspectives. *Japan Labour Review*, 10(1): 25–43.

Yuasa, M. (2005). Japanese women in management: getting closer to 'realities' in Japan. *Asia Pacific Business Review*, 11(2): 195–211.

18

Diversity in the Japanese firm

Stephanie Assmann

Introduction

Japan is a relative newcomer to the implementation of diversity management. Diversity management in Japan has so far focused primarily on the advancement of women. In recent years, a number of companies have implemented diversity management in their corporate culture. The automaker Nissan, under a management team run by Charles Ghosn from Renault, increased the proportion of women in managerial positions from 1.6 per cent in 2003 to 4 per cent in 2006 (Tanikawa 2006). Another example is the clothing retailer Uniqlo, which introduced family-friendly policies that include sending employees home at 7 pm so that they have time to devote to their families (Tanikawa 2006).

These headlines concern a limited number of companies, which raises the question of how far diversity management practices have been implemented in Japan. Under the current prime minister, Shinzo Abe, who has developed a growth and revitalization strategy dubbed Abenomics, three arrows target monetary policy, a flexible fiscal policy, and a new growth strategy. In particular, the reforms targeted by the third arrow of Abenomics relate to diversity management. The objectives of the growth strategy are to increase labour mobility and to change the Dispatch Worker Law (*Rōdōsha haken-hō*)[1] by removing all limitations on using temporary staff. A further goal is the advancement of the employment of women and skilled foreigners (North 2014).

This chapter first introduces the concept of diversity management, and then gives an overview of diversity management in Japan. I will discuss the implementation and advancement of diversity management practices with regard to gender, cultural diversity, disability, age, and, finally, employment status.

Diversity and diversity management

Diversity in its most basic sense is defined as a 'set of attributes which make an individual different from others' (Klarsfeld 2012: 395). Attributes of difference include concepts such as gender, race, age, education, knowledge, religion, civil status, and disability (Klarsfeld 2012: 395). The acknowledgement of diversity has its roots in the United States, in the Civil Rights Movement of the 1960s. The beginnings of diversity management in companies, which acknowledges the inclusion of difference as a positive force, which can indeed be conducive to corporate culture, emerged in the United States with the publication of *Workforce 2000* in 1987 by the Hudson Institute, an independent think-tank.[2] This report foresaw challenges in the labour market at the beginning of the twenty-first century, such as a decrease in younger workers and an increase in women, migrants, and older people in the workforce, and suggested that these challenges could only be met through effective human-resource policies such as flexible working hours, child-care programmes, and diversity training.

Apart from the United States of America, various countries have acknowledged the challenges of globalization and the need to manage diversity. Diversity-management policies are addressed in Human-Resource Management (HRM). However, a unifying approach to managing diversity is difficult: 'Although researchers have examined several aspects of diversity, no comprehensive model exists' (Shen *et al.* 2009: 235). There are three reasons for that. First, the implementation of diversity management intersects with other equal-employment policies such as affirmative action programmes and positive action programmes. The concept of corporate social responsibility (CSR) also emphasizes the significance of managing diversity. Second, the concept of diversity needs to be seen in country-specific contexts. Klarsfeld *et al.* (2012) contend that gender equality remains the most significant diversity issue worldwide (Klarsfeld 2012: 396; see also Shen 2009: 235), but various countries approach diversity and diversity management in different ways. For example, in India, managing diversity with regard to ethnicity and religion is a pertinent issue. European countries such as France and Sweden focus on diversity with regard to the integration of migrants (Klarsfeld 2012: 396). In the United States and South Africa, the diversity of race is significant (Shen *et al.* 2009: 235). Third, attitudes towards the implementation of diversity management vary. Shen *et al.* (2009) contend that the acceptance of diversity in firms ranges from intolerance, to acceptance, to the appreciation of diversity (Shen *et al.* 2009: 236). They stress that it is not sufficient to merely tolerate diversity, but that it is vital to turn diversity into a positive force: 'The question is not, therefore, one of accepting that individuals are different but creating an atmosphere of inclusion and making a commitment to valuing diversity' (Shen *et al.* 2009: 236).

Gender

As mentioned earlier, in Japan, diversity management has predominantly focused on the advancement of gender equality in the workplace – more precisely on the advancement of women. Taguchi (2013) and Shiraki (2013) stress that approaching the concept of diversity from the angles of age, race, ethnicity, nationality, or religion is rare in Japan, while equal-employment policies that specifically target women are more significant.

Japan is lagging behind with regard to gender equality in employment. On the positive side, the employment rate of women rose significantly between 1975 and 2013, depending on age group and marital status. Whereas in 1975, employment rates for women were 61.5 per cent for women aged 45–49 years, and 42.6 per cent for women aged 25–29 years, these figures have changed. In 2013, 76.1 per cent of all women aged 45–49 and 79.0 per cent of all women aged 25–29 years were in employment (MIC 2014). However, the data from 2013 also show that the discrepancy between the employment rates of married and unmarried women persists. In 2013, 91.6 per cent of all unmarried women between the ages of 25 and 29 years were working but only 56.9 per cent of all married women in the same age group. This gap lessens but persists in the age group of 45–49-year-old women: whereas 83 per cent of all unmarried women work, this figure amounts to 73 per cent for married women (MIC 2014). An additional problem is the fact that rising employment of women coincides with a significant increase in female part-time employment since the early 1990s. The share of women who are enrolled in part-time employment increased from 51.1 per cent in 2004 to 54.4 per cent in 2012 (Ministry of Internal Affairs and Communications 2013: 3). Part-time employment often results in low salaries of two million yen, or even less for 60 to 70 per cent of the women who work part-time (Kuba 2011: 9).[3] Furthermore, women are underrepresented in law, politics, and academia. Only 16.5 per cent of all judges and 16.3 per cent of lawyers are women. Only 7.2 per cent of all management positions in enterprises (i.e. companies with more than 100 employees) are occupied by women (Tsujimura 2011: 4).

There are two laws that seek to improve the situation of women in the workplace and aim to establish gender equality. The Equal Employment Opportunity Law (EEOL) (*Danjo koyō kikai kintō-hō*), which was enacted in 1986 and underwent two reforms in 1997 and 2006, provides a comprehensive legal framework. The EEOL applies specifically to the private sector. After the reform in 2006, the EEOL includes positive-action programmes and measures against sexual harassment and indirect discrimination (MHLW 2007: 20–22). Together with the Basic Law for a Gender-Equal Society (*Danjo kyōdō sankaku shakai kihon-hō*), which was enacted in 1999 as a guideline for creating a society in which both men and women participate on an equal basis in all areas of life, these two programmes seek to establish gender equality. The strong emphasis on gender equality also becomes evident in the Abenomics policy, which incorporates the support of women in the workplace as one part of a multidimensional growth strategy (Taguchi 2013: 37).

Despite the reforms in 1997 and 2006, the implementation of gender equality has been slow. There are three reasons for that. First, the EEOL remains largely ineffective, because employers who do not comply with the EEOL are not sanctioned. Furthermore, employers have found loopholes to evade the law, through creating two career tracks within a firm: the management track (*sōgō shoku*), which, predominantly, men apply for, is based on a training-on-the-job programme, which includes rotations of appointments within a given firm and the acceptance of nationwide transfers. In contrast, the clerical track (*ippan shoku*), which is primarily sought after by women, consists of administrative and secretarial duties that leave no room for significant career development (North 2014). Second, the gendered two-track-career system perpetuates itself and leads to more women working in clerical positions, who find themselves in unstable work conditions, in particular after they return to the labour market after a period of family responsibilities. Third, women themselves make a choice between family responsibilities and employment, which is reflected in the fact that employment of women declines upon marriage and childbirth.

Ethnic diversity

On the surface, Japan appears to be a rather homogeneous society. According to the *CIA Factbook* (2014), 98.5 per cent of Japan's inhabitants are Japanese. But ethnic diversity does exist in Japan: 0.5 per cent of Japan's citizens are of Korean descent, whereas 0.4 per cent are ethnically Chinese. Other ethnicities account for 0.6 per cent. The Ainu are the indigenous people in Hokkaido.[4] Okinawans reside in Okinawa, in Taishō Ward in Osaka City (where approximately 20,000 residents are Okinawan migrants or their descendants (Rabson 2012)), and in Kyūshū, in the south of the country. A further ethnic group are the *Nikkeijin* – Brazilians and Peruvians of Japanese descent, many of whom returned to Japan in the 1990s.

As of 2014, Japan's population consists of 127 million people of Japanese nationality, but, according to data made available by the Ministry of Justice, merely 2.2 million migrants of non-Japanese descent (*zairyū gaikokujin*) were living in Japan as of December 2012 (MOJ 2014).

A look at the data reveals that migrants who are employed in Japan are often employed as 'foreign workers' (*gaikokujin rōdōsha*), who are considered temporary migrants as opposed to being long-term residents in Japan. According to data collected by the Ministry of Health, Labor and Welfare (MHLW) for the year 2012, the largest group of working migrants consisted of 296,388 Chinese migrants (43.4 per cent). The second largest group was of Brazilian nationality (101,891 persons, 14.9 per cent), followed by Filipinos (72,867 persons, 10.7 per cent), and nationals of the G8 nations and Australia and New Zealand (51,156 persons, 7.5 per cent). In addition, 31,780 Korean migrants (4.7 per cent), 23,267 Peruvians (3.4 per cent) and 26,828 Vietnamese migrants (3.9 per cent) were working in Japan. The remaining 78,273 persons (11.5 per cent) came from different countries (MHLW 2014: 2). Examining the industries that migrants are working in, the data reveal that 28.8 per cent of all migrants were employed in the manufacturing industry, followed by 16.1 per cent in the wholesale and sales industry, 13.3 per cent in hotels and gastronomic businesses, and 7.6 per cent who were employed in the service industry. Only a minor percentage of 4.8 per cent were employed in the information-technology industry; and only 3.7 per cent were employed in education (MHLW 2014: 4). The remaining 25.6 per cent were employed in different occupations (MHLW 2014: 4). Migrants tend to concentrate in Japan's major cities. Some 25.9 per cent of all migrants live in Tokyo, followed by 11.8 per cent who reside in Aichi Prefecture, 5.9 per cent in Kanagawa, 5.4 per cent in Shizuoka, and 5.2 per cent in Osaka (MHLW 2014: 6).

The inclusion or integration of non-Japanese people into the Japanese workplace poses a particular challenge. Lee (2010) gives one example of arbitrary treatment of migrants. During the 1980s, and starting in the 1990s, the Japanese government initiated programmes to attract Brazilians and Peruvians – *Nikkeijin* – with Japanese roots to come to Japan with the objective of long-term integration (Lee 2010: 69). Many *Nikkeijin* worked for automobile companies such as Toyota in Aichi Prefecture and for Mitsubishi (Lee 2010: 69). However, the financial crisis of 2008 resulted in lay-offs of manual workers, amongst them workers of Peruvian and Brazilian descent, who were paid a lump sum of 300,000 yen per person when they agreed to return to South America and not come back to Japan (Lee 2010: 69).

Against the background of an ageing society, the Japanese government has recognized the need to welcome migrants. In 2008, the liberal-democratic government under Prime Minister Yasuo Fukuda announced a shift from the strict control of immigration towards the establishment of an 'immigrant nation' (*imin kokka*) (Lee 2010: 76). However, the government seeks to attract highly skilled professionals in particular. In 2012, Japan reformed the immigration policy and introduced a points system for highly skilled foreign professionals. Points are calculated on the basis of age, work experience, academic qualifications, annual wages, and Japanese-language skills. For people who score more than 70 points, immigration requirements were relaxed with regards to receiving permanent residency (Nakatani 2013).

It will be a challenge to make a genuine commitment to the already existing ethnic minorities in Japan and to the long-term integration of migrants. So far, migrants are welcome as long as they are either highly skilled and/or are based in Japan on a temporary basis. But ethnic diversity includes the integration of future generations of migrants who have decided to stay in Japan and build families.

Disability

The integration of persons with disabilities into the workforce is strongly welfare-oriented in Japan, and concentrates on anti-discrimination policies and a minimum-requirement rate of employment. The Japanese government differentiates between persons with physical disabilities (*shintai shōgaisha*), persons with intellectual disabilities (*chiteki shōgaisha*), and persons with mental disabilities (*seishin shōgaisha*). According to data provided by the Cabinet Office of the government of Japan for the year 2010, 3.66 million persons in Japan were physically impaired, while a smaller number of 540,000 persons were intellectually impaired, and 3.23 million were suffering from mental disabilities.[5] According to data collected by the Ministry of Health, Labor and Welfare (MHLW), as of June 2010, the number of persons with disabilities (*shōgaisha*) who were employed by private companies (*minkan kigyō*) stood at 343,000 people. This figure has risen from 253,000 employed persons with disabilities who were in employment in 2000 to 303,000 employed persons in 2007, to 333,000 persons with disabilities in 2009.[6]

The Basic Act for Persons with Disabilities (*Shōgaisha kihon-hō*), which was enacted in 1970, stipulates that it is unlawful to discriminate against the rights of persons with disabilities. However, in a similar way to the enforcement of the Equal Employment Opportunity Act (EEOL) mentioned earlier, this legal framework remains rather ineffective, since compliance with the law is merely encouraged, but non-compliance with the law is not sanctioned. A more powerful tool for enforcing the inclusion of persons with disabilities in the workforce is the *Act on Employment Promotion of Persons with Disabilities* (*Shōgaisha koyō sokushin-hō*), which was enacted in 1960. Up to date, this law has been amended frequently: in 1976, in 1987, in 1997, in 2005, and again in 2008 (Hasegawa 2010). Compared with *The Basic Act for Persons with Disabilities*, this law is more effective, since it charges a penalty to employers who do not fulfil the quota and supplies financial benefits to employers that employ more disabled persons than the minimum-requirement rate mandates (Hasegawa 2010: 35).

In particular, after the amendment in 1976, the *Act on Employment Promotion of Persons with Disabilities* became a powerful tool, with the provisions as follows:

1   A quota system, which requires companies to fulfil a mandatory minimum employment rate. Currently, the quotas stand at 2.1 per cent for public corporations and at 1.8 per cent for private companies.
2   The law contains a payment system for people with disabilities.
3   The law stipulates a double counting system, which regards the employment of one person with severe disabilities as the employment of two people with disabilities.
4   The law also includes a disclosure system, which discloses the names of companies that do not fulfil the mandatory minimum-requirement rate of disabled persons. This act of publicly shaming companies that do not fulfil the legal requirements is supposed to help to ensure that the quotas are met.
5   Finally, the law includes a notification system, according to which employers must report the firing of a disabled person (Hasegawa 2010: 30). The amendment of 2005 strengthened the employment of people with mental disabilities, while the most recent revision in 2008 promotes the employment of disabled persons in medium-sized and small companies, and aims to establish the number of working hours over 20 hours per week but below 30 hours per week for people with physical and intellectual disabilities.[7]

Age

Against the background of an ageing workforce, the Japanese government has recognized the need to secure employment opportunities for people beyond the ages of 60 and 65 years. The question of the inclusion of employees who continue to be in employment beyond the age of

65 years, is becoming more significant as the baby-boomers (*dankai no sedai*) who were born between 1947 and 1949 approach retirement age (JILPT 2011: 4).

The major legal framework, which targets the employment of older employees, is the *Act Concerning Stabilization of Employment of Older Persons* (*Kōnenreisha nado no koyō no antei nado ni kansuru hōritsu*). This law emerged from the *Act for Promoting Employment of Middle-aged and Older Persons*, which was enacted in 1971. After a review of the law in 2004, employers were not only prohibited from setting a mandatory retirement age below 60, but were, in addition, required to create possibilities of continuing employment beyond the age of 60 (Fujimoto 2008: 60). In the fiscal year 2013, the mandatory retirement age was raised from 60 years to 61 years. Until 2025, the mandatory retirement age will increase at the rate of one year of age every three years, until the mandatory retirement age reaches 65 in 2025 (Schreiber 2013).

The results of the 'Survey on the Employment Status of the Ederly', which was conducted by the Japan Institute for Labor Policy and Training (JILPT) in the fiscal year of 2009/2010 show that companies have implemented the amendment of 2004 and continue to employ persons beyond the age of 60. Data from the Ministry of Health, Labor and Welfare (MHLW) confirm this. Japanese seniors are now more active on the labour market. The number of employees between 60 and 64 years of age increased from 3.17 million in 2005 to 4.59 million in 2013, whereas the number of employees aged 65 to 69 years who continued working increased from 2.28 million persons in 2005, to 3.05 million persons in 2009 (Takayama 2013), and to 3.75 million persons in 2013 (Cabinet Office 2014).

A considerable challenge with regard to employment of senior employees is the adjustment of mandatory retirement and the age at which employees receive pension-benefit payments. Japan has a two-tier social security pension system. The first tier provides a flat-rate benefit for all residents of Japan, whereas the second tier provides an earnings-related benefit for regular full-time employees who have worked for 30 hours or more per week for a time period of 25 or more years (Takayama 2013: 2). In principle, benefit payments begin at age 65, which Takayama (2013) refers to as the normal pensionable age (NPA). But, under certain conditions, it is possible to receive advanced benefit payments (Takayama 2013: 2). The principal programme for private enterprises is the *Kōsei Nenkin Hoken*, which set the age for receiving pension benefits at 55 for men in 1942. Since then – as Takayama (2013) discusses in depth – life expectancy has been rising, and it became necessary to close the income gap between the mandatory retirement age and the age of eligibility for pension benefits. Therefore, it is essential to secure employment for older age groups on the basis of a certain level of earned income, which motivates senior citizens to continue to work and enables them to defer the receipt of pension-benefit payments as long as possible. According to the demands of trade unions that this gap between retiring and starting to receive pension payments should be closed, employers have applied a variety of employment measures that target employees between the ages of 50 to 59 years. For instance, employers have transferred employees of this age group to smaller branch offices or have continued to re-employ people who have reached the retirement age on a contract basis, which entails shorter working hours and a reduction in salary (Takayama 2013: 6).

Further results of the research report by JILPT[8] have shown a correlation between educational history and vocational-skills development. The research report emphasizes the need to sustain an income beyond the age of 60, the significance of lifelong learning, and the importance of deferring pension payments, or of shifting pension payments towards providing medical care. However, little mention is made of managing intergenerational work environments, which is essential when implementing age-diversity practices. It will be vital to investigate how older employees can be successfully integrated in a society that places high importance on hierarchies based on age and seniority. In this context, economist Yumi Nishioka (2013) has pointed out that the employment of employees beyond the age of 60 years appears to be a form of diversity, but that the hierarchical principle by which senior employees pass on their knowledge and skills to younger employees (*sedai keishō-sei*) remains in place (Nishioka 2013: 18).

Sexual orientation: the situation of lesbian, gay, bisexual, and transgender individuals (LGBT)

Same-sex behaviour has been legal in Japan since 1880. In particular, in metropolitan areas like Tokyo and Osaka, vibrant LGBT communities exist. The Tokyo Rainbow Pride is the nation's largest festival for the LGBT community, and holds an annual parade in April with the aim of raising awareness of sexual minorities in Japan (Kim 2014, Tokyo Rainbow Pride Website). Cases of discrimination on the basis of sexual orientation remain rare in Japan. LGBT individuals can work in all professions. The Self-Defense Forces declared that sexual preference posed no barrier to being admitted into employment (Lunsing 2006: 146).

However, in the workplace, many LGBT individuals remain silent about their sexual orientation. Gay and lesbian individuals do experience difficulties. The pressure to conform to societal expectations and start a family is strong in Japan; LGBT individuals will feel this pressure. The legal situation leaves room for improvement. The discrimination against members of sexual minorities is not explicitly prohibited. Same-sex marriage is not legal in Japan (Lunsing 2006: 147). Article 24 of the Japanese constitution defines marriage as a union of two persons of the opposite sex. Same-sex partners cannot be included as spouses in the family register (*kōseki*). Discussions on whether to expand the EEOL to include equal-employment opportunities for sexual minorities have not yielded positive results.

Japanese society has been more sympathetic to persons who feel a need to change their gender identity, which is considered an illness (*shōgai*) and therefore needs to be cured (Lunsing 2006: 146). In 2004, the Act on Special Cases in Handling Gender for People with Gender Identity Disorder (*Seidō itsusei shōgaisha no seibetsu no toriatsukai no tokurei ni kansuru hōritsu*) was enacted, which allows transgender persons that are defined as having a Gender Identity Disorder to change their sex and legally change their gender. Changing the status of gender in the family register is essential, because problems might arise if the gender documented in the family register is different from the gender status that the individual has attained after the sex-change surgery (Lunsing 2006: 146). In order to undergo sex reassignment, very specific conditions must be met. Individuals who undergo sex reassignment:

1   must be at least twenty years or above;
2   must not be married at present;
3   must not have children who are under age;
4   must not have reproductive organs; and
5   must have the external genital features of the opposite sex.[9]

According to data compiled by the General Incorporated Association Japan People with Gender Identity Disorder [*sic*] (*Nihon seidō itsusei shōgai to tomoni ikiru hitobito no kai*), as of 2013, sex reassignment of 4,353 individuals has been approved.[10] MTF (male-to-female) transgender people who undergo sex-change surgery are likely to face similar discrimination to that experienced by women in the workplace (Lunsing 2006: 147).

The legal situation in particular for transgender people has improved, but effective laws that prohibit discrimination against sexual minorities are desirable in order to integrate people into the workforce, regardless of their sexual preference.

Diversification of employment patterns

When addressing diversity in the Japanese firm, it is essential to discuss the diversification of employment patterns. Based on the assumption of a predominantly male and native core workforce, post-war human resource management in Japan was characterized by three pillars: (1) lifetime employment (*shūshin koyō*); (2) payment and promotion based on seniority (*nenkō joretsu*); and (3) enterprise trade-unions (*rōdō kumiai*) (Aoki *et al*. 2012: 3).

However, after the collapse of the bubble economy around 1990, and after the global financial crisis in 2008, human–resource management in Japan underwent significant changes. First, payment schemes that are based on individual performance (*seikashugi*) as opposed to seniority and length of service, have gained greater significance (Benson *et al*. 2007: 895; Debroux *et al*. 2012: 623–625). Second, neoliberal employment policies such as the reforms of the Labor Dispatch Law (*Rōdōsha haken-hō*) have led to a deregulation of the labour market and an increase in atypical workers (Benson *et al*. 2007: 894), such as temporary workers who are employed on limited contracts and paid on an hourly basis. Part-time employment is also rising in Japan. The current percentage of part-time employees amounts to 37.1 per cent in 2015 (MHLW 2015). In 2010, the overall rate of part-time employees in Japan amounted to 34.3 per cent, compared with 16.4 per cent in 1985 and 32.6 per cent in 2005 (MIC 2013).[11] According to data collected by the Ministry of Health, Labor and Welfare (MHLW), in 2014, 32.88 million employees were regular employees (*seiki shain*), whereas 19.09 million employees were non-regular employees (*hiseiki shain*). Amongst these employees, 9.44 million were working part-time; 3.75 million were enrolled in temporary jobs (*arubaito*), 1.14 million were dispatch workers (*haken shain*), and 2.77 million were contract workers (*keiyaku shain*).

Aoki *et al*. (2012) make a connection between relations in the workplace and employment patterns. They stress that the Anglo-American model, which is based on universalistic relations and favours change and flexibility of employment, contrasts with the Japanese model, which is based on particularistic relations that emphasize group orientation and the favourable treatment of insiders. In contrast, particularistic relations result in continuity of employment and long-term service to a company (Aoki *et al*. 2012: 6). In other words, whereas Japanese firms maintain commitment to the principles of lifetime employment and payment schemes on the basis of seniority for their core workforces, contract workers and temporary employees are facing unstable employment conditions.

Conclusions and outlook

Perhaps the most effective step towards diversity management has been made with regard to employees beyond the ages of 60 and 65 years. The gradual increase in the mandatory retirement age to reach 65 in the year 2025 is a significant step towards the inclusion of older employees. Employment in this age group is rising, but further discussion of how to sucessfully create an intergenerational workforce in a society that equates age with higher hierarchical status is essential for sucessfully managing age diversity.

The implementation of gender diversity – albeit a priority in Abenomics – is lagging behind, as women are subjected to a gendered career system and frequent part-time work that leave little or no room for professional development. Comprehensive legal frameworks that aim to prevent discrimination against women, older employees, and employees with disabilities do exist. However, frameworks such as the EEOL and the *The Basic Act for Persons with Disabilities* are only partially effective, since their enactment was the result of Japan's aim to conform to international expectations. Furthermore, employers are merely encouraged to comply with these frameworks, and are not sanctioned when they do not obey them.

Attitudes towards non-Japanese nationals will need to change from the perception of temporary migrants or highly skilled foreign nationals towards a long-term commitment to ethnic diversity. A further step is the acknowledgement of the various ethnic and indigenous groups that reside in Japan. The increasing diversity of employment patterns poses a particular challenge. Advocated in Abenomics as neoliberal work policies that help to create flexibility on the labour market, temporary work conditions are also a source of instability, which needs to be countered by creating more stable work environments in terms of length of service and payment.

In the future, the inclusion of women, employees beyond the mandatory retirement age of 61, and the inclusion of non-Japanese employees will continue to be of importance as Japan faces the crippling effects of an ageing society. Given the demographic crisis, these measures will need to be implemented more quickly and more effectively, in order to secure employment. Furthermore, a more open attitude towards diversity will be necessary to shift the perception of diversity management from a utilitarian tool towards a genuine commitment to diversity.

Notes

1 The Labor Dispatch Law was enacted in 1986, and has undergone a number of reforms with regard to the expansion of applicable occupations and the duration of temporary employment (Yuasa 2008: 108). At the time of enactment, the law was limited to thirteen professions and expanded to twenty-six applicable professions in 1996. In 1999, the law applied to all occupations except the manufacturing industry (*seizōgyō*); the construction industry (*kensetsugyō*); lawyers; and doctors. In 2004, the Koizumi government moved even one step further in lifting the last remaining ban on temporary work in the manufacturing industry.

2 See for more information: United States General Accounting Office (GAO) (ed.) (1992). *The Changing Workforce. Demographic Issues Facing the Federal Government*, Washington, D.C.

3 The recent reform of the EEOL coincides with the revision of the part-time law (*tan-jikan rōdōsha no koyō kanri no kaizen-nado ni kansuru hōritsu*) in June 2006. The part-time law was enacted in 1993 and defines part-time work as 35 working hours per week (Broadbent 2005: 6). The reformed part-time law stipulates that part-time workers who do the same work as full-time employees must earn the same wages, and prohibits discriminatory treatment of part-time employees (*sabetsuteki taigū no kinshi*). The reformed law also requires the promotion of temporary employees to regular employees (*sei shain-ka sokushin*).

4 The Ainu had to go through a long struggle to be officially recognized by the Japanese government as an indigenous people (*senjū minzoku*). In 1997, the Japanese government acknowledged the existence of indigenous peoples and recognized the Ainu as an indigenous people, which led to the recognition of the *Ainu Cultural Promotion Act* (CPA) as a law in 1997 (Siddle 2009: 33–34).

5 Cabinet Office, Government of Japan (ed.), *The Situation of Disabled Persons* (*Shōgaisha no jōkyō*), http://www8.cao.go.jp/shougai/whitepaper/h25hakusho/gaiyou/h1_01.html, last accessed 18 October 2015.

6 Ministry of Health, Labor and Welfare (MHLW) (2010). *Employment of Disabled Persons* (*Shōgaisha koyō no jōkyō*), www.mhlw.go.jp/bunya/koyou/shougaisha/dl/shougaisha_genjou01.pdf. Accessed on 18 October 2015.

7 Further amendments of the *Act on Employment Promotion of Persons with Disabilities* (*Shōgaisha koyō sokushin-hō*), which followed in 1987 and 1997, expanded the scope of the definition of disabilities and included people living with intellectual and mental disabilities. The amendment of 1997 included mandatory employment not only of persons with physical disabilities but also with intellectual abilities, and raised the minimum employment rate of persons with disabilities at private companies from 1.6 per cent to 1.8 per cent, which is the current required quota.

8 The Japan Institute for Labor, Policy and Training (JILPT) (2011). *Study of the Current Status of Employment Among the Elderly, Research Report*, No. 137, June 2011. www.jil.go.jp/english/reports/documents/jilpt-research/no.137.pdf, last accessed 17 October 2015.

9 The content of the act is accessible at: Legislative Bureau House of Councillors (*Sangiin hōsei kyoku*) (2003), *Act on Special Cases in Handling Gender for People with Gender Identity Disorder* (*Seidō itsusei*

shōgaisha no seibetsu no toriatsukai no tokurei ni kansuru hōritsu), 16 July 2003, Law 111, http://hous-eikyoku.sangiin.go.jp/bill/outline007.htm, last accessed 27 October 2014.

10 General Incorporated Association Japan People with Gender Identity Disorder [sic] (*Nihon seidō itsusei shōgai to tomoni ikiru hitobito no kai*) (2014), Number of persons who have changed their sex according to the Act on Special Cases in Handling Gender for People with Gender Identity Disorder (*Seidō itsusei shōgaisha tokurei-hō ni yoru seibetsu no toriatsukai no henkō-sū no suii*), http://gid.jp/html/GID_law/index.html, last accessed 27 October 2014.

11 According to data compiled by the Ministry of Health, Labor and Welfare (MHLW) and the Ministry of Internal Affairs and Communications, non-regular employment includes part-time work, jobs (*arubaito*); dispatch work and contract-based work; and other non-defined forms of part-time employment (Ministry of Internal Affairs and Communications 2013).

References

Aoki, Katsuki, Delbridge, Rick, and Endo, Takahiro (2012). Japanese human resource management in post-bubble Japan. *The International Journal of Human Resource Management*, 25(18): 1–22.

Benson, John, Yuasa, Masae, and Debroux, Philippe (2007). The prospect for gender diversity in Japanese employment. *International Journal of Human Resource Management*, 18: 890–907.

Broadbent, K. (2005). Pawaa Appu! Women only unions in Japan. *Electronic Journal of Contemporary Japanese Studies* (ejcjs), 31 October 2005, available at: www.japanesestudies.org.uk/articles/2005/Broadbent.html, last accessed 30 October 2015.

Cabinet Office, Government of Japan (ed.) (2014) *White Paper on the Ageing Society, Employment of Elderly People (Heisei 26 Nenpan Kōrei Shakai Hakusho, Kōreisha no Shūgyō)*, http://www8.cao.go.jp/kourei/whitepaper/w-2014/zenbun/s1_2_4.html, last accessed 30 October 2015.

Cabinet Office, Government of Japan (ed.) (2015) *The Situation of Disabled Persons (Shōgaisha no jōkyō)*, http://www8.cao.go.jp/shougai/whitepaper/h25hakusho/gaiyou/h1_01.html, last accessed 17 October 2015.

Central Intelligence Agency (CIA) (2014). *The World Factbook, Country Profile Japan*, https://www.cia.gov/library/publications/the-world-factbook/geos/ja.html, last accessed 31 October 2015.

Debroux, Philippe, Harry, Wes, Hayashi, Shigeaki, Jason, Huang Heh, Jackson, Keith, and Kiyomiya, Toru (2012). In: Brewster, Chris and Mayrhofer, Wolfgang (eds), Japan, Korea and Taiwan: issues and trends in human resource management. *Handbook of Research on Comparative Human Resource Management*, Edward Elgar: Cheltenham and Northampton, 620–643.

Fujimoto, Makoto (2008). Employment of older people after the amendment of the act concerning stabilization of employment of older persons: current state of affairs and challenges. *Japan Labor Review*, 5(2): 59–88.

General Incorporated Association Japan People with Gender Identity Disorder [sic] (*Nihon seidō itsusei shōgai to tomoni ikiru hitobito no kai*) (2014). Number of persons who have changed their sex according to the Act on Special Cases in Handling Gender for People with Gender Identity Disorder (*Seidō itsusei shōgaisha tokurei-hō ni yoru seibetsu no toriatsukai no henkō-sū no suii*), http://gid.jp/html/GID_law/index.html, last accessed 17 October 2015.

Hasegawa, Tamako (2010). Japan's employment measures for persons with disabilities: centred on quota system of 'Act on Employment Promotion of Persons with Disabilities'. *Japan Labour Review*, 7(2): Spring 2010: 26–42.

Japan Institute for Labor, Policy and Training (JILPT) (2011). *Study of the Current Status of Employment Among the Elderly*, Research Report No. 137, June 2011. www.jil.go.jp/english/reports/documents/jilpt-research/no.137.pdf, last accessed 17 October 2015.

Kim, Sang Woo (2014). Parade aims to raise awareness of sexual minorities. *The Japan Times*, 23 April 2014, www.japantimes.co.jp/news/2014/04/23/national/parade-aims-raise-awareness-sexual-minorities/#.VE8hurT4CYY, last accessed 15 October 2015.

Klarsfeld, Alain, Combs, Gwendolyn M., Susaeta, Lourdes, and Belizon, Maria (2012). International perspectives on diversity and equal treatment policies and practices. In: Brewster, Chris and Mayrhofer, Wolfgang (eds), *Handbook of Research on Comparative Human Resource Management*, Edward Elgar: Cheltenham and Northampton, UK, 393–415.

Kuba, Yoshiko (2011). The current women's work: 25 years since the Equal Employment Opportunity Law enacted. *Josei Rōdō Kenkyū (Society for the Study of Working Women)*, 55: 7–23.

Lee, Suim (2010). Nihon ni okeru Daibashiti Maneejimento no kanōsei to kongo no kadai. Gaikokujin jinzai no katsuyō no genjō to mondai-ten o tsūjite (Possibilities and future tasks of diversity management in Japan. Approaching the current situation and problems of employment of foreign human resources). *The Journal of Business Studies Ryukoku University*, 2010(3): 68–82.

Legislative Bureau House of Councillors (*Sangiin hōsei kyoku*) (2003). Act on Special Cases in Handling Gender for People with Gender Identity Disorder (*Seidō itsusei shōgaisha no seibetsu no toriatsukai no tokurei ni kansuru hōritsu*), 16 July 2003, Law 111, http://houseikyoku.sangiin.go.jp/bill/outline007. htm, last accessed 17 October 2015.

Lunsing, Wim (2006). LGBT Rights in Japan. *Peace Review: a Journal of Social Justice*, 17(2–3): 143–148.

Ministry of Health, Labor and Welfare (MHLW) (*Kōsei Rōdōshō*) (2007). *Danjo kikai kintō-hō no aramashi* (Outline of the Equal Employment Opportunity Law) (2007) www.mhlw.go.jp/general/seido/ koyou/danjokintou/dl/danjyokoyou_a.pdf, last accessed 17 October 2015.

Ministry of Health, Labor and Welfare (MHLW) (*Kōsei Rōdōshō*) (2010). Employment of Disabled Persons (*Shōgaisha koyō no jōkyō*), www.mhlw.go.jp/bunya/koyou/shougaisha/dl/shougaisha_genjou01.pdf, last accessed 17 October 2015.

Ministry of Health, Labor and Welfare (MHLW) (*Kōsei Rōdōshō*) (2011). *Heisei 22 nenpan. Hataraku josei no jitsujō* (The Situation of Working Women 2010), *I hataraku josei no gaikyō* (Chapter I: Overview of Working Women), Press Release, 20 May 2011. www.mhlw.go.jp/bunya/koyoukintou/josei-jitsujo/ dl/10c.pdf: page 3, last accessed 17 October 2015.

Ministry of Health, Labor and Welfare (MHLW) (*Kōsei Rōdōshō*) (2014). *Gaikokujin koyō jōkyō no todokede jōkyō* (Notification status of foreigners' employment situation) as of October 2012. www.mhlw.go.jp/ stf/houdou/2r9852000002ttea-att/2r9852000002tthv.pdf, last accessed 17 October 2015.

Ministry of Internal Affairs and Communications (MIC), Statistical Office (Sōmushō tōkei-kyoku) (2013). *Rōdō-ryoku chōsa (shōsai shūkei) heisei 24 nen heikin (sokuhō) kekka no yōyaku* (Labor Force Survey (Summary of Details), Summary of Results (Preliminary Report) for the Year 2012), www.stat.go.jp/ data/roudou/sokuhou/nen/dt/pdf/index1.pdf, last accessed 30 October 2015.

Ministry of Internal Affairs and Communications (MIC), Statistical Office (Sōmushō tōkei-kyoku (2014). *Heisei 26 nenpan. Jōhō tsūshin hakusho no pointo* (Characteristics of the White Paper on Information Technology 2014), http://www.soumu.go.jp/johotsusintokei/whitepaper/ja/h26/html/nc141210. html, last accessed 30 October 2015.

Ministry of Internal Affairs and Communications (MIC), Statistical Office (Sōmushō tōkei-kyoku) (2015). *Rōdō-ryoku chōsa (shōsai shūkei) heisei 27 4–6 gatsuki heikin (Sokuhō)* (Labor Force Survey (Preliminary Report) for April to June 2015), http://www.stat.go.jp/data/roudou/sokuhou/4hanki/dt/pdf/2015_2. pdf, last accessed 30 October 2015.

Ministry of Justice (Hōmushō) (MOJ) (2014). *Zairyū gaikokujin tōkei (kyū Tōroku gaikokujin tōkei) tōkei- hyō* (Statistics of Foreign Residents (Previously: Statistics of Registered Foreigners) Overview), www.moj. go.jp/housei/toukei/toukei_ichiran_touroku.html, last accessed 17 October 2015.

Nakatani, Iwao (2013). Drastic change in immigration policy off the Japanese election agenda. *East Asia Forum*, 21 July 2013, www.eastasiaforum.org/2013/07/21/drastic-change-in-immigration-policy-off-the-japanese-election-agenda/, last accessed 17 October 2015.

Nishioka, Yumi (2013). Daibashiti manajemento no aratana kaidan – jinzai manajemento no shiten kara (A new phase of diversity management – from the viewpoint of human resource management). *Eruda*, *[Elder]*, 35(3): 12–18.

North, Scott (2014). Limited regular employment and the reform of Japan's division of labour. *The Asia-Pacific Journal*, 12(15): No. 1, 14 April 2014, www.japanfocus.org/-Scott-North/4106, last accessed 17 October 2015.

Rabson, Steve (2012). Being Okinawan in Japan: the diaspora experience. *The Asia-Pacific Journal*, 10(12), No. 2, http://japanfocus.org/-Steve-Rabson/3720/article.html, last accessed 30 October 2015.

Schreiber, Mark (2013). Mandatory retirement takes a leap forward. *Japan Times Online*, 24 March 2013, www.japantimes.co.jp/news/2013/03/24/national/media-national/mandatory-retirement-takes-a-leap-forward/#.Uo6abS5mDc, last accessed 17 October 2015.

Shen, Jie, Chanda, Ashok, D'Netto, Brian, and Monga, Manjit (2009). Managing diversity through human resource management: an international perspective and conceptual framework. *The International Journal of Human Resource Management*, 20(2): 235–251.

Shiraki, Mitsuhide (2013). Daibashiti manajemento to gaikokujin shain (Diversity management and foreign employees). *Sangyō kunren*, 2013(10): 4–8.

Siddle, Richard M. (2009). The Ainu: indigenous people of Japan. In: Weiner, Michael (ed.), *Japan's Minorities: the Illusion of Homogeneity*. Sheffield Centre for Japanese Studies/Routledge Series, 2nd edn, 2009, 21–39.

Taguchi, Seiko (2013). *Mitsui Sumitomo Ginkō no daibashiti shuishin ni kansuru torikumi* (Approach of Mitsui Sumitomo Bank to the advancement of diversity), Ippan shadan hōjin zenkoku ginkō kyōkai (ed). *Kin'yu*, 797, 20 August 2013: 37–46.

Takayama, Noriyuki (2013). *Closing the Gap Between the Retirement Age and the Normal Pensionable Age in Japan*. Research Institute for Policies on Pension and Aging, http://takayama-online.net/pie/stage3/Japanese/d_p/dp2012/dp583/text.pdf, accessed on 2 November 2015.

Tanikawa, Miki (2006). Japanese companies embrace diversity. *New York Times*, 1 June 2007, www.nytimes.com/2007/06/01/business/worldbusiness/01iht-wbjapan.1.5956210.html?pagewanted=alland_r=0#, last accessed 17 October 2015.

Tokyo Rainbow Pride Website, http://tokyorainbowpride.com, accessed October 30 2015.

Tsujimura, Miyoko (2011). *Pojitebu Akushon. 'Hō ni yoru byōdō' no gihō* (Positive Action. 'Equality through Law'). Tokyo: Iwanami.

United States General Accounting Office (GAO) (ed.) (1992). *The Changing Workforce. Demographic Issues Facing the Federal Government*. Washington DC: US GAO.

Yuasa, Makoto (2008). *Han-hinkon: 'Suberi-dai shakai' kara no dasshutsu*. (Against Poverty: the Escape from the 'Sliding Society'). Tokyo: Iwanami.

Part V
The Japanese market

19

Japanese consumer behaviour

Emi Moriuchi

Japanese consumer behaviour

Japan has one of the largest economies in the world by nominal GDP (Census 2010). Despite the evidence of Japan's corporate recovery (www.nytimes.com), consumer spending was still considered the weakest link in the 'Abenomics' development (Tabuchi 2013). Although the amount of consumer spending in Japan has fallen, economists are confident of the continuation of up-trend consumption (www.nytimes.com). Therefore, what are the current consumption habits of Japanese consumers? In this chapter, we will discuss the impact of culture on Japanese consumer behaviour, the Japanese preference for the country-of-origin products; the types of advertising that appeal to them; and the correlation between product choice and societal status. In conclusion, we will look at the new breed of luxury shoppers; how these Japanese consumers interpret luxury in the twenty-first century; and the role of working women in the Japanese consumer market.

Culture

Culture has a ubiquitous influence over all aspects of social behaviour and interaction. It is a multi-layered facet of human life. The view of culture, however, is dependent on how individuals perceive and interpret the phenomenon. But there is no unanimous decision on how to define culture (Craig and Douglas 2006). McCracken (1986) defines this phenomenon as the 'blueprint' of human activity. Sojka and Tansuhaj (1995) grouped culture within the marketing context into three major elements: values and belief systems; artefacts, symbols and rituals; and communication links, all of which propagate a cultural system. In the past, these three major elements were often researched independently. However, due to the evolving dynamic forces of the communication process, these three elements were discovered to be intertwined. For example, artefacts such as clothes may be an expression of an intangible belief, and at the same time highlight one's self-identity and membership of a group. For example, when individuals wear Japanese traditional clothing such as the kimono, these individuals are expressing their self-identity as Japanese, indicating that they belong to the Japanese ethnic group. These material aspects of culture symbolize an individual's membership in this global culture. The interdependence of the three elements is prevalent, especially within the technologically driven lifestyle that is emerging throughout the world. This is visible through people's behaviour towards communicating via different media that create shared values (e.g. collectivism). Next, we will discuss culture in detail, touching upon Japanese cultural orientation, gift-giving, and loyalty as traits of the Japanese culture.

Cultural orientation

Aaker and Maheswaran (1997) stressed that cultural orientation has been a central construct used in psychology and other social sciences. The main purpose of focusing on individuals' cultural orientation is to examine their cognition and cognitive processes, specifically to investigate how this cognitive complexity differs from one culture to another. According to Hofstede's cultural dimensions, countries were grouped into different exemplars of either individualist or collectivist societies. As these exemplars represent different cultural dimensions in each respective country, it is believed that the cognitive processes leading to a particular behavioural pattern will differ. The US society is commonly known as individualist, and at the opposite end of the continuum is Japan (i.e. a collectivist society). Although Japan has generally been regarded as a collectivist society, Japanese individuals have gradually acculturated into Western culture, leading them to follow the individualist society's behavioural patterns. The contributing factor for such an acculturation is due to the massive exposure of Western influence through media (e.g. Hollywood movies) and the educational emphasis on English-language learning (www.japantoday.com; Chavez 2013), as well as the importance of being globally competitive in the globalized Japanese workforce (Katsumura 2011; McNeil 2011). Furthermore, the ability to speak and comprehend English serves as a pathway to promotion. In fact, Japanese companies have incorporated English-language skills as part of the hiring criteria (chronicle.com, www.reuters.com). Although individualism is gradually taking hold in Japan, the majority of Japanese consumers are still categorized as collectivistic individuals. In comparison to their Western counterparts, the Japanese are proud of their homogeneity and their purity (Larke 1994). The reason behind this conformity is due to a pressure towards social uniformity. This pressure thus separates Japanese consumption patterns from those of other non-Japanese consumers.

Gift-giving

Gift-giving in Japan is 'rife with intricately prescribed behaviour' (Gehrt and Shim 2003: 11). Japanese gift-giving, unlike that in the US, is a form of obligation which individuals have to follow in order to maintain their social status in Japanese society. Feelings of obligation and intricate rules of prescription are at the root of Japanese gift-giving. Gift-giving in Japan is highly ritualized, a tradition that is viewed as an important aspect of an individual's interdependence in the social group (Lee and Kim 2009). Thus, gift-giving in Japan involves more than just the gift itself, but rather is the observation of the purpose of the gift. For example, a gift choice will differ depending on the season and the purpose of the gift. The difference depends on whether the gift is intended to serve as a gesture of gratitude or friendship, such as a Christmas gift, or is intended for a traditional Japanese formal gift-giving season such as *Ochugen* and *Oseibo*. The latter refers to a Japanese customary tradition where the motive behind this gift-giving practice is to broaden one's relationships with others, including co-workers, teachers, the boss, etc. Gift-giving is not limited to these two seasons, but rather it is a year-round ritual that is observed by Japanese. Apart from these formal gift-giving seasons, gift exchanges actually occur regularly. For example, Japanese culture does not permit one to show up at a friend's or affiliate's residence empty-handed. Bringing a gift is prescribed behaviour, and if the visitor has nothing to offer to the host, then this is often perceived as rude or ignorant. Stemming from the development of the Japanese language, there are many levels of honorific personal pronoun. These multiple levels of honorific language signify formality, which is a prevalent aspect of the Japanese culture, and it impinges on behaviour, which includes gift-giving practices (Jensen *et al.* 2003). Gift-giving is also a way of displaying gratification. This is known as *orei*, which serves to 'achieve this temporary restoration of equilibrium' (Ohashi 2009).

Loyalty

Japanese have a strong sense of loyalty to brands and stores. They view 'the store reputation as a guarantee for product performance' (Johansson *et al.* 1985; Johansson 1986: 38; Johansson 1989). However, as the ongoing European recession has reinforced concerns about the global economic downturn and cast a cloud over Japanese growth, Japanese consumers have changed their way of collecting 'intelligent' information. This change in consumerism, however, has led to contrary conclusions from researchers. An ongoing '*Fukkatsu*: Japan Rebuilds' study found that Japanese consumers are turning their loyalty domestically to boost the Japanese economy (McCaughen 2011), but some claim otherwise, stating that 'Japanese consumers are not overly patriotic to domestic brands, meaning the retail landscape is primed to host foreign brands' (www.epsilon.com 2012). Regardless of whether there is a high inclination towards domestic or foreign products, there has been an increase in public spending and personal consumption that has briefly helped to boost the economy (www.epsilon.com).

Japanese consumers will stay loyal to a brand only if they perceive the three components (i.e. price, quality, and good customer service) to be present. Top examples of deal-breakers for a Japanese consumer to stay loyal include poor customer service and incorrect billing. Customer engagement is extremely important for Japanese consumers, especially when Japanese society is driven heavily by its collectivistic culture. Furthermore, in Japanese culture, caring for customers has a heavy emphasis placed on empathy.

Loyalty can be associated with emotional attachment. For Japanese consumers, once loyalty is established between the business and consumers, this relationship will be long lasting, as trust has been gained. Loyalty to products and services differ in each age category. Younger consumers (25 to 34 years old) tend to have allegiances towards clothing and grocery brands, whereas older consumers (55 to 64 years old) spread their loyalties between financial services and travel brands (www.epsilon.com).

Loyalty makes a major contribution towards engaging consumers in the Japanese consumers. Despite many types of loyalty programme existing in Japan, the most effective form of loyalty programmes are coupon or discount programmes. In order to keep Japanese consumers loyal to their brand/products, companies need to offer products that are identical or better than their competitors' offerings. In essence, to capture Japanese consumers' loyalty, companies need to offer quality products at a reasonable price, with valued customer service.

Preference for Japan-made products

Holt (1998, 2002) asserted that brands serve as cultural cues. This suggests that there is a set of meaning associated with the brand name (Joy 2001). Nagashima (1970) found that Japanese students favour their own countries' products, in particular, automobiles, relatively more than a foreign brand. In addition, as reported by a recent survey (www.epsilon.com 2012), Japanese consumers have slightly higher preference for made-in-Japan products, especially within the grocery and financial services categories.

Nonetheless, Japanese consumers' preference for made-in-Japan products is dependent on their country of residence. Japanese consumers, like Japanese companies in Japan, tend to rely on word-of-mouth sources which they perceive as being authoritative, and then remain fiercely loyal to the products recommended. The reason for such a tie can be related to *giri* (obligations), a prominent part of Japanese culture. However, as society changes, young Japanese consumers are turning towards Western culture for shopping tips, and therefore developing a different type of consumer culture. For these modernized Japanese consumers, loyalty to a brand seems to be diminishing. They are gradually experiencing the need to feel individualistic and more self-expressive. In other words, they start to embrace new values and social diversification, which erases the traditional Japanese values of being loyal. Therefore, there is a need to segregate the type of Japanese consumers demographically in order to target marketing accurately.

Moriuchi (2013), in contrast with Nagashima (1970), found that Japanese immigrants (e.g. permanent residents) living in Hawaii (USA) had a preference for American products over their own country's products. The assumption is that immigrants want to assimilate into the local culture, hence the overwhelming preference for American products. Despite the tremendous influence of a 'made-in' cue on the acceptance and success of a particular product, consumers' knowledge of the country-of-origin (COO) cues has been miscalibrated (Balabanis and Diamantopoulos 2008; Carpenter *et al.* 2013). Furthermore, Usunier and Cestre (2008) argued that COO are no longer relevant in consumers' purchasing processes, as COO information has become increasingly difficult for consumers to ascertain. This is due to the changing labelling requirements; global sourcing; or even global companies' reluctance to emphasize the origin of the product. Essentially, the perceived COO may be inaccurate with respect to the true origin of the product.

Advertising in Japan

Due to the collectivistic nature of Japanese culture, Japanese consumers exhibit differences in appreciating the content and message of an advertisement. Foreign companies that try to market and promote their products in Japan have to understand Japanese culture and the distinctive characteristics of Japanese advertising. A helpful suggestion in determining the nature of Japanese preference towards advertising is to highlight the difference between a Japanese and a Western advertising ritual. In comparison to American adverts, Japanese ads often use celebrity endorsements. Japanese ads are also more subtle and indirect when the content of the ad messages are being discussed. They are overall less assertive compared with Western ads. Kilburn (1998) found out that celebrity use is highly evident in Japan; approximately 70 per cent of Japanese commercials feature a celebrity. Praet (2001) and an advertising company known as Milward Brown, however, argued that if the advertisements were to be examined based on whether celebrities are endorsing a product or service, then the percentage drops to around 40 per cent. This suggests that celebrity endorsement is a highly persuasive method of conveying the intended message (Hsu and McDonald 2002). Celebrities (e.g. actresses) in Japan play a different role to those in America. Celebrities in Japan are well known to Japanese society, and this familiarity is transferred to the trustworthiness of the product. Consumers are more likely to gain confidence in the product if the celebrity has a positive image and is extremely well known in Japanese society. In America, athletes are often the endorsers of a product. Unlike American ads, Japanese ads do not normally contain statistical figures to prove brand superiority. Due to the high-context nature of the Japanese culture, Japanese consumers have a strong preference for creative images. These images link the relationship between the people and their feelings in the products that are being sold. Essentially, Japanese ads are more image oriented and appeal to the sentiments of the audience (di Benedetto *et al.* 1992: 40).

Indirect message

Japanese ads are commonly expressed in written and spoken form, in an abstract way which is difficult to translate exactly into English. In fact, what is important about advertising in the Japanese community is not about what the ad is explicitly intending to say, but rather what is implied by the speaker or writer. Perhaps another reason for a preference for an indirect message is that 'Japanese consumers process information in more detail but also less systematically than American consumers' (Johansson 1986: 38).

Relatedness

A well-known advertising agency in Japan stated that 'Japanese commercials are very emotional' (Helming 1982). Unlike the American advertising firms, which focus on pushing one's brand above the rest (e.g. comparative ads), the Japanese prefer ads that conform to unity and have brief narrations, with a minimal explanatory content. There is little relationship between the ad content and the product. In essence, Japanese commercials do not place as much emphasis on the brand name in their ad; and neither do they focus on the price of the product. Due to the underpinning of the Japanese culture, information processing seems to be influenced heavily by how the society has set a behavioural norm. Commercials in Japan definitely play down the attributes of the product and hype it up with more music and entertainment. The main reason for such downplay is to highlight the emotional appeal of a particular product that is being offered.

Emotionally driven

Mueller (1987, 1992) consistently found that Japanese advertisements use soft-sell appeals, despite the increased exposure of Western culture in Japanese advertisements. Johansson (1994), however, asserted that culture alone is insufficient in drawing a conclusion as to why Japanese consumers are more responsive towards advertisements with soft-sell appeal than advertisements with hard-sell appeal. He claims that the unique established arrangements that exist in the Japanese agency world, as well the cost-effectiveness of producing an advertisement in the Japanese marketplace, are also factors. On the contrary, Okazaki, Mueller and Taylor (2010a, 2010b) discovered that, in their Japanese sample, hard-sell appeal was more favourable than soft-sell appeal. The cause of such an attitude was assumed to be the recession that Japan had been facing. To stay afloat in a competitive market, the use of a direct, hard-hitting appeal seems logical in order to produce an immediate increase in sales. Nonetheless, there is still a consensus that, assuming that the economy is stable, the Japanese will be more likely to be responsive towards soft-sell appeals, and that this is because 'soft-sell appeals may be more effective in transmitting global brand quality, social responsibility, prestige, and relative price in a symbolic and explicit form' (Okazaki *et al.* 2010: 31).

The authors De Mooij and Hofstede (2011) assert that Japanese advertising is based on building a relationship between the company and the consumer. The reason behind this relationship is to allow consumers to be dependent on the company's product and/or services. This dependence is also known as *amae* in the Japanese language. It is a result of how these Japanese consumers feel towards the advertisement, which can be determined by the outcome of their behaviour (e.g. to purchase the product or to disregard it). In other words, Japanese consumers may not have most of the information on the product prior to their initial purchase, generally because they make their purchasing decision based on their feelings. Miracle (1987) theorized these characteristics as a 'feel–do–learn' approach.

Knight and Kim (2007) and other researchers (Babin and Babin 2001; Kim *et al.* 2009) found that emotional value had a significant, positive effect on consumers' purchase intentions. Japanese consumers are attracted to products that send emotional messages. Supphellen (2000) defined consumers' perceived 'emotional value' as their affective reactions to a brand. Humour is used to create a bond of mutual feelings. Morris *et al.* (2002) added that products that can emit emotions will attract consumers, as an emotional response is a strong indicator of purchase intentions. Ultimately, because consumers are overwhelmed with the commercial messages about a product, as long as the advertisement is designed to evoke viewers' emotions, the companies could expect a significant increase in sales.

Word-of-mouth

According to Nielsen (2013), word-of-mouth (WOM) from friends and family carry more weight than those messages that companies put out on their behalf (www.nielsen.com). Eighty-nine per cent of their respondents worldwide stated that they would rely on WOM when making their purchasing decisions. Interestingly, despite the growing popularity of online advertising, WOM triumphs over any other form of communication (e.g. TV, branded websites, newspaper ads, permission marketing (where emails are sent to customers who are subscribed to receiving news and advertising updates from the respective companies), editorial content in newspaper and ads in magazines), receiving an increase of 6 per cent over the past six years (Neilsen 2013). Particularly in the Asia-Pacific region, WOM seemed to be a more trustworthy source compared with in Europe or America. Overall, in the Asia-Pacific region, there is high confidence in earned media, such as 'recommendations from friends and family' (94 per cent) and 'consumer opinions posted online' (76 per cent).

Japanese consumers in search of their identity

Japanese consumers are known to be status conscious. This social status is tied in with their sensitivity towards prestige. Prestige sensitivity is a favourable perception of the price cue, based on feelings of prominence and status that higher prices signal to other people about the purchaser (Lichtenstein *et al.* 1993). Consumers who are victims of prestige sensitivity relate to more socially visible consumption behaviours (McGowan and Sternquist 1998). Sproles and Kendall (1986) added that consumers who seek high prices tend to be brand conscious and sensitive to prestige. These consumers tend to favour expensive and well-known national brands over cheap and localized brands. Snyder and Fromkin theorized that this behaviour (1980) represents the consumer's need for uniqueness. This theory explains that Japanese consumers are attracted to goods that express their uniqueness (Solomon and Rabolt 2004). Despite the deep-rooted conformist culture in Japan, some Japanese consumers, especially youngsters, are willing to risk social disapproval so that they can establish their uniqueness. This exemplification of uniqueness is done by choosing products that deviate from the group norms (Tian *et al.* 2001). In fact, this behaviour has an effect in boosting their self-image. Regardless of whether Japanese consumers choose to express their socially accepted uniqueness, i.e. their counter-conforming unique choice, the choice of unique products is either foreign-brand products, vintage products, or prestigious or exclusive brands (Knight 1999; Knight and Kim 2007).

Johansson (1986) added that 'Japanese consumers view products much more as valuable in and of themselves' (p. 37). In other words, Japanese view products as having an intrinsic value which can be appreciated in its own right (Johansson 1986). Thus, regardless of the demands of any situation, Japanese can be generalized as a group of consumers who are brand conscious and price sensitive, as these are the visible product cues that represent their social status. This is largely due to the reason that Japanese belong to a collectivist culture. The 'self', according to the Japanese culture, cannot be separated from others and the surrounding context. In other words, the self is interdependent of the social relationship of others. For example, in the situation of gift-giving, Japanese tend to favour high-priced products and known brands as a gift choice. This is not only to show their social status, but also because their definition of feeling good encompasses the need to associate with their interpersonal situations (De Mooij and Hofstede 2011). The Japanese believe that well-known brands come with high price, which is accompanied by superior packaging for excellent presentation.

Products' quality indicators

Japanese consumers often correlate price with the quality of the product. Lichtenstein, Ridway and Netemeyer (1993) agreed that it is a generalized belief amongst consumers, as they often use price as a cue to determine the quality of a product. This generalization is known as the price/quality schema. The schema serves as a short cut for consumers during their decision-making process, especially when there is no non-price information in determining an unfamiliar product's level of quality. In addition, individuals who have strong price/quality schema are highly likely to seek expensive products (Lichtenstein *et al.* 1998). Sternquist *et al.* (2004) highlighted that there are many variables involved in the relationship between price and consumers' purchasing intent. However, if there is no available price cue, then consumers are likely to use a product's appearance (e.g. packing) and brand names (e.g. country of origin), as alternatives for a non-price information, in assessing the quality of the product. According to Sternquist *et al.* (2004), the Japanese commonly equate price with quality, believing that there is a reason why a product has been assigned a particular price tag. Johansson (1986) argued that Japanese superior product quality is the result of responding to the quality consciousness of Japanese consumers' demands.

McGowan and Sternquist (1998) added that Japanese perceive inexpensive products as low quality. Although some may argue that Japanese are more loyal to Japanese-made products, Japanese products are often more expensive. Thus, there is an increasing demand for 'made in Japan' labels on products. However, in order to have a sustainable spending habit for the future, the Japanese are starting to turn to more inexpensive products, which are often made in other Asian countries (e.g. China) (Ahmed and d'Astous 1993).

Value or brand-named products?

McCreery (2000) and others (e.g. Ikeno 2010) assert that, generally, Japanese shoppers were perceived as the world's most avid consumers of local and global brands, and scholars saw Japanese culture becoming the very epitome of post-modern pastiche (p. 14). Since the economic depression, older-generation consumers have started to spend on things they want and not just things they need (www.nytimes.com). Younger consumers, on the other hand, have made frugality part of their life. Thus, they favour the inexpensive products.

Japanese consumers are meticulous when they shop for products. In fact, Japanese are known to be consumers who avidly support high-quality products. They appreciate not only the functionality of a product, but also the appearance, size and packaging. The reason behind the cultivation of this behaviour is the competitive situation in Japan, which forces compliance on the part of the companies, and allows the consumer to be perceived as king (Yoshino 1971). However, Japanese consumers' preference for products (e.g. brand named versus low price) changes dramatically according to the state of the Japanese economy (Magnusson 2011). Although the Japanese have long been known for their preference for high-end products (e.g. Louis Vuitton), their shift towards cheaper products was apparent when there was a 'new climate for domestic and foreign competitors alike as parallel imports, private brands, and generic products claim a growing share of many markets' (Shill *et al.* 1995: 32). This new climate emerged when the fast-growing bubble economy collapsed and the Japanese yen strengthened over the years.

As an antidote to luxurious brands, a low-cost segment has emerged in Japanese markets. Currently, value, as perceived by Japanese consumers, is not only about the price and quality, but also having good customer service. According to a recent survey (www.epsilon.com), the majority of the consumers will stay loyal when the product offers the best value for money. Retailers such as Daiso, a hundred-yen retail store, have been gaining popularity in Japan. Don Quijote and other major retailers are also cutting their prices to stay competitive in the market. These retailers have a reputation for 'value-for-money' and affordable products.

Moore and Smith (2004), however, argued that luxury goods still have their place in the Japanese market. Profitability and uniqueness are the attributes of this Japanese market. With a large population and a GDP of $3.5 trillion, this economy makes Japan a critical market for many global companies. Due to the long-known preference for high-end products, the global brands that have acquired success in the Japanese market are the luxury brands. Moore and Smith (2004: 29) support this claim, as they state that 'Japan represents 20 per cent of Gucci Group's worldwide revenue'. According to De Mooij and Hofstede (2011), 'prestigious' is a characteristic attributed to 'global brands in high-power-distance cultures (p. 184). (A high-power-distance culture, as defined by Hofstede, refers to a culture where people in the society accept and expect that power is being distributed unequally. In other words, the ownership of a luxurious brand indicates high social status in the society, whereas the ownership of no brand-named products indicates otherwise.) 'Trustworthy', on the other hand, is most attributed to strong brands in high-uncertainty-avoidance cultures (p. 185).

A new breed of luxury shoppers

Japanese consumers are amongst the world's greatest spenders and are often known as brand-conscious consumers. According to Salsberg (2009), Japan's luxury market is worth fifteen billion to twenty billion dollars. The Japanese market is second in rank compared with the world's largest retail market (i.e. the US). Unlike many markets, in Japan, the consumers of luxury goods are those with a middle-class lifestyle rather than an upper-class lifestyle. Therefore, it is natural for Japanese fashion magazines and department stores to target Japanese's middle-class consumers. Japanese consumers habitually skimp on daily expenses or expensive meals so that they can afford designer bags and apparel and even overseas travel. Despite the unpredictable economy, consumers pursue this face-saving type of behaviour in order to follow the trend towards appreciating luxury goods.

The trend for luxury goods is no longer just the high-end, expensive products. To search for greater individuality, Japanese women defy conformity and are now much more confident in creating their own style. In order for these emerging group of consumers to find their own style, they start to mix and match cheap and expensive products. Brick-and-mortar stores are also no longer the sole source for retail. Rather, shopping channels such as 'click-and-mortar', or purely online stores such as Rakuten, have gradually grown to dominate the consumer market in Japan.

Luxury has broadened its definition to include service experiences rather than a tangible product. This includes spa treatments or a vacation at a foreign high-end hotel. While consumers perceive luxury from a broader perspective, the traditional luxury consumer demographics (35 to 55-year-olds) are starting to lose their interest in owning luxury goods, as they feel that luxury goods are not as special as they used to be. There is not only an abundance of luxury products to purchase, the price is also a contributor to greatly intensified competition for a share of the luxury consumers' spending.

Women shoppers

The perception of social status has changed as the Japanese have gone through a decades-long recession. As the Japanese societal norm changes, women are gradually taking on a larger role in the Japanese workforce. The increasing number of women entering the job market has debunked the stereotype of the dutiful housewife in Japan. This change is directly affected by the rapid drop in the Japanese birth rate, combined with the ageing population (MacKellar and Horlacher 2000). Due to the drastic drop in birth rates in Japan, the government is increasing its efforts to open up more jobs to Japanese women, in order to compensate for the net labour loss (Hosni and Kobayashi 1993). Bolwijn and Brinkman (1987) claimed that the increased number of women in the Japanese workforce is due to cost reductions in the manufacturing sector. Despite the need for women to enter the workforce, Japan remains a society that abides by its traditions, culture and values. In other words, the glass-ceiling phenomenon is still prevalent for women who are competing with their male counterparts.

The evolution of women's working opportunities in Japan has been improving. *Jun-sogoshoku* is a career track developed by companies to accommodate married women who plan to stay employed even after they are married. It has been noted that Japanese women are more pragmatic and tend to 'gravitate to second-tier companies and foreign-owned companies that pay well' (Bolwijn and Brinkman 1987: 47). These characteristics add a new dimension to the Japanese working landscape, which is an area that marketers should definitely concentrate on.

As a number of Japanese women step into the workforce, the desire to get married or have children is no longer on women's priority list. As unmarried women gradually attain a degree of wage equality in comparison to their male counterparts, the amount of disposable income available to spend on consumer goods for their individual pleasure should become ubiquitous. This is definitely a growing market that has the potential to maximize the sale potential by adjusting products to match this reality (Ishikawa 1990). Furthermore, Higashi and Lauter (2012) added that more than 47 per cent of all housewives hold at least a part-time job. The rise in female employment in Japan has definitely provided Japanese women with more income, emphasizing their importance as consumers while generating changes in spending habits.

Conclusions

New generations of consumers have gradually gained dominance in the Japanese market. In fact, an increasing amount of attention has been devoted to targeting Japanese women (Dallmann 2001). In the twenty-first century, the traditional characteristics and collectivistic attitude of Japanese consumers are slowly being replaced with Americanized-individualized consumption behaviour. Younger generations of consumers will inevitably have different needs and wants. With the nation's reputation as a fashion icon, creativity and innovative ideas will be necessary to juggle the perception of values and quality, and to keep consumers satisfied at the same time.

References

Aaker, J. L. and Maheswaran, D. (1997). The effect of cultural orientation on persuasion. *Journal of Consumer Research*, 24(3): 315–328.

Ahmed, S. and d'Astous, A. (1993). Cross-national evaluation of made-in concept using multiple cues. *European Journal of Marketing*, 27(7): 39–52.

Babin, B. J. and Babin, L. (2001). Seeking something different? A model of schema typicality, consumer affect, purchase intentions and perceived shopping value. *Journal of Business Research*, 54(2): 89–96.

Balabanis, G. and Diamantopoulos, A. (2008). Brand origin identification by consumers: a classification perspective. *Journal of International Marketing*, 16: 39–71.

Bolwijn, P. T. and Brinkman, S. (1987). Japanese manufacturing: strategy and practice. *Long Range Planning*, 20(1): 25–34.

Carpenter, J. M., Moore, M., Alexander, N., and Doherty, A. M. (2013). Consumer demographics, ethnocentrism, cultural values, and acculturation to the global consumer culture: a retail perspective. *Journal of Marketing Management*, 29(3–4): 271–291.

Chavez, Amy (2013). English education and English sheepdogs. *The Japan Times: Community*. 25 May 2013, www.japantimes.co.jp/community/2013/05/25/our-lives/english-education-and-english-sheepdogs/#. UqD9jSfORlk, last accessed 18 October 2015.

Craig, S. C. and Douglas, S. P. (2006). Beyond national culture: implications of cultural dynamics for consumer research. *International Marketing Review*, 23(3): 322–342.

Dallmann, Katharina M. (2001).Targeting women in German and Japanese magazine advertising: a difference-in-differences approach. *European Journal of Marketing*, 35(11–12): 1320–1341.

De Mooij, M. and Hofstede, G. (2011). Cross-cultural consumer behavior: a review of research findings. *Journal of International Consumer Marketing*, 23(3–4): 181–192.

di Benedetto, C. A., Tamate, M., and Chandran, R. (1992). Developing creative advertising strategy for the Japanese marketplace. *Journal of Advertising Research*, 32(1): 39–48.

Gehrt, K. C. and Shim, S. (2003). Situational segmentation in the international marketplace: the Japanese snack market. *International Marketing Review*, 20(2): 180–194.

Higashi, C. and Lauter, P. G. (2013). *The Internationalization of the Japanese Economy*. Springer Science and Business Media.

Holt, Douglas B. (1998), Does cultural capital structure American consumption. *Journal of Consumer Research*, 25 (June), 1–25.

Holt, D. B. (2002). Why do brands cause trouble? A dialectical theory of consumer culture and branding. *Journal of Consumer Research*, 29(1): 70–90.

Hosni, D. E. and Kobayashi, T. (1993). Japan's labour shortage. *Computers and Industrial Engineering*, 24(4): 607–613.

Hsu, C.-K. and McDonald, D. (2002). An examination on multiple celebrity endorsers in advertising. *Journal of Product and Brand Management*, 11(1): 19–29.

Ikeno, Shinpei (2010). *Changing Values and Buying Behavior: Survey of 10,000 Consumers Shows the Transition of Japanese People* (September, Vol. 13). Japan: Service Industry Consulting Department, Nomura Research Institute, Ltd.

Ishikawa, K. (1990). *Introduction to quality control*. Japan: Productivity Press.

Japan Today (2013). Gov't plans to increase number of foreign English teachers to 10,000 (24 April 2013). www.japantoday.com/category/business/view/govt-plans-to-increase-number-of-foreign-english-teachers-to-10000, last accessed 17 October 2015.

Jensen, T., Kees, J., Burton, S., and Turnipsees, F. L. (2003). Advertised reference price on an internet environment effects on consumer price consumer price perceptions and channel search intentions. *Journal of Interactive Marketing*, 17(2): 20–33.

Johansson, J. K. (1986). Japanese consumers: what foreign marketers should know. *International Marketing Review*, 3(2): 37–43.

Johansson, J. K. (1994). The sense of 'nonsense': Japanese TV advertising. *Journal of Advertising*, 23(1): 17–26.

Johansson, J. K., Douglas, S. P., and Nonaka, I. (1985). Assessing the impact of country of origin on product evaluations: a new methodological perspective. *Journal of Marketing Research*, 22(4): 388–396.

Joy, Annamma S. (2001). Gift giving in Hong Kong and the continuum of social ties. *Journal of Consumer Research*, 28 (September): 239–256.

Katsumura, M. (2011). Fear for jobs ignites English crisis in Japan, 22 September 2011. www.reuters. com/article/2011/09/22/uk-japan-english-idUSLNE78L02A20110922, last accessed 17 October 2015.

Kilburn, D. (1998). Star power. *Adweek Eastern Edition*, 39(2): 20.

Kim, E. Y., Knight, D. K., and Pelton, L. E. (2009). Modeling brand equity of a U.S. apparel brand as perceived by generation Y consumers in the emerging Korean market. *Clothing and Textiles Research Journal*, 27(4): 247–258.

Knight, D. K. and Kim, E. Y. (2007). A path analytic exploration of consumer information search in online clothing purchases. *Journal of the Korean Society of Clothing and Textiles*, 31: 1721–1732.

Knight, Gary A. (1999). Consumer preferences for foreign and domestic products. *Journal of Consumer Marketing*, 16(2): 151–162.

Larke, R. (1994). *Japanese Retailing*. London: Routledge.

Lee, H.-H. and Kim, J. (2009). Gift shopping behavior in a multichannel retail environment: the role of personal purchase experiences. *International Journal of Retail and Distribution Management*, 37(5): 420–439.

Lichtenstein, D. R., Ridgway, N. M., and Netemeyer, R. G. (1993). Price perceptions and consumer shopping behavior: a field study. *Journal of Marketing Research*, 30(2): 234–245.

Lichtenstein, D. R., Bloch, P. H., and Black, W. C. (1998). Correlates of price acceptability. *Journal of Consumer Research*, 15: 243–252.

McCaughen, D. (2011). *How Japanese Consumer Habits Have Changed Since the Earthquake: From Fears Over Food Sourcing to Rise in Online Shopping, Citizens Rethink What and How They Buy*. http://adage.com/article/agency-viewpoint/japanese-earthquake-changed-consumer-habits/228124/, last accessed 19 October 2015.

McCracken, G. (1986). Culture and consumption: a theoretical account of the structure: a theoretical account of the structure and movement of the cultural meaning of consumer goods. *Journal of Consumer Research*, 13(1): 71–84.

McCreery (2000). *Japanese Consumer Behaviour: From Worker Bees to Wary Shoppers. An Anthropologist Reads Research by the Hakuhodo Institute of Life and Living*. Honolulu, University of Hawaii Press.

McGowan, K. M. and Sternquist, B. J. (1998). Dimensions of price as a marketing universal: a comparison of Japanese and US consumers. *Journal of International Marketing*, 6(4): 49–65.

MacKellar, L. and Horlacher, D. (2000). Population ageing in Japan: a brief survey. *Innovation: the European Journal of Social Sciences*, 13(4): 413–430.

McNeill, D. (2011). Global economy exposes Japan's shortage of English-speaking graduates. 1 November 2011, http://chronicle.com/article/Global-Economy-ExposesJapans/129596/, last accessed 19 October 2015.

Magnusson, P., Westjohn, S. A., and Zdravkovic, S. (2011). What? I thought Samsung was Japanese: accurate or not, perceived country of origin matters. *International Marketing Review*, 28(5): 454–472.

Miracle, G. E. (1987). Feel-do-learn: an alternative sequence underlying Japanese consumer response to television commercials. In: *Proceedings of the 1987 Conference of the American Academy of Advertising*. Columbia, SC: University of South Carolina. pp. R73–R78.

Moore, K. and Smith, M. (2004). Taking global brands to Japan. *Across the Board*, 41(1): 39–42.

Moriuchi, E. (2013). *Who Am I? A Cross-Cultural Study on Japanese-American Biculturals' Consumption Preference Towards Hedonic and Utilitarian Products. Strategy*. Manchester, University of Manchester. Unpublished Doctoral Thesis.

Morris, J. D., Chongmoo, W., Geason, J. A., and Jooyoung, K. (2002). The power of affect: predicting intention. *Journal of Advertising Research*, 42(3): 7–17.

Mueller, B. (1987). Reflections of culture – an analysis of Japanese and American advertising appeals. *Journal of Advertising Research*, 27(3): 51–59.

Mueller, B. (1992). Standardization vs. specialization: an examination of westernization in Japanese advertising. *Journal of Advertising Research*, 32(1): 15–24.

Nagashima, A. (1970). A comparison of Japanese and U.S. attitudes toward foreign products. *Journal of Marketing*, 34(1): 68–74.

Neilsen (2013). Under the influence: consumer trust in media and entertainment. *Advertising. Nielsen*. www.nielsen.com/us/en/newswire/2013/under-the-influence-consumer-trust-in-advertising.html, last accessed 19 October 2015.

Ohashi, J. (2009). Natural conversation reconstruction tasks: the language classroom as a meeting place. *PORTAL Journal of Multidisciplinary International Studies*, 6(1): 1–15.

Okazaki, S., Mueller, B., and Taylor, C. R. (2010). Global consumer culture positioning: testing perceptions of soft-sell and hard-sell advertising appeals between U.S. and Japanese consumers. *Journal of International Marketing*, 18(2): 20–34.

Okazaki, S., Mueller, B., and Taylor, C. R. (2010). Measuring soft-sell versus hard-sell advertising appeals. *Journal of Advertising*, 39(2): 5–20.

Salsberg, B. S. (2009*). Japan's Luxury Shoppers Move On*. McKinsey and Co. Report. www.mckinsey.com/insights/consumer_and_retail/japans_luxury_shoppers_move_on, last accessed 2 November 2015.

Shill, W., Guild, T. and Yamaguchi, Y. (1995). Cracking Japanese markets. *McKinsey Quarterly*, 3: 32–40.

Snyder, C. R. and Fromkin, H. L. (1980). *Uniqueness: the Human Pursuit of Difference*. Plenum Press New York.

Sojka, J. and Tansuhaj, P. S. (1995). Cross-cultural consumer research: a twenty-year review. *Advances in Consumer Research*, 22: 461–474.

Solomon, M. R. (1983). The role of products as social stimuli: a symbolic interactionism perspective. *Journal of Consumer Research*, 10(3): 319–329.

Solomon, M. R. and Rabolt, N. J. (2004). *Consumer Behavior in Fashion*. Upper Saddle River, NJ: Prentice-Hall.

Sproles, G. B. and Kendall, E. L. (1986). A methodology for profiling consumers' decision-making styles. *Journal of Consumer Affairs* 20(2): 267.

Sternquist, B., Byun, S.-E., and Jin, B. (2004).The dimensionality of price perceptions: a cross-cultural comparison of Asian consumers. *The International Review of Retail, Distribution and Consumer Research*, 14(1): 83–100.

20

Japanese consumer rights

Mariko Morimoto

Consumerism in Japan: historical perspective

The beginning of Japanese consumerism took place after the Second World War. Since then the movement has become mature and active, and it is estimated that approximately 2,400 consumer organizations now exist in Japan (Oto *et al.* 2007).

The first notable consumer movement in Japan dates back to the 1940s, when Japanese consumers suffered from severe poverty due to Japan's defeat in the war. This phenomenon led to a major consumer protest by 250,000 people, demanding food – particularly a Japanese staple, rice – in front of the gate of the Imperial Palace in 1946 (Oto *et al.* 2007). While Douglas MacArthur, the General of the United States Army and General Headquarters and the Supreme Commander for the Allied Powers (GHQ), issued a cease-and-desist order to this protest, the trend among consumers demanding fair prices for fine-quality products was continuously carried out mainly by housewives in Japan during this era (Harayama 2011). The driving force of these ordinary Japanese housewives was poverty coupled with inflations and black-market prices that had pressed their household spending significantly.

Consumer activities by Japanese housewives were indeed a grassroots movement. The beginning of these housewives' activities took place in Osaka, where three housewives made a formal request for rationing of rice and other food, arguing that their families and children were on the verge of starvation. This small effort evolved into the foundation of Kansai Housewives' Alliance (*Kansai Shufu Rengōkai*), a key player in consumerism in the Kansai region in later years (Harayama 2011). From that point, several networks of citizens' groups were established throughout Japan, and several notable organizations, such as the Housewives' Alliance, started voluntary inspections of merchandise and products. As a result, the Japan Consumers' Alliance (*Zenkoku Shōhisha Dantai Rengōkai*) was founded in 1956, and this network of consumer protection alliances has become quite influential on policy making (Oto *et al.* 2007). In particular, the introduction of the Declaration of Consumers in 1957 by the Japan Consumers' Alliance is regarded significant in the history of consumers' rights, as it reinforced the voice of resistance from consumers against the increasing trend of monopolistic and oligopolistic capital in Japanese society (Hanzawa 1997). These alliances raised awareness among the public of the potential revision of the Antitrust Law in 1957, and this effort resulted in the scrapping of the proposed revision (Oto *et al.* 2007).

While the initial trend in consumerism in Japan after the war placed an emphasis on fair prices and better product quality, the decades of 1950s and 1960s were the era of rising concerns for product safety. Two incidents that highlight this tendency are (1) the Morinaga powdered-milk case in 1955; and (2) the thalidomide case in 1961.

In the Morinaga case, over 13,000 infants who consumed Morinaga powdered milk were poisoned with arsenic, and approximately 130 infants died from this incident (Museum of Morinaga Arsenic Milk Poisoning Incident 2014). The investigation revealed that arsenic was mixed with other ingredients during production (Hiroo 2012). To preserve the freshness of the powdered milk, Morinaga used dibasic sodium phosphate taken from industrial waste. However, the extracted chemicals also contained lethal amounts of arsenic (Museum of Morinaga Arsenic Milk Poisoning Incident 2014). A similar food product incident was the Kanemi Oil PCB poisoning case which caused serious illness and death among a large number of consumers, due to the mix of polychlorinated biphenyl in the product (rice oil) at the time of production (Katō 2007; Hiroo 2012). This incident was caused by a leak of polychlorinated biphenyl into the plumbing systems, a chemical used as a deodorant and a heat medium during the production of rice oil. The heated polychlorinated biphenyl became an extremely toxic substance known as dioxin, and mixed with the rest of the ingredients in the production process. This was the world's first food-poisoning incident caused by dioxin. The victims suffer from symptoms that have lingered on for forty years since the reporting of the first case. As of 2012, the number of victims recorded by the Japanese government is 1,966 people, of which 596 have already died (Kyushu Asahi Broadcasting 2014).

The thalidomide case in 1961 presents a similar story in the pharmaceutical area. Pregnant women taking over-the-counter cold medicines containing thalidomide gave birth to babies with severe disabilities (Hiroo 2012). Thalidomide was initially introduced to the Japanese market in the late 1950s as a sleep aid, but later on as a cure for gastritis. In Japan, this drug was promoted as a safe medicine for pregnant women and sold for the purpose to alleviate nausea and morning sickness (Ishizue 2014). However, in 1963, victims brought a lawsuit against the pharmaceutical company responsible, Dianippon Pharmaceutical Co. and the Ministry of Welfare, with the case eventually settled in 1974. The Japanese government has officially acknowledged 309 victims from this incident (Ishizue 2014). These cases – from the food and pharmaceutical fields – shed light on the possibility of serious physical harm to the general public and opened their eyes for their rights as consumers.

While the concerns among consumers regarding the safety of food and drugs continued into the 1970s, this decade was characterized by consumers' sensitivity toward unethical and deceptive sales practices, contracts, and price issues. For example, Britannica Japan was known for its aggressive door-to-door sales methods. Representing consumers claiming monetary damages, Japan Consumers' Alliances negotiated with Britannica Japan and came to an agreement to compensate the injured parties (Tōyama 2012). Another vicious sales method used in the 1970s was the pyramid scheme. The Tenka Ikka no Kai (The Society of One Family) incident, with over a million members, is a well-known example of this method, with the largest debt/damage in the Japanese history, leading to the enactment of the Act on Prevention of Pyramid Sales (Tōyama 2012).

Meanwhile, the oil crisis in the 1970s triggered price increases among a variety of goods and services, including utilities and household items. Many marketers took advantage of the crisis and increased prices unnecessarily, or they simply became engaged in price gouging. Consumer protests became active during this period, and many consumer groups and organizations filed lawsuits with the liable marketers in order to confront these price issues (Katō 2007). Such movements raised awareness among the general public, leading them to call for the establishment of solid consumer rights as well as consumer-protection policies.

The 1980s and 1990s were two decades of deregulation in Japan, and the trend in consumer movements in Japan slowed down to some degree. Coupled with the bubble economy in this time period, which improved consumers' economic conditions, the number of consumerism-related issues continued to increase. Examples include the emergence of consumer-financing firms offering loans with outrageously high interest rates (Katō 2007); product-safety issues in food; deceptive and forceful door-to-door sale practices; and price cartels (Oto *et al.* 2007). To battle against these malpractices, the consumers that were affected filed official claims to consumer-protection centres nationwide and brought serious issues to the court to seek remedies – which, since the 1970s, has become a common practice by consumers in Japan in order to tackle unethical business conduct. From the late 1980s, an argument that advocated further strengthening of the Competition Law to enable fair competition, emerged from Japanese society due to Japan–US trade friction (Oto *et al.* 2007). While this trade friction facilitated further deregulation concerning imported foods, it also left several serious concerns for consumers' safety. Issues like post-harvest pesticides on imported lemons from the US in the early 1990s, and genetically modified potatoes and soy beans in the late 1990s have made headlines in the mass media in Japan, making the general public even more concerned about product safety (Tōyama 2012).

Activities facilitated by consumer groups have evolved from campaigning/grassroot movements to actual proposals for regulations in the 1990s. The proposal for the establishment of the Products Liability Act clearly illustrates this trend (Oto *et al.* 2007). It is noteworthy to point out that these product-liability regulation drafts proposed by groups of attorneys, political parties, and scholars undoubtedly reflected the collective voices and opinions of various consumer alliances that had continuously demanded making consumer safety the first priority (Mitsui and Inō 1995). Another example of active involvement by consumer-alliance groups in policy making was the legislation of the Consumer Contract Act in 2000. In this case, the All Japan Consumer Groups' Liaison Association played an important role in organizing an interest group consisting of scholars and specialists in order to maximize the level of consumer protection regarding business contracts (Oto *et al.* 2007; Tani 2008).

Throughout the 2000s, the trend in consumer rights was still based on the principles of consumer safety. However, the advancement of electronic commerce (e-commerce) raised another concern from consumers: the rights to privacy. Consumers became worried about collection of their personal information via online means, such as collection without consent and misuse (or unauthorized use) of personal information (Sakusa 1998; Guo 2012). To fight against this misconduct by marketers, consumer groups in Japan collaborate with other consumer groups worldwide to form alliances and make collaborative efforts in policy making. Such efforts include collaboration with consumer groups in the European Union (EU) and North-eastern Asian countries (Oto *et al.* 2007). This type of international cooperation appears to continue beyond the area of consumers' online safety, and active exchanges of opinions and information by consumer groups from around the world are taking place in the field of food safety, consumer fraud, and environmental issues.

Regulations for consumer protection

The principles

Consumer rights in Japan are based on the Consumer's Bill of Rights, first introduced by President John F. Kennedy in the form of a speech to the US Congress in 1962 (Shufurengokai

2014). The Bill of Rights includes: (1) the right to safety; (2) the right to be informed; (3) the right to choose; and (4) the right to be heard (Fueroghne 2007). Based on these basic rights, in 1968 the Japanese government enacted the Consumer Protection Fundamental Law, which clearly specified the following eight consumer rights:

1 the right to have their basic demands satisfied;
2 the right to secure a healthy living environment;
3 the right to security/safety;
4 the right to choose;
5 the right to receive necessary information;
6 the right to consumer education;
7 the right to have one's opinions reflected in consumer-related policies; and
8 the right to be remedied from injuries (Shufurengokai 2014).

These principles remain in the amendment of the Consumer Protection Fundamental Act, which eventually became the Consumer Basic Act legislated in 2004.

Consumer-protection-related regulations

Consumer Basic Act

The Consumer Basic Act is considered the basic framework for consumer policies in Japan, since the act clearly addresses the roles that the government, local governments, businesses, and consumers are expected to play (Tani 2008). The act, a revision of the Consumer Protection Fundamental Act, was introduced to help consumers make rational purchase decisions based on accurate product information provided by marketers. This amendment provided consumers with the power to have fair and equal relationships with marketers. The act illustrates the directions for: (1) consumers' rights and safety including remedies for damages due to any unlawful and deceptive advertising claims; (2) consumer education; (3) responsibilities for marketers; and (4) consumer organization (Okada and Yanase 2006).

The Consumer Basic Act requires businesses to include material information essential for purchase decisions in promotional claims. Claims made by manufacturers and service providers are also prohibited from making deceptive claims (Yabe 2009). This approach is often used to regulate advertising claims in conjunction with the Act against Unjustifiable Premiums and Misleading Representations, which is discussed in the following section. In a nutshell, this act is regarded as the guiding principle to protect welfare, benefits, and safety for consumers from unlawful and deceptive actions and claims by marketers.

Act against unjustifiable premiums and misleading representations

This act was introduced in order to supplement the Antimonopoly Act (Okada and Yanase 2006). It is the Japan Fair Trade Commission (JFTC) that is actually responsible for enforcing the administrative regulations associated with this act (Tani 2008; Yabe 2009). Specifically, the JFTC can restrict the maximum value of a premium according to this act (or the total amount of premiums that a business may offer). In addition, this act prohibits deceptive and/or misleading promotional claims and exaggerated giveaways to induce purchase; in addition, the act allows the JFTC to issue cease-and-desist orders to violators (Morimoto 2014).

Consumer Contract Act

The Consumer Contract Act was legislated in 2000 in order to set civil rules on contract-related issues. This act is applicable to every contract between consumers and businesses (Takizawa 2009). It specifies that a consumer can revoke his/her obligation to fulfil a contract under certain situations, such as fraudulent concealment, deceit, and negligent misrepresentations (Tani 2013). Specifically, if consumers are at a disadvantage under a contract, due to lack of information or misleading material information – essential information to make purchase decisions such as quality, use, conditions of payment, etc. (Fueroghne 2007), then they can void the contract. However, this is only possible when there is intentional deception made by businesses (Takizawa 2009). The act also states that a consumer can void the contract when the negotiation takes place in his/her residence and the business party refuses to leave the place despite requests from the consumer (Takizawa 2009).

A significant amendment was made to this act in 2006. The amendment now allows consumer organizations to file injunctions against inappropriate business actions concerning contracts; specifically, the revision grants a certified consumer organization the right to file lawsuits against responsible business operators to stop their solicitations (Tani 2013). This is a notable point, since it provides more power to consumers to battle against the malpractices by businesses, both individually and collectively.

Product liability

In Japan, the Product Liability Act was enacted in 1995. The act specifies that if a consumer's life, body, or property is damaged due to a defect in a product, the manufacturer will be liable for the damage and is required to compensate the consumer for the loss (Japan Consumer Affairs Agency 2014b). Initially, the act defined 'product' as any moveable property (Cohen 1997). However, in 2007, the Supreme Court expanded the definition of 'product' to include immoveable 'buildings' in the category of products (Hiroo 2012). This ruling provided a wider coverage of protections for consumers in case of injuries due to product defects.

At the same time, the Product Liability Act provides two defences for manufacturers. The first exemption from the liability is when a manufacturer cannot detect a defect, given the state of scientific or technical knowledge at the time of the product's delivery (Cohen 1997; Japan Consumer Affairs Agency 2014b). Another situation is where a product is used as a component or raw material of another product; in this case, the manufacturer of the component will not be liable for the defect of the product as a whole (Japan Consumer Affairs Agency 2014).

There are time limits for filing lawsuits according to this act. A plaintiff must file suit within three years from the discovery of the defect (Cohen 1997). In addition, a plaintiff cannot bring a cause of action more than ten years after he/she received the product (Cohen 1997; Japan Consumer Affairs Agency 2014b).

The significance of the Consumer Affairs Agency in consumer protection

When it comes to consumerism and consumer protections in Japan, the Consumer Affairs Agency (CAA) plays a very critical role. This agency, a part of the Cabinet Office, is a relatively new agency, established in September 2009 to facilitate a society where ordinary consumers can play a leading role in protecting themselves (Consumer Affairs Agency 2014a). Prior to the establishment of this agency, each ministry was responsible for placing legal sanctions on conduct related to industries/products that they had regulated. However, there was a lack of coordination among these ministries, which caused delays in responding to consumer complaints. Many consumers did not know where to bring their complaints regarding purchases and consumption, which also contributed to the issue of slow responses by these government offices. There was no central office or system that collects complaints and enquiries from consumers, which was another factor contributing to slower handling of consumer complaints (Consumers Affairs Agency 2014a). The CAA was founded to overcome these difficulties, so that the government can take a more active initiative to protect consumers. Such an attempt is reflected in the authority given to this agency – it has the power to plan new consumer protection policies as well as handle any consumer problems that cannot be governed or regulated by other ministries (Morimoto 2014).

One of the major contributions made by the CAA thus far is enactment of the Consumer Safety Act in 2009. This act prevents harm and ensures safety for consumers and also allows the Prime Minister to form basic policies related to consumer safety (e-Gov 2014). It also enables local governments to perform administrative functions for consumer-affairs consultations as well as to establish centres for the purposes of risk prevention and information sharing (Soda 2009). However, this act does not address potential reparations for a victim's loss of their possessions and properties, and instead specific acts and laws are required to fully protect consumer safety. While the CAA is a stand-alone organization specializing in consumer protection, cooperation with other government ministries and agencies is vital to better serve the consumer's welfare. In order to overcome this weakness, the CAA also works closely with other government ministries and offices such as the Ministry of Economy, Trade, and Industry (on product labeling associated with household items); the Food Safety Commission (concerning the Food Safety Basic Law); the Ministry of Internal Affairs and Commissions (concerning the Act on Regulation of Transmission of Specific Electronic Mail); and the Ministry of Agriculture, Forestry and Fisheries (on the Japan Agricultural Standard Act (JAS Act)) (Morimoto 2014).

Although this agency handles various consumer related issues, currently its focus is on establishing structured regulations for food labeling, such as enforcing requirements for clear and accurate ingredient identification and product origins for processed food (Japan Consumer Affairs Agency 2014a). Its goal is to eventually introduce and operate a single legal system concerning food labels. Because the organization is still in the development phase, the range of its responsibilities and roles in consumer protection is expected to expand in the future (Morimoto 2014).

The role of Japan Fair Trade Commission (JFTC)

Japan Federal Trade Commission (JFTC) was established in 1947, with the main responsibility of enforcing and facilitating fair market competition (JFTC 2014).

It is independent from other governmental administrative organizations, and it has the authority to give cease-and-desist orders for any illegal acts prohibiting fair competition and surcharge payment orders for price curtails (JFTC 2014). Although the original intent of the JFTC's foundation appears not to have a direct impact on consumer protection, since the focus is more on preserving a fair and competitive environment for businesses, the JFTC is intensively involved in monitoring and correcting product labelling for the benefit of consumers, along with unsubstantiated claims by businesses, which are often seen in advertising (Okada and Yanase 2006).

Moreover, the JFTC requires marketers to make their claims in promotional messages clear and easy to understand for general consumers. For instance, the JFTC has guidelines for clear advertising claims that include (but are not limited to):

1   repeating/restating important claims for purchase;
2   clearly stating information on additional charges and conditions; and
3   using advertising layouts that can be easily followed and understood by consumers (Okada and Yanase 2006).

Ministries and their specific areas of regulations for consumer protection

In conjunction with the CAA and the JFTC, other regulations concerning consumer protection are enforced by specific ministries. For example, the Ministry of Internal Affairs and Commission (Sōmu-sho) handles intellectual property and e-commerce related issues, and the Ministry of Justice is responsible for Commercial Law, the Constitution, and Civil Law concerning product liability. Health-related promotional claims are regulated by the Ministry of Health, Labor, and Welfare, and based on the Pharmaceutical Affair Act and Health Promotion Act (Okada and Yanase 2006). Food-related promotional claims are regulated by the Ministry of Agriculture, Forestry and Fisheries. Also the Ministry of Economy, Trade and Industry (METI) oversees the Japan Patent Office, direct marketing practices, and unsolicited commercial e-mail practices (Mutel 2002). As these examples show, with the coordinating initiative of the CAA, various ministries are also involved in protecting consumers' rights and benefits.

New approaches to consumer protection in Japan

With consumption styles changing due to advances in technology, new approaches to consumer protection are also called for in order to accommodate this change. Soda (2009) identifies three main areas that require amendments and/or reinforcements in existing regulatory approaches:

1   diversification in the enforcement of consumer protection-related laws;
2   recognition of the importance of advertising and promotion-related regulations;
3   more emphasis on remedies for unfair agreements outside of sales contracts.

From these three issues, a major trend has surfaced: consumer behaviour has become more varied in the twenty-first century. In conjunction with the ever-growing popularity of the Internet used as a means to perform transactions and communication between businesses and consumers, the needs of consumer protection are diversifying as well.

Enforcement of consumer-protection laws exists in a variety of formats. For example, in France, such laws are often enforced with administrative penalties, while civil relief, which includes lawsuits brought by consumer alliances, is usually the norm in Germany (Soda 2009). In the United States, consumer-protection laws are regulated by independent government agencies such as Federal Trade Commissions (FTC), in order to protect fair competition in a marketplace; this is under the basic assumption that preserving fair competition among businesses will lead to more options for consumers (Fueroghne 2007). Scandinavian countries utilize the method of alternative dispute resolutions intervened in by local governments, in order to handle consumer disputes (Soda 2009). For Japan, consumer protection consists of a combination of these aforementioned approaches.

In Japan, trades in specific industries have been traditionally regulated by the METI (in a form of administrative penalties), and issues regarding sales contracts and product liabilities have been handled through civil relief, including lawsuits. The JFTC oversees monopolistic and oligopolistic business practices based on the similar approaches of the FTC in the US. Any untouched consumer-protection issues are then run through the National Consumer Affairs Center, serving as a mediator between businesses and consumers for settlements – a form of alternative dispute resolution (Soda 2009). This multi-faceted approach is crucial to reinforce consumer protection in Japan as globalization in business practices become more prominent, which in turn affects Japanese consumers. Therefore, further research concerning consumer laws across the world is called for in order to cater more effectively to the welfare of Japanese consumers.

Conclusions

The development and protection of Japanese consumers' rights have come a long way, particularly in the twentieth century. Moreover, numerous government initiatives regarding consumer protection were introduced in the 2000s, due to concerns about product mislabelling, particularly in the food and health-related product categories. At the same time, the legal trend is moving toward deregulation in the field of marketing communication, including advertising. This phenomenon may appear contradictory at first; however, deregulation can benefit consumers when making product selections. Previous research by Sakurai (1995) found that Japanese housewives, often the primary purchase decision-makers, tend to rely on TV commercials when making purchasing decisions for low-priced products; for more expensive items they tend to rely on print ads and newspaper inserts.

For consumers to make rational purchase decisions, it is necessary to have access to a sufficient amount of information (Rotzoll et al. 1996). This idea is related to one of the basic consumer rights – to be informed. One way that marketers can contribute to this aspect is to deliver comparative information about products in their promotional activities. The trend in deregulation in advertising has led marketers to open the door for comparative advertising in Japan. This type of advertising was not common in Japan before; however, it was officially permitted, based on the idea that it provides more options for consumers and facilitates competition among advertisers (Shimamura 2000).

Of course, such an assumption is based on a principle that marketers provide fair and accurate product information to aid consumers' decision-making processes. It is expected that government initiatives, particularly ones led by the Consumer Affair Agency, will play a critical role in enhancing consumers' rights and enriching consumers' welfare in Japan.

References

Cohen, J. F. (1997). The Japanese product liability law: sending a pro-consumer tsunami through Japan's corporate and judicial worlds. *Fordham International Law Journal*, 21: 106–189.
Consumer Affairs Agency (Japan) (2014a). For a Society with Security, Safety, and Comfortable Living, http://www.caa.go.jp/en/pdf/caa.pdf, last accessed 19 October 2015.
Consumer Affairs Agency (Japan) (2014b). The Product Liability Act, www.consumer.go.jp/english/pla/index.html, last accessed 19 October 2015.
e-Gov (2014). *The Consumer Safety Act.* http://law.e-gov.go.jp/htmldata/H21/H21HO050.html, last accessed 30 December 2014.
Fueroghne, D. K. (2007). *Law and Advertising.* Pasadena, CA: Yellow Cat Press.
Guo, M. (2012). A comparative study on consumer right to privacy in e-commerce. *Modern Economy*, 3: 402–407.
Hanzawa, H. (1997). The establishment of Japan Consumers' Association. In: National Consumer Affair Center of Japan (ed.), *Sengo Shohisha Undo Shi* (The History of Post-War Consumer Movements). Tokyo: The Research Dept., National Consumer Affairs Center of Japan, pp. 44–47.
Harayama, K. (2011). *Shōhisha no Sengoshi: Yamiichi kara Shufu no Jidai W* (The Post-war History of Consumers: From the Black Market to the Era of Housewives). Tokyo: Nihon Keizaisha.

Hiroo, S. (2012). Private enforcement of consumer law: a sketch of the Japanese landscape. *Shinsedai Hōseisakugaku Kenkyu*, 16: 63–80.

Ishizue (2014). *Saridomaido to Yakugai* (Thalidomide and its Harmful Effects), www008.upp.so-net.ne.jp/ishizue/aboutthalidomide.html, last accessed 17 October 2015.

Japan Fair Trade Commission (2010). For fair and free market competition. Japan Fair Trade Commission, http://www.jftc.go.jp/en/about_jftc/role.files/1009role_1.pdf, last accessed 23 October 2015.

Katō, M. (2007). The concept of the consumer as seen through Japanese consumer acts. *Keiei Keizaigaku Kenkyu Hen*, 12: 17–28.

Kyushu Asahi Broadcasting (2014). *Kanemi Abura Sho.* (About the Kanemi Oil PCB Poisoning Case), www.kbc.co.jp/tv/kanemi/, last accessed 17 October 2015.

Mitsui, T. and Inō, K. (1995). *PL no Chishiki* (The Knowledge of Products Liability). Tokyo: Nihon Keizaisha.

Morimoto, M. (2014). Japan. In: Shaver, M. A. and An, S. (eds), *The Global Advertising Regulation Handbook.* Armonk, NY: M. E. Sharpe.

Museum of Morinaga Arsenic Milk Poisoning Incident (2014). *Morinaga Hiso Miruku Chudoku Jiken* (About the Morinaga Arsenic Milk Poisoning Incident), http://ww3.tiki.ne.jp/~jcn-o/hiso.htm, last accessed 19 October 2015.

Mutel, G. (2002). Japan revises law to stem flow of unsolicited e-mails. *Precision Marketing*, 14: 9.

Okada, Y. and Yanase, K. (2006). *Kōkoku Hoki* (Advertising Law and Ethics). Tokyo: Shojihomu.

Oto, Y., Mo, G., Chung, M., and Kim, J. (2007). Japan's consumer movements and consumer organizations in media coverage. *Communications Research*, 37: 101–132.

Rotzoll, K. B., Haefner, J. E., and Hall, S. R. (1996). *Advertising in Contemporary Society: Perspectives Toward Understanding.* Urbana, IL: University of Illinois Press.

Sakurai, K. (1995). *Kōkoku No Hōteki Imi* (The Legal Meaning of Advertising: Economic Effects of Advertising and Consumer Protection). Tokyo: Keiso Shobo.

Sakusa, K. (1998). Electronic commerce and privacy. *Technical Report of the Institute of Electronics, Information and Communication Engineers*, 98: 13–18.

Shimamura, K. (2000). Japanese trends of advertising regulation and the factors affecting them. *The Waseda Commercial Review*, 385 (June): 195–213.

Shufurengokai (2014). *Shōhisha no Kenri* (Consumers' Rights), http://shufuren.net/modules/tinyd14/, last accessed 19 October 2015.

Soda, T. (2009). *Shoshisha Hō no Shintenkai* (New Development of Consumer Law). Tokyo: Keio University Press.

Takizawa, M. (2009). Consumer protection in Japanese contract law. *Hitotsubashi Journal of Law and Politics*, 37: 31–39.

Tani, M. (2008). *Japan's Consumer Policy*. Research Institute of Economy, Trade and Industry, www.rieti.go.jp/en/special/policy-update/031.html, last accessed 19 October 2015.

Tōyama, K. (2012). 1970 nendai no shōhisha mondai (Consumerism in the 1970s), Shōhishamondai to Tokuteishōtorihikihō Nadono Hōritsu (Consumer Protection Laws and the Specified Commercial Transaction Act), http://consumer-road.com/history.html, last accessed 15 October 2015.

Yabe, J. (2009). Regulation of advertising claims based on the Antimonopoly Act. In Iju, H. and Yabe, J. (eds), *Kōkoku Hyoji Kisei Hō* (Advertising Claim Regulations). Tokyo: Seirin Shoin.

21

Consumer/market research

Emi Moriuchi

A multidimensional perspective is essential when researching the Japanese consumer market. Recent international programmes have been focusing on the health of the Japanese market. For example, NHK World broadcast (February 2014) a session known as the Global Debate WISDOM (www.nhk.or.jp). In this session, there was a panel of experts discussing Japan's current affairs, enquiring about Japan's path to recovery after the 2011 earthquake and tsunami. Specifically, discussions were on Japanese's economy and how the implementation of Prime Minister Shinzo Abe's economic policies (i.e. *Abenomics*) has an effect on the recovery of the Japanese market. The discussion focused on various subtopics, including working people's demographics, foreign imports, and wage increments. From those discussions, it suggested that when conducting research on the consumer market in Japan, it is essential to look at various areas of enquiry, as they are all interlinked. Some of the major and most prevalent areas to look at are the health of the economy, Japan's approach to internationalization, and Japanese e-commerce. Most importantly, however, is what drives all these business movements in the Japanese market. These movements stem from the traditional Japanese culture that is embedded in the business practices. To have a better understanding of how to conduct market research in the current consumer market, this chapter will cover a variety of topics: Japanese culture, value and belief systems; changes in Japanese society; Japanese cultural influence on consumer research; an overall understanding of the Japanese market; Japanese marketing; the Japanese approach to international business; the distribution system; and lastly we will be exploring the booming online industry of Japanese e-commerce.

Japanese culture, values, and belief systems

'How did Japanese companies make their products known to the world?' This is a pervasive question to ask while conducting market research in Japan. In response to this question, we will need to first look at the underlying motivator in the Japanese market – the culture. According to Sojka and Tansuhaj (1995), culture can be categorized into three major streams: abstracts of culture such as the values and belief systems; material aspects of culture such as artifacts, symbols, and rites; and the communication process that links the cultural systems.

Societal values and belief systems have an influential role in characterizing a society and how its culture guides people's behaviour in that society. In Japan, value-systems are examined at the level of the society or organizations within that society. However, as the nation turns towards Westernization, the level of value at the individual level has gradually gained more attention. The concept of self (e.g. self-construal), behaviour towards others (e.g. public vs. private consumption) or relative to specific areas of life (e.g. requesting paid holidays but feeling awkward when doing it) or purchasing intentions (e.g. gift-giving traditions) are all domains that the Japanese have in their value orientations.

Unlike its American counterparts the consumer market in Japan is still largely dominated by Japanese residents. Even though there is an increase in expatriates, sojourners, and visitors from foreign countries, companies are still focusing on their prime consumers – individuals who are born in Japan and are ethnically Japanese. What lies underneath this successful Japanese market is the balance of a collectivistic and individualistic approach to understanding the consumers in Japan. As Japanese consumers, especially the younger generations, receive influences from the Western countries (e.g. individualism), the need to be unique is a trend in the consumer market. In fact, many foreigners (e.g. French people in the West and the Taiwanese in Asia) are trying to adopt this uniqueness in their country.

Barnlund (1975) compares the culture of the United States and Japan and calls it 'polar extremes' (p. 55) with regard to the way that Americans and Japanese communicate and interact. The qualities that the Japanese society nurture (e.g. reserve, formality, and silence) are discouraged in the US due to the difference in the set of qualities being observed (e.g. self-assertion, informality, and talkativeness. Traditionally, Japan observes a collectivistic culture. What that means is that there is an emphasis on interdependence in human relationships. Markus and Kitayama (1998) theorized this phenomenon as interdependence self-construal. Unlike Western culture, the Japanese culture does not consider autonomy and independence of developmental goals (Shibusawa 2001), rather the Japanese instil in their adolescents an expectation to adapt to group norms and function as social beings. Another significant cultural characteristic is the Japanese attitude towards tolerance (*gaman*). Tomita (1998) asserted that Japanese see this as a strength of character, enduring difficulties posed by the environment. Japan has a culture that fits into the high-context category. This is why Japanese are often observant of what others are trying to communicate from the context and the way it is being communicated, rather than the literal words. Japanese may be seen as people who are not affectionate, but this is only due to the fact that the Japanese culture does not promote physical expressions.

However, as Japanese, especially youngsters, are exposed to Western culture; the Japanese culture gradually adopts cultural differences based on each generation. Ironically, as Japan turns to Western culture, certain parts of the US still embrace the traditional Japanese culture. For example, in Hawaii, Japanese-Americans still maintain elements of traditional Japanese culture from the Meiji period. In fact, Japanese tourists feel that Japanese-Americans know more about Japanese culture than youngsters in Japan. Despite being a melting pot, the culture that exists in Hawaiian society is none other than the dominant Japanese culture of the Meiji period. McDermott, Tseng and Maretzki (1980) assert that modern Hawaii can provide glimpses of rural Japan in the Meiji and pre-Meiji eras. In actual fact, in their research, they found that tourists in Hawaii noticed that the Japanese-Americans in Hawaii 'unknowingly perpetuate minor practices, verbal expression, and attitudes that seem incredibly old-fashioned' (p. 18). What about Japan? As Japan adopts Western culture, the consumer market continues to discover new target markets and new consumption preferences. The next paragraph discusses how the impact of globalization has changed Japanese society over the years.

Changes in Japanese society

In recent years, Japan has encountered a number of changes in its society. These changes triggered the creation of new values and growing social divergence. These changes include the increase in discretionary income, the rise of material standards of living, and more significantly is the shift of *hitonami* – consciousness which results in a de-emphasizing of traditional values and the emergence of greater individuality and freedom of self-expression (Douglas 1987; Jenkins and Pepper 1988; Aaker 1999). Other parallel developments include new segments of consumers: working couples with children, and single young adults. With the increasing standard of living and minimal to no increase in income, couples seemingly need to both work to maintain a comfortable living. According to the Japan Institute for Labor Policy and Training (2012), women accounted for more than 48 per cent of the Japanese workforce. And, according to a recent World Bank report (2013), the number of women who participate in the workforce increased by 1 per cent in recent years. As the female consumer segment broadens, apart from purchasing traditional household and food items, the culture (e.g. domestic and international travel), fitness and health, and leisure industries have been targeting this new emerging female market.

On the other hand, the number of young adults have increasingly chosen to either stay single for a longer period of time or choose to marry at a later age. This is an important market segment, because they have a high purchasing power without having heavy family obligations, which translates to more disposable income. They have also begun to break away from the traditional values of Japanese society and how they should determine their life patterns. Furthermore, the term 'lifetime employment' does not seem to be applicable to this market, as they feel that they don't want to be tied down to a single company.

Consumption patterns

According to Salsberg (2010), Japanese consumers are changing their consumption patterns, following those of the Europeans and Americans. Generally known to be brand and quality conscious, Japanese are not willing to sacrifice quality and convenience for discounted and online purchases. Japanese consumers pick and choose their products differently. For example, they have a preference for shopping in malls and stand-alone specialty shops to shopping at department stores in their neighbourhood. Their reasons for such a change in behaviour is due to their strong preference for being able to shop at their own pace, and more importantly, being able to undertake several activities at one location. Larke (2014) asserted that there was a general increase in consumer demand for specialty apparel retailing in the fiscal year 2012.

Shopping experience

A reason why consumers in Japan loathe purchasing online products is because they value luxury. Luxury is not only perceived as high-end products, but is actually accompanied by the shopping experience. The top two reasons why Japanese consumers value the luxury in-store shopping experience are first because they feel that the staff are kind, and second, the way that the staff are able to deliver their knowledge on the product. Convenience shopping or 'click' shopping may be desirable especially in this hectic working society, but Japanese consumers are still fond of experiencing the in-store shopping ambience and the sense of ownership of the product.

Japanese culture and its influence on research

The dynamics of culture have inevitably influenced the way that research is being conducted. Craig and Douglas (2005) assert that 'new sources of cultural influence are permeating and changing society' (p. 323). Due to the complexity of culture, there are various definitions that constitute how culture should be interpreted. McCracken's (1986) approach to defining culture is more incorporating. He argues that culture is based on an individual's subjective view. In other words, McCracken perceives culture from an individual level, which determines the interaction between a social action and a product activity of an individual's overall behaviour. On the contrary, Leung *et al.* (2005) segregate culture at different levels, such as global, national, organizational (e.g. within a company), and group culture (e.g. membership of an informal group). These types of segregation differ between individuals. As globalization takes place, greater emphasis is placed on social and group processes (Craig and Douglas 2005) especially when culture is converging and diverging in different countries. However, according to Craig and Douglas (2005), in this current era, cultural embracement is viewed as 'partial globalization rather than cultural convergence' (p. 324).

So what is the role of culture on research? Culture, when used as a holistic concept, is deemed too extensive as a main motivation on any research agenda. Meek (1988) utilized anthropological terminology labelled as 'cultural derivatives' to break down this holistic concept of culture into digestible portions. These portions include 'symbol, myth, ideational systems and rituals' (p. 466). A symbol, as explained by Meek (1988) includes language, architecture and artefacts which may be viewed as a stimulus with a learned meaning and value. Bagozzi (1975) had an extended definition, he asserted that symbols are generally defined where 'an object, action, word, picture, or complex behaviour is understood to mean not only itself but also some other ideas of feelings' (p. 36).

Now that we know the general role of culture in research, we will go deeper and unfold the role of culture on consumer psychology in market research. Solomon (1983) used the symbolic interactionism theory to explain the process by which individuals understand their world. According to Rose (1962), the response received from an individual towards the stimulus is based on the learned meaning and value, and generally does not correspond with its effect upon the person's physical sense organs. Similarly, Blumer (1962) asserted that people interpret the actions of others rather than simply reacting to them. This is because humans live in a symbolic environment and individual's actions are accompanied by meanings. Furthermore, symbols are a form of reference, as they provide meanings, serve as emotional triggers, and compel individuals to action (Cohen and McKay 1984). Language is an example of a symbol. Regardless of what language it is, it has the ability to mystify knowledge, and its meaning adds more value to the respective user (e.g. the jargon used by academics, military personnel). Other symbols include artefacts such as the Japanese national flag flown by the navy during the Second World War (which symbolizes aggression and imperialism) and architecture such as a temple which symbolizes a uniting of the faithful and practising a good faith). Symbolic interactionism theory explains patterns of symbolic discourse and that this theory has a consensus definition which emphasizes the social nature of the self and its importance for the individual's interaction patterns (Blumer 1969). It proposes that an individual's self-concept is based on their perceptions of responses of others, and it functions to direct behaviour (Kinch 1967). This self-concept is believed to have many roles (e.g. the social self, spiritual self) which encourages individual analyses of each social role we perform. In essence, marketing companies take advantage of symbols to trigger consumers' self-concept during their decision-making process, ultimately manipulating their purchasing intentions.

Due to such a culture embedded in Japanese society, Western researchers find it a challenge to obtain *honest* data. It may be assumed that the Japanese are more positive and polite when it comes to public consumption (e.g. face-saving) rather than private consumption, and that such an attitude bleeds over to their opinions. In other words, there is a tendency for the Japanese to be hesitant in giving their true opinion, even if they think that it is negative.

Despite the successful sales of Japanese products within the domestic and international markets, market research has not been the main focus in Japanese enterprises. Most product developments were achieved via a *hit-and-miss* process or *trial and error*. However, slowly and gradually, while learning from other foreign companies, especially for their international market expansion, Japanese companies see the importance of research. These Japanese companies see the need to learn about local culture and habits through market research, while developing new products to cater to these local markets. Market research has become especially important for Japanese companies that venture overseas, especially when their target markets have consumers who have extreme differences in consumption behaviour. For example, in a NHK episode on UNIQLO's foreign venture in Bangladesh, the team that was sent to this underdeveloped country was tasked to sell products that were offered at the headquarters. The challenge that this team had was to maintain the company's motto and vision while selling to consumers with a different consumption preference. Initially, the team was struggling to attract locals to buy their product, despite a decrease in price. The pricing of each product was in fact in ratio of what each working individual would get. In other words, the products offered were affordable for the locals. However, there were certain clothes that were not selling, and those were ladies' T-shirts. Due to such a setback, the research team decided to do more market research and find out what local preferences were. They realized that these women and girls do not wear T-shirts in public; rather they choose to wear their traditional garments (saris). T-shirts are worn only in the comfort of their own homes. With that research data, the team then designed T-shirts that resemble Saris so as to capture more local female consumers.

This episode tells us that Japanese companies have come to realize that product-development research may not be necessary domestically, but it is tremendously important in a foreign market. With a difference in culture and consumption habits, Japanese companies need to know how these non-Japanese consumers are different from typical Japanese consumers.

Understanding the Japanese market

Globalization has been a topic analysed extensively in the economic or political world. There is a growing understanding that 'globalization lies at the heart of modern culture and the practices lie at the heart of globalization' (Tomlinson 1999: 1; Tomlinson 2003). Many foreigners (e.g. companies and independent researchers) conveniently assume that the Japanese consumer market is homogeneous with other Asian markets. Unfortunately, that is an incorrect assumption. For foreign businesses to succeed in the Japanese market or foreign researchers to obtain good-quality data, it is vital to have a strong understanding of the local culture, language, customs, and business protocol and government relations. All companies and researchers need to recognize the significance of cultural diversity in the country they operate. This understanding of culture is a pre-eminent way of knowing what appeals to their potential customers. Understanding Japanese culture is one thing, but why are foreign companies struggling to get access to the Japanese market? One of the main reasons is a deep-rooted culture that cannot be studied through books, but rather can only be experienced in real-life situations.

Foreign researchers and their challenges

The most challenging aspect for foreign (e.g. Western) researchers who decide to obtain Japanese data through market research is an understanding of Japanese culture. Due to the strong presence of collectivism and Shintoism in Japanese culture, Japanese individuals often have a different perspective when it comes to beliefs and values (Lebra and Lebra 1986). For example, the Japanese are not accustomed to say 'no' to a request, an offer, or an invitation. So how do Japanese reject an offer? They would reply with a humble statement such as *Thank you for asking, I'll think about it*. For foreigners, such a statement indicates a possibility that the offer will be accepted, even if it was only a very slim chance of accepting the offer (www.jetro.go.jp). They would never assume that such a response means otherwise (e.g. rejection). For foreigners, especially individuals with a Western background, rather than beating around the bush, a flat 'no' would be a preferred response (Stening and Hammer 1992). However, to Japanese, that is a sign of rudeness. Japanese nuance is something that is distinct in the Japanese culture, and which is difficult to explain (Lebra and Lebra 1986; Markus and Kitayama 1991; www.nature.com). Thus, due to such a cultural difference, Western researchers often encounter cultural shock with their research participants. Often, they doubt the responses of their participants, suspecting that some of these responses are not sincere.

So, what are the challenges that researchers face during their data collection? First, it is important to be aware that there are two main types of research methods: quantitative and qualitative (Miles and Huberman 1994; Bernard 2012). Both types of methods require the development of surveys/questionnaires. Quantitative research is more straightforward (e.g. the Likert scales questionnaire), whereas qualitative research requires more understanding of Japanese nuances, due to its narrative nature. However, this does not mean that researchers should seek a quantitative method; rather they should pay extra attention while analysing the qualitative data. When developing questions for either of the research methods, the whole set of surveys would require translations by bilinguals who understand the nuances and hidden meanings of those stated sentences. I had first-hand experience when I was conducting several pieces of research with Japanese respondents. Despite the clear and straightforward questions written in English, when they were translated directly into Japanese the intended meanings were lost. Often, when the questions are translated into meaningful Japanese sentences, the questions would be longer, due to the nature of the language. While trying to contain the main ideas and meanings from the English survey, the Japanese sentences need to make sense to Japanese native. The translation process is tedious, as the researchers not only need to be sensitive towards Japanese culture, but also questions asked need to be sensible from the viewpoint of a regular Japanese person (i.e. no technical terms). If the questionnaires are directly translated without any consideration of the cultural meanings and nuances, the perceived meaning of the sentences would be different when read by Japanese respondents. Sometimes it may draw in negative responses, which could contaminate the data.

The same applies for qualitative studies (e.g. in-depth interviews). When an interviewer carries out an interview, he/she must not only be fluent in the Japanese language but also in *how* the questions should be asked, as well as what questions are being asked. Like attending a Japanese meeting, Japanese etiquette must be observed from the beginning to the end of the interview session (www.jetro.co.jp). Occasionally, a gift is presented to the interviewee in order to thank them for their effort and time for participating in the interview. As for the foreign researcher, he/she has also to observe Japanese etiquette when asking for a favour, especially if the respondents need to take time off from their work. If the foreign researcher is not fluent in the Japanese language, an accompanying translator would be beneficial in making the interview process fruitful (www.nature.com).

When the data are collected, researchers will then analyse and interpret those data. When collaborating with foreign researchers, I noticed that foreign researchers are often challenged with the interpretation of the data. Although there is the desire for researchers to have their research propositions and hypotheses supported, due to nuances and cultural differences in language structure, the responses might differ from what is expected. This is especially true for qualitative research methods. For example, during an interview process, the body language, hand gestures, facial expressions are all part of the data-collection process. While analysing those data, researchers need to understand what those non-verbal communications actually mean. Although every culture has their own distinctive non-verbal communication, Japanese are especially expert in expressing themselves through their facial expressions and body movements (www.jetro.co.jp). In addition, a part of the non-verbal fillers are essential in analysing the truth of the received responses. A foreign researcher can only obtain, hopefully, near true data by combining all the non-verbal, verbal and nuances when analysing the data (Giorgi and Giorgi 2008).

Despite the downturn of the Japanese economy due to the Great East Japan Earthquake in 2011, the economic situation in Japan is slowly but gradually picking up. This has encouraged the commissioning of more and more market research (Levine 2011). Research institutions such as the Center for International Research on Japan Economy (CIRJE) and many more have been established to support research activities within Japan. Regardless of international and domestic researchers, these researchers are trying to understand how Japanese society works and how their research could contribute towards improvements in the consumer market. As foreign researchers continue to face challenges in the accuracy of their data obtained in Japan and the interpretation of those data, these researchers have started to put more effort into understanding Japanese consumer behaviour, rather than just accepting the surface (e.g. superficial) answers.

Conclusions

Drawing on recent literature on the consumer market in Japan, individuals' preference for products, as well as their shopping habits, have changed dramatically over the past decades (Moriuchi and Jackson 2011). Constant research is necessary in order to keep up with the ever-changing attitudes and mindsets of consumers, which are continuously driven by the constant change in the social demographics. However, despite the need for more rigorous research to examine the Japanese consumer market, cultural barriers seem to be a hindrance in seeking *true* data (Matsumoto and Jones 2009). In other words, data that are not polluted by external attributes such as cultural beliefs. Foreign researchers, occasionally, in collaboration with foreign companies, are constantly working hard to achieving near-perfect data for analysing the Japanese consumer market. This chapter has highlighted the importance of the common practices, culture and behaviour, and challenges that foreign researchers faced in their market research in Japan. The topics discussed in this chapter may not be adequate for a full understanding of the Japanese market, but the intention is to cover the fundamentals of the need to know about the Japanese consumer market.

Bibliography

Aaker, J. L. (1999). The malleable self: the role of self-expression in persuasion. *Journal of Marketing Research*, 36(1): 45–57.

Bagozzi, R. P. (1975). Marketing as exchange. *The Journal of Marketing*, 39(4): 32–39.

Barnlund, D. C. (1975). *Public and Private Self in Japan and United States: Communicative Styles of Two Cultures*. Tokyo: Simul Press.

Bernard, H. R. (2012). *Social Research Methods: Qualitative and Quantitative Approaches*. London: Sage.

Blumer, H. (1962). *Society as Symbolic Interaction*. In: Rose, A. M. (ed.), *Human Behavior and Social Processes: An Interactionist Approach*. Boston, MA: Houghton Mifflin.

Blumer, H. (1969). *Symbolic Interactionism: Perspective and Method*. Englewood Cliffs, NJ, Prentice-Hall.

Cohen, S. and McKay, G. (1984). Social support, stress and the buffering hypothesis: a theoretical analysis. In: Baum, A., Singer, J. E., and Taylor, S. E. (eds), *Handbook of Psychology and Health*. Vol. 4, Hillsdale, NJ: Erlbaum, pp. 253–267.

Craig, S. C. and Douglas, S. P. (2005). Beyond national culture: implications of cultural dynamics for consumer research. *International Marketing Review*, 23(3): 322–342.

Douglas, S. P. (1987). Emerging consumer markets in Japan. *Advances in Consumer Research*, 14: 1.

Euromonitor International (2009). *Current and Expected Landscape of Mail Order/E-commerce Business in 2008–2009*, December 2009. Fuji-Keizai; Research on utilization in Japan 2008. Japanese Ministry of Economy, Trade, and Industry (METI); McKinsey analysis.

Giorgi, A. P. and Giorgi, B. (2008). Phenomenological psychology. *The SAGE Handbook of Qualitative Research in Psychology*, London: Sage, pp. 165–179.

Hofstede, G. (2011). Dimensionalizing cultures: the Hofstede model in context. *Online Readings in Psychology and Culture*, 2(1): 8.

Itō, M. (1991). Two types of distribution system and access to the Japanese market (table 6.4). *The Japanese Distribution System and Access to the Japanese Market*, Chicago, IL: University of Chicago Press, pp. 175–190.

Japan Institute for Labor Policy and Training (2012). *Japanese Working Life Profile 2011/2012: Labor Statistics (2012)*. Tokyo: Japan Institute for Labor Policy and Training, http://www.jil.go.jp/english/jwl/2012-2013/index.html, last accessed 23 October 2015.

Japan Market Resource Network (JMRN) (2007). *Japan's Changing Consumer: Drivers of Change for Luxury Brands*. Tokyo: Japan Market Resource Network.

Japan Retail News (2009). *Market Reports Japan: Retail and Consumer Goods Japan. G and S International*, http://www.japanretailnews.com/list-japan-market-reports.html, last accessed 23 October 2015.

Jenkins, A. and Pepper, D. (1988). Enhancing students' employability and self-expression: how to teach oral and groupwork skills in geography. *Journal of Geography in Higher Education*, 12(1): 67–83.

Jeremy, M. and Robinson, M. E. (1989). *Ceremony and Symbolism in the Japanese Home*. Manchester, UK: Manchester University Press.

JETRO (1999). Communication with Japanese in business. www.jetro.go.jp/costarica/mercadeo/communicationwith.pdf, last accessed 18 October 2015.

Jiji Press (2013). Japan September jobless rate falls to 4 per cent. 29 October 2013. Retrieved on 5 November 2013 from http://newsonjapan.com/html/newsdesk/article/105132.php, last accessed 17 October 2015.

Kau, Ah Keng, Uncles, Mark, Ehrenberg, Andrew, and Barnard, Neil, (1998). Competitive brand-choice and store-choice among Japanese consumers. *Journal of Product and Brand Management*, 7(6): 481–494

Kinch, J. W. (1967). A formalized theory of self-concept. In: Manis, J. G. and Meltzer, G. N. (eds), *Symbolic Interaction: a Reader in Social Psychology*. Boston, MA: Allyn and Bacon.

Krugman, P. (ed.) (1991) *Trade with Japan: Has the Door Opened Wider?* Chicago, IL: National Bureau of Economic Research: University of Chicago Press.

Kurihara, T., Tanaka, K., and Maeda, K. (2013). An optimization method for designing ecological and economical procurement logistics system. In: Stjepandić, Josip, Rock, Georg, and Bil, Cees (eds), *Proceedings of the 19th ISPE International Conference on Concurrent Engineering*, pp. 63–71.

Larke, R. (2014). Specialty Apparel FY 2012: Gaining further ground. *Japan Consuming*. www.japanconsuming.com, last accessed 17 October 2015.

Lazer, William, Murata, Shoji, and Kosaka, Hiroshi (1985). Japanese marketing: towards a better understanding. *Journal of Marketing*, 49 (Spring): 69–81.

Lebra, T. and Lebra, W. P. (1986). *Japanese Culture and Behavior: Selected Readings*. Honolulu, Hawaii: University of Hawaii Press.

Leung, K., Bhagat, R. S., Buchan, N. R., Erez, M., and Gibson, C. B. (2005). Culture and international business: recent advances and their implications for future research. *Journal of International Business Studies*, 36: 357–378.

Levine, Alaina, G. (2011). Internationalizing Japan's scientific landscape. Retrieved from http://sciencecareers.sciencemag.org/legacy/getfile/aaas/files/uploaded-files/pdf/503db333-a642-45b0-89a1-b35cc44f94a1/science.opms.r1100107.pdf, last accessed 17 October 2015.

McAlister, L. and Rothschild (eds) (1993) *Advances in Consumer Research*. Association for Consumer Research; Provo, Utah, 22: 461–474.

McDermott, J. F., Tseng, W.-S., and Maretzki, T. (eds) (1980). *People and Cultures of Hawaii: A Psychocultural Profile*. USA: University of Hawaii Press.

Markus, H. R. and Kitayama, S. (1991). Culture and the self: implications for cognition, emotion, and motivation. *Psychological Review*, 98(2): 224.

267

Markus, H. R. and Kitayama, S. (1998). The cultural psychology of personality. *Journal of Cross-cultural Psychology*, 29(1): 63–87.

Matsumoto, D. and Jones, C. A. L. (2009). Ethical issues in cross-cultural psychology. *Handbook of Social Science Research Ethics*, London: Sage, pp. 323–336.

Meek, V. L. (1988). Organizational culture: origins and weaknesses. *Organization Studies,* 9(4): 453–473.

Miles, M. B. and Huberman, A. M. (1994). *Qualitative Data Analysis: An Expanded Sourcebook*. London: Sage.

Moriuchi, Emi and Jackson, Paul R. (2011). *The Role of Product Type and Foreign Brand Names in Bicultural's Purchasing Intentions* (September 29, 2011). Available at SSRN: http://ssrn.com/abstract=1862683, last accessed 17 October 2015.

NHK World (February 2014). Japanese economy: seeking future economic models (television programme). In: *Global Debate WISDOM*. Japan, Tokyo: NHK (Japan Broadcasting Corporation). www.nhk.or.jp/wisdom/140125/theme_en.html, last accessed 17 October 2015.

Rose, A. M. (ed.) (1962). *Human Behavior and Social Processes: An Interactionist Approach*. Boston, MA, Houghton Mifflin.

Salsberg, B. and Morita, Y. (2012). *Consumer and Shopper Insights: Online Retail in Japan: Too late for New Entrants?* July 2012, Tokyo: McKinsey & Company.

Sato, S. and Asahi, Y. (2012). A daily-level purchasing model at an e-commerce site. *International Journal of Electrical Computer Engineering*, 2(6): 831–839.

Shibusawa, T. (2001). Japanese American parenting. In: N. B. Webb (ed.), *Culturally Diverse Parent–Child and Family Relationships: A Guide For Social Workers and Other Practitioners*, pp. 283–303. New York, NY: Columbia University Press.

Sojka, J. and Tansuhaj, P. S. (1995). Cross-cultural consumer research: a twenty-year review. *Advances in Consumer Research*, 22: 461–474.

Solomon, M. R. (1983). The role of products as social stimuli: a symbolic interactionism perspective. *Journal of Consumer Research*, 10(3): 319–329.

Stening, B. W. and Hammer, M. R. (1992). Cultural baggage and the adaptation of expatriate American and Japanese managers. *MIR: Management International Review*, 32(1): 77–89.

Stjepandić, J., Rock, G., and Bil, C. (2012). Concurrent engineering approaches for sustainable product development in a multi-disciplinary environment. *Proceedings of the 19th ISPE International Conference on Concurrent Engineering*, pp. 63–71.

Tabuchi, H. (2013). Economic expansion slows down in Japan. *New York Times*, 11 August 2013, http://www.nytimes.com/2013/08/12/business/global/economic-expansion-slows-down-in-japan.html?_r=0, last accessed 17 October 2015.

Takada, H. and Jain, D. (1991). Cross-national analysis of diffusion of consumer durable goods in Pacific Rim countries. *Journal of Marketing*, 55(2): 48–54.

Tomita, S. K. (1998). The consequences of belonging: conflict management techniques among Japanese Americans. *Journal of Elder Abuse and Neglect*, 9(3): 41–68.

Tomlinson, J. (1999). *Globalization and Culture*. Chicago, IL: University of Chicago Press.

Tomlinson, J. (2003). Globalization and cultural identity. In Held, D. and McGrew, A. (eds), *The Global Transformations Reader*. Cambridge, UK: Polity Press, pp. 269–277.

Vernon, R. (1966). International investment and international trade in the product cycle. *Quarterly Journal of Economics* May 1966.

Winsted, K. F. (1997). The service experience in two cultures: a behavioral perspective. *Journal of Retailing*, 73(3): 337–360.

World Bank (2015). *Labor Force Participation Rate, Female (% of Female Population Ages 15+) (Modeled ILO Estimate)*. http://data.worldbank.org/indicator/SL.TLF.CACT.FE.ZS?order=wbapi_data_value_2013+wbapi_data_value+wbapi_data_value-last&sort=asc, last accessed 23 October 2015.

Yano Research Institute (April 2009). *Luxury Import Accessories Market in Japan 2009*. Retrieved from https://www.yanoresearch.com/press/pdf/1100.pdf, last accessed 15 October 2015.

yStats.com GmbH and Co. KG (2010). *Research on International Markets (April 2010). Japan B2C E-Commerce Report 2010*, www.ystats.com/uploads/report_abstracts/1021.pdf, last accessed 17 October 2015.

22
Japanese marketing

Yumiko Toda

Introduction

Japanese marketing practices began in 1955, when a team from the Japan Production Center (JPC) visited companies in the US to learn marketing concepts and practices. Upon its return, the team rapidly and extensively distributed the knowledge learned throughout Japanese industry. However, marketing historians have revealed that some Japanese company histories show evidence of early marketing practices even before the Second World War.

In this chapter, the author illustrates a brief history of marketing in Japan from the early 1920s. This chapter contains six sections. The second section addresses pioneering marketing practices in the pre-war period. The third section mentions the social background of marketing in the post-war period. The fourth section discusses the development of marketing management in the post-war period from the mid-1950s to the 1970s. The fifth section details the globalization of Japanese companies from the mid-1970s to the 1980s. The final section discusses the rise of big retailers and the development of strategic alliances between manufacturers and retailers since the 1990s to present day. This historical overview of Japanese marketing reveals the sector's unique characteristics.

Pioneering marketing practices in the pre-war period

The end of the Edo period in the late 1860s also brought to an end the 200 year-long era of isolationism. Japan opened to the world, and the new Meiji government took a bold step in introducing Western culture. Products like milk, bread, Western confectionary, and beer appeared on the Japanese market for the first time. Oil lamps became commonplace, and electric lamps were available for use. From the Meiji period (1868 to 1912), the Taisho period (1912 to 1926), and until the start of the Second World War, elements of Western culture gradually penetrated daily life, including new products in food, clothing, and housing (Maeda 1977: 163). Additionally, Table 22.1 shows that as social infrastructure and services, such as transportation; the railway system; the water and sewerage system; electricity; and education, developed in urban areas, the proportion of the population living in cities rapidly increased from the end of the Taishō period to the beginning of the Shōwa period (1926 to 1989).

Yumiko Toda

Table 22.1 The proportion of people in urban areas to total population

	Total population	City population with more than 10,000 people	Percentage of city population with more than 10,000 people, to total population (%)	City population with more than 100,000 people	Percentage of city population with more than 100,000, to total population (%)
1903	48,543,000	10,049,000	20.7	–	–
1913	55,131,000	15,244,000	27.7	–	–
1920	55,963,000	18,035,000	32.2	6,753,000	12.1
1930	64,450,000	25,291,000	39.2	10,481,000	16.3
1940	71,933,000	36,891,000	51.3	21,291,000	29.6

Source: Ando (1979: 6)

The standard of living in Japan progressively increased with the effects of Westernization, urbanization, and social-infrastructure development during the mid-1930s (Kohara 1994: 7–8). As income levels increased, expenditure for food decreased, and other expenses, including housing, utilities, clothing, health care, and education increased (cf. Table 22.2). Salaried workers in urban areas, who received a higher education and engaged in white-collar jobs, played a central role in the changes in consumer life in the 1920s, and were called the 'new middle class' (Nihon Research Sōgō Kenkyujō 1988: chapter 6). However, the new middle class at that time was not large enough to generate a mass-consumption society, which would develop in earnest after the 1950s.

Moreover, although the chemical and heavy industries achieved remarkable development from the 1910s to the 1920s, economic growth in the pre-war period was dominated by light industries centred on textiles. The consumer goods industries remained under development, with little impact on the national economy (Kohara 1994: 8). Most consumer goods companies depended on wholesalers and retailers, although some innovative consumer goods manufacturers set out to intervene in the distribution process by implementing sales practices to increase sales, prevent price slumps, and control brand image (Maeda 1977: 164). Examples include Ajinomoto's artificial flavouring production; Calpis' condensed dairy beverages; Suntory and

Table 22.2 Changes in personal consumption in the pre-war period (million yen, (%))

Date	Food	Clothing	Housing	Utility	Others (including education, entertainment, etc.)
1880	589 (68.7)	71 (8.2)	50 (5.8)	34 (4.0)	114 (13.3)
1890	664 (66.3)	72 (7.3)	88 (8.8)	33 (3.3)	144 (14.3)
1900	1,366 (61.7)	222 (10.0)	174 (7.9)	68 (3.1)	383 (17.3)
1905	1,610 (63.5)	201 (8.0)	209 (8.2)	80 (3.2)	433 (17.1)
1910	2,060 (61.3)	311 (9.3)	326 (9.7)	118 (3.5)	544 (16.2)
1915	2,268 (59.9)	348 (9.2)	377 (10.0)	159 (4.2)	632 (16.7)
1920	7299 (61.7)	1,473 (12.5)	754 (6.4)	543 (4.6)	1,748 (14.8)
1925	7,843 (59.0)	1,353 (10.2)	1,422 (10.7)	502 (3.8)	2,156 (16.3)
1930	6,057 (53.5)	1,101 (9.7.)	1,549 (13.7)	494 (4.4)	2,124 (18.7)
1935	6,575 (50.3)	1,671 (12.8)	1,534 (11.7)	559 (4.2)	2,742 (20.9)
1940	9,955 (48.9)	2,247 (11.0)	2,656 (13.1)	916 (4.5)	4,584 (22.5)

Source: Ando (1979: 9)

Kirin's wine, whiskey, and beer production; Kagome's tomato ketchup; Janome's sewing machines; Morinaga and Meiji's Western confectionery;[1] Shiseido's cosmetics; Lion and Kao's soaps and toothpaste; and Matsushita's electrical products. These companies share some common characteristics – their products were new, companies used mass advertising in newspapers and magazines extensively, and marketing strategies evolved from a partial dependence on traditional wholesalers to a gradual selection of superior companies and the organization of their own direct distribution channels. These characteristics form a part of what is known today as the marketing mix or the '4Ps' (McCarthy 1960) of product, price, promotion, and placement strategies. Without the concept of marketing or the recognition of innovative marketing practices, these marketing-oriented companies emerged during the pre-war period. The companies focused primarily on advertising and channel management, although their practices were not adequately integrated or managed. Therefore, some leading manufacturers in the emerging Japanese consumer goods industry engaged in marketing practices, albeit with restricted development.

The social background of marketing in the post-war period

The pioneering marketing practices developed in the pre-war period were suspended at the outbreak of the Second World War and the struggle for recovery in the period afterwards. In this section, the author analyses the underlying conditions for the development of marketing in the post-war period.

Economic growth and the consumption revolution

The encouragement of the transfer of new technologies from foreign countries prompted manufacturers to invest in technological innovations (Kohara 1994: 63, cf. Table 22.3). The government aggressively promoted heavy chemical industrialization based on the mass production of durable consumer goods. The main industries modernized production facilities. Moreover, new industries emerged, including artificial fibre production, home electrical appliances, and automobiles; the mass-production system made steady progress (Maeda 1977: 172).

After the post-war reconstruction period, Japan achieved rapid and remarkable economic growth, increasing national income by the mid-1950s, with the economy recovering at a level 13 per cent above the pre-war baseline. The White Paper of 1956 declared the end of the post-war period (Economic Planning Agency 1956), and income levels doubled between 1955 and 1960. Additionally, narrowing income gaps led to changes in Japanese class consciousness. Most Japanese began to consider themselves middle class (cf. Table 22.4).

These economic factors resulted in high consumption levels and changes in consumption patterns. The mass-consumption culture was established by the end of the 1950s, when the consumption of electric appliances such as washing machines, refrigerators, and black-and-white televisions dramatically increased during the 1950s and 1960s (cf. Table 22.5). These three products were consumed in imitation of 'sanshu no jin-gi', the three sacred imperial treasures. Additionally, with the development of chemical fibres such as nylon, clothes made from these new fibres were produced, consumed, and made available to most people at reasonable prices. Western clothing increased in popularity and was considered more fashionable than in the pre-war period. During the 1960s and 1970s, an increase in the availability of credit led to the 3Cs – colour TVs, cars, and coolers (air conditioners) – as new 'sacred imperial treasures' and symbolizing mass consumption in Japan. During the period of high economic growth from the mid-1950s to the mid-1970s, consumption was no longer limited to the rich but was enjoyed

Table 22.3 Number and percentage of technology transfer from foreign countries

	1955–1961		1962–1965		1966–1973		1974–1979	
	Number	%	Number	%	Number	%	Number	%
Electronics	295	23.8	465	24.9	2,138	21.0	1,622	17.7
Communications devices	148	12.0	155	8.3	665	6.5	389	7.3
Electric machines	–	–	–	–	337	3.3	392	7.3
Transportation vehicles	78	6.3	57	3.1	533	5.2	482	5.1
Precision machines	–	–	88	4.7	290	2.8	368	3.9
Metallic machine tools	17	1.4	71	3.8	360	3.5	187	2.0
Special and general industrial machines	–	–	–	–	1,599	15.7	1,323	14.1
Metals	119	9.6	210	11.3	648	6.4	442	4.7
Chemicals	298	24.1	338	18.1	1,598	15.7	1,010	10.7
Medicines and agricultural chemicals	48	3.9	38	2.0	301	3.0	323	3.4
Organic and inorganic chemicals	188	15.2	222	11.9	713	7.0	367	3.9
Textile spinning	64	5.2	5	2.6	766	7.5	1,241	13.2
Petroleum	28	2.3	31	1.7	236	2.3	125	1.3
Total	1,238	100.0	1,864	100.0	10,177	100.0	9,416	100.0

Source: Yamamoto (1992: 209)

Table 22.4 Changes in Japanese class consciousness (%)

	1958	1961	1964	1967	1968	1969
Upper	0	0	1	1	1	1
Upper middle	3	4	1	6	8	7
Middle	37	42	50	53	51	52
Lower middle	32	31	31	29	28	30
Total of middle classes	72	77	87	88	87	89
Lower	17	13	9	7	8	8
Unknown	11	11	3	4	4	3

Source: Economic Planning Agency (1970: 5)

by most people on a national level. The advent of a mass-consumption society was an essential factor in the development of marketing in the post-war period (Kohara 1994: 70–71, Maeda 1977: 173).

Marketing as an imported idea from the United States

Pioneering manufacturers engaged in marketing practices as early as the 1920s, although these practices were not recognized as marketing. Most business practitioners were not aware of the term 'marketing' before the Second World War. Marketing concepts were imported through the Japan Productivity Center (JPC), established in 1955 as a central industrial organization to promote the Productivity Movement with financial support from the US. The movement

Table 22.5 The penetration of durable consumer goods (%)

	Sewing machines	Cameras	Electric fans	Electric washing machines	Black-and-white TVs	Colour TVs	Electric refrigerators	Vacuum cleaners	Air conditioners	Automobiles
1958	64.2	38.5	27.6	24.6	15.9	–	3.2	–	–	–
1959	68.3	43.4	28.6	33.0	23.6	–	5.7	–	–	–
1960	69.5	45.8	34.4	40.6	44.7	–	10.1	7.7	–	–
1961	74.1	49.2	41.9	50.2	62.5	–	17.2	15.4	0.4	2.8
1962	75.8	51.8	50.6	58.1	79.4	–	28.0	24.5	0.7	5.1
1963	79.1	56.4	60.6	66.4	88.7	–	39.1	33.1	1.3	6.1
1964	76.2	43.8	49.9	61.4	87.8	–	38.2	26.8	1.8	6.0
1965	77.4	49.4	59.6	68.5	90.0	–	51.4	32.2	2.6	9.2
1966	76.6	52.9	65.7	75.5	94.4	0.3	61.6	41.2	2.0	12.1
1967	81.7	57.3	69.1	79.8	96.2	1.6	69.7	47.2	2.8	9.5
1968	82.6	59.8	75.6	84.8	96.4	5.4	77.6	53.8	3.9	13.1
1969	84.6	62.7	80.1	88.3	94.7	13.9	84.6	62.6	4.7	17.3
1970	84.5	64.1	83.2	91.4	90.2	26.3	89.1	68.3	5.9	22.1
1971	84.4	67.0	85.0	93.6	82.3	42.3	91.2	74.3	7.7	26.8
1972	83.0	69.8	89.3	96.1	75.1	61.1	91.6	79.8	9.3	30.1
1973	84.6	72.7	91.8	97.5	65.4	75.8	94.7	85.2	12.9	36.7
1974	84.2	75.6	93.3	97.5	55.7	85.9	96.5	89.6	12.4	39.8
1975	84.7	77.4	94.3	97.6	48.7	90.3	96.7	91.2	17.2	41.2

Source: Economic Planning Agency (1991: 52–55)

was expected to reinforce economic recovery. The JPC consisted mainly of academic scholars and representative members of industrial organizations, such as the Japan Business Federation, the Japan Committee for Economic Development, the Japan Chamber of Commerce and Industry, and the Japan Management League. Through this movement, business principles and technologies that had been developed in the US were actively introduced to Japanese industries, and marketing concepts were imported as one technique to improve business productivity. In 1955, the JPC organized a group called the 'Top Management Mission', composed of practitioners, academic scholars, and public officers. The group dispatched their representatives to the US to inspect US company business practices. When Taizo Ishizaka, then the Chairman of the Japan Business Federation and the head of the mission, returned to Japan, he stated, 'marketing is a scientific method to resolve market problems, and Japanese companies need to learn the theory and principles of marketing more seriously and adopt them into their practices'. His speech was widely reported in both general newspapers and technical journals, and 'marketing' became a catchphrase amongst practitioners. The following year, the 'First Marketing Mission' was newly organized, concentrating on marketing practices (Yokota 1987).

The team imported two fundamental principles. First, the idea of consumer-centrism or placing consumer demand at the centre of marketing activity, as expressed by the phrase 'the consumer is King'. Second, the team learned principles of managerial marketing, which emphasized the scientific market research of consumer demand and the integrated management of marketing tools such as product planning, pricing policies, distribution channel management, and promotion policies later conceptualized in the 4Ps marketing mix (McCarthy 1960).

Subsequently, the JPC hosted seminars to teach marketing, inviting prominent marketing scholars from the US as guest speakers; publishing marketing journals; and even producing radio programmes featuring marketing lectures (Japan Marketing Association 2007: 5–7). Through these efforts, marketing concepts spread rapidly across industries (Shirahige 1967: chapter 4). Unlike the history of marketing in the US (Bartels 1962; Tedlow 1990), marketing in Japan was introduced intentionally rather than spontaneously.

While practitioners were driven to learn marketing principles, they soon realized that US marketing techniques were similar to the business practices of Japanese pioneering companies such as Shiseido and Morinaga during the pre-war period. Practitioners understood that these companies had, in fact, practised marketing management. However, US marketing principles emphasizing the integration and management of the marketing mix offered a new perspective. Japanese industries eventually adopted this perspective as a component of their practices.

Common characteristics of marketing in the post-war period

Marketing in the post-war period developed particularly with respect to the durable consumer goods industry, which employed marketing strategies such as full product line-ups, frequent model changes, quality improvements, cost reductions, lower prices derived from mass-production-scale advantages, the establishment of exclusive sales channels for manufacturers, mass advertising, and the adaptation of other promotional tools (Kohara 1994: 141). Eventually, these practices spread to other industries, with extensive dissemination of marketing management ideas. Between the late 1950s and the 1970s, manufacturers of durable goods typically strengthened their integration of marketing tools to avoid severe price competition and to protect their brand image.

Branded products and advertisements

Table 22.3 shows that Japanese manufacturers formed alliances with foreign companies and incorporated advanced technologies to speed up innovation efforts. The electrical appliance and automobile industries led during periods of high economic growth. For example, Matsushita Electric Industrial formed an alliance with Royal Phillips of the Netherlands, Nissan with The Austin Motor Company of the UK, and Isuzu with The Rootes Motors Group (Kohara 1994: 134–135). These companies concentrated technological development and improved product quality. Manufacturers like Kashiyama Company Limited, a clothing company in the semi-durable goods industry, also actively introduced new artificial-fibre technology and design through alliances with foreign apparel companies (Kinoshita 2010).

Moreover, many manufacturers in the consumer goods industries, including medicine, cosmetics, artificial fibres, plastic products, confectionary, and electrical-appliance manufacturers, established product-development departments for technological development, design, and product planning. For example, from the late 1950s to the mid-1960s, electrical-appliance companies expanded their product lines annually (cf. Table 22.6) to respond to different consumer needs.

As technological cycles accelerated with the advance of technical innovation, product life-cycles shortened for clothing, cameras, automobiles, and electrical appliances. Marketers adopted planned obsolescence strategies to reduce the cycle intentionally through frequent product model changes (Maeda 1977: 174–175). Product planning became the focus of marketing strategy, stimulating consumption using obsolescence strategies.

Electrical products were sold under company brand-names such as Matsushita, Toshiba, and Sanyo. These manufacturers provided major home electrical appliances representing '*sanshu no jin-gi*', with their company name serving as quality assurance during the consumption revolution. Company brands and individual product lines were used to differentiate companies from competitors. Companies successfully used newspapers, magazine, radio, and TV advertising. Figure 22.1 shows the growth in total advertising expenditure. TV advertising surpassed newspaper expenditure after the mid-1970s.

Advertisements played an important role in the growth of company brands and product lines, and consumer goods manufacturers leveraged them to increase brand awareness, successfully blending product and promotion strategies.

Table 22.6 Product-line expansion at Matsushita Electric Industrial Company Limited

1956	Automatic rice-cooker, vacuum cleaner, juicer, electric blanket, electric frying-pan, and germicidal lamp
1957	Transistor radio, battery clock, flash-lamp, and reflector camera flash-lamp
1958	Stereo, tape recorder, *kotatsu* (table with heater), table hot-plate, gas heater, and room cooler
1959	Stereo amplifier, electric cooking pot, hand-towel steamer, hot-plate, siphon pot, electric drying machine, and garbage disposer
1960	Colour television, television containing transistors, electric oven, and infrared *kotatsu*
1961	Transceiver, oil heater, tape recorder, cooling fan, air conditioner, and cathode-ray television
1962	Egg cooker, trouser press, kitchen sink, kitchen table, shredder, sodium-vapour lamp, and silicon optical transistor
1963	Electronic organ, electric can opener, electric air filterer, and microwave oven
1964	Video tape-recorder, electric heater, and gas hot-plate (for cooking) for the table.

Source: Matsushita Electric Incorporated (1985)

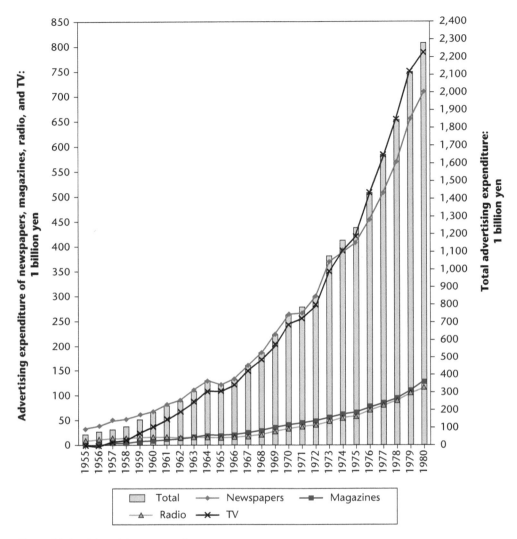

Figure 22.1   Advertising expenditures

Source: Dentsu Incorporated, chronological table of advertising

Keiretsu *in marketing channels and price maintenance*

During the war, prices were strictly regulated and business activities severely limited; however, the government lifted these controls in the late 1940s. Manufacturers of durable consumer goods were allowed to transact freely, and many reorganized their marketing channels. Most manufacturers still depended on existing independent wholesalers to sell their products, but some manufacturers gradually organized their own sales companies (*hansha* in Japanese) to reinforce the sales function. Matsushita founded its own sales company in 1950, Toshiba in 1953, and Hitachi in 1955, establishing an exclusive marketing channel at the wholesale level and establishing the basis of a mass-sales system through these companies. For example, in 1955,

Matsushita owned 110 sales companies. On the other hand, it still maintained 41 joint ventures with wholesalers and kept contracts with another 65 independent sales agents (Shirahige 1967: 55). However, by 1965, Matsushita reorganized and cut ties with the joint ventures and independent sales agents, integrating all wholesaling functions into its own sales company (Kohara 2010: 84).

At the same time, companies also controlled retailing activities. Matsushita graded retailers according to the in-store share of the manufacturer's product. Retailers whose coverage of Matsushita merchandise (branded as National) was over 80 per cent were designated as National Shops; retailers with 50 per cent to 79 per cent coverage were designated as a National Shop Associations (National Tenkai in Japanese); and retailers with 30 per cent to 49 per cent coverage were designated as National League Shops (National *renmei-ten* in Japanese). National Shops received favourable terms, including volume and other discounts for buying merchandise from Matsushita (Shirahige 1967: 57). This direct retail control was called '*keiretsu* in the marketing channel'.[2] Manufacturers of automobiles, electrical appliances, medicines, cosmetics, and detergents adopted a similar vertical *keiretsu* system. These manufacturers did not invest capital in these retailers, because they were principally independent organizations. *Keiretsu* in the marketing channel avoided intense price competition by selling at extremely low prices as a loss leader to protect the manufacturer's brand image. Representative examples of *keiretsu* in marketing channels are found in the business practices of Matsushita and Shiseido.[3] Products were principally sold at the same price across *keiretsu* retail stores. *Keiretsu* retailers cooperated with the manufacturer's strategic direction and followed the manufacturer's suggested retail prices, although the retailers were not forced to do so. In return, manufacturers maintained superior relationships with *keiretsu* retailers or dealers, and established win–win relationships during the period 1950 to 1980. During the economic growth period, sufficient consumer demand for branded goods from these manufacturers allowed retailers to benefit from cooperating with leading manufacturers.

Thus, channel management through *keiretsu* and pricing strategies was integrated to maintain prices and protect manufacturers' brand image. While *keiretsu* in the marketing channel were primitively formed in the pre-war period (cf. Usui 2005), they spread extensively across industries in the post-war period. As new products with identifiable brands entered the consumer market and manufacturers advertised directly to consumers, manufacturers needed to secure stable marketing channels that they could actively manage to prevent prices from collapsing. *Keiretsu* in the marketing channel were an innovative device to shift competition from pricing to non-price factors such as branding or product differentiation. Thus, the integration of marketing strategies using product, price, place, and promotion factors characterized marketing strategy in the post-war period.

The development of international marketing in the 1970s and 1980s

Japan is not rich in natural resources, and was an export-oriented economy before the Second World War. Silk, cotton textiles, and light-industrial products were the primary Japanese exports. At that time, Japanese-manufactured products had a bad reputation, and were considered 'cheap and shoddy'.

As the textile industry declined, and the chemical and heavy industries prospered, durable consumer goods became the primary export items (see Figure 22.2). Manufacturers of durable consumer goods such as Honda, Sony, Matsushita, Canon, Yamaha, YKK, and Kikkoman began to export overseas as early as the 1960s (Kohara 1994: 169). These companies addressed the poor reputation of Japanese products by improving product quality through continuous technological innovation. For example, Honda and Sony established sales subsidiaries in the US ahead of other Japanese companies. Honda introduced a 500 cc motorcycle, the Super Cub, to the US market in 1959. This model had been a success in the Japanese market; therefore, Honda attempted to sell it in the US. At that time, large motorcycles, such as the Harley-Davidson models, dominated the market, but Honda focused on the niche market for small motorcycles. Honda introduced this motorcycle as a new product, developed new marketing channels, and sold them through sporting equipment shops, hobby shops, and motor-boat shops (Kohara 1994: 172). By winning international automobile races in the 1960s, Honda demonstrated the excellent performance of their engines, and proved that their motorcycles and automobiles were of high quality. This raised their reputation and gained them worldwide brand recognition in the 1970s (Kohara 1994: 173).

Sony also demonstrated innovative capabilities and product quality. The company introduced new products such as the world's smallest transistor radio, the Pocket Radio TR-63, in 1957; the world's first transistor television in 1959; and the world's smallest and lightest television, the Micro TV, in 1962, selling these products in Asia, Europe, and the US. Sony established a strong brand image that represented 'good quality, good price' by selling innovative products worldwide during the 1970s (Kohara 1994: 177).

After the shift to the floating exchange-rate system and a revaluation of the Japanese currency, and through the oil crisis of the 1970s, the US and Japan experienced serious trade friction. To decrease the country's export dependency, Japanese manufacturers were required to expand direct investments in the US in the 1970s. Companies established production and marketing subsidiaries in the US (Kohara 1994: 160). Japanese manufacturers steadily transferred production bases overseas, including other Asian countries, in response to the rise in value of the yen against the dollar following the 1985 Plaza Accord (Kohara 1994: 161).

Kotler and Fahey (1982) analysed Japanese marketing strategies in the US, and found four features of the market-entry stage. First, Japanese manufacturers typically entered the market with a low-priced technologically superior product, capturing a large market share Kotler and

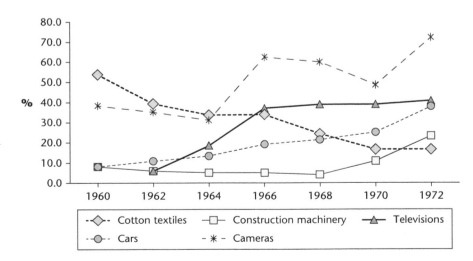

Figure 22.2 The export rate of primary products

Source: Ando (1979: 166)

Note: export rates = amount of export/amount of production.

Fahey (1982: 6). Second, as Honda had avoided head-on competition with Harley-Davidson, Japanese firms did not enter and compete with strong firms already serving the market, but chose segments where competitors were unable and/or unwilling to respond aggressively to their entry. This pattern is evident with radio and television product introductions by Sony and Panasonic; motorcycles from Honda and Yamaha; and smaller copy machines from Canon and Sharp (Kotler and Fahey 1982: 6–7). Third, Japanese companies emphasized quality and service and established an adequate number of service centres where products could be repaired quickly. Finally, Japanese companies integrated distribution into the marketing mix, and frequently offered higher commissions to intermediary agents in order to generate product push (Kotler and Fahey 1982: 7). As Japanese companies organized *keiretsu* in the marketing channel domestically, they similarly focused on securing stable marketing channels in foreign markets.

After gaining a market foothold, the next stage focused on expanding market share and maintaining competitive leadership. Japanese companies concentrated on product development strategies in the form of product improvements, product upgrades, and product proliferation; and market development strategies, including market segmentation, sequencing, and flexibility (Kotler and Fahey 1982: 8). Japanese companies committed to continuous improvements in product performance, features, style, and quality. Companies also broadened product ranges to reach the upper end of the market, while not abandoning the lower end, offering dozens of product versions to appeal to different end-users and income classes.

In summary, Japan's market entry strategy involved the following: market segmentation; targeting underserved segments; product design for a particular market segment; entering the market with a low price; offering high quality and service; developing strong distribution; and backing the product with heavy promotion and advertising (Kotler and Fahey 1982: 8). Although this represents textbook marketing, the Japanese practised these principles thoroughly, and better than most US companies (Kotler and Fahey 1982: 5).

Kotler and Fahey (1982) noted that Japanese manufacturers closely followed the principles of marketing management learned from the US in the mid-1950s. Following these marketing principles, Japanese manufacturers such as Ajinomoto, Honda, Kikkoman, Nissan, Olympus, Panasonic, Sanyo, Sony, and Toyota gained a solid foundation as international companies and dominated the market in the 1980s. Japanese marketing has a distinctive nature in order to respond precisely to the various customer needs of different cultures, offering original, quality products at reasonable prices and organizing stable distribution channels. Consequently, Japanese products overcame their reputation for being 'cheap and shoddy' and, by the 1980s, 'made in Japan' came to symbolize good quality at reasonable prices.

The rise of big retailers and the progress of strategic alliances between manufacturers and retailers since the 1990s.

When the asset-inflated economic bubble collapsed at the beginning of the 1990s, the Japanese economy struggled in a prolonged recession in the post-bubble times. The sluggish economy persisted into the 2000s and was called the 'lost decade' or even the 'lost two decades'. Corporate performance deteriorated because of chronic depression and consumers who sought lower-priced goods. However, since the 1990s, the Japanese government has proceeded with regulatory reforms in various fields, and the regulations concerning big retailer operations were not exceptional. The Large-Scale Retail Store Law[4] was established in 1973 to protect small-scale retailers from larger competitors. The law severely regulated the hours of business, regular holidays, and store floor space of big retailers, which caused them substantial difficulties in opening new big retail stores during the 1980s. However, in 1989, Japanese business customs such as cross-shareholdings, *keiretsu* corporate grouping, and the Large-Scale Retail Store Law were harshly criticized by the US in the Japan–US Structural Impediments Initiative talks. Following the talks, the Japanese government decided to deregulate the law and revise the regulations in 1991 (Mimura 1996: 42). After the deregulation, a wide variety of discount stores[5] emerged in various product areas, such as home electrical appliances; men's formal clothing; casual clothing; cosmetics and drugs; and DIY merchandise. These volume-sales speciality stores attracted consumers with extremely low prices, and the Japanese retail industry experienced a remarkable drop in prices, known as 'price destruction' (Kubomura and The Institute of Distribution Research 1996).

Price reduction caused a squeeze in profits and damage to products' brand image. Consumers typically perceive product quality from price, not quality itself. The price symbolizes the quality. So manufacturers had to manage price destruction. The *keiretsu* system was developed to avoid price competition, but it has weakened since the 1990s as large-scale retailers rapidly grew and gained massive buying and bargaining power over manufacturers. The *keiretsu* retailing system was based on the business relationship between big manufacturers and small retailers. Since the beginning of the 1990s, instead of practising manufacturer-leading types of marketing such as the *keiretsu* system, manufacturers began to form strategic alliances with large-scale retailers[6] in order to optimize efficiency in physical distribution and the co-development of original products (Noguchi 1996).

Since the mid-1980s, retailers began to adopt information technologies such as EDI (electronic data interchange) and an EOS (electronic ordering system) with manufacturers in order to introduce electronic ordering/receiving systems. Additionally, POS (point-of-sales) systems were also introduced to retailers such as convenience chain-stores and discount stores. POS enabled retailers to collect sales information for all items and improve efficiency. Consumers could order the best-selling products, and lost sales opportunities were reduced through merchandise sales data. Before the 1990s, manufacturers had always held a superior position and led marketing activities in the distribution channels, but retailers used POS and other information technologies to directly collect consumer information, and obtained a powerful weapon against large manufacturers. Manufacturers were eager to access the POS data that retailers obtained, and offered the joint development of new products with retailers while using and analysing the consumer data (Kaketa 1996). PB strategy was actively promoted through strategic alliances between retailers and manufacturers. In most cases, these jointly developed products were marketed under the retailer's own brand; that is, a private brand (PB). The PB products deployed in supermarkets, convenience stores, and discount stores were usually 20 per cent to 30 per cent cheaper than manufacturers' products, and consumers supported PB products during the recession.

Moreover, the PB strategy brought benefits for both retailers and manufactures. As long as retailers sell manufacturers' products, they are easily led to competition for lower prices amongst retailers, as other competitive retailers also sell the same manufacturers' products and the competition should be based on price. However, in the case of PB, merchandise is planned and developed by retailers themselves, who maintain sufficient margins, even though the prices are inexpensive. Additionally, these PB products are sold only to limited retailers as differentiated and original products. The PB strategy enables retailers to prevent severe low-price competition and manufacturers to avoid market risk through a contract with retailers to provide their PB products. The retailers purchase the product, and manufacturers obtain secure profits effectively utilizing idle plant facilities. Thus, strategic alliances for joint product development between manufacturers and retailers rapidly expanded in the Japanese market in the mid-1990s.

More recently, Seven-Eleven Japan, a major convenience chain-store, introduced a new concept to their PB strategy in 2007, symbolized by the new brand name 'Seven Premium'. The company emphasized high-quality PB products or value for money, not low prices. Seven-Eleven also introduced new brand categories such as Seven-Premium Gold, which are higher-quality products than the standard PB and manufacturers' lines, and are more expensive. Because the leading manufacturers avoid emphasizing low price or price competition, they willingly cooperate with Seven-Eleven. Other convenience stores are following similar strategies, and PB strategy is recognized as an essential factor in retail marketing. Retailers have obtained unprecedented power and have seized the initiative from manufacturers in distribution and marketing channels in recent years.

Conclusions

This chapter offers a brief history of Japanese marketing. Marketing strategies were practised as early as the 1920s in Japan, but these activities were not recognized as marketing until the concept was imported through a Top Management Mission to the US in the mid-1950s. After the reconstruction in the post-war period, Japan experienced rapid economic growth and a dramatic increase in the standard of living – a society of mass consumption was born. Manufacturers of durable consumer goods enthusiastically integrated marketing management. New, branded products were advertised through mass media, including newspapers, radio, and television. Manufacturers collaborated with wholesalers and retailers to avoid price competition by establishing their own sales companies, internalizing some existing wholesalers and organizing *keiretsu* retailers. Strategies based on the marketing mix were practised coherently in the post-war period. In the 1970s, manufacturers searched for new markets and expanded internationally. Common characteristics of Japanese companies in the 1980s included market entry with unique, low-priced products, higher-quality products, and extended product lines. Thus, Japanese manufacturers consolidated their positions as high-quality global brands. After the economic bubble burst at the beginning of the 1990s, large-scale retailers rapidly grew, and these demonstrated a strong ability to collect consumer information using a variety of information technologies. Retailers have had a hegemony or a position of leadership over manufacturers in marketing activities in recent years.

Space limitations prevent more detailed case studies of Japanese marketing companies and a more thorough exploration of Japanese marketing. Research studying the history of marketing in Japan began with the establishment of the Japan Society for the Study of Marketing History in 1988. Since then, historical studies on marketing have developed in earnest. This research area has a rather short history compared with other marketing study fields, and is still lacking in quantity. This chapter offers an introduction to an understanding of Japanese marketing, and the author hopes that students and practitioners will gain interest in Japanese marketing historical research.

Notes

1 For details of Morinaga's channel management in the pre-war period, see Usui (2005).
2 The term '*keiretsu*' has two dimensions – horizontal and vertical. Vertical *keiretsu* include *keiretsu* in production (*seisan keiretsu*) exemplified by the just-in-time production systems of Toyota and *keiretsu* in distribution, or *keiretsu* in the marketing channel (*ryūtsu keiretsu*), which includes the relationship between the manufacturer and wholesalers and/or retailers (Usui 2005: 309). In this section, *keiretsu* refers to *keiretsu* in the marketing channel. For more detailed definitions of *keiretsu*, see Usui (2005).
3 Some product categories, including soaps, cosmetics, men's shirts, medical products, and published books were allowed by the Japan Fair Trade Commission (JFTC) to maintain resale prices from 1953 to 1959.

Yumiko Toda

From the mid-1960s, the JFTC gradually rescinded the designation, but cosmetic and medical goods remained until 1993. Shiseido, a cosmetic manufacturer, grew under the protection of resale-price maintenance, and had good reason to manage *keiretsu* retailers to legitimately maintain retail prices.

4 For more detailed discussion of the Large-Scale Retail Store Law, see Larke (1994).

5 Before the development of discount stores in the 1990s, some independent retailers had developed nationwide store networks with self-service systems since the mid-1960s. Self-service chain stores such as Daiei and Itō-Yōkado sold food items; processed meat products; daily necessities; cosmetics; drugs; and clothing. These self-service stores were called general supermarkets in order to distinguish them from self-service stores that sold only food (Usui 2014: 120). These general supermarkets were called self-service discount department stores (SSDDS). The SSDDSs emphasized a wide product assortment, but speciality discount stores focused on assortment depth.

6 The strategic alliance is generally called *Sei–Han Dōmei*. 'Sei' means manufacturers and 'Han' means retailers; *Dōmei* means alliance.

Bibliography

Ando, Y. (1979). *Catalogue of Economic History in Modern Japan* (Kindai Nihon Keizai-shi Yoran), 2nd edn. Tokyo: Tokyo University Press (in Japanese).

Bartels, R. (1962). *The Development of Marketing Thought*. Homewood, IL: R. D. Irwin.

Dentsu Incorporated (n.d.) *Chronological Table on Advertising*, www.dentsu.co.jp/books/ad_nenpyo/index.html (in Japanese), last accessed 15 October 2015.

Economic Planning Agency (1956). *White Paper on the Growth and Modernization of the Japanese Economy* (Nihon Keizai Seicho to Kindaika). Tokyo: Economic Planning Agency (in Japanese).

Economic Planning Agency (1970). *White Paper on National Lifestyle* (Kokumin seikatsu Hakushō). Tokyo: Economic Planning Agency (in Japanese).

Economic Planning Agency (1991). *The Consumer Behavior Survey* (Shōhisha Dōkō Chōsa Nenpo). Tokyo: Economic Planning Agency (in Japanese).

Gordon, A. (2012). *Fabricating Consumers: The Sewing Machine in Modern Japan*. Berkeley, CA: University of California Press.

Ishikawa, K. (2011). *The Dynamics of Marketing in the Japanese Automobile Industry* (Waga-kuni Jidōsha Ryūtsū no Dynamics). Tokyo: Senshu Daigaku Shuppan-kyoku (in Japanese).

Japan Marketing Association (2007). *Japan Marketing Association, 50 Years of History* (Nihon Marketing Kyokai, 50 nen no Ayumi). Tokyo: Japan Marketing Society (in Japanese).

Kaketa, Y. (1996). Distribution issues in the age of information-oriented society (Jōhō ka shakai no ryūtsū mondai). In: *The Second Distribution Revolution, Further Tasks Rest in the 21st Century* (Dai Niji Ryūtsū Kakumei, 21 seiki he no Kadai). Tokyo: Nihon Keizai Shimbunsha, pp. 241–252 (in Japanese).

Kinoshita, A. (2010). Marketing of Onward, the branding and internalization of retailing function (Onward no marketing, brand kōchiku to kōri kinō no hōsetsu). In: *Marketing of Japanese Companies* (Nihon Kigyō no Marketing). Tokyo: Dōbunkan Shuppan, pp. 113–135.

Kohara, H. (1994). *History of Japanese Marketing, the Historical Structure of the Modern Distribution System* (Nihon Marketing-shi, Gendai Ryūtsū no Shiteki Kōzu). Tokyo: Chūō Keizai-sha (in Japanese).

Kohara, H. (2010). Marketing practice of Panasonic (Matsushita Electric, Inc.) (Panasonic no marketing). In: *Marketing of Japanese Companies* (Nihon Kigyō no Marketing). Tokyo: Dōbunkan Shuppan, pp. 76–94.

Kotler, P. and Fahey. L. (1982). The world's champion marketers: the Japanese. *The Journal of Business Strategy*, Summer, 3(1): 1–13.

Kubomura, R. and The Institute of Distribution Research (1996). *The Second Distribution Revolution, Further Tasks Rest in the 21st Century* (Dai Niji Ryūtsū Kakumei, 21seiki he no Kadai). Tokyo: Nihon Keizai Shimbunsha (in Japanese).

Larke, R. (1994). *Japanese Retailing*. New York: Routledge.

McCarthy, E. J. (1960). *Basic Marketing: Managerial Approach*. Homewood, IL: Richard D. Irwin.

Maeda, K. (1977). Marketing. In: Miyamoto, M. and Nakagawa, K. (eds), *Japanese Management: the History of Japanese Management* (Nihon-teki Keiei: Nihon Keiei-shi), Vol. 5, pp. 159–183 (in Japanese).

Matsushita Electric Incorporated (1985). *50 years of History, Matsushita Electric, Inc., as a Pioneer of International Trade* (Matsushita Denki Boueki 50 Nen no Ayumi: Kaden Boeki no Pioneer wo Mezashite). Osaka: Matsushita Electric Incorporated.

Mimura, Y. (1996). Super Chain from now on (Korekara no Super Chain). In: *The Second Distribution Revolution, Further Tasks Rest in the 21st Century* (Dai Niji Ryūtsū Kakumei, 21seiki he no Kadai). Tokyo: Nihon Keizai Shimbunsha, pp. 40–53 (in Japanese).

Nakauchi, I. (2007). *My Discounting Philosophy* (Waga Yasuuri Tetsugaku). Tokyo: Chikura Shobō (in Japanese).

Nakauchi, J. and Mikuriya, T. (2009). *Nakauchi Isao, His Life and Distribution Revolution* (Nakauchi Isao, Ryūtsū Kakumei ni Shōgai wo Sasageta Otoko). Tokyo: Chikura Shobō (in Japanese).

Nihon Research Sogo Kenkyūjō (ed.) (1988). *Historical Research of Living Standards* (Seikatsu Suijun no Rekishi Bunseki). Tokyo: Sōgō Kenkyū Kaihatsu Kikō (in Japanese).

Noguchi, T. (1996). Strategic alliance from the perspective of manufacturers (Maker no tachiba kara mita Sei-Han Doumei). In: *The Second Distribution Revolution, Further Tasks Rest in the 21st Century* (Dai Niji Ryūtsū Kakumei, 21seiki he no Kadai). Tokyo: Nihon Keizai Shimbunsha, pp. 193–204 (in Japanese).

Shimizu, A. (1974). *Marketing Theory, Principles and Cases* (Marketing Tsū-ron, Genri to Jirei). Tokyo: Dōbunkan Shuppan (in Japanese).

Shirahige, T. (1967). *The History of Japanese Marketing* (Nihon Marketing Hatten-shi). Tokyo: Bunkasha (in Japanese).

Takeda, S. (1985). *International Marketing of Japanese Companies* (Nihon Kigyō no Kokusai Marketing). Tokyo: Dōbunkan Shuppan (in Japanese).

Tedlow, R. S. (1990). *New and Improved: The Story of Mass Marketing in America*. New York: Basic Books.

Usui, K. (2005). An origin [*sic*] early version of the 'keiretsu' retail store: marketing of western-style sweets by Morinaga before the Second World War in Japan. *Proceedings of the 12th Conference on Historical Analysis and Research in Marketing*, pp. 301–311.

Usui, K. (2014). *Marketing and Consumption in Modern Japan*. Abingdon, UK: Routledge.

Yamamoto, Y. (1992). *Economic History of Modern Japan* (Kindai Nihon Keizai-shi). Kyoto: Minerva Publishing (in Japanese).

Yokota, S. (1987). A Memorandum regarding the Marketing Mission in 1956, the historical material in the beginning of marketing in Japan (Marketing shisatsu dan ni kansuru oboegaki). *Keiei Ronshu* (Meiji University), 34(3–4): 115–135 (in Japanese).

Yoshino, M. (1971). *The Japanese Marketing System: Adaptation and Innovations*. Cambridge, MA: MIT Press.

23

Japanese retailing

Kazuo Usui

The Japanese retail industry has two significant features. The industry still retains an old format, such as the existence of many traditional small-sized retailers, while modern retail formats develop so well that they overwhelm the market. The traditional features, however, have been in transition. In the meantime, modern retail formats, which originated in Western countries, have been introduced, but with large modifications in order to suit them to Japanese business practices and consumer culture.

Changes in small-sized retailers

A stereotypical description of Japanese retailing is that there is 'a profusion of tiny retail shops', which are supported by the traditional shopping behaviour of homemakers, who shop several times a week at neighbourhood establishments (Armstrong and Kotler 2000, p. 346). However, this is only half true.

An indicator which demonstrates the high number of many tiny shops is the density of retail outlets as measured by the number of retail outlets per thousand inhabitants. It was recognized even by Japanese scholars (e.g. Tajima and Miyashita 1985; Minamikata 2009) that this indicator was remarkably high in Japan compared with many Western countries. Calculating the data by Euromonitor (2014), Japan had 6.75 retail outlets per thousand inhabitants in 2012, while the USA had 2.85, the UK 4.36, Canada 4.68, Germany 3.61, and France 5.21. Nevertheless, not all European countries have lower densities of small retailers. For instance, the Netherlands and Belgium had almost the same density as Japan, 6.32 and 6.36 respectively; and Italy, Spain, and Greece had a much higher density at 14.74, 11.00, and 11.58 correspondingly. Many Asian countries also had a higher density, such as India 11.66, Indonesia 11.57, the Philippines 9.23, South Korea 10.11, Taiwan 11.63, Thailand 13.48, and Vietnam 8.62, while some Asian countries had a relatively smaller density, as exemplified by China 4.40, Singapore 5.16, and Malaysia 5.23.

Therefore, it seems to be a myth that Japan is unique in terms of having a myriad of tiny shops. We should consider in depth the socio-economic, cultural, and historical background of the density of retail shops in each country. In the case of Japan, it would be undeniable that consumers' preferences for ingredients with a short shelf-life, such as *sashimi* (raw fish), *tōfu* (soybean curd), and some leafy greens, have encouraged frequent shopping and immediate consumption rather than large weekly shopping trips with storage in the fridge for a week or more, and that this type of cultural consumer behaviour has tended to support tiny neighbourhood retail shops. Despite this tendency, however, it should be noted that the structure of the Japanese retail sector has been through a major transformation.

Japan conducts a Census of Commerce, which enumerates all wholesale and retail establishments throughout the country. This began in 1952, when surveys were made every two years; from 1979 onwards every three years; and from 1997 onwards every five years, with supplementation by the simple census survey two years after the main one, and from 2012 investigated in the Economy Census, with a recent decision that the Census of Commerce will be conducted two years after the Economy Census. Figure 23.1 shows the changes in the number of retail establishments.

The concept of 'establishment' is defined as a single demarcated area in which economic activities are carried out under a single entity of management on a continual basis. In the case of retailing, a retail establishment is the same as a retail outlet, and different from a retail enterprise,

The number of establishments

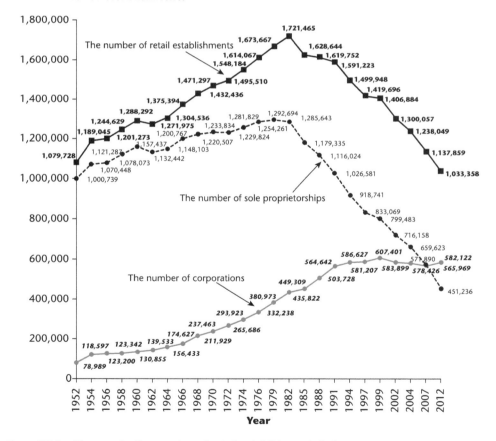

Figure 23.1 Changes in the number of retail establishments in Japan

Sources: Statistics Bureau website (1952–2004); e-Stat website, Economic Census (2007–2012)

which can hold many retail establishments or outlets. The figure reflects two fundamental features of Japanese retailing.

First, the total number of retail establishments or outlets simply increased from 1952 to 1982, and then decreased consistently up until the present day. This change can be said to be structural, because the increase and decrease had nothing to do with the business cycles. For instance, although the period from 1986 to 1991 encompassed the tremendous economic boom usually called 'the bubble economy', the number of retail outlets was constantly decreasing, and now stands at a lower figure than in 1952 when the survey began.

Second, when the retail establishments are divided into 'sole proprietorships' (establishments that are not incorporated and are owned and managed by individuals or under the joint management of individuals) and 'corporations' (establishment that are incorporated in various manners, such as joint-stock companies, limited companies, limited and unlimited liability partnerships, and so forth), the figure clearly shows that it is the sole proprietorships that have been decreasing sharply since 1979; in contrast, the number of corporations has actually increased. By 2012, the number of corporations was larger than that of sole proprietorships. As the sole proprietorships are assumed to be composed of small- and medium-sized retail outlets, this fact means that the number of small retail outlets has been consistently decreasing, despite Japan's image of small-scale retail. The increase in retail corporations suggests that modern retailers have been occupying the retail market. Clearly, the structure of the Japanese retail sector has changed.

Modern retail formats as the Japanese style

The dominant force in the Japanese retail industry is the modern type of retailer. These develop their strategies and operations on the basis of modern retail formats, such as department stores; superstores or 'sūpā'; convenience stores; speciality stores; DIY stores; pharmacists; and non-store retailing through catalogues, vending machines, TV, and the Internet. While the original ideas of modern formats were born in the West, Japanese retailers have successively introduced them since the early twentieth century, but with major revisions, in order to fit Japanese business and consumers (see Usui 2014). This section will explore the four major retail formats: (1) department stores, (2) sūpā or superstores, (3) convenience stores, and (4) e-retailing. As Table 23.1 shows, some of them have grown to be world-class retailers in terms of sales volume.

The department store

The modern retail format of department stores was introduced to Japan as early as in the 1900s and 1910s. The earliest founders were the traditional merchants of silk fabrics for *kimono* called 'ōdana' (large merchant houses), who started their business in the seventeenth and eighteenth centuries. They directly observed Western department stores in the late nineteenth and early twentieth centuries, and changed their store formats to the modern department stores by discarding the traditional ways of selling such as 'zauri' (sales to customers kneeling on *tatami*-mats), expanding the assortments of products, and constructing modern multi-storey buildings with window displays. Typical stores were Mitsukoshi Department Store, Daimaru Department Store, Matsuzakaya Department Store, and Takashimaya Department Store. In the 1920s and 1930s, newcomers appeared by establishing department stores connected to the large railway stations. The Hankyu Department Store, based on the development of the network of private electric railways and many housing-lots adjacent to the railway lines, was successful in targeting

Table 23.1 Top ten retailers in Japan (FY 2012)

Ranking	Name	Main format	Sales volume (million yen)	World ranking*
1	Aeon	*Sūpā*	5,685,303	13
2	Seven & i Holdings	Convenience store, *sūpā*	4,991,642	17
3	Yamada Denki	Speciality store	2,153,600	44
4	Isetan-Mitsukoshi Holdings	Department store	1,701,489	64
5	J. Front Retailing	Department store	1,332,291	81
6	Uny Group Holdings	*Sūpā*	1,030,258	80
7	Fast Retailing	Speciality store	928,699	45
8	Takashimaya	Department store	870,332	103
9	Daiē	*Sūpā*	831,293	100
10	Amazon Japan	Non-store retailing	730,000	(16)

Source: Nikkei MJ (2013)

Note:
* Data by Deloitte (2014). Some rankings are different from Nikkei MJ (2013) because they come from a different data source. The world ranking of Amazon is based on total sales volume around the world

the passengers/consumers who lived along the railway lines and used the hub stations. This model was followed by the Hanshin, Keio, Tobu, Tokyu, Odakyu, and Seibu department stores before and after the Second World War. The powerful department stores monopolized the retail market in major cities, accompanied by the emergence of a strong anti-department-store movement by traditional retailers. A result was the enforcement of the first Department Store Law in 1937 (see in detail, Usui 2014, chapter 4).

This first law was abolished in 1947 when the Anti-Monopoly Law started to be enforced, but soon the second Department Store Law was enacted in 1956. While the department stores enjoyed powerful status at the time, they caused serious conflicts with vendors regarding returning unsold goods to the suppliers and forcing the vendors to dispatch sales clerks to supplement sales in store (Ōtomo 1959). Since then, these trade practices have been controversial in terms of the Anti-Monopoly Law and fair trade in retailing. Nevertheless, some clothing suppliers began to take advantage of these requirements to establish their original marketing strategies. They positively accepted the returned products in order to enhance their sensitivity to market trends and consumers' preferences, and dispatched sales clerks at their own expense to supervise their sales spaces occupying some part of the sales floors of department stores, and to keep direct contacts with key customers. As a result of these practices, some clothing suppliers grew to be large-sized manufacturers (Kinoshita 2011). These trade customs generally spread amongst Japanese department stores. According to the survey by the Japan Department Stores Association (JDSA), while buying products without returns (*kaitori shiire*) accounted for 34.0 per cent of the total amount of buying by department stores in 1997, buying on consignment (*itaku shiire*) accounted for 29.9 per cent, and buying on condition that it can be recorded only after actual selling was made (*shōka shiire*) accounted for 34.0 per cent (Suzuki and JDSA 1998). Also, JDSA (2009) data showed that there were about 90,000 regular employees hired in department stores in 2008 and about 75,000 short-contract employees, while there were more than 250,000 sales clerks dispatched by manufacturers or vendors to the sales floors of department stores. These features have been debatable as a retail strategy, because the stores lost the opportunity to display attractive assortments of products for consumers, while reducing costs and market risks in the short run.

Another Japanese feature is that department stores tended to depend on what is called 'the out-of-store sales (*gaishō*)' – the door-to-door sales by sales clerks of department stores to high-value customers including wealthy individual families and business offices. The longer the history of the department store and the more expensive the items that they sell, the larger is their percentage of out-of-store sales. While precise data are hard to establish, it is generally believed that around 20 per cent to 40 per cent of sales volumes tend to come from the out-of-store sales in each major department store. In addition, many Japanese department stores organize Friendship Clubs (*tomono-kai*), in which each member of the Club saves a certain amount of money every month for a particular department store, then almost 10 per cent interest and the principal is repaid to the customer in vouchers after one year. As the interest rate is higher than for the usual bank savings accounts and tax is not be deducted from the interest, this scheme may be attractive to some wealthy customers, despite the repayment in vouchers, not money, that can be used only at a particular department store or group of department stores. Many stores provide additional services, such as special bargain sales only for club members and special discounts at specific hotels, restaurants, museums and/or exhibitions, in order to attract these customers.

Finally, the basement of Japanese department stores is usually for expensive foods, not for a bargain floor as seen in some countries. Rather, the basement of department stores, called '*depa chika*' in the Japanese abbreviation, has become the epitome of a sales floor for luxury ingredients, ready-to-eat foods, sweets, and gifts. Isetan Department Store developed a new format of self-service supermarket, Queen's Isetan, which only provides expensive foods, based on the image of the department-store basement.

In the twenty-first century, a new feature appeared in the world of Japanese department stores. Some powerful stores merged aggressively into groups. Mitsukoshi Department Store (founded in 1673) and Isetan Department Store (founded in 1886) established Isetan-Mitsukoshi Holdings Ltd. in 2008 in order to compensate for their individual weaknesses, and were ranked as the top of department stores by FY 2012. The group ranked fourth in terms of sales volume amongst Japanese retailers (Nikkei MJ 2013). As Table 23.1 above shows, this group ranked sixty-fourth in the world retail business in 2012 (Deloitte 2014), higher than J. C. Penney (seventy-fourth place) and Nordstrom (eighty-sixth) in the USA. Another case was that of the Daimaru Department Store (founded in 1717) and the Matsuzakaya Department Store (founded in 1611), which established J. Front Retailing in 2007, ranked fifth in Japan and eighty-first in the world. The largest four groups, these two plus Takashimaya Co. Ltd. (founded in 1831) and Sogō and Seibu Co. Ltd (established in 2003 by the merger of the Sogō Department Store and Seibu Department Store, and further merged to Seven & i Holdings in 2006), are now the key players in the Japanese department-store industry.

The 'sūpā' or superstore

Although some Japanese commentators were familiar with the concept of self-service as early as the 1920s, because of their knowledge of Piggly Wiggly Stores in the USA (Usui 2014, p. 117), the first self-service store, Kinokuniya, opened for the first time in Japan in 1953, with support by NCR Japan and after direct observation by the owner of self-service stores inside the bases of the American occupying army. In the 1950s, self-service stores gradually increased, mainly in food retailing, but a major change occurred in the early 1960s. The concept of SSDDS (the self-service discount department store) introduced by a Japanese expert (Kitazato 1962) spread rapidly and became the principal format. Self-service or semi-self-service stores with several storeys, selling a full range of products at a discount price, became known as 'general supermarket', 'general sūpā (sōgō sūpā)' or simply 'sūpā' in Japanese. The term came to mean a Japanese-style self-service store that customers equated to the American supermarket, although it is totally different.

The general *sūpā* aggressively adopted the principle of chainstores. They developed nation-wide networks of large stores with central buying offices, and became the dominant retail format in the 1960s to 1990s in Japan. Daiē was the top player in this format, followed by Itō-Yōkado, Seiyu (now under the umbrella of Walmart), Jusco (now Aeon), Nichii (later Mycal and merged with Aeon), and Uny. The year 1972 was epoch-making, because the sales of Daiē, which at that time only had a fifteen-year history (it was founded in 1957), surpassed that of Mitsukoshi Department Store with its almost three-hundred-year history from 1673. This symbolized the change in the dominance of modern retail formats in Japan from the department store to the *sūpā*. It was the *sūpā* that led the so-called 'Revolution of Distribution' (Hayashi 1962), which was a popular phrase in the business world in the 1960s. Along with the shift in dominance, the conflicts between modern retail formats and traditional retailers also changed. As *sūpā*, not the department stores, aggressively developed their store networks into many local cities, the movements by traditional merchants against new openings of *sūpā* became a focal political issue in many cities. Because *sūpā* could not be classified as department stores, it was difficult for the Department Store Law to regulate the expansion of *sūpā*. Therefore, the Large-scale Retail Store Law replaced the Department Store Law in 1974. The new law defined premises with $1,500\,m^2$ or more of sales-floor space ($3,000\,m^2$ or more in metropolises) as 'the large-scale store', no matter what kind of retail format the store had, and further defined premises with $500\,m^2$ or more sales floor space as 'the type II large-scale store' in 1978. The Law required pre-coordination amongst interest groups, including the company intending to open a new large-scale store; the existing retailers in the city involved; and some representatives of the consumers, before the new store could open. This Law continued until 2000, when it was discarded. Despite the strong regulations, the Law did not basically prohibit the new establishment of stores, so *sūpā* continued the expansion of their store networks, although the pre-coordinating talks were often protracted. As a result, the problem of new *sūpā* openings became a more serious political issue in many local cities.

The background to the rapid development of *sūpā* was the changes in consumption patterns after the Second World War (see Usui 2014, chapter 5). The demand for Western-style every-day clothing was so strong because Japanese consumers entirely changed their everyday clothes to the Western style for the first time in history, although Western-style clothing had begun to be introduced in the mid-nineteenth century and was gradually adopted by specific classes of consumers on specific occasions before the Second World War. This demand was supported by the changes in the supply side, which began to provide synthetic fibres on a massive scale as the useful raw materials for low-priced clothing, and expanded the offers of ready-made cloth-ing. *Sūpā* became an effective link between this changing demand and supply. The leading *sūpā* were good at dealing with clothing, because almost all of them originally began as clothing merchants, not food merchants – except Daiē, which started its business as a pharmacy, and Seiyu, a subsidiary of Seibu Department Store. Dealing with clothing, therefore, was an essential feature of large-sized *sūpā*. Retail marketers of clothing, however, were always tempted to 'trade up' assortments, because they could not ignore the trends of fashion and vogue, and many speciality stores became their competitors.

Although the early philosophy of the *sūpā* was symbolized by the book *Discount is My Philosophy* (Nakauchi 1969), published by the founder of Daiē, the aggressive low-price policy was gradually disappearing. In turn, the leading *sūpā* became absorbed in the strategy of diver-sification, leading them to be 'conglo-merchants', covering the full line of retail formats from department stores to discount stores, and a variety of service companies such as restaurants, travel agencies, hotels, fitness clubs, financial companies, real estate companies, and so forth. The slogan 'the comprehensive life industry' (Saison Corp. 1992), suggesting that they would be involved in every aspect of consumers' lives, became their main philosophy.

This strategy was a trap, however. Some leading *sūpā* and their subsidiaries accumulated tremendous losses, due to speculation in land and real estate where prices rose steeply during the period of the bubble economy'(1986–1991) but fell dramatically after the bubble burst. A result was that the leading *sūpā* were divided into the winner group (Itō-Yokadō, Aeon and Uny) and the loser group (Daiē, Seiyu, and Mycal). The loser groups were dissolved and their companies were liquidated or bought by other companies.

In the twenty-first century, the Large-scale Retail Law was discarded, and the winner group began to develop large-sized shopping centres in suburban areas. As shown in Table 23.1, Aeon was at the top and Seven & i Holdings (Itō-Yōkado and Seven-Eleven) was second in terms of sales volume in fiscal year 2012, and thirteenth and seventeenth respectively in the world ranking in 2012.

The convenience store

Since the 1970s to 1980s onwards, the format of convenience stores has dominated the retail industry of Japan. As is known (Liles 1977), the original idea of this format was created by Southland Ice Co., Dallas, Texas. As early as the 1960s, some Japanese businesspeople recognized the spread of this format in the USA, and, in the early 1970s, Itō Yōkado, a Japanese *sūpā*, was successful in getting the exclusive international area licence to develop Seven-Eleven stores in Japan. Itō Yōkado and its subsidiary Seven-Eleven Japan (at first called the York Seven Co.) developed their franchise network of convenience stores from 1974 onwards. Soon after this event, the competitors, Daiē and Seiyu, also began to develop convenience store chains.

Despite the original expectation by the SMEA (Small and Medium Enterprise Agency) of the Japanese government and some businesses that this format could be helpful to revitalize small-sized retailers, the fact was that the subsidiaries of large-sized *sūpā* who entered this field have dominated, as shown by the original parent companies in Table 23.2. A reason was that the Large-scale Retail Store Law (1974–2000) regulated not only development of new stores, but also operating hours (large-sized stores had to close the stores at 6.00 pm; this was relaxed to 7.00 pm in 1990 and 8.00 pm in 1994, and continued until the law was abolished in 2000) and closing dates (the stores had to have 44 closing days; later this was relaxed to 24 days in 1994 and continued until the abolition of the law), while a convenience store usually had $100\,m^2$ to $200\,m^2$ of sales-floor space, and never reached the category of large-sized store. This meant that only the convenience stores could freely operate longer hours, even twenty-four hours, seven days a week; a possibility which was quite attractive for large-sized *sūpā*.

Japanese convenience stores have created the Japanese method of strategy, mainly initiated by Seven-Eleven Japan (see Usui 2014, chapter 7). The first is the unique location strategy. They set a circle from the store with a radius of 500 m as the 'primary trading area', with the expectation that consumers living within this circle would come to the store to buy something anytime, but those living outside the circle would be unwilling to walk further. Once one convenience store opened in a certain area, new stores would be opened not far from the first store, i.e. densely located in this area. This strategy clearly assumed that the consumers would generally visit the convenience stores on foot. This was in contrast with the assumption by their American counterparts that customers would come by car. Because of strict zoning regulations on land use, US residential areas usually had no retail shops, so that consumers would visit shops by car; therefore, many convenience stores were located at petrol stations because this is

Table 23.2 Top five convenience stores in Japan (FY 2012)

Ranking	Store name	Original parent company[1]	Current parent company*	Number of stores†	Percentage of franchise stores‡	Sales volume (million yen)†
1	7-Eleven	Itō-Yōkado (*sūpā*)	Seven & i Holdings (convenience stores, *sūpā*)	15,072	94.4	3,508,444
2	Lawson	Daiē (*sūpā*)	Mitsubishi Corp. (general trading company)	10,976	n.d.	1,906,547
3	FamilyMart	Seiyu (*sūpā*)	Itochu Corp. (general trading company)	8,772	95.7	1,584,558
4	Circle K, Sunkus	Uny (*sūpā*)	Uny Group Holdings (convenience store, *sūpā*)	5,329	97.3	876,204
5	Mini Stop	Jusco (*sūpā*)	Aeon (*sūpā*, convenience store)	2,168	95.8	352,687

Notes:
* Each parenthesis shows the main type of retail format or business of the parent company.
† The number of stores and sales volume excludes those in the local sub-franchise systems, although all of the top five except Seven-Eleven develop the sub-franchise systems locally.
‡ By calculation of the data of sales volume.
Source: Nikkei MJ (2013)

a convenient place for many consumers. Thus, the concept of 'nearness' was totally different between Japan and the USA, i.e. near *on foot* and near *by car*. This location factor, in addition to the difference in the legal circumstances, can explain why Japanese convenience stores could enjoy advantages over their competitors, while the US counterpart could not. In the US, there was no regulatory law regarding operating hours and closing dates, so many supermarkets could operate long hours each day. In these conditions, even if the consumers recognized that convenience stores were open at the local petrol station, they could easily drive further to supermarkets, where the assortments of products were wider and the prices were cheaper. In contrast, in Japan, there was no *sūpā* operating long hours, and the consumers, who came on foot were not generally willing to walk further to another convenience store, even though it was located relatively nearby. Japanese convenience stores could thus capture the consumers residing inside the primary trading area.

Second, the Japanese convenience stores developed 'fast foods' made to Japanese recipes, and so suitable for Japanese consumers. These included items such as box lunches with rice (*obentō*); rice balls (*onigiri*); *daikon* radish and other ingredients stewed in a thin soy soup (*oden*); and steamed buns filled with sweet bean-paste (*an'man*). Unlike the processed foods that were already controlled by large-sized manufacturers, production of these recipes was rather easily organized by convenience stores, which could in turn enjoy larger gross margins from these goods. The assortment of this type of fast foods was strongly supported by Japanese consumers.

Third, these fast foods and other perishable products were frequently delivered by the local distribution centres to each franchised store; in many cases three times a day! This system was called just-in-time delivery. The aim was to reduce the inventory and maintain the freshness of foods. As a basis of this delivery system, the Japanese convenience stores readily introduced the EPOS and other electronic information systems. It was the convenience stores (subsidiaries), not *sūpā* (parent companies), that took the lead in introducing advanced information systems. *Sūpā* tended to introduce them only after the experiments by the convenience stores were successful.

Finally, the systems of Japanese convenience stores were heavily supported by salespeople, who frequently visit the franchisees' stores. In the case of Seven-Eleven Japan (Seven-Eleven 1991), they were summoned to the headquarters in Tokyo every Tuesday to be given a variety of information and knowledge on the policies of the headquarters, possible assortments of products, newly introduced products, etc., and then travelled around each local area, in which one salesperson was responsible for seven to eight stores. The salespeople relayed information and knowledge, gave a variety of support to the owners, and checked the conditions of each store.

A result of these strategic measures produced the epoch-making event in 1991, in which Seven-Eleven and Itō Yōkado, the latecomers, acquired Southland Corp., the originator, based on a requirement by Southland itself. In the meantime, as *sūpā* were divided into winners and losers, the parent companies in the losers' group sold the profitable convenience stores out to general trading companies to offset their huge losses. Thus as Table 23.2 shows, the current parent companies of these convenience stores were different from the original parent companies. In addition, the business of convenience stores was becoming so mature around the turn of the twenty-first century that new strategies were emerging. One was to arrange alliances with large-sized manufacturers and introduce private brands. The second was beginning to publicize lower prices in order to attract the homemakers who usually chose the cheaper products at *sūpā*. The third was to create a new formula for convenience stores, such as the stores focusing on vegetables, fish, meat, and perishable products, called 'fresh foods convenience stores'. The fourth was to launch a home-delivery system, especially of foods, in order to serve elderly consumers who had difficulty coming to the shops. Finally, many convenience stores introduced several new services to their shops, such as e-money and automatic teller machines. The retail format of convenience stores was still attempting to progress.

E-retailing

Recently remarkable attention has been paid to the format of e-retailing. The METI (Ministry of Economy, Trade and Industry) has undertaken an estimate of the market size of e-commerce since 1998, in collaboration with some private research agencies (METI 1998–2014). According to this survey, the market of BtoC (business-to-consumer) transactions over the Internet in 2013 expanded to become 197 times larger than in 1998. BtoC transactions over the Internet increased from 65 billion yen in 1998 (0.02 per cent in total BtoC transactions) to 12.8 trillion yen in 2013 (4.4 per cent), although the market size was apparently larger for BtoB or wholesale e-commerce, including all computer-mediated transactions like EDI outside the Internet, as these were reported to be 8.62 trillion yen (1.5 per cent in total BtoB transactions) in 1987 and 280.17 trillion yen (26.5 per cent) in 2013.

This tendency has naturally occurred in parallel with the increasing Internet penetration. According to a survey by the MIC (Ministry of Internal Affairs and Communications), the Internet penetration rate amongst homes was 11 per cent in 1998, but rose rapidly to 84.9 per cent by the end of 2013 (MIC 1996–2013). A recent feature has been the increasing access to the Internet via smartphones; representing 16.2 per cent of all Internet access in 2011 and growing to 42.4 per cent in 2013, while the access by PCs at home decreased moderately from 62.6 per cent in 2011 to 58.4 per cent in 2013. In the case of Rakuten, the largest e-shopping mall in Japan as described below, smartphones, tablets, and feature phones accounted for 47 per cent of orders as of the first quarter of 2015 (Rakuten 2015), perhaps soon surpassing the orders via PCs. As the number of so-called 'digital natives', who 'are all "native speakers" of the digital language of computers, video games and the Internet' (Prensky 2001, p. 1; ITU 2013, p. 129), is also increasing in Japan (see Hashimoto *et al.* 2010; Kimura 2012) like other countries, e-retailing is generally expected to continue expanding.

The content of e-retailing can be divided into three major groups: tangible products, intangible goods or services, and digital products. As of 2013, the largest share of e-retailing by value was in the sales of tangible products, accounting for 53.2 per cent of all e-retailing sales (6.8 trillion yen), while services accounted for 35.0 per cent of e-retailing (4.5 trillion yen). E-retailing of digital goods was just 11.8 per cent (1.5 trillion yen), although its growth rate was highest, i.e. a 14.6 per cent increase compared with the previous year; while growth in tangible goods was 13.5 per cent and services was 10.1 per cent (METI 2014, p. 45). As shown in Table 23.3, sales of travel services made up the largest share (19.7 per cent) of all e-retail transactions; followed by clothing and related products (10.4 per cent); and domestic electrical appliances, audio-visual systems, and PCs (10.3 per cent). Amongst digital products, online games enjoyed by far the biggest share (79.7 per cent in digital goods but 9.7 per cent for all products).

The top marketer in e-retailing in Japan is Rakuten, the developer of an e-shopping mall. Founded in 1997, the company rapidly grew based on a strategy of '*omotenashi*', the Japanese traditional concept of providing high quality and intimate personal services (Mikitani 2013). From the outset, Rakuten recruited many small-sized retailers, who had never ever thought to open their shops on the Internet. The company taught them everything, including how to set up the computers, install the software and connect with the Internet (*KC* 2000); how to improve the designs of websites; and how to be successful in the e-shopping mall business. Gatherings of shop owners have been held regularly, sponsored by Rakuten. The founder rejected the idea that each shop within this e-shopping mall would be an automatic vending machine on the Internet or the idea that only the algorithms could give automatic recommendations to the consumers. Rather, Rakuten has respected 'human being's recommendations', so that the company has sought the hybrid approach of the algorithms and services by humanity on the Internet (Mikitani 2013, p. 80). As a result of, in a sense, such a very Japanese approach and effort, Rakuten grew to host 40,000 different businesses and services and to be considered 'one of the biggest Internet companies in the world' (*Fortune* 2013). Now Rakuten is in the quest to globalize all of their business. A recognized symbolic indicator of their globalization strategy is that Rakuten has decided to change the official language used inside the company from Japanese to English.

An emergent feature in e-retailing is exploring so-called 'omni-channel retail'. While similar concepts have already existed such as 'click and mortar' and 'multichannel retail', the omni-channel retailers should serve 'the "omni-channel" shopper, an evolution of the multichannel consumer who wants to use all channels – store, catalog call centre, Web, and mobile – simultaneously, not each channel in parallel' (Ortis 2010, p. 1). Japan saw the boom of 'omni-channel retail' in 2014 (METI 2014, p. 49). An example is Seven & i Holdings, one of the two top runners in the Japanese retail industry.

This group has already embraced the nationwide 'real' store networks, including Seven-Eleven (convenience stores), Itō Yōkado (a general *sūpā*), York Benimaru (a food *sūpā*), Seibu a (department store), Sogō (department store), Loft (a speciality store selling high-quality miscellaneous goods for everyday life), Akachan Honpo (a speciality store for maternity and baby

Table 23.3 Sales shares in e-retailing in terms of sales volume (2013)

Product category	Percentage in three major categories	Percentage in all categories
Tangible products		
Foods, beverages, and liquors	17.5	9.6
Domestic electrical appliances, audiovisual systems, and PCs	18.7	10.3
Books, CDs, and DVDs	13.2	7.2
Cosmetics and pharmaceuticals	6.5	3.6
Miscellaneous goods, furniture, and interior-related products	17.0	9.4
Clothing and miscellaneous goods related to clothing	18.8	10.4
Automobiles, motorbikes, and their parts	2.6	1.5
Stationery	2.3	1.3
Others	3.3	1.8
Subtotal	100.0	54.9
Intangible products		
Travel services	60.0	19.7
Restaurant services	2.3	0.8
Theatre tickets	7.0	2.3
Financial services	15.8	5.2
Others (medical, insurance, hairdressing, residence-related, educational and other services)	14.8	4.9
Subtotal	100.0	32.9
Digital products		
E-books	8.4	1.0
Online music	2.9	0.4
Online movies	4.2	0.5
Online games	79.7	9.7
Others	4.8	0.6
Subtotal	100.0	12.2
Total		100.0

Source: Calculated from METI (2014)

products), Pia (selling theatre tickets), and Denny's (a family restaurant). The group has also introduced several e-commerce services via 7-Net, which provided home-delivery services of box lunches and meals with many recipes from each Seven-Eleven store (called 7-Meal), selling theatre tickets (called Ticket Pia), travel services (called 7-Travel Net), and Internet sales of their *sūpā* (called net *sūpā*), department stores (called e-department stores) and the speciality store Akachan Honpo. In addition, this group operates Seven Bank, which has cash machines installed in Seven-Eleven and Itō Yōkado shops and provides Internet banking services. The group has bought Nissen as well, a leading mail-order retailer through catalogues basically issued five times a year.

Seven & i Holdings decided in 2014 to make the omni-channel strategy 'the second stage of inauguration' of the group. Leveraging the network of approximately 18,000 'real' stores receiving about 19.5 million visitors per day in total, customers can take advantage of searching, ordering, purchasing, collecting, and/or delivery of the products for customers' seamless and simultaneous use of any channel including the Internet through smartphones, PCs, etc., call centres, the traditional catalogues and the 'real' stores (Seven & i Holdings Co., Ltd. 2014; *Weekly Tōkyō Keizai* 2014a, 2014b). This strategy has been prepared and piloted with partial starts with a full-scale launch planned for autumn 2015. Thus, the omni-channel approach is becoming a core strategy of top Japanese retailers. This is the most significant development in e-retail in Japan.

Bibliography

Armstrong, G. and Kotler P. (2000). *Marketing: An Introduction*, 5th edn. Upper Saddle River, NJ: Prentice Hall.

Deloitte (2014). *Global Powers of Retailing 2014: Retail Beyond Begins*, Deloitte LLP, PDF version, www.reasonwhy.es/sites/default/files/Deloitte-lideres-comercio-mundial-ReasonWhy.es_.pdf, last accessed 23 October 2015.

Enjōji, Kon (1917). *Policies to Increase Sales Power (Hanbai-Ryoku Zoshin-saku)*. Tokyo: Sato Shuppan-bu (in Japanese).

e-Stat website (2012). *Economic Census 2012, Wholesale and Retail Establishments*, PDF version, www.e-stat.go.jp/SG1/estat/List.do?bid=000001051403&cycode=0, last accessed 23 October 2015.

Euromonitor (2014). *World Retail Data and Statistics 2014*. London and Chicago: Euromonitor International.

Fortune (2013). Rakuten: the biggest e-commerce site you haven't heard of, 22 March 2015, http://fortune.com/2013/03/22/rakuten-the-biggest-e-commerce-site-you-havent-heard-of/, last accessed 23 October 2015.

Hashimoto, Yoshiaki, Oku, Ritsuya, Nagao, Yoshihide, and Shōno, Tōru (2010). *The Birth of Neo-Digital Natives (Neo Digital Native no Tanjo)*. Tokyo: Diamond-sha (in Japanese).

Hayashi, Shuji (1962). *The Revolution of Distribution: Products, Channels and Consumers (Ryūtsū Kakumei)*. Tokyo Chūōkōron-sha (in Japanese).

ITU: International Telecommunication Union (2013). *Measuring the Information Society*, Geneva, Switzerland, PDF version, https://www.itu.int/en/ITU-D/Statistics/Documents/publications/mis2013/MIS2013_without_Annex_4.pdf, last accessed 23 October 2015.

JDSA (Japan Department Stores Association) (2009). *A Research Report of Strategies for Enhancement of Corporate Values (Kigyō-kachi Kōjō Senryaku Kenkyū no Hokokusho)*, PDF version, www.meti.go.jp/policy/intellectual_assets/pdf/kigyoukachihoukokusho%20honnbun.pdf (in Japanese).

KC: Kigyōka Club (2000). The future of the EC kingdom established by the support systems. *Kigyōka Club*, 27 October: 12–17 (in Japanese).

Kimura, Tadamasa (2012). *The Age of Digital Natives (Digital Native no Jidai)*. Tokyo: Heibon-sha (in Japanese).

Kinoshita, Akihiro (2011). *Marketing History in the Apparel Industry: Creating Brands and Subsuming the Retail Functions (Apparel Sangyō no Marketing-shi: Brand Koōhiku to Kouri Kinō no Hōsetsu)*. Tokyo: Dōbunkan (in Japanese).

Kitazato, Uichi (1962). A turmoil over the selling revolution in the USA: emergence of large-sized discount department stores. *The Economist*, 28 August: 6–19 (in Japanese).

Kuwatani, Teiitsu (1912). Policy of retailers to expand the markets. *The Business World (Jutsugyō-kai)*, 4(2): February: 102–120 (in Japanese).

Kuwatani, Teiitsu (1913). *Commercial Artifices (Shō-ryaku)*. Tokyo: Dōbunkan (in Japanese).

Liles, Allen (1977). *Oh Thank Heaven! The Story of the Southland Corporation*. Dallas, TX: The Southland Corporation.

METI: Ministry of Economy, Trade and Industry (1998–2014). *Survey on Actual Condition and Market Size of Electronic Commerce (Denshi Shō Torihiki ni Kansuru Shijō Chōsa)* (in Japanese), PDF version. www.meti.go.jp/policy/it_policy/statistics/outlook/ie_outlook.html, last accessed 23 October 2015.

MIC: Ministry of Internal Affairs and Communications (1996–2013). *Communications Usage Trend Survey (Tsūshin Riyō Dōkō Chōsa (Setai-hen))* (in Japanese), PDF version, www.soumu.go.jp/johotsusintokei/statistics/statistics05b1.html.

Mikitani, Hiroshi (2013). Rakuten's CEO on humanizing e-commerce. *Harvard Business Review*, November: 47–50.

Minamikata, Tatsuaki (2009). A comparative study of the structure of food retailing between Japan and the UK. *The Review of Osaka University of Commerce (Ōsaka Syōgyō Daigaku Ronshū)*, 5(2): 21–37 (in Japanese).

Nakauchi, Isao (1969). *Discount is My Philosophy* (*Waga Yasuuri Tetsugaku*). Tokyo: Nihon Keizai Shimbunsha (in Japanese).

Nikkei, MJ (2013). *Nikkei Marketing Journal Resource of Information of Trends 2014* (*Nikkei MJ Trend Jōhō-gen 2014*). Tokyo: Nihon Keizai Shuppansha (in Japanese).

Ortis, Ivano (2010). Unified retailing – breaking multichannel barriers. *IDC Retail Insight*, September, PDF version, http://info.hybris.com/rs/hybris/images/IDC-Multichannel-EN.pdf.

Ōtomo, Kenji (1959). Survey of dispatched sales clerks to the department stores and issues from now on. *Fair Trade* (*Kōsei Torihiki*), 103, April: 28–33 (in Japanese).

Prensky, Mare (2001). Digital natives, digital immigrants. *On the Horizon*, 9(5) October: 1–6, PDF version, www.marcprensky.com/writing/Prensky%20-%20Digital%20Natives,%20Digital%20Immigrants%20-%20Part1.pdf, last accessed 23 October 2015.

Rakuten (2015). *The Explanatory Materials of Financial Accounts for the First Quarter of 2015*, PDF version, http://global.rakuten.com/corp/investors/documents/pdf/15Q1PPT_E.pdf, last accessed 23 October 2015.

Saison Corp (ed.) (1992). *The Comprehensive Life Industry* (*Seikatsu Sōgō Sangyō-ron*). Tokyo: Libro Port (in Japanese).

Seven-Eleven Japan (1991). *Seven-Eleven Japan: Endless Innovation* (*Seven-Eleven Japan, Owarinaki Innovation*). Tokyo: Seven-Eleven Japan Corporation (in Japanese), [not for sale].

Seven & i Holdings Co. Ltd. (2014). *Annual Report 204: Every Day, in Every Way . . . Preparing for the Omni-Channel Era*, PDF version (in English) www.7andi.com/dbps_data/_template_/_user_/_SITE_/localhost/_res/ir/library/ar/pdf/2014_all.pdf, last accessed 23 October 2015.

Statistics Bureau website (2015). Historical Statistics of Japan, www.stat.go.jp/english/data/chouki/index.htm, last accessed 23 October 2015.

Suzuki, Yasuaki and JDSA (Editorial Committee of Books for the 50th Anniversary of the Founding of the JDSA) (eds) (1998). *Record of the History of Department Stores* (*Hyakka-ten no Ayumi*). Tokyo: JDS (in Japanese).

Tajima, Yoshihiro and Miyashita, Masahusa (1985). *An International Comparative Study of the Distribution System* (*Ryūtsū no Kokusai Hikaku*). Tokyo: Yūhikaku (in Japanese).

Usui, Kazuo (2014). *Marketing and Consumption in Modern Japan*. Abingdon, UK: Routledge.

Weekly Tōkyō Keizai (2014a). Seven & i: the whole picture of omni-strategy. *Weekly Tōkyō Keizai* (*Shūkan Tōkyō Keizai*), 26 April: 50–53 (in Japanese).

Weekly Tōkyō Keizai (2014b). An interview with Toshifumi Suzuki, CEO of Seven & i Holdings. *Weekly Tōkyō Keizai* (*Shūkan Tōkyō Keizai*), 26 April: 54–55 (in Japanese).

Part VI
Manufacturing and logistics

24

Japanese production management and just-in-time systems

Yacob Khojasteh

Introduction

Japanese production management, especially Toyota's production management system, became a leading worldwide influence in the field of production management in 1980s, and knowledge of its main elements became known beyond Japan. The Toyota production system is one of the world's most innovative production systems. When it was introduced, it opened up the world to a new production approach that decentralized mass production. Although the traditional mass-production system lowers the unit cost, it increases the cost of customization, causing an inherent loss of flexibility and ability to customize.

This chapter aims to give an overview of Toyota production management and its core concepts. First, the Toyota production system and its two components Jidōka and Just-in-time (JIT) systems are described. Then, *kanban* and *kaizen*, as two techniques of JIT, are described. Also, production systems and the differences between pull and push production systems are presented. Finally, the adaptation of the Toyota production system into Western companies is outlined.

The Toyota Production System

The Toyota Production System (TPS) was developed and promoted by Toyota Motor Corporation, which is being adopted by many Japanese companies. Outside of Toyota, TPS is often known as being 'lean' or 'lean production'. The main purpose of the TPS is to make products with effective tools and techniques in order to maximize profit. To achieve this purpose, the primary goal of the TPS is cost reduction as well as productivity improvement. Costs include not only manufacturing cost, but also costs related to sales, administration, and capital. The elimination of waste is the way that the TPS plans to reduce costs. Waste (*muda* in Japanese) is anything that does not add value to the product or service from the customer's point of view.

Monden (2011) classified waste in manufacturing production operations at four levels:

1   excessive production resources;
2   overproduction;

3   excessive inventory;
4   unnecessary capital investment.

The primary waste is the existence of *excessive production resources* such as excessive workforce, excessive facilities, and excessive inventory. An excessive workforce leads to unnecessary human-resource costs; excessive facilities lead to unnecessary depreciation costs; and an excessive inventory (in the form of raw material, work-in-process, finished goods, etc.) leads to unnecessary inventory holding costs. Moreover, holding those excessive resources can lead the management to fully use those resources when they are not needed, which causes the secondary waste: *overproduction*. Overproduction means to continue working when this is not required by the market. This causes the third type of waste: an *excessive inventory*, which requires more human resources, more equipment, and more floor space to store and manage it. This causes the fourth type of waste, *unnecessary capital*, which can bring several costs: such as the cost of building a new warehouse to store the extra inventory; the cost of hiring extra workers for transportation; and also the costs of managing the inventory. Management must focus mostly on the primary wastes in order to avoid the others (Monden 2011).

Types of waste can be classified differently as follows. This can apply not just to manufacturing and production cases, but to product development, order taking, and the office (Ōno 1988; Liker 2004).

- *Overproduction:* producing more than the customer orders, or producing early (before it is demanded).
- *Queues/waiting:* waiting for material, information, equipment, tools, etc.; also, idle times (operator waiting for the machine, or machine/materials waiting for the operator).
- *Transportation:* moving material between plants or between work centres and handling it more than once.
- *Overprocessing:* effort such as reworking, which adds no value to a product or service. A technique called Value Stream Mapping (VSM) is frequently used in order to help identify the overprocessing steps in the process (for both manufacturers and service sectors).
- *Inventory:* unnecessary raw material, work in process, and finished goods.
- *Motion:* unnecessary movement of equipment or people, which is caused by poor workflow, poor layout, housekeeping, and inconsistent or undocumented work methods (VSM is also used to identify this type of waste).
- *Defective product:* returns, warranty claims, rework, and scrap are waste.

Ōno (1988) described two key concepts of *jidōka* and *just-in-time* as two pillars to support the TPS. The following two sections describe those two concepts.

Jidōka

The basic structural feature of the TPS is autonomation. The autonomation system (in Japanese, '*ninben no aru jidōka*', which often is abbreviated to '*jidōka*') is another unique concept innovated by Toyota, which integrates the human workforce into the screening process to increase efficiency in ways that couldn't be done by a machine itself. *Jidōka* is interpreted as autonomous defects control. It supports JIT by never allowing defective units from a preceding process to flow into and disrupt a subsequent process (Monden 2011). The Toyota term '*jidō*' is applied to a machine with a built-in device for making judgements, whereas the regular Japanese term '*jidō*' (automation) is simply applied to a machine that moves on its own. *Jidōka* refers to 'automation with a human touch', as opposed to a machine that simply moves under the monitoring and supervision of an operator (Toyota 2015).

Jidōka can prevent the production of defective products by focusing on identifying the problems in order to ensure that they never happen again. Every worker has the authority and the responsibility to stop an entire production line when a problem arises. The purpose is to bring some attention to the problem and to focus effort on it. This results in a permanent solution.

Just-in-time

Just-in-time (JIT) is a set of principles, tools, and techniques that allows a company to produce and deliver products in small quantities, with short lead times in order to meet specific customer needs. It is an inventory strategy to increase efficiency and decrease the work-in-process inventory, thereby reducing the inventory costs. It originated in Japan, and its introduction as a recognized technique or philosophy is generally associated with Toyota.

JIT basically means to produce the necessary parts in the necessary quantities at the right time. That means that only the specifically requested items in the right quantity move through the production system when they are needed. Supplying what is needed; when it is needed; and in the right quantities, can eliminate waste, inconsistencies, and unreasonable requirements, resulting in improved productivity. Through this method, Toyota successfully discovered a way to eliminate waste in order to reach the ultimate goal of reducing production time and costs.

JIT flow requires a very smooth operation system. If materials are not available when a workstation requires them, the entire system may be disrupted. If JIT is realized in the entire firm, then unnecessary inventories in the factory will be completely eliminated, making warehouses unnecessary (Monden 2011).

JIT objectives

The goals of JIT can be described in terms of the seven zeros, in order to achieve zero inventories (Edwards 1983; Hopp and Spearman 2008):

- *zero defects*: to avoid disruptions of the production process due to defects;
- *zero lot size*: to replenish the storage of all parts quickly enough to avoid delays;
- *zero set-ups*: to lower set-ups in order to achieve small lot sizes;
- *zero breakdowns*: to avoid halting the whole production-line;
- *zero handling*: to avoid extra moves to and from storage;
- *zero lead time*: to have a perfect parts flow providing the required parts to a downstream station immediately;
- *zero surging*: to avoid unnecessary work-in-process buffers.

Two concepts are embodied in JIT: *kaizen* (continuous improvement), and inventory reduction. JIT emphasizes inventory reduction. Indeed, it sees inventory as an evil in many aspects. First, the inventory is an investment; it has a financial cost that affects price competitiveness. Second, it is used to hide problems such as poor quality of products, process inefficiencies (machine breakdowns, long set-up times, large batch sizes, etc.), inefficient layout, an unreliable supplier, and difficulties with respect to due dates, etc.

Often, people working on JIT use the metaphor of a company floating as a boat on a sea of inventory. Lowering the sea (inventory) level uncovers rocks (problems). The idea emphasized by the JIT philosophy is that the sea level should be gradually lowered, and the rocks uncovered should be removed. The JIT technique for lowering the inventory is pull production (such as the *kanban* system), and the technique for removing the rocks is *kaizen*. These techniques are described in the following two sections.

Kanban – *a 'pull' production system*

Kanban is a tool to achieve JIT production. It is a unique production control system, which plays a significant role in the JIT production system. The word *kanban* is Japanese for *card*. It is a card (or a signal) containing all the information required for production/assembly of a product at each stage, and details of its path of completion. In a *kanban* system, production is triggered by a demand. When a part is removed from an inventory point (which may be a finished-goods inventory or some intermediate buffer) the workstation that feeds the inventory point is given authorization to replace the part. This workstation then sends an authorization signal to the upstream workstation to replace the part that it just used. Each workstation does the same thing, replenishing the downstream void and sending authorization to the next workstation upstream. Therefore, production authorization cards, called *kanbans*, are used to control and limit the release of parts into each workstation (Hopp and Spearman 2008). It is a system that enables designated parts to be delivered from a specified location to another specified location, at a specified time, in the specified quantity. It is often referred to as the subsystem of the TPS, for its dominant role in facilitating the JIT system. Through the *kanban* system, Toyota was able to eliminate stock, and thus produce diversified products in the exact desired quantities.

Figure 24.1 illustrates a *kanban* control system. It shows the Activity Interaction Diagram (AID) of a simple *kanban* system with four workstations. An AID is a diagram that has three kinds of components: *activities*, *queues*, and *connecting arrows*. Activities should be connected with queues, and vice versa (Sato and Praehofer 1997). The manufacturing/assembling processes (activities) and buffers (queues) at each workstation are drawn as squares and ovals, respectively. M represents the raw-material buffer, and b represents the finished products buffer. Queue K_i contains station i's kanban. Queue b_i is the output buffer of station i containing both finished parts and station i's kanbans. Solid lines represent material flows, and dashed lines indicate information flows, which can be demand information or production authorizations.

The *kanban* system developed at Toyota made use of two types of cards to authorize production and movement of product: a withdrawal *kanban* and a production–ordering *kanban*. A *withdrawal kanban* specifies the kind and quantity of product which the subsequent process should withdraw from the preceding process, while a *production-ordering kanban* specifies the kind and quantity of product which the preceding process must produce. The production-ordering *kanban* is often called an in-process *kanban*, or simply a production *kanban* (Monden 2011).

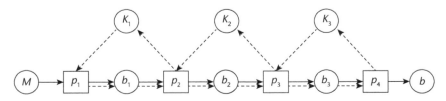

Figure 24.1   Kanban control system

Several other kinds of *kanban* were described in Monden (2011, p. 37). Two different types of *kanban* systems, single-card and two-card, were compared in Muckstadt and Tayur (1995). More definitions and applications of *kanban* can be found in Ōno (1988), Morgan and Liker (2006), Hopp and Spearman (2008), and Monden (2011).

Kaizen

In addition to *kanban* and *jidōka*, *kaizen* is another innovative concept practised in the JIT system of Toyota. Unlike the first two concepts, *kaizen* is a moral concept that is used by employees throughout the production system. *Kaizen* is a Japanese word, which literally means improvement: change (*kai*) for good (*zen*).

A major concept that must be understood and practised in implementing *kaizen* is the plan–do–check–act (PDCA) cycle. In fact, the PDCA cycle is a set of activities pursued for improvement. The first step is to study the current situation by gathering data to formulate a plan for improvement. After finalizing the plan, it is implemented. Then, the implementation is frequently checked to see if the expected improvement has been achieved. This is followed by a final action such as methodological standardization, which is taken to ensure that the introduced plans will be continuously performed to achieve improvements.

Kaizen, or '5S' is an improvement method that brings tools and techniques into a unified whole. It represents Japanese words *seiri*, *seiton*, *seiso*, *seiketsu*, and *shitsuke*. Translated into English, they all start with the letter 's': *sort*, *straighten*, *shine*, *standardize*, and *sustain*. The list describes how to organize a work-space for efficiency and effectiveness by identifying and storing the items used; maintaining the area and items; and sustaining the new order (Hirano 1995; Ho *et al.* 1995; Scotchmer 2008; Monden 2011; Imai 2012).

The five principles are:

- *Seiri*: to clearly separate all the unnecessary items in the workplace from the necessary ones and remove them;
- *Seiton*: to neatly arrange and identify things for ease of use;
- *Seiso*: to keep everything, tools and workplaces clean;
- *Seiketsu*: to make cleaning and checking routine;
- *Shitsuke*: to have the workers make a habit of always conforming to rules.

In fact, to have a successful *kaizen*, everyone in the company should be committed. All employees must accept the need to continually improve performance, accept the responsibility for, and participate in improving performance.

Production systems: pull vs. push

Production control systems can be mainly divided into pull and push systems. A pull system can be implemented in many ways. The well-known pull production control system is the *kanban* system described above.

The contrast between push and pull systems is illustrated schematically in Figure 24.2. A push system releases a part into a production process (factory, line, or workstation) precisely when called to do so by an exogenous schedule, and the release time is not modified according to what is happening in the process itself. In contrast, a pull system, such as *kanban*, only allows a part into the line when a signal generated by a change in line-status calls for it.

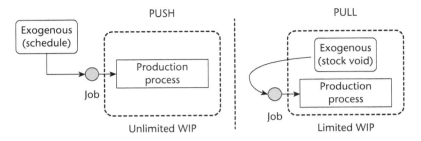

Figure 24.2   Push and pull mechanics (Hopp and Spearman 2008)

The push system seems to be a material requirements planning (MRP) system driven by demand forecasts. The MRP system computes ordering and production quantities and times by analysing the product's bill of materials, and assumes fixed lead times and unlimited capacities in the production system. Therefore, in a push system, work releases are *scheduled*, while in a pull system, releases are *authorized*. That is, pull systems authorize parts to be processed in response to the actual demand arrival. The difference is that a schedule is prepared in advance, while an authorization depends on the status of the plant. Another useful way to think about the distinction between push and pull systems is that a pull system establishes an a priori limit on the work-in-process in order to control it, while a push system does not (Hopp and Spearman 2008).

In fact, the worst type of inventory (as the third type of waste) is a work-in-process inventory, which includes all parts which have been released into the system but have not left the system yet. In other words, it includes all parts that still need more operations to become a finished product. The work-in-process inventory can be significantly reduced by employing a pull production control system such as *kanban*.

Western adaptation of TPS

Japanese production management, especially TPS, became a leading worldwide influence in production management in the 1980s. When the system was created, it opened up the world to a new production approach that decentralized mass production and offered a small-lot production system that made possible limited production of diversified products.

Many manufacturing companies in the US, Europe, and other countries tried to apply TPS practices. It was first described under a variety of names, for example, Hewlett-Packard called it 'stockless production'. In fact, such an adaptation by Western industry was based on informal analysis of the systems being used in Toyota and other Japanese companies, because, the books by Japanese authors (such as Ōno and Monden) detailing the development of TPS and JIT in Japan were not published in the West until the late 1980s (Schonberger 2007; Beasley 2014).

A generalization of the *kanban* system, called the constant work-in-process (CONWIP) control system, proposed by Professor Spearman in the early 1990s (Spearman *et al.* 1990), can be viewed as a single-stage *kanban* system. CONWIP uses a single type of card to control the total amount of WIP permitted in the entire line. In a CONWIP system, the cards traverse a circuit that includes the entire production line. A card is attached to a standard container of parts at the beginning of the line. When the container leaves the line, the card is removed and sent back to the beginning of the line, where it waits in a card queue to eventually be attached to another container of parts.

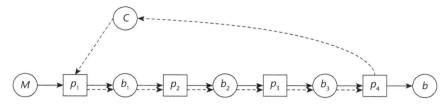

Figure 24.3 CONWIP control system

The AID of a CONWIP control system with four workstations is depicted in Figure 24.3. Queue C contains CONWIP cards. Even though there are four stages drawn here, CONWIP production control is executed only at the entry of the production line, and the intermediate buffers b_i play no control role.

The CONWIP is a very simple control mechanism that depends only on one parameter for the entire line: the total number of circulating cards. It influences both the transfer of finished parts downstream and the transfer of demands upstream through the line. There is no demand transfer between each workstation, except for the last and the first ones (Spearman *et al.* 1990; Hopp and Spearman 2008).

Although several studies shows that CONWIP is a superior control system to Toyota's *kanban*, nevertheless, many Japanese manufacturing companies still use *kanban* to control their production processes. For a comparison between *kanban* and CONWIP, see for example, Khojasteh-Ghamari (2009, 2012), Khojasteh and Sato (2015), and Khojasteh (2015).

References

Beasley, J. E. (2014). Just-in-time. http://people.brunel.ac.uk/~mastjjb/jeb/or/jit.html, last accessed 23 October 2015.

Edwards, J. N. (1983). MRP and kanban – American style. *APICS 26th Conference Proceedings*, pp. 586–603, no publisher given.

Hirano, H. (1995). *Five Pillars of Visible Workplace: the Source Book for 5S Implementation*, Cambridge, MA: Productivity Press.

Ho, S. K., Cicmil, S., and Fung, C. K. (1995). The Japanese 5-S practice and TQM training. *Training for Quality*, 3(4): 19–24

Hopp, W. J. and Spearman, M. L. (2008) *Factory Physics*, 3rd edn. New York: McGraw-Hill.

Imai, M (2012). *Gemba Kaizen: A Commonsense Approach to a Continuous Improvement Strategy*, 2nd edn. McGraw Hill, New York, USA.

Khojasteh, Y. (2015) *Production Control Systems, A Guide to Enhance Performance of Pull Systems*, Tokyo: Springer

Khojasteh, Y. and Sato, R. (2015). Selection of a pull production control system in multi-stage production processes. *International Journal of Production Research*, 53(14): 4363–4379.

Khojasteh-Ghamari, Y. (2009). A performance comparison between Kanban and CONWIP controlled assembly systems. *Journal of Intelligent Manufacturing*, 20(6): 751–760.

Khojasteh-Ghamari, Y. (2012). Developing a framework for performance analysis of a production process controlled by Kanban and CONWIP. *Journal of Intelligent Manufacturing*, 23(1): 61–71.

Liker, J. K. (2004). *The Toyota Way: 14 Management Principles from the World's Greatest Manufacturer*, New York: McGraw-Hill.

Monden, Y. (2011). *Toyota Production System: An Integrated Approach to Just-In-Time,* 4th edn. Boca Raton, FL: CRC Press.

Morgan, J. M. and Liker, J. K (2006). *The Toyota Product Development System: Integrating People, Processes, and Technology*. New York: Productivity Press.

Muckstadt, J. A. and Tayur, S. R. (1995). A comparison of alternative kanban control mechanisms: I, background and structural results. *IIE Transactions*, 27(1): 140–150.

Ōno, T. (1988) Toyota production system, beyond large scale production. Cambridge, MA: Productivity Press.

Sato, R. and Praehofer, H. (1997). A discrete event model of business system – a systems theoretic foundation for information systems analysis: Part 1. *IEEE Transactions on Systems, Man, and Cybernetics*, 27(1): 1–10.

Schonberger, R. J. (2007). Japanese production management: an evolution – with mixed success. *Journal of Operations Management*, 25: 403–419.

Scotchmer, A. (2008). *5S Kaizen in 90 Minutes*. Cirencester: UK: Management Books 2000.

Spearman, M. L., Woodruff, D. L., and Hopp, W. J. (1990). CONWIP: a pull alternative to kanban. *International Journal of Production Research*, 23: 879–894.

Toyota Motor Corporation (2015). www.toyotaglobal.com/company/vision_philosophy/toyota_production_system/jidoka.html, last accessed 23 October 2015.

25

Japanese supply chain management

Yacob Khojasteh and M. Reza Abdi

Introduction

Today, a large Japanese company, such as Hitachi or Sony, consists of subsidiaries, affiliates and joint ventures with subcontractors, suppliers, and service providers, as well as partners in strategic alliances worldwide. In fact, the value chain is broken down into a variety of operations, which are performed wherever they can be done more effectively. Japanese companies procure the required materials and parts from local suppliers as well as overseas suppliers. Therefore, like other countries, outsourcing and subcontracting in Japanese companies play an important role in achieving an effective supply chain management.

Japan is the world's third-largest economy and a vital supplier of parts and equipment for major industries like computers, electronics, and automobiles. Because of Japan's economic crisis in the 1990s, many Japanese companies shifted their key production facilities to low-cost countries such as China in order to reduce their production costs. In addition, the effects of globalization and rising competition have caused a shift of production facilities from Japan to overseas, especially Asian countries, in order to also be closer to the end-consumer markets.

This chapter presents an overview of supply chain management in Japanese companies. First, we will provide the definition and concepts of supply chain management. Then, we will classify the risks associated with supply chains, and outline the essentials of supply chain risk management. Finally, we will describe supply chain resilience, and the challenges faced by Japanese companies with their suppliers during supply chain interruptions such as natural disasters, followed by supply chain lessons from the catastrophic natural disasters in Japan.

Supply chain and supply chain management

In the literature, there is a consensus on the definition of 'supply chain' encompassing the views of many authors. For example, Lambert *et al.* (1998) proposed that the supply chain could be defined as the alignment of firms that brings product and services to market. Christopher (2011) defined the supply chain in a more-comprehensive way as a network of organizations, which are involved with different processes and activities, in order to produce value in the form of products and services to the ultimate customer through upstream and downstream linkages. Chopra and Meindl (2012) defined a supply chain in a customer-oriented way that comprises all parties, in order to meet the customer's needs directly or indirectly. It does not only include the manufacturers and suppliers, but also the warehouses, transporters, retailers, and customers themselves. Moreover, each organization within the supply chain (with all the functions such as marketing, operations, distribution, and finance and customer services) is involved to meet the customer's requests.

Supply chain management (SCM) is the design and management of flows of parts, products, and information throughout the supply chain. A supply chain can be classified, based on its complexity, into three different types (Mentzer *et al.* 2001) (see Figure 25.1): a *direct supply chain* (consisting of a supplier, a company, and a customer); an *extended supply chain* (consisting of a direct supply chain plus suppliers of suppliers, and customers of customers); and the *ultimate supply chain* (consisting of the upstream flows and/or the downstream flows of services, products, information, and finances from the ultimate supplier to the ultimate customer). The ultimate supply chain represents the complexity that a supply chain can reach. It has a financial provider, which provides the required financing and financial advice, and it has a logistics provider, which offers logistic activities between two companies, and a market-research firm that provides the necessary information about ultimate customer needs.

Evolution of the supply chain

The purpose of the evolution of the supply chain is not only to show how the improvement occurred in the supply chain over the past few years, but also to emphasize that the concept of supply chain risks is newly introduced. During the period from the 1950s to the 1960s, the manufacturers' primary operation strategy was reducing unit production costs through focusing on mass production while ignoring the product or process flexibility. In that period, the problem of bottleneck operations emerged, and manufacturers solved this problem by relying on the work-in-process (WIP) inventory having a balanced line-flow. The WIP inventory is all the parts which have been released into the system, but are not

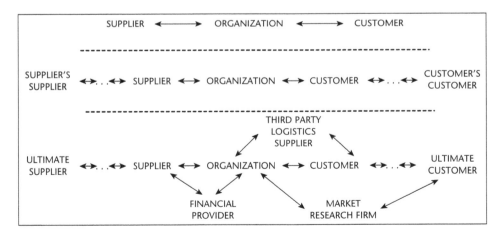

Figure 25.1   Direct, extended, and ultimate supply chains

Source: Mentzer *et al.* (2001)

completed yet. This has led to a huge investment on the WIP inventory, thus affecting the financial performance of factories. The concept of sharing technology and expertise with customers or suppliers was viewed as risky and unacceptable. Therefore, there was not any tendency to collaborate or to build strategic partnerships with buyers or suppliers (Tan 2001).

In the 1970s, introducing Manufacturing Resource Planning (MRP) helped manufacturers to understand the adverse impact of WIP on quality, product development, manufacturing cost, and delivery time. In the 1980s, because of fierce competition, manufacturers started thinking about providing customers with high quality and reliable products offered at low costs. To achieve that, Toyota introduced and used Just-in-Time (JIT) and the lean manufacturing technique, both of which improved manufacturing efficiency and reduced inventories and waste (Womack and Jones 2006). In addition to that, using these techniques helped manufacturers to realize the importance of building strategic partnerships with suppliers in order to achieve high-quality products offered at low cost. However, the lean supply chain failed in a volatile market where the demand is unpredictable.

In the 1990s during the Japan economic crises, the emergence of *agile supply* helped to solve the problem of unpredictable demand. Agile supply chains can respond quickly to sudden changes in supply or demand, and can handle unexpected external disruptions smoothly and cost-effectively with rapid recovery from shocks such as natural disasters. In 1995, the lean, agile supply chain was adopted to exploit the advantages of both agile and lean supply chains. In addition to agility, in order to gain sustainable competitive advantage, supply chains must be adaptable to market structure and align the interests of all the firms in the supply network (Lee 2004).

Supply chain relationships

Many companies are trying to find tools for performance improvement in response to turbulent business markets and for efficiently controlling their business activities. The objective of performance measurement is to improve the efficiency and effectiveness of a supply chain (Gunasekaran *et al.* 2001). Establishing and managing effective relationships at the tier of a supply chain is becoming the condition of business success in the diverse and uncertain global business environment

Suppliers' relationships

Making a supplier–supplier connection will encourage communication and coordination across the suppliers for product development and quality enhancement. In many industries, such as the automotive and electronic industries, the first-tier supplier plays a key role in integrating components to the higher-tier manufacturers. The manufacturing firms, which produce final products, need to integrate the parts produced by the first-tier suppliers into their product design. Therefore, interaction between the first tier supplier and the other suppliers (buyers of the first-tier suppliers) during product design and development is crucial.

By introducing new products that have shorter life cycles, information exchange and sharing resources across the suppliers become of greater importance, particularly during the product design and development stage. Trust plays a key role in a sustainable connection between suppliers and supply chain agility, and on the contrary, the lack of support will result in inadequate information transferred across the tiers, and thus a delay in product design, production, and delivery of products.

Japanese firms have recently been used their supplier relationship as a tool for innovating an agile supply chain while continuing to cut costs. However, disruptions and natural disasters such as earthquakes will damage the suppliers' partnership. For example, Japanese suppliers will need to recover from disruptions and disaster damage, and this will result in a delay in information exchange and parts delivery. As a result, Japanese suppliers may lose their buyers, e.g. the US manufacturing firms, who are encouraged not to wait for disaster recovery and to seek the domestic first-tier suppliers instead.

Supplier–buyer relationships

Supplier–buyer relationships in the supply chain are one of the key elements of supply chain integration. Establishing and managing effective relationships at every link in the supply chain is becoming the prerequisite of financial success. The buyer–supplier relationships with the purchasing process have become the key characteristic in relationship marketing and purchasing as well as business-to-business marketing. The supply chain in Asia has a special socio-economic environment in which small independent retailers with big international suppliers can dominate the market. High volatility in the retail industry reflects rapid fluctuations in customer demand and unpredictable market trends. In addition, environmental diversity reveals uncertainty in the global business environment. Facing market volatility and diversity, retailers are encouraged to develop relatively flexible relationships with multiple-channel partners in order to deal with unexpected market demands and thus reduce the dependence on the vendor (Ganesan 1994). The links between the relationship characteristics such as trust, cooperation, and the performance of the relationship need to be investigated (Olsen and Ellram 1997).

Most Western companies today are investing in supplier relationships that would require significant care and feeding for sustainability. Japanese companies' success is not only due to technology and process advancement but also due to enhancing supplier relationships as a tool for moving towards an agile supply chain while cutting costs. For example, the traditional *keiretsu* system was used in the 1980s for an arrangement in which buyers formed close associations with suppliers – it was the darling of business schools and the envy of manufacturers everywhere. Indeed, many people probably assume that *keiretsu* died when Japanese manufacturers initiated Western style cost-cutting tactics. Although there was some provisional movement in the West toward *keiretsu*-like supplier partnerships at the time, the rise of manufacturing in low-wage countries soon made cost the pre-eminent concern.

Some Japanese automakers have developed and reinvented *keiretsu*. For instance, Toyota provides an instructive example and has gained enormous benefits from the new *keiretsu*, with supplier relationships that are more open, global, and cost-conscious than they ever had. The new *keiretsu* has deepened trust, collaboration, and educational support – features which were the hallmarks of *keiretsu* in their earlier form (Aoki and Lennerfors 2013). In order to develop high-quality products while reducing costs and development time, the automaker requests that the supplier provide integrated systems of components instead of individual parts. Toyota encourages its suppliers to enhance their ability to provide integrated systems and to become involved in product development at the planning stage. It has also helped many suppliers meet its changing needs through providing support for operational improvements; organizing study groups; and dispatching engineers to help vendors improve efficiency and quality and bring prices down (Aoki and Lennerfors 2013). By dropping a supplier for a particular model, e.g. because of price, the relationship will not end, as other opportunities for the supplier, such as supplying parts for other models can be created.

Supply chain risk management (SCRM)

Supply chain management is responsible for the movement of materials all the way from initial suppliers through to end customers. Supply chain risk would be any unexpected event that might affect this movement and disrupt the planned flow of materials. Supply chain vulnerability can also be considered a risk factor, and can be defined as 'exposure to serious disturbance arising from supply chain risks and affecting the supply chain's ability to effectively serve the end customer market' (Mason-Jones and Towill 1998). The aim of supply chain risk management (SCRM) is to identify the potential sources of risk and implement appropriate actions in order to avoid or contain supply chain vulnerability (Narasimhan and Talluri 2009).

Supply chain disruptions have a significant impact on firms' business and financial performance. They might block deliveries, cause delays, damage goods, or somehow affect smooth operations. But these initial effects are only the beginning, and the consequences are generally much broader. A late delivery of raw materials might stop production; raise costs by forcing a move to alternative transport, materials, or operations; raise the WIP inventory; and make partners reconsider their trading relationships (Waters 2007).

Research carried out by Accenture in 2006 showed that 73 per cent of organizations have experienced a significant disruption in the past five years. Of those, nearly 32 per cent required more than one month to recover, and another 36 per cent took between one week and one month. The ability to meet the needs of customers and constituents was compromised in 94 per cent of these situations (Inagaki and Kuroda 2007). Hendricks and Singhal (2003, 2005) pointed out that sales typically fall by 7 per cent in the year after a major supply chain disruption; shareholder return falls by 7–8 per cent on the day that a disruption occurs; operating income falls by 42 per cent; and return on assets is down by 35 per cent. There are basically two kinds of risk to a supply chain.

Internal risks: these occur in normal operations, such as machine breakdowns, late deliveries, forecast error, supplier failure, supplier-quality problems, malfunction of IT systems, change in customer demand, transportation failure, human error, etc. They can be divided into *internal controllable* and *internal partially controllable risks*. Internal controllable risks originate from sources that are most likely to be controllable by the company; for example, the quality, cost, and on-time delivery of products. Internal partially controllable risks originate from sources that are partially controllable by the company; for example, a fire accident affecting the company (Wu *et al.* 2006).

External risks: these come from outside the supply chain, such as a natural disaster (earthquake, hurricane, tsunami, etc.), war, oil crises, terrorist attacks, the outbreak of disease, financial irregularities, crime, rising custom duty, etc. Wu *et al.* (2006) classified the internal and external risks as follows: *external controllable risks* originate from sources that are most likely to be controllable by the supplier company; for example, the selection of the next-tier supplier. *External partially controllable risks* originate from sources that are partially controllable by the supplier company; for example, legal claims by customers. *External uncontrollable risks* originate from sources that are uncontrollable by the supplier company; for example, natural disasters such as earthquake and tsunami.

An example of an external uncontrollable risk was the Great East Japan Earthquake that occurred in 2011. Risks were mostly ignored in the supply chain until 2011, when the Great East Japan Earthquake and floods in Thailand had a tremendous impact on Japanese manufacturing by causing production and delivery stoppages. Then the concept of risk in the supply chain was extended to include all parties in the supply chain, and external factors as well.

Effects of the Japanese earthquake and tsunami

The Great East Japan Earthquake hit the north-eastern parts of Japan (the Tōhoku region) on 11 March in 2011, and the scale of the earthquake was the largest in recorded history in Japan. It disrupted both domestic and global supply chains. It caused significant disruption in the supply chains, so that many companies and their part suppliers – often a single source – were unable to deliver products at expected volumes for several months. For example, it took at least six months for Toyota's supply chain to fully recover from the earthquake damage.

Japan has been a large manufacturer of parts and products worldwide, and a disruption in its supply chains can cause disruptions in supply chains globally. For example, Japan provides 60 per cent of the world's silicon, which is a main raw material for semiconductor chips. Japan is also the world's largest supplier of dynamic random-access memory and flash memory, which play an important role in supplying liquid-crystal displays (LCD), and LCD parts and materials. Right after the disaster, the prices for these components on the world market soared by 20 per cent, showing the world's strong dependence on the Japanese supply chain (Park *et al.* 2013).

Japan also supplies the world with certain vital chemicals, such as bismaleimide triazine (BT) resin, a critical raw material used in the manufacturing of circuit boards. Prior to the earthquake, two major Japanese suppliers, Mitsubishi Gas Chemical Company and Hitachi Chemical Co. Ltd, produced more than 85 per cent of the world's BT resin, dominating the market. The operation of some plants was suspended due to damaged infrastructure after the earthquake (Chiu 2011).

These catastrophic disruptions have had serious impacts on firms' performances. The devastating Japanese earthquakes sent aftershocks of another kind to the economy: the potential disruption of the flow of goods from Japanese suppliers to US high-tech manufacturers. However, the Obama administration and domestic companies decided not to wait for Japanese suppliers to recover from earthquake damage, and they took action to ensure that the US invested in growing the domestic stock of world-class suppliers, along with launching a national campaign to enhance supply chain partnerships in order to accelerate job creation (Kanter 2011).

Resilient supply chain

Supply chain resilience is the ability of a supply chain to cope with changes. Resilient supply chains should align their strategy and operations to adapt to risks that affect their capacities. It is not about responding to a one-time crisis or disaster. It is about continuously anticipating and adjusting to discontinuities. Strategic resilience, therefore, requires continuous innovation with respect to product structures, processes, but also regarding corporate behaviour (Wieland and Wallenburg 2013).

In 2011, major natural disasters, including the Great East Japan Earthquake and the floods in Thailand, had a tremendous impact on Japanese supply chains by halting production and delivery. Kureha, which provided 70 per cent of a crucial polymer used in the lithium-ion batteries of Apple's iPods, had to shut its factory in Iwaki – near the quake's epicentre – after the disaster struck. It was the only place where Kureha made this particular polymer (*The Economist* 2011).

The production plant of Xirallic pigments (speciality paints used in automobile painting) owned by Merck KGaA of Germany, located in Onahama in Iwaki Prefecture, was destroyed. It was the only plant in the world supplying pigments to automakers worldwide, and it was closed for almost two months after the disaster. The shutdown of the plant affected many of the world's automakers, including Ford, Chrysler, Volkswagen, BMW, Toyota, and GM (Park *et al.* 2013).

Renesas Electronics, a major global vehicle chip-maker, which before the earthquake produced about 40 per cent of the world's supply of automotive microcontrollers, was badly damaged. A reason for the industry's heavy reliance on Renesas is that it is the product of mergers involving three Japanese semiconductor companies. Hitachi and Mitsubishi Electric merged their semiconductor operations in 2003 to form Renesas Technology. Then, in 2010, Renesas Technology merged with NEC Electronics to form Renesas Electronics. Renesas plant operations stopped for nearly three months, and, after restarting production, it operated at only about 10 per cent of capacity (Matsuo 2015).

Panasonic, the nation's biggest maker of batteries, closed two plants in the area hit by the quake. For Sony, the most significant damage was to its Tagajo plant, in Miyagi Prefecture, that produced coating materials for magnetic tapes, touch-panel mobile devices and Blu-ray discs (Ohnsman *et al.* 2011). Toyota, more than its domestic competitors, experienced supply chain difficulties.

For two weeks after the earthquake, all the Toyota plants in Japan stopped completely. The problems were lack of parts, or not even knowing which parts would be missing when the plants resumed production. It is reported that it took a week for Toyota to list the 500 parts sourced from 200 locations which would be difficult to secure, and then recover to the normal production level. Although it grasped the availability of parts up to the second-tier suppliers, Toyota did not keep track of the suppliers of the third-tier parts or further down in general. Not only Toyota, but also most of the Japanese major assembling companies during the first week or two after the earthquake, worked frantically to list the missing parts in their entire supply chains. This is a period when one-of-a-kind-product companies like Fujikura Rubber, Ltd., which had 1,333 employees in 2010 and produced rubber parts that were used in some of Toyota's cars, became well known to the public. The number of missing parts remained at 150 items in April 2011 and at 30 items in May 2011 (Matsuo 2015).

Some companies affected by the earthquake developed plans that will dramatically lower their supply chain risks. For instance, in the wake of the earthquake, Toyota asked suppliers to stock several months' worth of key components such as computer chips, if those parts can be produced at only one location. It developed new plans regarding its suppliers, asking them to either spread production over multiple locations or to hold extra inventory stocks. Looking at more dual-sourcing of parts was another part of the plans. At about the same time, Nissan asked its suppliers to take similar steps, so that the company can get production lines back on stream more quickly in the event of disruption. Toyota pushed Japanese automakers to standardize some parts so that they can share common components produced in different factories.

Fujitsu developed the SCRKeeper system, a SCRM service to reduce supply chain disruptions. The system is able to evaluate and analyse a firm's business continuity capabilities in cases of natural disasters and other unexpected situations. It can provide damage forecasting and assessment for the regions where suppliers are located. The system's features are as follows (Fujitsu 2013):

1   The system evaluates and analyses the business-continuity capabilities of suppliers. It enables firms to perform quantitative analyses regarding the resumption of suppliers' operations; the amount of time required for recovery; damage projections; and the status of implemented countermeasures before a disaster occurs.

2   The system uses hazard maps to evaluate the geographical risks for suppliers. It uses the latest hazard maps with the addresses of suppliers' production facilities and offices, which

makes it possible to visually simulate the expected damage that will occur during a natural disaster.

3   It analyses the impact on the firm's own products. Based on an evaluation of the suppliers' business-continuity capabilities and the results of geographical risk evaluations, the system enables a firm to quantitatively analyse the impact of a disaster on its own products. For example, firms can estimate which products will be affected by production stoppages, and then can calculate when production will resume.

4   Finally, the system provides immediate damage-status updates on suppliers. When a disaster actually occurs, the system is immediately updated with reports from suppliers about the status of damage and the situation of their operations. This makes it possible for firms to check on the status of their suppliers in real time and overview their damage status, so that they can quickly respond to their suppliers or select alternative suppliers (Fujitsu 2013).

Supply chain lessons from Japan

Companies should challenge their suppliers to develop disaster plans so that they can make provisions to move to alternative sites for production, in the event that they are unable to produce a product at their main plant.

Suppliers who have near-monopolies on crucial parts and materials may be pressed to spread their production facilities geographically. Their customers may, as a precaution, also switch part of their orders to smaller rivals.

Companies should eliminate sole-source suppliers, and develop the capabilities of additional sources. It is obvious that having one supplier is too risky. One strategy would be to give the majority of the work to the primary supplier, and the rest to a secondary one that is located in another region.

Companies should analyse where suppliers are located, and limit the number of critical-component suppliers that are geographically situated in a risky area. The area that is currently considered highly risky in Japan is Tōkai. The probability of a magnitude 8 or greater earthquake along the Nankai Trough within the next forty years is about 80 per cent.

After the major disruption in Toyota's supply chain, the company revised the supply chain coordination mechanism of its production system, which addresses:

1   monitoring the information on all the suppliers of key parts/materials across the entire supply chain;

2   managing the inventory of key parts/materials across the entire supply chain;

3   ensuring the continuing supply of key parts/materials; and

4   increasing the standardization of key parts/materials and their production methods (Matsuo 2015).

Conclusions

This chapter has highlighted the main aspects of the supply chain, and described the types of supply chain, and supply chain management, with a focus on the Japanese context. The evolution of supply chains since the mid-twentieth century, through different concepts such as WIP, MRP, just-in-time, and agility, and their applications in Japan were highlighted. Two types of relationships amongst supply chain tiers, i.e. suppliers and buyers and the impacts on supply chain performance, were discussed briefly. In particular, the supplier relationships in Japan, for example via the *keiretsu* system in Toyota, were rationalized. Various risk sources occurred in a supply chain and their impacts on supply chain performance were classified and defined. The specific impacts of natural disasters such as the 2011 earthquake and tsunami on Japanese firms, and the consequent disruptions of supply chains, were outlined.

References

Aoki, K. and Lennerfors, T. T. (2013). The new, improved keiretsu. *Harvard Business Review*, September 2013: 109–113.

Chiu, Y. T. (2011). How Japan's earthquake is shaking up Taiwan's high-tech sector, IEEE Spectrum, available at: http://spectrum.ieee.org/semiconductors/memory/how-japans-earthquake-is-shaking-up-taiwans-hightech-sector, last accessed 23 October 2015.

Chopra, S. and Meindl, P. (2012). *Supply Chain Management: Strategy, Planning, and Operation*, 5th edn. Essex, UK: Prentice Hall.

Christopher, M. (2011). *Logistics and Supply Chain Management*, 4th edn. Harlow, UK: Prentice Hall.

The Economist (2011). Japan and the global supply chain: broken links. *The Economist*, 2 April 2011, not paginated.

Fujitsu (2013). 'SCRKeeper', Japan's first cloud-based supply chain risk management service, available at: http://jp.fujitsu.com/solutions/cloud/saas/application/scrkeeper/en/, last accessed June 2015.

Ganesan, S. (1994). Determinants of long-term orientation in buyer–seller relationships. *Journal of Marketing*, 58, 1–19.

Gunasekaran, A., Patel, C., and Tirtiroglu, E. (2001). Performance measures and metrics in a supply chain environment. *International Journal of Operations and Production Management*, 21(1–2), 71–87.

Hendricks, K. B. and Singhal, V.R. (2003). The effect of supply chain glitches on shareholder value. *Journal of Operations Management*, 21(5): 501–522.

Hendricks, K. B. and Singhal, V. R. (2005). An empirical analysis of the effect of supply chain disruptions on long-run stock price performance and risk of the firm. *Production and Operations Management*, 14(1): 35–52.

Inagaki, M. and Kuroda, K. (2007). Supply chain management in Japan. *Supply and Demand Chain Executive*, 8(3): 68.

Kanter, R. M. (2011). While waiting for Japan's recovery, let's enhance supplier competitiveness at home. *Harvard Business School Working Knowledge*, http://hbswk.hbs.edu/item/6703.html, last accessed 23 October 2015.

Lambert, D. M., Stock, J. R., and Ellram, L. M. (1998). *Fundamentals of Logistics Management*. New York: McGraw-Hill.

Lee, H. K. (2004). Supply chain triple A. *Harvard Business Review*, http://file.seekpart.com/keyword-pdf/2010/12/22/2010122294137780.pdf, last accessed 23 October 2015.

Mason-Jones, R. and Towill, D. R. (1998). Shrinking the supply chain uncertainty circle. *Control*, 24(7): 17–22.

Matsuo, H. (2015). Implications of the Tohoku earthquake for Toyota's coordination mechanism: supply chain disruption of automotive semiconductors. *International Journal of Production Economics*, 161(1): 217–227.

Mentzer, J. T., DeWitt, W., Keebler, J. S., Soonhoong, M., Nix, N. W., Smith, C. D., and Zacharia, Z. G. (2001). Defining supply chain management. *Journal of Business Logistics*, 22(2): 1–25.

Narasimhan, R. and Talluri, S. (2009). Perspectives on risk management in supply chains. *Journal of Operations Management*, 27(2): 114–118.

Ohnsman, A., McCombs, D., and Edwards, C. (2011). Toyota, Sony disruptions may last weeks after Japan earthquake. *Bloomberg Business*, 20 March 2011, http://www.bloomberg.com/news/articles/2011-03-19/toyota-sony-disruptions-may-last-weeks-after-japan-quake-power-power-shortages.

Olsen, R. F. and Ellram, L. M. (1997). Buyer–supplier relationships: alternative research approaches. *European Journal of Purchasing and Supply Management*, 6: 221–231.

Park, Y. W., Hong, P., and Roh, J. (2013) Supply chain lessons from the 2011 natural disasters in Japan. *Business Horizons*, 56(1): 75–85.

Tan, K. C. (2001). A framework of supply chain management literature. *European Journal of Purchasing and Supply Management*, 7(1): 39–48.

Waters, D. (2007). *Supply Chain Risk Management: Vulnerability and Resilience in Logistics*. London: Kogan Page.

Wieland, A. and Wallenburg, C. M. (2013). The influence of relational competencies on supply chain resilience: a relational view. *International Journal of Physical Distribution and Logistics Management*, 43(4): 300–320.

Womack, J. P. and Jones, D. T. (2006). *Lean Thinking: Banish Waste and Create Wealth in Your Corporation*, 2nd edn. London: Simon and Schuster.

Wu, T., Blackhurst, J. and Chidambaram, V. (2006). A model for inbound supply risk analysis. *Computers in Industry*, 57: 350–365.

26

'Hollowing-out' – Japanese production overseas

Patrick Bessler

The 'hollowing-out' of the Japanese industry – just a matter of perception?

As a major industrialized country, Japan has long seen a trend of large manufacturing companies investing abroad and offshoring their production capacities. Their targets mostly have been emerging Asian countries like China and the ASEAN states. While this is seen as necessary to keep up with rising competition amidst globalization, it also brings potential negative effects in the sense of a 'hollowing-out' of the domestic economy. As in other industrialized countries like Germany, there has been a controversial debate about the reasons, reality, and dangers of this 'hollowing-out'. The following chapter introduces the debate in Japan, as well as the history of *kūdōka*, as the phenomenon is termed in Japanese, and recent policies dealing with the issue.

Kūdōka, the 'hollowing-out' or 'de-industrialization'[1] of Japan's economy, has been discussed for many years. Amidst a new globalization movement exemplified in an increasing number of outbound M&As and a considerable growth in outward foreign direct investment (FDI) from Japanese companies since 2008/9 (see Figure 26.1), one would think that *kūdōka* also should be feared more than ever.

However, these days, it seems, the opposite is the case. Being the result of a shift of production facilities to less labour-cost-intensive countries, *kūdōka* is closely linked to globalization.[2] And globalization is, in the era of so-called 'Abenomics', considered to be Japan's last hope to remain amongst the leading global economic powers, as Japan's prime minister, Shinzo Abe, time and again stressed as part of his 'Japan is back' rhetoric since entering office in early 2013.

Nonetheless, the potential threat cannot be easily neglected. 'Hollowing-out' implies loss of jobs, loss of innovation potential, reduction of the domestic production base, and therefore an overall economic deterioration, including dwindling tax income and growing public debt.

Therefore this chapter focuses on the Japanese discourse on this phenomenon, which is torn between the fear of 'hollowing-out' on the one hand and the hope for the benefits of globalization on the other, as well as the industrial policy outcome thereof. It will first give an overview of the general understanding of 'hollowing-out' and its history in Japan. It will then introduce the major push-and-pull factors for offshoring of production capacities in the manufacturing sector. This is followed by an assessment of to what degree 'hollowing-out' is truly perceived

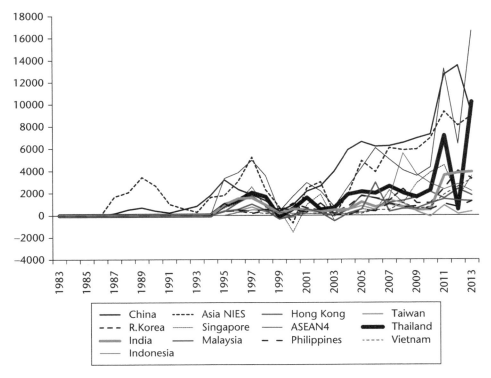

Figure 26.1 Japanese outward FDI flows (in millions of US dollars). Based on balance of payments, net

Source: JETRO (2014). Original data available

as an immediate threat. Finally, this chapter will give an overview of ways that the Japanese government tries to deal with the issue.

The question of how severe the *kūdōka* threat really is in Japan and how the country plans to cope with it are not only important ones, since Japan is the world's number-three economic power. It also matters because other countries face very similar challenges, or will probably do so in the near future. The USA, for example, shows similarities like close-to-zero interest rates, which lead to monetary policy being exhausted as a tool to boost the economy. In addition, both countries feature a huge degree of fiscal stimulus, which has led to budgetary deficits, also further strengthening 'hollowing-out' (Bosworth 2013).

What is 'hollowing-out'?

Kūdōka, or the 'hollowing-out' of an economy, generally describes the process of companies from one country moving their production facilities to another country, therefore creating negative effects in their home country, like job losses, reduced tax payments, or brain drain, with deteriorating effects on the overall economy in the form of a 'significant reduction in the industrial capacity of a nation brought on by the increasing weakness of the domestic manufacturing sector', as well as weaker 'overall economic growth, labour productivity and international competitiveness' (Simeon and Ikeda 2003: 1).[3] Accordingly, it is closely linked to globalization, which 'increases the interaction between nations and reduces the barriers to the free flow of capital and investments', and therefore 'can both intensify and accelerate the "hollowing-out" experience' (Simeon and Ikeda 2003: 1). However, as we will see later, most Japanese globalization advocates stress its positive effects on competitiveness as well as job creation and therefore often neglect this negative correlation to *kūdōka* (see, for example, METI 2013).

Factors propelling *kūdōka* in Japan

There are six major factors in Japan commonly understood to urge domestic companies to shift production abroad: a high corporate tax rate;[4] high labour costs and low mobility; strict greenhouse-gas targets; delays in reaching free-trade agreements (FTA); an extremely strong yen, especially until 2012; and post-earthquake power shortages (Kwan 2012). The latter could be described more generally as the danger of a disruption of production as a result of external factors, like natural catastrophes. In addition there are large distances to new, emerging markets and – as a factor that might have been beneficial to Japanese companies in the past, but is now growing to be a burden for them – overregulation. This is best illustrated through the health-care industry. While strong regulations and protectionism have kept outside competition out of the country for a long time, this is now seen as a major reason for the Japanese industry struggling to keep up competitiveness in the global market (Bessler 2013). However, this overregulation affects a wide range of industries and sectors. According to the 'ease of doing business survey' by the World Bank, Japan ranks only 23rd (World Bank 2014).

Other factors are long-term stagnation and demographic change. Japan today has a population of about 127 million, and this is shrinking. The working-age population will fall by 20 per cent between 2000 and 2030, according to OECD estimates (OECD 2014). At the same time, pension and health-care costs will rise and companies will face a growing challenge of establishing a work environment friendly to older employees.

Logistics are another factor. Most of the freight traffic within the country relies on its highways, and is therefore subject to petrol prices and highway tolls (Yanagihara 2013). Also, Japan's major harbours lack competitiveness compared with other Asian harbours, because of strict labour laws forbidding them to run 24 hours.

Besides these push factors, growing emerging markets in East and South-East Asia, North Africa, Middle and South America, and Eastern Europe are a major pull factor. The value of sales in these overseas markets is growing, while profits are rising (Saito 2013). To stay competitive, it is becoming more and more necessary to be close to the market.

Overall, corporations have increasing freedom and flexibility to move their production capacity to different locations around the world. Firms can avoid the impact of regulations, strong domestic currencies, land prices, and high wages, by moving to areas with cheaper labour, fewer regulations, and more available land (Simeon and Ikeda 2003).

Hollowing-out since the 1980s

However seriously they may be taken today, the concerns about hollowing-out have a long history in Japan. The first catalyst for Japanese outward foreign direct investment (FDI) came in the early 1970s, with a lifting of outward investment restrictions. This was but one result of a comprehensive industrial policy that focused on identifying 'national champions', building up their strong domestic base with the aim of finally helping them conquer global markets (Johnson 1982). The lifting of FDI restrictions helped Japanese companies 'shift [their] production activities offshore in order to enhance their bargaining power with labour and take subsequent advantage of lower labour costs, to overcome rising trade barriers and to compete strategically with their domestic and global rivals' (Bailey and Sugden 2007: 69).

The next significant jump came after the Plaza Accord in the second half of the 1980s. The yen began to rise, and major companies started to move their production facilities abroad. This was accompanied by a rise in international competition. Cheap labour, cheap land, and access to resources grew more and more important. Japan's FDI outflow rose from 6.5 billion US dollars in 1985 to 22.6 billion US dollars in 1995. By 1996, Japan's global outward FDI stock amounted to 285 billion dollars. However, this was only the beginning. In 2012, the numbers stood at over 1 trillion US dollars.[5] In addition, in the late 1980s the Japanese car manufacturers, by then already the motor of the economy, were restrained by export limits. 'Locating factories in abroad markets was a way to expand their sales over these limits. Once they began to do so, they learned that it was also a way to hedge against currency movements' (Schoppa 2008: 104).

It was not until the mid-1990s that 'hollowing-out' began to be perceived as a problem in Japan. Another steep rise in the yen in 1995 gave the starting signal for *kūdōka*-fear to slowly but steadily grow. The manufacturing costs in the country increased significantly. Industries like aluminium processing and textiles began to invest abroad. The automotive industry continued to do so as well. Between 1986 and 2000, the latter was responsible for more than 43.3 per cent of all of Japan's FDI. However, this expansion of overseas production facilities did not happen at the cost of domestic jobs, and was therefore not accompanied by protests at home. Not only did bureaucrats not see this as a problem, but they supported this rise in FDI (Schoppa 2008: 104). Still, in subsequent years, the term 'hollowing-out' began to appear in government reports, newspaper and magazine articles, and book titles. This is understandable against the backdrop of the overall economic situation at that time: After the economic bubble burst in the early 1990s, the economy faced stagnation and even deflation. A negative atmosphere was amplified by the 'Aum shock' and the Kobe Earthquake in the middle of that decade. The Ministry of International Trade and Industry (MITI, today the Ministry of Economy, Trade and Industry/METI) voiced concerns about a growing number of companies investing in transplants in East Asia – at the expense of domestic sites. Amongst them, China became an especially popular destination for Japanese FDI, where wage costs at that time were 'approximately 1/30th of those for comparable employment in Japan' (Kobayashi 2004: 28). Negative effects started to materialize:

> Since the early 1990s, all prefectures and industrial sectors have experienced a significant decline in real output, business activity and employment. The large industrial belts of Kanagawa, Tokyo, Osaka and Saitama [have] been particularly adversely affected. The industrial capacity of these regions fell dramatically throughout the 1990s, and they continued to experience higher levels of unemployment than the national average.
>
> *(Kwan 2012)*

Similarly, the number of workers in manufacturing has decreased significantly in these areas up until today, especially with regard to youth and elderly workers. In particular, the Southern Kantō region shows a significant gap between the number of new entries (100,000) and exits (390,000). However, the overall job decrease is similar in peripheral regions, but while it is – to some degree – being alleviated in the core regions through a significant increase in service-sector jobs, 'in the peripheral regions, the service sector was unable to absorb the job losses in the manufacturing sector, and the overall number of jobs decreased under the direct impact of the hollowing-out of industries' (Hamaguchi 2012).

Hollowing-out in the 2000s

By 2006, the share of total output produced overseas by Japan's MNCs had risen from 8.7 per cent in 1985 to 31.4 per cent. Japan's overseas production ratio stood at 3 per cent of domestic output in 1985 (Cowling and Tomlinson 2011). By 2012 it had risen to 32.9 per cent, according to METI (2013c) (see Figure 26.2).

The number of businesses with an overseas affiliate has increased steadily for at least 20 years. Nearly three times as many Japanese companies have an overseas operation now as compared with 1992, according to the Ministry of Economy, Trade and Industry. Home-electronics maker Toshiba now produces all of its televisions overseas, as well as 96 per cent of its home appliances. JVC and Kenwood feature similar shares for their car navigation systems abroad. Bridgestone produces about 70 per cent of its tyres overseas. Japan's major automotive companies produced 39.4 per cent of their output abroad in 2012. In the electronic parts and machinery industries, the value stood at 43.3 per cent, and it is broadly expected to rise in the future (Nakamichi 2014).

This, in fact, does go hand in hand with a steady reduction in the labour forces in these industries. While in the past Japan's manufacturing industries accounted for almost one-third of the country's workforce in the early 1970s, with a peak in the total number of employed persons in the early 1990s (almost 16 million people), the share had decreased to 16 per cent in 2012. In the same year, for the first time in over 50 years, the total number of employees in the manufacturing sector fell below 10 million (Hamaguchi 2012).

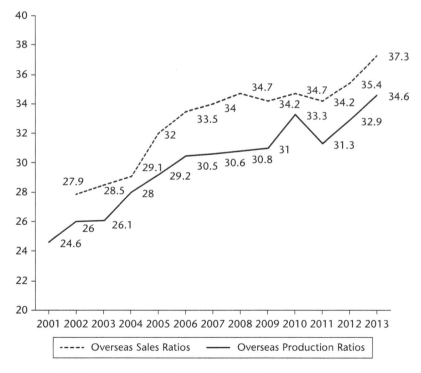

Figure 26.2   Ratios of overseas production and overseas sales

Source: JBIC (2013). Original data not available

A rather new trend is that a broad range of SMEs have already started to expand, or plan to expand, their overseas activities. According to a survey by the Japan Bank for International Cooperation (JBIC 2013) in 2013 some 74 per cent of Japan's SMEs from the manufacturing sector planned to expand their overseas activities in the next three years or so. In 2009 the number had stood at 52.8 per cent. For all manufacturing companies, the numbers were 82.5 in 2013 and 65.8 per cent in 2009.

After the 'Lehman Shock' hit in late 2008, followed by a global financial and economic crisis, Japan's MNCs began to invest heavily overseas, including major M&As. The triple disaster of March 2011 added further fuel to the fire. Outbound M&A deals by Japanese companies amounted to 68 billion US dollars in 2011, according to an Ernst and Young report (2012). That is an increase of 81 per cent on the previous year. The number of deals rose by 20 per cent to a total of 644.

The Great East Japan Earthquake, as well as the floods in Thailand in 2012 where many Japanese MNCs had some kind of production facilities, taught them a painful lesson that they had to diversify their supply chains. In addition, they had to fear power shortages in the wake of the Fukushima power plant meltdown and the subsequent shutdown of all of the country's nuclear plants. This happened at a time when competition from Japan's neighbouring countries had grown to truly daunting proportions. Add on a long-standing stagnation, and the Japanese government's description of the situation after the earthquake and tsunami as a 'crisis in the midst of a crisis' becomes very comprehensible (MOFA 2011).

In a nutshell, most of the push-and-pull factors for moving production abroad, as laid out earlier, have become more severe over the past decade. In a 2013 report, METI concluded, with regard to the offshoring in the automotive sector, that:

> Medium- and long-term deterioration in competitiveness cannot be denied. Overseas business expansion has diversified, and design and R&D bases, in addition to mass production bases, may be moved to foreign countries. We need to keep an eye on this trend to ensure that the key functions of Japanese companies – the source of their competitiveness – are not also.
>
> *(METI 2013b)*

Still, there are many observers and policy makers who challenge the threat of 'hollowing-out', especially as a negative backlash to globalization.

Is kūdōka *really a threat to the Japanese economy?*

'Outward FDI can lead to positive developments for corporations', conclude Ito and Tanaka (2014) after analysing firm-level data over twenty years, extending back to the mid-1990s, in order to examine the effects of Japanese outward FDI on the manufacturing sector and economy in general. According to their analysis, there is even a positive correlation between 'FDI starters' and the employment growth rate, with companies that do invest abroad creating more than three times as many jobs as those that do not. 'The positive employment effects of FDI are accompanied by positive effects on exports and domestic sales by the parent firms in Japan. This suggests that the relationship between domestic and overseas activities by Japanese firms is complementary' (Ito and Tanaka 2014).[6] These findings are in line with earlier study results based on empirical evidence (see Ramstetter 2002).

And even if Japanese manufacturers have been moving their capacities overseas efforts are still being made to ensure that at least one 'mother factory' remains in Japan as a production base [. . .] in an attempt to be able to respond to the loss of production know-how that is accompanied by the closure of production bases [. . .]. In addition, corporations are making efforts to regain their competitive advantage by producing high value-added goods.

(Nakamura 2001)

In fact, the share of GDP of value added through the manufacturing industry has decreased by only a few points, according to data by the World Bank. While in 1994 it stood at 22 per cent, in 2004 it stayed at 20 per cent and went down slightly to 18 per cent in 2013.[7]

Also, some of the negative factors like decline of employment in total numbers need to be put in perspective. While labour-force employment in the production sector has decreased, in the service sector it went up. While in 1985 about half of Japan's labour force worked in the service sector, today it is about 75 per cent (see Figure 26.3).

The total unemployment rate in Japan has been stable, with the rate standing at a relatively low 3.7 per cent as of April 2014. In fact, a shortage of skilled labour can already be observed. A shortage of less-skilled labour is also slowly materializing. Both of these factors are far bigger concerns to the Japanese government. As of mid-2014, the job openings-to-applicants ratio stood at 1.09 – the highest figure in two decades.

For some economists the shift of low-value-added production to overseas facilities is not only necessary but very much to be desired. One proponent of this is Ozawa Terutomo, who further developed the so-called flying geese model as introduced by Kaname Akamatsu. This model suggested that the offshoring of certain production activities helped a developed country like Japan (the leading 'goose') focus on more competitive and higher value-added sectors, while at the same time supporting the development of less-developed countries (those 'geese' that fly behind, slowly catching up).

In this process, each country aims to advance its industries in accordance with its stage of development, while exporting products in which it possesses a comparative advantage. This has worked as a key driver for the dynamic development of the Asian region as a whole, in which both the countries that are catching up and those that are being caught up actively facilitate changes to their industrial structure.

(Kwan 2012)

In fact, one can argue that the very high level of sophistication in Japanese manufacturing industries and the concomitant need for *monodukuri* values makes a strong argument for the complementary nature of their overseas business activities and domestic activities. Many companies state that their product cannot (yet) be produced abroad, since the necessary conditions for their production with regard to the skill level of the workers or consistency of a high-level work environment are not provided in newly industrializing economies (Bessler 2012; Bessler 2014). A similar argument goes for many MNCs, which still have their R&D centres in Japan and plan to continue to do so: 'Even as we continue to grow and advance our capabilities in the U.S., Japan remains the critical base for our global R&D, purchasing, and production/engineering capabilities,' says Charles Ernst, Chief Engineer, Honda North America Engineering Center, who argues that his company has been very successful in the US in the past few years, which did not hurt its Japanese operations or manufacturing base (Ernst 2013).

Last but not least, the industrial structure of Japan is undergoing a general change. While the manufacturing industry's output as well as job numbers are decreasing, the service sector grows. This mitigates the negative effects of de-industrialization in the manufacturing industries and is

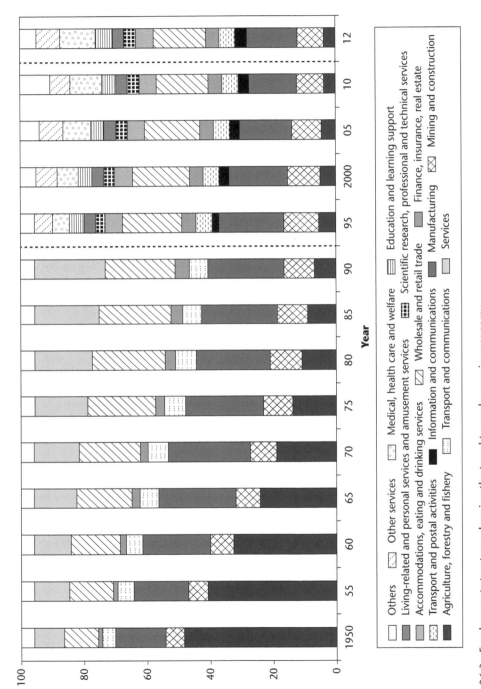

Figure 26.3 Employment structure, showing the trend towards a service economy

Source: MHLW (2013). Original data not available

a 'normal' development for industrialized countries: The rise of a service-based post-industrial economy is a phenomenon common to developed countries, and must be distinguished from an industrial hollowing-out (Kwan 2012).

Still there are as many arguments that stress the severity of hollowing-out.

Negative effects of *kūdōka* for the Japanese economy

As Simeon and Ikeda (2003:1) argue, 'as the manufacturing sector declines, there is a substantial loss of high paid manufacturing jobs. Although new jobs can be found in the service sector, they are usually at much lower wages with fewer chances for advancement'. Also the growth in service jobs cannot make up for the loss in manufacturing jobs, as one observer from the Research Institute of Economy, Trade and Industry argues: 'As such, Japanese service industries are far from being powerful enough to absorb the labor force [. . .] and lead the entire national economy into growth' (Hamaguchi 2012).

The result is a decline in private purchasing power, and thus domestic demand. According to their analysis, the growing globalization and outward FDI of Japan's companies are in fact 'primarily a substitute for domestic production rather than to support complementary production activities' (Simeon and Ikeda 2003: 1).

In Japan, the potential negative effects are accelerated as a result of the traditional structures and characteristics of the industry, namely the *keiretsu* structures and the high level of dependency of SMEs on multinational principals. 'Japanese assemblers are extensively engaged in the multiple sourcing of components, which places their smaller *keiretsu* partners – three-quarters of whom typically depend upon one assembler for over 50 per cent of their orders – in a significantly weaker bargaining position in contract negotiations' (Coffley and Tomlinson 2002). For Cowling and Tomlinson (2011), it is clear that Japan's SMEs have long stood to bear the negative effects of hollowing-out: 'Since the early 1990s, the exit rate of firms in Japanese manufacturing has significantly exceeded the number of business start-ups [as a] result of industrial restructuring and "hollowing-out". The long-standing inter- and intra-firm "close ties" and "mutual trust", that have been said to be unique to the "J-Firm" are now at stake – to the detriment of Japan's SMEs'.

The vast majority of these firms have no overseas business of their own. Neither do they have any experience or the necessary capacities to work in an international environment. While in the past Japan's MNCs were known for protecting these relationships, under the pressure of globalization they have started to look for new partners and suppliers abroad, for many of these SMEs are just not fit to follow them in overseas markets at all. Consequently, these companies are at a high risk of losing their domestic business (Bessler 2012). The overseas production ratio for SMEs lies at 22 per cent, while large companies boast about 66 per cent. Amongst these major companies, only 34 per cent do not have overseas production at all. Amongst Japan's SMEs the figure is 80 per cent. 'So, the key is when, and how, and whether these SMEs are moving out of Japan or not' (Yanagihara 2013).

Kūdōka after 2013: policies

As described earlier, there is a strong trend to emphasize the need for and benefits of Japanese companies globalizing, including their investments abroad. Ever since the Abe administration took office in early 2013, this has been its mantra. It has been one of the primary targets after 2013, and has been supported by all major government bodies and business associations. Asked whether they were torn between helping Japanese companies to globalize on the one hand and protecting those on the other hand, that cannot – i.e. the vast majority of Japan's SMEs – one Japanese government official explained: 'Yes. It is a problem. But globalization is our priority'.[8]

This, however, is not to say that the government has not realized the aforementioned potential negative effects of Japanese companies' shifting of production facilities abroad. Especially since 2013 it has been eager to identify new ways to promote what Germany calls its '*Mittelstand*' – globally successful and largely independent SMEs – and therefore help Japanese SMEs catch-up. The German Chamber of Commerce and Industry in Japan has time and again been contacted by representatives from METI and other official bodies in this matter. When Prime Minister Shinzo Abe visited Germany for the first time in his tenure in April 2014, he put the topic at the top of his agenda.

However, Japan had already started to tackle the problem through its industrial policy prior to this, trying in various ways to alleviate the push factors introduced at the beginning of this chapter.

One example is a massive change in the domestic labour market. To push down high labour costs and low flexibility in Japan, the government has been liberalizing labour over the past decade, with accelerated reforms after 2008. As an effect, the share of non-regular workers has nearly doubled since 1990, to 34 per cent of total employment in 2012 (OECD 2014). While this has led to more opportunities for employers to flexibly adapt to changes in the global economy, it is seen as a major challenge to Japan's social system – since for non-regular workers, wage levels are considerably lower, and their job security is also low.

To keep Japanese production facilities inside the country and facilitate domestic investment, the government has set up subsidies for establishing new plants in Japan. Following the Great East Japan Earthquake (also known as '3/11'), METI provided subsidies reaching approximately 300 billion yen to over 500 firms to remain in the country (Tanaka 2013). While these efforts shortly after '3/11' – and under the government run by the Democratic Party of Japan (until December 2012) – were framed as measures against 'hollowing-out', in the following years the term appeared much less in official reports like METI's annual strategy paper. Matsumoto Takashi, Vice-Minister of the Cabinet Office, put this in direct correlation to the alleged early success of his superior's policy: 'It has been eight months since the Abe administration was inaugurated. Its catchphrase "Japan is back" is steadily being embodied, which is confirmed by the fact that the term "hollowing-out" has disappeared from media such as television and newspapers' (Matsumoto 2013).

Still, one of the central policy tools of Abenomics has directly aimed at alleviating one major push factor for offshoring production facilities – the strong yen. The shift to overseas production had strongly accelerated 'after the yen's 50 per cent jump against the dollar between 2007 to 2011, weighing heavily on the bottom lines of Japanese firms. Rises in the yen reduce the value of overseas profits when converted into the home currency' (Nakamichi 2014). A quote by Toyota Motors received wide attention in Japan, saying that 'each 1 yen move in the dollar has a 40 yen billion impact on annual operating profit' (Nakamichi 2014). Aggressive monetary easing, one of the three 'arrows' of the Abe government's economic policy has successfully aimed at weakening the yen. However, as explained earlier, this has, until mid-2014, failed to raise actual production output, and there is broad scepticism as to whether a weaker yen can be successful as an alleviating factor with regard to 'hollowing-out' in the long run, or whether this offers 'only a short breathing space' (Saito 2013).

High hopes are also laid upon regional free trade. As METI argues, there is 'an urgent need in correcting [the Japanese economy's] high-cost structure [through] economic partnerships, such as the TPP, the [. . .] RCEP, and the Japan–China–Republic of Korea Free Trade Agreement'

(METI 2013). Often, Japanese companies have no choice but to switch from 'manufacturing products in Japan and exporting them to China' to 'manufacturing and selling products locally in China', because of the presence of trade barriers. A typical example is automobiles, on which China imposes a high import duty of 25 per cent. The presence of trade barriers is one of the main causes of the 'hollowing-out' of industry in Japan' (Kwan 2012).

As of late 2015, Japan, China, and South Korea have returned to talk about a trilateral FTA against the backdrop of a general warming in their often tense relationship. The reason for this might also be the successful conclusion of the TPP talks in October, as well as the planned start of the ASEAN Economic Community (AEC) in January 2016, both excluding China and South Korea. However, these large agreements, of twelve member states, respectively, are still far from successful implementation.

To upgrade its industry and avoid a 'hollowing-out', Japan should actively encourage inward FDI. The entry of foreign capital not only facilitates the transfer of technologies and management resources, but also creates jobs and encourages competition (Kwan 2012). The Abe administration shares this understanding and has launched a massive 'invest in Japan' campaign. At present, however, Japan's inward FDI is low by global standards. According to a 2010 estimate by UNCTAD 'the net receipt of direct investments stood at [. . .] 9.9 per cent of GDP in China, and 23.5 per cent of GDP [. . .] in the United States'. By contrast, it reaches only [. . .] 3.9 per cent of GDP [. . .] in Japan' (Kwan 2012).

Another way to tackle the problem is through comprehensive deregulation. Known as the 'third arrow' of 'Abenomics', deregulation has been a hot topic after 2013. The introduction of so-called 'special economic zones' has aimed at solving the problem of overregulation, while at the same time not shaking up the whole regulatory system. In these geographically limited zones, certain companies can benefit from certain deregulations like less-strict employment laws or accelerated approval procedures for new technologies. In this sense, they are supposed to grant a more favourable business environment and promote local innovation potential. This is seen as a potential way to boost competitiveness, which would be most necessary, according to Saito (2013) since 'Japan's national innovation system [. . .] cannot meet the current needs' any more.

Deregulation is one of the key-terms for the industry when it comes to the question of how the domestic environment can be optimized so that manufacturing companies see less need to move production abroad. Japan's most influential business association, *Keidanren*, is much in favour of creating an environment that supports the global competitiveness of Japanese companies.[9] As of 2014, the government plans to act accordingly, e.g. through lowering corporate taxes.

However, really promoting liberalizations for the sake of strengthening domestic competition seems to be a rather recent trend. While outward FDI promotion is not new and the Japanese government has spent heavily on economic stimulus since the bursting of the bubble in 1990, 'most of this spending has gone to protecting declining industries such as agriculture and construction, rather than to cultivating new ones' (Kwan 2012). One reason for this, as Schoppa argues, is that in the past those firms that have stood to benefit the most from globalization have been 'reluctant to exert pressure on the Japanese government to do so [. . .] which in turn led to the government doing the opposite: strengthening protectionism to protect the firms that have [stayed] and adhere to their vested interests' (Schoppa 2008: 99).

Today as in the past, if we believe Schoppa, hollowing-out is seen as a problem – but not as an urgent one: 'The government official's ambivalence about whether to define "hollowing-out" as a problem [. . .] has been inextricably intertwined with their views on the policies that might be used to address the problem' (Schoppa 2008: 110).

Notes

1 According to Simeon (2011) the terms 'de-industrialization', 'hollowing-out', and the Japanese term kūdōka are similar and can be used in parallel. Since in the Japanese context the terms 'hollowing-out' or kūdōka are most widely used, this chapter will stick to these.

2 For the sake of simplicity, this chapter will define the 'globalization' of the Japanese economy as the growth of international business activities and better integration of Japanese overseas affiliates in their respective markets. For just one of a vast number of definitions of 'globalization', see: http://stats.oecd.org/glossary/detail.asp?ID=1121, last accessed 23 October 2015.

3 Although there is no singular definition of 'hollowing-out', the one introduced by Simeon and Ikeda (2003) can be understood as a broad consensus. However, some distinguish between 'hollowing-out' in a broad sense on the one hand, which 'implies a state of industrial decline demonstrated by a decline in the domestic market caused by increased imports'. On the other hand, 'hollowing-out' in a narrow sense 'implies lowered employment levels in domestic industries caused by direct foreign investment by Japanese manufacturing companies, establishing a local head office in a specific country' (Horaguchi 2004).

4 At about 39.5 per cent, Japan has some of the highest corporate taxes amongst the world's industrialized countries. Although, as some argue, only about one-third of all Japanese companies pay these taxes at all (since there are far-reaching tax exemption schemes for companies that have reported losses or at least no profits in the past), representatives of major business organizations like *Keidanren* have been emphasizing the gravity of this matter. Foreign companies in Japan support this view. Therefore the government of Prime Minister Shinzo Abe has made lowering corporate taxes one of the key issues of its economic policy.

5 JETRO (2014): FDI flow – based on reports and notifications, gross. www.jetro.go.jp/en/reports/statistics/, last accessed 26 October 2015.

6 A similar study can be found for the service industry, which seems to be often neglected in the debate about *kūdōka*. Japan's outward FDI has also risen rapidly in the service sector. In a study analysing firm-level data between 2000 and 2011, Sakura and Kondo (2014) identify a 'positive employment effect [. . .] in the wholesale and transportation industries'. In the service industry in general, 'outward FDI has been beneficial for Japan's economy from the viewpoint of domestic job creation' (Sakura and Kondo 2014).

7 http://data.worldbank.org/indicator/NV.IND.MANF.ZS?page=3, last accessed 23 October 2015.

8 Conversation with the author (not dated).

9 https://www.keidanren.or.jp/english/journal/jou003.html and www.keidanren.or.jp/en/policy/2014/027.html, both last accessed 24 October 2015.

References

Bailey, David and Sugden, Roger (2007). Kudoka, restructuring and possibilities for industrial policy in Japan. In: Bailey, David, *Crisis or Recovery in Japan*. Cheltenham, UK: Edward Elgar Publishing.

Bessler, Patrick (2012). Interviews with Kaneko Manufacturing Co., Ltd. and Noguchi Seiki Co., Ltd. *Japanmarkt*, September 2012: 15–16.

Bessler, Patrick (2013). Gesund ins neue Jahr? (A healthy new year?). *Japanmarkt*, January 2013: 6–15.

Bessler, Patrick (2014). Interview with the CEE-BEE Chemical Co., Ltd. *Japanmarkt*, September 2014: 28–29

Bosworth, Barry P. (2013). Japan's Economic Performance: Relevance for the United States. Presentation held at *The Hollowing-Out of Japan's Economy: Myths, Facts and Countermeasures, Symposium at the Brookings Institution*, 20 February 2013, www.brookings.edu/events/2013/02/20-japan-economy, last accessed 23 October 2015.

Coffley, Dan and Tomlinson, Philip R. (2002). Globalisation, vertical relations and the J-mode firm. *Seventh International Post-keynesian Conference*, 29 June to 3 July 2002, Kansas City, Missouri, USA, www.cfeps.org/events/pk2002/confpapers/coffeytomlinson.pdf, last accessed 23 October 2015.

Cowling, Keith and Tomlinson, Philip R. (2011). The Japanese model in retrospective: industrial strategies, corporate Japan and the 'hollowing out' of Japanese industry. *Policy Studies*, 32(6): 569–583, http://dx.doi.org/10.1080/01442872.2011.601208, last accessed 24 October 2015.

Ernst, Charles (2013). Presentation held at *The Hollowing-Out of Japan's Economy: Myths, Facts and Countermeasures, Symposium at the Brookings Institution*, 20 February 2013, www.brookings.edu/events/2013/02/20-japan-economy, last accessed 23 October 2015.

Ernst and Young (2012). *Hunting Growth: Japanese Outbound M&A on the Rise*. http://www.eytas.co.jp/tas-library/reports/2012/pdf/Issue-11.pdf, last accessed 23 October 2015.

Hamaguchi, Nobuaki (2012). Japan's manufacturing employment falling below 10 million: a lesson from the U.S. reshoring experience. *Nihon Keizai Shimbun*, 21 March 2013. www.rieti.go.jp/en/papers/contribution/hamaguchi/02.html, last accessed 23 October 2015.

Horaguchi, Haruo (2004). Hollowing-out of Japanese industries and creation of knowledge-intensive clusters. Paper presented for the international symposium: *Globalization and Revitalization of Industrial and Regional Employment: Comparison of Germany and Japan*. Tokyo: The Japan Institute for Labor Policy and Training. www.jil.go.jp/english/events/documents/keynote_report.pdf, last accessed 24 October 2015.

Itami, Noriyuki (2004). *Keiei to Kokkyo* (Management and National Boundary). Tokyo: Hakutō Shobo.

Ito, Keiko and Tanaka, Ayumu (2014). The impact of multinationals' overseas expansion on employment at suppliers at home: new evidence from firm-level transaction relationship data for Japan. *RIETI Discussion Paper Series* 14-E-011. Tokyo: Research Institute of Economy, Trade and Industry. www.rieti.go.jp/jp/publications/dp/14e011.pdf, last accessed 23 October 2015.

JBIC (Japan Bank for International Cooperation) (2013). *Survey Report on Overseas Business Operations by Japanese Manufacturing Companies*. www.jbic.go.jp/wp-content/uploads/press_en/2013/11/15929/FY2013_Survey2.pdf, last accessed 23 October 2015.

Johnson, Chalmers (1982). *MITI and the Japanese Miracle*. Stanford, CA: Stanford University Press.

Kobayashi, Hideo (2004). *Responses of South Korea, Taiwan and Japan to the Hollowing Out of Industry*. Tokyo: Waseda University. https://dspace.wul.waseda.ac.jp/dspace/bitstream/2065/790/1/031120_kobayashi_eng.pdf, last accessed 24 October 2015.

Kwan, Chi Hung (2012). Overcoming the hollowing out of Japan. *Allatanys Newspaper Guide*, 6 January 2012, www.rieti.go.jp/en/china/12011001.html, last accessed 24 October.

Matsumoto, Takashi (2013). Abenomics and Takahashi policy – aiming to revitalize the Japanese economy' (translated from 'Abenomikusu to Takahashi Zaisei') *Chūōkoron*, October 2013, pp. 82–87, www.japanpolicyforum.jp/en/archives/economy/pt20131125171855.html, last accessed 24 October 2015.

Ministry of Economy, Trade and Industry of Japan (METI) (2013a). *White Paper on Manufacturing Industry (Monodzukuri) 2013*. www.meti.go.jp/english/report/index_whitepaper.html, last accessed 24 October 2015.

Ministry of Economy, Trade and Industry of Japan (METI) (2013b). *White Paper on International Economy and Trade 2013*. www.meti.go.jp/english/report/index_whitepaper.html, last accessed 25 October 2015.

Ministry of Economy, Trade and Industry of Japan (METI) (2013c). *Quarterly Survey of Overseas Subsidiaries* (October–December 2013). www.meti.go.jp/english/statistics/tyo/genntihou/h2c3n30e.html, last accessed 25 October 2015.

Ministry of Health, Labor and Welfare of Japan (MHLW) (2013). *White Paper on the Labor Economy 2013 Summary*. www.mhlw.go.jp/english/wp/l-economy/2013/index.html, last accessed 25 October 2015.

Ministry of Foreign Affairs of Japan (MOFA) (2011). *The Guideline on Policy Promotion for the Revitalization of Japan*. www.mofa.go.jp/announce/jfpu/2011/5/0520_2_1.html, last accessed 25 October 2015.

Nakamichi, Takashi (2014). Japan's 'hollowing-out' means weaker yen not helping much. *Wall Street Journal*, 4 February 2014. http://blogs.wsj.com/japanrealtime/2014/02/04/japans-hollowing-out-means-weaker-yen-not-helping-much/, last accessed 25 October 2015.

Nakamura, Yoshiaki (2001). What are the issues surrounding hollowing out of industry? *RIETI Column 0013*. www.rieti.go.jp/en/columns/a01_0028.html, last accessed 25 October 2015.

Organization for Economic Cooperation and Development (OECD) (2014). *OECD Economic Surveys JAPAN*. www.oecd.org/eco/surveys/Overview%20Japan%202013%20English.pdf, last accessed 25 October 2015.

Ramstetter, Eric D. (2002). *Is Japanese Manufacturing Really Hollowing Out?* Working Paper Series Vol. 2002-24 September 2002, The International Centre for the Study of East Asian Development, Kitakyushu, Japan. www.icsead.or.jp/user03/927_190.pdf, last accessed 25 October 2015.

Saito, Jun (2013). What model for Japan's future? Overcoming the hollowing-out syndrome. Presentation held at *The Hollowing-Out of Japan's Economy: Myths, Facts, Countermeasures, Symposium at the Brookings Institution*, 20 February 2015. www.brookings.edu/~/media/events/2013/2/20%20japan%20economy/20%20japan%20economy%20saito.pdf, last accessed 25 October 2015.

Sakura, Kenichi and Kondo, Takashi (2014). *Outward FDI and Domestic Job Creation in the Service Sector*, Bank of Japan Working Paper Series, No.14-E-3, February 2014. www.boj.or.jp/en/research/wps_rev/wps_2014/data/wp14e03.pdf, last accessed 25 October 2015.

Schoppa, Leonard J. (2008). *Race for the Exits: The Unraveling of Japan's System of Social Protection*. Ithaca, NY: Cornell University Press.

Simeon, Roblyn and Ikeda, Yumi (2003). The hollowing out phenomenon in Japan. *Journal of Business and Economics Research*, 1(6). www.journals.cluteonline.com/index.php/JBER/article/view/3017/3065, last accessed 25 October 2015.

Tanaka, Ayumu (2013). Is the negative impact of FDI real? Empirical evidence from Japan. www.voxeu.org/article/outward-fdi-and-domestic-jobs, last accessed 25 October 2015.

World Bank (2014). *Ease of Doing Business Index (1=Most Business-Friendly Regulations)*. http://data.worldbank.org/indicator/IC.BUS.EASE.XQ, last accessed 25 October 2015.

Yanagihara, Tsunehiko (2013). Push and Pull Factors for Japanese Manufacturing Companies Moving Production Overseas, presentation held at *The Hollowing-Out of Japan's Economy: Myths, Facts and Countermeasures*, Symposium at the Brookings Institution, 20 February 2013. www.brookings.edu/events/2013/02/20-japan-economy, last accessed 25 October 2015.

27

Kaizen: concepts and strategies

Yacob Khojasteh

Introduction

Kaizen is a Japanese word that literally means improvement: change (*kai*) for good (*zen*). *Kaizen* is the most important concept in Japanese management and in fact is the key to Japan's competitive success. Imai (1986) defines the meaning of *kaizen* as follows:

> '*kaizen*' means continuous improvement in personal life, home life, social life, and working life. When applied to the workplace, *kaizen* means continuous improvement involving everyone – managers and workers alike. The *kaizen* philosophy assumes that our way of life should focus on constant improvement efforts. It is a gradual, unending improvement, doing little things better, setting and achieving ever higher standards.

In fact, to have a successful *kaizen*, everyone in the company, from top management downwards, should be committed. All employees must accept the need to continually improve performance, accept responsibility for it, and participate in improving it.

Kaizen and management

In the context of *kaizen*, management has two major roles: *maintenance* and *improvement* (Figure 27.1). Maintenance refers to activities directed towards maintaining current technological, managerial, and operating standards. However, 'improvement' refers to activities aimed at elevating current standards. Management develops policies, rules, directions, and procedures called standard operating procedures (SOP) for all major operations that need to be followed by every employee. If employees are unable to follow those policies, then appropriate training should be provided; or the standards should be reviewed and revised so that the employees can follow them. However, if employees are able to follow the policies but they don't, then management should introduce discipline. *Maintenance* refers to maintaining those standards through training and discipline, and *improvement* refers to improving the standards (Imai 2012).

Imai (2012) indicated that improvement can be classified as either *kaizen* or innovation (Figure 27.2). *Kaizen* signifies small improvements as a result of ongoing efforts. Innovation

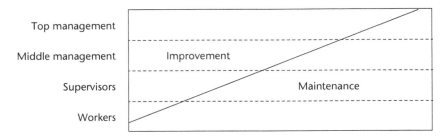

Figure 27.1 Japanese perception of job functions (Imai 2012)

involves a drastic improvement as a result of a large investment of resources in new technology or equipment. Most means of improvement that managers consider implementing in companies are costly and related to high technology. On the contrary, *kaizen* is a common-sense low-cost approach to improvement, since it emphasizes human efforts, morale, communications, training, teamwork, involvement, and self-discipline.

The major kaizen *system*

A major concept that must be understood and practised in implementing *kaizen* is the plan–do–check–act (PDCA) cycle. The PDCA cycle is also known as the Deming cycle/wheel, or Shewhart cycle, or continuous-improvement spiral. It is a continuous quality-improvement model, consisting of a logical sequence of four repetitive steps for continuous improvement and learning (Figure 27.3). The plan is to establish a target for improvement. 'Do' is to take some steps in controlled circumstances to improve the plan. 'Check' is to determine whether the planned improvement is achieved, and, finally, 'Act' is to improve the process by taking proper actions. In fact, the PDCA cycle is a set of activities pursued for improvement. The first step is to study the current situation by gathering data to formulate a plan for improvement. After finalizing the plan, it is implemented. Then, the implementation is checked frequently to see if the expected improvement is achieved. This is followed by a final action, such as methodological standardization, which is taken to ensure that the introduced plans will be continuously performed in order to achieve improvements.

Before one starts working on PDCA, any current process must be stabilized, in a process often referred to as the standardize–do–check–act (SDCA) cycle. In fact, the SDCA cycle standardizes and stabilizes the current process, whereas the PDCA cycle improves it. SDCA refers to maintenance, and PDCA refers to improvement; these become the two major responsibilities of management (Imai 2012).

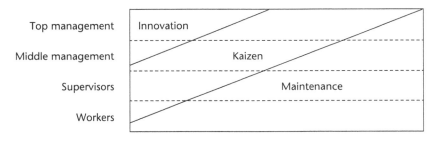

Figure 27.2 Improvement broken down into innovation and *kaizen* (Imai 2012)

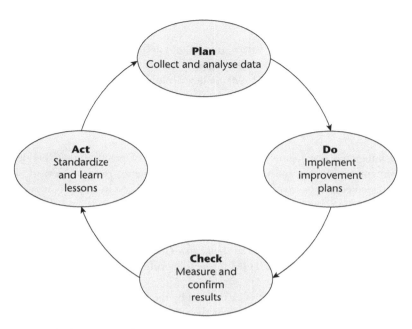

Figure 27.3   Deming's PDCA cycle (Deming 1994)

Bessant *et al.* (1994) defined the *kaizen* concept as an organization-wide process of focused and sustained incremental innovation. As an organization-wide process, *kaizen* requires the efforts of all employees at every level. Among the major potential benefits of *kaizen* are: increased business performance (in terms of reduced waste, set-up time, stock, handling, breakdowns, and lead time) and 'people performance', in the form of improved development, empowerment, participation, involvement, and quality of work-life of employees, all of which address contemporary societal needs. (Hyland *et al.* 2004).

Although there are different definitions in the literature for *kaizen*, the following characteristics can be highlighted (Sanchez and Blanco 2014):

- *Kaizen* is a cycle; it is not just one act. Therefore, it is a constant activity that must be done over time. It should not be an independent activity.
- All people from the organization should participate in the *kaizen* cycle.
- The *kaizen* aim is, precisely, to improve. In order to do so, the organization should focus on eliminating waste and identifying new areas of improvement.

Berger (1997) defined the standardization and organizational designs of *kaizen*. He suggested that improvement tasks can be integrated into the regular work of individual employees, and that, depending on product design and process choice, *kaizen* must be adapted to the degree of standardization involved. Lindberg and Berger (1997) described strategies for designing, organizing, and managing systems for *kaizen* implementation. They identified four basic strategies for the design and organization of *kaizen*, of which three are team-based strategies and one is an individually based strategy. They pointed out that the design largely depends on the definition of the process, goals, and content of the improvement tasks.

The components of *kaizen*

In order to successfully implement a *kaizen*, Imai (1986) defined the *kaizen* umbrella that covers some techniques (Japanese practices), including total quality management (TQM); just-in-time (JIT); total productive maintenance (TPM); policy deployment; suggestion system; and small-group activities (SGA). The following is a brief description of each technique.

TQM

TQM is an integrated management philosophy and a set of practices that, besides continuous improvement, emphasizes meeting customers' requirements; reducing rework; long-range thinking; increased employee involvement and teamwork; process redesign; competitive benchmarking; team-based problem-solving; constant measurement of results; and closer relationships with suppliers (Ross 1993). It emphasizes improving the overall management performance and quality, and involves everybody in the company.

The Deming Prize Committee, in *The Application Guide for the Deming Grand Prize 2015 for Companies and Organizations*, defines TQM in the following way:

> TQM is a set of systematic activities carried out by the entire organization to effectively and efficiently achieve the organization's objectives so as to provide products and services with a level of quality that satisfies customers, at the appropriate time and price.

JIT is one of the key components of the Toyota Production System (TPS), which is to produce the necessary parts in the necessary quantities at the necessary time. It was designed and implemented at Toyota by Taiichi Ōno in the late 1970s. Its ultimate goal is to eliminate waste (any non-value-adding activity from the customer's point of view), and to achieve a lean production system flexible enough to accommodate fluctuations in customer orders. For more on TPS and JIT, see Ōno (1988) and Monden (2011).

TPM is a maintenance system that involves a newly defined concept for maintaining plants and equipment. It focuses on improving equipment quality, and seeks to maximize equipment efficiency through a total system of preventive maintenance. It involves everyone in all departments and at all levels. It motivates employees to participate in plant maintenance through small-group activities, and involves such basic elements as developing a maintenance system, education in basic housekeeping, problem-solving skills, and activities to achieve zero breakdowns (Imai 2014).

Policy deployment (*hoshin kanri* in Japanese) is a process of achieving corporate objectives by establishing policies, targets, and priorities. The management sets clear targets to guide everyone, and provides leadership for all *kaizen* activities directed towards achieving the targets. *Hoshin kanri* refers to the process by which top management's targets and agendas are promoted throughout the organization (Tennant and Roberts 2001; Imai 2012).

The *suggestion system* is a formalized mechanism that encourages employees to contribute constructive ideas for improving the organization in which they work. Japanese management usually makes a significant effort to involve employees in *kaizen* via suggestions. Therefore, the suggestion system is a highly integrated part of *kaizen* in Japan. Japanese-style suggestion systems emphasize morale-boosting benefits and positive employee participation over economic and financial incentives (Imai 1986).

Small-group activities are a method for problem-solving in teams. The team members learn to use techniques such as the cause-and-effect diagram (or the fishbone diagram) to structurally search for the root causes of problems and then eliminate them.

In addition to the JIT system, many Japanese companies employ the *jidōka* (*autonomation*) system, introduced by Ōno as a part of the Toyota Production System. *Jidōka* supports JIT by never allowing defective parts from a proceeding process to flow into and disrupt a subsequent process (Monden 2011). That is, machines will stop automatically whenever a problem occurs. At Toyota, for instance, all machines are equipped with automatic stop mechanisms. Each time a defective item is produced, the machine stops immediately and the entire line shuts down. A thorough adjustment must be made to prevent a recurrence of the same mistake.

5S kaizen

5S *kaizen* is an improvement method that brings tools and techniques into a unified whole, with 5S forming the base that links all the other methods together. 5S is the name of a workplace-organization method that uses a list of five Japanese words: *seiri, seiton, seiso, seiketsu,* and *shitsuke.* Translated into English, they all start with the letter '*s*': *sort, straighten, shine, standardize,* and *sustain.* The list describes how to organize a workspace for efficiency and effectiveness by identifying and storing the items used; maintaining the area and items; and sustaining the new order (Hirano 1995; Ho *et al.* 1995; Scotchmer 2008; and Imai 2012).

- *Seiri (sort):* separate all the unnecessary items in the workplace from the necessary ones and then remove them;
- *Seiton (straighten):* put the necessary items, tools and equipment in order and label them in such a way that everyone knows where to find them and where to return them after use;
- *Seiso (shine):* keep everything – tools and workplaces – clean;
- *Seiketsu (standardize):* make cleaning and checking routine;
- *Shitsuke (sustain):* keep everything in working order, and do this without being told.

For 5S to be effective, workers must make a habit of placing things near at hand for easy access. Workers must practise 5S over and over, and having only the knowledge of 5S is not enough. It should become a spontaneous, natural act of their own volition, rather than something that they are forced to do (Monden 2011).

Kaizen in practice

Imai (1986) classified a well-planned programme of *kaizen* into three major segments, depending on the complexity and the level of *kaizen*: (1) management-oriented *kaizen*; (2) group-oriented *kaizen*; and (3) individual-oriented *kaizen*.

Management-oriented kaizen

The most important segment of the *kaizen* is management-oriented *kaizen*. It is the most important because management-oriented *kaizen* deals with the critical strategic issues to keep up progress and morale. Problem-solving expertise, as well as professional and engineering knowledge, are amongst the requirements. The seven basic tools of quality are used for analytical problem-solving: the cause-and-effect diagram (also known as the fishbone or Ishikawa diagram), check sheets, control charts, histograms, Pareto charts, scatter diagrams, and stratification (or flow charts) (ISO 9004-4 1993; Tague 2004).

Group-oriented kaizen

Group-oriented *kaizen* involves quality-control (QC) circles and small-group activities, as well as permanent and continuous use of the PDCA cycle. Team members in QC circles identify problems and their causes; analyse the causes; implement and test countermeasures; and establish new standards and procedures. Small-group activities strengthen teamwork; help members share and coordinate their roles; improve communication between workers; improve morale; help workers develop new skills, knowledge, and cooperative attitudes; and improve labour-management relations (Imai 1986).

Individual-oriented kaizen

Individual-oriented *kaizen* focuses on *suggestion systems* and the idea that employees should work smarter, not necessarily harder. Individuals provide suggestions on how to improve their work areas. The key to success is to provide employees with the education needed for quality suggestions. Employees need problem-solving skills to make their jobs easier; safer; more productive; and less time- and cost-consuming.

Essential key criteria

Kaye and Anderson (1999) made a model based on ten essential key criteria and supporting elements of best practice, as a planned and integrated approach for achieving continuous improvements in an organization.

1   senior management commitment and involvement;
2   leadership and active commitment to continuous improvement should be demonstrated by managers at all levels;
3   focusing on the needs of the customer;
4   integrating continuous improvement activities into the strategic goals across the whole organization, across boundaries, and at all levels;
5   establishing a culture for continuous improvement and encouraging high involvement in innovation;
6   focusing on people;
7   focusing on critical processes;
8   standardizing achievements in a documented quality-management system;
9   establishing measurement and feedback systems;
10 learning from continuous-improvement results – the automatic capturing and sharing of learning.

The ten key criteria are illustrated in Figure 27.4.

Kaizen *evolution*

Caffyn (1999) developed a self-assessment tool to help companies establishing *kaizen* to make an objective assessment of continuous improvement in the company. It was designed to be used by any organization, regardless of size, industry, length of time working with *kaizen*, and the particular approach taken. Used appropriately, the tool can help firms monitor where they are with continuous improvement and how they progress over time. The results of the assessment can also provide useful input in planning the further development of continuous improvement. Bessant *et al.* (2001) proposed an evolutionary model of *kaizen* behaviour. They emphasized the impossibility of one step leading to a successful *kaizen*. From the behavioural perspective, they proposed a five-level evolution, from trying out the idea; through structural and systematic *kaizen*; strategic *kaizen*; autonomous innovation; and, finally, to becoming a learning organization. According to their model, the successful *kaizen* target can be achieved after the conclusion of those five levels.

Wu and Chen (2006) developed an integrated structural model towards a successful *kaizen* activity. They proposed a system that places a pyramid made up of: (1) a problem; (2) models and tools; and (3) promotion, at its core. The system can analyse a firm's improvement ability from the presentation of cases and find the proper regenerative input from the failure status. Abdolshah and Jahan (2006) described how to use *kaizen* tools in the different life periods of an organization. Through studying several cases, they reported that some *kaizen* tools in an organization were not employed just because they were not efficient. Therefore, organizations are facing the problem of which *kaizen* tool should be used during different stages and life periods of the organization. They discussed some methodologies of applying both quantitative and qualitative tools in different life periods of an organization.

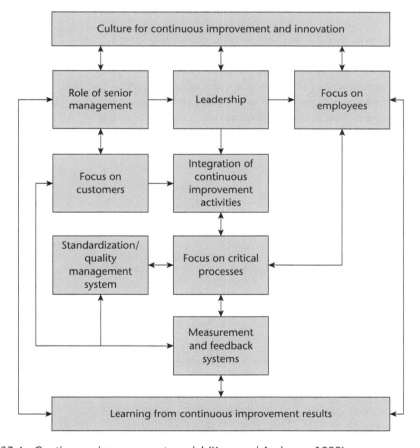

Figure 27.4   Continuous-improvement model (Kaye and Anderson 1999)

Brunet and New (2003) studied *kaizen* in Japanese companies by taking Nippon Steel Corporation as a base model. They compared the empirical findings with the data from other Japanese companies. They concluded that *kaizen* evolves uniquely within each organization, following changes to the organization's business environment.

Gemba *kaizen*

In Japanese, *gemba* means 'real place – the place where work is done'. When a problem arises, *kaizen* says 'go to the *gemba* first'. This is the first rule out of the five golden rules of *gemba* management defined by Imai (2012). Many managers still spend little time outside their offices. Even in today's open work environments, they prefer their own desk. However, going to the *gemba* forces management and workers to work together, at the place where the error is occurring. The second rule is to check the *gembutsu*. '*Gembutsu*' in Japanese means 'something physical or tangible'. In the context of the *gemba kaizen*, the word can refer to a broken-down machine; a reject; a tool that has been destroyed; returned goods; or even a complaining costumer. When a problem or abnormality occurs, managers should go to the *gemba* and check the *gembutsu* (Imai 2012). The other three rules are: take temporary countermeasures on the spot, find the root cause, and standardize to prevent a recurrence.

Kaizen events

A *kaizen event* is a focused and structured improvement project, using a dedicated cross-functional team to improve a targeted work area, with specific goals, in an accelerated timeframe (Farris *et al.* 2008). *Kaizen* events are often associated with lean production that can result in substantial improvements in technical system outcomes, such as lead time, work-in-process inventory, and productivity, as well as in social system outcomes, such as employee knowledge, skills, and attitudes aligned with continuous improvement (Aken *et al.* 2010). Melnyk *et al.* (1998), Bodek (2002), Montabon (2005), Doolen *et al.* (2008), and Farris *et al.* (2008, 2009) addressed different cases of *kaizen* events.

References

Abdolshah, M. and Jahan, A. (2006). How to use continuous improvement tools in different life periods of organization. *IEEE International Conference on Management of Innovation and Technology*, 2: 772–777, Singapore: IEEE.

Aken, E., Farris, J., Glower, W., and Letens, G. (2010). A framework for designing, managing, and improving Kaizen event programs. *International Journal of Productivity and Performance Management*, 59(7): 641–667.

Berger, A. (1997). Continuous improvement and kaizen: standardization and organizational designs. *Journal of Integrated Manufacturing Systems*, 8(2): 110–117.

Bessant, J., Caffyn, S., and Gallagher, M. (2001). An evolutionary model of continuous improvement behaviour. *Technovation*, 21(3): 67–77.

Bessant, J., Caffyn, S., Gilbert, J., Harding, R., and Webb, S. (1994). Rediscovering continuous improvement. *Technovation*, 14(1): 17–29.

Bodek, N. (2002). Quick and easy Kaizen. *IIE Solutions*, 34(7): 43–45.

Brunet, P. B. and New, S. (2003). Kaizen in Japan: an empirical study. *International Journal of Operations and Production Management*, 23(12): 1,426–1,446.

Caffyn, S. (1999). Development of a continuous improvement self-assessment tool. *International Journal of Operations and Production Management*, 19(11): 1138–1153.

Deming, W. E. (1994). *Out of the Crisis*, 2nd edn. Cambridge, MA: MIT.

Doolen, T. L., Van Aken, E. M., Farris, J. A., Worley, J. M., and Huwe, J. (2008). Kaizen events and organizational performance: a field study. *International Journal of Productivity and Performance Management*, 57(8): 637–658.

Farris, J., Van Aken, E. M., Doolen, T. L., and Worley, J. (2008). Learning from less successful Kaizen events: a case study. *Engineering Management Journal*, 20(3): 10–20.

Farris, J., Van Aken, E., Doolen, T., and Worley, J. (2009). Critical success factors for human resource outcomes in Kaizen events: an empirical study. *International Journal of Production Economics*, 117(1): 42–65.

Hirano, H. (1995). *Five Pillars of Visible Workplace: The Source Book for 5S Implementation*. Cambridge, MA: Productivity Press.

Ho, S. K., Cicmil, S., and Fung, C. K. (1995). The Japanese 5-S practice and TQM training. *Training for Quality*, 3(4): 19–24.

Hyland, P. W., Milia, L. D., and Terry, R. S. (2004). CI tools and technique: are there any difference between firms? *Proceedings, 5th CINet Conference*, Sydney, Australia.

ISO 9004-4:1993 (1993). *Total Quality Management, Part 2. Guidelines for Quality Improvement*. Geneva: ISO.

Imai, M (1986). *Kaizen: The Key to Japan's Competitive Success*. McGraw Hill, New York, USA.

Imai, M (2012). *Gemba Kaizen: A Commonsense Approach to a Continuous Improvement Strategy*, 2nd edn. McGraw Hill, New York, USA.

Imai, M. (2014). *Kaizen Institute*, available at: http://www.kaizen.com/knowledge-center/glossary-2.html#takt, last accessed 23 October 2015.

Kaye, M. and Anderson, R. (1999). Continuous improvement: the ten essential criteria. *International Journal of Quality and Reliability Management*, 16(5): 485–506.

Lindberg, P. and Berger, A. (1997). Continuous improvement: design, organisation and management. *International Journal of Technology Management*, 14(1): 86–101.

Melnyk, S., Calantone, R., Montabon, F., and Smith, R. (1998) Short-term action in pursuit of long-term improvements: introducing Kaizen events. *Production and Inventory Management Journal*, 39(4): 69–76.

Monden, Y. (2011). *Toyota Production System: an Integrated Approach to Just-In-Time*, 4th edn. Boca Raton, FL: CRC .

Montabon, F. (2005). Sing kaizen events for back office processes: the recruitment of frontline supervisor co-ops. *Total Quality Management and Business Excellence*, 16(10): 1139–1147.

Ōno, T. (1988). *Toyota Production System, Beyond Large Scale Production*. Cambridge, MA: Productivity Press.

Ross, J. (1993). *Total Quality Management: Text, Cases and Readings*. Delray Beach, FL: St Lucie Press.

Sanchez, L. and Blanco, B. (2014). Three decades of continuous improvement. *Total Quality Management and Business Excellence*, 25(9–10): 986–1001.

Scotchmer, A. (2008). *5S Kaizen in 90 Minutes*. Cirencester, UK: Management Books 2000.

Tague, N. R. (2004). *Seven Basic Quality Tools: The Quality Toolbox*. Milwaukee, WI: American Society for Quality Press.

Tennant, C. and Roberts, P. (2001). Hoshin Kanri: a tool for strategic policy deployment. *Knowledge and Process Management*, 8(4): 262–269.

Wu, C. W. and Chen, C. L. (2006). An integrated structural model toward successful continuous improvement activity. *Technovation*, 26(5–6): 697–707.

28

Consumer goods distribution and logistics in Japan

Hendrik Meyer-Ohle

One of the main characteristics of Japan's industrial structure is a multi-layered distribution system with goods passing through several stages before reaching the final user. On the one hand, trading intermediaries include gigantic so-called general trading companies that played a major role in the internationalization of Japanese manufacturing by procuring raw materials and providing the necessary support in selling finished products overseas. Intermediaries in domestic distribution, on the other hand, vary widely in size and in the role that they play in the distribution chain, with goods often being passed through several layers of wholesalers, some of them being very closely affiliated with specific manufacturers. The Japanese wholesale system gained some prominence in the trade conflicts of the 1980s, where it was frequently mentioned as a non-tariff trade barrier. Foreign companies found it difficult to find distributors for their products, and even if they overcame this hurdle they had to adjust to a complicated set of trade practices, such as the right to return unsold merchandise, as well as myriad rebates that honoured long-term relationships more than trade volume or guaranteed fixed margins across the different levels of the distribution chain.

This chapter provides an overview of the intermediary trade sector in Japan, with a focus on consumer goods distribution. Outlining the underlying rationales and discourses, it argues that, while the intermediary sector has lost some of its importance, this has not happened suddenly and disruptively. Rather, change has been slow and evolutionary and in parallel with the growing influence of certain retail formats, companies, and business models. While it was previously manufacturers that sought exclusive relationships, it is now retailers that strive for advantages by exerting influence on manufacturers to develop and supply products for exclusive sales in their stores. At the same time, in order to stay relevant, wholesalers have been broadening their business capabilities, so that they can serve manufacturers and retailers beyond distributing and supplying goods. Consequently, this has led to new models of commerce where forward and backward integration, as well as new ways of distributing functions, have further blurred the lines between the different actors in Japan's distribution system.

Complex and growth-driven distribution structure

General trading companies

So-called general trading companies (*sōgō shōsha*) are the most prominent and, in an international comparison, they are the most distinct representatives of the Japanese wholesale sector. They emerged with the industrialization of Japan, as the trading arms of Japan's industry-spanning family conglomerates (*zaibatsu*), by taking care of group members' needs to import raw materials and export finished products. Re-established after the Second World War, they played a major role in the internationalization of Japan's industries through their extensive network of international offices that provided, for many Japanese companies, access to foreign markets, either by handling goods directly or by introducing partners and providing information. Manufacturers eventually emancipated themselves from the services of the general trading companies and developed international sales and marketing capabilities of their own (Yoshino and Lifson 1986), yet general trading companies continue to play a major role in the raw material and commodity trade. Here they have acquired substantial interests in the extraction of raw materials and food production as well as logistics, and they also engage in significant trade not involving Japan. General trading companies have diversified into other areas such as finance, risk management, project management, or infrastructure projects, and play a very active role in the development of new businesses and markets. Many of their investments in companies worldwide are related to trading activities, but, increasingly, general trading companies invest as shareholders for dividend returns or to grow the value of companies (Shimada 2003; Tanaka 2013). General trading companies control powerful subsidiaries in domestic logistics, food, and textile wholesalers, and have intensified their interest in retailing by having taken stakes in major convenience store and supermarket chains. Finally, they represent many foreign retail brands and have driven their expansion in Japan (Meyer-Ohle 2004; Larke and Davies 2007). The activities of general trading companies account for a significant portion of overall wholesale revenues in Japan, and the fact that much of their business is very high volume and low margin needs to be considered in any quantitative evaluation of the Japanese wholesale sector (Table 28.1).

Diverse wholesale sector

Apart from the general trading companies, Japan's intermediary sector is very diverse in terms of size of establishments, main procurement sources, customers served and of course merchandise handled. The 2007, and, as of 2015, still the most current survey of distribution channels (METI 2009) lists 273,400 establishments employing 3.35 million people. This number included 43,000 establishments employing 440,000 people that mainly procured merchandise from wholesalers

Table 28.1 Major general trading companies, 2014

Name	Total trading volume (billion yen)*	Revenues (billion yen)†	Subsidiaries and affiliated	Employees (consolidated)
Mitsubishi Corporation	21,950.1	7,635.2	622	68,383
Mitsui & Co. Ltd	11,155.4	5,731.9	426	48,090
Sumitomo Corporation	8,146.2	2,727.8	860	74,638
Itochu	14,566.8	5,530.9	354	102,376
Marubeni	13,633.5	7,055.7	459 consolidated	39,465
Toyota Tsusho	7,743.2		500+	50,423
Sojitz	4,046.6	1,803.1	419	16,132

Notes: Revenues as for the year ending 31 March 2014. Employers and affiliates: information from websites as available in March 2015.
* Includes intra-group trading and it remains a popular measure in Japan in order to rank trading companies.
† Revenues calculated by US accounting standards which are increasingly being applied.
Source: Corporate websites as of early 2015

to then sell it on to other wholesalers, pointing to at least three wholesale levels in the flow of merchandise from producer or importer to final user. Roughly 50,000 establishments with about 500,000 employees bought mainly from wholesalers and then sold on to retailers, putting at least two wholesale levels into the flow of merchandise. The number of establishments and employees procuring from wholesalers and selling on to manufacturers is roughly the same as those selling to retailers. Finally, there were 24,000 wholesale establishments that sold from manufacturers to other manufacturers, and 20,000 establishments that sold goods from manufacturers to retailers and whose business thereby did not involve another wholesaler.

Strong position of manufacturers through complex trade practices

Japan's complex intermediary distribution structure has been related to a number of factors. On the producer side, consumer goods manufacturing was very fragmented, regionally dispersed, and distanced from the large consumer markets, and this allowed a wholesale sector to develop that collected goods and then distributed them to an equally fragmented small-scale retail sector. When larger consumer goods manufacturers developed, most of them did not strive to develop integrated sales and distribution functions, but instead began to rely on the wholesale sector to distribute to a still fragmented retail sector. Over time, manufacturers increased their interest in distribution and began to affiliate and control larger wholesalers through capital linkages, with some first-tier wholesalers eventually becoming quasi-sales companies of large manufacturers. Eventually, manufacturers strived to control marketing activities down to the retail level. To ensure the loyalty of smaller downstream wholesalers and retailers, they developed the abovementioned complex set of trade practices. Trade practices included granting exclusive licences for certain products or areas and especially a complex system of rebates and price maintenance that regulated the activities of wholesalers and retailers. This rebate system normally did not prioritize trade volume or acknowledge who was performing specific trade functions, such as warehousing and transportation. Instead, manufacturers provided rebates that honoured loyalty. This included rewards for the achievement of certain sales targets or a high relative share of a manufacturer's products to overall sales of a wholesaler or retailer. Other trade practices included enforcing strict pricing structures that wholesalers and retailers had to follow, for example that the wholesale price always had to include delivery to the retailer's store, and could not be adjusted if this was not the case. Commission sales and the delegation of personnel to retail shops were common, as was the right to return unsold merchandise to manufacturers. Manufacturers took control over sales channels to different degrees. In some industries, like cosmetics, cameras, or household appliances, manufacturers eventually controlled networks of thousands of formally independent, yet factually tightly integrated small retail stores; these stores mainly carrying their products and prominently displaying the controlling manufacturer's name. This type of organization became known as *ryūtsū keiretsu*, the largest being maintained by Matsushita and, in the early 1990s, still consisting of 28 wholesale companies and 27,000 retail stores (Mishima 1993; Shimotani 1995; Niida 2002). For the distribution side, these networks mirrored the multi-level supplier networks that major manufacturers were maintaining on the production side. This practice provided leading manufacturers with several advantages, such as reaching high levels of market penetration, avoiding price competition, and being able to manufacture and sell a broad assortment of products, even if the products were not superior in terms of innovativeness or functionality. Newcomers were blocked from entering the market, and niche manufacturers were kept small – be those domestic or international (Itō *et al.* 1991). Government policies recognized the need to modernize the distribution system, especially at a time when it was thought that the wholesale and retail sector was hoarding labour that could be deployed otherwise more productively. Yet government policies did not challenge the strong product specialization that characterized the system, but rather looked at improving infrastructure and communication between the actors on the different distribution levels. Support measures promoting product-specific investments in facilities such as warehousing or communication infrastructure thus reinforced existing patterns even further (Bartlett 2000).

Introduction of new retail formats

Manufacturers thus largely controlled the activities of wholesalers and retailers, and their strong position was not challenged by the emergence of new large-scale retail formats. Before the Second World War, department stores had handled procurement themselves, yet already with the possibility of returning unsold merchandise. After the war, department stores changed to a system whereby wholesalers provided merchandise on commission and often also deployed the sales floor staff to sell their goods. Initially, when rebuilding and expanding operations, this helped department stores to overcome a financial crunch and also a shortage in qualified personnel. Later, these practices significantly reduced the risk of ending up with unsold merchandise in ever-expanding stores, as well as the costs of employing and training knowledgeable sales staff, especially since department stores followed a decentralized business model where each department was responsible for its own procurement and operations, with no centralized support from headquarters. Wholesalers offered these services in order to gain a foothold in department stores and also to profit from the information that they received from the direct contact with customers (Imaizumi 2010). The introduction of new retail formats, such as food supermarkets and general merchandising stores, by fast-growing entrepreneurial companies such as Daiei, Jusco, Seiyu, or Ito Yokado, happened in Japan from the 1950s onwards. Initially it was thought that this development would lead to significant changes in the intermediary distribution sector, with large centrally organized retailers dealing directly with manufacturers and taking over the functions previously performed by wholesalers (Hayashi 1962). Indeed, some spectacular conflicts between retailers and manufacturers developed, especially over the right to set retail prices, and this led to the refusal of some manufacturers and wholesalers to supply certain retailers and, consequently, the early attempts of some retailers to develop and manufacture their own products (Meyer-Ohle 2003). However, manufacturers refused to change their practices. Here, they could rely on their continued strong hold over a large number of very resilient small stores, which allowed them to argue that they could not disadvantage their small partner stores by offering different terms of sale to the new superstores. Superstore operators eventually learned to live with or even to use the existence of strong wholesalers to their own advantage. The main focus of retailers was less on profitability than on quickly growing store networks and expanding market share. Thus, retailers realized the value of a capable wholesale sector that was willing to stock new stores on generous credit lines; provided product expertise; and, as for department stores, helped to reduce the risk of introducing new product lines by providing products on commission and even deploying the personnel to handle sales. Eventually, companies in general merchandising and in food retailing managed to establish formats that attracted consumers via the wide choice and quality of their products rather than their low prices. Where retailers experimented with discount formats, they had to rely on procurement channels outside of the official supply routes in order to stock stores, and so could not guarantee stable assortments, thus finding it difficult to grow the store network (Goldman 1991; Yahagi 1993; Meyer-Ohle 2003; Imaizumi 2010).

Japan's intermediary trade structure and practices did not receive much international attention until the trade conflicts between Japan, the US, and Europe in the 1980s. They were then identified as non-tariff trade barriers to the entry of foreign products and retailers into Japan, as well as the reason for high consumer prices that were seen as standing in the way of Japan developing from an export-driven economy to a consumption-oriented one (Ishida and Haley 1983; Ross 1983). Academically, this led to a discussion about the economic legitimacy, rationality, and efficiency of the wholesale system and trade practices. Some academics pointed to sectoral and structural differences, such as spatial constraints on the sales floors or storage space of retailers; the shopping habits of consumers; or the fact that aggregated margins were not always necessarily higher than in countries with shorter distribution channels. The discussion also challenged accepted standards of measuring efficiency, by pointing out that the Japanese distribution system very reliably provided Japanese consumers with a high diversity of products of high quality and freshness very close to their homes, and was thereby largely a reflection of the needs and wishes of Japanese consumers (Ito and Maruyama 1990; Goldman 1992).

Incremental instead of radical change

The Japanese wholesale sector still accounts for significant sales and employment, and it also has maintained some of its complexity, with many products still being passed through multiple distribution levels. Yet, change has taken place. This change has not been radical, but rather it has been incremental, following the changing interests and power structures in the distribution system, as well as advances in logistics and information technologies.

The introduction of convenience stores into the Japanese market demonstrated the limitations of the Japanese food distribution system. The concept of the convenience store was brought into Japan in the 1970s from the US, when leading Japanese retailers looked to diversify their businesses by introducing a small-store concept that, in its development, was not limited by increasingly tighter government regulations for large-scale retail outlets. In the process of introducing the convenience store format into Japan, Japanese retailers made several adaptations in terms of product assortments or shop locations, yet kept to the main concept of the convenience store, which is to sell a relatively broad assortment of fast-moving products in a small sales space close to and for quick consumption by consumers. This concept necessitates constant replenishment of stocks, yet there were no wholesalers who had the capabilities to do so efficiently. Instead, retailers had to deal with wholesalers that only handled a certain product group, such as dairy products, confectionery, beverages, or household goods and, even within their specialization, did not carry the products of major competing manufacturers. Early convenience store franchisees therefore had to deal with as many as seventy different wholesalers, which, in return, faced the challenge of having to deliver very small quantities at high frequencies (SIJ 1992; Yahagi 1994).

Convenience store operators, such as Seven-Eleven Japan, Lawson, or FamilyMart, eventually came to agreements with wholesalers, and from thereon initiated changes in their favour. This happened incrementally and pragmatically, and in tandem with the growing importance of convenience stores in Japan's retail industry. This stood in stark contrast to the demands of some foreign retailers, such as Carrefour, which, when entering the Japanese market, despite no proven business success in Japan, immediately asked for radical changes, such as direct dealings with manufacturers. While Carrefour failed in changing the system (Nishimura 2005), it needs to be acknowledged that Toys 'R' Us was, for the toy sector, more successful by relying on its international buying power over Japanese toy manufacturers (Takahashi 1994).

Japanese convenience store companies at first managed to convince wholesalers to collaborate by physically delivering goods together to stores or into distribution centres, while keeping commercial dealings separate. To do so, they could utilize the relationships between their parent companies and wholesalers. Operators also helped wholesalers to increase delivery efficiency by spatially concentrating their new store openings. Later, convenience store companies collaborated closely with wholesalers in the quality control of services, coding of merchandise, and the introduction of temperature-controlled deliveries. Pre-cooked lunch sets contribute significantly to the revenues of convenience stores. To ensure consistency in quality between the various local suppliers from which the franchisees sourced the lunches, the franchise headquarters promoted collaboration between manufacturers, and even organized the joint procurement of ingredients for these companies. These initiatives were supported through the introduction of advanced logistics and information systems. Rapidly rising demand also encouraged some manufacturers to deliver directly into the distribution centres serving the convenience store industry, yet they usually left commercial transactions with wholesalers (SIJ 1992). In the 1990s with increasing integration in the wholesale sector and manufacturers also looking at streamlining distribution processes, some companies finally managed to unite physical distribution and commercial transactions by initiating wholesalers to set up joint companies for supplying them. The shift to a retail-led procurement structure thus only happened after convenience store chains had become the largest sellers of food in Japan. Operators of supermarkets and superstores followed in streamlining procurement, and, instead of direct deliveries by wholesalers to stores, the goods are now supplied through distribution centres that are either operated jointly by wholesalers or by retailers through third-party providers. A continuously declining number of small stores further forced manufacturers and wholesale companies to align themselves with the needs of convenience store companies and supermarkets (Maruyama 2004).

New models of commerce

Dawson (2007) has argued for the emergence of new models of commerce that blur the traditional hard lines between manufacturing, wholesaling, and retailing. Within these developments, he highlights non-price competition and socially constructed relationships as becoming more important; the increasing merger of the sales of goods and services; the formation of horizontal and vertical alliances; multi-channel and multi-segment strategies; change driven by technology; striving for organizational scope and scale; and finally the inclusion of international activities.

Dawson (2007) uses general trading company Mitsubishi's ventures into the retail sector as a major case in point for recent change. However, the above outline of the state of Japan's distribution sector shows that, for Japan, the lines between manufacturing, wholesaling and retailing had been blurred all along, such as the way in which wholesalers operated sales floors for department stores; manufacturers affiliating with wholesalers and retailers; or general trading companies having interests in production and logistics as well as retailing. Therefore, the more recent developments in Japanese consumer goods distribution that will be outlined below, while seemingly falling into Dawson's new paradigm, can alternatively be interpreted as a continuation of existing practices.

Widening scope and reach of wholesalers

In the distribution of grocery and household goods, wholesalers have merged or taken over other companies in order to develop from specialized wholesalers into general ones, and to extend their spatial reach. They have often done this with the backing of general trading companies. This has allowed retailers to further reduce the number of supply sources. Wholesalers that previously saw themselves as the sales agents of manufacturers are increasingly positioning themselves as the buying agents of retailers. Here they strive to manage the supply chains for retailers, and also to provide other sorts of retail support (Maruyama 2004; Rawwas *et al.* 2008).

Forward and backward integration in apparel retailing

In apparel retailing strong companies have emerged that control supply chains from design to sales and see this as their main competitive advantage. Under the concept of speciality store retailer of private label apparel (SPA), these are either retailers that have taken control over upstream activities, such as Fast Retailing (UNIQLO), or wholesalers or manufacturers such as World or Onward Kashiyama that have been threatened by these retail activities and have begun to develop their own retail concepts. Supply chains are operated in close collaboration with business partners – be this independent logistics providers or manufacturers. This development has not happened independently, but in line with similar developments in apparel distribution around the world. Japanese companies have been following these examples, and are developing their own business models (Fernie and Azuma 2004; Kim 2010; Urakami and Wu 2010).

Private brands

In many other countries, retailers have introduced their own private labels to challenge the power of manufacturers, and often the private labels eventually developed into brands in their own right, with a significant market share. In Japan, with the continuing strong position of manufacturers, a lesser focus on price competition and a reliance of retailers on wholesalers, private brand development has been comparatively slow. Yet, with the increased size of retailers, the need to differentiate assortments in saturated markets; the increased price sensitivity of consumers; and also with the threat of the entry of foreign retailers with strong private labels, the interest of Japanese retailers in private brands has increased. Leading superstore and convenience store chains have increased the emphasis on the development of private brands. This again involves collaboration and not necessarily confrontation, with some manufacturers having taken to producing products for retailers' brands without disguising their role, or under their own brand exclusively for certain retailers.

Developments in logistics

As for the distribution sector, Japan's logistic sector is very diverse, with an array of large and small specialized service providers on the one hand, and the affiliated logistics operations of large companies on the other hand. While systems still differ considerably from company to company, the state of physical distribution of goods has been gradually evolving, from a situation in the 1960s, when functions like warehousing and transporting were not integrated, and manufacturing and logistics were separated. Most manufacturers only developed an interest in the state of the physical distribution of their products in the 1970s, when they realized cost-saving potentials and new information technologies became available. This led from the establishment of specialized logistics departments in headquarters; to the foundation of logistics subsidiaries with comprehensive facilities in the 1980s; and then eventually to the introduction of the principles of supply chain management (Li 2002). However, the market has been changing again, with more and more companies giving up their logistics operations to focus on their core business, spinning of logistics subsidiaries so that they can take on additional business from outside of corporate groupings, and outsourcing the organization of logistics to specialized providers. Within this development, third-party logistics providers that aim to fulfil the complete logistics needs of their clients have been growing in importance, with companies also increasingly seeking to integrate their domestic and international logistics needs. These third-party providers also serve the large retailers by increasingly integrating information flows from retailers to manufacturers. While the development of strong third-party logistic providers is ongoing, Japan already has a highly efficient structure for home deliveries, with some companies specializing in this area. The service standards provided by these companies, and the underlying managerial processes, have received international acclaim early on (e.g. Sekita 1990), and these companies have substantively contributed to the development of Japan's e-commerce sector.

Overseas expansion

With domestic markets shrinking, Japanese retailers are again forced to look at overseas expansion, and companies have been working on bringing their successful formats, such as food supermarkets, convenience stores, or the general merchandising stores overseas. Japanese restaurant chains are also expanding, and, in addition, the Japanese government hopes to expand exports of Japanese agricultural products. Here, distribution and logistics have been identified as a major bottleneck by players in the industry as well as policy makers. As outlined above, Japanese retailers have come to rely on the support of capable logistics providers and suppliers, and can only bring their competitive advantages to other markets properly if high standards of logistics and product supply are available. The fact that convenience stores run by Japanese companies outside of Japan are significantly different in appearance from those in Japan has thus not only been related to different consumer expectations or the preferences of relatively independent licence holders, but also to the fact that reliable logistics for fresh products or pre-cooked meals were not available. The relatively slow expansion of Japanese supermarkets in China has also been related to a stronger dependence of Japanese store formats on the existence of temperature-controlled logistics and high-frequency deliveries, when compared with the less-demanding hypermarket concepts of European, American, or local competitors, which mainly seek to attract consumers by selling packaged merchandise in bulk at attractive prices. This also extends to e-commerce. Japanese companies hope to acquire a high share in the e-commerce markets in the quickly developing other markets in Asia, yet again find that the highly reliable door-to-door delivery services available in Japan are lacking in those countries. Recently, Japanese logistic providers have been substantially expanding their operations in other Asian countries, and it will be interesting to see whether (as in the manufacturing sector, where whole supplier networks have moved to Asia, together with their customers) the same will happen in the consumer goods distribution sector (Larke 2005, Meyer-Ohle 2014).

The distribution system and the 2011 Great East Japan Earthquake

The great Tohoku earthquake of 2011 demonstrated how far retail companies became reliant on just-in-time and pull-based systems. Retailers had minimized inventories in their stores; and in their distribution centres they had shortened lead times. The collapse of physical and information infrastructure after the earthquake thus quickly led to a breakdown in product supplies. Companies struggled to set up available alternative supply routes and to change to push-based systems that did not rely on sales data from automated information systems. The earthquake also demonstrated to some retailers the continued value of working with wholesalers. While regional retailers that relied on their own or third-party-managed distribution centres and logistics had problems re-establishing supplies, wholesalers with nationwide networks could re-establish supply quicker by extending the reach of non-affected distribution centres. Still, some wholesalers

Hendrik Meyer-Ohle

commented that they might have driven centralization of warehousing too far, having considerably widened the areas that single warehouses had to serve.

Market entry

It has been shown that much of the interest in the Japanese intermediary distribution system in the past was due to the issue of market entry by foreign companies, market access for exports, and trade conflicts. Indeed, multiple levels and specializations, complicated trade practices; complex ownership structures and affiliations; and an emphasis on continuous long-term relationships have made it difficult to enter the Japanese market and access the distribution system, yet it has to be reemphasized that this has not only been the case for foreign companies but also for domestic newcomers. With the long stagnation in Japan and the fast growth in other markets, interest in the Japanese distribution system has decreased, yet Japan continues to be a large market and the question of market entry remains. Therefore, with regard to the distribution system, the following points can be formulated. First, when looking at potential business partners or competitors, companies need to carefully assess the business network and relationships of these companies and the functions that they fulfil for each other. For example, retailers might show interest in a product, but might point to a wholesaler as the only possible supply route. The value that a product delivers might need to be assessed within the context of the larger supply network. Second, the Japanese distribution sector is still in a period of intensive reorganization with companies aiming to improve their positions through mergers, acquisitions, and collaborations, or trying to develop new functions or shedding others. This might come with opportunities for foreign companies but might also lead to sudden changes in the position of existing or potential distribution partners. Finally, foreign companies increasingly can work with independent and specialized service providers in the areas of supply chain management, with some of these companies offering services that extend beyond Japan.

Bibliography

Bartlett, B. L. (2000). Product specialization among Japanese wholesalers: the role of policy and consequences for market access. In: Czinkota, M. R. and Kotabe, M. (eds), *Japanese Distribution Strategy*. London: Business Press/Thomson Learning, pp. 164–178.

Dawson, J. (2007). Wholesale distribution: the chimera in the channel. *International Review of Retail, Distribution and Consumer Research*, 17(4): 313–326.

Fernie, J. and Azuma, N. (2004) The changing nature of Japanese fashion. *European Journal of Marketing*, 38(7): 790–808.

Goldman, A. (1991). Japan's distribution system: institutional structure, internal political economy, and modernization. *Journal of Retailing*, 4(2): 154–183.

Goldman, A. (1992). Evaluating the performance of the Japanese distribution system. *Journal of Retailing*, 68(1): 11–39.

Hayashi, S. (1962). *Ryūtsū kakumei* (Revolution in distribution). Tokyo: Chūō Kōronsha.

Imaizumi, F. (2010). Chūkan ryūtsū no shōaku to sono rekishiteki tenkai (The control of the intermediary distributors and its development). In: Imaizumi, Fumio, Uehara, Yukihiko, and Kikuchi, Hiroyuki (eds), *Chūkan ryūtsū no dainamikksu* (Dynamics of intermediate distribution). Tokyo: Sōfusha, pp. 13–27.

Ishida, H. and Haley, J. (1983). Anticompetitive practices in the distribution of goods and services in Japan: the problem of distribution keiretsu. *Journal of Japanese Studies*, 9(2): 319–334.

Itō, M., Matsushima, S., and Yanagawa, N. (1991). Ribeeto to saiban kakaku iji kōi (Rebates and measures to control resale prices). In: Miwa, Y. and Nishimura, K. (eds), *Nihon no ryūtsū* (Japanese Distribution). Tokyo: Tokyo Daigaku Shuppankai, pp. 131–157.

Ito, T. and Maruyama, M. (1990). *Is the Japanese distribution system really inefficient?* NBER Working Paper No. 3306. Cambridge, MA: National Bureau of Economic Research.

Kim, M. (2010) Marketing strategy and the current status of global SPA brands. *Journal of Fashion Business*, 14(3): 35–51.

Larke, R. (2005). Expansion of Japanese retailers overseas. *Journal of Global Marketing*, 18(1–2): 99–120.

Larke, R. and Davies, K. (2007). Recent changes in the Japanese wholesale system and the importance of the Sogo Shosha. *International Review of Retail, Distribution and Consumer Research*, 17(4): 377–390.

Li, R. (2002). Nihon kigyō no butsuryū shisutemu no keisei to hatten (Formation and development of logistics system in Japanese corporation). *Kokusai kaihatsu kenkyū fōramu*, 22 (September): 179–205.

Maruyama, M. (2004). Japanese distribution channels: structure and strategy. *Japanese Economy*, 32(3): 27–48.

METI (Keizai Sangyōshō) (2009). *Heisei 2007 Shōgyō tōkeihyō – Ryūtsū keirobetsu tōkei hen* (2007 Census of commerce, distribution channels), available at: www.meti.go.jp/statistics/tyo/syougyo/result-2/h19/index-ryudata.html, last accessed 23 October 2015.

Meyer-Ohle, H. (2003). *Innovation and Dynamics in Japanese Retailing – from Techniques to Formats to Systems*. Houndmills, Basingstoke: Palgrave Macmillan.

Meyer-Ohle, H. (2004). Walking with dinosaurs: general trading companies in the reorganization of Japanese consumer goods distribution. *International Journal of Retail and Distribution Management*, 32(1): 45–55.

Meyer-Ohle, H. (2014). Japanese retailers in Southeast Asia: strong local partners, shopping malls, and aiming for comprehensive internationalization. *The International Review of Retail, Distribution and Consumer Research*, 24(5): 500–515.

Mishima, M. (1993). Ryūtsū keiretsuka no ronri (Theory of the systematization of distribution channels). In: Ariga, K. (ed.), *Nihonteki ryūtsū no keizaigaku* (Economics of Japanese Distribution). Tokyo: Nihon Keizai Shimbunsha, pp. 207–254.

Niida, H. (2002). The distribution of household appliances: a keiretsu distribution system. In: Miwa, Y., Nishimura, K. G., and Ramseyer, J. M. (eds), *Distribution in Japan*. Oxford, UK: Oxford University Press, pp. 77–98.

Nishimura, J. (2005). The linkage of trades in terms of wholesale business formats in Japanese distribution systems. *Journal of Global Marketing*, 18(1–2): 167–186.

Rawwas, M., Konishi, K., Kamise, K., and Al-Khatib, J. (2008). Japanese distribution system: the impact of newly designed collaborations on wholesalers' performance. *Industrial Marketing Management*, 37(1): 104–115.

Ross, R. E. (1983). Understanding the Japanese distribution system: an explanatory framework. *European Journal of Marketing*, 17(1): 5–13.

Sekita, T. (1990). Value added distribution of parcels in Japan. *Long Range Planning*, 23(6): 17–22.

Shimada, K. (2003). Sōgō shōsharon no kaitō to tenbo (Revolving faces of the theoretical discussion on GTC and outlook). In: Shimada, K., Kō, K., and Tanaka, A. (eds), *Sōgō hōsha* (General Trading Company). Tokyo: Minerva, pp. 21–52.

Shimotani, M. (1995). The formation of distribution *keiretsu*: the case of Matsushita electric. *Business History*, 37(2): 54–69.

SIJ (Sebun-Irebun Japan) (1992). *Sebun-Irebun Japan – owari naki inobeeshon* (Seven-Eleven Japan – never ending innovation). Tokyo: Sebun-Irebun Japan.

Takahashi, Y. (1994). Toys 'R' Us fuels changes in Japan's toy-distribution system. *Journal of Marketing Channels*, 3(3): 91–112.

Tanaka, A. (2013). The changing business models of postwar Japan's Sōgō Shosha. *Japanese Research in Business History*, 30: 65–84.

Urakami, T. and Wu, X. (2010). Specialty store strategy within Japanese apparel wholesalers: an empirical analysis. *Journal of Fashion Marketing and Management*, 14(4): 634–647.

Yahagi, T. (1993). Ryūtsū chaneru no hendō (Changes in distribution channels). In: Nikkei Ryūtsū Shinbun (ed.), *Ryūtsū gendaishi* (Modern History of Distribution). Tokyo: Nihon Keizai Shimbunsha, pp. 119–149.

Yahagi, T. (1994). *Konbiniensu sutoa shisutemu no kakushinsei* (Revolutionary features of the convenience store system). Tokyo: Nihon Keizai Shimbunsha.

Yoshino, M. Y. and Lifson, T. B. (1986). *The Invisible Link: Japan's Sogo Shosha and the Organisation of Trade*. Boston, MA: MIT Press.

Part VII
Interaction and communication

29

Japanese negotiation styles and decision-making processes

Parissa Haghirian

Introduction

Japanese management teams have a very particular way of negotiating and making decisions. This style of coming to conclusions and making corporate decisions draws strongly on Japan's cultural roots, and the tendency to respect others and include their opinions has given rise to a group-oriented decision-making and negotiation style which is quite contrary to Western approaches. In cross-cultural negotiations, the differences between the different styles can often become the cause of misunderstanding and even conflict.

This chapter explains Japanese negotiation and decision-making processes. First, I will describe the cultural foundations of this form of negotiation and communication. After this, I will explain the peculiarities of negotiation and decision-making as they are practised in Japan. A major topic of this chapter is the *ringi* system, which is used in Japanese organizations to make decisions at both staff and management levels. The final part of the chapter will review the advantages and disadvantages of the Japanese negotiation and decision-making style, and its relevance in the modern J-Firm.

Cultural foundations of Japanese negotiation styles and decision-making processes

Japan's unique culture of communication has a strong effect on management as well as on the style of negotiation within the corporate environment.

Group orientation

Japan is widely considered to be a group-oriented culture (Haghirian 2011). In group-oriented societies the individual has a strong concern for the well-being of their group or team, or for the people surrounding them. Group-oriented societies prefer to focus on these surroundings, meaning that the individual is supposed to put the well-being of the group members first, and only after this attend to his or her personal preferences. Not surprisingly, in Japan a group-oriented person is considered superior to a person who focuses on individual issues (Haghirian

2011). This makes the Japanese negotiation style fundamentally different from that in the West. Japanese negotiations are not considered to be confrontations in which two opposing opinions are exposed to each other, but rather as a circular communication process in which both parties seek to reach a goal together.

Team spirit plays a very important role, and also affects interpersonal relationships (Reischauer and Jansen 2005). Group membership also plays an important role when developing trust through interaction with other individuals. In general, Japanese feel more secure in stable and well-established relationships, but show more distrust when dealing with outsiders (Yamagishi *et al.* 1999). The strong dedication towards the other members of a group or an organization is naturally reflected in communication and interaction processes. Japanese negotiators, preferring group-oriented decision-making, try to avoid on-the-spot decisions (Shinnittetsu 1992, in Adachi 1997, p. 5).

This attitude also leads to a holistic approach when discussing the minutiae of a decision or project. Japanese negotiators gravitate towards holism in decision-making, and believe that nothing is settled until everything is settled. Concessions are therefore typically provided at the very end of a negotiation process (Hendon *et al.* 1996).

Harmony

At the root of Japanese philosophy is the quest for oneness and harmony (Holden 2002). Harmony, or the process of making sure that all relationships inside a group remain intact, is considered one of the most important concepts in Japanese organizations. Japanese people try to avoid taking inappropriate positions in relation to others, as this would destroy the harmony of society. Organizational harmony and group orientation cannot tolerate procedures and communication processes which have winners and losers (Craig 1975). Therefore, Japanese generally try to avoid conflict between parties in order to sustain harmonious relationships between all members (Adachi 1997). Modest forms of expression are respected in Japan (Kameda 2014).

Communication styles

Group orientation, and the desire to maintain enduring and harmonious relationships with all the other members of the group, has given rise to specific communication styles.

Japanese are said to prefer an indirect communication style (Kameda 2014), and make greater use of the techniques of communication without language – what Hall refers to as 'high-context communication' (Hall and Hall 1990). Vagueness is seen as a virtue (March 1989, p. 15); Reischauer and Jansen even claim that the Japanese 'have a positive mistrust of verbal skills, thinking that these tend to show superficiality in contrast to inner, less articulate feelings that are communicated by inference or nonverbal means' (p. 136). They explain this as being an expected feature of relatively homogeneous societies such as Japan or other South and West Asian countries.

Japanese negotiators do not seek to specify things down to the last detail, and do not feel a need to go into great detail when speaking with each other. It is incumbent upon the listener to decipher the parts that have been left unsaid (Kameda 2014).

Hierarchy

Vertical interpersonal relationships dominate in Japan, and people have different ranks based on gender, age, rank, and occupation (Nishiyama 2000). Power accrues mostly based on seniority, and in a business context this means time spent in the corporation. It is therefore crucial for a

Japanese negotiator to determine the rank and positions of the counterparties. Japanese negotiators need to know who has higher social status, and where they themselves stand in relation to the other people involved in the negotiation.

The relationship is determined by the size of the companies. If the companies have a similar status, then the title and age of the other negotiators are taken into account (Adachi 1997). Hierarchy is most visible in seating arrangements. Each seat in a meeting room is assigned to a particular person, and is chosen based on this person's rank and experience in the firm. This allows the participants in a meeting to understand the other parties' rank and status (Nishiyama 2000).

The role of negotiations in Japanese corporations

In Western management literature, negotiations are seen as the interaction between two parties which have differing objectives. In the course of this interaction, the two parties present their opinions and make proposals for the outcomes of the negotiation. After this, they start the negotiating process, in which they try to persuade or convince the other party to change its mind or make concessions. This mode of interaction can easily lead to conflict. The final part of a negotiation consists of making compromises and concessions, leading to a result which is the conclusion of the process.

In the West, meetings and negotiations are usually held to come to a conclusion or to develop an agreement between two parties. In any event, the key thing is that there should be a result. Here, the Japanese meeting culture is strikingly different, and it strongly reflects the cultural aspects explained above. Japanese meetings do not carry the same meaning as meetings in a Western context. Many Japanese meetings have a more informative function, being designed to exchange information and to get to know the other party. A Japanese meeting (*kaigi*) can be considered as an unofficial consultation session, before coming to a decision which needs formal approval by all members of an organization. It can also be considered a form of ceremony, which differs according to the different levels of the organization or the ranks of the participants (MacColl 1995).

Indeed, the very term *negotiation* itself varies in meaning between the Japanese and Western contexts. In Japanese the word 'negotiation' is usually translated as *kosho,* a word that has connotations of fighting, conflict, strategy (*senryaku*), and verbal debate (*iiau*) (March 1989). The English word 'negotiation' lacks these overtones, and usually suggests discussion, concessions, and conferring accordingly, 'businessmen who think of negotiation as *kosho* or *iiau* will, not surprisingly, enter the meeting with a more aggressive intent than those who view it as "negotiation" ' (March 1989, p. 84).

A Western–style negotiation process, in which different opinions confront each other, can be seen in Japan as a rupture of harmony. In the West, the counterparties apply strategies to reach their goals: they bargain; try to convince the other side; and present their ideas in the negotiation phase in a very direct manner. This can be stressful even for Westerners; for the Japanese it is often perceived as flatly aggressive.

The peculiarities of Japanese negotiations
Relationship-building and trust

The Japanese negotiation process is thus founded on the idea of maintaining harmonious relationships with the other party and developing relationships that lead to long-term mutual benefits (Martin *et al.* 1999). Social activities are often part of the negotiation process, and when negotiating on their home turf the Japanese negotiators are often very hospitable (Hendon *et al.* 1996). In addition, the Japanese put more weight on their relationships with the other party and the trusting ties between them, rather than on the information on the table (Adachi 1997). Accordingly, direct confrontation is avoided, even when outright mistakes have been made. Kameda describes how situations like this are usually taken care of:

> Japanese speakers tend to use a number of traditional proverbs and phrases (such as *shikata ga nai* to mean 'something has gone wrong and perhaps it cannot be helped' – even if an error could have been avoided, this phrase politely avoids blame) that allow a few words to communicate detailed feelings and ideas without expressing them in personal terms.
>
> *(Kameda 2014, p. 100).*

Team size and membership

Perhaps surprisingly, negotiation teams in Japan are rather large. They include various experts in the relevant fields, and usually comprise five males, with one serving as the chief negotiator (Martin 1999, p. 66).

Sharing

Japanese negotiators resist fast decision-making, because they prefer to rely on a large amount of information (Abramson *et al.* 1993). The way that information is communicated also differs strongly from Western communication styles. Japanese begin with general explanations or background information, and only after such introductions do they follow up with the point that they wish to make (Kameda 2014).

'Reading the air'

Japanese negotiations make use of a number of very special skills. The ability to 'read the air' (*kūki o yomu*) – in other words, to understand the atmosphere in a group, meeting, or institution – is a highly valued skill in Japanese society (Maemura 2014, p. 104). Many authors have seen this emphasis on the 'air' or 'atmosphere' (*kūki*) as revealing the importance of group dynamics in a 'high context culture' like that of Japan (Maemura 2014, p. 117).

Japanese negotiators prefer to accent group values, affiliation, harmony, and interpersonal warmth during their negotiation and decision-making processes (Abramson *et al.* 1993). New ideas, disagreement, or agreement are often indicated by indirect or vague implications (Reischauer and Jansen 2005). The *kūki* or atmosphere can therefore be seen as the guiding element in Japanese social interactions, as well as in negotiations (Maemura 2014). Reading the air also means that many clues are given in a non-verbal manner, where the other party is expected to be able to understand unspoken information and tacit signals. This is often a problem for non-native speakers of Japanese, who, in particular, may have difficulties understanding the various signals indicating 'no' or an objection. To do so they need to be not only linguistically competent (Adachi 1997), but also to possess a lot of bicultural knowledge. Westerners should be warned that Japanese negotiators may quickly feel threatened or victimized by aggressive negotiation tactics or behaviour (Adachi 1997).

The use of go-betweens

To avoid conflict and support group solidarity, Japanese negotiators often use a *chukaisha*, a person to mediate between the different sides. In business negotiations, a neutral mediator can give both parties a chance to articulate their expectations, which helps each party to keep face even if the negotiations are terminated (Reischauer and Jansen 2005).

Process orientation

Japanese negotiators prepare an agenda, and bring it with them into the negotiations. As a consequence, 'The Japanese are more flexible about the order of topics, but much less flexible about the choice of topics' (Martin *et al.* 1999, p. 66).

Challenges and opportunities for Japanese negotiation

Skills in foreign languages and effective communication are seen as the key desiderata for improving communication in management contexts (Yoshida *et al.* 2013), as well as in negotiation processes. Most multinational Japanese corporations offer company-sponsored English classes and support their employees to speak English (Nishiyama 2000). In Japan, many Japanese find it difficult to practise their English with native speakers (Nishiyama 2000).

Japanese decision-making processes

The form of decision-making is closely related to culture (Kerlinger 1951). As we have noted, Japan is a group-oriented society: decisions are made in groups, and negotiation processes are group-oriented and involve a large number of people. This tradition has its roots in Japan's feudal period, when a large proportion of the Japanese population was engaged in rice farming – something which is more easily done by strong communities where all members work together. Decisions were made in the same manner, although older members played a notably more important role in the process (Kopp 2012).

Japanese decisions centre on the goals and best interests of the group to which the decision-makers belong, and the wider society within which they are embedded (Asongu *et al.* 2007). Decisions should be based on consultation and committee work; one-person decrees are resented (Reischauer and Jansen 2005). In Japanese organizations, decision-making processes are not set up to flow from the top downwards, but begin at a lower level. In these 'bottom-up' decision-making processes (Fetters 1995; Kameda 2014), successive rounds of negotiation on all levels of the organization are intended to lead to an organization-wide decision. The discussion starts at a subunit, which is expected to reach an agreement before the process spreads to the superior units, eventually reaching the higher management levels (Ballon 1970). The overall idea is that all members should benefit from the decisions made by a group or team, and so, even if where are power differences between members of a decision-making group, a single person's opinion cannot always influence the outcome of the process, even if that person is a notable power holder. This is also the case for high-level managers. Company presidents in Japan do not have the authority to make quick and independent decisions on their own, except for those who are founders or who own a majority of company stocks. Even the managing director, who is officially in charge of corporate decisions and operations, needs the president's and other executives' approval for any decision made (Nishiyama 2015, p. 268).

The reason for this lies in the nature of Japanese power structures. Within a corporation, each department acts as an individual power centre. The *buchō* (or department chief) supervises a number of *kachō* (section managers) (Chen 2004), who take care of day-to-day management processes and so are close to the shop-floor; being at the base of the business, they are often the ones to initiate new projects, and so can be an effective source of new ideas.

Japanese group decision-making therefore does not resemble Western group decisions, which are mostly based on voting. As early as 1951, Kerlinger observed that there is not even an appropriate word for the concept of voting in the Japanese context. The result of a vote may offend a group member (Kerlinger 1951), or leave some members who are against the outcome of a vote feeling stressed and not integrated into the group.

Japanese decision-making tools

Nemawashi

The *nemawashi* process is a fundamental feature of the communication and interaction processes that operate within a Japanese firm. The term *nemawashi* translates literally as 'to dig around the root of a tree' (Kameda 2014, p. 104). Just like trees in a garden, Japanese business relationships and communication processes require a lot of care (Chen 2004). '*Nemawashi* is a semi-formal but systematic and sequential consensus building procedure in Japan by which the approval of a proposed idea or project is sought from every person in a significant organization position' (Fetters 1995, p. 375). The *nemawashi* process is a standard procedure in Japanese organizations (Chen 2004, p. 156), and still plays a major role in decision-making, even in international organizations.

In the *nemawashi* process, a decision is prepared by asking very many members of a department or organization about a possible new idea or relevant decision and including them in the discussion. This can happen by going from one office to another, or by informal conversations over drinks, dinners, or games of golf (Nishiyama 2000). During the *nemawashi* process, all members are informed about a new development, and can give feedback and share their concerns about it. The feedback and possible ideas for improvement are then implemented into the final decision. In the *nemawashi* process, an idea can be tested unofficially without the risk of full commitment (Nishiyama 2000). In a final meeting, the idea is then presented to all the members who have already discussed it informally. The meeting and the process of asking for support for a decision is thus preceded by long and intense discussion beforehand. In some cases there are also votes (that are often unanimous) that confirm the decision (this is a personal observation by the author).

Nemawashi is 'a lobbying mechanism used by any individual or group wanting to get a project through the system' (Nishiyama 2000, p. 123). It secures the consent of members before the final decision is made. Objections and concerns about the new idea or the project are taken care of beforehand in private discussions. The *nemawashi* process is often invisible to Western observers, who can get the impression that democracy is neglected in Japanese meetings. In an article from 1951, Kerlinger describes a semi-formal group decision-making method which he calls '*Suisen–Sansei–Igi Nashi*'. He describes his observation in Japanese corporations, and explains that if there is a need for a company decision and a recommendation for how to solve a problem by a prominent person in the group, then the reactions of the others will come in the form of a *sansei* (agreement). Even if they are asked directly whether they have any concerns about this proposal, the reaction of the team members will be '*Igi nashi*', which means no objection.

What he did not see was the *nemawashi* process that had taken place before the final meeting. It may seem that all members are required to agree to a proposal in the final meeting, but in fact there have been numerous *nemawashi* activities performed before the group comes to a conclusion that is finally agreed by consensus.

The *ringi* system (*ringi seido*)

Another famous concept is the *ringi-seido* or *ringi* system. This refers to a more structured approach to organizational decision-making in Japanese organizations, which can involve more than ten people. The word *ringi* can be translated as 'circle discussions' and 'is the system of circulating an intra–office document (*ringishō*) in order to obtain approval for a proposed course of action' (MacColl 1995, p. 377). It is widely seen as the most popular and commonly used decision-making process in Japanese organizations (e.g. Nishiyama 2000).

The *ringi* process is initiated by a *kiansha* (plan initiator), who is responsible for the *ringi-shō* (the *ringi* proposal or *ringi* in a written form) (Nishiyama 2000). The *kiansha* starts the *nemawashi* process, in which he or she starts by discussing the proposal with various other executives and managers. The *kiansha* then collates their feedback and ideas for improvement and drafts a proposal document, the *ringi-shō* (Nishiyama 2000). Once the managers approve of the proposal, they stamp the document with their *hanko* (name seals) in the prescribed place. If they disapprove of the proposal, then they can pass on the documents without stamping them with their seal. However, the employment of the *nemawashi* process at the beginning of the whole procedure should avoid this (Kameda 2014). Depending on the importance to the organization of the decision to be made, the *ringi-shō* is eventually presented to top managers, who also affix their stamps (if they agree). After this, the document is returned to the initiator of the process to be implemented (Ala and Cordeiro 1999). The consulting process has various stages. MacColl (1995) presented a model of the *ringi* process, which contains five stages of negotiations, starting with *chotto ippai*, an informal get-together after work to discuss the proposal in a relaxed setting such as a restaurant. The next step is *hanashiai* a discussion amongst managers related to the topic, and after this a number of meetings (*kaigi*) take place until the final *ringishō* (the *ringi* document) can be signed by all participants in the process. This is the official agreement of all members of the organization involved in the decision-making process, and marks its conclusion. An overview of the process is shown in the graphic in Figure 29.1.

The model shows how the initial idea is presented and then improved by the involvement of an increasing number of people. It is first introduced in an informal setting, and then gains acceptance in other parts of the organization with the participation of all the staff-members concerned. In the model, MacColl cites interpersonal interactions as the basic mechanism at work within these negotiations, referring to such techniques as *haragei*, the use of indirect words to indicate a desire to negotiate, and *suriawase*, indirect negotiations and concessions being made to all the other parties involved to smooth the process and unify the opinions presented (MacColl 1995).

The *ringi* system plays an important role in Japanese corporations and meets various socio cultural expectations of the members of staff (Nishiyama 2015). Craig (1975), however, argues that the *ringi* system as such cannot be called a decision-making tool at all, since it only confirms the decision and the results of informal meetings held beforehand. He argues that informal consultation is hard to see, whereas the *ringi* processes are quite visible, but are mainly used to communicate and circulate information about decisions that have already been taken (p. 24).

Consensus or unanimous decision-making in Japanese firms

The building of a common position often also has an effect on the outcome of the decision (Craig 1975), and although this is commonly portrayed as arriving at '*consensus*', this is often misinterpreted in Western literature as meaning that everyone in a Japanese team or group has to have the same *opinion*. Kerlinger, for example, reports that a Japanese unit seems to feel the need to present a solid front to the world, and says that conformity within the group is often what leads to unanimity in group decisions (Kerlinger 1951).

In reality, however, the notion of consensus does not have this exact meaning in Japanese business contexts. My personal observations, based on working for more than 15 years in

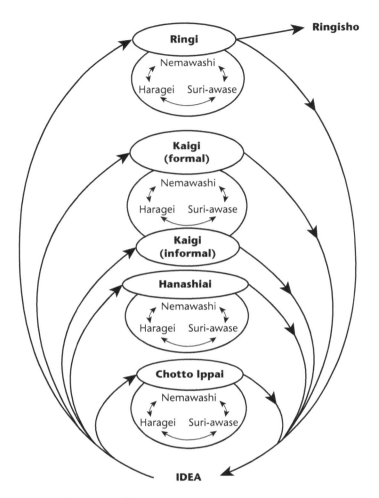

Figure 29.1 Japanese decision-making

Source: MacColl (1995: 381)

Japanese organizations, suggest that consensus in the Japanese context means all members being able to *accept* a certain solution, even if they do not fully *agree* with it.

In discussions concerning possible solutions, it is perfectly possible to state one's individual opinion; however, in the long and non-confrontational process of discussion of a topic, a solution is found by integrating the opinions of most of the members of the group. The overall idea is to develop a solution that all members can accept. This means that final decisions are often smoothed out to accommodate all the decision-makers. Members of the group making the decision are also expected to adapt their views and ideas to support the group in coming to a final decision. Open resistance is unwelcome, and even if every individual who opposes the conclusion may get a hearing, in the end everyone will be asked (or persuaded) to understand and support the conclusion that the group has made. This agreement is very important for all group members to continue good cooperation and keep a friendly climate in the team or work group.

Advantages and challenges of Japanese decision-making

Low resistance and inclusion of all company members

The group-oriented decision-making style has many advantages. It includes all members of the team or organization, and allows all members to feel included and part of the decision that is finally reached. It reduces the fear of being excluded from the group, and makes it less likely that corporate leaders make a decision that has a negative effect on the employees and on the company as a whole. It is a means of sharing responsibility and of allowing all members to improve and support the decision that is finally taken.

Despite these advantages, Japanese decision-making processes have been the focus of criticism in recent years, and are often portrayed as one of the reasons why radical changes cannot be implemented within the J-Firm.

Time

Group decision-making is rather time-consuming, and standardized processes like the *ringi* system involve many sections of the firm and many people, and call for a great many meetings. The *ringi* process thus becomes a complicated and time-consuming process (Abramson *et al.* 1993), which can take several weeks to complete (Ala and Cordeiro 1999). Chen (2004) refers to a survey of the Japanese Management Association, which found that Japanese managers spend about 40 per cent of their time in meetings and conferences. Japanese companies have long claimed to have expedited these processes, but without obvious improvements being seen (Nishiyama 2015). The long time needed to make a decision may lead to business opportunities being lost (Chen 2004).

Relationship orientation

The group decision-making process is also very relationship-oriented. Although the *ringi* system allows discussion between all participants, the outcome of these discussions are often influenced by power structures within the firm, as well as by the specific character of the relationships between the discussants. The whole process may often turn out to be nothing more than a process of confirmation, not a process in which contradictory opinions are aired and discussed (Chen 2004).

Radical versus group-oriented results

Most decisions in a Japanese organization require confirmation from other group members. Even a small decision needs to be discussed and approved by most members of a team or department. The *ringi* system is mainly used when a decision will have an organization-wide effect, or possesses a political dimension (Ala and Cordeiro 1999). It ensures that relevant members of the organization are involved in the decision; they are informed about the background and take an active part in shaping it. Resistance after the *ringi* process is completed is therefore minimal (Ala and Cordeiro 1999); yet the *ringi* process rarely leads to surprising or radical solutions or issues in major strategic changes.

Responsibility

The *ringi* systems is said to diffuse responsibility (Kameda 2014). Managers affixing their stamp to the *ringi* document incur only limited responsibility for themselves (Ala and Cordeiro 1999).

It is not uncommon to have a *ringi* document stamped by thirty or more people (personal observation by the author). Decisions made by groups of this size are naturally not radical, but often try to accommodate all members of the group or the organization.

Conclusions

Japanese negotiation tactics draw upon cultural assumptions that are very different from those in the West. The concept of harmony is often cited as the basis for communication and negotiation processes. Japanese negotiators work in teams and make decisions together, while seeking to keep their relationship with the other party intact. In recent years, these decision-making processes have been blamed for the slow pace of change in Japanese companies. The cultural foundations and the strong orientation to the group impede radical decisions in favour of mass-oriented solutions. However, there remains an understanding within the J-Firm that the decision-making processes need to get faster, and need to open up to more radical results. Whether Japanese corporations can implement these ideas in their daily practices remains to be seen.

The question thus arises of whether Japanese decision-making processes will change in the future. As early as 1995, MacColl had already remarked that, even while such group-oriented practices seem to be dominant in most Japanese companies, there are different decision-making processes at work in companies that are owner-controlled and -managed. In such firms, contrary to the wider Japanese style, decision-making is highly centralized, and strategic decisions are made by the president or highest-ranked executive (MacColl 1995, p. 385). In the Japanese economy of today, many owner-controlled companies practice a mixture of Japanese and more centralized decision-making styles, and show a high degree of flexibility, as well as success in the market. Well-known examples of founder-managed corporations include Softbank, led by Masayoshi Son; Rakuten managed by its founder Hiroshi Mikitani; and UNIQLO, whose owner Tadashi Yanai has turned the company into one of Japan's major brands (Haghirian 2010). It remains to be seen whether these new styles will also be applied in the new J-Firm.

References

Abramson, N. R., Lane, H. R., Nagai, H., and Takagi, H. (1993). A comparison of Canadian and Japanese cognitive styles: implications for management interaction. *Journal of International Business Studies*, 24(3): 575–587.

Adachi, Y. (1997). Business negotiations between the Americans and the Japanese. *Global Business Languages*, 2(4), http://docs.lib.purdue.edu/gbl/vol2/iss1/4, last accessed 23 October 2015.

Ala, M. and Cordeiro, W. P. (1999). Can we learn management techniques from the Japanese Ringi process? *Business Forum*, 24(1–2): 22.

Asongu, J. J., Ho, C., and Marr, M. (2007). *Doing Business Abroad: A Handbook for Expatriates*. Lawrenceville: Greenview Publishing Company.

Ballon, R. J. (1970). *Doing Business in Japan*. Tokyo: Sophia University Press.

Chen, M. (2004). *Asian Management Systems*, 2nd edn. London: Thompson Learning.

Craig, A. M. (1975). Functional and disfunctional [*sic*] aspects of government bureaucracy. In: Vogel, E. (ed.), *Modern Japanese Organization and Decision Making*. Tokyo: Tuttle Company.

Fetters, M. D. (1995). *Nemawashi* essential for conducting research in Japan. *Social Science and Medicine*, 41(3): 375–381.

Haghirian, P. (2010). Wer is hier der Boss? *Japan Markt*, September 2010: 30–32.

Haghirian, P. (2011). *Successful Cross-cultural Management: A Guide for International Managers*. New York: Business Expert Press.

Hall, E. T. and Hall, M. R. (1990). *Hidden Difference: Doing Business with the Japanese*. New York: Doubleday, Anchor Books.

Hendon, D. W., Hendon, R. A., and Herbig, P. (1996). *Cross-cultural Business Negotiations*. Westport: Greenwood Publishing Group.

Holden, N. (2002). *Cross-Cultural Management: A Knowledge Management Perspective*. Harlow, UK: Financial Times, Prentice Hall.

Kameda, N. (2014). Japanese business discourse of one-ness: a personal perspective. *International Journal of Business Communication*, 51(1): 93–113.

Kerlinger, Fred N. (1951). Decision-making in Japan. *Social Forces*, 30(1/4): 36–41. Chapel Hill, NC: University of North Carolina Press.

Kopp, R. (2012). The Japanese decision making process in Japan. *Japan Intercultural Consulting*, 2 April 2012, www.japanintercultural.com/en/news/default.aspx?newsid=154, last accessed 23 October 2015.

MacColl, M. D. (1995). A model of Japanese corporate decision making. *The International Journal of Organizational Analysis*, 3(4): 374–393.

Maemura, Y. (2014). Humor and laughter in Japanese groups: the *kuuki* of negotiations. *Humor*, 27(1): 103–119.

March, R. (1989). *The Japanese Negotiator: Subtlety and Strategy Beyond Western Logic*. Tokyo: Kodansha International.

Martin, D., Herbig, P., Howard, C., and Borstorff, P. (1999). At the table: observations on the Japanese negotiation style. *American Business Review*, 17(1): 65–71.

Nishiyama, K. (2000). *Doing business with Japan; successful strategies for intercultural communication*. Honolulu, Hawaii: University of Hawaii Press.

Nishiyama, K. (2015). Japanese style of decision making in business organizations. In: Samovar, L. A., Porter, R. E., McDaniel, E. R., and Sexton Roy, C. (eds), *Intercultural Communication: A Reader*, 14th edn. Boston, MA: Cengage Learning.

Reischauer, E. O. and Jansen, M. B. (2005). *The Japanese Today: Change and Continuity*. Tokyo: Tuttle Publishing.

Shinnittetsu (1992). *Nippon: The Land and its People*. Tokyo, Japan: Shinnittetsu.

Yamagishi, T., Kikuchi, M., and Kosugi, M. (1999). Trust, gullibility, and social intelligence. *Asian Journal of Social Psychology*, 2(1): 145–161.

Yoshida, T., Yashiro, K., and Suzuki, Y. (2013). Intercultural communication skills: what Japanese businesses today need. *International Journal of Intercultural Relations*, 37: 72–85.

30

Knowledge management in Japan

Parissa Haghirian

Introduction

Knowledge is widely recognized as a primary organizational resource, and as a company's only enduring source of advantage in an increasingly competitive world (Drucker 1992; Birkinshaw 2001). The problem that corporations encounter is to manage knowledge in a way that creates and sustains effective competitive advantage. The *management of knowledge* refers to all aspects of creating, examining, distributing, and leveraging knowledge (Haghirian 2003).

The management of knowledge has been a crucial topic in management research over recent decades, and Japanese approaches to knowledge management have played an influential role in shaping this discussion. The main difference that is commonly cited between Japanese companies and Western ones, is that the Japanese company is less concerned with financial assets and focuses more on growth. This is achieved through keeping the focus on people, talents, and knowledge (Ōnishi 2009). This chapter will provide a short overview of the topic of knowledge management, explaining Japanese ideas and approaches in this field.

Knowledge management

As Nonaka (1996, p. 167) has observed, 'Knowledge is a multifaceted concept with multilayered meanings'. From the perspective of a knowledge-based theory of the firm, knowledge is seen as the most important resource and as the base of long-lasting competitive advantage. Knowledge is thus a strategic asset, and the management and dissemination of knowledge plays a major role in modern organizations (Holden 2002).

Knowledge in organizations is used in a variety of ways: the overall goal, however, is always to use knowledge and information to develop new products, increase profits, and sustain competitive advantage. 'Knowledge management in a business organization means managing the activities of knowledge workers, which is achieved through facilitating, motivating, leading, and supporting knowledge workers and providing or nurturing a suitable working environment' (Gao *et al.* 2008, p. 13). To keep and sustain its competitive advantage, the firm needs to access the knowledge within it, and to share that knowledge with all the members who can make further use of it (Haghirian 2010).

Knowledge management revolves around the concept of the firm as a social institution that attempts to use its intellectual assets as effectively as possible. Knowledge is accumulated in organizations as a result of research and development and the kind of problem-solving that accompanies day-to-day operations (Wikström and Normann 1994). To use and implement knowledge effectively, companies and their members have to develop appropriate mechanisms and rules, which will underpin the structures and systems that enable knowledge sharing (Birkinshaw 2001). Knowledge management can thus be seen as the methods, instruments, and tools that contribute to the promotion of core knowledge processes. In a corporate context, this refers to generating, storing, distributing, and applying knowledge in all areas and levels of the organization (Mertins *et al.* 2001).

Research in knowledge management investigates the efficient creation, transfer and implementation of knowledge, and also examines the determinants of effective knowledge flows in organizations (Hedlund and Nonaka 1993; Nonaka 1994; Szulanski 1994). Just like other corporate assets, knowledge can and should be multiplied within the organization.

Knowledge-management practices

Knowledge-management approaches can be divided into two groups – the *hard* track, and the *soft* track, corresponding with whether they employ methodologies, approaches, and tools related to *hard* technology (the application of science to industrial or commercial objectives, like industrial R&D) or *soft* technology (related to software, database, information, patents, or copyrights, which have clear objective criteria in their corresponding professional communities) (Gao *et al.* 2008). Both approaches should be used interactively to leverage knowledge and information in the most effective way. The main goal in managing knowledge is the development of knowledge-based and innovative products, and at a good pace: companies always run a risk of being too slow in the market and so losing business (Leipold *et al.* 2002).

Effective management of knowledge in corporations can be divided up into four processes: (1) Finding Knowledge, (2) Sharing Knowledge, (3) Receiving Knowledge, and (4) Applying Knowledge. The outcomes of these processes should be directed towards increasing the competitive advantage of the firm. In a first step, the knowledge which is relevant for overall corporate success has to be identified. After this, knowledge needs to be shared with other individuals in the corporation who need it to improve their own management processes (Haghirian 2010). A business organization should attempt to perform these processes in the best way possible. To do so, it needs the strategic capability to exploit, accumulate, share, and create new knowledge (Nonaka and Takeuchi 1995). The knowledge-sharing process is of particular relevance because it allows knowledge to be used in various ways, and also to multiply. The sharing or transfer process can happen via communication between employees, or via training programmes or other teaching activities. Finally, the recipient of knowledge accepts the knowledge and interprets and applies it further. Successful transfer of knowledge is considered a prerequisite for a modern firm to be successful (Becerra-Fernandez and Sabherwal 2001).

Nonaka and knowledge management in the J-Firm

The Japanese approach to knowledge management is strongly influenced by the Japanese philosophical tradition, which itself shows the strong influence of Chinese thinking, as well as of Confucianism and Indian religious systems, notably Buddhism (Haghirian 2010). In the management science literature, Japan is generally seen as a unique country which has developed an equally unique culture (Kranias 2000). This viewpoint is also common in the discussion of

Japanese knowledge management (Nonaka and Takeuchi 1995). For many Japanese companies, knowledge management, particularly concerning how best to share, transmit, and keep knowledge in the company, has always been a natural component of doing business, and likely has deep roots in Japanese culture (Ōnishi 2009).

It is no surprise that collecting information, without giving any of it away, is seen as a strength of Japanese businesses. Information gathering and collection is institutionalized within Japanese culture and Japanese business. Unlike Westerners, Japanese do not question or pass judgement on the usefulness of this information right away, but first collect it – without always knowing about its usefulness (March 1990).

In their work on learning in a Japanese–American alliance, Crossan and Inkpen (1995) refer to an American manager who reported that Japanese employees were not afraid to ask questions and that they spent a lot of time doing just that. He recalled that there were always Japanese people visiting, both from Japanese parent divisions and from the Japanese parent world headquarters, and it was not always clear what they were there for: sometimes they just observed, other times they would ask a lot of questions. Japanese knowledge management does not only consist of data or information that can be stored in the computer: it also involves tacit knowledge such as emotions, values, and hunches (Takeuchi 2001). Japanese corporations have developed intensive knowledge-sharing practices – including awareness-building programmes such as singing the company song and performing exercises every day – along with rigorous induction, that often require several months in which the new employees spend time together on group assignments or outdoor activities (Choi and Lee 1997).

Ikujiro Nonaka is the most influential researcher on the topic of knowledge management. He introduced Japanese knowledge management to a Western audience in the 1990s, and, after this, Japanese knowledge management became a role model for Western corporations.

The concept of 'ba'

Nonaka's concept of knowledge management stresses the group as the base for knowledge creation in the Japanese firm. Knowledge is not developed and created by an individual, but collectively, by several members of a group or organization. At the time that the West encountered this, it was seen as a striking new approach, since knowledge was strongly seen as an individual resource, to be developed and taken care of by specific persons within the firm. Another new aspect of Nonaka's approach was the focus on human beings as knowledge providers and carriers. This was a marked contrast to the focus on technical aspects of knowledge management, such as databases and knowledge storing, that dominated the Western discussion on the topic at that time.

Nonaka also presented the concept of *ba* (meaning 'place', but not only in the physical sense, but also in terms of time and space) in the knowledge-creation process. *Ba* refers to the 'shared context that knowledge is shared, created, and utilized in' (Nonaka and Teece 2001, p. 22), and it is absolutely essential, as it supplies not only the place, but also the energy and quality needed to stimulate the conversions within the knowledge spiral (Nonaka and Konno 1998; and Nonaka *et al.* 1998). This ultimately results in *ba* being the place where information is transformed into knowledge (Nonaka and Teece 2001, p. 22): '*ba* can be thought of as a shared space for emerging relationships. This space can be physical (e.g., office, dispersed business space), virtual (e.g., e-mail, teleconference), mental (e.g., shared experiences, ideas, ideals), or any combination of them' (Nonaka and Konno 2008, p. 40). Knowledge is created during interactions, conversations, and discussions amongst individuals, and not by any one person alone.

Tacit vs. explicit knowledge

Nonaka also introduced different knowledge types into the academic discussion of the time (Nonaka *et al.* 2000). Knowledge can be divided into *tacit* knowledge and *explicit* knowledge. Explicit knowledge is the most articulable and most context-free type of knowledge, and exhibits the highest degree of fit between the knowledge and the way that it is represented to others (Doz and Santos 1997). This kind of knowledge can be separated from its owner, and is expressed in a formal and systematic language (Nonaka 2000), learned by observation and study (Doz and Santos 1997), and can be shared in the form of data, scientific formulas, specifications, manuals (Nonaka and Teece 2001), patents, technical blueprints, computer software, etc. (Doz and Santos 1997). Because of its expressive form, explicit knowledge can easily be processed, transmitted, and stored (Nonaka 1994; Nonaka *et al.* 2001). Explicit knowledge plays an increasingly large role in organizations, and has the most important role in the knowledge economy (Zack 1999). Explicit knowledge is mainly based on creating a separation between the individual that holds the knowledge and what is known. However, this does not mean that explicit knowledge is simple to handle. Articulation and codification of explicit knowledge may require specific languages or codes, and an ability to understand the meaning of this knowledge (Haghirian 2010).

Tacit knowledge, on the contrary, is based on an identity between the person who owns the knowledge (Scharmer 2000). Tacit knowledge is deeply rooted in action, commitment, and involvement in a specific context (Nonaka 1994). Polanyi (1985) observed that, although people may be *able* to perform certain tasks, they may not be able to *articulate* the way that they perform these. Performing an activity is not the same as explaining the very same action. Tacit knowledge is therefore not only strongly connected to the knowledge owner, but also located within an individual. It refers to knowledge that is not easily articulated, and can be described as know-how that is acquired via learned behaviour and procedures (Howells 1996). In fact, knowledge can never be fully explicit, and always shows a certain degree of tacitness. Even if knowledge can be separated from its owner and put down in words or other explicit forms, there is still a part of it which stays tacit and cannot be extracted and therefore cannot be easily shared (Haghirian 2010).

The Japanese preference for tacit knowledge

East and West further differ in the types of knowledge that they prefer. Japanese knowledge management is strongly dependent on tacit knowledge, embedded in individuals (Haghirian 2010). The tradition of communication without language is called *isshin denshin* in Japanese, and has been strongly influenced by Zen Buddhism. It is believed that the most important things cannot be communicated in language, and indeed that language is only useful for rather secondary or trivial messages (Scollon and Wong-Scollon 1995).

Japanese managers therefore put more emphasis on tacit knowledge (Takeuchi 2001), and Japanese employees understand exactly what to do without being told explicitly. Business practices also make relatively greater use of tacit understanding: for example, written contracts are kept simple or do not even exist, whereas a Western firm would expect a great deal of articulation. Social situations have to be 'read' with great precision, and a talent for working with tacit knowledge is important (Hedlund and Nonaka 1993).

The idea that not all knowledge needs to be articulated and that people are the main carriers of knowledge strongly influences the way that knowledge is perceived in Japanese management, and information flows freely in Japanese firms. The emphasis is on stored rather than on transmitted information. Furthermore, channels are seldom overloaded, because people stay in constant contact. Interpersonal contacts take precedence over everything else (Hall and Hall 1990). Japanese firms use various means such as symbols, analogies, and similar means to codify tacit knowledge: these represent a codification of tacit knowledge which is only understood by them (Dutrénit 2000). The idea of viewing people as a long-term investment was a major part of what enabled many Japanese companies to grow and prosper. Because of this, employees and workers became storehouses for information and knowledge that was often highly specific to the company for which they worked, and was seen as more important than the possession of a specific skill-set such as accounting or welding (Ōnishi 2009).

For Japanese companies and their employees, this emphasis on personnel is not a problem, since many companies still practice lifetime employment and can expect their employees to stay with them for many years. As a consequence, in many Japanese companies the processes are not documented at all, and can only be managed by involving experienced staff members (Haghirian 2010).

Western firms, on the other hand, do not expect their employees to spend a lifetime with them, and Western knowledge-management activities focus on the individual as a knowledge creator. Western firms prefer explicit knowledge, or knowledge which is abstracted from people and can be stored easily in databases, or other forms such as process documentation and activity reports. The corporation thus becomes independent from their employees, who may leave and take their knowledge with them.

The SECI process

In his work, Nonaka describes how Japanese companies gain competitive advantage by their use of tacit knowledge (Nonaka and Takeuchi 1995). The famous SECI model developed by Nonaka sets out knowledge creation as a spiral process of interaction between explicit and tacit knowledge. Nonaka's (1996) spiral refers to the interrelationship between the epistemological and ontological dimensions of knowledge creation. The combination of the two categories makes it possible to conceptualize four conversion patterns (*socialization*, *externalization*, *combination*, and *internalization*: hence the name 'SECI model'). The first step, socialization, involves the sharing of tacit knowledge between individuals (Nonaka and Konno 1998). This stage is the start of the SECI process: the employees empathize with their colleagues and customers, diminishing barriers and setting the stage for the sharing of knowledge (socialization). Then, once the individual is committed to the group, and becomes one with the group by aligning their intentions and ideas with that of the group (externalization, where tacit knowledge is made explicit by communicating it to the other) the new knowledge created through externalization is made available to the group through digital or analogue signals (combination). Here explicit knowledge leads to more explicit knowledge. Finally, the individual can then access the knowledge of the group, and even the entire organization (internalization). At this stage, explicit knowledge becomes tacit once again (see Nonaka and Teece 2001, especially page 21).

New product development

Knowledge management also plays an important role when developing new products, and, again, Japanese corporations undertake this in a manner that is different from their Western counterparts. Nonaka and Takeuchi (1995) describe the distinct approach adopted by knowledge managers and new-product developers in Japan. Interaction between the individuals involved in the process naturally plays an important role in leveraging and developing new ideas (Nonaka 1996). New-product development is undertaken by large, multifunctional teams. These teams are made up of internal representatives from different departments of the firm, such as engineering, production, and marketing, and external representatives from suppliers and subcontractors (Dobi and Bugar 2008). The exchange between tacit and explicit knowledge also plays a very important role in these processes.

Cultural differences in knowledge management

Japanese and Western approaches to knowledge management thus differ greatly. These differences in how to deal with and implement information and knowledge in the firm have attracted a lot of interest from Western researchers and managers. An overview of these two concepts is given in Table 30.1.

The first difference refers to the type of knowledge preferred respectively in Japan and in Western countries. Japanese corporations prefer group knowledge, and think that knowledge which is developed by a team or group and which supports all its members is superior to knowledge developed by an individual. Western organizations, on the other hand, show a preference for individual knowledge, and see it as a power source. Their employees tend to focus on improving their personal skills and knowledge to support their careers and improve their competitive position within the firm and in the labour market. Western employees and managers therefore have a tendency to share knowledge only very carefully, and often do not share it. Sharing too freely may be seen as a danger for one's career.

Japanese employees, on the other hand, see their knowledge as supportive for their team or corporation. Since they often prefer to stay and work in companies for many years, they do not use knowledge as a means to strengthen their position in the firm, and so share knowledge more frequently. Based on these differences, employees also take different roles in knowledge acquisition. In Western companies, employees take an active role in acquiring knowledge and skills, and they use these skills to manage their careers. In a Japanese company, employees are often overwhelmed with knowledge and find it very difficult to deal with the quantity of it. They do not take an active part in acquiring it, but share it freely.

Table 30.1 Knowledge as a source of power in the West and Japan (Haghirian 2010)

Western knowledge management	Japanese knowledge management
Individual knowledge is thought to improve an individual's position or future in the company	Group knowledge is considered to improve the group's or organization's power and consequently its members' position too
Employees attempt to gain specialized and individual knowledge to increase their personal competitive advantage within the company or on the job market	Employees do not attempt to gain specialized and individual knowledge to increase their personal competitive advantages within the company
Employees may block knowledge-sharing and knowledge-transfer activities	Employees support knowledge-sharing and knowledge-transfer activities
Employees always take responsibility for knowledge acquisition, and actively search for and investigate new knowledge for their personal use	Employees do not always take responsibility for individual knowledge acquisition, and often passively wait to receive knowledge from their group or organization

Parissa Haghirian

Sharing knowledge within the Japanese organization

One of the major aspects of managing knowledge concerns transferring it effectively between various members of the corporation. The different roles that knowledge has in the East and West are also reflected in how it is shared within the firm.

Western organizations try to make their employees exchange and share knowledge. This often proves to be a very difficult undertaking, however, since in Western companies employees fear a loss of power or are afraid of becoming redundant if they share too freely (Haghirian 2010).

Trust-based relationships in the Japanese firm allow easier sharing of knowledge. Group ideas are best accepted and can be used without major conflicts (Tudor et al. 1996). The firm is able to maintain a competitive environment while decentralizing much of the internal information, reacting quickly to changes in the market or problems on the shop-floor using an autonomous problem-solving and group-consensus mentality (Aoki 1988, p. 49–50).

When sharing knowledge within a multinational corporation or a multinational team, these differences become even more obvious. Japanese employees and their Western counterparts have differing understandings of how to share knowledge with their colleagues and amongst partners (Inkpen 1996), and also about receiving and implementing knowledge from different sources. As remarked above, knowledge managers in Japan share knowledge more easily than their counterparts in other industrialized countries. Communication between individuals in high-context countries[1] (Japan) and low-context countries (e.g. Germany) differs significantly with respect to the amount of information transferred (Li 1999).

In knowledge-transfer relationships, interlocutors who are members of different cultures communicated less information than those who were members of the same culture, but low-context/low-context communication relationships do not differ from high-context/high-context relationships in this respect. These differences in communication between high-context and low-context cultures have led to tremendous losses of relevant knowledge within the transfer process between these groups (Li 1999). Richter (1995) reports that, due to cultural differences, many German foreign investors in Japan are capable of accessing corporate knowledge located in their subsidiaries, but do not manage to transfer it back to Germany and successfully implement it. To assure effective knowledge transfer, the knowledge sent needs to be couched in a format that can be understood by the receiver (Thomas 2002). This is difficult where the sender and the receiver of the knowledge have different cultural backgrounds, because often knowledge cannot be considered universal, but rather is culture-specific (Roth 2001).

These differences can also be observed in cases of cross-cultural knowledge transfer between Japanese and Western managers. Japanese managers show a higher acceptance when receiving this knowledge from non-Japanese sources than Western managers do upon receiving knowledge from foreign sources (Haghirian 2010). And we can also see that Japanese managers have a high capability to integrate and accept knowledge without being unduly influenced by its origins. Japanese managers, as knowledge-management literature has long pointed out, have a very open approach to knowledge (Nonaka and Takeuchi 1995). Indeed, the origin of the knowledge may not play a very important role at all. Inkpen and Crossan (1995) showed that Japanese corporations are more willing to invest in the creation and the transfer of knowledge from overseas partners, and may be better fitted to recognize the benefits of these knowledge-transfer processes.

Conclusions

In a time where the rapid market introduction of innovations and new ideas can decide the future of a company, knowledge management has become a major management discipline for multinational corporations.

Japanese knowledge management was introduced to Western researchers and managers by Ikujiro Nonaka in the 1980s. Its approach differed from Western approaches at that time, which focused on knowledge as an asset to be managed mainly in the form of databases and other knowledge-storage assets.

The Japanese approach, on the other hand, stresses the importance of the members of an organization as the main carriers of knowledge and information. Because of this, Japanese corporations have a stronger focus on knowledge based in people, and have developed specific knowledge-management practices which allow them to leverage this tacit knowledge and use it to develop a sustainable competitive advantage. Knowledge-creation processes are therefore seen as interactions between members of an organization. New product development in Japan is also based on these principles. Knowledge is created via metaphors and circular communication processes encompassing all the members of the development team.

Western organizations try to make their members share and communicate knowledge; and often their members are rather reluctant to do this, since, in a Western context, knowledge is power – and sharing too much of it may have a negative effect on the individual's position in a company. Japanese companies have a different approach. Here, knowledge sharing is a frequent practice, and is more supported by Japanese managers. This also extends to sharing processes within multinational firms, where Japanese managers are more open to knowledge that comes from outside sources or foreign units than the typical Western manager.

Incontestably, the Japanese approach to knowledge management, considered so unorthodox when it was first introduced to the West, has come to exert a powerful influence on Western research and management approaches in this field.

Note

1 Li (1999) refers to Hall's concept of high-context and low-context countries: see Hall, E. T. and Hall, M. R. (1990): *Understanding Cultural Differences*. Yarmouth, MD: Intercultural Press.

Bibliography

Aoki, Masahiko (1988). *Information, Incentives, and Bargaining in the Japanese Economy*. Cambridge, UK: Cambridge University Press.

Becerra-Fernandez, I. and Sabherwal, R. (2001). Organizational knowledge management: a contingency perspective. *Journal of Management Information Systems*, 18(1): 23–55.

Birkinshaw, J. (2001). Why is knowledge management so difficult? *Business Strategy Review*, 12(1): 11–18.

Casrnir, F. L. (1999). Foundations for the study of intercultural communication based on a third-culture building model. *International Journal of Intercultural Relations*, 23(1): 91–116.

Choi, C. J. and Lee, S. H. (1997). A knowledge-based view of cooperative interorganizational relationships. In: Killing, P. J. (ed.), *Cooperative Strategies*. San Francisco, CA: New Lexington Press.

Crossan, M. and Inkpen, A. C. (1995). The subtle art of learning through alliances. *Business Quarterly*, 60(2): 68–85.

Crystal, D. (1997). *English as a Global Language*. Cambridge, UK: Cambridge University Press.

Dobi, S. and Bugar, L. (2008). Japanese Management Strategies. *Proceedings of the MEB 2008 – 6th International Conference on Management, Enterprise and Benchmarking*, May 30–31 2008, Budapest, Hungary. Budapest: MEB 2008.

Doz, Y. and Santos, J. F. P. (1997). *On the Management of Knowledge: From the Transparency of Collocation and Co-setting to the Quandary of Dispersion and Differentiation*. INSEAD Working Paper Series, Vol. 97/119/SM, Fontainebleau, France: INSEAD.

Drucker, P. F. (1992). The new society of organizations. *Harvard Business Review*, 70(5): 95–104.

Dutrénit, G. (2000). *Learning and Knowledge Management in the Firm*. Cheltenham, UK: Edward Elgar.

Gao, Fei, Li, Meng, and Clarke, Steve (2008). Knowledge, management, and knowledge management in business operations. *Journal of Knowledge Management*, 12(2): 3–17.

Haghirian, P. (2003). *Communicating Knowledge within Euro-Japanese Multinational Corporations.* Vienna University of Economics and Business Administration: Unpublished Dissertation.

Haghirian, P. (2010). *Multinationals and Cross-Cultural Management: The Transfer of Knowledge within Multinational Corporations.* Abingdon, UK: Routledge International Business in Asia Series.

Hall, E. T. and Hall, M. R. (1990). *Understanding Cultural Differences.* Yarmouth, Maine: Intercultural Press.

Hayashi, K. (2003). Current intercultural issues and challenges in Japanese business interfaces: blending theory and practice. *Management Japan*, 38, www.iijnet.org.jp/imaj/mj/hayashi35.pdf.

Hedlund, G. and Nonaka, I. (1993). Models of knowledge management in the West and Japan. In: Lorange, P. (ed.), *Implementing Strategic Processes: Change, Learning and Co-operation.* Oxford, UK: Basil Blackwell, pp. 117–144.

Holden, N. (2002) *Cross-Cultural Management: A Knowledge Management Perspective.* Harlow: Financial Times, Prentice Hall.

Howells, J. (1996). Tacit knowledge, innovation and technology transfer. *Technology Analysis and Strategic Management*, 8: 91–105.

Inkpen, A. C. (1996). Creating knowledge through collaboration. *Californian Management Review*, 39(1): 123–140.

Inkpen, A. C. and Crossan, M. M. (1995). Believing is seeing: joint ventures and organization learning. *Journal of Management Studies*, 32(5): 595–618.

Johanson, J. and Vahlen, J.-E. (1977). The internationalization process of the firm – a model of knowledge development and increasing foreign market commitments. *Journal of International Business Studies*, 8(1): 23–32.

Kameda, N. (2000). Communication competency of Japanese managers in Singapore. *Corporate Communication: An International Journal*, 5(4): 204–209.

Kim, Y. (1988). *Communication and Cross-Cultural Adaptation: An Integrative Theory.* Clevedon, UK: Multilingual Matters.

Kranias, D. S. (2000). Cultural control: the case of Japanese multinational companies and their subsidiaries in the UK. *Management Decision*, 38(9): 638–648.

Leipold, M., Probst, G. J. B., and Gibbert, M. (2002). *Strategic management in the knowledge economy.* Erlangen, Germany: Publicis and Wiley.

Li, H. Z. (1999). Communicating information in conversations: a cross cultural comparison. *International Journal of Intercultural Relations*, 23(3): 387–409.

Maasdorp, C. (2001). *Bridging Individual and Organizational Knowledge: The Appeal to Tacit Knowledge in Knowledge Management Theory.* www.hds.utc.fr/~barthes/ISMICK01/papers/IS01-Maasdorp.pdf, last accessed 23 October 2015.

March, R. M. (1990). *The Japanese Negotiator: Subtlety and Strategy Beyond Western Logic.* Tokyo: Kodansha International.

Mertins, K., Heisig, P., and Vorbeck, J. (2001). Introduction. In: Vorbeck, J. (ed.), *Knowledge Management: Best Practices in Europe.* Heidelberg, Germany: Springer.

Nonaka, I. (1994). A dynamic theory of organizational knowledge creation. *Organization Science*, 5: 14–37.

Nonaka, I. (1996). A dynamic theory of organizational knowledge creation. In: Starkey, K., Tempest, S., and McKinley, A. (eds), *How Organizations Learn.* London: Thomson Learning, pp. 165–201.

Nonaka, I. and Konno, N. (1998). The concept of 'ba': building a foundation for knowledge creation. *California Management Review*, 40(3): 40–54.

Nonaka, I. and Takeuchi, H. (1995). *The Knowledge Creating Company: How Japanese Companies Create the Dynamics of Innovation.* New York: Oxford University Press.

Nonaka, Ikujiro and Teece, David J. (2001). *Managing Industrial Knowledge: Creation, Transfer, and Utilization.* London: Sage Publications.

Nonaka, I., Reinmöller, P., and Senoo, D. (2000). Integrated IT systems to capitalize on market knowledge. In: Von Krogh, G., Nonaka, I., and Nishiguchi, T. (eds), *Knowledge Creation: A Source of Value.* London: Macmillan.

Ōnishi, A. (2009). Knowledge management. In: Haghirian, P. (ed.), *J-Management: Fresh Perspectives on the Japanese Firm in the 21st Century.* Bloomington, NY: Iuniverse Inc.

Patterson, P. G., Johnson, L. W., and Spreng, R. A. (1997). Modeling the determinants of customer satisfaction for business-to-business professional services. *Journal of the Academy of Marketing Science*, 25(1): 4–17.

Polanyi, M. (1985) *Implizites Wissen.* Frankfurt am Main: Suhrkamp Verlag.

Porter, M. E. (1985). *Competitive Advantage: Creating and Sustaining Superior Performance*. New York: Free Press.

Probst, G., Raub, S., and Romhardt, K. (1998) *Wissen Managen*. Frankfurt am Main: Frankfurter Allgemaine Zeitung, Gabler.

Richter, F.-J. (1995). Transfer von Kenntnissen und Erfahrungen zwischen Zentrale und Auslandsniederlassung. *Zeitschrift für Planung*, 6: 227–240.

Richter, F.-J. (1996). *Organizational Learning between Subsidiaries and Headquarter: The German Experience in Japan*. Working Paper. Berlin: Ostasiatisches Seminar: Free University, Berlin.

Rosengren, K. E. (2000). *Communication: An Introduction*. Thousand Oaks, CA: Sage Publications.

Roth, K. (2001). Material culture and intercultural communication. *International Journal of Intercultural Relations*, 25: 563–580.

Scharmer, C. O. (2000). Organizing around not-yet-embodied knowledge. In: Von Krogh, G., Nonaka, I. and Nishiguchi, T. (eds), *Knowledge Creation: A Source of Value*. London: Macmillan.

Schulz, M. and Jobe, L. A. (2001). Codification and tacitness as knowledge management strategies: an empirical exploration. *Journal of High Technology Management Research*, 12: 139–165.

Scollon, R. and Wong-Scollon, S. (1995). *Intercultural Communication*. Oxford: Blackwell Publishers.

Szulanski, G. (1994). *Unpacking Stickiness: An Empirical Investigation of the Barriers to Transfer Best Practices Inside the Firm*. Fontainebleau, France: INSEAD Working Paper 1995/37/SM.

Takeuchi, H. (2001). Towards a universal management concept of knowledge. In: Teece, D. (ed.), *Managing Industrial Knowledge: Creation, Transfer and Utilization*. London: Sage Publications, pp. 315–329.

Thomas, D. C. (2002). *Essentials of International Management: A Cross-Cultural Perspective*. Thousand Oaks, CA: Sage Publications.

Tudor, T., Trumble, R., and George, G. (1996). Significant historic origins that influenced the team concept in major Japanese companies. *Journal of Applied Business Research*, 12(4): 155–128.

Wikström, S. and Normann, R. (1994). *Knowledge and Value: A New Perspective on Corporate Transformation*. London: Routledge.

Zack, M. H. (1999). Managing codified knowledge. *Sloan Management Review*, 40: 45–58.

31
Strategic management

Parissa Haghirian

Introduction

Strategic management plays an important role to strengthen the position of a company, and it is used to develop sustainable competitive advantages. Management literature sees strategy development as a means to develop competitive advantages and earn above-average results. Japanese companies certainly have the same goals. Their strong point was traditionally to manufacture high-quality products, leveraging on the high process orientation and high level of perfectionism of the Japanese workforce. These ideals and attitudes have allowed them to develop very cost-effective processes in manufacturing. In using this core competency, Japanese companies have developed very particular strategies in order to compete internationally. Japanese management strategies and the research into this subject therefore focus mainly on improving work processes and new product development.

This chapter discusses the development and particularities of Japanese strategy development. It will further show how structural developments influence the development and implementation of strategies. The chapter closes with Japanese international strategies and the implementation of international strategic alliances which deepen the usage of core competencies and help to leverage economies of scale.

Strategic management

A strategy refers to a set of procedures or plans which are be developed and used in order to achieve a desired goal in the future of the company or to solve an existing problem with the use of available resources. Organizational strategy is used to reach corporate objectives (e.g. profit, revenue or sales targets) in order to achieve sustainable competitive advantages or lead the company away from a critical situation (Haghirian 2013). A strategy includes an outline of the mission, a goal, and a basic direction for the strategy to be developed, as well as a structure and a code of behaviour (Kono 1984). Strategies encompass the business vision and mission and long-term goals or can be developed at a more granular level to reach performance targets, plans, and schedules for operation (Chungyalpa and Bora 2015). Strategies can be developed based on ideas, and may be simply the logical extension of one's usual thinking processes. Strategies are a matter of long-term philosophy and not of short-term expedient thinking (Ōmae 1975).

Strategic management practices therefore describe the development of visions and goals, as well as the implementation of decisions and actions to achieve or maintain strategic competitiveness, in order to obtain long-term above-average returns for the firm. In this process, in-house resources and expertise should be used as the best possible way to support these processes (Haghirian 2013).

Strategy types and levels

Strategies can be defined at various levels. Generally, strategies are divided into corporate strategies, business strategies, and functional strategies (Thompson and Strickland 2001).

Corporate strategies

This term describes strategies that operate on the corporate or inter-corporate level. Corporate strategies are mainly concerned with growth and the business fields in which the companies operate. Corporate strategy is also applicable to the Japanese firm, which is a company with multiple divisions and operative in many different business fields at the same time. A corporate strategy involves management at the highest level (the top executive level). It deals with long-term strategic issues, such as: in which business fields should the firm compete; how can the corporation improve growth processes; and how can the corporation improve its competitive position and overall profitability. It further makes decisions regarding the use of resources and investments (Chungyalpa and Bora 2015). These strategies can include alliances, mergers, and acquisitions. Japanese corporate strategies traditionally focused on internationalization processes, new product development, and innovation management, as well as strategic alliances.

Business-level strategies

These are strategies levelled at the company's business units or departments. Here the goal is to achieve a long-term competitive position in the market (Thompson and Strickland 1992). These processes focus on cooperation between different departments and resources of the firm and aim at combining and bundling them in the best possible way. This can be done in the form of a business plan. In the Japanese context, business strategies mainly refer to competitive strategies and successful strategies to internationalize Japanese organizations.

Functional strategies

These focus on the everyday activities in a firm and how they are performed. Functional strategies are strategies designed at the functional level of a business, supporting the business strategy. They mainly refer to activities within departments of the firm such as production, marketing, finance, human resources, etc. Functional strategies are designed to achieve the departmental objectives and goals (Chungyalpa and Bora 2015). Functional strategies can be found at the department level of the Japanese firm. Here we can find a strong process orientation, an attitude that can generally be observed on all strategic levels. Japanese organizations are a strong unit with a solid hierarchical structure. These groups also have very clear rules, and expect all members to abide by them. To guarantee harmonious and long-lasting relationships, Japanese employees have developed a strong sense of duty, and are very dedicated to their tasks. Rules and regulations play an important role in a Japanese workplace and must be followed at all costs in order to avoid problems for other team members. Japanese companies have therefore developed a very strong process orientation and a work environment where rules and regulations play a very important role. All procedures in a Japanese firm are practised very carefully and sequentially. This concept is called *shikata*, or the proper way of doing things (Haghirian 2010a). In daily management processes and when developing functional strategies, the preference for processes and rule-based work processes come in handy. In particular, the famous Japanese management practices such as just-in-time or *kaizen* benefit from these attitudes. In this chapter, however, we will investigate how strategies are implemented in the Japanese organization.

Strategic management in Japanese corporations

The Western approach to management and corporate leadership sees companies as being in constant competition with other companies. In order to survive in this competition, a company must use its resources, expertise, and staff as efficiently as possible. The goal of any business is to get a long-term competitive advantage, i.e. in the long term to be more attractive for the customer or end consumer than their competitors (Haghirian 2013). These attitudes cannot always be recognized in Japanese organizations, and the question occurs as to whether Japanese management is strategic and how Japanese strategies are developed, which has led to a discussion in management literature. Drucker (1979) notes that 'the business strategy of Japanese enterprise while indeed different from American or European business, is not "mysterious" or "non-rational" nor "culturally conditioned". It optimizes, in perfectly rational fashion, the specific structural realities in which Japanese businesses operate' (p. 229). Kono (1992a) mentions that Japanese management techniques do not originate in the uniqueness of Japanese culture, but in the positive integration of new theories, methods, and the interest in continuous improvement. He finds structural explanations for the development of Japanese management strategies; he also considers that institutional shareholders are not putting very much pressure on Japanese managers, constitute the basis for strategic development processes in Japanese firms (Kono 1992a).

It is obvious, however, that Japanese strategies traditionally focused on new product development and innovation management. This can be explained by the historical relevance and dominance of manufacturing firms in Japan, which were not only high in number but also world leaders in their respective industries until the 1990s. Their main focus was to internationalize, to improve their manufacturing, and to develop new products to sell on international markets during the international expansion period (Kono 1992a).

However, many of these companies did not develop high-risk strategies, but concentrated rather on a strong sense of stability. This stability was often valued more highly than profit, which explains why Japanese companies often showed a much lower rate of profitability than corporations in the USA and Europe (Drucker 1979), and always show a strong growth orientation and a tendency towards long-range goals (Kono 1992a).

Corporate strategies in the Japanese firm

Centralized decision-making

Japanese corporations have a tendency to set long-term goals and centralize decision-making. About 80 per cent of Japanese large corporations have formal long-range planning. Also on the governmental level, long-range economic plans have been published since the 1950s (Kono 1992a). These processes are highly centralized and delegated to those who have the necessary knowledge and information, and the ability to make decisions. In the case of the Japanese company, these are upper-level or top managers (Kono and Clegg 2001). The process is divided into four phases (see Figure 31.1).

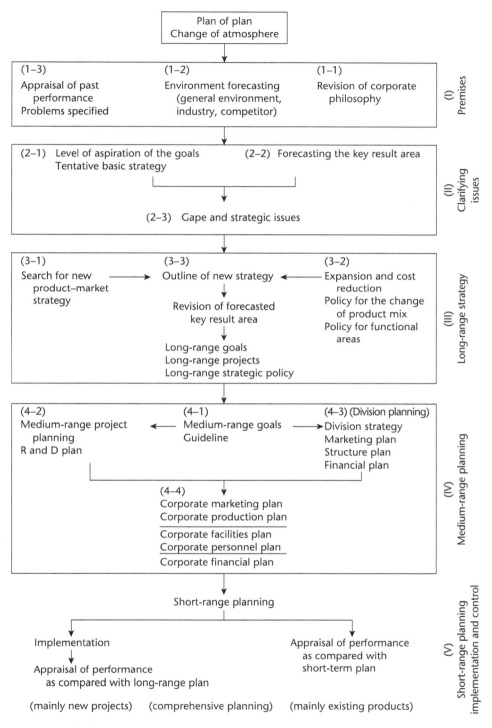

Figure 31.1 The long-range planning process in the Japanese firm (Kono 1984, p. 257)

In the first phase, premises are established. As Japan is a group-oriented culture (Haghirian 2010a), all stakeholders and owners of key resources need to be informed and listened to. At this stage, information on competitors, past performance, and the overall market environment is collected, and opportunities and challenges are being discussed.

In the second stage, major issues that may hinder the new strategy are being clarified. Here, overall goals such as the expected growth rate are developed and compared with forecasts. In cases where gaps are discovered, at this stage strategies should be developed to close these gaps.

The third stage is the long-range planning phase. Here, all the differences between the forecast and the goals are taken care of. This stage involves market research, vertical integration, and the possibility of joint ventures. This happens to ensure that the goal to which the company aspires can actually be achieved. If the gap between the forecast and the goal cannot be closed, then the process needs to be revised again.

The last phase is about medium-range planning. After establishing long-range goals, medium-range goals are developed. This includes project planning; the planning by new product groups with regard to the new product mix; and corporate functional planning by the functional department (Kono 1984). This activity would be called marketing planning in a Western corporation.

The process is interesting for a number of reasons. First, it is a highly group-oriented process and involves many members of the organization. This is partly based on the need to have the support of all members to have a new idea or strategy implemented. It also differs from Western strategic processes, which tend to be more individualistic and promote the development of new and different ideas. Companies with big and strong headquarters seem to be more successful in developing strategies, because they have more resources and more power to diffuse the idea or strategies to other parts of the firm (Kono and Clegg 2001).

The second interesting aspect is the fact that the strategy development phase is already highly structured and involves a lot of structured processes. It is time-consuming, and may not always lead to the implementation of radical new ideas.

These planning processes were mainly used in new product development and are a typical procedure of Japanese companies in the manufacturing field. These companies, however, dominated the Japanese market and also had a great influence in international markets until the 1990s. Japanese strategy development therefore mainly refers to these kinds of strategic goals and strategy-planning processes. The Japanese long-range planning process is focusing on satisfactory performance but not on maximizing performance (or profits). It is based on the fact that Japanese managers have a lot more managerial autonomy because most of the shareholders in a Japanese firm are institutional shareholders and are not interfering with management procedures as much as American investors (Chen 2004).

Strategic alliances

Strategic alliances are popular inside Japan to reinforce core competencies and produce economies of scales in production (Kono and Clegg 2001). Strategic alliances define business cooperations, in which two or more independent organizations form a cooperation or partnership to leverage a mutual strategic advantage (Miller and Dess 1996). In the Japanese context, this cooperation can already be found in the typical *keiretsu* structure, which is still dominant in the Japanese market. Japanese researchers stress or exaggerate the solidarity amongst those alliances (Kono and Clegg 2001). Ōmae (1975) states that a *keiretsu* is a diversified company that is trying to exploit synergies across various businesses in order to achieve cost and quality leadership over its single business competitors, whereas a conglomerate that also consists of different companies in various businesses can be seen as a portfolio manager of these companies (Ōmae

1975). In fact, there is no controlling centre and no regular meetings or coordination between the presidents of the respective firms, however, there is an active trading and financial connection with non-members or non-affiliated corporations (Kono and Clegg 2001). However, the idea of strategic alliances became prominent in the overseas activities of Japanese firms, which were seen as a successful means to support global and regional strategies. In particular 'strategic alliances' with foreign partners are used to spread the cost of development amongst a number of business partners (Hook 1998).

Organizational structure and strategy

In Japanese organizations, strategic planning is strongly supported by company structure. The main strategies are developed in the head office, where the central planning department is one of the most relevant players because it is responsible for the study and implementation of corporate strategy. It further collects strategic information and looks for new business opportunities. On the other hand, it plans the developed strategy and coordinates its implementation amongst the operating units (Kono and Clegg 2001). This centralized policy and strategy development can also be found at the government level, where the Prime Minister's Office, the Economic Planning Agency, the Ministry of Finance, and the Ministry of Economy, Trade and Industry (METI) gather a large number of intellectuals, such as engineers, natural scientists, and technicians, in order to provide input in regional- and urban-planning decisions (Passin 1975).

In the companies, project teams are developed at various corporate levels, such as product-development level or at the research and development department, and these have the goal of researching new products and collecting other data (Kono 1992b). These project teams focus on new product development, and consist of members of different departments, and are multifunctional teams (Nonaka and Takeuchi 1995). Once the project is completed, the team is dissolved and the members return to their departments (Kono 1992b).

Internal venture teams, on the other hand, are not so common in Japanese companies. An internal venture can be formed by an individual who has developed a new idea. In this case, this individual becomes the project manager, taking the idea on an organizational level and making it into a new product (Kono 1992b). More common are incubator departments, which are in charge of developing new products. After being developed in a research group or department, a product is then transferred to the incubator department, where cost calculations and the further promotion of the product within the company are taken care of. A long-term perspective can be developed by this department, even if the product may not provide immediate profits (Kono and Clegg 2001).

Business-level strategies

Me-too strategy

Japanese business strategies are not developed in the same way as Western strategies. Western strategies intend to be different and develop originality; Japanese strategies on the other hand do have a strong orientation towards others. Ōmae's (1975) definition of strategy differs from the Western idea of strategy. According to him, the term 'strategy' should be 'reserved for actions aimed directly at altering the strength of the enterprise relative to that of its competitors' (p. 37). In Japan, however, including the rival's actions in strategic development is part of the strategy development. Many Japanese companies developed risk-averse strategies, such as the me-too strategy, which refers to the fact that, even if they are in the same industry, companies will pursue the same strategy. Examples can be found in the motorcycle, computer, semiconductor, and automotive industries. These companies developed a similar product mix, whereas Western companies would focus on developing differentiated and innovative products (Kono and Clegg 2001). Even today we can find very similar products from various different Japanese manufacturers when visiting big retailers in Japan.

Japanese competitive strategies in international markets

The overseas expansion of Japanese corporations was a reaction to strong competition in the Japanese market. Therefore to be and stay competitive they had to improve the quality of their products and introduce professional large-scale production systems to produce them at low cost. Products developed in these conditions also proved successful on the world market (Kono 1984). Japanese companies developed very successful and Japan-specific strategies in order to exploit their competitive advantages. They were extremely successful in leveraging their manufacturing advantages and using technology to develop innovative and customer-oriented products (Chen 2004). During the peak period of Japanese exports, 'everyone thought the Japanese possess some special magic that enables them to run rings around their competitors in world markets' (Ōmae 1975, p. 1). During the prime time of Japanese management, overall interest was also focusing on how Japanese companies could be so successful in foreign markets. In fact, Japanese organizations moved from producing reliable and cost-efficient products to developing highly innovative brand products in almost every industry (Ōmae 1975). Japanese process orientation supported these developments, because they improved manufacturing and production processes (Haghirian 2010a).

Functional strategies

Strategy implementation – hoshin kanri

Japanese state their missions and goals very clearly, which motivates employees and allows the easy introduction of innovation (Kono 1992a). This preference can be also observed in strategy-implementation processes. The best-known practice in the field is *hoshin kanri* (HK), which is a quality planning and management method that was developed in Japan by Yokogawa Hewlett-Packard in the early 1970s (Jolayemi 2008, p. 295), and which also spread to Western companies. *Hoshin kanri* is a form of corporate-wide management that combines strategic management and operational management by linking the achievement of top-management goals with daily management at an operational level (Witcher and Butterworth 2001). The word '*hoshin*' means 'policy' or 'plan', and refers to a long-term strategic direction that also includes the anticipation of competitive developments. The word '*kanri*' refers to a control system for managing the process. Blending these two elements into an integrative management process to achieve a shared purpose is the basis of the *hoshin kanri* process (Su and Yang 2015).

The *hoshin kanri* has the overall goal of supporting the implementation of strategic goals developed at top-management level. Policy is used to support the organization on key priorities and corporate goals throughout the whole organization, and to ensure that objectives are translated into operational goals (Witcher and Butterworth 2001).

The process starts with a thorough assessment and analysis of the current situation of the company and its working climate. This is carried out by collecting data and by daily control of processes. Data are provided by various sources within and outside the company (Wood and Munshi 1991). The process then breaks down the goals and objectives for all employees, to ensure that all employees are focused on the same vision and the same goals of the company.

During the implementation of the strategies, the process is constantly supervised, and, if necessary, improved. Regular process reviews are held to support these attempts.

The implementation of the new idea is supported by detailed and frequent reviews of the progress towards achieving a target (Marsden and Kanji 1998). A main feature of *hoshin kanri* is the fact that targets initiated at the corporate level are subject to feedback from lower management levels in the firm (Wood and Munshi 1991). This is the so called 'catchball', which allows two-way communication that is both strategically top-down and bottom-up and thus engages all parts of the organization in the conversation (Su and Yang 2015). It allows these levels to contribute to the final plan, and leads to full ownership and understanding throughout the whole corporation (Wood and Munshi 1991). Feedback of this information is used to inform the next phase of the planning process and to assess progress (Marsden and Kanji 1998).

There is perhaps nothing new about this, except that the approach in general is more participative than many conventional Western approaches (Witcher and Butterworth 2001). Also, involvement with the organization is higher (Kono 1992a).

The interactions and the high level of communication and information within the company enable Japanese organizations to leverage technological and market opportunities in domestic and global markets (Dobi and Bugar 2008).

Challenges for Japanese strategy development

Japanese corporations face the following challenges: globalization; ever-changing consumer attitudes; more international and new rivals; and new technologies – all of which also require traditional and successful companies to make faster and more effective decisions to stay competitive. Japanese companies are no exception. Strategic decisions and their consequences determine the company's future. However, many Japanese strategies still seem to be stuck in the industrialization phase of the economy when Japanese firms grew rapidly. These strategies also have their flaws. In the 1990s, Kono (1992b) was already describing which factors are problematic regarding the Japanese tendency for long-range planning and centralized decision-making. Uncontrollable factors or consequences, as well as difficulties in forecasting, are pressing issues. Kono also refers to other problems, for example, top management is not willing to participate and support the planning, and often wrong goals are being developed and ideas are accepted too quickly. He also mentions poor coordination as a major problem for the Japanese strategic decision-making processes (Kono 1992b, p. 357ff.).

Modern Japanese companies more than ever feel the weak points of their strategic development. Traditionally, Japanese corporate strategies were focusing on the development of new products and the improvement of organizational processes. However, management and strategic processes became even more complex when Japanese companies were expected to enter a post-industrialized, services- and knowledge-based economic phase. These problems have increased over the past two decades. Many Japanese companies in the manufacturing industry have so far not managed to develop strategies that are adequate for these economic changes and growing global competition. It is only recently that Japanese enterprises are trying to recover their international competitiveness by restructuring their processes. They are reducing the number of employees, and reducing their complex business activities and speculative overseas operations (Dobi and Bugar 2008).

Conclusions

During post-war economic development, Japanese corporations developed particular strategies to succeed and expand internationally. This was based on a strong focus on cost-efficient manufacturing and improving the quality of their products. These developments also convinced consumers outside Japan, and set the stage for the unprecedented success story of the Japanese economy after the Second World War. The reasons for this can be found in the way that Japanese companies and managers have strong preferences for processes. This is based on the Japanese tradition of *shikata*, or doing things the right way, and is accompanied by a positive idea of perfectionism and strong group orientation.

Japanese companies have shown that they possessed successful strategies during the industrialization phase of their economy. But, whereas Japanese managers could concentrate on the professional organization of business processes and the coordination of operations until a few years ago, the current global business environment forces them to face very new challenges. Today Japan is a post-industrialized country, and therefore management strategy goes beyond production and quality alone.

Modern strategic decisions include making long-term, sustainable decisions, ensuring the profitability and competitiveness of the company. Strategic decisions are taking place mainly in the following areas: corporate vision, mission, and goals; market selection; mergers; product selection; positioning; the product portfolio; and responding to competitors and the behaviour of competing companies. In these areas, making bold strategic moves is of utmost relevance. Strategy development and implementation of strategic decisions, therefore, play an increasingly important role in modern management, especially for companies that operate internationally.

Group decision-making processes do not always allow these moves, but tend to favour group- and customer-oriented outcomes. Today, many formerly successful companies in the Japanese manufacturing industry are outperformed by faster and more marketing-oriented Asian rivals. Many Japanese strategies are not seen as very adequate for navigating Japanese companies through turbulent and global challenges. It remains to be seen whether Japanese corporations can move away from the past process-oriented planning and strategy-developing practices and develop consumer-based strategies that allow fast reactions to market changes.

Bibliography

Chen, M. (2004). *Asian Management Systems*. London: Thompson Learning.

Chungyalpa, W. and Bora, B. (2015). *Towards Conceptualizing Business Strategies*, 02(1), January–February 2015, p. 73.

Dobi, S. and Bugar, L. (2008). Japanese management strategies. *Proceedings of the MEB 2008 – 6th International Conference on Management, Enterprise and Benchmarking*, May 30–31 2008, Budapest, Hungary. Budapest: MEB 2008.

Drucker, P. (1979). Economic realities and enterprise strategies. In: Vogel. E. (ed.), *Modern Japanese Organization and Decision Making*. Tokyo: Tuttle Company, pp. 228–248.

Haghirian, P. (2010a). Ist japanisches Management strategisch? (Is Japanese management strategic?) *Japan Markt*, February 2010: 22–24.

Haghirian, P. (2010b). *Understanding Japanese Management Practices*. New York: Business Expert Press.

Haghirian, P. (2013). Strategisches Management. In: Laske, S., Orthey, A., and Schmid, M. (eds), *PersonalEntwickeln (Loseblatt)*. Köln: Wolters Kluwer.

Hook, G. D. (1998). Japanese business in triadic regionalization. In: Hasegawa, H. and Hook, G. D. (eds), *Japanese Business Management: Restructuring for Low Growth and Globalization*. London and New York: Routledge.

Jolayemi, J. K. (2008). Hoshin kanri and hoshin process: a review and literature survey. *Total Quality Management*, 19(3): 295–320.

Kono, T. (1984). *Strategy and Structure of Japanese Enterprises*. Houndmills, Basingstoke, UK: Macmillan.

Kono, T. (1992a). *Strategic Management in Japanese Companies*. Oxford, UK: Pergamon Press.

Kono, T. (1992b). *Long-Range Planning of Japanese Corporations*. Berlin, New York: de Gruyter.

Kono, T. and Clegg, S. (2001). *Trends in Japanese Management; Continuing Strengths, Current Problems, and Changing Priorities*. Houndmills, Basingstoke: Palgrave.

Liker, J. K. (2004). *The Toyota Way: 14 Management Principles from the World's Greatest Manufacturer*. New York: McGraw-Hill.

Marsden, N. and Kanji, G. K. (1998). The use of hoshin kanri planning and deployment systems in the service sector: an exploration. *Total Quality Management*, 9(4–5): 167–171.

Miller, A. and Dess, G. G. (1996). *Strategic Management*. New York: McGraw-Hill College.

Misumi, J. (1990). The Japanese meaning of work and small group activities in Japanese industrial organizations. *International Journal of Psychology*, 25: 819–832.

Nonaka, I. and Takeuchi, H. (1995). *The Knowledge Creating Company: How Japanese Companies Create the Dynamics of Innovation*. New York: Oxford University Press.

Ōmae, K. (1975). *The Mind of the Strategist*. Tokyo: Tuttle Company.

Passin, H. (1975). Intellectuals in the decision making process. In: Vogel, E. (ed.), *Modern Japanese Organization and Decision Making*. Tokyo: Tuttle Company, pp. 251–283.

Su, Chao-Ton and Yang, Tsung-Ming (2015). Hoshin Kanri planning process in human resource management: recruitment in a high-tech firm. *Total Quality Management and Business Excellence*, 26(1–2): 140–156.

Thompson, A. A. Jr and Strickland, A. J. III (1992). *Strategic Management: Concepts and Cases*, 6th edn. Boston: Irwin/McGraw Hill.

Thompson, A. A. Jr and Strickland, A. J. III (2001). *Strategic Management*, 12th edn. New York: Irwin/McGraw Hill.

Witcher, B. J. and Butterworth, R. (2001). Hoshin Kanri: policy management in Japanese-owned UK subsidiaries. *Journal of Management Studies*, 38(5): 651–674.

Wood, G. R. and Munshi, K. F. (1991). Hoshin Kanri: a systematic approach to breakthrough improvement. *Total Quality Management*, 2(3): 213–226.

Part VIII
The future of Japanese management

32

Emerging topics in Japanese management research

Michaela Blahová, Parissa Haghirian, and Přemysl Pálka

Introduction

The research was undertaken by two academic teams from the Czech Republic and Japan in order to establish a multi-perspective view in the context of global and business trends.[1]

Focus on Japanese management research – an overview

Although it is easy to forget now, Japan was once considered an economic miracle. A country with scant natural resources, little financial capital, and few areas of technological expertise, Japan was the first Asian nation to modernize and compete with the West (Lehmberg *et al.* 2013). Since that time, Japan has been renowned for its economic superpower status and global automotive and electronic-appliance manufacturers, such as Toyota, Nissan, Honda, Mitsubishi, Mazda, Sony, Panasonic, Canon, Toshiba, Fujitsu, NEC, and Sanyo. The miraculous transformation of Japan from an insulated, island-based agrarian state to a highly industrialized nation, and subsequently from a war-torn state to a country with superpower status, has captured much attention (Chatterjee and Nankervis 2007). But keeping a system in perfect balance is never easy, and Japan was no exception.

Japan's amazing growth from 1950 to 1973, and its emergence as one of the world's leading nations, was almost unprecedented. With an annual average growth rate of nearly 10 per cent during that period, the size of the Japanese economy expanded fivefold. It was during this period that Japan's economy surpassed those of France, Germany, and the United Kingdom for the first time (OECD 2014). Until the end of the 1980s, the Japanese economy was seen as the most successful economic model in the world (Drucker 1971; Hayes 1981; Pudelko and Haak 2005). One major aspect influencing economic success was the strong connection between government and economy. Stability was one of the main goals behind this cooperation, and it supported technological and innovation processes (Lukas and Saito 2009).

However, after a major boom in the 1970s and 1980s, in the 1990s and the 2000s the Japanese management system started to be considered a model of the past (Porter *et al.* 2000). During this period, much of the attention shifted away from Japan to newly developing countries, such as South Korea, China, and India (Lehmberg *et al.* 2013). Numerous factors contributed to this, including the long-lasting stagnation of the Japanese economy, ill-advised macroeconomic policies, delayed microeconomic reforms, etc. The bursting of the speculative 'bubble economy' – and the longest recession in Japan's post-war history that followed it – plunged the Japanese economy into crisis and called many of Japan's idiosyncrasies into question, particularities which, until that time, had been seen as factors in the success of Japanese businesses (Schmidt 1997).

Even when the Japanese economy started to recover at the beginning of the twenty-first century, the image of Japanese management did not improve. Lifetime employment, the seniority system, and group-oriented decision-making have been strongly criticized as holding Japanese companies back (Firkola 2006; Pudelko 2009; Haghirian 2010a; Pudelko and Harzing 2011; Arai *et al.* 2013). But, as Peter Drucker, a well-known management expert, cautioned, 'Don't underestimate the Japanese . . . once they reach a critical mass of consensus . . . they have an incredible ability to make brutal, 180-degree, radical changes overnight' (Weston 2014).

Despite the problems that the Japanese economy has had to face, it has still kept its strongest competitive advantages in car manufacturing; the production of machinery and equipment; and the fabrication of radio, TV and communications equipment (Witt 2006). Currently, Japan still remains the world's third-largest economy and a major exporter of capital.

Nowadays, many researchers, as well as practitioners, have been discussing the key role of change in the Japanese corporate sphere (Firkola 2006; Chatterjee and Nankervis 2007; Pudelko 2009; Abe 2010; De Mente 2012; Blahová and Zelený 2013; Haghirian 2010a; Keizer *et al.* 2012; Lehmberg *et al.* 2013; Blahová *et al.* 2014; Shimizu 2014; Blahová *et al.* 2015; and many others). Change is brewing that could lead to a rebound for Japan, although the Japanese management style remains deep-rooted. Moreover, Prime Minister Shinzo Abe, who took office in December 2012, has started to address the current challenges by launching his 'three arrows' strategy – a bold monetary policy, flexible fiscal policy, and a growth strategy that encourages private-sector investment (OECD 2014). Many scientists have observed various trends influencing Japan and Japanese companies recently. For example, Shimizu (2014) has noticed the following developments – a resurgence in confidence (Japanese companies were able to recover quickly from the devastating damage wreaked by the Great East Japan Earthquake and the Fukushima Daiichi nuclear-plant accident, both of which occurred in 2011), a shift in decision-making and acceptance of responsibility (e.g. three electronics companies – Sony, Panasonic and Sharp – have announced that their top executives may be replaced due to past poor corporate performance), increased accountability, and moves to more clearly defined responsibilities.

To sum up, since the emergence of the Japanese model, important changes have been made in the management practices of Japanese firms, changes that have had an enormous influence on the corporate sphere. Nowadays, as Lehmberg *et al.* (2013) point out, Japan still faces an uncertain future in a number of ways, but it remains an important country worthy of attention. Chatterjee and Nankervis (2007) expect Japanese management to continue to play an important role in providing solutions to the challenges now faced in the maturing processes of the global economy. Although it can be difficult for outsiders to completely grasp the Japanese situation, the opportunities that it offers make up for the effort required.

Emerging topics in Japanese management research

Japanese management practices are to be considered as a complex system that is not easily categorized. From the outside, Japanese management seems to be more united than it actually is. Although many observers believe that the traditional Japanese management system has to be transformed to a Western-oriented system that seems much more flexible especially in terms of communication, decision-making processes, a fast response to the market, leadership, etc. in order to stay competitive, the Western style of management and the Japanese style of management are still two different things and two contrasting ideas.

Haghirian (2010a) mentions that Japan has been changing only in its own Japanese way. Japanese corporations are expected to change in a Western way, finally accepting a more shareholder-value-oriented attitude, putting profit before relationships and increasing profitability. However, the concept of change differs greatly between Japan and the West. The Japanese way of business has proved highly resilient to change, as Hasegawa and Noronha (2009) point out. This is most visible in economically bad times, such as the 'lost decade' of low economic growth in the 1990s. Normally, economic pain leads to structural reforms. However, in the case of Japan, there is little evidence of truly fundamental changes (Witt 2006).

Change from the Western perspective is mostly radical; things really have to be drastically different from previous conditions (Haghirian 2010a). In Japan, however, the principle of *kaizen* (continuous change) dominates. Change takes time, and does not always mean the elimination of old and successful ideas, or breaking relationships that have grown over a long time. The key determinant in the future success of Japan is to be open-minded, but at the same time not to forget what works.

Therefore, although a number of issues having impacts (not only positive) on Japanese companies have been addressed in the literature in the past few years, so far only a few changes have been adopted by Japanese companies. More time is needed to implement all the necessary changes that Japanese people consider relevant to their businesses.

The following main trends and practices have been identified as the drivers of change of the traditional Japanese management model within the recent practical research. Each of these trends, however, contains specific practices that interact with each other, shape, and give strength to each individual category. Trends that have only appeared in the literature have been ignored for the time being, although they may continue to gain traction in the future.

This chapter provides an overview of the research that has involved assembling key academic and other literature on trends in strategic management in Japan. We supported these results with a series of semi-structured interviews with managers within manufacturing companies located in Japan. The following section describes the key topics that will drive change in the future, as identified by both academics and businesses.

Integrating women into the workforce

Japan's potential growth rate is steadily falling with the ageing of its population. Population projections suggest that the share of the population over age 65 will rise to 36 per cent in 2040 (Steinberg and Nakane 2012) (it was only 9 per cent in 1980). A shrinking population already has implications for the workforce. Currently, some 16 million Japanese people are in their twenties. This number will shrink by 3 million over just the next decade. By 2030, demographers say, Japan will have just two working-age people for each retired one; by mid-century, short of a rapid and unlikely return to fecundity, the ratio will rise to three for every two retirees (*The Economist* 2007). Figures 32.1 and 32.2 show the projections of the Japanese population in 2015 and 2050.

Prime Minister Shinzo Abe is aware of the critical situation that needs to be changed. In April 2013, he announced that allowing women to 'shine' in the economy was the most important part of his 'Abenomics' growth strategy. Raising female labour participation to the level of that of men could add 8 million people to Japan's shrinking workforce, potentially increasing GDP by as much as 15 per cent, according to Goldman Sachs, an investment bank (*The Economist* 2014).

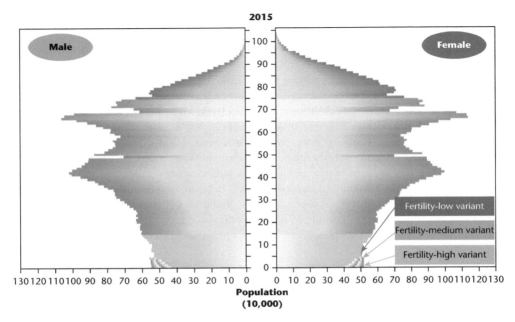

Figure 32.1   Census (1920–2010) and 'Population Projections for Japan 2011–2060'
(2015–2060). National Institute of Population and Social Security Research

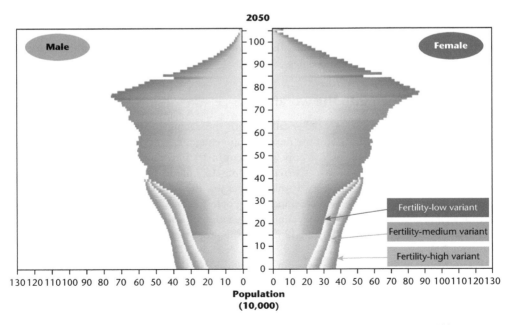

Figure 32.2   Census (1920–2010) and 'Population Projections for Japan: 2011–2060'
(2015–2060), National Institute of Population and Social Security Research

Japanese companies still have a comparatively low number of female staff and female managers. An extensive study performed by McKinsey (Süssmuth-Dyckerhoff *et al.* 2012) and focused on gender composition in companies in Asia showed that, in recent years, the numbers of women graduates and of women at entry-level positions in companies have increased, although the proportion of women sitting on corporate boards and executive committees in Asian companies is strikingly low as compared with Europe and the United States. Japan enacted an equal-employment-opportunity law in 1985, but the reality is far from what is stipulated by this law. Japanese society is still highly male-dominated, and this is especially true at the workplace (Yuasa 2005; Magoshi and Chang 2009). This is supported by the following statement: 'Diversity in our company is really low. Most of our employees are men and there are very few women in management. However, this situation has been changing. Women achieve higher performance in some business areas and, therefore, are very important for the company' (Blahová *et al.* 2015).

Other research results (United Nations 2008; Haghirian 2010b; McKinsey, 2012) indicate that only around 10 per cent of managerial positions are held by women in Japan, compared with 42 per cent in the United States and 35 per cent in the United Kingdom. As a result, Abe announced that women shall occupy at least 30 per cent of all 'leadership' positions – which would include members of parliament, heads of local government and corporate executives – by 2020.

Eventually, the number of women staff, as well as number of women in management positions, will increase in the coming years. The majority of researched companies stated that an increase in women staff and women managers is anticipated in their company in the near future.

Globalization of the Japanese firm

The internationalization of Japan is one of the pillars of Prime Minister Shinzo Abe's growth strategy at a time when a shrinking domestic market is forcing more businesses to look overseas for profits. However, more than 70 per cent of Japanese companies with global operations face challenges in hiring and educating a suitable workforce, according to a government survey (*The Japan Times* 2014a).

Since the end of the bubble economy, Japanese society has clearly opened its doors for long-term residents, even though it has the reputation of being closed to foreigners. Japan is in desperate need of workers from overseas to support its ageing population. However, as Haghirian (2009) points out, the number of foreigners working in Japan has not so far been sufficient to perform this role. Hidenori Sakanaka, a former director of the Tokyo Regional Immigration Bureau, confirms that if the working population keeps shrinking, then this will keep pushing down consumption, and the country will be unable to maintain economic growth. In short, this means that the growth strategies of 'Abenomics' cannot be successful without accepting immigrants (*The Japan Times* 2014c).

At the end of October 2013, the number of foreign workers in Japan reached 717,504, up 5.1 per cent from the year before. The number was the highest since employers started regularly submitting reports on foreign employees to the ministry in 2007. The increase also reveals that Japanese workplaces are internationalizing just as workplaces worldwide are doing. However, Japan is far behind most other advanced countries in the percentage of workers who come from other countries. The foreign percentage of Japan's labour force stands at about 1 per cent, compared with 36 per cent in Singapore (*The Japan Times* 2014b).

Amongst the various policies on foreign workers that have been applied recently, there seems to be a consensus for moving towards accepting more highly skilled foreign professionals

Michaela Blahová *et al.*

(Saito 2014). In order to support the immigration, the government of Prime Minister Abe passed a revision to the Immigration Law in 2014 that enables foreigners with advanced skills to be eligible for permanent residency after staying in Japan for three years instead of ten years for most foreigners (or five in some cases where certain conditions were fulfilled). On the other hand, policies focusing on unskilled workers are more controversial. Saito (2014) mentions that, as in other countries, there will always be fears that foreign workers will take jobs that might otherwise have gone to Japanese citizens. However, Japan's declining population implies a shortage of labour, so there should be increasingly less competition for work.

In our research, the respondents considered integration of foreigners into their workforce as one of the measures to professionalize and internationalize Japanese corporations. Many workplaces are now starting to accept diversity, changing past expectations of homogeneity, as the following statement confirms: 'Our company focuses not only on gender equality but on nationality equality, too. My boss is an English man and the company is also trying to employ more people from overseas' (Blahová *et al.* 2015).

Changes in traditional Japanese management practices

Since the collapse of the bubble economy, the conventional Japanese management practices have been increasingly internally and externally challenged. The corporate Japanese system has been under pressure primarily because of the long-term implications of labour costs and inherent inflexibility (Mroczkowski and Hanaoka 1989; Debroux 2003). Rethinking lifetime employment necessarily entails rethinking the traditional seniority-based wage and promotion system. Inherent in the system are wage increases related to the worker's age and length of service, regardless of his or her real productivity and contribution (Watanabe 2000).

The change in the labour market gained pace in the 1990s, as Japan's economic woes forced companies to scale back employees' benefits dramatically. Increasingly, many firms hired new staff on short-term or part-time contracts rather than treating them as members of the corporate family. Moreover, a big generational shift is taking place. Today's young professionals refuse to make work the centre of their lives or to accept the hardships and corporate paternalism of earlier decades (*The Economist* 2008).

More and more Japanese companies have started to focus on replacing full-time employees with part-time, contract, and temporary workers. The seniority-based lifetime employment system made it difficult to cut the wages of older full-time workers. Therefore, employers shifted their focus on hiring more part-time workers, who can be paid much less, with few or no benefits (*Nikkei Weekly* 2007).

Japanese management is at a turning point and is currently undergoing change. However, as statistics and examples of companies show, it is not merely a switch from one set of management strategies, that is, the three pillars of life-time employment, seniority-based wages, and labour unions, to Western standards, with employees switching jobs freely and merit-based wages. The traditional three pillars of Japanese management are still very much in place. But change is happening, and management is choosing between traditional and new trends that have been introduced via globalization (Haghirian 2009). This is supported by the following statement from the interview series: 'Although lifetime employment brings a lot of benefits, there are also problems occurring from it. In today's global economy more flexibility in hiring people is required' (Blahová *et al.* 2015).

The changes in employment practices can be considered part of a wider development – moving from long-term relationships towards a greater marketization and internationalization of the Japanese economy. For example, the introduction of performance-related pay means that the basis for remuneration has shifted away from the long-term development of skills towards short-term results. Performance-related pay can be considered a new standard in the management of regular workers amongst Japanese firms and has introduced important changes to their evaluation and remuneration. Seniority often remains as a criterion for evaluation, but it no longer defines the Japanese wage system (Keizer *et al.* 2012), as the following statement of an interviewee confirms: 'Our company is trying to pursue a well-organized wage system without considering the difference of culture and language. If a person has skills, then s/he will get paid higher. However, this also means that if a person does not show a satisfactory result, then s/he will get paid lower'.

Conclusions

The Japan of today is different. Just looking at the current social environment, it can already be observed that the country is in a state of change, whether it is cultural or corporate (Haghirian 2009).

Until the economic bubble burst, the Japanese economy had been successful mainly due to its unique and traditional methods of management (Haghirian 2009). According to Hasegawa and Noronha (2009), the Japanese business system developed as one of the world's most powerful, especially in industries requiring high levels of technical skill in manufacturing; the building of globally significant brands; complex organizational coordination at high levels of efficiency; and an ability to engage workers in product improvement and quality assurance.

However, when the economic crisis hit the country, many institutions were called into question, and the demand for reforms became louder. The Japanese system seemed to have become dysfunctional for a mature economy in a global environment and facing stronger international competition (Kwan 2000). As the economy developed, many industries rose and sunk again as their comparative advantages shifted. This brought changes to corporate, employment, and industrial structures (Sakakibara 2003).

This chapter has aimed to address the emerging topics in Japanese management research that have been influencing Japanese management practices in recent years, and their consequences for the corporate world. Amongst the most important topics are those listed below:

1 integrating Japanese women into the workforce, due to the demographic changes that have been taking place in Japanese society recently, and the implications of this for business management;
2 the globalization of the Japanese firm, including attracting more foreigners to work in Japan;
3 introducing overall changes in traditional Japanese management practices, such as changes in working and more time-efficient management styles; and
4 rethinking the traditional seniority system and lifetime employment practices, while introducing productivity and performance appraisals as well as cultural and social changes.

Note

1 The research was supported by the research grant No. 14-18597P from the Czech Science Foundation ('Creating Strategic Performance Model Framework Based on Utilization of Synergy Effects of Selected Management Systems') and grant no. CZ.1.07/2.3.00/20.0147 from the Operational Programme Education for Competitiveness, co-funded by the European Social Fund (ESF) and the national budget of the Czech Republic (Human Resources Development in the Field of Measurement and Management of Companies, Clusters and Regions Performance).

Michaela Blahová *et al.*

References

Abe, M. (2010). Introduction: Japanese management in the 21st century. In: Haghirian, P. (ed.), *Innovation and Change in Japanese Management*. Basingstoke, UK: Palgrave Macmillan, pp. 1–11.

Arai, K., Kitada, H., and Oura, K. (2013). Using profit information for production management: evidence from Japanese factories. *Journal of Accounting and Organizational Change*, 9(4): 408–426.

Blahová, M. and Zelený, M. (2013). Effective strategic action: exploring synergy sources of European and Asian management systems. *Human Systems Management*, 32(3): 155–170.

Blahová, M., Pálka, P., and Zelený, M. (2014). Contemporary trends in Japanese business environment: a review of existing empirical evidence. *Human Systems Management*, 3(3): 57–70.

Blahová, M., Haghirian, P., and Pálka, P. (2015). Major factors affecting contemporary Japanese business environment. *International Journal of Productivity and Performance Management*, 64(3): 416–433.

Chatterjee, S. R. and Nankervis, A. R. (2007). *Asian Management in Transition: Emerging Themes*. Basingstoke, UK: Palgrave Macmillan.

Debroux, P. (2003). *Human Resource Management in Japan: Changes and Uncertainties*. Farnham: Surrey, UK.

De Mente, B. L. (2012). *Japan: Understanding and Dealing With the New Japanese Way of Doing Business*. London: Phoenix Books.

Drucker, P. F. (1971). What we can learn from Japanese management. *Harvard Business Review*, 49(2): 110–122.

The Economist (2007). Japan's changing demography: cloud, or silver linings? 26 July 2007, www.economist.com/node/9539825, last accessed 6 November 2015.

The Economist (2008). Sayonara, salaryman. 3 January 2008, www.economist.com/node/9539825, last accessed 23 October 2015.

The Economist (2014). Holding back half the nation. 29 March 2014, www.economist.com/node/10424391, last accessed 23 October 2015.

Firkola, P. (2006). Japanese management practices past and present. *Economic Journal of Hokkaido University*, 35: 115–130.

Haghirian, P. (2009). *J-Management*. Bloomington, IN: iUniverse.

Haghirian, P. (2010a). *Innovation and Change in Japanese Management*. Basingstoke, UK: Palgrave Macmillan.

Haghirian, P. (2010b). *Understanding Japanese Management Practices*, New York: Business Expert Press, LLC.

Hayes, R. H. (1981). Why Japanese factories work. *Harvard Business Review*, 59(4): 56–66.

Hasegawa, H. and Noronha, C. (2009). *Asian Business and Management: Theory, Practice and Perspectives*, Basingstoke, UK: Palgrave Macmillan.

The Japan Times (2014a). Ministry official knocks down barriers to overseas study. 2 February 2014, www.japantimes.co.jp/news/2014/02/02/national/ministry-official-knocks-down-barriers-to-overseas-study/#.Vj0n_Ycnwmx, last accessed 6 November 2015.

The Japan Times (2014b). More foreigners working in Japan. 15 February 2014, www.japantimes.co.jp/opinion/2014/02/15/editorials/more-foreigners-working-in-japan/#.Vj0o_ocnwmx, last accessed 6 November 2015.

The Japan Times (2014c). Success of 'Abenomics' hinges on immigration policy. 18 May 2014, last accessed: www.japantimes.co.jp/news/2014/05/18/national/success-abenomics-hinges-immigration-policy/, last accessed 6 November 2015

Keizer, A. B., Umemura, M., Delbridge, R., and Morgan, G. (2012). Japanese management 20 years on: the contemporary relevance of Japanese management practices. *AIM Executive Review*, 1: 1–24.

Kwan, C. H. (2000). Revitalizing the Japanese economy. 22 December 2000, www.brookings.edu/research/papers/2000/06/globaleconomics-kwan, last accessed 6 November 2015.

Lehmberg, D., Dhanaraj, C., and Funai, A. (2013). What do we make of Japan? *Business Horizons*, 56(2): 219–229.

Lukas, M. and Saito, M. (2009). Structural and economic changes. In: Haghirian, P. (ed.), *J-Management: Fresh Perspectives on the Japanese Firm in the 21st Century*, Bloomington, IN: iUniverse, pp. 45–72.

McKinsey and Company (2012). *Women Matter: An Asian Perspective. Harnessing Female Talent to Raise Corporate Performance*, www.mckinsey.com, last accessed 23 October 2015.

Magoshi, E. and Chang, E. (2009). Diversity management and the effects on employees' organizational commitment: evidence from Japan and Korea. *Journal of World Business*, 44(1): 31–40.

Mroczkowski, T. and Hanaoka, M. (1989). Continuity and change in Japanese management. *California Management Review*, 31(2): 39–53.

Nikkei Weekly (2007). Firms recognizing importance of part-time workers. 4 July 2007.

OECD (2014). *OECD Japan's 50th Anniversary*, www.oecd.org/about/secretary-general/japan-50th-anniversary-symposium-opening-remarks.htm, last accessed 6 November.

Porter, M. E., Takeuchi, H., and Sakakibara, M. (2000). *Can Japan Compete?* New York: Basic Books.

Pudelko, M. (2009). The end of Japanese-style management? *Long Range Planning*, 42(4): 439–462.

Pudelko, M. and Haak, R. (2005). *Japanese Management: The Search for a New Balance Between Continuity and Change*, Basingstoke, UK: Palgrave Macmillan.

Pudelko, M. and Harzing, A. (2011). Japanese human resource management: inspirations from abroad and current trends of change. In: Bebenroth, R. (ed.), *International Human Resource Management in Japan*, London: Routledge, pp. 28–60.

Saito, J. (2014). Is immigration a solution for Japan's plummeting population? *East Asia Forum*, 31 December 2014, www.eastasiaforum.org/2014/12/31/is-immigration-a-solution-for-japans-plummeting-population/, last accessed 23 October 2015.

Sakakibara, E. (2003). *Structural Reform in Japan*, Brookings Institution Press, Washington DC.

Schmidt, A. (1997). *Management der Human-Ressourcen und Restrukturierung in Japan*, St Gallen, Switzerland: University of St Gallen.

Shimizu, S. (2014). *Japanese-Style Management: From Crisis to Reformation in the Age of Abenomics*, London: LID Publishing Ltd.

Steinberg, C. and Nakane, M. (2012). *Can Women Save Japan?* International Monetary Fund, Working Paper, WP/12/248.

Süssmuth-Dyckerhoff, C., Wang, J., and Chen, J. (2012). Women matter: an Asian perspective. Harnessing female talent to raise corporate performance, June 2012, www.mckinsey.com/~/media/mckinsey%20offices/japan/pdf/women_matter_an_asian_perspective.ashx, last accessed 23 October 2015.

United Nations (2008). *Gender Empowerment Measure*, available at: www.un.org/womenwatch/directory/statistics_and_indicators_60.htm, last accessed 20 October 2015.

Watanabe, S. (2000). The Japan model and the future of employment and wage systems. *International Labour Review*, 139(3): 307–333.

Weston, M. (2014). *Giants of Japan: The Lives of Japan's Greatest Men and Women*. New York: Regina Ryan Publishing Enterprises Inc.

Witt, M. A. (2006). *Changing Japanese Capitalism: Societal Coordination and Institutional Adjustment*, Cambridge, UK: Cambridge University Press.

Yuasa, M. (2005). Japanese women in management: getting closer to 'realities' in Japan. *Asia Pacific Business Review*, 11(2): 195–211.

Index